'The great merit of Trevor Royle's superb n[...] presents this catalogue of horrors unflinchi[...] So absorbing and stimulating is Royle's b[...] racing . . . [His] pen-portraits of the *drama*[...] magnificent history cannot be mistaken for a[...] McLynn, *Independent on Sunday*

'Trevor Royle's new book has many virtues . . . for almost 900 pages, we gallop the length and breadth of the British Isles, careering from skirmish to battle with the narrative élan of a cavalry charge . . . This book provides a vivid account of the fighting [and is] masterly in its control of military detail' John Adamson, *Sunday Times*

'A full and ambitious narrative . . . Royle comes into his own with the story of the military campaigns . . . His brisk, well-written narrative skilfully weaves together the events' Kevin Sharpe, *Independent*

'A lively narrative' Ronald Hutton, *The Times*

'This is a superb history of the cataclysmic convulsions which brought much death, destruction and devastation to Scotland, England and Ireland . . . This is history as Thomas Babington Macaulay, the most readable and celebrated of all British historians, wrote it – and I mean that as high praise. Indeed, Royle's writing, with its verve, dynamism and colour, frequently reminds one of the master. Further . . . his descriptions of battles – and he has many to describe – are masterpieces of clarity . . . But the essential merit of this fine book is its consistent lucidity. The events he describes were complex; he steers them with a smooth and steady hand' *Sunday Herald*

'An enthralling, magisterial study' *Scotsman*

'A long, graphic, ably controlled narrative' *Guardian*

'[A] large-scale examination of the conflict . . . rich in detail and clearly presented . . . the volume is essential reading. In addition, Royle brings out well the religious intensity of the time' *Herald*

'This is a splendid account, highly impressive, lucid, readable, a wonderfully organised history for the common reader' *Catholic Herald*

'A top-notch investigation of the wars that shaped the present-day British Isles, this is a scholarly, compelling, even entertaining read. Recommended' *Good Book Guide*

'Trevor Royle's book is a battlefield in itself, rich in its portrayal of Puritan and Royalist forces and the ideals for which they fought . . . Royle's intricately layered book . . . is as powerful as Cromwell in his prime and as expansionist as the political forces raging throughout Britain in the 17th century' *Oxford Times*

Trevor Royle is a highly respected writer on the history of wars and empire. His recent books include *Winds of Change: The End of Empire in Africa*, *Orde Wingate: Irregular Soldier* and *Crimea: The Great Crimean War 1854–1856*.

He is a Fellow of the Royal society of Edinburgh. As a journalist, he is an associate editor of the *Sunday Herald* and a regular commentator on international affairs for BBC radio.

By the same author

We'll Support You Ever More: The Impertinent Saga of
Scottish Fitba (ed., with Ian Archer)
Jock Tamson Bairns: Essays on a Scots Childhood (ed.)
Precipitous City: The Story of Literary Edinburgh
A Diary of Edinburgh (with Richard Demarco)
Edinburgh
Death Before Dishonour: The True Story of Fighting Mac
The Macmillan Companion to Scottish Literature
James and Jim: The Biography of James Kennaway
The Kitchener Enigma
The Best Years of Their Lives: The National
Service Experience, 1945–1963
War Report: The War Correspondent's View of Battle
from the Crimea to the Falklands
The Last Days of the Raj
A Dictionary of Military Quotations
Anatomy of a Regiment: Ceremony and Soldiering
in the Welsh Guards
In Flanders Fields: Scottish Poetry and Prose of the
First World War (ed.)
Glubb Pasha: The Life and Times of Sir John Bagot Glubb,
Commander of the Arab Legion
The Mainstream Companion to Scottish Literature
Orde Wingate: Irregular Soldier
Winds of Change: The End of Empire in Africa
Scottish War Stories (ed.)
Crimea: The Great Crimean War, 1854–1856

CIVIL WAR

The Wars of the
Three Kingdoms
1638–1660

TREVOR ROYLE

ABACUS

ABACUS

First published in Great Britain by Little, Brown in 2004
This paperback edition first published by Abacus in 2005
Reprinted 2005, 2006, 2007

A CIP catalogue record for this book
is available from the British Library.

ISBN 978-0-349-11564-1

Papers used by Abacus are natural, recyclable products made from
wood grown in sustainable forests and certified in accordance with
the rules of the Forest Stewardship Council.

Typeset in Garamond by M Rules
Printed and bound in Great Britain
by Clays Ltd, St Ives plc
Paper supplied by Hellefoss AS, Norway

Abacus
An imprint of
Little, Brown Book Group
100 Victoria Embankment
London EC4Y 0DY

An Hachette Livre UK Company

www.littlebrown.co.uk

Contents

PART THREE
The Second and Third Civil Wars 1648–1651

PART FOUR
The Protectorate 1653–1659

PART FIVE
RESTORATION 1660

List of Maps

Preface and Acknowledgements

These words are being written some 360 years after two rival English armies faced one another across the rolling patchwork countryside of south Warwickshire at a place called Edgehill. On a late summer's day they engaged in a battle which left 1500 dead and many more wounded; ahead lay other battles which would scar the English landscape as warfare swept from the centre of the country to the north and the west, creating casualties, ruining lives and destroying property. This is the traditional starting point for a conflict which has long been known as the English Civil War, the bloody internecine confrontation between those who supported the Crown and those who backed the claims of parliament. But in both armies there were Scottish and Irish soldiers, and although the Battle of Edgehill began the conflict in England, the war also raged in the adjoining kingdoms of Scotland and Ireland. Far from being purely an 'English' civil war, these were the wars of Charles I's three interconnected kingdoms, and the bloodshed in all three would continue right up to the restoration of King Charles II in 1660.

In recent years historians have begun putting the events of 1638–1660 into a British context. Instead of viewing the conflict as purely English they have examined it as a train of events which also involved Scotland and Ireland and to which all three kingdoms made a contribution. Wales, too, was involved. Although some experiences were different in each of the component kingdoms and although the violence in the Celtic fringes was often isolated from the main events, there is sufficient linkage to regard the war as an inclusive conflict. This is not to deny the fact that the fighting in England between 1642 and 1645 was a violent struggle between two groups of Englishmen who supported either King Charles I or the parliament. On that level it was a civil war as bitter as the earlier Wars of the Roses or the later American Civil War. Rather, it is impossible to view the conflict in its entirety without taking into account events in Scotland and Ireland;

by the same token Scottish and Irish history cannot be read without understanding the English and wider British contexts. And, throughout, there are the linking figures of the two Stewart kings, Charles I and Charles II, whose actions provoked reactions in all three kingdoms.

The seventeenth-century wars in Britain have produced a huge bibliography, and it would have been impossible to attempt a new work without a thorough reading of the writers and historians who have illuminated the period. It would be invidious of me not to recognise their labours and to thank them for the learning and inspiration they provided during an invigorating period of research. In particular, I would like to thank and acknowledge the following authors whose books are listed in the bibliography and are mentioned in the notes and references: John Adair, Gerald Aylmer, T. C. Barnard, J. C. Beckett, Martyn Bennett, Keith Brown, John Buchan, Nicholas Canny, Bernard Capp, Charles Carlton, Thomas Carlyle, Edward J. Cowan, Peter Donald, Frances Dow, Christopher Durston, William Ferguson, Charles Harding Firth, Antonia Fraser, Edward M. Furgol, Samuel Rawson Gardiner, Peter Gaunt, J. T. Gilbert, Roger Hainsworth, Christopher Hibbert, Christopher Hill, Ronald Hutton, Edward Hyde (Earl of Clarendon), John Kenyon, Mark Kishlansky, Maurice J. Lee, Allan I. Macinnes, Rosalind Mitchison, John Morrill, the editors and contributors to the New History of Ireland, Vol. III, Jane Ohlmeyer, Richard Ollard, Michael Perceval-Maxwell, Tom Reilly, Ivan Roots, Conrad Russell, Kevin Sharpe, Roy Sherwood, David Stevenson, Lawrence Stone, C. V. Wedgwood, Austin Woolrych, Blair Worden, Peter Young. Austin Woolrych's *Britain in Revolution 1625–1660* (2002) was published after the completion of my text and was not consulted.

The fighting also produced a large number of memoirs, letters and diaries written by men and women who recorded their experiences or wrote about them later. In the spirit of remembrance, therefore, it is fitting to acknowledge the shades of the following writers whose works provided so many keen personal insights from that bygone age: Richard Atkyns, John Aubrey, Richard Baxter, Robert Baillie, Robert Blair, Sir Richard Bulstrode, Bishop Thomas Burnet, Margaret Cavendish, Duchess of Newcastle, Sir Hugh Cholmley, Lady Anne Clifford, Sir Symonds D'Ewes, Sir Henry Ellis, John Evelyn, Lady

Ann Fanshawe, James Gordon of Rothiemay, Patrick Gordon of Ruthven, Richard Gough, Lady Anne Halkett, Lady Brilliana Harley, John Hodgson, Sir Ralph Hopton, Lucy Hutchinson, Sir Archibald Johnston of Wariston, John Lister, Edmund Ludlow, Sir Samuel Luke, Adam Martindale, Jean de Montereul, Sir John Oglander, Samuel Pepys, John Rushworth, Walter Slingsby, James Somerville, John Spalding, Joshua Sprigge, Sir William Springate, Henry Townshend, Sir James Turner, Robert Venables, Nehemiah Wallington, Sir Philip Warwick, Nehemiah Wharton, Bulstrode Whitelocke. In the interests of accessibility most of the texts have been reproduced in modern English.

Thanks are also due to those editors and antiquarians who ensured that the memoirs, letters and journals were edited and published, many of them in the nineteenth century. It would be wrong, too, not to remember the societies which promoted much of that work, among which may be mentioned the Bannatyne Club, the Camden Society, the Irish Archaeological and Celtic Society, the Maitland Club, the Navy Records Society, the Scottish History Society, the Spalding Club, the Wodrow Society. In more recent times John Adair and Charles Carlton helped to point the way to other readings in their books, respectively, *By the Sword Divided* and *Going to the Wars*.

For their customary help and advice in locating texts I want to thank the staffs of the National Library of Scotland and the Public Record Office, Kew.

My publisher, Alan Samson, must take the credit for suggesting the book in the first place and I hope I have repaid his enthusiasm and support with interest. John Bright-Holmes edited the text with a skill and precision which I hope I do not take for granted: he has my warmest thanks, as does Stephen Guise of Time Warner Books who was a tower of strength during the production process. Once again I am indebted to Alan Palmer for casting an expert eye over the typescript and for making many useful comments and corrections. It goes without saying that I am responsible for any remaining errors or mistakes in interpretation.

Trevor Royle
Edinburgh
January 2004

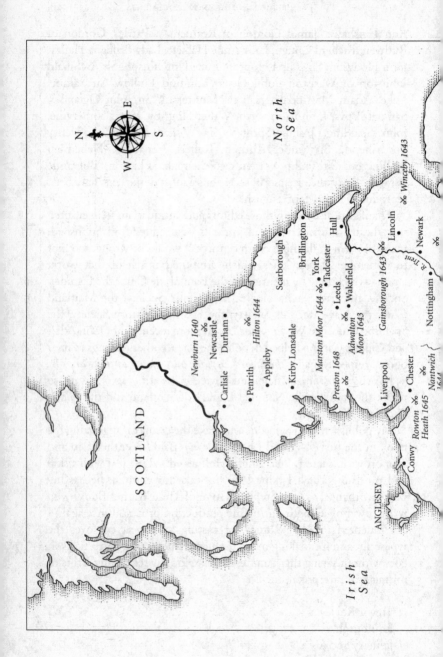

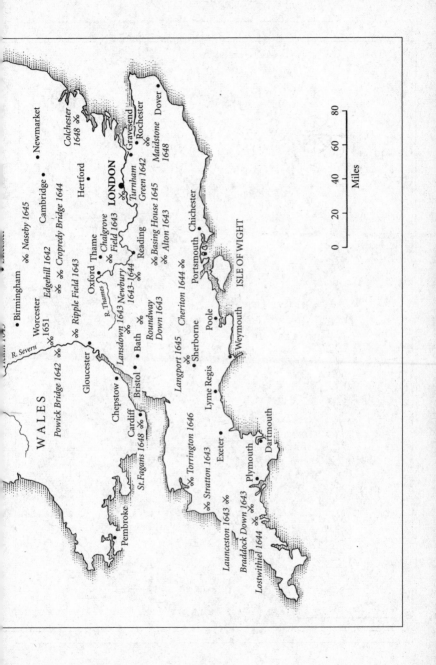

WALES

R. Severn

Birmingham

Worcester
⚔ 1651

Powick Bridge 1642 ⚔

Gloucester •

Ripple Field 1643 ⚔

Chepstow •

Cardiff •
St. Fagans 1648 ⚔

Pembroke •

Lansdown 1643 ⚔
Bath •
Bristol •

Roundway
Down 1643 ⚔

Langport 1645 ⚔
Sherborne •

Torrington 1646 ⚔
Exeter •
Lyme Regis •

Launceston 1643 ⚔

Braddock Down 1643 ⚔
Plymouth
Lostwithiel 1644 ⚔

Dartmouth

Stratton 1643 ⚔

• Newmarket

Colchester
1648 ⚔

Cambridge •

Hertford •

Edgehill 1642
⚔ ⚔ Cropredy Bridge 1644

Naseby 1645 ⚔

LONDON

Gravesend
⚔ Rochester Dover
Turnham Maidstone
Green 1642 1648

Oxford Thame
⚔ Chalgrove
Field 1643

R. Thames

Reading •

Newbury
1643-1644

⚔ Basing House 1645
⚔ Alton 1643

Cheriton 1644 ⚔

Portsmouth Chichester •

Poole •

Weymouth •

ISLE OF WIGHT

0   20   40   60   80

Miles

ORKNEY

Pentland Firth

Thurso •

Dunbeath •

North Sea

LEWIS

ASSYNT

Carbisdale ⚔
1650   • Dornoch

SKYE

Inverness •   Auldearn ⚔
                1645

Spynie ⚔   Banff •

                                    Turriff 1639 ⚔
                                    Towie-Barclay ⚔
Balvenie ⚔ Strathbogie ⚔   Fyvie ⚔
1649   1644

KNOYDART

BADENOCH

Strathdon ⚔   Alford ⚔
1645   1645

R. Spey

MORAR   Inverlochy ⚔
         1645

Mingary ⚔

R. Dee   Aberdeen •
                    Brig o'Dee ⚔
                    1639
            Megra Hill ⚔
            1639
Dunottar ⚔

Dalnaspidal ⚔
1654

ATHOLL

Blair Atholl ⚔

Careston ⚔
1645   • Montrose

MEARS

Alyth ⚔
1651

MULL

Lagganmore ⚔
1646   Inveraray •

Craignish ⚔

Tippermuir ⚔
1645   Perth •

Dundee •

St Andrews •

LORNE

Dunoon •   Dumbarton ⚔

Inverkeithing ⚔
1651
R. Forth
Stirling •

Burntisland •

Dunbar ⚔
1650

Skipness ⚔

Greenock •

Kilsyth ⚔
1645   Edinburgh • Leith •
        • Glasgow   Musselburgh ⚔
                         1650
                              Dunglass ⚔

Duns •

Berwick •

ISLAY

Hamilton ⚔
1650

R. Tweed

Kelso •

Coldstream •

Irvine •

Mauchline ⚔
1648

Dunaverty ⚔

• Ayr

Philiphaugh ⚔
1645

Dumfries • Annan Moor ⚔
            1645
Threave ⚔ Caerlaverock ⚔

• Carlisle

0   10 20 30 40 50
Miles

ENGLAND

N

W   E

S

*Rathlin Island
1642*

• Coleraine

ULSTER

*Scarriffhollis
1650*

Londonderry

Letterkenny

Carrickfergus

Bangor

*Lough
Neagh*

Belfast

Enniskillen

*Benburb
1646*

Armagh

*Newry
1642*

• Sligo

Carlingford

Cavan

Dundalk

*Irish
Sea*

Westport

CONNACHT

Longford

R. Boyne

Inishbofin

Roscommon

*Drogheda
1649*

Trim

Athlone

*Dungan's Hill
1647*

R. Liffey

Galway

DUBLIN

R. Shannon

Kildare

*Rathmines
1649*

*Atlantic
Ocean*

*Kilrush
1642*

Wicklow

Ennis

Carlow

LEINSTER

*Limerick
1651*

Cashel

Kilkenny

MUNSTER

Tipperary

Listowel

New Ross

*Wexford
1649*

*Liscaroll
1647*

*Clonmel
1650*

*Waterford
1649*

R. Blackwater

Dungarvan

Killarney

*Knockanuss
1647*

*Macroom
1650*

Cork

Youghal

0   10   20   30   40   50

Miles

CIVIL WAR: THE WARS OF THE THREE KINGDOMS

1638–1660

Prologue

LÜTZEN, 1632

'More sad or Heavie Tydings hath not in this Age been brought since Prince Harries Death to the True Hearts of England.'

John Bradshaw, later to be the presiding judge at the trial of King Charles I, on hearing the news of the death of King Gustavus Adolphus on 16 November 1632

There was no doubt about it, the saviour of the Protestant cause was dead, the right-hand side of his face shattered by a stray musket ball which had entered his head between right eye and ear. Other bullet wounds and deep cuts on his body told those who found him that death had come in dreadful close-quarter combat. Naked, King Gustavus Adolphus of Sweden lay at the bottom of a pile of anonymous bodies, having shared the fate of the men whom he had led from their northern fastnesses to the killing grounds of southern Germany. Earlier on that damp November day of 1632, amid the smoke and confusion of battle, the king's horse had been seen careering around riderless and maddened by the pain of a gashed neck. His awe-stricken soldiers had feared the worst but, as they hacked their way towards the burning town of Lützen, many refused to believe that the supernatural armour which seemed to surround their commander had failed him in the hour of victory. Now, in the flickering torchlight of that early winter evening, they could no longer hide their worst fears. 'The ship that carries me cannot sink' had been the Swedish king's proud boast; but amid the shipwreck of the charnel house outside an insignificant small town in Germany Gustavus Adolphus had proved himself to be as mortal as any other man.

It was an unnecessary death which did little to change the course of the Thirty Years War, that long and aimless conflict between the forces of the Habsburg-inspired Counter-Reformation and of Protestantism which devastated most of Germany and swept into many other corners of central Europe. By the time Gustavus Adolphus intervened on the Protestant side in 1630 the fighting was in deadlock and the German princes looked to him as towards the morning sun. They had good reason to seek salvation, for, on the imperial side, Count Albrecht von Wallenstein had assembled a huge and powerful mercenary army whose maintenance came from plunder, and by 1629 it had all but ended the opposition of the German princes still loyal to the Protestant cause. It was to save central Europe from the threat of Habsburg Catholic domination that Gustavus Adolphus entered Germany with the backing of funds from France.

Outside the village of Breitenfeld, north of Leipzig, on 18 September 1631 the Swedes did just that, crushing the imperial forces led by the previously invincible Count Tilly. Suddenly it seemed that the threat of Catholic domination was at an end, that never again would the Protestant Germans have cause to fear the Habsburg armies. Their celebrations were not misplaced, for this 'first great test and trial of the new tactics against the old, and therefore the first great land battle of the modern age'[1] had introduced new and terrifying tactics to the battlefield. Gustavus Adolphus's army won because the cumbersome, static and well-drilled lines of the imperial army were no match for its mobile columns and concentrated firepower. Breitenfeld was a declaration: the ponderous slow-moving masses of imperial cavalry and infantry which had crushed their opposition underfoot could be defeated by the flexibility and firepower of manoeuvrable horsemen armed with matchlock pistols which were discharged at the gallop and usually at point-blank range.

Although the Swedish victory rattled the Habsburg cause it did not break it. In the following year Gustavus Adolphus hoped to reach Vienna but was forced to protect his rear from Wallenstein, now intent on forcing a battle which both men knew would be decisive.

Displaying his usual recklessness, Gustavus Adolphus once had his horse shot from under him, and when rebuked by his courtiers he responded that there was no sense in keeping him in a box. His optimism seemed to be rewarded by further success. Tilly was mortally wounded at the River Lech and the Bavarian cities of Augsburg and Munich were soon in Swedish hands. Then, with winter fast approaching, came the fateful confrontation at Lützen.

Knowing that Wallenstein had been weakened by the absence of his main cavalry force under the command of Count Pappenheim, Gustavus Adolphus determined to press home the advantage, using the tactics which had served his army so well. This time, though, Wallenstein was waiting for him with his musketeers hidden in a long ditch from which they could shoot upwards as the attacking Swedish cavalry charged over them. With his overstretched forces lined up in traditional formation, the cavalry on the wings, the infantry in the centre, he waited to receive the Swedish assault. In the hard-fought struggle which followed the Swedish brigades succeeded in breaking the imperial line, but amid the smoke and confusion Gustavus Adolphus was mortally wounded while encouraging his men forward. The battle ended in a close-quarter struggle which left the Swedes victorious but at a dreadful cost:

> When his corpse was embalmed there was found in it five shots and nine wounds, so are we to our unspeakable grief deprived of the best and most valorous commander that ever soldiers had, and the church of God with her good cause of the best instrument under God, we because we was not worthy of him, and she for the sins of her children, and altho' our loss who did follow him shall be great, yet questionless the church her loss shall be much greater, for how can it be when the head which gave such heavenly influence unto all the inferior members that never any distemperature or weakness was seen in them; how can it be since that head is taken from the body, but the members thereof shall fall unto much fainting and confusion.[2]

The grief-stricken author of that letter, composed almost a fortnight later, was one of Gustavus Adolphus's most respected and bravest brigade commanders, a tough and battle-scarred Scot called Alexander

Leslie. He had been in Swedish service since 1605 and was knighted twenty years later following his skilful breaking of the siege at Danzig. A brilliant field commander and a hardy campaigner, Leslie often boasted to his friends that he had never troubled to learn the alphabet beyond the letter 'G', but his dictated letter, written to his fellow Scot, the Marquis of Hamilton, spoke for just about every soldier who served Gustavus Adolphus.

As the news of the king's death filtered back through his army's rank and file in small shockwaves of grief, men hardened by battle had difficulty fighting back their tears. For the Swedes it was a hammer blow. Gustavus Adolphus was their beloved ruler, the Lion of the North, the defender of the Protestant faith, a latter-day Gideon with seven armies and 80,000 men under his command. For the others in his army, a curious collection of soldiers of fortune – English, German, Irish and Scots – the loss was equally grievous. He was their patron, a god of battles whom they knew to be fearless and resolute, a commander who had scattered the imperial forces of his previously invincible opponents: in the words of another Scots mercenary, Robert Monro, he was 'the king of Captains and the Captain of Kings . . . Illustrissimus among Generals'. Money and a soldier's life had taken men like Monro to Lützen, but like every man in Gustavus's army they were also fighting for the Protestant cause against the imperial forces of the Catholic Holy Roman Emperor, Ferdinand III. The war had already lasted fourteen years, and despite the victory at Lützen it would continue for another sixteen, a savage and debilitating conflict which put Germany and its people on the rack between 1618 and 1648.

Among those mercenaries who huddled down so disconsolately by their campfires that night were two men whose paths would cross again as enemies, serving in another war which would also be fought on grounds of religious conscience. One was Sir Arthur Aston, of Fulham in Middlesex, who had also served the crowns of Russia and Poland; the other was Alexander Leslie, the dour Scots soldier from Perthshire who had articulated the army's shared sorrow. Both were far from home and both were united in grief for their fallen commander, but before the decade was out they would find themselves in opposing armies as King Charles I of Great Britain plunged his kingdoms into another long-drawn-out and bloody conflict which pitted a Church against the Crown. As another soldier of the time put it, Leslie 'took up the trade of killing men abroad and now is returned to kill, for Christ's sake, at home'.[3]

Leslie was not alone. Indeed, the Scottish contingent in the Swedish army was integral to its success. Scots made good fighters, and in common with many other minorities on Europe's fringes – the Croat cavalry in Wallenstein's army, for example – they exported their skills to the highest bidder, becoming soldiers of fortune who gave good value for money. At least 25,000 were in the service of Gustavus Adolphus, and half as many fought for the king of France, often confronting their fellow countrymen on the field of battle. One, Sir John Hepburn, scion of an old Scottish Catholic family, fought in the Swedish and the French armies and rose to become a Marshal of France, having raised the formation which lives on today as The Royal Scots, the 1st of Foot and the senior line infantry regiment in the British Army's order of battle. Trusted as one of the bravest of Gustavus's brigade commanders, he had lost the confidence of the Swedish king prior to Lützen and had departed his camp with the reproachful words: 'And now sire never more shall this sword be drawn in your service; this is the last time I will ever serve so ungrateful a prince!'[4] Ironically, the Scottish contingent was held in reserve during the battle, the first time it had not been in the vanguard during the entire campaign in southern Germany.

When war summoned the soldiers of fortune back to their country in 1638 they returned with military skills learned during the Thirty Years War honed to a fine art. Leslie would lead the Scottish forces in the opening rounds of the war against King Charles I and would go on to be a central figure in the parliamentary army. Robert Monro would command the covenanting armies in Ireland, where his opponent would be an Irish soldier of fortune who had served the Habsburgs, Owen Roe O'Neill,* a veteran of the fighting in the Low Countries. Other survivors of Lützen plumped for the Royalist cause. As Lord Eythin, James King would hold the centre for King Charles I at Marston Moor in 1644 while Leslie commanded the opposing parliamentary army. But for the most part those grizzled veterans

---

* Properly Eoghan Ruadh (Red Owen) O'Neill, but the anglicised form is generally used.

came back to their homeland to support the same Protestant cause which had taken them across the plains and valleys of Germany.

The English, too, were prominent under Gustavus Adolphus in southern Germany. Some followed Aston into the king's army. Sir Jacob Astley of Melton Constable in Norfolk had given his sword to Christian IV of Denmark when the Danes seemed to be the best hope of making a decisive intervention in Germany in 1625, and had then served in Gustavus Adolphus's army. Others opposed King Charles I and rose to prominence in the parliamentary forces, fighting like most of the Scots for the Protestant cause. The greatest of their number was Sir Thomas Fairfax, 'Black Tom', the inspiration behind the creation of the New Model Army, and others of his ilk included George Monck, the Earl of Essex, Sir Philip Skippon and Sir John Hotham. There was also Sydenham Poyntz, who had been on the opposing imperial side at Lützen and who went on to produce a racy memoir about his time as a mercenary soldier.

When they came back to fight in Britain they brought with them not just their experience but also their understanding of modern warfare. The Thirty Years War might have devastated Europe, but it also introduced new standards in warfare. Musketeers firing matchlock weapons advanced in orderly files, cavalrymen shed their armour and rode into battle armed with pistols and swords, while artillery was deployed in support of infantry attacks. These were decisive advances and they left their mark on the British mercenaries who served in Europe. King Charles I managed to keep his country out of the Thirty Years War – lack of funds and an unwillingness to be sucked into the quarrel saw to that – but British soldiers did fight as mercenaries in Europe and their experience was to stand them in good stead when war broke out in their own countries. In that sense at least the European conflict was to influence events in Britain after the disastrous defeat of Gustavus Adolphus at Lützen. Within eight years Astley and Leslie were to be at daggers drawn, together with thousands of other soldiers, English, Irish and Scottish, who found themselves fighting against one another in the wars which ravaged the three kingdoms of King Charles I.

PART ONE

THE DESCENT TO WAR
1638–1642

Chapter One

The Illustrious Hope of Great Britain

> 'I will end with a rule that may serve for a statesman, a courtier or a lover – never make a defence or apology before you be accused.'
>
> *King Charles I to Lord Wentworth, 3 September 1636*

For a prince who would become the second king of Great Britain and the monarch who would shoulder the main responsibility for plunging his kingdoms into twenty-two years of civil strife, the birth of Charles Stewart, Duke of Albany and Earl of Ross, was a muted affair. He came into the world on Wednesday 19 November 1600 in the bleak surroundings of the Scottish Royal Family's residence in Dunfermline, Fife, after a difficult birth which left his mother, Anne of Denmark, exhausted. No bonfires were lit (the traditional welcome for the birth of a son), not a bell tolled in his honour and his father James was not even present. He was on the other side of the River Forth in his capital city of Edinburgh reasserting his authority in the aftermath of a coup mounted against him earlier in the year by the Gowrie brothers,* who had plotted to murder him in their tower house near Perth. It was as if Charles did not even exist, a weak and

---

* John Ruthven, 3rd Earl of Gowrie, and his brother Alexander Ruthven, both of whom were killed in the aftermath. Their motives remain unclear and have never been given a satisfactory explanation.

sickly baby, who was after all only second in line to the throne of Scotland, one of the lesser Crowns in Europe.

Five weeks later young Charles was taken to Edinburgh to be christened in Holyroodhouse, and that austere royal palace was to be his home for the next three years. It was a curious yet formative time. The young prince did not flourish physically as Prince Henry, his much adored older brother, had done. He suffered from rickets, stammered, had difficulty holding down his food, was slow in growing, and it was something of a miracle that he survived, for his mother lost five out of the eight children who were born to her. There was also an emotional absence in his young life, although his early childhood experiences were mild compared to those endured by his Stewart forebears – James I (of Scotland) was captured by the English at the age of twelve and remained in captivity until he was eighteen, James V was kept under lock and key by his stepfather, Archibald Douglas, 6th Earl of Angus, while Charles's own father, James VI of Scotland, had been brought up and educated by a series of regents following the abdication of Mary Queen of Scots. In April 1603 James hurried south to succeed Queen Elizabeth and in so doing to become the first king of Great Britain. Within a month Charles's mother and two surviving siblings followed, leaving the young prince in the care of his governess Lady Ochiltree and her team of nurses. Under the tutelage of the Scottish Lord Chancellor, Lord Fyvie, the young boy's health began to improve and by the summer of 1604 he was considered strong enough to make the long journey to London by coach. It took over six weeks for the two coaches to take the royal party over the four hundred miles of indifferent roads which connected the two capital cities, and if it was a leisurely progress it was also an agreeable one, with several stops at the homes of the royal family's aristocratic friends.

Once in the English capital Charles was put in the care of Sir Robert Carey, an experienced courtier whose wife Elizabeth became something of a surrogate mother to him. While he remained physically small he enjoyed tolerable physical health, and in an age when medical care was in its infancy he proved to be sufficiently sturdy to survive. He had to be robust because the treatment meted out to him was severe by modern medical standards: he wore iron boots to strengthen his legs, and to try to cure him of his speech impediments, thought was given to the possibility of cutting the cord under his tongue. By his teenage years he was strong enough to hunt, a passion he shared with his father, and he proved to be an able swordsman. Although slight and short in stature he was well enough made and carried about his person an elegance which was much admired by visiting dignitaries.

His mental health was another matter. Charles had a painful stammer which only emphasised his sensitivity and shyness, drawbacks which were not helped by his mother's impatience with him. Queen Anne made it clear that she preferred her first son and, worse, she made little secret of her favouritism. (Paradoxically, though not untypically, she too had been ignored as a child by her father because she was not a boy.) While she would sing Henry's praises, Charles was 'a fool' who was in need of improvement. She also seems to have spent little time with her children, but her behaviour was in keeping with the spirit of the age, it being considered not unusual for royal children to be farmed out to others during their childhood years. Even so, that absence of maternal love helped to turn an awkward boy into a grave young man who found friendships difficult and was especially gauche in the company of women.

His sensitivities were also offended by the grossness of his father's court, the boisterous heavy drinking and coarse overfamiliarity which sat so uneasily with his growing intellectual and cultural interests. Whereas Henry shone at court and was widely admired for his easy charm and his mettlesome behaviour, Charles was thought a dullard who deserved to be the butt of his brother's jokes. There was also a closeness between Henry and his sister Elizabeth from which the younger brother was excluded. Constantly rebuffed, Charles tried to ingratiate himself, and his childhood letters betray a naive affection which was all the more pathetic because it was held in disdain. 'I will give anything that I have to you; both my horses, and my books, and my pieces, and my crossbows, or any thing that you would have,' he wrote in his earliest surviving letter. 'Good brother love me and I shall love and serve you.'[1]

In vain did the younger boy try to win his sibling's attention: the more Charles tried to curry favour the more Henry poured scorn upon him. The older brother even cheated him of his future, one which might have been spent among books and field sports, when he fell ill and died of typhoid fever in November 1612 – to the dismay of everyone at court. From being a royal prince and something of a nonentity at court, Charles suddenly found himself heir to the throne of Great Britain and in an entirely different relationship with his father.

He was to have a difficult apprenticeship. While Charles remained in his teenage years – he was slow to mature physically – he was kept in the background, and it was not until the death of his mother in 1619 that James began to include him in affairs of state. However, his father's influence was already being felt in other and more fundamental ways. Charles's conscience, already highly developed, was heightened by his religious leanings, which were distinctly High Church, as were his father's. He also delighted in studying the nature of the divine right of kings and came to believe in it implicitly. Particularly dear to him was the advice provided by his father in his book on kingship and statecraft, the *Basilikon Doron*. Written for Henry in the summer of 1598 and published the following year, it provided Charles with a thorough grounding in the theory of the divine right:

> Being born to be a king you are rather born to ONUS than HONOS: not excelling all your people so far in rank and honour as in daily care and hazardous pains-taking for the dutiful administrations of that great office that God has laid upon your shoulders: laying a just symmetry and proportion between the height of your honourable place and the heavy weight of your great charge, and consequently in case of failure (which God forbid) of the sadness of your fall, according to the proportion of that height.[2]

Charles proved a ready learner and the notion that kings were God's anointed was to be a lifelong obsession, one which commanded his own view of his relationship to those whom he ruled. It was during this fertile period in his life when he was still a boy yet growing into manhood that he fell under the baleful influence of his father's favourite, George Villiers, the scion of a distinguished Leicestershire family. James had always had an eye for young men who would do his bidding – homosexual attraction was one driving force, the need for simple affection another – and a succession of virile sycophants had provided him with a sheet-anchor in the busy affairs of state. Villiers, 'the handsomest bodied man in England', was his latest and last craze and he was to emerge as the leading light of James's court, perhaps even the most powerful man in the land. Within three years he had been promoted Master of the Horse, appointed Knight of the Garter and awarded estates with sufficient income to allow him to live in spectacular style. Raised to the peerage as the Earl of Buckingham in 1617 (six years later he would be a duke), Villiers was denied nothing by his patron.

To begin with, Charles was kept outside his father's charmed circle, but Buckingham was no fool. He realised that the old king's years were numbered and he was keen to embrace the successor, taking the opportunity to draw the young man into a triumvirate in which all three men had nicknames – Baby Charles, Steenie (Buckingham, on account of his likeness to St Stephen) and Dear Dad (James). For his part Charles was delighted to have the friendship of such a flamboyant, energetic and good-looking man and the feelings induced were so potent that he failed to recognise the paragon's faults. The trouble with Buckingham was that, for all his brash self-confidence, he was not a good judge of events. At the very moment when he was rising to prominence Britain found itself in danger of being sucked into European affairs with a crisis in Germany.

In 1618 Frederick IV, the Elector Palatine, was chosen by the Protestant princes as the new king of Bohemia. Five years earlier he had married James's spirited daughter Elizabeth, and that bond made Britain a natural ally when in the following year Ferdinand of Styria, the new Holy Roman Emperor, engaged Maxmilian of Bavaria to drive Frederick from his kingdom. The people of Britain were aghast at these events: not only did Elizabeth enjoy considerable popularity but the unfolding crisis was viewed as a confrontation between the Spanish-sponsored Catholic Counter-Reformation and the Protestant Church, a struggle in which Britain had an obvious stake. When Frederick's army was routed at the White Mountain in 1620 those voices became ever shriller. 'I most humbly entreat your Majesty to take care of the King and myself by sending us help,' wrote Elizabeth to her father as she fled into exile. 'Otherwise we shall be entirely ruined.' In fact she was as much the author of her misfortunes as her impetuous husband, having declared that she would rather eat sauerkraut off a humble plate as a queen than continue dining off gold plate as the wife of an elector.[3]

Much as James loved his daughter, whose short reign earned her the name of the 'Winter Queen', he was loath to intervene, not for lack of backbone but because he did not possess the forces or the funds to mount any full-scale European military operation. An army 30,000 strong would cost £2 million to raise and would then be a continuing drain on the exchequer at a time when Britain could ill afford it. Besides, to get approval for any funds James would have to go to parliament, and that was an option he was not prepared to take, being of the belief that his rule was best served by keeping that potentially troublesome body at arm's length. Nonetheless, in order to quell the growing clamour, he had to act and at the beginning of February 1621 he summoned his third parliament. While its members fretted, as did Charles, who dreamed romantically of marching off to the rescue of his sister, James preferred a diplomatic solution involving Spain. If Charles married the sister of King Philip IV of Spain, the Infanta Maria, then he could put pressure on his Habsburg cousin Ferdinand to end the fighting in Germany, or, even better, Spanish forces would restore Frederick to his throne.

As a piece of realpolitik it was thoroughly practical: in pursuit of a match British diplomats had already begun negotiations as early as 1608, with Henry in mind as the Infanta's suitor. The aim was the same: Britain would gain a powerful European ally, albeit one of Catholic persuasion. When the Palatinate was threatened ten years later it was a simple matter to transfer the suit to Charles. However, there was one sticking point: the arrangement would entail the heir to the throne of Britain marrying a Catholic, and that was a step which neither parliament nor the bulk of the population could tolerate. When James's third parliament opened it stood resolutely against the marriage and ended its session with a remonstrance deploring the situation facing Frederick and Elizabeth, by then in exile in the Netherlands. Finally, it criticised what it held to be a growing Catholic influence at home and abroad. Stung by its 'unruly' attitude, James ordered parliament not to discuss foreign policy any further and in January the following year he dismissed the body without further ado.

It was not the end of the matter. Early in 1623 Buckingham and Charles embarked on a hare-brained and hugely expensive plan to ride across Europe to Madrid in disguise so that the prince could woo the Infanta in person. At first King Philip IV seemed to be delighted, if surprised, by Charles's quixotic action – as, judging by her blushes, was the Infanta – and on 15 July Charles was able to report to his father that 'I, your baby, have, since this conclusion, been with my mistress, and she sits publicly with me at the plays, and within these two or three days shall take place of the Queen as the Princess of England'.[4] As the summer progressed, though, the Spanish king put increasingly unworkable conditions into the marriage treaty. The children of the union would have to be raised as Catholics and the Infanta would have a chapel in London which would be open to anyone who followed her faith. Difficult to swallow, these conditions were made unpalatable when King Philip's advisers let it be known that Spain had no intention of restoring Frederick's position in the Palatinate. The pope, too, had to be involved, as no marriage could take place without his dispensation, but Gregory XV would not issue this without extracting concessions for English Catholics. There were further delays when he died and his successor Urban VIII insisted that the marriage could only take place provided that new Catholic churches were built in every English county.

Charles was clearly infatuated with the Infanta – by then she was less sure of the match to a heretic, saying that she would prefer to enter a convent – but the English delegation was already being badly outmanoeuvred. The high-summer atmosphere in Madrid became so poisonous that Philip insisted that Charles dismiss all his Protestant advisers; this followed an incident when one English courtier, Sir Edmund Verney, later to be Charles's Standard-Bearer, punched a Spanish priest in the face. At the summer's end Charles and his party returned to London amid much national rejoicing in Britain that the marriage would never take place, fear of European papacy being stronger than a royal match. In his history of the period the Earl of Clarendon (the courtier Edward Hyde) described the scenes of jubilation as 'the loudest and most universal over the whole kingdom that the nation had ever been acquainted with'.[5] It was one of the few occasions in British history when a disastrous foreign policy was hailed at home as a wild success.

Such was the air of defiance within the country that when parliament met next in 1624 it voted funds for a limited naval war to be waged against the Spanish, whose long-running conflict with the Dutch had broken out again. Moneys were also found to provide a badly managed expedition to relieve Breda on the island of Walcheren, but under the command of a mercenary called Count Mansfeld it soon foundered and did nothing to discomfit the Habsburg forces. The attempt to take the war to Spain fared little better. As Lord Admiral – he had been appointed to the post in 1618 – Buckingham was put in charge of the operations but, although he had proved to be a skilful administrator who increased the size of the navy from twenty-three to thirty-five serviceable ships, he showed a less sure hand in devising plans to attack Spain.

An amphibious expedition was planned against the Spanish port of Cadiz in October 1625 which hoped to emulate the great victory of the Elizabeth period, but it proved to be an abject failure. Although the fleet managed to get the army ashore the men quickly succumbed to illness and drink, one officer reporting that 'they became so drunk that in my life I never saw such beastliness'.[6] By then James was dead, having succumbed to a stroke in March 1625. By then, too, Charles was king, and in pursuit of a French alliance had married Henrietta Maria, the fifteen-year-old sister of King Louis XIII and a daughter of Henry of Navarre. Still little more than a girl, the French princess had difficulty adapting to her new life and her new role, and the marriage did not get off to a good start, a result of Henrietta Maria's undisguised unhappiness and Charles's unease in her company. In the early months the union was not a thundering success – Henrietta Maria had a foul temper which she refused to curb – but on the credit side it did give Britain an important ally and had allowed Charles to persuade parliament to grant funds for the ill-fated expedition against Cadiz.

During those tense early days of their marriage, Henrietta Maria's presence in London reawakened fears that Charles was guilty of being more Catholic than was wise for his office. His actions had only served to fuel those suspicions. He had married a Catholic princess who brought with her to England a retinue of priests and confessors and then, on his marriage day, he had ordered that the English recusancy laws should be relaxed, thereby removing the necessity for Catholics to attend services conducted by the Church of England. Not unnaturally this caused great offence in parliament. The house's

anger was only assuaged by members anxious to get home to escape
the plague which swept through London in the winter of 1625 and the
spring of 1626.

It was not just his wife whom Charles could not control. He also
experienced difficulties with the 1626 parliament, where the problems
largely centred on one man, Sir John Eliot, a Cornish member who
had emerged as a severe critic of the Cadiz fiasco and was therefore
antagonistic to further military adventures. Once a friend of
Buckingham's – they had spent their youth journeying in Europe –
Eliot was typical of the landowning classes who were becoming
increasingly wearied by the king's handling of parliament. Sincere,
articulate, unbending and prepared to go to prison for his beliefs, he
was a leading light in the impeachment of Buckingham in the
summer of 1626, when parliament tried to charge the king's favourite
with mismanagement of the country's maritime affairs. For their pains
two of the leading members in the move, Eliot and Sir Dudley Digges
(another thorn in Charles's side), were briefly arrested but
Buckingham escaped censure, largely due to the king's undisguised
support. Charles stood beside him in the dock and during the
proceedings connived at Buckingham's appointment as chancellor of
the University of Cambridge.

These moves, and parliament's refusal to supply funds for further
European campaigns, thoroughly irritated Charles, and he began to
display a characteristic which was to remain with him throughout his
life – an exasperated impatience with anyone or anybody who
opposed his wishes. In his reign parliament did not enjoy the
executive powers over the Crown which it would win for itself in the
future, but it was even so an influential body – the House of
Commons had tax-raising powers and was a petitioning body while
all legislation required the consent of the House of Lords. Financial
necessity was the main reason for summoning the Commons, it
having been conceded as early as 1407 that any money bill must have
its origins in parliament and not the Crown, and for that reason James
had been loath to summon parliament too frequently. Charles was
inclined to take a similar course, and as he knew that no parliament
could meet without his summons or remain in being after he
dismissed it, to save Buckingham he dissolved the body in the
summer of 1626. At the same time he decided to act against his wife's

increasingly intemperate espousal of her religion by ordering her French attendants to return to France without further ado. The task was given to Buckingham in a letter dated 7 August:

> I command you send all the French away tomorrow out of the town. If you can by fair means (but stick not long in disputing), otherwise force them away; driving them away like so many wild beasts, until you have shipped them; and so the devil go with them! Let me hear no answer but of the performance of my command.[7]

It was a sullen little party which travelled down to Dover leaving only six servants – her nurse, dresser, baker, pantryman, tailor and cook – to attend the queen – and the expulsion inevitably caused a rift in relations with France. In retaliation Louis XIII ordered the English population in Calais to be arrested and, egged on by Buckingham, Charles began to think in terms of going to war against his brother-in-law, not because his wife was a shrew but because it offered a chance for a Protestant country to strike at the forces of the Counter-Reformation. Quite how a war against the two main Atlantic powers would help the cause was not clear, but for Charles and Buckingham it was a matter of honour and during the early summer of 1627 an amphibious force was assembled to relieve the Huguenot garrison in La Rochelle which was being besieged by French forces under the command of Cardinal Richelieu. All might have been well had Buckingham's force succeeded – a victory usually wipes out bad debts – but, once again, a British army blundered into an ignominious defeat which one contemporary account called 'the greatest and most shamefulest overthrow the English have received since we lost Normandy'. Only 3000 of Buckingham's army of 8000 made it back to English shores.

Shocked by the appearance of so many discharged servicemen, mostly diseased and wounded, on the streets of the country's main ports, members of parliament turned their attention to placing restraints on the Crown's right to wage war. They also vented their wrath once more on the much-hated figure of Buckingham, whom Eliot had cursed as 'the grievance of grievances', and they might have succeeded in unseating him had not a disgruntled officer called Felton assassinated him in Portsmouth a few months later. Not many mourned his passing. Even Charles seemed at first sight to be unmoved, showing complete mastery over his emotions when the news was brought to him at Southwark, but that was for public display. He ordered that the household's morning prayers should continue and only when the service had come to an end did he lock himself away in his chamber, his courtiers noting that he had taken the duke's death 'very heavily'. He was also dismayed by the general rejoicing which accompanied the news and failed to understand why his personal grief had not been replicated by his subjects. This inability to understand the public mood would surface again and again during Charles's lifetime.

The only winner from Felton's assassination was Buckingham's enemy and rival, Sir Richard Weston, a capable if imperious bureaucrat, who was appointed Lord Treasurer in July 1628. His introduction of economies helped to lessen the financial crisis facing the Exchequer by reducing the national debt and he established himself as a powerful figure at court at a time when the king's relations with parliament were faltering. Perhaps in memory of his dead friend, Charles decided to stick to his policies, and in so doing he embarked on the disastrous course which would make his confrontation with parliament even deeper and more intractable. He had already caused outrage by trying to raise money through enforced loans from landowners and imprisoning those who refused to pay, basing his policy on a dubious interpretation of Tudor law. When five of those imprisoned applied for a writ of habeas corpus it was refused because the King's Bench found that it could not be employed against imprisonment ordered by the king ('per speciale mandatum domine regis'). This led to the framing of the Petition of Right, a legal document drawn up by Sir Edward Coke, a member of parliament of the same kidney as Eliot, in response to the confrontation between Crown and parliament over the extent of the royal prerogative. Basically, it forbade the levying of taxes without parliamentary consent, put a stop to arbitrary imprisonment and placed restrictions on martial law. Although Coke declared himself to be 'almost dead for joy' when the petition was accepted in 1628 Charles soon convinced himself that he was simply confirming age-old rights and was not conceding anything new.

Another point of conflict was the king's religious observation, particularly his tendency to support the High Church policies being pursued by William Laud, the ambitious, some would say aggressive and meddlesome, bishop of London. Laud's short stature belied his authority, for he had curried his way into royal favour and, three years into the reign, had emerged as the only churchman of any prominence to have the king's ear. From a modest background he had shone at Oxford, where his antipathy to Puritanism was balanced by his solid learning and piety. He also attracted patrons and progressed steadily through a number of positions to become a privy councillor in 1626 and bishop of London two years later. He encouraged Charles in his trust in the divine right of kings, describing the king as 'the sun' and telling his congregation during one sermon in 1626 that there would be chaos if that order were removed. That same year he caused even greater offence at the state opening of parliament by magnifying the king's authority in both state and Church.

Early in his career, while still at Oxford, Laud had made it clear that in his view Presbyterians were almost as bad as Catholics. It came as little surprise, therefore, that as a bishop he advanced the belief that the Puritans – extreme Protestants opposed to rule by bishops – were dangerous radicals and that the true safety of the Church of England lay in strengthening its episcopacy and creating uniformity of liturgy along Anglican lines. In Church matters he wanted to introduce measures of 'purification' such as moving the communion table from the nave to the east end of the church and placing rails round it, in the Roman style. With the king's support he was able to influence appointments, and he always made sure that successful candidates shared his interests in Arminianism, then currently fashionable as an antidote to the Calvinist belief in predestination (the heresy that individuals are saved or damned before birth).

Named after the Dutch theologian Jacobus Arminius, it ruled that Jesus Christ had died to save all men and that divine sovereignty is compatible with man's free will. Because it rejected Calvinism it had split opinion in the reformed Church and its supporters were held to be 'popish', that is, inclining their beliefs to the Catholic Church and therefore contrary to the spirit of the Reformation. In the eyes of those who distrusted the king, the fact that Charles had a close relationship with Laud and his Arminian beliefs could only mean one thing: that he was a closet supporter of Catholicism. Why else would he marry a popish wife (who was so rigid in her belief that she refused to defile her beliefs by attending his coronation); and why else had he refused to make more effort to assist the Protestant cause in Europe?

With parliament turning its face against him, with religious observation changing from a question of faith to a point of confrontation, and disasters multiplying in Europe, Charles was about to face the first crisis of his reign, one which had already been foreseen by the Earl of Bristol, Britain's ambassador in Madrid who had been recalled by Charles in the aftermath of the Infanta debacle for being overfamiliar with the Spanish court:

> In all our enterprises lately we have been as he that shoots against marble, whose arrow rebounds back upon himself. The Lord has not gone forth with our armies. We have been like the broken staff of Egypt to all that have relied upon us.[8]

The first check came on 2 March 1629, when the third parliament in four years refused Charles's injunction to adjourn in order to continue a heated debate about the king's right to collect customs duties which the members held to be contrary to the Petition of Right. Their anger had been fuelled by the growing public disquiet over Laud's policies and the language of the members became increasingly intemperate – Catholics were castigated as 'the enemy' and bishops were dismissed as 'spiritual dogs'. As matters got out of hand Black Rod tried in vain to gain entry to the chamber while the Speaker, Sir John Finch, was held in his chair by two prominent members, Benjamin Valentine and Denzil Holles, their aim being to make sure that the debate continued. The members' arrogant behaviour enraged Charles, who ordered that parliament be dissolved, and such was his anger that many people thought that this time the rupture might be terminal. On 10 March 1629 Charles set down his reasons in a lengthy proclamation which reminded the people of England that while 'princes are not bound to give account of their actions, but to God alone', he wanted to reveal the 'truth and sincerity' of his actions:

> We do not impute these disasters to the whole House of Commons, knowing that there were among them many religious, graver and well-minded men; but the sincerer and better part of the

House was overborne by the practices and clamours of the other, who, careless of their duties, and taking advantage of the times and our necessities, have enforced us to break off this meeting; which, had it been answered with like duty on their parts as it was invited and begun with love on ours, might have proved happy and glorious both to us and this whole nation.[9]

Warrants were issued for the arrest of Holles, Valentine and Eliot, who were all fined heavily for their roles in the fracas. Eliot refused to pay and tried to use parliamentary privilege when he was examined. Condemned to the Tower of London, he died of consumption in 1632 and was interred where he spent his final days, Charles having refused his family's petition for the release of his body for burial in Cornwall. He was the first casualty in the king's long-drawn-out quarrel with parliament.

Chapter Two

THE PERSONAL RULE

'How elegantly your Majesty doth dispose your vacant hours,
with your joy in chivalry and the use of the Great Horse.
Musick, both instrumental and vocal, under you grows every
day more regular, and in hunting, the image of war, you exercise
your vigorous spirits.'

Sir Henry Wotton, A Panegyrick of King Charles, *1633*

In taking the decision to dismiss parliament in March 1629 Charles
introduced a period which came to be known by his supporters as his
'personal rule', a time when the king governed England by royal
prerogative with the support of his privy councillors. To others who were
sceptical of the king's policies, his popish leanings and his insistence on
the divine right of kings it was the beginning of a time which was also
described as the 'eleven years' tyranny', for it would not be until 1640 that
the king was forced to summon the House of Commons to help raise
funds for another war, this time to be waged against his Scottish subjects.
In fact the personal rule got off to a reasonably good start in England.
The Puritans might have thought Arminianism the work of the devil,
but many ordinary people responded to the more formal approach to
their religion and happily embraced Laud's changes. Others thought that
parliament had overreached itself, but there was also universal relief that
the quarrel with Spain and France had been ended with the passing of
peace treaties in 1629 and 1630. Even the war in Europe seemed to be less
of a problem as it slumped into stalemate after the death of Gustavus
Adolphus at Lützen in 1632.

The mood was marked by a thaw in Charles's marriage with Henrietta Maria. Perhaps the absence of Buckingham had something to do with it, or perhaps by dismissing her French courtiers Charles had displayed a mastery of temperament hitherto lacking in the relationship, but the decade of the personal rule proved to be a happy one for the couple. Her English improved and she became more gracious in dealing with the manners and customs of her adopted country. She fell pregnant, too, and although the first child miscarried she gave birth to a strapping boy in May 1630, the occasion being greeted with great rejoicing in London and bonfires lit across the three kingdoms. He was christened with his father's name. Another six children followed and the royal family became further extended when Charles agreed to look after Buckingham's brood. At the time there was thought to be little passion in the marriage, the evidence consisting of Charles's refusal to take a mistress and the decorous ambience he encouraged at court, but this is hardly borne out by Henrietta Maria's recollections of that period. 'I was the happiest and most fortunate of queens, for not only had I every pleasure the heart could desire,' she wrote in later years when she was a widow in France, 'I had a husband who adored me.'[1]

However, given the queen's attachment to the Catholic Church there was always going to be an insurmountable problem in convincing doubters that she was not using her position for missionary-cum-strategic purposes. Under the terms of her marriage settlement the queen was permitted freedom of worship in her own chapel, but there was a suspicion, difficult to erase, that she was more committed to her religion than a British queen should be. Her eldest child Charles accompanied her to mass, as did her second son James, who was born in 1633, and she was surrounded by a number of Catholics, all charming and therefore all thought to be influential. Gregorio Panzani, the pope's emissary, was one of that number, George Con, his Irish successor, another. Following the treaty with France in 1630 Henrietta Maria was also allowed to have twelve Capuchin priests in her household, and they proved to be ready promoters of their faith, winning over a number of courtiers' wives with a mixture of godliness and seductiveness which the ladies concerned found utterly compelling. Even Charles was moved by the priests' style and the passionate intensity which visiting preachers such as the bishop of Angoulême brought to the services. As one of the Capuchins, Father Cyprien, reported to his superiors, the masses and the beauty of the interior of the queen's chapel had a great effect on court life:

> After dinner [on 10 December 1636] Her Majesty went to attend vespers, compline and the sermon. The musicians, having perceived the satisfaction with which the charming melody of their singing afforded the Queen, were animated to such a degree that they far surpassed what they had done in the morning. After vespers Monsignor de Peron [Bishop of Angoulême] ascended the pulpit, and delivered a very learned, very eloquent and very pathetic sermon on this text of the Psalms: 'This is the Lord's doing, and it is marvellous in our eyes'. He dwelt with wonderful force upon the grace which God vouchsafed to the Queen to have a Catholic Church, with liberty to have the whole divine service performed here, after it had been abolished and forbidden for so many years in all England, Ireland and Scotland. The sermon being finished with the satisfaction of the Queen, with the applause of the whole audience, which was very large, her Majesty retired. Those who were in the chapel had great difficulty to leave it on account of the crowd of people who were bent on forcing their way to see the magnificence displayed there. The crush lasted so long that it was impossible to close the doors of the church till the third night, when the King gave orders that it should be cleared of strangers, for he was desirous to be himself a spectator of that magnificent representation.[2]

All might have been well had Charles been able to counter his wife's proselytising and keep it under control and discreet, but in his diffident way he let matters be, one reason being that he liked his wife's Catholic courtiers and could relax in their company. He was not a Roman Catholic himself, nor did he ever come close to embracing the faith: when he used the word 'Catholic' of himself and his beliefs he was using it in the sense of belonging to the Church universal. The Capuchins might have deluded themselves into believing that one day the king would take England back into the fold of Rome, but that was pure fantasy. Charles indulged Catholics and did nothing to discourage his wife's crypto-Catholic missionary activities; it also cannot be denied that he was an enemy of Puritanism, but that polarity of interests – tolerance of Catholicism and dislike of Calvinism – did not mean that he was leading the country down a 'popish' road. Rather, as he admitted on the scaffold at the end of his life, his sole concern had always been with the maintenance of doctrine and discipline within the Anglican Church. As the defender of faith and head of the Church of England he wanted to uphold uniformity of worship and rule by bishops.

Some of the king's more attractive personal qualities also became apparent during the decade. He emerged as a patron of the arts and added substantially to the royal collection by purchasing the paintings of the Dukes of Mantua, a good decision which brought to London the work of Raphael, Titian (*Entombment*), Correggio (*Marriage of St Catherine*) and Mantegna (*Triumph of Julius Caesar*). In so doing his agents managed to outbid Richelieu by spending a grand total of £18,200, quite a coup considering that the cardinal was no mean collector himself. That Charles had a discerning eye was made clear by his later purchase of the Raphael cartoons, and he was encouraged in his cultural tastes by Peter Paul Rubens, who came to London as a diplomatic representative of Spain and whose painted ceiling of the Banqueting House in Whitehall is a wondrous celebration of the power and glory of kings.

By then in middle age, Rubens was one of the great European figures of his day, an artist who was also a diplomat, an aesthete who was also a man of action. Ideally Charles would have liked him to stay in London as court painter, but Rubens was too grand and too restless to remain for long in one location. Instead, in 1632, the position went to Anthony Van Dyck, a young Flemish painter whose name became inseparable from Charles's. An indefatigable worker, 'the picture drawer' produced a string of portraits of the royal family, and in so doing bequeathed to history a good idea of their physical looks and the settled dignity of life at court. Dismissed by many as a flatterer who was only intent on lining his pockets, Van Dyck's portrait of the king in three positions – in profile, full face and half face – rises above that criticism to give probably the best representation of Charles in mid-life, conveying as it does the king's known sensitivity and, not least, the famous elongated Stewart nose.

As a renovator of the royal residences, albeit a modest one, Charles also encouraged architecture. At Greenwich Inigo Jones designed a pavilion for Henrietta Maria, creating a Palladian building in sprawling parklands which was both severely attractive and functional. Somerset House was restored and his father's Banqueting House in the warren of royal apartments in Whitehall was changed out of all recognition by the addition of the Rubens ceilings. The classical style matched the sense of order which Charles encouraged at his court: in place of his father's bawdy behaviour and the atmosphere of licence there was new 'splendour and liberality' which visiting ambassadors and courtiers applauded. There was a substantial household and the costs were high – around half of his annual income of £500,000 was spent on maintaining the court to a standard which reflected Charles's sense of order and personal decorum. Suddenly etiquette became very important, and according to Rubens strict rules – much more rigidly exacted than in any other European court of the day – became the order of the day. During the trial of the Earl of Castlehaven on charges of rape and sodomy Charles was so disgusted by the proceedings that he banned women from attending them 'upon pain of ever after being reputed to have forfeited their modesty'.

In a sense the imposition of new standards of behaviour was as much a declaration of intent as anything else. Ever fastidious and shy of close friendships, the close platonic relationship with Buckingham being an exception, Charles liked having people around him but they had to keep their distance and betray no familiarity; he valued his privacy and was concerned to protect it. As fond of the hunt as his father ever was, he made a regular progression round stately homes in the great hunting counties of Northamptonshire, Leicestershire and Huntingdonshire, where he insisted that the meets and the subsequent entertainment should be kept within sensible proportions. Gone was the grossness of his father's court, and excess gave way to the restraint which Charles encouraged his court to practise at all times.

The theatre, too, became a craze and Charles's court was renowned throughout Europe for the lavishness of its masques, some of the best of which had been fashioned by the playwright Ben Jonson and the poet Thomas Campion, a favourite of his father's era. A combination of opera, drama and, above all, the decorative arts, masques were sumptuous and expensive private affairs which delighted the senses by emphasising themes such as courtly love and pastoral or mythological relationships. In their time they were deservedly popular, not least because parts were often played by members of the court and spectators were usually encouraged to participate in the dancing. For Charles, the cultivated side of his life was supposed to mirror the blessings of his public rule and, catching the mood, an army of Royalist poets put the new sense of optimism into verses which spoke of harmony, courtly gallantry and graceful wit. Encouraged by the example of Ben Jonson, who died in 1637 before Charles's reign ran into trouble, the so-called 'Cavalier poets' included Thomas Carew, Richard Lovelace, Sir John Suckling, Edmund Waller and Robert Herrick.

Outside the court life was equally harmonious, and while Clarendon was probably overindulging himself when he wrote that the decade of the personal rule was one of 'universal tranquillity' there is literary evidence to suggest that England enjoyed a period of sufficient peace and prosperity for it to be remembered fondly as a golden age.[3] Partly, the sentiment was enhanced by the decade of civil strife which followed. Partly, too, there is a tendency for writers, especially poets in receipt of patronage, to make the king the subject of grandiose praise-poems and to indulge in nostalgia for calmer and more prosperous times, but there is also much substance in their literary conceits. Albeit hardly a disinterested observer, Father Cyprien was fulsome in his praise for his adopted country. He told his superiors in France that 'England is an abundant country, and has no taxes; the inhabitants lead a luxurious life, far removed from the poverty of other places'.[4] Compared to what was happening in Germany, still ravaged by the depredations of the conflicting armies, England was enjoying what Thomas Carew called 'halcyon days' – words also used in several contemporary diaries to describe that period of Charles's reign:

> Tourneys, masques, theatres better became
> Our halcyon days; what though the German drum
> Bellow for freedom and revenge, the noise
> Concerns not us, nor should divert our joys;
> Nor should the thunder of their carabins
> Drown the sweet air of tun'd violins.[5]

The absence of war fuelled the feeling enunciated by Carew and others. At the beginning of the 1630s Gustavus Adolphus's victories and the treaty with France had eased fears that England would be the next country to fall victim to the powers of the Counter-Reformation. This was not just paranoia: through popular and widely read publications such as the *Swedish Intelligencer* people were remarkably well-informed about the events in Europe, making the Thirty Years War not just a distant drum but a conflict whose echoes were being heard much closer to home. One of its many readers was a young Huntingdonshire squire, Oliver Cromwell, who, in common with others of his class and generation, regarded Gustavus as a total hero and the banner-bearer of the Protestant cause.

Unfortunately the certainties were not so evident in the king's attitude to those who served him, the statesmen closest to the throne. In 1633 he appointed William Laud archbishop of Canterbury, a move which gave the meddlesome churchman tremendous authority which he used, inter alia, to root out Puritanism and to support his belief in the Church Catholic. In addition to reforming the Church of England and pushing through the innovations which frightened those of a Puritan disposition who believed that they were being introduced as a preliminary to returning to the fold of Rome, Laud's voice was heeded and feared. At his behest the Court of the Star Chamber mounted a series of vituperative prosecutions against arch-Puritans and opponents of the episcopacy and outlawed justification by faith and Sabbatarianism, both tenets of the reformed churches. While some of the cases were trivial or merely bizarre, one prosecution conducted in 1637 became infamous. It involved three defendants, all of whom had had brushes with authority – John Bastwick, a doctor from Colchester, a half-cracked lawyer called William Prynne, whose book *Histriomatix* had wildly attacked any form of enjoyment, and Henry Burton, who had preached against 'advancers of popery, superstition and idolatry'.

Earlier, in February 1634, Prynne had been sentenced to have his ears cropped, and this savage punishment was repeated for all three men, who were also sentenced to periods of imprisonment. The terrible torture and the forbearance shown by the three defendants had a somewhat different effect to what Laud and his colleagues in the Star Chamber might have anticipated. Even outside the Puritan community Bastwick, Prynne and Burton were treated as martyrs, many holding to the view that the trial and punishment displayed a vindictiveness which ill became the spiritual head of the Church of England. But the most prophetic voice belonged to the Venetian ambassador. He thought that 'this pest may be the one which will ultimately disturb the kingdom'.[6] Not that Catholics were spared by the court. A year later, one William Pickering was fined £5000 and had his tongue pierced with an awl after he had accused all Protestants of being heretics and devils. Laud was nothing if not consistent.

Backed by his friend and protégé Bishop William Juxon of London, who had been appointed Lord Treasurer, the Primate of All England also exercised considerable temporal power. Laud was a member of the Privy Council and a commissioner of the Treasury and he used his influence to become, in reality, Charles's first minister, a position which led some to think of him as England's Richelieu, Louis XIII's cardinal and statesman. In fact the comparison is unfair for, whereas Richelieu's policies created the power which gave substance to the French throne and provided France with a commanding position in Europe, Laud was more concerned with details than with the wider picture. To his credit, though, Laud had a reformer's instincts and used his appointment as Chancellor of Oxford University in 1630 to push through long-lasting and beneficial changes in the institution's statutes and management. Among his innovations was the creation of a chair in Arabic.

Secure in the king's support, yet never a close friend, he also believed in his own omnipotence and, fatally, he took little interest in winning over those who differed from him. For all his loyalty, his hard work and his incorruptibility, he could appear donnish and self-righteous and was unhappy about taking advice from others, reserving a sarcastic tongue for those who differed from him. As a recent historian described him, in military terms he was more of a sergeant-major than a major-general, more intent on chasing up policies than directing them.[7] For example, while he supported the expansion of the navy and the collection of ship money to pay for it, his reasons had less to do with Britain's maritime pretensions in the wider world than with the need to scourge the curse of piracy around Britain's coasts.

Admittedly piracy was endemic around England's southern

coastline. Hardly a week went by without some outrage and the authorities were powerless to halt the depredations. Just as bad was the practice of selling captured English men and women into slavery which had become such a lucrative business in the Mediterranean. While Turkish and Algerian pirates prospered, Britain was impotent, and the need to create a modern navy had become too obvious to be ignored, chiefly because it was essential to protect the country's growing trading interests. Charles was sufficiently convinced to insist that the navy be expanded and equipped with modern vessels, and he took a great interest in the construction, manning and training of the fleet.

To raise the necessary funds the powers of the Ship Money system of taxation were extended in 1634. Devised as a communal means of defence, it enabled coastal communities to combine to construct ships to defend themselves, and as the charges were assessed on property and land it was held to be generally fair. However when Charles, supported by Laud, extended its collection to inland areas it became unpopular, though not so odious as the famous resistance of John Hampden would make later generations believe. An unyielding parliamentarian who had played a prominent part in the creation of the Petition of Right, Hampden challenged the imposition of Ship Money in the Court of Exchequer in 1637, a move which cemented his reputation as a champion of individual liberties. In fact his case was lost and the law was upheld, but that did not detract from the symbolism of a commoner, albeit a landowner, taking on the might of majesty and questioning Laud's assertion that the tax was 'the most necessary and most honourable business that ever was set on foot in my memory'.[8]

Laud's main ally was another man who would have a profound effect on the course of the king's reign: Sir Thomas Wentworth, a Yorkshire landowner and member of parliament who had been a leading supporter of the Petition of Right before coming to the conclusion that the country's good governance could only be maintained through respect for the king and the dignity of the Crown. Not only did he come to terms with Charles's personal rule but he extolled it as 'the keystone which closeth up the arch and order of government, which contains each part in due relation to the whole, and which once shaken and informed, all the frame falls together into a confused heap of foundation and battlement, of strength and beauty'. An industrious bureaucrat who could be as hard on himself as he was on those who served him, Wentworth took little heed of the opinions of others. (Clarendon said of him 'he wholly relied upon himself, and discerning many defects in most men, he too much neglected what they said or did'.)[9] One word marked everything that he did or thought. Wentworth based his political beliefs on a policy which he called 'thorough' – the complete disregard of private interests with a view to the establishment, for the good of the whole community, of the royal power as the embodiment of the state – and it was to take him far. Tellingly, he had also attracted the attention of Richard Weston, Earl of Portland and the Lord Treasurer. The two men shared a belief that Spain should be an important ally; it was Weston who attacted Wentworth into the orbit of the court in 1628, following the proroguing of parliament. (Later that support drained away as Weston began to believe, not without cause, that Wentworth coveted his job.) Appointed a baron, Wentworth rose quickly, becoming Lord President of the North in 1631, a position he used to display his competence as a man of affairs. Two years later, in the year that Laud was raised to the see of Canterbury, Wentworth was sent to Ireland as Lord Deputy, the king's representative with plenipotentiary powers.

It was an appointment which would have long-lasting repercussions. Despite the difference in their background and age – Wentworth was twenty years younger than Laud – the two men became allies. The Irish appointment drew them closer together as Laud became the conduit for Wentworth at court, often softening Wentworth's letters to the king, for the Lord Deputy was a prickly man who was not altogether sure if Charles entirely trusted him. (He was right to feel that way, and not just because Henrietta Maria complained to her husband that Wentworth had ugly hands. Throughout his time in Ireland Wentworth bombarded the king with demands to be raised to the peerage to silence his critics, but he had to wait until 1639 before he was made Earl of Strafford.) In return for the archbishop's helping hand Wentworth supported Laud's attempts to bring the Protestant Church of Ireland into line with Anglican usages by forcing them to surrender their Calvinist canons stressing predestination in favour of a new set based on the Thirty-Nine Articles. Needless to say, it was not a popular move.

Ireland did not figure very highly in Charles's ambitions; indeed he had never set foot in the country. His attitude was governed as much by political necessity as by history, for Ireland had proved to be a troublesome possession ever since it had come into the Crown's hands during the reign of Henry II. Not until the 'Flight of the Earls' in 1607 had the country been completely subdued and brought under British control when the heads of the great native Ulster families of O'Neill and O'Donnell fled from their lands in Donegal, Tyrone, Cavan, Fermanagh and Armagh, leaving them to be occupied by English and Scottish 'planters'. This new process of plantation, the latest in a long line of English colonial expansionist policies, had begun two years after the Ulster chiefs left Ireland. The methodology was encapsulated in the Articles of Plantation which offered cheap land to be sold in parish-sized lots of one to two thousand acres, mainly in the country between Derry and Coleraine.

Over a third of the country was still owned by Old English families of Norman extraction, Catholic in faith yet owing their loyalty to the Crown. They were prepared to accept the new order and could have been natural allies, but the main thrust of English policy lay in the plantations, forcing out the wild native Irish with their Gaelic tongue, their Catholicism and their dangerous links to the European Counter-Reformation, and replacing them with Presbyterians. Some Gaels managed to stay on as labourers and tenants, an abject underclass, sullen and waiting for any chance to strike back. Colonising Ireland in this way was a simple act of faith and one which attracted Wentworth's approval: if the Irish would not embrace Protestantism, then the Protestants would swallow up Ireland and turn it into an industrious and God-fearing society. By 1638 there were 20,000 Scottish settlers in Ulster alone, although the number may have been higher.[10]

Being an administrator at heart, Wentworth warmed to the task of governing Ireland, even though he admitted to friends that he was dismayed at finding himself 'in the society of a strange people' and depressed by Dublin's shabby streets. The distance between the two capitals also helped him by providing the illusion that he had plenipotentiary powers: letters could take up to a fortnight to arrive and travelling by ship and coach produced a tiring journey lasting anything up to three weeks. Because Wentworth had been given direct powers he was able to act without too much recourse to London, and his first step was to introduce a system of government which would divide the main power groups. In so doing he contrived to upset everyone. The Old English quickly found that they could no longer use parliament to defend themselves against unwelcome policies, as they had contrived to do so often in the past: when that largely inoffensive body was convened in 1634 Wentworth made sure that its agenda was laid down by himself. Unable to provide any opposition, the Old English faction were discomfited further by Wentworth's repudiation of the 'Graces', the guarantees and concessions on land ownership promised by Charles to the Old English families in 1628 in return for loans to fund his futile campaigns against Spain. Even the new landowners suffered through taxation on their (admittedly large) profits.

In pursuit of the policy of forcibly removing the native Irish from their lands and sweeping away their customs, language and religion, further plantations were planned in Connacht. As an example of Wentworth's 'thorough' policies, this systematic colonisation of Ireland made sense, for not only did it extend royal authority but it could also be a civilising influence. As the Lord Deputy told his king, 'plantations must be the only means under God and your majesty to reform this subject as well in religion as in manners'.[11] In addition to extending the plantations he also made it his business to challenge land titles whenever they became available. Only in Galway was the process halted when the Earl of Clanricarde succeeded in pleading with Charles to have his lands excluded.

Many of the newcomers also suffered, for under Laud's guidance Wentworth was equally hard on any religion which smacked of Puritanism. In Ulster the Presbyterian Church, which had been imported from Scotland, had restrictions placed on it as a result of its anti-episcopalian leanings and ministers were excluded from their parishes if they did not accept the new articles. In addition, many of the planters were fined for not keeping to the conditions by which they received their grants of land. Wentworth's policy was clear: he kept any opposition divided yet, with an optimism that would not be confirmed by subsequent events, he hoped that the day would dawn when the Irish people would learn to live in harmony. In return he promoted the Irish linen trade, regularised customs taxes, built up a powerful army and took steps to extirpate piracy around Ireland's coasts, just as he had promised Charles he would do shortly after taking up his position:

> The reasons which moved me were the consideration of our commodious situation; the increase of trade and shipping in these parts of your dominions, which seem now only to want foreign commerce to make them a civil, rich and contented people; and consequently more easily governed by Your Majesty's ministers and the more profitably for your Crown than in a savage and poor condition.[12]

Those aims were largely achieved but the improvements were outweighed by his capacity to alienate just about every section of Irish society. He might have promised Charles that all was well in Ireland and that its people were 'well satisfied, if not delighted' by the measures being taken on their behalf, but beneath that apparent tranquillity the country was seething. Not for the first or last time, an English ruler had severely misjudged the mood of the Irish.

Charles had the opportunity to appoint Wentworth Lord Treasurer when Weston died in 1635, and had he been permitted to pursue his 'thorough' policies in England, the country's finances might have been better ordered than they were during the personal rule. It was not to be. The king never warmed to Wentworth, partly because he did not altogether trust him and partly because he was exasperated by his constant demands for advancement, and the appointment eventually went to Bishop Juxon, who was faced with a thankless task. In the absence of parliament Charles had to raise revenues through the Privy Council's interpretation of the law, and inevitably the process led to acrimony. The granting of monopolies and patents caused widespread discontent, as did the taxation of knighthoods and forestry. Ship Money, too, had been unpopular and its collection by sheriffs' writ had been inefficient and widely resented. A three-year cycle of plague between 1636 and 1639 also dampened spirits and added to local financial burdens. While none of these impositions was sufficient to create unrest, they did provide an undertow of rancour which lay uneasily beneath the certainties of court life with its patronage and strict courtesies.

As yet, though, there was neither an identifiable constitutional opposition to the regime in England nor any hint that unrest was in the offing. Most historians of the period are agreed that during Charles's personal rule England was a secure and homogeneous society and that it was hardly the tyranny which critics have made it out to be – as late as May 1640 Wentworth was able to reassure Charles that 'the quiet of England will hold out long'. Despite the complaints about taxation and the concerns about religious toleration (especially the opposition of Puritans to episcopalianism), moderation was still the order of the day – except in Ireland, where Wentworth's policies of divide and rule were shortly to have disastrous consequences. However, the first assault on Charles's personal rule, the spark which started the conflagration, came not from Ireland, which plunged into an orgy of arson and massacre in 1641, but from his other Celtic kingdom, Scotland.

Chapter Three

THE CROWN AND THE KIRK

'How could the Scots and we be enemies Grown?'

*Abraham Cowley, lines on King Charles's return
from Scotland, July 1633*

For a ruler who was born in Scotland and who had in James Stewart
a thoroughly Scottish father, Charles was never attracted to his fellow
countrymen. Apart from close aristocratic friends such as his cousin
the Duke of Lennox and the anglicised Duke of Hamilton, he had
little time for his northern subjects and made few attempts to
understand them or to give substance to their political and religious
aspirations. There was also a question of style. Despite his heritage –
Charles could write and speak in his native tongue with the best of
them – the Scots seemed to be an alien people, their nobles rough-
mannered and uncouth, so different from the formality of the court
in London. In short, Charles considered the Scots to be boorish,
almost comically so, and he shied away from their overfamiliarity,
finding them backward, sullen and lacking in courtly manners. Just
as bad, he did not trust them, especially the wild Highlanders who,
he felt, would be better off settled in distant Nova Scotia.

Charles's views ill became the monarch of a kingdom whose crowns
his father had united with so little rancour. Had his feelings been
confined to personal antipathy he might have been excused, but all

too often Charles allowed his emotions to overcome good sense, with alarming results for his authority. After coming to the throne he made his preferences perfectly clear by putting off his acceptance of the Scottish Crown, thereby causing great offence to his northern subjects. By the time he came to remedy that defect eight years after his accession the stage seemed to be set for a political and religious confrontation which Robert Baillie, a young Scots minister and diarist, feared might turn into a 'a bloody civil war' of the kind that was ravaging Europe.[1] The tragedy was that the events were set in train by Charles's refusal to take seriously a country which should have been a natural supporter of his rule.

At the time of his succession Scotland had been relatively docile and peaceful, a state of affairs that was very different from the internecine squabbling and anarchy which had been its lot in the previous century. Then the Stewart kings had had good reason to fear for their succession, such was their nobles' propensity to indulge in bullying and blackmail, not to say abduction, to get their own way. For the first time in many years the once all-powerful nobility had put aside violence in favour of an uneasy coexistence with their lord and master the king, the parliament was under royal control and, despite economic stagnation and a recent period of famine, there was a general air of contentment and stability. That the country should have been in a such a happy state of affairs owed everything to its previous king, James VI of Scotland and I of Great Britain. Following the union of the two crowns in 1603 he might have ruled from London but his writ ran over the border and, vitally for his authority, it was heeded. 'This I must say for Scotland and truly vaunt it,' he boasted famously four years later. 'Here I sit and govern with my pen: I write and it is done: and by a Clerk of the Council I govern Scotland, which others could not do by the Sword.'[2]

There was much to his bold contention, for James was schooled in that most vital of the sovereign arts, realpolitik. Flexible in his approach, he promoted a closer union between his two kingdoms but he still allowed Scotland to retain provisions for the law, religion and civil administration – privileges which were jealously guarded north of the border. A Privy Council managed Scottish affairs and he kept the old-established nobility happy through the skilful manipulation of court patronage. He also possessed a sure touch. The Church was brought under stricter control through an episcopate which was within the gift of the Crown but, despite his personal belief that bishops should govern the Church, James knew when to leave matters as they were. In 1618 he forced a General Assembly of the Church of Scotland to accept the Five Articles of Perth, which insisted on changes in liturgical practice including kneeling at communion and observance of the Christian year. However, when this innovation caused such outcry that it smacked of 'papist tendencies', James was forced to back down and the limitations were never introduced.

For the most part, James's Scottish subjects were proud of the fact that there was a Scottish king sitting on the throne of a united Britain, and after his death in 1625 Scots looked back with genuine regret to the rule of 'the wisest fool in Christendom'. A prolific author, James produced works on political theory, witchcraft, and on the evils of tobacco, and he was a proficient poet who gave patronage to a school of court poets known, somewhat self-consciously, as the Castalian Band. He was also responsible for the creation of the Authorised Version of the Holy Bible which appeared in 1611. It remains one of his finest monuments.

As a ruler James had come through a hard school of knocks. His reign had begun badly, in that he had been raised to the throne by the same nobles who had demanded his mother's, Mary Queen of Scots', abdication, and he had to endure a number of indignities during his youth and education. A boyhood favourite, his cousin Esmé Stewart, was thought to be influencing him towards Catholicism, and as a result James was held in solitary confinement for the better part of a year. Although he had to contend with further plots and disruption he showed considerable dexterity in checking the power of the leading Scottish families, and by the beginning of the seventeenth century had emerged as master of his destiny. His succession to Elizabeth's throne only served to increase his prestige and gave him the security and peace of mind that had been absent in his younger years. Shrewd and intelligent, James was able to keep his two kingdoms separate but equal and, to a great extent, reasonably contented.

His son, from the very outset, displayed an uncertain touch in dealing with the prickly civic and religious leaders of his northern kingdom. Like his father he continued to govern through the Privy Council led by a triumvirate of trusted magnates, the Earl of Mar

(Lord Treasurer), Thomas Hamilton, Earl of Melrose and from 1627 Earl of Haddington (President of the Court of Session), and Sir George Hay of Kingfauns (Lord Chancellor), but his relationship with that body, which met in Edinburgh, was distant and secretive. The council simply carried out the wishes of the absent monarch and its members resented the fact that they had no active part in governing the country. They also came to suspect interference in their affairs from London, and although this was unfair, as Charles did not allow the English Privy Council to discuss Scottish business, a belief grew that their counsels counted for nothing. The fact that Charles lived in, and operated from, distant London did not help matters, the exchange of letters being a poor substitute for personal contact and debate. At best it took a week for letters to reach Edinburgh from London. Increasingly, the English court was felt to be the focus of power and as time went by the Scottish nobility felt excluded from it. True, the country's interests were represented by a Scottish Secretary of State, but as the holder of that post, William Alexander, Earl of Stirling, a career politician and minor poet, lived in London, he could hardly be said to be in touch with everyday Scottish affairs of state.

All this might not have mattered had Charles felt any affection for Scotland or had he displayed some of his father's earthy, hard-drinking love of life and the sly intelligence which appealed to the Scots nobility, but as Angelo Correr, the Venetian envoy to London, noted after the succession, 'King James made much of the Scots while his son is close-fisted with them'.[3] Nervous and unsure of himself, Charles could appear cold and aloof, character flaws which were heartily disliked by the Scots, who mistook his formal public manner for rudeness. In his witty and anecdotal autobiography *History of My Own Times*, Gilbert Burnet* captured the contrasts in the style of the two courts:

> [Charles] was much offended with King James's light and familiar way, which was the effect of hunting and drinking, on which occasions he was very apt to forget his dignity, and to break out

---

*Gilbert Burnet, 1643–1715, was educated in Aberdeen and was minister of Saltoun in East Lothian. Dismissed as Charles II's chaplain he went into exile and on the accession of William of Orange was appointed bishop of Salisbury.

into great indecencies: on the other hand the solemn gravity of the court of Spain was more suited to his own temper which was sullen even to a moroseness.[4]

There were other and more fundamental differences. Charles was a firm believer in the divine right of anointed kings, but whereas his father had known when to trim his beliefs, Charles held them absolutely. Worse, he began his reign by attempting to introduce a number of policies north of the border which did nothing but cause trouble, mainly because he betrayed his own ignorance of Scottish susceptibilities. Just as bad, he was under the impression that he understood the Scots, 'our ancient and native kingdom', and that the changes were in the best interests of the country. He was also badly advised by his closest English counsellors, notably and fatefully by Archbishop Laud, and he took little account of local opposition even when he realised that his policies were causing offence.

First, there was the vexed and confused question of the revocations, a legal process which permitted a new king to revoke grants and gifts made to the nobility during his minority. At the time this was accepted practice, not least because during the previous two centuries every Scottish monarch had succeeded as a minor, but Charles decided to take the matter further by extending the revocations to all gifts made since 1542, the accession of Mary Queen of Scots, which could be claimed by the Crown. Whatever the rights or the wrongs of the matter – Charles believed that he was restoring order to a confused legal situation – such a sweeping decision was guaranteed to upset the Scottish nobility, mainly because it entailed the surrender of lucrative property and incomes.

The Scottish nobles were outraged further by the secretive manner in which the decision was taken. Whereas James had always been open to debate and met regularly with his subjects at court, his son could appear distant and, to his proud Scottish nobles at least, discourteous. To be legal the revocations had to be passed before Charles reached his twenty-fifth birthday in November 1625, which meant that he had to introduce the act shortly after his accession to the throne in March that same year. Even so he could have stilled fears by explaining his intentions, but when his Scottish privy councillors travelled to London to discuss the matter in January 1626 they were disconcerted to discover that they were being presented with a fait accompli. Unused to the new courtly manners, they were discommoded by being asked to remain standing while Charles sat and had to kneel before speaking, behaviour which was unknown north of the border. The net result produced the impression that the king was merely holding an audience to announce a decision.

At stake was a huge amount of Church property which the king wanted to be taken out of the hands of the nobility to provide a machinery which would give adequate stipends for the clergy. However, in addition to bringing some financial benefit to the Crown it would inevitably lead to a reduction in the nobility's land holdings; among those who stood to lose most were men like Haddington, upon whom Charles depended for the good governance of Scotland. Although there was much sense in the proposals, which were by no means as radical as they were made out to be, for the Church property was not to be completely surrendered but would be held by the Crown 'upon reasonable conditions', such was the suspicion created by the revocations that Charles only succeeded in alienating a class of people who should have been supporting him. As it turned out, few nobles surrendered land and in February 1627 Charles was forced to concede that Crown leases would be repurchased over ten years, the profits being used to subsidise Church stipends. Nonetheless the nobles never forgave Charles, and a feeling grew that his 'mischief' had led to the 'alienation of the subjects hearts from their prince, and laid open a way to rebellion'.[5]

More was to follow during that first winter of Charles's reign. First he insisted that members of the Privy Council could not also be judges in the Court of Session (the main civil court), at one stroke removing many astute legal minds from the council. Although the move allowed the councillors to concentrate on their own work while freeing the Court of Session from nobles who had little understanding of the law, it caused great resentment in Edinburgh, most particularly among the seventeen men who sat on both bodies. Once again Haddington was the loser: not only was he president of the Court of Session but two of his brothers were also members. From Charles's point of view he was breaking the influence of the great landowners in a court in which key decisions would be taken; at the same time he wished to weaken the purpose of the Privy Council and to hamper its opposition to the revocations. But to the legal profession, many of whose members belonged to the nobility, the king was guilty of removing judges for no other reason than that he wanted to do so. It also did not escape their notice that the reform would entail them losing their exemption from paying tax.

To rub salt into an already raw wound, the king ordered that henceforth judges of the Court of Session had to ride to hearings on horseback, a difficult and dangerous procedure in the Scottish capital's narrow and precipitous streets. James would never have done that. When the Scottish nobility complained about the changes to the administration of their courts of law, which they felt were as much an affront to their dignity as an encroaching anglicisation of their institutions, Charles retorted that he had been 'just and fair' and that, moreover, the means had been 'lawful'. After their acrimonious fortnight in London at the beginning of 1626 the Scottish representatives left 'in great choler'. Haddington was particularly vexed because he knew that the power given to him by James was on the point of being removed.

The changes were not long in coming and they were accompanied by the introduction of two new bodies: a commission for grievances, which one courtier described as 'the star chamber court of England under another name come down here to play the tyrant' and an exchequer commission whose presidency was granted to John Spottiswood, the increasingly influential archbishop of St Andrews.[6] By then in his sixty-first year, he had been close to James and prominent in his support of the king's plans for episcopalian Church government – he was Moderator of the General Assembly in 1618 when the Five Articles of Perth had been introduced. For Charles that earlier support alone made Spottiswood an attractive personality, and the new king used his patronage to give the archbishop precedence over the chancellor, Hay, a move bound to infuriate the nobility.

The new council was constituted on 23 March 1626. It was led by John Graham, fourth Earl of Montrose, an unassuming and retiring aristocrat who was best known for his love of golf and his addiction to tobacco, the latter providing him with the poor health which the sport failed to cure. His political leadership was anonymous, just as Charles hoped it would be, and power gradually ebbed away from the triumvirate who had served his father so well. Haddington had already been sidelined, in 1627 Mar was replaced by the Earl of Morton, and Hay was bought off with a title – he was raised to the nobility as Viscount Dupplin in 1627 and repaid the king's patronage by doing as he was told. In their place came councillors who owed their positions to the king and who knew how to bow to his wishes. Among their number were the Earl of Nithsdale, a quarrelsome and untrustworthy Catholic; Sir John Scot of Scotstarvet 'whose covetous-ness far exceeded his honesty' (according to his contemporary Sir James Balfour, Lord Lyon King of Arms); Patrick Lindsay, the garr-ulous bishop of Ross; and Alexander Strauchan of Thornton, who had scandalised Scotland by first seducing the wife of the fifth Earl Marischal and then proceeding to plunder the cuckold's castle at Dunottar. As far as the governance of Scotland was concerned, it was the end of the Jacobean system and the beginning of a long season of discontent.

All this had been foreseen half a dozen years earlier by Sir Robert Gordon of Gordonstoun when he wrote to his nephew, the Earl of Sutherland, warning him that it stood to reason that a London-based king would do all that he could to 'curb the nobility of Scotland'. Now it had come to pass:

> It is not now with our noblemen as when our king was resident in Scotland. Hardly then could the king's majesty punish any of our greatest nobility when they had offended, by reason of their great dependencies and friendship. But now, he [James] being absolute King of all Great Britain, the cause is altered. He may, when he listeth, daunt the proudest and mightiest of you all.[7]

Once again Charles had failed to recognise the sense of resentment which was building up within Scotland. For a time the darkening mood was held in check by the emergence of William Graham, Earl of Menteith, like Wentworth a capable bureaucrat, who became Charles's principal manager of Scottish affairs in January 1628. Nominated to take Spottiswood's place during one of the archbishop's increasingly frequent bouts of illness, Menteith took advantage of the advancement by making himself indispensable to the London court, so much so that he quickly became regarded as Charles's agent in Scotland and held powers that equalled

Wentworth's in Ireland. It also helped that he liked travelling: by commuting regularly between Edinburgh and London – his journeys by coach took up to four weeks in both directions – he was able to explain the king's thinking to the Scottish counsellors while keeping him informed about political developments in Scotland. In short he was a fixer who enjoyed the confidence of both sides, Charles because he liked him personally and admired his capacity for getting things done; the majority of the Scottish nobles because he was one of their number and could be trusted.

However, in common with many men who rise to power quickly, Menteith was vainglorious and ambitious. He also had a loose tongue. An interest in his family's genealogy led him to lay claim to the earldom of Strathearn, which lay vacant. His request was perfectly sound – he was the direct heir of David, eldest son of the second marriage of King Robert II, who was the first earl of Strathearn and whose daughter Euphemia married Patrick Graham, Menteith's lineal ancestor – but it proved an unwise move. Although Menteith announced that he made no claim on the lands of Strathearn, his ambition to hold the title appeared to have an ulterior motive because unresolved doubts about the validity of Robert's marriages seemed to question the royal succession.

To his enemies, who had grown in number and were centred on the equally ambitious Sir John Scott of Scotstarvet, it seemed that Menteith was actually making a challenge for the throne. True, he had surrendered the lands of Strathearn but it was noted that he had not renounced his claim to be David's successor. At a time when Scottish property rights were under threat from the revocations this seemed suspicious; when Menteith drunkenly boasted that he had 'the reddest blood in Scotland' his move smacked of treason. Charles had supported his friend's action and had created him Earl of Strathearn in July 1631, but he was enough of a believer in the divine right of kings to understand the threat to his own authority posed by Menteith's distant relationship to Robert II. What followed next was all too typical of the ferocious internecine squabbling which runs through Scottish political affairs. With the help of leading grandees such as the Earl of Haddington and the Duke of Hamilton (whose family also entertained aspirations to the Scottish throne), Scotstarvet began a whispering campaign. Even Menteith's brother-in-law, the melancholic and reclusive poet William Drummond of Hawthornden, joined in with a polemic against upstarts who thought themselves better than their rightful king. The inference was obvious: Charles should rid himself of the meddlesome Menteith family.

However, the king chose to ignore the advice. While he expressed shock at his favourite's behaviour he was not yet minded to sack him and in December 1632 he was happy to accept Menteith's apologies. The matter seemed to be settled early in the following year when Menteith exchanged his new earldom for Airth and the Court of Session formally declared that the king was the rightful heir of David, Earl of Strathearn. But this being Scotland, Scotstarvet was not satisfied and the rumour-mongering continued. Slowly, Menteith was becoming isolated, while his genealogical investigations had run him into debt. Now he was that dangerous beast, a politician at bay faced by angry creditors. In May Charles had no option but to investigate Menteith, who was forced to retire from public life – for ever, as it turned out.

If Menteith's removal was a victory for his enemies it was also a terrible defeat for the king. Not only had Charles lost an ally but he was not powerful enough to protect his protégé. Nor did he grant Menteith an audience during his visit to Edinburgh to celebrate his coronation. Charles had finally decided to journey north, thereby putting an end to his continual prevarications about his coronation, a delay which had led the poet William Lithgow to complain:

> Say, if he come this year say he come not,
> Yet time shall praise me for a loving Scot.[8]

Lithgow was an odd praise-poet, having travelled lengthily in Europe, during which time he had become a perfervid anti-Catholic propagandist – his account of his experiences, *The Rare Adventures and Painful Peregrinations,* was held to be a pack of lies – but he was one of those rare poets who were able to give a public voice to his countrymen's feelings. It was not until July 1628 that the king gave any hint that he would travel north to be crowned, and in the period that had passed since his accession the rumour had grown that, far from wanting to travel to Scotland, Charles insisted that the Scottish crown be brought to him in London. The tittle-tattle was untrue but it stuck, and it was to be another five years before Charles made the journey to Edinburgh to be crowned in the bleak confines of Holyrood Abbey, which had been carefully spruced up for the occasion.

In fact from the moment he entered the city through the West Port on 15 June 1633 Edinburgh was *en fête*. The nymph Edina welcomed the king and his retinue with the presentation of the keys and the Lord Provost and his councillors, clad in scarlet, were on hand to lead the royal retinue down the lavishly decorated main street, now known as the Royal Mile, towards the Royal Palace of Holyroodhouse. The elaborate and expensive pageantry was matched by the pomp and solemnity of the crowning of Charles which was held two days later and which was organised by the Lord Lyon King of Arms, who was moved to say that it was 'the most glorious and magnifique coronation that was ever seen in this kingdom'. Perhaps it was too gaudily done for, far from assuaging everyone's feelings, the coronation ceremony seemed to contain too many elements which were deemed to be 'popish'. The service was conducted by Archbishop Spottiswood and David Lindsay, bishop of Brechin, delivered the sermon, but both these pre-eminent Church leaders were obliged to wear English vestments and the proceedings, which lasted four hours, seemed to be more Anglican than Presbyterian in nature. The Aberdeen chronicler, John Spalding, noted with some distaste that the altar had been covered with 'a rich tapestry wherein the crucifix was curiously wrought; and as these bishops who were in service passed by this crucifix they were seen to bow their knee and beck, which, with their habit, was noticed, and bred great fear of inbringing of Popery'.[9]

Genuflection and an adorned altar: together with the use of English vestments this could only signal one thing, namely that the king was hell-bent on imposing Anglican rituals and liturgy on the Presbyterian Church of Scotland. The impression was not improved during the Sunday after the coronation when Charles instructed two of his chaplains to conduct an Anglican service in the High Church of St Giles. Before leaving the city on 18 July the king also announced that Edinburgh would become an episcopal see and that its bishop would take precedence next to the archbishops of Glasgow and St Andrews. Furthermore St Giles, the main parish church, would become a cathedral. These gestures were hardly likely to please the anti-ritualistic Presbyterians who dominated the city council, but, as in all of his dealings with the Scots, Charles was blissfully unaware that he was causing any offence, not least because the city had been forced to pay dearly for the privilege of crowning their new king. He did, however, manage to meet his Scottish parliament, a feat which would have been impossible in London.

It met between 18 and 28 June and its agenda had been laid down in advance by the king with the assistance of his secretary of state. Legislation on the royal prerogative concerning religion and the vexed matter of clerical dress was carried narrowly – Charles made great play of noting down the names of those who opposed him – as were moves to increase taxation. Both caused resentment, the religious impositions because they struck at the heart of the country's Presbyterian traditions and the taxes because they hit the moneyed classes whose support the king needed. The most disliked measure was the infamous 'two-in-ten', the imposition of a tax introduced in England in 1624 whereby interest on loans was reduced from 10 per cent to 8 per cent with 2 per cent being paid to the Crown.

Interfering in religious procedures and increasing taxation were hardly the most sensitive ways of dealing with a people who were not only of independent mind but notoriously prone to feuds and jealousies, often over quite petty matters. Speaking from his deathbed a year later, Sir John Gordon of Lochinvar, Viscount Kenmure, lamented his inability to oppose the liturgical innovations with words which echo that class's distaste for the king's meddling: 'I think, and am persuaded in my conscience, they are superstitious, idolatrous and anti-Christian, and come from hell; and I repute it a mercy that my eyes shall not see the desolation that shall come upon this poor church. It's plain Popery that's coming among you.'[10]

For all its pageantry – the parliamentary proceedings had been enlivened by a game of football between barons and gentlemen – Charles's visit to Scotland was not a success. To a people worried about encroaching anglicisation the religious ceremonies had hinted at the introduction of popish practices, the Scottish bishops appeared to be enjoying too much power, and Charles himself had appeared haughty and insensitive, characteristics which marked him as irredeemably English. The king, though, remained ignorant of the strong feelings he had engendered. He left Edinburgh convinced that he had done his duty and that he had achieved everything that was necessary to keep his northern kingdom happy, especially by forcing its Church to conform with the practices of the Church of England. On his return to London the crowds turned out in force to welcome him back and his secretary of state, Sir John Coke, was moved to note that there was 'much satisfaction to his Majesty in every point'.

Perhaps Charles had failed to understand the hidden resentments, or perhaps he really did believe that his visit had been a triumph, but Scotland marked a turning point in his attitudes. No sooner had he returned to London than he wrote to Bishop James Wedderburn of Dunblane, the new dean of the Chapel Royal, informing him that henceforth the services at Holyrood should be conducted according to the English liturgy. Then, a year later, the Lords of Session were told that it was their duty to take sacrament twice a year and that in so doing they should kneel, according to the precepts of the Perth Articles. Worse, Laud took a hand in these changes and began dealing directly with the Scottish bishops as if he were their primate and not Spottiswood. His aim was quite simple: he wanted to produce a new Book of Common Prayer and canons which would reflect the 'uniformity of the discipline' of the Church.

This was entirely in keeping, for during that period the ambitious cleric was at the height of his powers, and in matters of conscience he had the king's ear. A committed Anglican, he was determined to introduce a uniform religious liturgy throughout the three kingdoms and he was in constant contact with the Scottish and Irish bishops about the necessity of maintaining a common form of worship based on his Church's principles. This inevitably made him a bogeyman figure among the ministers of religion who opposed his views, and in Scotland the feeling grew that Laud alone was responsible for the swing towards Rome. Later, when he was fighting for his life in the Tower of London, he fell back on the excuse that he was merely carrying out his master's orders, but his letter books show that it was his zealousness that was largely responsible for the attempted introduction of a new-fangled form of Church service.

In Scotland, at least, it would always be damned as 'Laud's Liturgy', even though its main executants were Wedderburn and other equally anglicised bishops such as John Maxwell, the new incumbent at Ross, and Adam Bellenden of Aberdeen. For two years they laboured, always encouraged by Laud, who continually reminded them of the king's interest in the project, and the first draft was ready by October 1636. By then, Charles had issued a book of canons intimating radical changes to the way services were conducted and announcing that the Scottish Church was to come under his governance. By then, too, rumours was already circulating about the contents of the Book of Common Prayer: the general feeling was that the new liturgy was not just an Anglican imposition but that it contained traces of Roman Catholic thinking. Even conservative churchmen feared that it was 'little better than the Mass' and contained too many unwelcome popish rites. 'I am greatly afraid that this apple of contention have banished peace for our poor Church hereafter forever,' wrote Robert Baillie, the young and recently appointed minister of Kilwinning in Ayrshire. 'I am sore afraid that there is a storm raised which will not calm in my days.'[11]

It was a prescient comment, but the storm did not break until the following year, and when it did it would sweep along men like Baillie, who was no enemy of the king's but a committed Royalist, as well as the many arch-opponents of 'popery and Arminianism' in Scotland's reformed Church who regarded the new liturgy as a betrayal of the Reformation. This was a raw nerve, for there had long been friction between the rival claims of the presbytery and the episcopacy and any strengthening of the latter was regarded as a leaning towards Catholicism. Before the king began interfering in Scottish religious affairs ministers and bishops had coexisted quite happily; indeed the episcopate generally supported the ideals of the Reformation and were not as powerful – spiritually or politically – as their opposite numbers in England. Even the Canterburians, those appointed by Charles and largely responsible for drafting the new prayer books, were not the powers that Laud thought them to be.

It was on that score that Charles underestimated the authority of his bishops in Scotland. Although they had been permitted to revise and amend the English Prayer Book to make it acceptable to their fellow countrymen, and despite the fact that it had been through many drafts, the new liturgy was still regarded as an alien creation which had not been authorised by the General Assembly, the Church of Scotland's governing body. As Drummond of Hawthornden's biographer put it: 'Had the book been immaculate in its kind, had it been the work of a joint-committee of Cherubim and Seraphim, it would not have been accepted in Scotland.'[12] Even Baillie was forced to admit that the atmosphere in his area was so heated that 'the whole people thinks Popery [is] at the doors'. As the various drafts shuttled between Edinburgh and London Charles was reported to be 'well pleased' with the results and trusted that they would settle the Church. He could not have been more wrong.

Chapter Four

'THAT GLORIOUS MARRIAGE OF THE KINGDOM WITH GOD'

'No man may speak anything in public for the King's part, except he would have himself marked for a sacrifice to be killed one day. I think our people possessed with a bloody devil, far above anything that ever I could have imagined.'

Robert Baillie, letter to William Spang, 4 October 1637

Opposition to the new liturgy was not long in finding a common voice. Although the bishop of Ross had begun using the new prayer book in 1636, and although Bishop William Juxon forecast that the initial hostility would give way to acceptance, there was a growing groundswell of antagonism to its implementation. Not only was the imposition resented, but the Scots simply did not want their Church to be ruled by bishops and the king, preferring instead the existing establishment of parish kirk session and regional synods or presbyteries. The opposition came from a broad spectrum, too, uniting the nobility and the landed gentry with the ministers of the Church in rejecting the offending publication. When the various opponents met they were obliged to keep their discussions secret, but through the correspondence of men like Baillie and Samuel Rutherford, minister of Anwoth in Galloway and one of the most outspoken critics of the king's religious policies, it is possible to see that the revolt was widespread in Scotland and also included disaffected ministers in Ulster.

The minds of those evangelical Presbyterians were concentrated further when the Privy Council received a letter from Charles ordering the publication of the new prayer book. As a result, on 20 December 1637 the council issued a proclamation for each parish to have the new liturgy in use by Easter the following year. Insult was added early in the new year when Charles ordered the Kirk to use a new translation of the Psalms. As these were partly the work of his father they might have been acceptable, but for many ministers this was further evidence that the king was hell-bent on bringing the Church of Scotland under his personal control. The Kirk seemed to be in mortal danger, leading Rutherford to warn that it was about to be subverted by the hated prelacy:

> We are in great fears of a great and fearful trial to come upon the Kirk of God; for these, who would build their houses and nests upon the ashes of mourning Jerusalem, have drawn our King upon hard and dangerous conclusions against such as are termed Puritans, for the rooting of them out. Our prelates (the Lord take the keys of this house from those bastard porters) assure us that, for such as will not conform there is nothing but imprisonment and deprivation.[1]

The murmuring grew louder as the date of implementation approached. In April two radical ministers, Alexander Henderson of Leuchars and David Dickson of Irvine, emerged as the focus of the Kirk's resistance and they had the support of the Lord Advocate, Sir Thomas Hope, as well as Lord Balmerino, who had narrowly escaped the death sentence in the previous year for possessing a copy of the supplication to Charles outlining the Church's grievances. (The charge was 'lease-making' or slandering the king.)

The two ministers had further meetings in Edinburgh, where the opposition was already coming out into the open. At a meeting of the local synod on 31 May when the bishop of Edinburgh, David Lindsay, chose the moment to promote the new book several ministers showed their disgust by walking out and refusing their copies. Similar scenes were enacted elsewhere, but the bishops pushed ahead with their plans to introduce the book on 23 July, the intimation being given during services on the previous Sunday. Matters were moving to a head – as Baillie noted, throughout that week the Scottish capital was agog with 'murmurs and grudges'. As the day approached, the opposition, led by Henderson and Dickson, put the final touches to their plot for a series of public demonstrations against the introduction of the new liturgy. As it turned out they were spectacularly successful, not least because it was agreed that women should take the lead in the protests.

The most famous of these took place in St Giles in Edinburgh, recently and significantly elevated as the cathedral church of the diocese, when the dean, James Hanna, attempted to lead his service from the 'black popish superstitious service book'. In a well orchestrated riot members of the congregation threw their stools at Hanna and the bishop; according to one contemporary account angrily denouncing Lindsay as 'false Anti-Christian wolf, beastly bellygod and crafty fox' (the writer added helpfully that these were 'the best epithets'). The magistrates, who were present in number together with other notables including Archbishop Spottiswood, ordered the church to be cleared, and the service continued behind closed doors, but that could not save Hanna and Lindsay when they left St Giles. Both had to flee for their lives, and even when they reached the street outside the tumult continued:

> His [the dean's] gown was rent, his service book taken from him, and his body pitifully beaten and bruised so that he cried often for mercy and vowed never afterward to give his concurrence to such clagged [polluted] devotion. The bishop in the same time thought to have removed himself peaceably to some house but no sooner was he seen upon the streets when the confused multitude rushed violently in upon him and enragedly pursued after him with railing and clodding [mud-throwing], and if their hand could have been as active as their minds were willing, they had doubtless demolished the great butt [target] which they aimed at.[2]

Lindsay was rescued by the arrival of the Earl of Roxburgh in his coach. His skin was saved but, as there had also been equally turbulent riots in the nearby Old Kirk and Greyfriars, long-lasting damage had been done. The following day the Privy Council met and on Spottiswood's advice the introduction of the prayer book was suspended; but far from cooling tempers the aftermath of the riots introduced a new season of discontent. The nobility blamed the bishops for miscalculating the mood of the country while the bishops countered that they had received no support from those in authority. At the same time the council exchanged insults with the baillies, or magistrates, of Edinburgh over the arrest of troublemakers and the prevention of further riots. As for the recalcitrant ministers, they wisely kept their heads below the parapet, arguing that the riots were caused by the imposition of a flawed liturgy and that the blame for this lay with the bishops, though not as yet with the king.

Even so, despite their protestations, the crisis seemed to be set fair on a collision course with the Crown. David Stevenson, the historian of the period, notes presciently that it was fast becoming 'a crisis by monthly instalments'.[3] Charles reacted with dismay to the news of the rioting, and predictably he ordered the council to round up and punish the ringleaders and to support the bishops until such time as the new form of service had been accepted. Equally predictably this led to renewed opposition. Backed by the nobility, ministers from Fife and the west of Scotland, the most disaffected areas, sent petitions or supplications with supporting letters to the Privy Council denouncing the prayer book as a plot to destroy the Kirk. This was very much a community-based protest, with ministers taking the responsibility for drafting the papers while the nobility and the gentry lent support to it by raising subscriptions and ensuring that the petitions reached Edinburgh. Egalitarian the movement might have been, but it placed the Privy Council in an impossible position when it met on 25 August 1638. Its members, many of whom were in sympathy with the revolt, were honour-bound to support the king's fiat, yet they could hardly ignore the feelings of antagonism which the prayer book had aroused. Unwilling to press ahead with its introduction without further guidance from the court, the council sent a letter to London revealing the widespread disquiet which was rising in an unstoppable tide of condemnation 'from diverse parts and corners of the kingdom'.

Undeterred by the news and encouraged by the stout resistance displayed by Laud, who feared that any slackness in Scotland would encourage the English Puritans, Charles continued to insist that the prayer book had to be introduced and its opponents punished. Matters now began to move fast. On 20 September the Privy Council met again and agreed to forward the petitions to the king through the good offices of the Duke of Lennox, who was visiting the Scottish capital to attend his mother's funeral. Redrafted by the new Lord Treasurer, the Earl of Traquair, who argued that a moderate approach to Charles had a better chance of succeeding, the new version repeated the Church's condemnation of the prayer book. At the same time the dissenting ministers took steps to widen their support by encouraging parishes in other parts of Scotland to lend their voices to their protest. As John Spalding noted with some alarm, even the north-east, traditionally an episcopalian stronghold, was affected, so much so that the bishop of Brechin was forced to read the new prayer book equipped with two loaded pistols and surrounded by armed retainers. As it was the precautions did the bishop little good:

> In this month of November Mr William Whiteford, bishop of Brechin, upon one Sunday within the kirk of Brechin, using this English service as he had often times done before, but impediment [opposition or objection] in that kirk the people got up in a mad humour detesting this sort of worship, and pursued him so sharply that hardly had he escaped out of their hands unslain and forced for the safety of his life to leave his bishoprik and flee the kingdom.[4]

So successfully was the opposition organised that a steady stream of people, united by dislike of the prayer book, began to converge on Edinburgh in anticipation of the king's next move. A flavour of that intense preoccupation with the need to preserve Scotland's Kirk can be found in the diaries of Archibald Johnston of Wariston, an ascetic young Edinburgh lawyer with aristocratic connections who was convinced that he had been elected to God's glory and that no deviation of purpose could be permitted: 'it came in to mind that if we licked up this vomit of Romish superstition again, the Lord in his wrath would vomit us out. The Lord engraved in my mind that of the prophet, "There is poison in the pot".'[5]

It was an unreal time, bordering on hysteria. The day for moderation had long passed, the atmosphere was heavy with the possibility of revolution and events unfolded with casual inevitability. There was further rioting in Edinburgh on 18 October, an incident considered so serious in London that Charles ordered the Privy

Council and the Court of Session to remove themselves to Linlithgow, to the west of the capital. The decision only inflamed the situation, however: Edinburgh was left as a hive of revolutionary activity, with petitioning ministers and their supporters protesting against royal policy in the crowded confines of the city centre. So far the revolt had been driven by petition but, as the days shortened, passions were running higher, leaving Traquair to ask: 'Shall I give way to the people's fury, which, without force and the strong hand, cannot be opposed?'

Weak-willed but arrogant, another of Charles's magnates who believed that they could control events, Traquair had the unenviable task of standing between the 'supplicants' (with whom he had some sympathy) and the king (to whom he owed his loyalty) and of explaining the wishes of each to the other. As is always the case with such trimmers, he failed to reach a compromise, and when he was called to London later in the year he was forced to admit that 'it was already grown difficult to keep the King and them [supplicants] too'.[6] By then too Scotland had become well-nigh ungovernable. The Privy Council did not meet in Linlithgow until 14 November and it did so without any real knowledge of what was happening in Edinburgh which, to all intents and purposes, had been abandoned to the disaffected ministers and their supporters. Among them was an increasingly worried Robert Baillie, who feared that the protest would lead to violence:

> The Lord save my poor soul! for as moderate as I have been, and resolve in the spite of the devil and world, by God's grace to remain to death. For as well as I have been beloved hitherto by all who had known me, yet I think I may be killed, and my house burnt upon my head; for I think it wicked and base to be moved or carried down with the impetuous spate of a multitude; my judgement cannot be altered by their motion, and so my person and state may be drowned in their violence.[7]

To retrieve the situation Traquair was deputed to return to the capital accompanied by the Earl of Lauderdale and Archibald Campbell, Lord Lorne. It was a forlorn hope: the supplicants were adamant that, legally and morally, their actions were justified and that they were proceeding to select commissioners who would be responsible for dealing with the king's response to the petitions. This would change everything: from being an amorphous, though by no means inchoate, mass of protesters the supplicants would be transmogrified into an organised party of opposition. The following day the three councillors together with the bishop of Edinburgh and Lord Advocate Hope met with a deputation of thirteen supplicants, representing each of the three 'estates'* – four nobles and three each drawn from the gentry, burgesses and ministry. Their agenda was conducted on five 'desires' posed by the supplicants, repeating the call for restitution of regular church services and an end to unwanted innovations, requesting the council to intercede with the king, who they believed had not been 'rightly informed', and finally calling for the nationwide election of commissioners as an executive body to argue their cause. Traquair was far from sure if he was in a position to authorise any such action, but following the intervention of Hope, who advised (to the Lord Treasurer's dismay) that the elections would be lawful, it was agreed that the supplicants should disperse to choose what would in effect become an alternative form of government made up of commissioners representing all the nobility, one minister from each presbytery, two landed gentry from each county and one or two burgesses from each burgh.

Thus were born the 'Tables', the administrative system by which the supplicants would conduct their future discourse and which would later become the instrument for governing Scotland. Five in number, each representing one estate with the fifth fulfilling an executive function, they were essentially committees and according to John Row, the historian of the Church of Scotland and a contemporary witness of events, they were called Tables because each estate met separately 'sitting in four several rooms at four several tables in the Parliament House'.[8] They met formally on 6 December and instituted a process of consultation and debate both to maintain solidarity and to codify their demands, which they believed the king,

---

* 'The estates of the realm were composed of those who held land directly from the king as tenants-in-chief and had the right and duty to be represented in parliament to advise and assist the king in governing. There were three estates, those of the lay tenants in chief (nobles and lesser barons or lairds), the clergy, and the royal burghs.' Stevenson, *Scottish Revolution*, 18.

once fully briefed on the subject, would have no other option but to meet. Five advocates were also chosen to test the legality of the Tables' actions; the most notable of these was Johnston of Wariston, who quickly emerged as the spiritual guiding force behind the revolt. Single-minded to the point of being a zealot, he believed passionately in the certainty of God's providence not only to himself but also to his country. Intolerant of others, remote and austere, he could be an uncomfortable companion, yet, as one of his prayers reveals, he could also be touchingly human and frail: 'O Father, Saviour and sanctifier, take Archie Johnston – a poor, silly, imprudent, ignorant, improvident, passionate, humorous, foolish, ungrateful, diffident body – in unto Thy thoughts, and know him by name and surname, and make him know yet that Thou art the Lord God and his God and the God of his seed both in Thy words and works.'[9]

Between them Wariston and Baillie represented the two extremes of the opposition raised against the introduction of the prayer book. The first was the pupil of the other, Baillie having acted as a teaching regent in Glasgow while Wariston was a student of divinity, and a dozen years separated their births, but both were destined to play central roles in the events of the coming two decades as they unfolded after the dramas of 1637. At the request of the Fifth Table Wariston started work on a declinator – a formal, usually written, declining or refusal – which advised the council that the commissioners were not prepared to countenance the presence of bishops while their grievances were debated. Realising that his control over events was slipping away, Traquair was reluctant to grant the commissioners a formal meeting until later in December. His council was divided, and the advice he had received from the king had been unhelpful – he ordered the issue of a proclamation condemning 'popery' yet he also insisted on the arrest of the rioters, an impossible task. It was not quite open rebellion but, as Baillie noted, events were moving rapidly towards an impasse and the time had come to take sides: 'I am glad to join with them [the supplicants] in opposition to a common enemy, since no way is left, but either to swallow down all that the Canterburians can invent, or else oppose them plainly in their lawless practices'.[10]

When the council eventually did meet a delegation of commissioners on 21 December, Traquair and his associates were forced to concede that the matter would now have to be referred to the king. They had little choice. Led by John Campbell, Earl of Loudoun, the twelve commissioners produced a solid and well-argued case for reversing the new ecclesiastical order which was anathema not just to the national good but also to reformist belief. While the argument was designed as much to convince as to put the supplicants in a good light – Loudoun was quick to remind the council of the patience and forbearance shown by the supplicants (the rioting in Edinburgh notwithstanding) – it was presented calmly and logically. Theirs was no revolt over small matters, he explained, but a reasoned objection to proposals which would wreak fundamental changes in the character, substance and future direction of the Church of Scotland.

Loudoun ended his peroration with an attack on the bishops and pushed home the point of Wariston's declinator, namely that there had to be a debate. He was followed by James Cunningham, minister of Cumnock in Ayrshire, who reminded the councillors of their God-beholden duty to uphold the spiritual desires of their fellow countrymen. Then Loudoun handed over the national supplication together with the supplications of 20 September and 18 October and asked that they be forwarded to Charles together with a copy of the declinator. With a heavy heart Traquair accepted them and made ready to leave for London to face his wrathful master, who was determined to 'risk everything' (Laud's advice) rather than surrender to his rebellious northern subjects.

To Charles the resistance in Scotland amounted to little more than 'a needless noise' against royal authority, and he chose to ignore the fact that the supplicants had based their argument on a point of principle from which they would not budge. Personal stubbornness was one reason for his decision. The necessity of maintaining the authority and dignity of his Crown was another, for he realised that to bow to the supplicants' demands would represent such an undignified challenge to his kingship that his authority would be damaged permanently. The stability of his reign was indeed a factor in his thinking. During the years of the personal rule England had been a peaceable place, and although there had been opposition to Ship Money and rumbles of discontent from Puritan clerics, Charles was in the happy position of being a monarch at ease with himself and his country, telling his nephew the Elector Palatine in the summer of 1637 that 'he was the happiest King or prince in all Christendom'.

That absence of any foreboding certainly played a part in lulling him into thinking that the unrest in Scotland was little more than a summer squall which would disappear as quickly as it had appeared. In vain did Traquair argue that the prayer book should be withdrawn. Charles was determined to enforce it, and he sent the Lord Treasurer back to Edinburgh with an uncompromising proclamation to do just that. 'We can never conceive that the country is truly quiet when regal authority is infringed,' he explained in a covering letter of admonition to the council, 'for although it may have a seeming settlement at first, it cannot so long continue when the King's true authority is not truly preserved.'[11]

Traquair recognised that an uphill task lay ahead of him. Among those who had combined to defend the cause of their Church, there existed a unity which went beyond simple obstinacy: the supplicants were determined, whatever the costs, not to bow to rule by bishops and to fight for the right of ministers to preach and pray as the spirit took them and not to be bound to a prescribed form of service. The mood was caught by Samuel Rutherford, who wrote from Aberdeen reminding Loudoun that he was doing God's work and deserved nothing but praise and support for 'purging of the Lord's house in this land and plucking down the sticks of Antichrist's filthy nest'.[12]

The letter, and many others of a similar nature, reveal the extent of the spiritual pressure which the clergy could exert on the leadership of the supplicants, but apart from their talk of the pope as the Antichrist there is more to them than the fanatical outpourings of fundamentalist belief. However obscure Rutherford's observations might sometimes have been, they give some indication of the strength and unity of those members of Scotland's polity who were determined to resist royal control of the Church.

Being friends with many of their number, Traquair knew how deep-rooted were the supplicants' beliefs, and on his return to Scotland he delayed as long as possible before ordering the proclamation to be read. It was to no avail. The supplicants had been forewarned about the nature of the king's message and by the time that the proclamation was made – in Stirling on 19 February 1638 and on subsequent days in Linlithgow and Edinburgh – Wariston had already drafted a riposte. As Traquair had warned, the proclamation produced expressions of outrage and disappointment at the king's refusal to listen to their grievances and his threat to punish them – having first patronised the supplicants by claiming that he believed they had only acted out of 'preposterous zeal', Charles had gone on to warn them that any further meetings would be held to be treasonable. The response was predictable. Following the proclamation in Edinburgh John Leslie, Earl of Rothes, dispatched a notice to all the supplicants urging them to converge on Edinburgh 'with all possible diligence' for a mass meeting to make a legal challenge to the king's reply. 'Speaking generally what was to be done,' remembered Rothes, 'they [the Tables] fell upon the consideration of a band of union to be made legally; also, after his Majesty was supplicated, and would not return an answer, a declaration was thought on as the last act.'[13]

The result was the creation of the National Covenant, a formal document of protest or manifesto, to which all church-going communicants would subscribe, on behalf of themselves, their families and followers and in so doing would make themselves responsible for upholding its precepts. The Covenant's authors were Wariston and Henderson, who created it 'for the maintenance of religion and the King's Majesty's authority, and for the preservation of the laws and liberties of the kingdom'[14]: in so doing they produced a compact for the Scottish people not just with God and their king but also with each other. This was an important point for, although the National Covenant came into being as a result of nationwide protests about religious innovations, it also had a political element in that it united that opposition in common cause.

For a revolutionary document which was supposed to appeal to popular sentiment, the language of the Covenant was remarkably restrained and its argument was drafted with legal shrewdness to avoid the possibility that it might provoke allegations of treason. That does not reduce its effectiveness as a declaration of intent. It opens by rehearsing the terms of the Negative Confession which James VI and his advisers signed in 1581, pledging their commitment to the Protestant religion at a time when it was thought that their allegiance to the Reformation might be wavering. The inference was clear: just as fear of Catholicism had forced the Negative Confession, so was the National Covenant a petition against the imposition of 'all contrary religion and doctrine'. There follows a listing of laws passed by parliament suppressing all forms of Catholicism and ensuring the ascendancy of Protestantism – here the hand of Wariston can be seen. Again the inference was clear: rule by bishops and the introduction of a new liturgy were not just moves against the spirit of the reformed Church, they had no legal justification. Instead, the liturgy should be withdrawn and the rule of bishops replaced by free general assemblies to safeguard the liberties and freedoms of the 'true Church of God'.

Having made a statement of loyalty to the Crown – albeit grudgingly given, for the underlying assumption was that by insisting on the changes Charles, an absentee monarch, had not provided good governance for Scotland – the document ended with a protestation of loyalty to God and the king:

> We promise and swear, that we shall, to the uttermost of our power, with our means and lives, stand to the defence of our dread Sovereign, the king's Majesty, his Person and Authority, in the defence of the foresaid true Religion, Liberties and Laws of the Kingdom: As also to the mutual defence and assistance, every one of us another in the same cause of maintaining the true Religion and his Majesty's Authority.

It reads like a vote of confidence for Charles, but the allegiance offered by those who signed the National Covenant – thereafter known as Covenanters – was conditional. Loyalty there was in plenty for the king, but only if he defended the people's right to worship as they saw fit. If not, then the people pledged to combine to defend that right. As recent Scottish historians have shown, the National Covenant was not just a religious manifesto but a profoundly political document which 'upheld the corporate right of the people to resist a lawful king who threatened to become tyrannical', and in taking that course of action they pledged to take responsibility for ensuring that its conditions were met.[15] This was far removed from the doctrine of divine right of kings that personified Charles's personal rule; instead, he was being asked to submit his will to the direction of his subjects.

The first draft was completed on 23 February, and on the following day it was revised by Balmerino, Loudoun and Rothes before being passed to almost 300 representatives of the ministers who were meeting in the Tailors' Hall in the Cowgate. Moderates such as Baillie were alarmed lest the Covenant contain phrases directly attacking bishops or demanding their removal, and at their request these were dropped, for the last thing needed by the covenanting movement was a schism before it began. Then, on a momentous day in their country's history, 28 February 1638, the people of Scotland began putting their names to the National Covenant to pledge their solidarity and commitment to the common good. The proceedings began in Greyfriars Kirk in Edinburgh with Wariston reading the document's 4300 words before it was signed by the nobles and the lairds; it proved to be a long-drawn-out affair which lasted until eight o'clock in the evening. Throughout the following three days the ministers put their names to it, followed by the people of Edinburgh before copies were sent out for signature in 'every shire, balzierie [regality], stewartry or distinct judicatory'.

It is doubtful if all those who added their names to the document had actually read it, but they certainly understood its message and the signing of the National Covenant was accompanied by scenes of incredible enthusiasm and religious exaltation. A fast day was proclaimed on Sunday 18 March, and throughout the Lowlands, the area most affected by the excitement, some Sunday services were gripped with evangelical fervour. After family prayers Wariston went to service at Currie, a village outside Edinburgh, to hear its minister John Chairtres introduce and explain the meaning of the Covenant. Having done so Chairtres asked the congregation to lift their hands in assent, a request which was answered by a display of mass emotion bordering on hysteria:

> In the twinkling of an eye there fell such an extraordinary influence of God's spirit upon the whole congregation, melting their frozen hearts, watering their dry cheeks, changing their very countenances, as it was a wonder to see so visible, sensible, momentous a change upon all, man and woman, lass and lad, pastor and people, that Mr John, being suffocated almost with his own tears, and astonished at the emotion of the whole people, sat down in the pulpit in amazement, but presently rose again when he saw all the people falling down on their knees to mourn and pray and he and they for a quarter of an hour prayed very sensibly with many sobs, tears, promises and vows to be thankful and fruitful in the time to come.[16]

Wariston was much moved, for this was a people obviously at one with their God. The wave of emotion continued throughout the month, binding the signatories together in such a harmony that there could now be no hope of imposing the prayer book. It was the first blast against Charles's rule, and not for the first or last time in Scotland's history unpopular policies emanating from London were resoundingly dismissed. Not everyone was enamoured – the burghs of Aberdeen, Crail and St Andrews refused to sign, and in the western Highlands and in the largely Catholic and Episcopalian north-east there was trenchant resistance to the outbreak of Presbyterian zeal. Inspired by the teachings of the 'Aberdeen Doctors', six moderate ministers and academics who recognised the authority of the king and rejected the National Covenant,* the city of Aberdeen held out until March 1639 and not even the arrival of a delegation which included James Graham, the attractive Fifth Earl of Montrose, could make them change their minds. Recently returned from the Continent, this 'Presbyterian cavalier' had been elected to the Tables and was destined to play one of the leading roles in the drama that was to unfold once Scotland had embraced the National Covenant.

By then, to all intents and purposes the Privy Council had ceased running Scotland, having written to Charles to inform him of 'the true state of the country', and the political initiative had passed to the Covenanters. The leadership, too, was in tatters: having tried to be all things to all men Traquair found that his authority had evaporated as power passed from him to the Tables, and as it did so he made the feeble promise that he would not give offence to anyone. If Charles wanted to retrieve his position he had to act quickly and decisively, but to do so would have gone against his character. His response was unhurried and it would take another four months before he decided what must be done. In the meantime Traquair was ordered to journey south once again, this time carrying with him papers drawn up by Wariston and Henderson outlining conditions which would 'settle

---

* They were: William Leslie, principal of King's College; John Forbes, Professor of Divinity at King's; Alexander Scoggie, minister of St Machar's Cathedral; Robert Baron, Professor of Divinity at Marischal College; James Sibbald, minister of St Nicholas's Kirk, and the Reverend Alexander Ross.

this church and kingdom in a solid and durable peace'. Briefly stated, this amounted to the withdrawal of liturgy, the ending of obedience to the Five Articles, and the guarantee of annual general assemblies to ensure that such detested innovations would never again be visited on the Church in Scotland.

It was an unwelcome message and Charles recognised it as such, for he was not normally in the position of being forced to face demands from his subjects. On the question of the prayer book and canons, he was in fact prepared to temporise, but he was certainly not going to play his hand until the Covenanters had disbanded, for in his book it ill became an anointed king to deal with an illegal and perhaps treasonable assembly. He would listen to Traquair but he would also issue commands directly to the Covenanters so that they would recognise his intentions: to do this Charles decided to send a diplomatic mission, his emissary being his 'true friend and loving cousin', James, Third Marquis of Hamilton. A courtier who enjoyed the affections of the king and a soldier who had served under Gustavus Adolphus, Hamilton was a type who was to become well known in the years to come – a leading Scottish magnate who knew that real power was not vested in Edinburgh but resided at court in London. Loyal, slyly intelligent and something of an aesthete, he undertook the mission unwillingly, not just because his wife had just died, but because he understood the temper of his fellow countrymen.

With him he took two proclamations which, though worded differently, amounted to the same message. Both promised that the prayer book and canons would only be imposed through legal instruments, but the first promised a pardon provided that the Covenanters disbanded, while the second threatened arrest if they did not. If necessary Hamilton was empowered to raise the necessary forces, but how he would have done so is open to doubt, for the Covenanters were fast solidifying their grip on the country. St Andrews and other recalcitrant northern burghs had given up their resistance, and throughout the country ministers appointed by bishops were being replaced, while those who had not signed faced threats of violence. This was religious fervour backed by political intent; the mood was bellicose, revolutionary, faintly hysterical and driven by the conviction that the people of Scotland were 'riding in Jerusalem to triumph'. It was given expression in a sermon which came to be known as the Red-Shankes Sermon or Pockmantie Preaching, which was given by the Rev. James Row in St Giles Church in Edinburgh in April 1638. Row, the son of John Row, the Church historian, likened the bishops' treatment of the Church to Balaam's ass carrying a 'pockmantie' [portmanteau] 'stuffed full of popish trash and trinkets'. To prevent that fate being visited on Scotland those who had refused to sign the National Covenant had to combine; unless they did so, he warned his congregation, they were not 'fit for the kingdom of heaven':

> You have a fashion here in the southern parts of Scotland, that when you come to the ford of a river, the poor post man must venture over upon his little nag, to see whether it be deep or no, and then the Laird comes mounted on his gay steed and he passes over. This is not good fashion where ever you had it. We that are highlanders have a better than that our selves. We usually go on foot, and when we come to a ford, we are loath to lose a man. Therefore, we join arm in arm, and all go in together, so that the strong supports the weak and drown one drown all. So, out your hand to the Covenant and either live or die with the rest.[17]

James Row's tone is optimistic, yet strangely compelling, and all over Scotland people were heeding its call.

Chapter Five

THE ASSEMBLY IN GLASGOW

'The king good subjectes can not save: then tell
Which is the best, to obey or to rebell?'

William Drummond of Hawthornden, Epigram 242, 1639

On a June morning in 1638 the Marquis of Hamilton was provided with ample evidence that, just as he had feared, his mission to Scotland was not going to be a smooth progression. As his party approached Edinburgh on the coastal road running from Berwick-on-Tweed, they were met by a reception committee which demonstrated the unity and strength of the Covenanting cause. Well outside the walls of the city, on the shores of the Forth estuary between the port of Leith and the town of Musselburgh, near present-day Portobello, Hamilton was greeted by a sight which confirmed all his worst fears. As the representative of the king he expected to be treated with respect and consideration, his position as one of Scotland's leading magnates also demanded it, but the crowd which had turned out, though numerous, was unsettling. First the nobility welcomed him, then followed the gentry 'standing all in ranks along the sea-side till very near the end of the sands, being a mile and a half long', and beyond them stood five hundred ministers with their psalm-singing certainty. Between Leith and Edinburgh crowds had also materialised but they were quiet and subdued, brought together more by hostile curiosity than any desire to offer the King's Commissioner a warm welcome:

> In his entry at Leith I think as much honour was done to him as ever to a King in our country. Huge multitudes as ever was gathered in that field set themselves in his way. Nobles, gentry of all shires, women a world, the town of Edinburgh, all at the Watergate; but we were most conspicuous in our black cloaks, above five hundred on a braeside on the links.[1]

Among those watching clergymen were Robert Baillie, who recorded the scene, and one William Livingstone, 'the strongest in voice and austerest in countenance', who attempted to preach a fiery sermon, but Hamilton would have none of it, gently reminding the minister that it would breach protocol as 'harangues in field were for princes' and not for their emissaries. It was not the first time that Hamilton had been gripped by a feeling of unease. No sooner had he reached the Scottish border than he had been told that the Covenanters were unlikely to accept any concession which the king might be prepared to make. Hamilton was too canny a diplomat to be dismayed by the rumour, but what did worry him was new information that the leadership might be prepared to carry out the National Covenant's threat unilaterally to summon a general assembly to protect its interests. To Hamilton such a move would be a direct challenge to the king's authority, and in some alarm he wrote urgently to Charles advising that he should begin preparations to send armed forces to Scotland to restore the rule of law. His disquiet increased when a message arrived from the Covenanting leadership telling him to proceed directly to Edinburgh to confer at Holyroodhouse instead of the palace at Dalkeith.

As it turned out, though, the first meeting on 12 June was propitious. Baillie thought Hamilton's 'speeches so fair, that we were in good hopes for some days to obtain all our desires' but the king's commissioner was merely playing for time, anxious not to publish the king's proclamation in case it provoked further demonstrations. Throughout the month the two sides bartered, but while Hamilton reassured the Covenanters that their demands for a general assembly and parliament would be met, this was balanced by the king's wish that in exchange the

Covenant would have to be rescinded. This the Covenanters refused, as to do so would have been a betrayal of their spiritual values. Following two weeks of negotiation and playing for time, Hamilton was left with no other option than to return to London to confer with an increasingly exasperated king. By then he already knew of the king's displeasure – Charles had written to inform him that while 'the damnable covenant' was in force he [Charles] had 'no more power in Scotland than as a Duke in Venice'. Before Hamilton left Edinburgh the king's proclamation was published on 4 July promising that the liturgy would not be introduced unlawfully and stressing Charles's willingness to call a free assembly and parliament 'which shall be indicted and called with Our best convenience'.[2]

Far from satisfying the Covenanters, the proclamation prompted the preparation of another legal challenge by Wariston (who, for once, had been wrong-footed by the suddenness of its publication), and Hamilton left for London with a heavy heart, telling the king on his arrival that he could see 'see no possibility to save . . . the country from ruin'. He was right to entertain such gloomy thoughts, for both sides were already beginning preparations which could only lead to military confrontation. For the Covenanters this meant purchasing arms from the Low Countries, and the first supplies started being shipped in through the port of Leith that summer. Lacking a standing army, or even an extensive militia (there had been no warfare in the country for over half a century), the Covenanters had to look to their own material resources, and these proved to be not insubstantial. A rollcall was ordered of all those with military experience who had signed the National Covenant, especially anyone who had 'been abroad and is able to do any service in wars'. Local lairds were also ordered to draw up lists of available armaments, horses and other military equipment. This was not just a precaution: as Baillie told his cousin William Spang, minister at Veere in the Netherlands, it was the beginning of a national armed resistance movement:

> Certainly our dangers were greater than we might let our people conceive, but the truth is we lived by faith in God . . . we knew the goodness of our cause; we were resolved to stand by it upon all hazards whatsoever; we knew the worst, a glorious death for the cause of God and our dear country.

Always we resolved no longer to be idle. In all the land we appointed noblemen and gentlemen for commanders, divided so many as had been officers abroad among the shires, put all our men who could bear arms to frequent drillings, had frequent both public and private humiliations before God in whom was our only trust. Everyone, man and woman, encouraged their neighbours.[3]

The Covenanters were to be especially well provided for in trained soldiers through the support provided by mercenaries who had been fighting in Germany under Gustavus Adolphus, but it was not just professionalism which fired the creation of the Covenanting army. Those who had signed the National Covenant drew comfort from its clarion call to protect the true religion and from the inference in many of the sermons of the day that Scotland was the new Israel, a beleaguered tribe struggling to do God's great work by extirpating all traces of popery and superstition. 'I do not believe our Lord will build his Zion in this land upon this skin of reformation,' wrote Samuel Rutherford to his English Puritan friend John Fennick. 'So long as our scum remains and our heart-idols are kept, this work must be at a stand, and our lord must yet sift this land and search us with candles.'[4] Fear of future retribution also played a part in encouraging men to join the Covenanting army, not least because it was being raised by the Tables, a form of government which had no legal standing – as James Row had preached in Edinburgh, 'drown one drown all'. Charles's most recent proclamation had made it clear that the act of signing the National Covenant was illegal and would result in punishment: that was a powerful inducement for those who already believed that right was on their side.

The drums were not just sounding in Scotland. If Charles was to carry out his threat to punish the Covenanters, or 'rather die than yield to those impertinent and damnable demands', he too needed an army, for with no standing army he had to look to the militia system which had been evolved in Tudor times to raise local trained bands to protect the national interest. Until the reign of Queen Elizabeth it had been a useful force, well armed and trained and provided with leadership and discipline sound enough to give a good account of itself in the field. By the 1600s, though, the system had fallen into disrepair. Training days were few and far between, equipment was not maintained, and as one colonel reported while Charles was trying to raise an army, no one seemed to realise that service in the militia had become a joke:

> As trainings are now used, we shall, I am sure, never be able to make one good soldier; for our custom and use is, nowadays, to cause our companies to meet on a certain day, and by that time the arms be all viewed, and the muster master hath had his pay (which is the chiefest thing many times he looks after) it draws towards dinner time; and, indeed, officers love their bellies so well that they are loath to take too much pains about disciplining of their soldiers.[5]

From unpromising material of that kind Charles had to find men who would not just be prepared to put down a northern revolt about which many of his English subjects knew nothing and cared even less, but who would also have the daunting task of facing the professionally led forces of the Covenanting army. Neither factor was conducive to recruiting an army which would be capable of taking on the Scots, but there were other assets on which the king could call. Within Scotland itself he controlled the strategically important castles at Edinburgh and at Dumbarton in the west. The former dominated the capital and the latter covered the upper Clyde estuary, which could be used to import men and supplies. He also enjoyed the support of several powerful Scottish families such as the Gordons of the north-east, led by the Marquis of Huntly, the Ogilvys of Airlie in Angus, and a number of Highland clans which were traditional enemies of the Campbells, whose leader, the Marquis of Argyll, was on the point of siding with the Covenanters. In Ulster he could rely on Ranald McDonnell, the Second Earl of Antrim, and crucially, he could call on the Royal Navy to transport forces north or to enforce a blockade of Scottish ports. Charles was not without allies.

As matters stood in August those preparations were only contingency plans for an uncertain future, but as attitudes hardened on both sides of the border the peace process was already in jeopardy. When Hamilton returned again to Edinburgh in the middle of the month he carried with him instructions to surrender any point rather than break off the talks, but the king's instructions had been framed in such a way that they would never be amenable to the Tables' demands. First, Charles believed that a third way could be found by granting a general assembly on condition that bishops should be admitted and that church elders should not be allowed to vote for the commissioners who would attend the assembly. Second, he insisted that the Covenanters should sign the confession of faith of 1581, the so-called Negative Confession which bound the signatory to maintain the authority of the king in clerical matters. Neither would be acceptable, the first because it allowed the king to control the election of delegates, elders being elected mainly from the ranks of the nobility and the gentry, both of which supported the Covenanters, and the second because it abrogated the National Covenant.

Once again the Covenanters mounted a challenge, arguing that as they were ecclesiastical matters only an assembly could decide them, and once again Hamilton was obliged to return to London with an unwelcome message for his master. Like Traquair, he had also been playing a double game. There is evidence from Henry Guthry, later to be bishop of Dunkeld, that Hamilton advised the Tables through Montrose to show resolution by sticking to their principles, for 'if you faint and give ground in the least, you are undone'.[6] Such a comment would have been in keeping with Hamilton's feline approach to his mission – adamant that he had to do the king's business but anxious not to offend his fellow countrymen – but it certainly did not mean that he was about to throw in his lot with the Tables. On the contrary, while in Scotland he made contact with potential allies, notably the leaders of Clan Donald, who were sworn enemies of the Argylls, and it was he who proposed enlisting the support of Antrim. It was a shrewd move, as the Ulster magnate laid claim to traditional Macdonald lands in Islay and Kintyre which were then under the control of the Campbells, and Hamilton knew that any outbreak of hostilities would encourage Antrim to support the king in the hope of scoring points off an old enemy. It was not a particularly edifying process, but not for the last time in Scotland's history, clan enmity would play a leading role in deciding loyalties and creating alliances.

On 22 September Charles finally played his hand when a royal proclamation was read at the Mercat Cross in Edinburgh giving permission for a General Assembly to be summoned in Glasgow in November and withdrawing ('discharging') the offending prayer book, canons and Articles of Perth which were 'to have no force nor effect in time coming'. In return the Covenanters would be obliged to sign the Negative Confession, an act which Wariston condemned as 'atheism' and therefore not to be tolerated. Before leaving Edinburgh at the end of another inconclusive mission Hamilton entreated the Covenanters not to make preparations for electing commissioners to the General Assembly, but he was preaching to deaf ears. Although the Privy Council approved the concessions and signed the Negative Confession, now known as the King's Covenant, and issued a warrant that the assembly would be held in Glasgow, Wariston and others questioned the king's word and a protest was produced in Montrose's name. Briefly, this rejected the King's Covenant because to sign it would not only deny the dignity of the National Covenant but it would make a nonsense of a solemn oath made with God. Signature would also imply acceptance of the new liturgy and recognition of bishops, and since they had 'no warrant for their offices in this Kirk' the Covenanters restated their insistence that in any General Assembly bishops should have 'neither place or voice'.[7]

The battle lines had now been firmly drawn. Charles had made concessions, but the more extreme Covenanters doubted his sincerity and they were right to do so, for Charles had already informed Hamilton that there were plans to send an artillery train north towards the border with Scotland. He also taken the advice of Wentworth, who had written to the Duke of Newcastle proposing the settlement of Scotland along the Irish pattern: the country would be subdued by force, the Privy Council dismissed, the prayer book imposed and the country ruled by a deputy, moves which would 'curb [the] insolences' of this 'miserly nation'.[8] Not that the Scots were holding back and waiting the outcome of events. In some burghs military training had already begun, and amid 'continual rumours of the King's preparation for war'[9] a system of warning beacons had been laid across the Lowlands in readiness for any attack by the Royal Navy.

Baillie's fears about the country's security were matched by his growing alarm at the possible emergence of internal divisions over the elections of the assembly. Many ministers disagreed with the call to allow elders to join ministers in voting for commissioners and some had indicated their willingness to sign the King's Covenant, believing that Charles's concessions were fair and equitable. Among their number was the Principal of Glasgow University, Dr John Strang, who had been a reluctant signatory of the National Covenant, only changing his mind at Baillie's behest. There was also the continued opposition of the Aberdeen Doctors, whose doctrinal refusal to sign the National Covenant must have played a part in encouraging 12,000 people in the north-east to sign the new confession of faith. (Ironically, though, the Aberdeen clerics were just as reluctant to sign the new covenant, believing that to do so would compromise their support for the status quo.) These confusions did not dilute the Covenanters' cause in the autumn of 1638, but they did help to create tensions when the presbyteries began electing commissioners to the General Assembly, for not every part of the country was minded to allow elders to vote.

As it turned out, though, all opposition came to nothing, such was the Covenanters' grip on the country. In October the Tables demonstrated that they were in control and the king was not when they announced that attendance at the General Assembly was compulsory for all nobles who had signed the National Covenant. To increase their authority over the assembly they also introduced a system of assessment by which their placemen would also attend, not to vote but to 'advise' the commissioners. Against this Hamilton could only summon the Privy Council, but it was by no means united in its opposition to the Covenanters, a factor which made it more or less impossible to form a dependable Royalist party in Scotland. The response to the King's Covenant had been disappointing: despite the rally in the north-east, there were only 28,000 signatures and the hoped-for support in Glasgow was also looking increasingly doubtful.

The city had been chosen for two reasons. Its presbytery had shown its independence by taking its time to hold elections – 'the first open door to division' according to Baillie – and only did so under compulsion when a delegation of Covenanters arrived from Edinburgh to stiffen their resolve. Hamilton was also heartened by reports of local support for the King's Covenant, but above all he hoped that the city's position just to the north of his landed estates in Clydesdale would bring local backing for his cause. In neither case was Hamilton to be proved right. While it was true that the city had been lukewarm in its response to the National Covenant, there was as yet no coherent opposition, and any that existed had bowed to the coercion of the Edinburgh ministers. The much-vaunted Hamilton influence also failed to materialise, not least because his mother, the dowager marchioness Anna Cunningham, had thrown in her lot with the Covenanters and her authority in the west of Scotland proved to be decisive.[10] Besides, the Covenanters were too well organised. Not only had they rigged the elections by laying down the rules for the presbyteries' elections, but through religious intimidation they had made it almost impossible for any party to oppose them.

One other factor favoured Glasgow: it was large enough to house the delegates and it could afford the additional costs of hosting the assembly, great care being taken by the town council to ensure that all lodgings were inspected so that 'every one may be lodged according to their quality and ability of this city'.[11] Although in its infancy, trade was beginning to enrich Glasgow and a new breed of merchants was exploiting links with Ireland, France and the Scandinavian countries as well as continuing the older agricultural trading connections with the Highlands and western islands. One English visitor described Glasgow as 'handsomely built . . . one of the most considerablest [sic] burghs of Scotland' while another, Sir William Brereton, made much of the university, 'a good handsome foundation' with a decent library. Founded in 1450, the university was a centre of Presbyterian teaching, many of its academics having trained at the French Huguenot college at Saumur – among their number was Zachary Boyd, whose kinsman, Lord Boyd, was a leading Presbyterian magnate and the youngest peer to have signed the National Covenant. While this concentration of Presbyterianism should have made Glasgow a hotbed of Covenanting fervour there was also a strong local feeling, especially in the university, in favour of Charles, and Baillie was not far wrong when he wrote that 'the greatest opposites in the west to this subscription are our friends in Glasgow'. At first this moderate cleric had been disinclined to attend the Assembly, fearing that to do so would be a treasonable offence, but having had his mind put at rest by the king's proclamation he decided that this was indeed God's will:

> If God be with us, we hope to have our Church and State put in
> a better case than it has been these thirty years bygone; but if he
> desert us, we cannot avoid presently to fall into great danger to be

a field of blood, and, thereafter a poor slaved province, at the devotion, both in religion and laws, of a faction which to us is extremely suspect of wicked designs: between this great hope and great fear now we hang.[12]

The General Assembly promised to be an electrifying occasion and, as it turned out, it did not disappoint the expectations of those who believed and trusted that it would finally abolish episcopacy and lay down firm foundations for the reconstruction of a Presbyterian form of Church government. Delegates started arriving in the city a week before it was due to begin on 21 November 1638, and most were impressed with the arrangements that had been made, considering them to be 'above all men's expectation'. Of their number 140 were ministers of the Church and all had signed the National Covenant, as had the accompanying 98 lay elders, who appeared in Glasgow with their friends and followers. Presaging what was to follow, few troubled to conceal their weapons – 'many swords but many more daggers' as Hamilton related to the king in some disgust at the end of the first day's proceedings – but there was present, too, a sense of unity and common purpose which went beyond intimidation. In effect the General Assembly was both the conscience of Scotland and a government in waiting and the only thing which stood in its way was the person of the king as represented by his commissioner.

Before proceedings opened, steps had already been taken to dissociate Scotland from episcopal rule: on 24 October the Tables had passed a bill demanding that the bishops be punished for the errors of their ways in introducing the new liturgy. Wisely, all the prelates decided to stay away from the proceedings and most, including Spottiswood, decided that it might be prudent to spend a short holiday in England. Knowing that he was outnumbered in his fight to save episcopacy ('my chief end and next endeavour'), Hamilton saw that his best hope was to carry out the king's wishes and delay the assembly's proceedings as best he could.

From the outset the atmosphere in Glasgow was intimidating, just as the Covenanters and their supporters meant it to be. A large crowd gathered in the precincts of the cathedral and many of the men were armed: if the mood was one of high expectation then it was tempered by a widespread belief that a struggle lay ahead. That much became clear during the first five days, which were taken up with procedural matters largely concerning the election of a moderator and clerk and the right of the bishops to declare the assembly illegal. Throughout the proceedings Hamilton did as best he could to hold up the proceedings, but the odds were stacked against him. As the king's commissioner he was granted some respect, sitting in the church with his six assessors in front of him, facing the massed ranks of Covenanters in the choir, but that confrontation alone must have unsettled him. Hamilton might have affected to understand his fellow countrymen but he was much more at home in court circles.

The Assembly began with a sermon given by the aged Dr John Bell on the text of the Seven Golden Candlesticks from the first chapter of The Revelation of St John the Divine, although so infirm was he that it was only heard by those sitting close to the pulpit. Hamilton then read the king's commission, and so began a succession of delaying tactics, each one being countered by the Covenanters' arguments. First Hamilton attempted to halt proceedings by claiming that the Assembly could not be constituted until its membership had been agreed, then he demanded that a letter be read from the bishops protesting against the Assembly. He also tried to block the elections, but on the second day Alexander Henderson was voted moderator and Wariston his clerk. Both being original subscribers to the National Covenant and its leading instigators, they made a formidable team. Wariston was also able to produce registers of the General Assembly back to 1560, documents which provided him with legal precedents from a period before the rule of bishops.

Worn down by the tireless responses to his argument and realising that the king's wishes were being denied, Hamilton took the only course open to him. Late in the day on 28 November, with the candles flickering in the gloom of the cathedral, the king's commissioner rose to declare the Assembly dissolved, telling the delegates 'that nothing done here in this Assembly shall be of any force to bind any of his Majesty's subjects; and I in his Majesty's name discharge this Court to sit any longer.'[13] It was nobly said, but it made little difference to the proceedings. A formal protest at his action was read out, and to add insult he was forced to sit and listen to it, as the cathedral door was locked and the key concealed.

Once the door had been forced open and Hamilton allowed to

depart, the Assembly had to decide whether or not to heed the king's commissioner's words. Had they done so they would have broken their sacred word, but to stay in place meant that they were in effect disobeying the king's wishes as he had presented them through the person of his plenipotentiary. First Henderson spoke, and his words calmed minds that otherwise might have been unsure that they were acting for the good of the Church. Having reassured his fellow delegates that, although kings had the right to convene assemblies, they were bound too by Christ's wishes to protect the liberties of the Church, he bade them be of good cheer, that right was on their side:

> You all know that the work in hand has had many difficulties, and God has borne us through them all to this day; therefore, it becometh us not to be discouraged now by any thing that has intervened, but rather redouble our courage when we seem to be deprived of human authority.[14]

Other voices joined in to reinforce Henderson's message, arguing that they had no option but to continue, otherwise they would be guilty of apostasy. The question was put to the vote and, with only four declining (one being Strang), the Assembly took their first step to defy the king and to commit an act of open rebellion. It had in fact been a close-run thing, for if Henderson had not taken the initiative and others, including Dickson, had not spoken up in his support, the Assembly might well have swithered and plumped for the safer course. 'It was good we were all put to it presently,' noted Baillie, 'for if we had been delayed till morrow, it was feared many would have slipped away.'[15]

With Hamilton gone the Assembly was free to pursue its own agenda, and for the next three weeks – it finally dissolved itself on 20 December – its members set about the urgent task of reforming Church government in Scotland. They did so with a will. Within the space of its existence the Assembly set about dismantling the episcopalian system of Church government and restoring Presbyterianism. No half measures were tolerated. The bishops were deposed, the new liturgy was declared illegal, jurisdiction of the Church was returned to the presbytery, the synod and the General

Assembly, and the separation of Church and state was made complete by the prohibition of ministers holding public office, a decision which removed the clerical estate from the Scottish parliament. Before breaking up, the General Assembly's final decision was to meet annually. Previously James had designated the time and place of General Assemblies, but by deciding to meet again in Edinburgh the following summer the General Assembly struck a blow for its independence of action.

Before leaving Glasgow Hamilton convened the Privy Council to confirm his dissolution of the Assembly and ordered its members to leave Glasgow. Few obeyed and one of their number, Argyll, chose the moment to openly side with the Covenanters, a decision which would have momentous consequences. Then, before he departed for London the king's commissioner issued another proclamation declaring all acts of the Assembly null and void. To his monarch Hamilton had already written advising that military preparations should be increased 'to curb the insolency of this rebellious nation' and that steps should be taken to create a Royalist party led by Huntly in the north and Traquair or Roxburgh in the south.

As for the Covenanters, they left Glasgow with their hopes largely fulfilled. Earlier in the year they had set out to reform their Church with the king's blessing, but they had ended it by introducing the reforms of their own accord. It had not been easy – they had expected greater opposition from Hamilton and the bishops – but they had taken events into their own hands and become masters of their own fate. The process had not always been edifying. Intimidation was rife and the atmosphere in the high church so threatening that, with a few honest exceptions, including Baillie, who spoke out against the decision to make episcopalianism illegal, few ministers had dared to offer any objections. (For his pains and by his own admission Baillie earned the reputation of being 'a sour plum'.)

But the time for talking was rapidly passing. Henderson's next utterance came in his 'Instructions for Defensive Arms', in which he argued the Christian necessity of resisting tyranny and taking up arms to use them in the defence of a free national Kirk. Unless its religious liberties were defended, he warned, Scotland and its people could 'look for nothing but miserable and perpetual slavery'.[16] In England, too, preparations were in hand. William Juxon, the Treasurer, informed Charles that £200,000 was available as a war chest, and the year ended with Charles taking the first steps to raise the forces needed to crush the 'damnable, atheistical, puritanical crew of the Scotch Covenant'.[17]

Chapter Six

FOR CHRIST'S CROWN AND COVENANT: THE FIRST BISHOPS' WAR

'Next hell I hate this place.'

The Marquis of Hamilton to King Charles I, 28 November 1638

Charles was quite clear about the direction of his military preparations, and on paper at least they made sense. In the north-east of Scotland Huntly would raise a force drawn from those who supported the king, and Hamilton would command naval and ground forces which would land on the east coast; from Ulster Antrim would attack the west in Argyllshire and Wentworth would bring more men over from Ireland to land at Dumbarton. At the same time, Charles would raise an army of 20,000 which would muster at York before marching over the border at Berwick-on-Tweed to attack Edinburgh. This four-pronged attack would be sufficient to cow the Covenanters into submission or to defeat them in the field should they dare to offer battle. On 18 January 1639 letters were sent from the king to all his noblemen and supporters inviting them to offer aid and military assistance. A few weeks later other letters were dispatched to the Lords Lieutenant specifying the precise numbers of men each county should provide.

It was the first time that such a summons had been issued in almost a hundred years, and it was accompanied by a good deal of confusion.

Very few of the leading nobility had any military experience; arms and weapons, where they existed, were in poor condition, and apart from experienced mercenaries such as Jacob Astley, appointed Sergeant-Major responsible for York's defences, there was a complete absence of discipline or awareness of battlefield tactics. Of the 5000 men mustered by Hamilton to produce an amphibious force, only 200 could fire a musket with any hope of hitting the enemy. The Master Gunner reported that only four of his men were able to fire a mortar, and when the King's Standard-bearer Sir Edmund Verney reviewed the force at York he could only comment that 'there never was so raw, so unskilful, and so unwilling an army brought to fight'.[1]

Money too proved to be a problem. Charles decided not to recall parliament to support the conflict and relied instead on loans and the funds made available by Juxon, the Treasurer. Given the size of the forces about to be raised, the war exchequer (such as it was) proved to be insufficient, with the result that men were paid tardily or not at all and it proved difficult to persuade mercenaries to return from Germany. Eight thousand muskets were ordered from the Netherlands, but it was not an easy task to train men to use them and the Kentish contingent had to rely on their pikes, which were either too short or in parlous condition. The men, too, were not always of the best. Making use of the 'substitution' clause in the Militia Act, many of the soldiers sent to York were not trained men who were allowed to stay at home, but drawn from the lower orders and the dregs of society. The final blow came from Ireland when Wentworth reported that he was unable to raise an army before June 1639, by which time the Covenanters would have taken Dumbarton castle. This they did at the end of March.

Nonetheless, by April an army of 28,000 had assembled at York and Hamilton's force had embarked at Gravesend and Yarmouth. They were a motley bunch, for the most part untrained and badly equipped, but a handful of mercenary captains had returned from Germany and their presence not only stiffened resolve but offered the opportunity of instilling some discipline and weapons training before the army reached the border. Paradoxically, among them were a number of Scots. Some had been drawn back to Britain through their loyalty to the Crown; others because they had caught a ship to England instead of to Scotland, following the mercenaries' nostrum that it mattered not which master they served provided that they were paid. Among the latter was James Turner, a Scot, who having missed an English ship bound for Hull from Norway, took a second Danish ship to Leith and ended up fighting for the Covenanters:

> I had swallowed without chewing, in Germany, a very dangerous maxim, what military men there too much follow; which was, that so we serve our master honestly, it is no matter what master we serve; so, without examination of the justice of the quarrel, or regard to my duty to either prince or country, I resolved to go with the ship I first encountered.[2]

Had he been permitted to join the English ship, which sailed before his baggage arrived, Turner would just as surely have fought for Charles. But whatever their reasons for choosing a side, contemporary accounts speak of morale rising as the royal army made its way north and a growing confidence that the Scots were 'not so potent or strong as they brag of'. National animosity also fired the English army: Scotland was regarded with contempt as a barbarous and backward country and officers were not slow to encourage their troops to curse and make fun of the 'scabby, shitten, stinking, slovenly, snotty-nosed . . . insolent, proud, beggarly, impertinent' Scotsmen whom they would shortly meet in battle.[3]

At the beginning of May the campaign began in earnest when the amphibious force arrived in the roads of the Firth of Forth and Hamilton made ready to issue the king's proclamation upholding the concessions he had already made and ordering the Covenanting leaders to submit within eight days or to face the confiscation of their lands and possessions. This proved to be impracticable, as the local security forces made a landing impossible, and Hamilton was further discomfited by news that his mother intended to shoot him with her pistol if he set foot in Edinburgh. Instead of attacking Edinburgh and laying waste to the Lothians Hamilton was forced into the familiar position of sitting tight and negotiating with the Covenanters while the king decided his next move. By then, too, he had realised the impossibility of enforcing a blockade, such was the paucity of ships available to him.

In any case it was too late to make any impression on the

Covenanters without forcing a battle. While Charles had been raising his army, Scotland had been awash with military preparations. At the same time that the king had been writing to his nobles asking for help, a committee of leading Covenanters, including Rothes and Montrose, had met in Edinburgh to compose a similar dispatch to be sent around the country asking for men to rally to the call in the nation's hour of need. But whereas the English system had been haphazard the Scots had evolved an efficient system of recruitment and fund-raising. Committees of shires were formed to deal with such matters as recruitment, appointments, quartering and provision of the regiments raised. Reporting to the Tables they proved to be efficient and cost-effective. Men between the ages of sixteen and sixty were selected, armed and equipped, and in a far-reaching move which would later be developed when Cromwell's New Model Army was formed, the decision was taken to appoint experienced soldiers to positions of executive command. While many colonels of regiments were wealthy but inexperienced landowners, the lieutenant-colonel and the main under-officers were usually battle-hardened Scottish mercenaries from Germany, men like Turner, Alexander Hamilton and Sir Robert Monro, all of whom, according to John Spalding, 'came in great numbers upon hope of bloody war'.

The chance of battle was one reason, the fighting in Germany being in stalemate; money another, for the Tables had taken steps to raise funds through 'voluntary' contributions based on rents; but most of the mercenaries were sons of Covenanting families and felt honour-bound to help the militant Protestant cause. This did not make them anti-Royalists as such – the most prominent of their number, Alexander Leslie, spoke of his reverence for his 'dread sovereign' – but like all professional soldiers they were determined to give a lead to their men, many of whom were as unpromising and badly equipped as those marching from the south towards the Scottish border. The Scots' object was to defend their country from invasion and to uphold the National Covenant.

Overall command was given to the admirable Leslie, and there could have been no better choice. His experiences in Sweden and Germany gave him a pre-eminence which none could question, and his appointment avoided the necessity of appointing an aristocrat and thereby causing offence among the rest of the nobility. In fact Leslie may have been distantly related to his feudal superior Rothes, but even if he was not he had remedied that omission by marrying his son to Rothes's daughter. He also enjoyed a good relationship with Hamilton, with whom he had corresponded on the state of war in Europe, and might have been minded to accept a commission for further service abroad but for the summons from Rothes in the autumn of 1638. There is also little doubt that his mercenary instincts included a desire to be rewarded by his country, not just with money but with honours, and to make a nonsense of Spalding's description of him as 'a gentleman of base birth'.

It might seem strange to see this soldier of fortune pledging allegiance to two opposing forces – the Crown and the Covenant – but he and his fellow Covenanters saw no such clash. They were not fighting for independence or for the rupture of the union of the crowns but to uphold a form of worship which they devoutly believed to be under threat. Their main enemy was the episcopacy, not the person or office of the king, and most were quick to point this out to English friends. To their minds the settlement of the religious question would not weaken the relations between the two countries but strengthen them. If Charles had done wrong he had done so by acting as an absentee monarch and forcing unpopular policies on a distant country. To make their position clear the Covenanters published an 'Information' calling on the English parliament to judge their actions impartially and denying that they were treasonable troublemakers. (The king responded by saying that they were just that.) From St Andrews, where he had been moved, Rutherford wrote to his English friend Fennick explaining Scotland's position in terms of easily understood religious allegory:

> O what room is for your love, if it were as broad as the sea, up in heaven and in God? And what would not Christ give for your love? God gave so much for your soul, and blessed are ye if ye have a love for him and can call in your soul's love from all idols and can make a God of God, a God of Christ, and draw a line betwixt your heart and him. If your deliverance come not, Christ's preference and his believed love must stand as caution and surety for your deliverance till your Lord send it in his blessed time.[4]

The quarrel was not just about the religious well-being of the nation, it was as much concerned with the safety of the soul. Not that temporal measures were being ignored. Aberdeen had stuck to its guns and had not only refused to accept the decisions of the Glasgow assembly but had started taking military preparations to defend itself. The city fathers had high hopes of Huntly's support, but although he carried the king's commission, in common with so many of Charles's servants he was cursed with indecision and carried out to a fault the king's request not to act until the English forces had crossed the border. However, in that Huntly was a rallying point for disaffection he did pose a threat to the Covenanters, and to counter it Montrose received orders in February to raise a regiment from Perthshire and Angus which would then march north to prevent the Royalist party from winning control of the area. Accompanying it was General Leslie.

Montrose's first staging post was the Aberdeenshire town of Turriff, where the northern Covenanters were holding a meeting to select commissioners, and he had to move quickly to protect them because Huntly, too, was heading there with a sizeable force which included his sons and some local Gordon lairds. A confrontation seemed inevitable and, urged on by some local hotheads and much against his will, Huntly was persuaded to make a demonstration after he arrived on 14 February. The result was a humiliating farce. An envoy, Lord Findlater, was sent to parley with Montrose, who said that it was entirely acceptable for Huntly and his men to enter the town provided that they did not interfere with the Covenanters' meeting. Unwilling to provoke a fight yet indisposed to appear irresolute, Huntly took his force through the town 'without salutation or word speaking on either side' before riding off to the house of Sir George Ogilvy of Banff, one of the local lairds who had urged him to fight in the first place. So ended the 'Raid of Turriff', the first military confrontation involving Royalist forces in the wars of the three kingdoms.

From Banff Huntly moved to Aberdeen, some forty miles south, where a proclamation from the king was read out condemning the Covenanters' actions and reaffirming Charles's support of episcopacy. Encouraged by the king's words the city made ready for the expected attack from Montrose, but when the Covenanters arrived on 30 March the defences were not put to the test. Huntly withdrew and the well-armed Covenanting army marched into the city with its flag sporting the motto 'For Religion, The Covenant and the Countrie', each man wearing a blue bonnet and the cavalrymen a blue sash. From contemporary descriptions the soldiers were both well-disciplined and well-equipped and the force they served was rapidly becoming a proper army:

> They came in order of battle well armed on horses and foot, each horseman having five shots at the least, whereof he had a carbine in his hand, two pistols by his sides and the other two on his saddle pommel. The pikemen in their ranks [with] pike and sword; musketeers in their ranks with musket, staff, bandolier, sword, powder, ball and match. Each company both on horse and foot had their captains, lieutenants, ensigns, sergeants and other officers and commanders, all for the most part in buff coats and goodly order . . . they had trumpeters to each company of horsemen and drummers to each company of footmen. They had their meat, drink and other provisions, bag and baggage, carried with them all by the advise of his excellency Field Marshal [Alexander] Leslie whose council General Montrose followed in this business.[5]

This was a show of strength, a demonstration that the Covenanting army had all the big guns, and leaders to direct them. Even at this early juncture the Scots were garnering the fruits of their mercenaries' experience in the forward-looking Swedish army. Here were regiments of heavily armed cavalrymen who could act independently and here were musketeers with unwieldy matchlocks which were none the less capable of providing concentrated fire, if the men firing them were well drilled. As the Covenanters clattered into Aberdeen it must have been an imposing sight, but as they made their way to the links ostentatiously to eat their dinner in public, Montrose knew that more than a demonstration was needed, that he could not pacify the north-east until he had dealt with Huntly. A series of meetings followed in the nearby town of Inverurie and, finding that his support was dwindling, Huntly and his eldest son Lord Lewis Gordon were persuaded to go to Aberdeen, where Leslie apprehended them and sent them under arrest to Edinburgh. A soldierly decision it might have been, but it was a move which led to bitter recriminations later in the conflict as it seemed to Huntly that his safe-conduct had been forfeited.

Far from pacifying the area, Huntly's 'arrest' encouraged the local Royalists to sign a declaration 'in defence of the king's prerogative; and next for the duty, honour and service they owe to the house of Huntly'. With both the leading Gordons absent in Edinburgh – Huntly's brother Adam was held to be a simpleton and his son Viscount Aboyne was thought (wrongly as it turned out) to be too young – command was given to an able soldier of fortune, Lieutenant-Colonel 'Crowner' Johnstone, who successfully besieged the castle of Towie-Barclay to recover arms stolen from the Huntlys. During a brief but well-executed engagement one of the Gordons' retainers was killed by a stray shot from within the castle – this was David Prat, who has the unhappy distinction of being the first victim of the civil wars. Encouraged by the fall of the castle on 13 May Johnstone led his force to Turriff, where the Covenanters were surprised and forced to flee. Spalding, by no means an impartial witness, left some idea of the Covenanters' confusion as Johnstone's men mounted a surprise dawn attack which carried all before it:

> The Covenanters, whereof some were sleeping in their beds, others, some drinking and smoking tobacco, others, some walking up and down, hearing this dreadful noise of drums and trumpets, ran to their arms and confusedly to dress and compose themselves.[6]

The action was known as the 'Trot of Turriff', and while it was minor compared to the later battles of the civil war, such was the element of surprise engineered by Johnstone that the rout deserves to be counted as the first Royalist victory. It also gave the Huntly faction renewed hope, more so as they were soon joined by a force of Highlanders from Deeside and Glenlivet, armed with ancient muskets and swords.

In addition to providing the confrontation with its first military landmarks, the campaign in the north-east introduced tactics which would become drearily familiar to the non-combatants. The rival armies lived off the land, houses and farms were plundered, harvests destroyed and in some cases the opposition put to the sword. When William Keith, the Earl Marischal, retook Aberdeen on 25 May – for a short time it had been in Royalist hands – a heavy fine was levied, there was an outbreak of ransacking and the city's dogs were massacred for the only reason that their owners had thought it a good jest to make them wear blue Covenanting ribbons. In comparison with the atrocities committed in Germany during the same period this was small beer, but it left an unhappy legacy, not least because the incidents pitted Scot against Scot.

As yet there had been few casualties and the Royalist resistance was fanned by landowners who had no clear sense of direction but were fired by their unwillingness to sign the Covenant and to have their estates forfeited. On the Covenanting side Montrose showed a rare capacity to read events, and his interventions were responsible for keeping a lid on the violence, a fact that was admired by Wariston. He also knew that he had to prevent the north-east from becoming a hotbed of Royalist resistance. While recruiting men in June he received news that James Gordon, Viscount Aboyne, and other leading Royalists, including the Earls of Glencairn and Tullibardine, had landed at Aberdeen to rally the area for the king. Accompanied by a mercenary, William Gunn, who had been commissioned by Charles but who turned out to be more trouble than he was worth, their plan was to march south on 14 June with a combined force of Highlanders and men from the north-east. They got as far as the port of Stonehaven, to the south of Aberdeen, where a desultory artillery duel took place on the slopes of Megray Hill between Aboyne's and Marischal's forces.

Few were killed – the Covenanters were firing uphill – but the Highlanders broke and Aboyne's men were forced to retire to the Brig of Dee, where they were confronted by the main Covenanting force led by Montrose. To their credit the Aberdonians, encouraged by 'Crowner' Johnstone, had built stout defences, and with the Dee in spate Montrose had to capture the bridge if he were to have any chance of taking the city. In the initial stages of the battle, which began on 18 June, his artillery made little impression, and by the day's end there was stalemate, with the defenders having lost only one man, John Forbes. But this lone casualty was to be their undoing when a large number of Royalists abandoned the bridge to attend his funeral. Placing his cannons closer to the bridge Montrose renewed the assault at first light, but success came to him when he executed a manoeuvre which left Aboyne fruitlessly attempting to guess his intentions. With a party of horsemen Montrose made a feint westwards along the riverbank, a ruse which prompted Aboyne to shadow him. This left the bridge largely undefended and the Covenanters' artillery did the rest. By the end of the afternoon, following a frontal attack led by John Middleton, later to be a general and a noted Royalist, the bridge was in the hands of the Covenanters and so too was the hapless city of Aberdeen. Spalding claimed that the Aberdeen contingent was praised by the Covenanters 'for their service and ready fire' but many were jailed and the city itself was fined. Against the advice of his commanders Montrose decided not to raze the city, mainly because two days later, on 21 June, a ship arrived informing him that the war, such as it was, had already come to an end as a result of the king deciding to agree peace terms with the Covenanters.

Although the campaign in the north-east was a side-show compared to what would follow, it did serve a purpose. With good reason the Covenanters were concerned about Huntly's influence and the possibility of a landing by Royalist forces in the wake of Hamilton's presence in the Forth estuary. They knew, too, that Antrim posed a threat in the west and that this would be supported by the local enemies of the Campbells. While the invasion had not materialised – for the time being at least – and although Huntly's opposition remained a chimera, the Tables could not afford to allow a sizeable Royalist opposition to be created in this strategically important part of Scotland. That consideration at least made it worthwhile to curb Aberdeen's enthusiastic opposition to the National Covenant and by so doing to maintain a degree of national harmony. The campaign also helped to cement Montrose's reputation as a versatile soldier and forceful military commander – his rapid advance on Turriff, the feint at the Brig of Dee and, just as important, his decision to save Aberdeen from the torch.

At the same time the Covenanting stronghold of the south-west was secured against a possible invasion from Ireland through the intervention of forces led by the Earls of Cassilis and Eglinton, but the main thrust of the campaign was led by Leslie, who had returned to Edinburgh early in April. Inspired by Henderson's advice that resistance to the king was lawful if the compact between Crown and people had been broken, however inadvertently, the main Covenanting army was preparing at Dunbar in East Lothian to face the invasion which everyone in Scotland knew to be imminent – on 14 May Charles had issued a proclamation stating that the Scottish army would be destroyed if it moved up to within ten miles of the border, a move which would 'do a singular service both to his Majesty's honour and safety'.[7] The Scottish parliament was due to meet the following day, but with national resistance on everyone's minds this was an obvious and unnecessary diversion. Even so, the Covenanters knew that they would stand condemned if they refused to hold a sitting after the king had given them express permission, and this constitutional nicety placed them in a quandary. Release from it came from an unlikely source when a message arrived from the king postponing the opening of parliament until 23 July.

By then the English army had arrived in Berwick and camped at Birks to the west of Berwick, but although morale was good the men were still far from being ready for battle. Charles arrived on 30 May determined to make his way on to Scottish territory so that he could issue the proclamation which Hamilton had been unable to deliver. To the bemusement of the locals this was done the following day when the Earl Marshal, Thomas Howard, Second Earl of Arundel, and a small force entered the town of Duns in the foothills of the Lammermuir Hills and forced the local sheriff to proclaim the edict. It was as well that he acted when he did, for Leslie's force was already heading for Duns, where it would complete its muster by 5 June on the slopes of the neighbouring Duns Law. With them and serving in the Earl of Eglinton's Regiment was Robert Baillie, one of the many chaplains who accompanied the Covenanting army as it prepared to defend the faith of the Scottish people:

> Our regiments lay on the sides of the hill, almost round about: the place was not a mile in circle, a pretty round rising in a declivity, without steepness, to the height of a bow-shot; on the top somewhat plain; about a quarter of a mile in length, and as much in breadth, as I remember, capable of tents for forty thousand men. The colonels lay in canvas lodgings, high and wide; their captains about them in lesser ones; the soldiers all about in huts of timber, covered with a divot or straw.

Most of the men came from the south-west – 'stout young ploughmen', tenants of the great Covenanting lords and bound to them through ties of fealty and family – and Baillie was impressed not just by their discipline but also by their piety. This was the Lord's work and they were about to do it, under 'a brave new colour, stamped with the Scottish Arms and "For Chryst's Croun and Covenant" in golden letters'.

> Had you lent your ear in the morning, or especially at even, and heard in the tents the sound of some singing psalms, some praying, and some reading scripture, you would have been refreshed: true, there was swearing and cursing and bawling in some quarters, whereat we were grieved; but we hoped, if our camp had been a little settled, to have gotten some way for these misorders; for all of any fashion did regret, and all did promise to contribute their best endeavours for helping all abuses. For myself I never found my mind in better temper than it was all that time I came from home till my head was again homeward, for I was a man who had taken my leave from the world and was resolved to die in that service without return.[8]

And yet, for all that Leslie's army offered an imposing sight with its psalm-singing certainty and its Swedish discipline, it was not invincible. Shortage of numbers (it was some 10,000 shy of the 22,000 the Covenanters claimed), lack of training and a scarcity of provisions saw to that, but as Baillie insisted all was well because it was guided 'by a hand clearly divine'. If so, it was sorely needed, for Leslie knew that he could not remain long at Duns Law without receiving an adequate and steady flow of reinforcements as well as supplies to feed his men, admitting to Wariston that he was 'extremely perplexed' and 'brought low before God indeed'. On the night of 4 June Leslie wrote to the Covenanting leadership to warn them that, while he had placed his trust in God, he still needed worldly help: 'If our countrymen and fellow Covenanters, equally obliged with us, shall either withdraw themselves or come too late, it may be to the burying of our bodies, which with the cause itself might be saved by their speed, horse and foot, let them answer to God for it.'[9]

While Duns Law was a sound strategic position which enabled

Leslie to move his force to counter any English move from Berwick or the other possible point of attack, Kelso, he was acutely aware that he could do nothing to guard the western border near Carlisle should it be threatened (as was feared) by forces from Ireland. For all that, the Covenanting army was blessed with unshakeable confidence in its leaders and its own abilities and it was their good fortune that those same attributes were lacking in Charles's army. By then the king knew of the collapse of his support in the north-east and recognised that Hamilton would be unable to achieve anything in the Forth. There was also growing confusion about the size of the army they would be facing: one English commander complained that the Scots might as well have been in the Indies for all that was known about them or their capabilities. In an attempt to resolve that issue a small English force led by the Earl of Holland marched on Kelso and crossed the Tweed in broad daylight, only to retreat when Holland feared that he would be outnumbered by the Scots.

It was the closest the two sides would come to fighting, for already peace feelers were being put out by both sides, much to the later regret of '[English] men of good judgement [who] say that if his Majesty would have taken his advantage to punish their insolencies, he might have marched to Edinburgh and bred such confusion among them as that the common people must of necessity have deserted their nobility'.[10] That was wishful thinking, for the truth was that neither side had the stomach for unnecessary bloodshed, and on 6 June the king sent a page into Leslie's camp proposing talks. To this the Covenanters agreed and the following day the Earl of Dunfermline rode over to the king's camp carrying a supplication, requesting Charles 'to appoint some few of the many worthy men of your Majesty's kingdom of England who are well affected to the true Religion' to begin negotiations so that 'the two Kingdoms may be kept in peace and happiness under your Majesty's long and prosperous reign'.[11]

Charles's reply was given the next day by Sir Edmund Verney and it opened with the demand that his proclamation should be read out to the Scottish army. Once again the king failed to understand the temper of the Covenanters. If they had followed the king's command to the letter it would have been tantamount to declaring themselves traitors. However a compromise was reached whereby they agreed to read the document 'with much reverence' in private but not to publish it. This nicety having been agreed, a time and place was set for peace talks: six commissioners from each side would meet in Arundel's headquarters at Birks on 11 June, the Covenanters choosing to be represented by Rothes, Dunfermline, Loudoun, Henderson, Wariston and Sir William Douglas of Cavers, Sheriff of Teviotdale. With them they took precise demands including the ratification of the acts of the assembly and parliament, an agreement to hold yearly assemblies which would deal with all ecclesiastical matters, the withdrawal of the Royalist army, and 'to punish ignominiously and exemplarily those firebrands [the excommunicated bishops] who by their misinformations have brought him [Charles] to this extremity against his people'.[12]

When the Scots arrived – there had been a delay over the agreement for safe-conduct – they thought that Arundel would chair the meeting, but no sooner had the talks begun than Charles swept in to explain that he was required to clear his name of the slanders that been made against him in Scotland. His presence was both a challenge and a hindrance, to both parties. Having heard out Rothes, who justified the Covenanters' actions, Charles declared the Scots' demands to be 'too rude' and there followed a long and unproductive discussion on the legality of the Glasgow Assembly and the decisions it had reached. This ended with the Scots conceding a vague statement that their main desire was 'to enjoy our liberties according to our laws'. A formal memorandum was then prepared by Loudoun stating that the Scots only wanted religious freedom in return for their continued temporal loyalty to the Crown, and with that the talks concluded, the two sides agreeing to meet again two days later.

Once again the talks became bogged down in detail* but on this occasion the king cut through the discussion by saying that, if the sum of their demands was contained in the memorandum, then he would

---

* Some of it was farcical. When Charles asked if he was responsible to other than God for his actions Henderson replied that he was. 'Then,' answered Charles, 'David was mistaken who said, "against Thee *only* have I sinned".' Henderson then emended the minutes to read the correct text: 'against Thee *principally* have I sinned.' As Baillie noted, 'it is likely his Majesty's ears had never been tickled with such discourses'.

study it and give his opinion on 15 June, a Saturday. For the Scots it was a disappointment. Although Charles conceded the point that all ecclesiastical questions should be governed by assemblies which should meet annually or when occasion demanded, his wording was too unclear and imprecise to satisfy Wariston's legal mind. Another meeting was fixed for Monday but it, too, was inconclusive, leaving the Covenanters vexed and anxious. News had just reached them of Aboyne's landing at Aberdeen and they began to fear that Charles was stonewalling so that his army could be reinforced for an attack across the Tweed.

Aware that the king would not be moved on the matter of ratifying the decisions of the Assembly in Glasgow, and realising that their own military position was not as strong as it had been a week earlier, the Covenanters decided, fatefully, to compromise. In return for vaguely worded promises that ecclesiastical matters would be governed by assemblies and civil matters by parliament, the Scots agreed to withdraw their forces and return royal property. The Royalist army would also retire and an Assembly would meet in Edinburgh on 6 August followed by a sitting of parliament which would ratify its findings. Baillie thought the Treaty of Berwick a just outcome, 'that God had sent us a tolerable peace in a very fit time', Arundel was equally effusive, and on hearing the news in Cambridge young Abraham Cowley wrote the first of several praise poems:

> Others by war their conquests gain,
> You, like a God, your ends obtain,
> Who, when rude chaos for His help did call
> Spoke but the word and sweetly ordered all.[13]

Others were less sure. On hearing the news in London Laud was of the opinion that 'the King can have neither honour nor safety from it' and in Charles's camp there were fears that the Scots still posed a military threat. Even the ever dubious Wariston wondered if his party had been outmanoeuvred: in his diary he offered the lugubrious note that when the Covenanting leaders returned to Edinburgh they found 'many grieved with our proceedings'.

As was to become a familiar feature of his dealings with any opposition, Charles managed to reach compromise decisions which, being loosely defined and imprecise, failed to solve the issue at hand. Also, by refusing to accept the findings of the Glasgow Assembly, yet allowing another assembly which would simply rehearse and repeat the Glasgow proceedings, he was storing up trouble for the future. At least he had had the good sense to decide against presiding over the next Assembly in Edinburgh. In his place as commissioner would go Hamilton, but the king's favourite had had enough. Showing rare perspicacity Hamilton informed Charles that as he had become too odious to the Covenanters he should stand down both for his own and the Crown's good:

> The general hatred that is generally carried me, and in particular by the chief Covenanters, will make them (hoping thereby either to ruin me, or at least make my service not acceptable) stand more peremptorily on these other points of civil obedience, which your Majesty aims at, than they would do to one that is less hated. Since they are the same men I have formerly treated with, they cannot but find these particulars, which I have often sworn and said your Majesty would never condescend to, will now be granted: therefore they will give no credit to what I shall say thereafter, but will still hope and believe that all their desires will be given way to, thinking, as they have often said, that I had power to condescend to more, but would not, that I might endear myself to your Majesty, and be thought a deserving servant in procuring more than you was content to accept of.[14]

It was a fair point – his presence would be both unwelcome and unwise – but Hamilton was also covering his back, making sure that he did not lose royal favour by being involved in another hopeless mission for the king. Instead, Traquair was deputed to take his place, an appointment which was probably sensible but which was hardly guaranteed to please the Covenanters.

Chapter Seven

FOUL AND HORRID TREASON: THE SECOND BISHOPS' WAR

'We hear these people are as ready to relapse into their former disobedience as the devil can wish.'

Signet Clerk Edward Norgate to Robert Reade, 30 June 1639

The next General Assembly of the Church of Scotland opened in St Giles on 12 August 1639, and from the outset its members made their intentions clear by ratifying the decisions taken in Glasgow the previous year. They also passed an 'Act containing the Causes and Remedies of the bygone Evils of this Kirk' which condemned episcopacy as being both unconstitutional and against God's law, a move which was bound to put the Covenanters once more on a collision course with Charles: if bishops were illegal in Scotland they would also be so in England. In vain did Traquair attempt to change the wording of the resolution to ensure that its provisions would not extend to England: the Kirk would have none of it. The king's commissioner was under express instructions to avoid any possibility that the episcopacy might be declared illegal, but as usual he trimmed and consented to the act. If Charles's aim was to unite his kingdoms in one form of worship then the Covenanters' decision struck at the heart of any hope of unity.

On 30 August the Assembly dissolved itself after agreeing to meet again a year later in Aberdeen, and parliament was convened the following day. From the outset it was obvious that Traquair would be unable to exert influence, as any further hope of maintaining royal authority had already vanished with the enforced absence of the bishops from the parliamentary session. With the Covenanters firmly in control a new executive body, the Committee of the Articles, was elected by the remaining estates of the nobility, barons and burgesses and it proceeded to confirm the decisions of the General Assembly. In a further demonstration of independence it was agreed to impose a new tax to support the Covenanting cause and all adult males were ordered to sign the National Covenant if they had not already done so. All these decisions were assaults on the dignity of the Crown, but there was little that Charles could do in the short term. His army had been disbanded because there was no money to pay the soldiers, but the Scots had the necessary funds to keep many of Leslie's regiments in a state of readiness – another direct challenge to the peace agreement.

On Charles's orders and in some exasperation Traquair tried to prorogue the parliament in October, but his authority, already weakened, had evaporated and the order was ignored, Wariston arguing that there could be no dismissal unless warranted by the estates. This argument formed the basis of a remonstrance to the king, and in order to avoid further offence parliament dismissed itself, leaving a committee, virtually a continuation of the Tables, to maintain the status quo. Traquair then departed for London to explain matters to the king and, not unsurprisingly, met with a frosty welcome. By this time Charles was intent on punishing the Scots once and for all: 'I will rather die than yield to their impertinent and damnable demands,' he told Hamilton.[1]

That aim was helped by Wentworth's arrival from Ireland, ostensibly to deal with business matters, but he had already written advising Charles to play for time and to strike again the following year when he would be better prepared and in a position to punish the Covenanters. Given the circumstances, his advice could not be criticised, but the Lord Deputy's return to London proved to be a turning-point not just in Wentworth's life but also in the direction of the crisis. While his new authority placed him at the heart of Charles's inner councils – along with Arundel, Hamilton, Laud and Northumberland – this culmination of his ambitions was also a danger. Imperious, autocratic, single-minded and energetic (though enfeebled by gout), Wentworth was absolutely sure of his ability to deal with the 'Scotch business' which he characterised as a simple rebellion against the king. To his way of thinking the National Covenant was a treasonable document, and he believed that if it came to a fight the English would rally behind Charles because their traditional dislike of the Scots was stronger than any animadversion to the king's personal rule.

Shortly after Wentworth's arrival in London the tone of the communications with the Scottish parliament became less amicable. That was Wentworth's doing, but it did not take him long to realise that, while the king was anxious to reimpose his authority over Scotland, the Exchequer did not allow for the cost of raising the necessary forces. To do that effectively, to produce the estimated £900,000 thought necessary, parliament would have to be recalled, a move which Wentworth pushed through the Privy Council by arguing that the king's authority could only be upheld by 'an effectual war and no war to be made effectually but such a one as should grow and be assisted from the high counsel of parliament'.[2] Despite harbouring doubts Charles agreed, and on 5 December he advised his council that he would prepare for a war which would be financed by recalling parliament the following year.

Both decisions changed the complexion of the crisis. Charles was probably minded to be more resolute with the Scots shortly after signing the Treaty of Berwick, for not only did he take to quoting the old Scots proverb 'that bids you put two locks on your door after you have made peace with a foe' but he began to heed his advisers' warnings that the Scots were hell-bent on imposing Presbyterianism on the whole of Britain. Wentworth had gone further, writing from Ireland in the middle of March that the Scots' endgame might even be the destruction of Royalty itself.[3] What the king needed was a strong man able to do his bidding, and Wentworth seemed to fit the bill – but at a price. With Hamilton's and Laud's support Wentworth persuaded Charles to end his personal rule and offered the guarantee that, just as he had managed the Irish parliament, so too would he keep the recalled English parliament under control. By way of providing a good example the Irish parliament would meet beforehand in Dublin to vote subsidies. Encouraged by his Lord

Deputy's vigour – Wentworth returned to Dublin between 5 and 16 March – Charles issued a writ on 12 February 1640 to recall the first English parliament for eleven years.

Some time earlier, in November, the Scots had dispatched Loudoun and Dunfermline as commissioners to represent their case to the king in London, but they had been refused an audience and were forced to return to Edinburgh in high dudgeon. With the committee still sitting in lieu of parliament the Covenanters began preparing again for the war they knew would come. Not even the arrival of Traquair moved them: when the king's commissioner returned to Edinburgh he ordered the committee to disband on pain of treason and to nominate four commissioners to prepare to travel to London to explain the reasons for the Scottish parliament's actions. This would be the last chance of preserving peace, but by the time the Scottish mission – Dunfermline, Loudoun, Cavers and Robert Barclay, provost of Irvine – reached London in February Charles was not prepared to listen to their supplications because to all intents and purposes he was already in a state of war with the Scots. He had ordered Edinburgh Castle to be strengthened and reinforced and he had formed a committee to deal with Scottish affairs which was soon meeting regularly, with the forthcoming campaign dominating its agenda. All that remained was for the Irish and English parliaments to meet and vote the necessary funds.

Before they assembled, Charles was handed a useful piece of propaganda in the form of a letter from the Covenanting leadership to King Louis XIII of France, asking for his help in the struggle against England. It came to him through loyal friends in the Highlands who passed it on to Traquair and it reached London that February. Its contents were dynamite. Signed by Leslie, Rothes, Montrose and others, and addressed 'Au Roi',* as if Louis were the appellants' king and not Charles, it asked for French help in the confrontation with England at a time when it looked as if Scotland was about to be subdued by force. In fact the letter had been written the previous year, but it was not dated until 19 February 1640 and was sent to France through the hands of one William Colville. Unfortunately a second

_____

* Lack of fluency in French was probably to blame. Lauderdale had refused to sign the letter because its translation was so appalling.

copy had also been produced and this eventually found its way into Charles's hands. As it turned out, Louis had been advised by Richelieu to keep out of the British quarrel and had already instructed the French ambassador, Pompone de Bellievre, to resist the temptation – and his natural inclination – to make contact with the Covenanting leadership. But it mattered not. Charles had the letter and he was outraged by its contents which, for the time being, until parliament met, he decided to keep to himself.

The king's possession of the letter also gave him an extra card to play in his discussions with the Scottish commissioners, who were ordered not to leave London. Throughout the discussions Charles had become increasingly irked by their behaviour and comportment in his company, complaining that they did not show him due deference and were too direct in their approach, a characteristic which the commissioners refused to dilute as 'the Scots are more for realities in expressions of kindness than of words and gestures'.[4] At Wentworth's suggestion Charles decided to play for time, because in his hands he had Loudoun, one of the signatories of the ill-fated letter, whom he locked up in the Tower. As for the other signatories, Charles wrote to them summoning them to London to explain themselves, but as was only to be expected he received no reply. Colville arrived in France in April but his mission achieved nothing because, following Charles's publication of the Scottish correspondence, neither Richelieu nor Louis XIII was minded to intervene.

Parliament reconvened on 13 April 1640 with the good example of Ireland to inspire them, or so Charles imagined. True to his boasts, Wentworth had come back from Ireland with four subsidies of £45,000 each and the promise of a force of 8000 men commanded by James Butler, Earl of Ormond, who would be ready to cross over into Scotland by the middle of May. Hats had been thrown in the air as the decisions were made, the Irish parliamentarians being moved to declare themselves 'more bound [to the king] than we can with tongue or pen express'.[5] That the Irish were so prepared to cast in their lot behind Charles was due in no small measure to Wentworth's influence, and that happy spring in Dublin was probably the high point of his career. Before leaving England he had been created Earl of Strafford and promoted Lord Lieutenant of Ireland, and on his return to England, agreeably on a ship called *Confidence*, he still had high hopes that the English members of parliament would follow suit by voting subsidies. Although weakened by a bad attack of dysentery there was no lack of concentration on Strafford's part. From Chester, where he decided to rest before continuing to London, he wrote to the king promising that unless parliament fell into line he would give them something to remember.

But it was already too late for bluster, the time had come for action. Following the king's opening speech to the House of Commons Sir John Finch, by now Lord Keeper, had made a frank appeal for funds to punish the Scots for their 'foul and horrid treason' and enjoined the house to provide the funds for 'the common preservation' of the realm and the king's good name. Finch was not popular with everyone – he had been the primary author of the Ship Money judgements and had a notorious reputation for his ferocity in the Star Chamber – but he was heard out even though he ended with the churlish threat that the king was not looking for the members' advice but for the immediate grant of subsidies. At the end of his speech Charles then rose and revealed the contents of the Covenanters' letter to Louis XIII, a move which he hoped would reinforce Finch's entreaties. It was a good ploy but it failed to move those present.

Having elected a speaker, parliament started by making it clear that they would not be steamrollered into simply granting subsidies for the king's army. The turning-point came on 17 April when the member for Calne in Wiltshire rose to begin a speech which would set the tone for the rest of the sitting. John Pym was one of the most experienced parliamentarians of his day, a native of Somerset who had first been elected in 1614 and who had quickly emerged as a strong-willed opponent of the Crown's fiscal and religious policies. With his business interests – he was associated with the Providence Island Company, a mercantile venture for settling Puritans in the Caribbean – and his lawyer's training he was a mature and thoughtful figure whose word was heeded. What he said that April morning was to make a mockery of Strafford's belief that this parliament could be managed. In the space of two hours he rehearsed the grievances which he believed parliament should be discussing before the question of subsidies was addressed – the growth of Catholic influence and monopolies, the collection of import taxes (tonnage and poundage) contrary to the Petition of Right, and the despotism of the Star Chamber. It was a direct attack on the

Personal Rule, and to force the issue Pym made sure that his speech was printed and circulated to other members. It laid down the agenda which Pym thought that parliament should be following: grievances had to be discussed before subsidies.

In fact parliament was quite prepared to pay the subsidies, but it would not do so until action had been taken to address their concerns about the king's policies towards Church and state. As that debate would postpone the campaign against the Scots Charles decided to bypass parliamentary procedure. Spurred on by Strafford, on 24 April he took his case to the House of Lords, telling them that there could be no delay. Following three divisions the Lords approved the subsidies, but their decision was guaranteed to anger the Commons because it was a breach of privilege. The debate continued for a further week, but Charles was in no mood to compromise – a last-minute offer to abolish Ship Money in return for twelve subsidies came to nothing – and on 5 May he decided to dissolve parliament. 'Go on with a vigorous war as you first designed, loosed and absolved from all rules of government,' Strafford advised him. 'Being reduced to extreme necessity, everything is to be done that power might admit, and that you are to do. They refusing, you are acquitted towards God and man.'[6] The so-called Short Parliament had lasted only three weeks.

Charles had other reasons for taking such a precipitate decision. He felt secure in the advice given to him by his closest advisers, he had hopes, soon to be dashed, of raising funds from Spain, he feared, with good reason, that there was some sympathy in parliament for the Scottish cause, but above all he had to find money for the army which was being raised, and if that did not come from parliament there was no sense in keeping it in being. The king's thinking did not take place in a vacuum. Among his advisers he had absolute faith in Strafford, who promised that 'one summer well employed will do it' and was already in discussion with two envoys from the court of Spain about the possibility of leasing ships of the Royal Navy to guard Spanish transports in the Channel. Charles was right, too, to fear Scottish interference in English parliamentary matters. On 16 April the Covenanters had appealed to their English colleagues, insisting that their complaint was with the king's policies and not with England itself, and Pym had been due to raise that issue on the very day that Charles dismissed parliament. As for the king's impatience with the parliament's refusal to offer immediate support, that too cannot be denied. Within hours he was busily engaged with the details of financing and raising a force to conquer Scotland.

Money problems notwithstanding, the attempts to mobilise a disciplined army were no more successful than they had been in the previous year. This time the militias were to be raised from counties to the south of the River Trent, but they were soon exposed as broken reeds. Not only were most of the men uninterested in pursuing their king's quarrel with Scotland, but they soon turned that antipathy into mutinous and uncontrollable behaviour. Stories of desertions were rife, discipline in most regiments was notable by its absence, and officers who tried to maintain order were either ignored or attacked. Astley could not believe what he saw: under his capable command were 'all the arch-knaves of the kingdom', a motley crew which their commanding general Northumberland believed would be 'readier to draw their swords upon their officers than against the Scots' and counselled postponing the expedition for another year. Because the Petition of Right prevented the imposition of martial law the offenders who broke ranks, plundered and murdered superiors could not be punished. As Lord Conway saw the situation after he had been sent north to manage the defence of Newcastle with Astley, it would be an unequal struggle should his men ever have to face the Scots:

I am teaching cart-horses to manage and making men that are fit for Bedlam and the Bridewell to keep the ten commandments, [he wrote to the Countess of Devonshire] so that General Leslie and I keep two schools, he has scholars that profess to serve God, and he is instructing them how they may safely do perjury and all impiety; mine to the utmost of their power never kept any law either of God or the King, and they are to be made fit to make others keep them.[7]

Conway's one hope was that the quarrel would be solved by other means, but as early as January 1640 the Scots had begun remustering their regiments and Leslie had been given a fresh commission to lead the Covenanting army into England. Just as important, funds had been raised, but to balance that advantage the amounts were finite: to win the war the Scots would need a quick victory before their superior military strength began to deteriorate. As had happened in the previous year the Scots' first step was to pacify the potentially troublesome Royalist north-east. At the beginning of May, as a precaution, Aberdeen was occupied by Covenanting forces led by the Earl Marischal and Major-General Sir Robert Monro, the city council being obliged to pay a ransom of £4000 to prevent the men from plundering. The respite did not last and as would happen later in the war the local civilian population suffered from having troops quartered on them. From Aberdeen Monro's regiment set up camp in neighbouring Strathbogie, where they made themselves unpopular by living off the land, forcibly removing cattle and sheep and plundering houses such as Spynie Castle, the home of the bishop of Moray, and Dowhaugh, the home of Sir George Ogilvy of Banff, Huntly's great supporter.

Before anything else happened though, the Scottish parliament was due to meet in Edinburgh on 2 June, amid doubts that it would be legal to do so. In the previous November it had been prorogued to that date and Charles wanted to extend the period but, due to a gross and no doubt deliberate misunderstanding on the part of the Lord Advocate – Hope had always been sympathetic to the Covenanting cause – parliament met and decided forthwith that there was nothing to prevent it sitting. Its most important decision was to establish a committee of estates in succession to the Tables which would be responsible for directing the defence of the country and raising the necessary taxes to pay for it. Because general officers were entitled to attend meetings, and as half of the committee would accompany the Scottish army, this brought the military and the Covenanting cause into greater harmony. The governor of Edinburgh Castle, Sir Patrick Ruthven, now ennobled as Lord Ettrick, was ordered to surrender his charge and with it the Scottish regalia, but this doughty soldier did no such thing. His only reply to several requests (one shot by arrow) was 'Never!' Throughout that summer the city and the castle remained in a state of intermittent siege which cost around two hundred lives, and it only ended in September when Ettrick was forced to surrender due to lack of food. Ettrick's legs were so badly swollen through scurvy that he could scarcely walk, and he had lost all his teeth, a poor reward for his loyal defiance.

All this had taken place without the presence of the king, who was still integral to the Covenanters' concept of parliament and Crown working together. The members protested their loyalty to 'the sacred

and inviolable name of his Majesty and kingly authority' but it is hard
to avoid the impression that this was a revolutionary body intent on
creating a new order for the civil and religious governance of Scotland.
On the latter score the decisions of the 1639 General Assembly were
ratified and there were further acts upholding the keeping of the
Sabbath, banning observance of the Christmas holiday, and creating
new guidelines for the admission of ministers. Parliament took a mere
nine days to complete its business: 'the greatest change at one blow
that ever happened to this church and state these 600 years bypast; for
in effect it overturned not only the ancient state government, but
fettered monarchy with chains'. As one modern historian described
the momentous turnabout in the king's relationship with Scotland,
Charles had paid the penalty of his own ignorance and arrogance: 'his
Scottish subjects had broken the bonds which tied them to the
medieval world and had set about the creation of the new Zion'.[8]

One more decision was taken which would have momentous
consequences. Argyll was given a commission of fire and sword
against the Earl of Atholl, Lord Ogilvy, the Farquharsons in the Braes
of Mar and 'their accomplices and others, our enemies and opposites'
in Badenoch, Lochaber and Rannoch. All were enemies of the
Covenanters and supporters of the king and had to be 'brought to
their duty or rooted out and utterly subdued' – Ogilvy's father, the
Earl of Airlie, had already departed for London – and all were to pay
the price of that loyalty by having their property confiscated or
destroyed under the jurisdiction of the Committee of Estates. For the
ambitious Argyll, a Campbell, the commission was a godsend: here
was a chance to rekindle ancient enmities – the Campbells and
Ogilvys had fought a vicious clan war in the previous century – but
it also allowed him to add to his heritable holdings in Badenoch and
Lochaber, which he had received as security from Huntly. What
followed next was brutal and bloodthirsty. With 5000 men Argyll
marched into Lochaber, burning and looting their way into Badenoch
and the Braes of Mar before turning their attention to the Braes of
Angus. Guessing their fate, the local population had called on
Montrose for protection, as he was already recruiting in the area.
Being a friend of the Ogilvys, Montrose was happy to oblige by taking
Airlie Castle himself and putting it in the protection of one of his
officers; but when the Campbell force arrived outside Airlie Castle on

its well defended site high above the River Isla, Argyll expelled Montrose's officers and ordered his men to destroy the 'Bonnie Hoose o' Airlie' before going on to raze the Ogilvy farmlands between Alyth and Cortachy. This was clan revenge and, according to John Spalding, it was driven as much by a desire to plunder as a need to settle old scores:

> Argyll most cruelly and inhumanely enters the house of Airlie, and beats the same to the ground, and right so he does to Forter; then spoiled all the inside and plenishing in both houses, and such as could not be carried away they masterfully broke down and pitifully destroyed. Thereafter they fell to his grounds, plundered, robbed, and took away from himself, his men, tenants and servants, their whole goods, gear, corn, cattle, horses, nolts, sheep, inside plenishing, and all whatsoever they could get; and left nothing but bare bounds of such as they could consume or destroy or carry away with them, and such as could not be carried away, they spitefully burnt up by fire.[9]

The sacking of Airlie Castle was one of the most infamous incidents of the campaign – commemorated in a haunting folk song – and the bloodletting did not stop until 2 August, when Argyll set about laying siege to Dumbarton Castle, a more productive move which prevented Strafford's Irish army from landing in Scotland:

> The great Argyll raised five hundred men,
> Five hundred men and many,
> And he has led them down by the bonny Dunkeld,
> Bade them shoot at the bonnie house of Airlie.
> The lady was looking oer her castle-wa,
> And O but she looked weary!
> And there she spied the great Argyll,
> Come to plunder the bonnie house of Airlie.[10]

The song suggests that Lady Airlie was forced to watch the destruction of her bonnie house and has Argyll say that 'one kiss o his gay lady wad hae sav'd all the plundering of Airlie' but in fact, Lady Airlie was heavily pregnant and was allowed to leave before the Campbells set about the castle's destruction.

By then, though, the main theatre of operations for the Covenanters was at Duns, where Leslie's army was slowly taking shape. Obviously it had to have some objective, for as yet there was no military threat from the English side of the border and as long as the soldiers remained inactive they were an expensive liability. The waiting ended on 3 August when the decision was taken to invade England, not for territorial or any other kind of aggrandisement but to protect Scotland's religion and to help those in England – the Puritans – throw off episcopal rule. Papers were produced arguing that the Scots had no quarrel with the king but only with 'the crafty and cruel faction' which had offered him so much bad advice. That same day, Conway wrote to London from Newcastle informing the council that he did not 'believe that the Scots will come into England; this that they do is only to brag'.[11] His optimism did him credit, especially as he added that he could see 'no help' for Newcastle, but by the time his letter reached London Leslie's men were already crossing the River Tweed, the natural boundary between the two countries, and following the well-worn campaign trail used by feuding English and Scottish armies since the thirteenth century.

Leslie's objective was Newcastle and the rich coalfields on the Tyne which supplied the south with coal: if these could be captured and held to ransom the Covenanters would have a useful bargaining counter. On 17 August the first cavalry units led by Montrose crossed the Tweed at Cornhill, and soon the entire army was swarming across the unseasonably swollen river at Wark and Carham. Once in England they advanced to Wooler, passing the fateful field of Flodden on the way, and then on to Morpeth, carrying their colours proudly with the motto 'Covenant for Religion, Crown and Country'. Wearing blue bonnets and carrying musket and swords they made a brave sight, although, for the watching and wondering English north-countrymen, a discordant note was struck by the half-naked Highlanders armed with bows and arrows. Outlandish they might have looked, but they were all under the strict discipline enforced by Leslie and the progress into England was accomplished with little or no looting. Behind them came Alexander Hamilton's artillery train with its eleven nine-pounders and a variety of smaller field pieces, the baggage train and 10,000 sheep and 500 cattle. A contemporary English squib likened the move to Caesar crossing the Rubicon and, mixing metaphors, put into Leslie's mouth the thought that they were entering the promised land: 'Your turf cottages, you shall ere long exchange for stately houses, and let not the thought of your wives and bairns, and such like lumber which you leave behind trouble you, for having done your business, you shall have choice of English lasses, whereon you may beget a new and better world.'[12]

Their business was done sooner than the anonymous scribbler might have liked. Charles hurried north to York, which he reached on 22 August, but by then doubt was eating into Conway's mind and as reports reached him of the Scots' strength, erroneously put at 30,000, he began to fear that the opposition would 'fight devilishly'. In an attempt to defend the undefendable he split his forces and took his cavalry and a force of 2000 infantry north to shadow Leslie's army. Forced to retreat from Morpeth as the Scots advanced, Conway took up position by the River Tyne at the ford of Newburn, some ten miles north-west of Newcastle, where he ordered breastworks to be constructed on a flat stretch of ground known as the Stella Haugh for the battle which would surely follow. Throughout the morning of 28 August the two armies faced each other across the river, thankfully for the accompanying Scottish ministers 'without affronting one another or giving any reproachful language', but the Scots were in confident mood: that night Leslie had taken the measures which decided the course of battle. Alexander Hamilton's artillery had been moved into position in the surrounding wooded slopes, with some pieces placed on the steeple of Newburn church to fire directly into the English positions. As the tide began to ebb in the early afternoon, making the Tyne fordable, Leslie sent a messenger to Conway's camp explaining that he did not wish a fight but only wanted free passage to enable the Scots petition to be presented to the king.

Conway refused; to have done otherwise would have broken Charles's orders, but it left Leslie with no option but to attack. A small force of cavalry was ordered to cross the river to draw English fire and then it retired rapidly as Hamilton's hidden artillery pieces opened fire on the English positions. The onslaught was rapid, heavy and demoralising, so much so that the defenders in the breastworks began to panic as their officers were killed. As the shot continued to rain down on them they began to flee from the battlefield, leaving their weapons behind them. This gave Leslie the opportunity to advance his cavalry and a squadron of troopers drawn from the College of Justice Regiment, his personal bodyguard, forded the river to inspect the English positions. Although they encountered some English cavalry Leslie thought it safe to sound a general advance, and in the late summer afternoon the Scottish cavalry, led by Sir Thomas Hope of Kerse, poured across the Tyne, where they fought a brief skirmish with English troopers of Lord Wilmot's regiment. Again English resolve was broken by the superior Scottish numbers and the horse soldiers fled the field, after what Clarendon described as 'the most shameful and confounding flight that was ever heard of'.

Perhaps it was. The English soldiers did not behave well, but with the exception of Wilmot, who fought with some spirit, they were not well led. Conway's tactics were naive whereas Leslie brought his experience of European warfare to bear on the disposition of the artillery and the manoeuvring of the cavalry, a battle plan which the English could not counter. They were also outnumbered five to one – the Scottish army stood at 15,000 – and it is probably also true that Conway's men had no stomach for their cause. They were also fortunate that the Scots did not pursue them from the field – the casualties would have been much higher than the hundred or so killed during the artillery battle. However, the Scottish officers were under strict orders not to kill the fleeing Englishmen but to try to take them prisoner. Even so, Leslie had produced a military triumph, taking his army deep into enemy territory and inflicting on the English a decisive defeat before he turned his attention to Newcastle. Having given thanks to God for 'their safe passage, delivery and so good beginning' the Scots marched south again knowing that their next battle would be the investment of a major English city – a much more difficult proposition than anything they had faced at the encounter which came to be known in Scotland as the Newburn Fight. To gain any sort of advantage they also knew that they had to take it quickly because, as Baillie testified, they were quickly running out of supplies and 'in great straights'.

Had Newcastle been more rigorously defended, or if Conway had shown some resolve, the next stage of the campaign would have provided a more stringent test of Leslie's abilities, but when the Scottish army arrived outside the northern city on Sunday 30 August they found that Conway and Astley had departed, taking the remnants of the garrison with them. The mayor, Robert Bewick, had no option but to allow the Scots to enter and, as Leslie told the Committee of Estates a few days later, immediate arrangements were made to replenish the army.

> God mixes our proceedings with good success against our enemies, and evil carriage of our own soldiers, that both our hopes and fears are equal. It is the singular blessing of God that has put Newcastle in our hands, where there is so great store of corn above an ordinary measure, arms for many thousands.[13]

He also asked for reinforcements from the forces led by the Earl Marischal and Monro to guard the border area, for the English still held Berwick-on-Tweed, but his main task was to hold what he had captured. Newcastle received a garrison of 2000 troops and was put under the control of the Earl of Lothian; Durham was seized by the Earl of Dunfermline and the neighbouring towns of Shields, Tynemouth and Sunderland gradually came under the control of the Scots. It was all very orderly and reasonably civilised – looting was punished by the death penalty – for the English were still regarded as friends and potential supporters. The only exceptions were the leading Catholic families of the north-east, who were forced to hand over funds to help pay for Leslie's army of occupation. For the Scots it was the high point of their campaign: within a month they had captured Northumberland, and their pleasure was increased when first Dumbarton Castle and then Edinburgh Castle fell into their hands. Even though the military successes were modest the Scots allowed themselves some self-congratulation, secure in the belief that they were doing God's great work by maintaining the integrity of their covenant with him. Zachary Boyd, a Glasgow minister and a member of one of the great Presbyterian families of the city, caught the mood in a long and fanciful poem about the fight at Newburn:

> In Squadrons came like fire and thunder,
> Men's hearts and heads both to pierce and plunder
> Their errand was (when it was understood)
> To bathe men's bosoms in a scarlet flood.[14]

For the English these were difficult times. No one knew with any certainty if Leslie would continue the Scots' drive south and, if they did, there was little hope of finding forces to counter the invasion. Not even Strafford's arrival in York helped to calm nerves: sick and ill-tempered, the iron man caused more trouble than he solved by attempting to reassert his authority by feverishly persuading the king that all was not lost, that one more assault on the Scots would bring victory.* It was in vain. Having drawn up an army to punish the Scots, Charles now had to admit that the boot was on the other foot, that his opponents were in a position to cause him damage. He was also facing discontent within his own ranks – on the day that his forces were fleeing from the Newburn field he received a deputation of peers and members of the Short Parliament outlining grievances and requesting a peace treaty with the Scots. In some desperation he summoned a Council of Peers – an arcane body which raised money for King Edward III's wars – to meet in York and to consider the demands which the Scots had sent on 4 September restating their grievances and asking for the recall of the English parliament to ratify any peace treaty. Clearly the Scots were no longer prepared to accept the word of the king alone.

Charles now had no option but to summon parliament, and although part of him still believed that he could remuster his forces and march against Leslie's army the tide of opinion was against him. Writs were issued for parliament to meet on 3 November 1640 and commissioners were chosen to meet their Scottish opposite numbers at Ripon to work out a peace treaty. By the middle of October a deal had been struck, but the terms agreed were a humiliating blow to the king. The Scots demands would be discussed by parliament and Leslie's army would remain in Northumberland at a cost to the English exchequer of £850 a day. It was a far cry from Strafford's boast that 'one summer well employed' would see the Scots brought to heel and the king's authority re-established.

---

* Strafford also dreamed up a wild scheme to put pressure on the Covenanters by expelling the Scots from Ulster.

Chapter Eight

THE GATHERING STORM

'That long, ungrateful, foolish and fatal parliament.'

John Evelyn, Diary, *3 November 1640*

The Long Parliament, which would be in existence for an unprecedented twenty years,* opened in London amid widespread rumours of popish plots and a feeling that the country was plunging into an inexplicable crisis. Clearly the king had to reassert his authority, and in his opening speech he asked the members to lay aside their suspicions just as he would do, but the mood of the house was against words of comfort and bland reassurances. Most of the 493 members were keen to see the introduction of the kind of change which the influential John Pym had demanded in conversation with Edward Hyde, member for Saltash (and later in life the Earl of Clarendon): 'they must not only sweep the house clean below, but must pull down all the cobwebs which hung in the tops and corners, that they might not breed dust and so make a foul house hereafter'.[1]

---

* Apart from the lapse between 1653 and 1659 after Oliver Cromwell expelled the Rump. See Part Four, Chapter 7.

In common with other members Pym was still angered by the earlier dissolution of the Short Parliament and determined that this time its work should be businesslike to the point of ruthlessness. The lack of royal support in the house helped – fewer than 80 members could be counted as the king's men – but Pym was the main engine of reform. Restless, determined and blessed with a fine sense of timing, he was in a powerful position as leader of the house both to manage the agenda and to give the house a sense of direction. Parliament's main business was the resolution of the Scottish crisis, and that meant dealing with the terms of the pacification of Ripon as well as confronting the demands made by the Committee of Estates whose commissioners were already in London where, far from being treated as rebels, they were welcomed by many Puritans as defenders of the faith. Among their number was Robert Baillie, who wrote for his family and friends a commentary which is remarkable both for its colourful descriptions of London and for his shocked Presbyterian disapproval of its metropolitan way of life:

> From Kilwinning to London I did not so much as stumble; this is the fruit of your prayers. [He wrote to his wife on 18 November.] I was also all the way full of courage, and confronted with the sense of God's presence with my spirit. We were by the way great expenses; their inns are all like palaces; no nearest thing they extort their guests: for three meals, course enough, we would pay, together with our horses, fifteen or sixteen pounds Sterling. Some three dish of crayfish; like little partans [crabs], two and forty shillings Sterling.

The hardships of travel and the high cost of living notwithstanding, Baillie was convinced that the journey was worthwhile and that the Scottish delegation would prevail: 'Huge things are here in working: the mighty hand of God be about this great work!'[2]

The Scottish debate would continue over the winter, but from the outset it was clear that Pym had more important matters on his mind, namely the expulsion from public life and punishment of all of those whom he deemed to be responsible for the king's mistakes. In his sights were Laud, Finch, Secretary of State Sir Thomas Windebank and a number of bishops, but his main target was

Strafford. Recently raised to the Order of the Garter, the Lord Lieutenant of Ireland was now seen as the main author of the mismanaged campaign against the Scots but, more to the point as far as Pym was concerned, he was guilty of threatening to use his Irish army against England, a treasonable offence which the Scottish commissioners also wanted to be punished. Ironically, Strafford intended to turn the tables by charging Pym and others with the equally treasonable offence of dealing with the Scottish Covenanters throughout the recent crisis, but it was Pym who struck the first and the decisive blow.

On the evening of 10 November 1640 Strafford returned to London from York and the following day his fate was sealed in the House of Commons. His nemesis was Sir John Clotworthy, a Devon man with estates in Ulster who had already crossed swords with him over the Londonderry plantations, and he was in unforgiving mood. Having been briefed by Pym, who could also rely on the support of other members with Irish connections such as Lords Loftus and Wilmot, neither of whom bore Strafford any love, Clotworthy rose in the house to reveal that Strafford had claimed in the previous year that with an Irish army behind him Charles could 'have what he pleased in England'. The accusation opened a salvo of verbal attacks on Strafford, culminating in Pym's demand that the Lord Lieutenant be impeached as 'the greatest enemy to this country and the greatest promoter of tyranny that any age has produced'.[3]

At the time Strafford had been sitting in the House of Lords, which had been debating the terms of the treaty with the Scots, but he left in mid-morning to join Charles at Whitehall. Aware that Strafford had to be separated from the king, Pym urged the Commons to start the impeachment process – the charges had to be presented to the Lords – and the news of what was afoot quickly filtered back to Whitehall. Undeterred and showing considerable courage, Strafford returned to the Lords to find that once again Pym had outwitted him. Outside the chamber stood a crowd of Pym's supporters shouting 'Withdraw! Withdraw!' and he had to face the indignity of waiting in their midst while the Lords decided his fate. It did not take long, less than a quarter of an hour, but for a man as proud and unbending as Strafford it must have seemed a lifetime. The decision spelled his doom: called to the bar of the house by the Earl of Manchester, he was told that he would be sequestered and restrained until a formal hearing of the charges could be heard. His sword was removed by the Gentleman Usher of the Black Rod, James Maxwell, in whose house 'the greatest of England' was placed under arrest.

Strafford was not the first man of influence to be impeached – the Commons had tried and failed with Buckingham – but his closeness to the king and his direction of the failed policy against Scotland made him a marked man, one who had to be removed if parliament were to push through its reforms. His impeachment was followed by the arrest of Laud on charges of high treason, and the two unexpected events gave a revolutionary air to the opening months of the Long Parliament – Finch and Windebank fled to France before they could be arrested. However, as yet the moves were directed not against Charles himself but against his servants, who had to be eliminated. And it was not just the English who wanted to be rid of Strafford. His fall was welcomed in Ireland – before the arraignment proceedings Clotworthy had delivered a speech full of rebuke about the persecution of Protestants due to the Lord Lieutenant's policies – and in Scotland his life was also forfeit. In making their demands at Ripon the Covenanting leadership had accused Strafford of being 'this great incendiary' who had been responsible for attacking their liberties and religion and should therefore be brought to trial. Being good haters with long memories, they recalled, too, that Strafford had advised Charles to rule Scotland, like Ireland, as an English province. For Pym this was important support, as he realised that the presence of Leslie's army in the north was a powerful instrument in his cause: before the Scots could be paid off, loans had to be raised, and that could only be done by keeping parliament in being.

Despite the opening months of the Long Parliament being marked by confusion and diversions created by the impeachment of Strafford and the need to deal with common grievances raised by members, by February 1641 the main articles of the Treaty of London had been agreed with a speed and ease which suggested that the king was anxious to be rid of his Scottish problem so that he could turn his attention to his quarrel with parliament. The main demands to which he yielded were: an agreement to put his name to the acts passed by the last Scottish parliament, thereby agreeing to the resolutions of the two General Assemblies outlawing episcopacy; the royal castles of

Edinburgh and Dumbarton to be used only for defensive purposes; no Scots living in England to be condemned for signing the National Covenant; prosecution in Scotland of all 'incendiaries' responsible for creating the crisis; the return of all confiscated Scottish goods and all publications attacking the Scots to be suppressed. It was also confirmed that parliament would pay the Scots £300,000 as recompense for the invasion of England, 'a pretty sum' which the English parliament wrote off as 'brotherly assistance', Baillie noting with approval that 'the hearty giving of it to us, as to their brethren, did refresh us as much as the money itself'.[4]

This must have been a better outcome than the Scottish commissioners could have expected, but there were sticking points over demands for the limitation of the king's power in Scotland and the need to create a lasting alliance which would be more than a 'cessation of arms for a time, but peace for ever; and not peace only, but a perfect amity and a more near union than before'.[5] By this the Covenanters meant the provision of unity of worship in the three kingdoms, the abolition of episcopacy and its replacement by Presbyterianism. As this was opposed not only by the king but also by parliament and even by most Puritans, who certainly did not want to be instructed by the Scots on what form of worship they should use, that demand was dropped for later discussion. They were also lukewarm about Scottish proposals for closer civil and parliamentary links, and by the time the treaty had been drawn up in June most of the Covenanters' demands for union and unity of worship had been omitted or left vague. By then they were also outstaying their welcome. Having been greeted, at least by the Puritan faction, as the means of bringing about the end of episcopacy, more moderate voices were raised against them. Pride, too, was hurt. Here was an alien army being rewarded for occupying England while the English forces were neglected and left unpaid.

Besides, the Scots were also becoming truculent and troublesome. They wanted the king to concede that he or the Prince of Wales should spend an agreed amount of time each year in Scotland, and in late February the Scots commissioners caused great offence by privately printing a paper, written either by Henderson or Wariston, bitterly attacking episcopacy and demanding the punishment of Strafford and Laud. It was written to reassure Pym and others that the

Scots still supported them, but to many Englishmen it seemed a gross interference in their own affairs. Charles, of course, was so infuriated that he accused the Scottish commissioners of sedition and threatened to withdraw their safe conduct.

In fact the longer the discussion of the treaty continued the less likely were the Scots to retain their unity of purpose. Cracks were already appearing in the Covenanting leadership, with Montrose becoming increasingly disenchanted with what seemed to him to be a hardening of the anti-Royalist line in Scottish politics. He was also suspicious of Argyll's political ambitions now that he had emerged as the leading personality in the Covenanting leadership, an uncrowned 'King Campbell' who enjoyed both political and military authority. Before Leslie's army had departed for England there had been talk of deposing the king and replacing him with 'dictators' – Leslie in the field, Hamilton south of the Forth, and Argyll to the north. Alarmed by these steps 'by which the country was to be enslaved and reduced to all thraldom', Montrose had agreed with other moderates in August 1639 to sign the Cumbernauld Band, pledging 'all honest men who respected the Liberty of the Country and this Cause, to join themselves together to oppose those ways of tyranny, which in effect did tend to nothing less than the ruin of the Country, Liberty and personal freedom'.[6] Those concerns about Montrose's more extreme colleagues had prompted him to remain in communication with the king, assuring him of his loyalty and devotion, an activity which was bound to set him on a collision course with those Covenanters who believed that Charles was the sole author of the crisis.

In short, Montrose was facing the classic dilemma faced by any moderate caught up in a revolution. While he believed that it had been right to sign the National Covenant and to stand up for its precepts, throughout 1640 he began to entertain severe doubts about the legality and morality of taking up arms against a crowned king. Others supported him, most notably his brother-in-law Lord Napier,* and the presence of potential supporters in Scotland such as the Earls of Atholl and Mar helped to create an unofficial Royalist faction in

---

* Archibald Napier of Merchiston, son of John Napier of Merchiston, inventor of logarithms and 'Napier's Bones', the first attempt to produce a calculating machine.

Scotland. Even Rothes allowed himself to become a member of the royal household in June 1641, an appointment which brought a sharp rebuke from Baillie, who felt that this leading Covenanting nobleman would change out of all recognition: 'he is likely to be the greatest courtier either of Scots or English. Likely he will take a place in the bedchamber; and be little more a Scottish man.'[7] Rothes accepted the appointment, or, depending on the viewpoint, swallowed the bait, but he did not live long to enjoy the honour, dying suddenly a few months later.

Baillie's comments notwithstanding, Rothes had in fact been following a well trodden path: Scots courtiers were no strangers in the courts of James VI and Charles I, and as modern historians have shown,[8] they exerted considerable influence. Clarendon might have mocked them as parasites or as mere figureheads who enjoyed no influence or respect in Scotland, but men such as Hamilton were very close indeed to the king and enjoyed his confidence. Throughout the winter of 1640–41 as the process of impeaching Strafford proceeded apace, Northumberland noted that Hamilton had 'the sole power with the king' and his presence, together with the potential support of so many pro-Royalist Scottish aristocrats, were obvious factors in Charles's decision to travel north in the summer of 1641 to try to make his peace with the Covenanters.

The king's move made sense if he wanted to find fresh support in his dealings with the English parliament, but it ignored the fact that he had spent two years trying to subjugate Scotland by military means. It also added to the Covenanters' suspicions, for at the very moment that their demands were about to be met by the king, the unity which had characterised the Covenanting revolution was in danger of unravelling. Montrose had been interrogated at length by the Committee of Estates about his contacts with the king and his signing of the Cumbernauld Band. By the end of the year he was summoned as a 'delinquent' to explain his position and was briefly held in Edinburgh for his questionable loyalty to the Covenanting cause.

Charles had further reasons for seeking reassurance from other sources, because by the time that he visited Edinburgh he had lost the services of Strafford, who had promised to solve his difficulties with the Scots, and Laud, who was incarcerated in the Tower of London, a broken and forgotten man. Pym's persecution of Strafford had dominated everything in the early part of 1641. It was a life-or-death struggle between two strong and determined men, and the trial itself a compelling and dramatic process which enthralled all who witnessed it. For Pym it was all or nothing: he had to make the impeachment charges stick because his adversary was a dangerous man whose removal was essential if parliament were to gain the upper hand over the king. Strafford's very presence in London provided a danger, for here was a politician who knew all about crisis management and how to play off opponents against one another.

He was also supremely confident in his abilities and from the very outset doubted whether Pym would be able to harness the evidence needed to impeach him; even if he did, there were grounds for thinking that it would be difficult to substantiate the charge of high treason against the people. There was also the king's support to be taken into the equation and, even though Strafford was removed to the Tower of London at the end of November, he was still optimistic that the case against him would fail. Although sequestered, his life was not particularly onerous: he had a suite of rooms, visitors were welcome but, to prevent any possibility of escape, they were denied access during the hours of winter darkness. Only as winter began to bite did the conditions start affecting him, to the extent that he had to draw on all his reserves of stoicism and resilience. Left enfeebled by his earlier illness, he still managed to show old flashes of self-deprecating humour by choosing to sit in the same chapel seat once used by his old adversary, the crop-eared Prynne. According to his jailers he remained cheerful and considerate, a big man who had fallen from grace yet who still knew how to behave with equanimity.

All the time Pym was slowly assembling evidence against him, taking statements from witnesses and building up the indictment which would be sent to the Lords in the middle of January. If Strafford remained apparently equable about his fate, Pym was unshakeable in his determination, remarking that he would never leave his adversary alone 'while your head is on your shoulders'. Grudge mixed with moral and political rectitude guided Pym's actions, but other forces were also at work. Unwittingly Pym had touched the spirit of the age: Strafford – 'Black Tom Tyrant' – had become a convenient hate figure, the author of England's misfortunes, and had therefore to be punished. When he was taken to the House of Lords by boat in the late afternoon of 30 January the crowds were so large and menacing that he had to be protected by an armed guard. In the fading light the charges were then read out to him, but because he had been permitted legal counsel he asked if he could consider them before preparing a reply. Back in the Tower Strafford's mood lightened, for he could see that the indictment was flawed and might collapse in the face of a reasoned response. Relief was followed by a brief moment of jubilation:

> Sweetheart [he wrote to his wife that night], the charge is now come in, and I am now able, I praise God, to tell you that I conceive there is nothing capital; and for the rest, I know at the worst, his Majesty will pardon all, without hurting my fortune and then we shall be happy by God's grace. Therefore comfort yourself, for I trust these clouds will away and that we shall have fair weather afterwards.[9]

In his mind's eye, ahead lay acquittal and a happy retirement from public life in the company of his wife and family and the enjoyment of his not inconsiderable fortune. It was not a vain hope, for some of the charges were either vague (he was accused of calling the Scots 'rebels and traitors') or ludicrous (he was accused of betraying the English at Newburn) or created by personal malice (he stood condemned of creating a personal army in Ireland to punish his enemies). As Strafford and his legal team sat down to deal with each one individually – there were nine general changes backed by 28 accusations – they were confident they could rebuff them and knock down the charge of high treason.

When his trial opened on 22 March in Westminster Hall it was to be the sole political talking point for the next seven weeks. Throughout Strafford spoke with an eloquence and assurance that was remarkable considering that so much of the procedure was weighted against him. In so doing he won admirers as he dissected the case with a mixture of wit, sarcasm and forensic skill. One looker-on wrote to a friend telling him that it was worth coming a hundred miles to see 'so much bravery and modest courtship of both the houses' and even Baillie was moved to agree that Strafford's defence was 'exceeding brave', adding that 'doubtless, if he had grace or civil goodness, he is a most eloquent man.'[10]

As the trial progressed it was clear that Strafford had words and confidence in abundance and the arguments to reinforce them. He was able to refute or put into context most of the accusations made against him, including the charge that he intended to use the Irish army to subjugate 'this kingdom'. This was based on the memory of old Sir Henry Vane, a Secretary of State, whose words were reported by his son Harry, and not only were there well-grounded doubts about the accuracy of the recollection but it was impossible to prove whether the phrase alluded to England or Scotland.

By 10 April it was obvious that Pym's case had collapsed, but the war between the two men was by no means over. Foiled by the failure of the impeachment – and his opponent's skills – Pym turned to a new weapon, the terrible and little-used Bill of Attainder, which allowed parliament to put a man to death without recourse to law. Developed during the Tudor period, attainders were relatively rare – they had been used against the gunpowder plotters in 1605 – and were generally employed against enemies of the Crown who were guilty of high treason.

In the late spring of 1641 the instrument for attainting Strafford was a Leicestershire squire, Sir Arthur Hesilrige (according to Clarendon an 'absurd, bold man'), who introduced the bill in parliament, but the guiding force was still Pym, who saw that the only way of killing off his enemy lay in parliamentary legislation. Once passed, the bill would go to the Lords, who could vote for Strafford's death, and only the word of the king would be enough to save him. With London at fever-pitch and the atmosphere heightened with new rumours of popish plots and military intervention to save the Lord Lieutenant's life – according to Baillie 'in a clap all the city is in alarm' – the House of Commons voted overwhelmingly in favour of the bill (by 204 votes to 59) on 21 April and the process of slaughtering Strafford began. Although Charles promised Strafford 'upon the word of a king you shall not suffer in life, honour and fortune', the Lords passed the attainder just under three weeks later on 8 May.

This immediately placed Charles in the kind of quandary which would be companion to him in the years ahead, and his response to it was summed up by Laud, who saw his master as 'a mild and gracious prince, who knew not how to be, or be made great'. The choice was bleak: either he could keep his vow to Strafford, refuse to sign the bill and in so doing attract the wrath of parliament, or he could break his word, send his loyal servant to death and thereby appease Pym and his supporters. In vain did he take religious advice: his bishops insisted that he act upon his conscience and one of their number, John Williams of Lincoln, advised that while signing the attainder as a private man would harm his conscience, as a public man acting for the common weal he could do it in good faith. With an angry crowd making its displeasure known in the streets around Whitehall, Charles prepared himself to accept this bland assurance, but Williams was an odd choice of pious confidant: this former Lord Keeper and friend of Buckingham had just been released from imprisonment by parliament, having been charged by the Star Chamber in 1637 for breaking royal confidences.

There is little doubt that Charles did agonise about what to do. Equally he was well aware of the consequences of any decision he might take. In his possession he had a remarkable letter from Strafford releasing him from his promise, 'to set your Majesty's conscience at liberty' so that public order could be restored and the will of parliament satisfied. Perhaps it was a ploy to pass the responsibility back to the peers, but whatever its intent the letter's meaning was plain: Strafford was pleading for death, not life. As darkness fell on 9 May Charles gave way and signed the bill, adding the thought as he did so that his great servant's condition was happier than his. For all his prayers there were no words of comfort and, as the poet Thomas Stanley imagined, the moment would return to haunt the king for the rest of his life:

> Thou whose mercies know no bound,
> Pardon my compliant sin.
> Death in me the guiltless found,
> Who his refuge should have been.[11]

Three days later Strafford was done to death in front of a huge jeering crowd on Tower Hill; he met his end with exemplary dignity and courage, walking to the place of execution with the air of a conquering hero. The crowd of 100,000 was jubilant and few were to be found who did not express satisfaction at the removal from power of a such a malign influence over the king. The great tyrant had been beheaded, of that there was no doubt, but it was quite another matter if Baillie was right in his conviction that 'when we get his head off all things run smooth'. For all that Charles remained calm in the aftermath of 'great Strafford's' death, the initiative had already passed from him to a truculent parliament which was intent on pushing through a programme of radical reform.

Taxation by tonnage and poundage was abolished at the end of June; the Courts of the Star Chamber and High Commission disappeared at the beginning of July, the Triennial Act had already been passed, making it law for no more than three years to elapse between the dissolution of one parliament and the summoning of its successor (more radical was another act of May which forbade the parliament being dissolved other than by its own consent) and the first moves were being taken to reform Church government. Laud, too, had been indicted on fourteen counts of treason and had been given much the same treatment as Strafford: at the end of February 'the sty of all pestilential filth that hath infected the State and Government' had been committed to the Tower. Strafford had passed by Laud's window on his way to the block and had received his friend's blessing, but it would be another four years before the archbishop trod the same route.

The one shadow hanging over parliament was the militarised state of the country and the threat posed by the standing armies in England and Ulster. Charles had refused to disband the army raised by Strafford in Ireland, and the force raised for action against the Scots the previous year was still in existence in south Yorkshire. Unpaid and restless and loyal to Strafford, it posed a considerable threat, but it could not be paid off and disbanded until Leslie's army had left Northumberland. Until that happened there were continual rumours that the king intended to use the northern army to march on London to coerce parliament and the tension only increased when the king announced his intention to visit Scotland that summer. Quite what he hoped to achieve was open to doubt: the Scots were suspicious of his motives and if he hoped to use them as a counter in his struggle with parliament, as Montrose's correspondence seemed to suggest, he was to be much mistaken.

On his way north Charles stopped at Gateshead on 13 August to review the Scottish army, and he inspected it not as the monarch whose own forces had been defeated but as a visiting commander-in-chief. As if to underline the Scottish belief that the quarrel was not with Charles but with those incendiaries who had misadvised him, Leslie gave the king full honours: the army was drawn up in two divisions with Hamilton's artillery in the middle to fire a royal salute:

> And as the King passed along they gave such true fire as it is believed since the invention of guns never better was seen or heard, they discharged wondrous swift, but with as good a method and order as your skillfullest Ringers observe with Bells, not suffering the noise of the one to drown the other. The king received such contentment that whereas his dinner was appointed and provided at the Mayor of Newcastle, he yet went and honoured General Leslie with his presence at dinner.[12]

A week later the Scottish troops left Northumberland and tramped back over the border to be disbanded at Leith on the first anniversary of the Newburn fight. Only three regiments remained in being. Leslie was ennobled as the Earl of Leven by the same king whose forces he had humbled, but Charles was determined to put the past behind him. Once in the Scottish capital he attended parliament and allowed the acts passed the previous year to be published. He approved the National Covenant and attended lengthy church services according to Presbyterian rites, Baillie noting with approval that Charles heard 'all duly, and we hear none of his complaints for want of liturgy or any ceremonies'.[13] He invited Argyll to dine with him and encouraged his growing rapprochement with Hamilton, who had accompanied the royal party to Edinburgh. As soon as the Scottish commissioners returned from London he signed the Treaty of London, which concluded the process begun at Ripon and agreed that war could not be made against the Scots without the permission of the English parliament. He even played golf on Leith links, another move designed to put him in a good light with his hosts.

However, for all that Charles put on a good face and asked that the past 'unhappy mistaking' be put aside, the Covenanters remained suspicious of his motives. Their sticking point was the appointment of the main officers of state, councillors and lords of session who were due to be chosen in September. The Scots wanted them to be selected by parliament, but Charles insisted that that was a concession too far, that if he yielded on that point in Scotland Pym and his associates would demand the same for England. It also seemed to the king that no sooner had he granted favours, as he had spent the previous weeks doing, than the Covenanters asked for more or started introducing new conditions. On 16 September a compromise was reached whereby the king agreed that he would make the appointments but only after he had taken the advice of the Scottish parliament. Charles reasoned that this was only sensible, as he would not always know the background and worth of every candidate, but the reality was that he had surrendered more power than he might have wished – a determined parliament could quite easily refuse to accept any nomination which was unacceptable to them.

However, when it came to the appointments themselves there were further disagreements. The Covenanters wanted Argyll as chancellor but, given his ambitions and antipathy to the Crown, Charles could hardly agree. His choice was Morton, but this only prompted outrage, for not only was Morton considered to be too old and debt-ridden for the job but he had opposed the Covenant. After much jockeying for position it was agreed, with no little unease on the king's part (for he remembered the treasonable letter to Louis XIII), that Loudoun should be appointed. By then relations were growing more fractious within Scotland, and to add to the agitation the opponents of the Covenanters – committed Royalists and signatories of the Cumbernauld Band – began to grow more vociferous in public affairs. Their main target of disaffection was Hamilton, who seemed to them to be too thick with Argyll, prompting rumours that the two men hoped to divide and rule Scotland.

There was some truth to the allegation. Recognising the need to build up alliances in Scotland and to free himself of the suspicion that he was one of the incendiaries, Hamilton had built up a fair-weather friendship with Argyll while remaining in the king's party. How much Charles approved of the move is difficult to ascertain, for although he realised the need to cultivate friendships in Scotland he also relied completely on Hamilton. Whatever the reasons, and self-preservation must be high on the list, the sight of Hamilton combining with Argyll greatly aggravated the Scottish Royalist faction. The spark came on the night of 29 September when Lord Henry Ker, a vainglorious dipsomaniac and a son of the Earl of Roxburgh, issued a challenge to Hamilton, calling him 'a juglar with the king and a traitor both to him and to his country'. Nothing came of the provocation and Ker was forced to apologise, which he did abjectly and tearfully, but he had already ridden into Edinburgh with a troop of armed retainers, a practice followed by Covenanting leaders but until then not by Royalists. For the first time since the previous century it looked as if Scotland was about to return to the internecine warfare of the troubled years of the early Stewart period.[14]

Ker's challenge was only a distraction but it opened up the possibility of encouraging the factions to turn to violence. A fortnight later it led to an odd, though potentially disastrous, affair which came to be known as the 'Incident'. In common with most plots its beginnings are shadowy, but the intent was an ill-conceived idea to help the king by kidnapping or killing Argyll and Hamilton as well as the latter's younger brother, the Earl of Lanark. At its centre was a group of anti-Covenanting noblemen led by the Earl of Crawford, an ardent if blustering Royalist, who had agreed to be Ker's second in the challenge to Hamilton and who was determined to do away with the three men, declaring in his cups that he 'would have the traitors' throats cut'. Passion fuelled by alcohol pushed the plot forward. The agents were supposed to be two army colonels – John Cochrane and Alexander Stewart – who conspired with a number of other officers, but their indiscreet boastings in Canongate alehouses on 11 October meant that the rumours spread quickly through Edinburgh. Three officers, including Cochrane's lieutenant-colonel, Robert Home, reported the matter to the Earl of Leven. He passed on the warning and the three men went into hiding.

To add to the confusion Charles came to parliament on 14 October to declare his innocence of any involvement in the plot, an assertion which was untrue, as Cochrane had been in contact with him, but far from calming matters the king added to the tension by arriving with a heavily armed retinue. Fearing that Charles had come to arrest them the three noblemen fled the city and went into hiding at Kinneil, a

Hamilton residence near Linlithgow, a move which was understandable but which added to the king's fury. Later Hamilton tried to excuse his actions by claiming that they had left Edinburgh to prevent trouble brewing up between rival factions, but Charles refused to believe him and was mightily hurt by the suggestion made in a subsequent fawning letter that his friend believed his life to be in mortal danger:

> That I did refrain the place [court] for such a cause as the preservation of life, or that which is as dear to me, my liberty, is a misfortune beyond any I ever knew, for where should I find protection but from your sacred self and in your Court . . .[15]

Charles was not impressed and told Hamilton and his fellow fugitives that they must stay away from parliament until the matter was investigated, which it was – in private, and to the king's discredit. Not unnaturally, the Covenanters made the most of the Incident, seeing it as a further example of Charles's untrustworthiness and the treachery of his allies. To rub salt into the wound the three men were recalled to parliament on 6 November and Hamilton made the most of the occasion, comparing the Incident to the Armada and the Gunpowder Plot as one of 'the manifold plots against our Protestant religion'. Their presence was also needed because a new crisis had blown up – news had arrived from Ulster that the Irish Catholics were in open rebellion – but there is little doubt that the Covenanters were also demonstrating to the king that they enjoyed the upper hand.

Events in the Scottish parliament confirmed that that was indeed the case. Charles decided that he had outstayed his welcome and should return to London, but not before he completed a number of concessions to his enemies which all but destroyed his remaining power in Scotland. Argyll was created a marquis and there was a knighthood for Wariston, who was also made a lord of session. Hope, no friend, was confirmed as Lord Advocate and Balmerino and other opponents received places on the Privy Council. For those Royalists who had supported him and opposed the Covenant there was nothing, and for his pains in trying to secure the north-east Huntly was removed from the Privy Council. On Charles's last night in the

Scottish capital, 17 November 1641, he entertained Argyll and other nobles to a grand dinner in Holyrood and, deluded as ever, fondly thought that they were all his friends, either because he had bought them over or because they had learned to respect him. The following morning he rose early and set off for London. It was the last day he would ever spend in his northern kingdom.

Chapter Nine

IRELAND IN FLAMES

'The rebels march on furiously destroying all the English, sparing neither sex nor age, most barbarously murdering them, and that with greater cruelty than was ever used among Turks and infidels.'

Sir William Temple to King Charles I, from
Dublin Castle, October 1641

Strafford had been the glue which held Ireland together, but once he had departed the scene it was open season for those who were most discontented and whom he had repressed so severely – the Catholic Irish. When the revolt came, on 23 October 1641, it was a great shock to the English, for not only had Ireland been quiet since 1603 when Hugh O'Neill, Earl of Tyrone, had surrendered to Queen Elizabeth's Deputy, Lord Mountjoy, but Strafford had encouraged the belief that at long last the Irish had been civilised. Blind to reality, 'Black Tom Tyrant' had assured Charles that he need not worry about his Irish kingdom, that it was 'a conquered territory, and the king would do with it as he liked', but Strafford's policy of divide and rule had produced disastrous consequences, not least because in so doing he had managed to antagonise every shade of Irish opinion. That Strafford should have won the lasting enmity of the Irish peasantry was no surprise. These 'obstinate, senseless creatures' had been dispossessed and marginalised, not just by having land taken away from them and given to Protestant settlers, but by being treated as an unwanted underclass.[1] However, Strafford had gone further. The Scots planters in Ulster had been forced to swear their refusal to sign the National Covenant – the notorious 'Black Oath' – and the land holdings of the Old English families had been threatened, moves which only alienated two classes of people who should have been natural allies. To complicate matters, Strafford had limited most of his patronage to the New English settlers, ensuring obedience to the Crown but causing resentment outside their charmed circle. Of the 240 members of parliament in 1640 only 74 were Catholic.

That sense of being outcasts, fuelled as it was by Strafford's blatant prejudice against all Catholics, was to be instrumental in bringing the Old English and the Gaelic Irish into an uneasy alliance. Four years before his death Strafford had warned Charles that as long as the Irish 'continued popish, they are not a people for the crown of England to appear confident of'.[2] It was a piece of advice which had a more certain touch than his bluster that all was well in Ireland, but Strafford had failed to realise how his own heavy-handed treatment of the Catholics had only served to break all faith in him as the representative of the Crown. Repression of their religion and denial of their rights lay at the heart of their growing discontent, yet it was not inspired by any general hatred of Charles. Just as the Covenanters made it clear that their quarrel was not with the king but with those who had advised him so wrongly (in their view) over Church policy, so too did the Irish insurrectionists claim that they were guided by the need 'to preserve the freedom of this kingdom under the sole obedience of his sacred majesty'. Being pragmatists as well, they also declared that they were inspired 'to imitate Scotland who got a privilege by that course'. One Scottish minister, George Creighton, was told that he would be spared because the Scots 'had not oppressed them in government, and that if the Scots would be honest and had taken their parts, they would share the kingdoms among them: And they believed the Scots would not forget the great troubles that the English lately procured unto Scotland: Now it was their case with the English'.[3] Being Irish, the insurgents probably took comfort in the old adage about England's difficulty being Ireland's opportunity.

It was not just the constraints over religion which antagonised the Irish; land, too, was a contentious issue. Throughout his period in office Strafford had ridden roughshod over Irish sensibilities on land ownership and failed to understand the unease felt by a society whose hereditary status was under threat. (And not just feelings were hurt: when the Lord Lieutenant stayed with the Earl of Clanricard he caused great offence by soiling the bed with his dirty riding boots.) There had been the attempt to plant Connacht by confiscating land and unearthing older Crown lands, using the English freehold definition of property ownership which was unconnected to the Irish feudal system. Church lands, too, had been confiscated and at the same time Strafford had heightened the outrage by setting aside the principle of the Graces, the concessions over land ownership which had been made to the Old English families in return for their financial support earlier in Charles's reign. It was little wonder that the Old English families believed their rights had been infringed by an alien form of government, that – as one of their leaders, Lord Gormanston, put it – they had come to fear that the English would 'come into Ireland, with the Bible in one hand and the sword in the other, for to plant their Puritan, anarchical religion among us, otherwise utterly to destroy us'.[4]

With Strafford dead and his methods of rule exposed during his impeachment, parliament hoped that the Irish would be placated. The immediate problem was the power vacuum: there was no suitable replacement as Lord Lieutenant and the decision to share power between two rivals, Sir John Borlase and Sir William Parsons, both key figures in the plantation policies, only exacerbated discontent. A far better alternative would have been to appoint James Butler, the Earl of Ormond, one of the most powerful Irish magnates of his time and a member of an Old English family, whose presence, not to say that of the army he commanded, might have been a calming influence. Honourable, loyal and high-spirited, he was unusual in having been brought up a Protestant in London and was a natural Royalist, but Charles rejected the idea for fear of antagonising the Irish parliament. As had happened in both Scotland and England, the king was about to permit events in Ireland to get out of hand.

The unrest had begun after Strafford left Dublin in the spring of 1640 and it became more heated during the impeachment process which saw Gormanston, a Catholic, working with Clotworthy, an

Ulster Protestant, to bring down the despised Lord Lieutenant.* The Irish parliament was also in session and in November 1640 it passed a Remonstrance – a lengthy and detailed attack on Strafford and his policies and a plea for the restoration of the Graces – which was remitted to the English parliament with the appeal that it should be passed to the king, 'calling to mind the near links and great ties of blood and affinity between the people of this kingdom, and the famous people of England, from whose loins they are descended, and being therefore flesh of their flesh and bone of their bone, subjects to one gracious sovereign and governed by the same laws'.[5] It was a high-risk strategy. Just as the Scots had done, the Irish parliament dispatched commissioners to London in November 1640. These represented both the Old and the New English, but by cooperating with the London parliament they ran the danger of being subordinated to what was rapidly becoming, with the support of the Scots, an anti-Catholic body.

While the Irish commissioners were in London it would have been impossible for them to ignore the political tenor of the times – the growing truculence of the English parliament, the influence of the Scottish commissioners and the king's declining power – and that understanding would have given them pause for thought. The new anti-popish spirit also came as a surprise, and it was only natural that the Irish feared that it would soon be visited upon them. Gormanston said as much in a letter written to Clanricard once the rebellion had broken out:

> It was not unknown to your lordship how the Puritan faction in England, since by the countenance of the Scottish army they invaded the regal power, have both in their doctrine and practice laid the foundation of the slavery of this country. They teach that the laws of England, if they mention Ireland, are without doubt binding here, and the Parliament has wholly assumed the management of the affairs of this kingdom, as a right of pre-eminence due to it. And what may be expected from such zealous and fiery professors of an adverse religion but the ruin and extirpation of ours.[6]

---

* The distinguished historian Conrad Russell observes of this feat: 'Strafford appears to have achieved the distinction of being perhaps the only Englishman to have obliterated the religious divide in Irish politics'.

Gormanston's fears struck at the heart of Irish independence. The English parliament and its Scottish allies were perfervid Protestants, constituents of a northern European heresy to extinguish the Church of Rome, and if they decided to extend their influence to Ireland then Catholicism would be further suppressed and the plantations would continue with a vengeance. Also, and this emotion should not be underestimated, the native Irish had never reconciled themselves to the loss of land, especially in Ulster; the crisis in London must have encouraged their desire to retrieve their position, if need be by force.

In fact the early negotiations with Charles were reasonably successful. At the time, the spring of 1641, the king was facing up to the loss of Strafford and the increasing enmity of parliament and as a result was minded to offer concessions to the Irish. The Graces were granted for a second time and it was agreed to abandon the idea of planting Connacht. Taxation was reduced, trading agreements were reformed and the Court of High Commission was abolished, but the Old English were rightly suspicious that all of the king's concessions would be meaningless unless they were backed by law. Promises were not enough. Allied to this fear was a desire for the Irish parliament to play a more prominent and independent role in the governance of the country. This would entail repealing or changing the Poynings' Acts of 1494 which subordinated the Irish parliament to the English Privy Council, but on that score Charles refused to budge. As a result the granting of the Graces remained in limbo throughout the summer, a state of affairs which made any lasting agreement impossible. Blind to reality (or refusing to acknowledge it), Charles had left for Edinburgh believing not only that the Irish grievances had been addressed but that he could continue to rely on the support of the Old English magnates.

He was mistaken. While the negotiations were continuing in London plans were already being made locally to rise in armed rebellion both to protect Irish interests and to make good losses of property. The guiding light behind the uprising in Ulster was one of the leading disaffected local landowners, the member for Dungannon Sir Phelim O'Neill, a nephew of the Earl of Tyrone and cousin of his rival Owen Roe O'Neill. Together with neighbours and friends, all men of substance, he drew up a plan of action which would stand or fall on the ability of the insurgents to capture quickly key planter strongholds such as Newry, Armagh, Charlemont and Mountjoy. At the same time property would be repatriated either forcibly or, as O'Neill demonstrated, by social subterfuge: Charlemont Castle fell into his hands through the simple expedient of calling on its owner, Lord Caulfield, for dinner. (Another version had it that he was searching for lost cattle and used the ruse to take the castle.)

The element of surprise was the deciding factor. On the night of 22 October Ulster erupted and O'Neill's rebels soon had the principal objectives in their hands with an ease which demonstrates how unexpected the uprising was. (The plan to seize Dublin Castle was betrayed by treachery brought about by a drunken indiscretion.) The castles or fortifications at Armagh, Charlemont, Mountjoy, Tandagree and Newry all fell within days allowing O'Neill's men to take control of large parts of Tyrone, Armagh and South Down. By 31 October Dundalk had fallen and on 29 November, in the first pitched battle of the war, a government army sent to relieve Drogheda was defeated at Julianstown in County Meath by forces led by Rory O'More, another insurgent leader and the man behind the Dublin plot. From the outset O'Neill had made it clear that there was to be no massacre of Protestants – on 24 October he issued a proclamation from Dungannon stating that the insurgents were only protecting their liberties and that 'every person should make speedy return unto their own houses under pain of death, and that no further hurt be done anyone under like pain' – but it proved impossible to prevent bloodshed. When the Protestants attempted to flee to the unaffected towns – among them Londonderry, Coleraine and Carrickfergus – they were rarely shown any mercy when they were captured. Many were murdered in retaliation for past actions, an absence of discipline among the insurgents played a part and, with some priests urging that it was no sin to kill Protestants because they were already damned and beyond redemption, there was a fair degree of religious fanaticism. Among the many victims was the Reverend John Corbet, a religious pamphleteer who had been forced to leave Scotland for speaking out against the Glasgow Assembly of 1639 and had subsequently obtained the living of Killalan and Balintrubride. Hardly a Protestant extremist, his life was forfeit for being thought one: according to his erstwhile friend Robert Baillie he was 'hewed to pieces in the very arms of his poor wife'. Revenge was in the air and the dispossessed Catholics took their full measure.

Inevitably, too, the evidence of atrocities gave rise to wildfire rumours, many of them exaggerated, about the scale and intensity of the killings. A priest in Longford was reported to have torn apart a Protestant minister with his own hands; other stories spoke of popish beastliness as children were boiled alive; in Mayo cattle belonging to Protestant families were supposed to have been tried before being slaughtered; figures of 200,000 Protestant dead were readily believed and sank into folk memory.* Later this 'evidence' was recorded in depositions which were produced after the events, some of them at least a decade later, and given the timescale and the fact that they have a Protestant bias they are not completely reliable as corroboration that massacres took place or that the figures produced are accurate.[7] There was an ulterior motive, too: the depositions were collected for the specific purpose of assisting the efforts of Protestant officials in Ireland to identify and take revenge upon those Catholics who were involved with the onslaught during the winter and spring of 1640–41. However, their production helped to polarise opinion, and because the evidence was believed the depositions ensured that in the aftermath Protestants would be slow to forgive or to forget that their Catholic neighbours had taken the law into their own hands. For many years thereafter the Protestant community would offer special prayers each 23 October that they be spared the bestial behaviour of their Catholic neighbours. It would not be the last time in Irish history that enmity between the two religions would be fired by the memory of atrocity and suffering:

Many persons of good rank and quality, covered over with old rags, and some without any other covering than a little to hide their nakedness, some reverend ministers and others that had escaped with their lives sorely wounded. Wives came bitterly lamenting their murders of their husbands; ready to perish and pour out their souls in their mothers' bosoms; some over-wearied with long travel, and so surbated [footsore] as they came creeping on their knees;

---

* Most historians are agreed that the figure is much lower. In County Armagh up to 1300 were killed, some 25% of the population. See Jane Ohlmeyer's essay 'The Wars of Religion' in Bartlett and Jeffrey, *A Military History of Ireland*.

others frozen up with cold, ready to give up the ghost in the streets; others overwhelmed with grief, distracted with their losses, lost also in their senses.[8]

That eye-witness report and many other contemporary accounts published in England helped to create fears that this was a Catholic conspiracy and that innocent Protestants were being martyred by the forces of the Counter-Reformation. Most accounts were distorted or untruthful, but at a time of tension in London they were readily believed, not least because Ireland and rebellion were synonymous in many Englishmen's minds. For the members of the Long Parliament the Ulster uprising was also a distraction at a time when it was pressing on with its programme of reform. Clearly the challenge had to be met, but parliament was loath to raise an army in Ireland and then put it under Charles's control, perhaps for it to be used later against them. Their alarm on this score was increased when the rebels produced forged documentation that they were acting on the king's orders, producing as evidence a commission under the Great Seal of Scotland dated 1 October. Showing his usual vacillation, Charles failed to disown it immediately, thereby fanning fears that he was planning to encourage the Catholics to unleash the same horrors on England. Another widely believed rumour had it that Henrietta Maria was behind the 'horrid and execrable rebellion' and that under her baleful influence England would be reduced to popery.

As the revolt spread elsewhere – by November Leinster had risen and Drogheda was under siege – Charles took action from Edinburgh by appointing Ormond his lieutenant-general in charge of an Irish army of 2297 infantry and 943 horse. At the same time, without consulting the king, parliament voted on 12 November to send 2000 soldiers to Ireland and within a month negotiations were under way with the Scottish parliament to send the Covenanting army over to Ireland. It was an open door, for the Scots were already preparing: no sooner had the news reached Edinburgh than thought had been given to dispatching an army to intervene in Ulster. The Covenanters' motives were hardly altruistic. There was a pressing need to protect Scottish Presbyterian planters and to prevent a Catholic Irish victory which would threaten Scotland's position. Memories of the threat of invasion by the forces raised by Antrim and Strafford were still strong and there was a very real fear that the spirit of the insurrection might encourage Scottish Catholics in the Highlands to follow the lead taken by their Irish counterparts. Greed, the companion of opportunity, also played a part: by sending an army to Ireland the Covenanters would be able to extend their influence and benefit from the territorial acquisitions which would follow in the wake of any settlement.

Charles, too, wanted to encourage the Scots to intervene, as did the English parliament. In both cases it was a compromise. The king believed that by sending the Scottish army to Ulster he was relieving himself of a possible threat against him, while parliament wanted to see the rebels defeated quickly by an army which was not under the king's control. Of course it would have to be funded: while the Scots were nothing loath to intervene and were prepared to find the funds for raising an army 10,000 strong to be taken across St George's Channel, they were not prepared to pay for its upkeep. This would have to be borne by the English parliament, and the negotiations which began on 10 December were destined to drag on into the following summer, a delay which made Loudoun complain that 'all Ireland will be in the rebels' hands before any army can be sent over'.[9]

From a purely military point of view there were few difficulties in raising the force and dispatching it to Ulster. Three regiments of Leslie's army had remained in being and it would not take long to muster others, the crossing was short, and there was considerable enthusiasm within Scotland for the intervention. However there were understandable English fears that the Scots were simply intent on territorial aggrandisement. This was not just prejudice speaking: the Scottish commissioners in London had already insisted that their help depended on being given a share in further plantations and that the towns of Carrickfergus, Coleraine and Londonderry should be put under the control of the Scottish army for the duration of the operation. For the English this was 'hard digestion', but with no other option open to them parliament was forced to seek an accommodation with the Scots while it concentrated on its quarrel with the king.

It was not until March 1642, that the first Scots units began to arrive in Ulster after mustering at Ayr. Overall command had been given to Leslie, now the Earl of Leven, with the Earl of Lothian as his lieutenant-general. The latter had his own foot regiment drawn mainly from the Border counties which was commanded by its lieutenant-colonel, Walter Scott, but the over-arching military personality was the force's major-general, Robert Monro, the experienced mercenary commander who showed an early determination to put down the revolt as efficiently and as quickly as possible. From his base at Carrickfergus he ordered a succession of drives into land occupied by the rebels, the intention being to sweep out the Irish Catholics and to prevent them getting support from the local population. These search and destroy operations paid dividends because the Scots were better trained and better armed than the opposition and Monro was determined to maintain the initiative. By the middle of May most of Down had been pacified, but for the people of Ulster the price was high. Fired by the stories of Catholic atrocities, the Scots gave little quarter once men had surrendered and massacres were commonplace. Even hardened soldiers such as James Turner, who had witnessed similar atrocities in Germany, were shocked by the depravity shown by his men during the operations south of Carrickfergus to retake the town of Newry:

> In the woods of Kilwarning [Kilwarlin Wood, near Lisburn] we re-encountered some hundreds of rebels who after a short dispute fled. These who were taken got but bad quarter, being all shot dead. This was too much used by both English and Scots all along in that war; a thing inhumane and disavowable, for the cruelty of one enemy cannot excuse the inhumanity of another. And herein also their revenge overmastered their discretion, which should have taught them to save the lives of these they took, that the rebels might do the like to their prisoners.

The following day, 3 May, the Scots and English soldiers under the command of Conway entered Newry and recaptured its castle from the rebels; those who survived were lined up by the bank of the river and along with the local merchants were 'butchered to death, some by shooting, some by hanging, and some by drowning, without any legal process'. In vain did Turner gallop to the killing ground to stop the slaughter: by the time he reached the soldiers, pistol in hand, only a handful of civilians remained to be saved.[10]

With its strategic position in the Mourne Mountains and its proximity to the sea at Carlingford Lough, Newry had long experience of warfare and had been razed before, but the fact that O'Neill had seized the castle lent extra force to the Covenanting soldiers' zeal. As Turner noted, although he did not approve of the reprisals he could understand why the men under his command offered no quarter: 'the wild Irish did not only massacre all whom they could overmaster, but habitable houses, endeavouring to reduce, as far as their power could reach, all to a confused chaos'. In other places age-old animosities between rival families fuelled the urge to take revenge. Rathlin Island was garrisoned by Argyll's Foot under the command of Lieutenant-Colonel Sir Duncan Campbell of Auchinbreck, who actively encouraged his men, all Campbells, to take their revenge on the local MacDonnells. Ordered to expel or kill all rebels, they needed little incentive to choose the latter, and during the operations scores of local women were thrown from the clifftops. And it was not just Ulster which was ablaze: at the beginning of 1642 similar risings had taken place in all the Irish counties as the Old English Catholic families and their supporters joined the affray, all the while protesting that they were the king's 'loyal subjects' whose only concern was the protection of their legal and religious rights 'against Puritans and corrupt ministers of state'.

The result was the creation of the one thing which neither Charles nor parliament wanted: a union between the Gaelic Irish and the Old English aristocracy. Infuriated by the stalemate over the Graces, and encouraged by O'More's victory at Julianstown, where large numbers of weapons had been seized following the rout of the English cavalry, the two parties entered into talks with the insurgents, first at Knockcrofty near Drogheda and then at Kilkenny, where it was agreed to form an alternative form of government for Ireland. As Richard Bellings, the confederation's first secretary, put it: 'And so distrust, aversion, force and fear united the two parties which had since the conquest been most opposite'.[11] Together with Catholic Church leaders a confederation came into being which was held together by an oath of association, similar in intent to Scotland's National Covenant, asserting their rights as Charles's subjects and binding its adherents to restore Catholicism to Ireland. As such, national unity was its aim; its motto was *Pro Deo, Rege et Patria, Hibernia Unanimis* (For God, King and Homeland, Ireland United) and its main aim, albeit optimistic, was that 'there shall be no distinction or comparison betwixt old Irish, and old and new English, or betwixt septs or families, or betwixt citizens and townsmen and countrymen, joining in union, upon pain of the highest punishment'.[12] Its armies adopted a similar position, taking as their flag an Irish cross with the monogram CR and the motto *Vivat Rex Carolus* (Long live King Charles), and the opening words of the oath proclaimed its patriotic purpose:

> I, AB, do promise, swear and protest before God, and his saints and angels, during my life to bear true faith and allegiance to my sovereign lord Charles, by the grace of God, king of Great Britain, France and Ireland . . .

In the eleven years of civil warfare which lay ahead in Ireland, usually known as the Confederate War, 1641–53, that confident statement would be tested severely and frequently found wanting, but during the summer of 1642 the Confederation of Kilkenny seemed to the leaders of the uprising to be the best chance of promoting an already fragile unity. Aimed at restoring a semblance of law and authority, the confederation was founded as an alternative form of government with its own bureaucratic and military structure. Money was minted, arrangements were made for taxes to be collected and agents were sent abroad to try to raise funds from friendly Catholic countries, thereby adding fuel to not unfounded English fears that the members of the confederation were fermenting a counter-revolution to restore Catholicism in all three kingdoms. The first general assembly of civic and Church leaders was held in October and a supreme council of 24 members was elected with Lord Mountgarret – Ormond's grand-uncle – being elected president. Four regional army commands were formed and the military preparations were enhanced by the appearance of Colonel Thomas Preston and Owen Roe O'Neill, who took over from his cousin Sir Phelim whose forces had faltered before Drogheda.

With his experience of European warfare in Spanish service, Owen Roe O'Neill proved to be the confederates' most successful general at a time when the rebellion was in danger of collapsing – although his effectiveness was nullified by the rivalry between him and Preston. For

Charles, Ormond, having taken the king's commission, had rallied the government forces and his experienced commanders, notably Sir Charles Coote, had made large inroads into putting down the insurrection in Leinster. There were heavy defeats for the Irish at Swords outside Dublin and Kilrush in County Kildare, in Munster the Earl of Inchiquin had pacified much of the province, and the siege of Drogheda was raised, leaving the city in Royalist hands for the duration of the war. Only a shortage of funds, caused by the continuing quarrel between the king and the English parliament, prevented the campaign from being decided in the summer of 1642. Monro's army had been driven to the point of mutiny due to the slow arrival of pay and provisions; but they were calmed down by the Covenanting leaders who pointed out that 'if the Scots were away, it is feared that all Ireland should be ready to go upon Ireland at a call'. To all intents and purposes the Scottish army was reduced to fighting a guerrilla war against an enemy which melted away into the countryside after ambushes and rarely risked a fixed battle.[13] There were also problems with the high command. Monro frequently clashed with Conway, the marshal of the Irish Army – during the spring campaign they agreed to give orders on alternate days – and there were frequent allegations of Scottish looting in east Ulster.

Leven, too, had shown little interest in the campaign, his involvement being limited to leading two minor search-and-destroy operations from Carrickfergus, both of which angered Turner as he had to 'part with [our] hay, wine, beer and bread, which were not very well stored'. At the same time Leven had written to Owen Roe O'Neill expressing astonishment that he should have lent his support to a rebellion which threatened the king's position in Ireland. Back came a frosty reply from the Irishman saying that he was equally surprised to see Leven supporting the very king whose forces he had humbled during the recent Bishops' Wars. By the end of the summer Leven's first and last commission in the king's service had come to an end, having convinced himself that he had undertaken it only because the rights of Scots living in Ulster had been in hazard. Ahead for both men lay another decade of somewhat different and far more bloodthirsty warfare.

The rebellion in Ireland changed the complexion of the king's quarrel with parliament and made further unrest well-nigh inevitable.

First Scotland and then Ireland had risen in armed resistance to protect their interests against the king's policies, the first succeeding and the second taking heart from the outcome, so much so that the Catholics among them had eagerly risen to protect their rights. The creation of armies had also raised the temperature. The Covenanters had raised an army to protect their religious interests and to force concessions from the king; now under Monro it was doing the same thing in Ulster. It did not succeed in putting down the revolt, that was not its entire purpose, but by restoring order in Antrim and Down it gave the Covenanters a useful lever in their relationship with parliament. Not only were they acting as parliament's agents in Ireland but they were doing so in the knowledge that Charles had hoped to deploy Strafford's Irish army against them two years earlier. That provided grounds enough to strengthen their suspicions. Now parliament feared that Royalist forces in Ireland might also be used against them. That prompted the Scots and the English members of parliament to remain on friendly terms, however much some of the latter might have distrusted their Presbyterian allies. To cap it all, the confederates had three armies in the field in Ireland, as did the Royalists under the overall command of Ormond, and they were already at each other's throats: these were the sparks to the tinderbox.

Then there were the rumours: the news coming out of Ireland from those taking refuge from the uprising spoke of a great Catholic conspiracy and the massacre of English innocents which had to be put down for the greater good. 'Worse and worse news from Ireland' began a typical broadside of the day, and on 14 December the House of Commons was treated to a letter from Ireland which spoke only of carnage and bloodshed:

> All I can tell you is the miserable estate we continue under, for the rebels daily increase in men and munitions in all parts except the province of Munster, exercising all manner of cruelties, and striving who can be most barbarously exquisite in tormenting the poor Protestants, wheresoever they come, cutting of privy members, ears, fingers and hands, plucking out their eyes, boiling the heads of little children before their mothers' faces, and then ripping up their mothers' bowels, stripping women naked, and standing by them

being naked, while they are in travail, killing the children as soon as they are born, and ripping up their mother's bellies, as soon as they are delivered; driving men, women and children, by hundreds together upon bridges, and from thence cast them down into rivers, such as drowned not, they knock their brains out with poles, or shoot them with muskets, that endeavour to escape by swimming out; ravishing wives before their husbands' faces, and virgins before their parents' faces, after they have abused their bodies, making them renounce their religion, and then marry them to the basest of their fellows.[14]

Overblown that and other reports might have been, but they ushered in a climate of distrust which made a breakdown in order ever more likely – in the English parliament Pym, never a man to miss an opportunity, claimed that the rebellion in Ireland left England under threat from popery and, worse, the fault was the king's. For their part the Irish confederates were convinced that they were facing extinction at the hands of an English parliament which was determined to drag Ireland under the Protestant heel. They were not far wrong, for steps had already been taken to punish Ireland, if need be by what a later age would call privatisation: in February parliament had passed the Adventurers Act which advertised for private subscriptions to fund the repression of the rebellion in return for parcels of confiscated land. O'Neill's rebellion had begun to protect Irish rights, but now the English parliament was using a Scottish army and its own forces not just to put down the Catholics but, effectively, to reconquer Ireland. As Clarendon argued later when he came to write his history, by the beginning of 1642 the affairs of all three kingdoms were now inter-dependent on each other:

If this Scottish people had not, without any provocation, but their own folly and barbarity, with that bloody prologue engaged against the three kingdoms in a raging and devouring war; so that though Scotland blew the first trumpet, it was Ireland that drew the first blood; and if they had not at that time rebelled, and in that manner, it is very probable all the miseries which afterwards befell the King and his dominions had been prevented.[15]

In fact the first blood had been drawn two years earlier when the hapless David Prat had been killed at Towie-Barclay Castle as Huntly tried to protect the king's interest, but Clarendon was right: once O'Neill's men had swept through Ulster, killing and burning and sending hundreds of refugees across the sea to England and Scotland, the quarrel between Charles and his parliament was now incapable of remedy.

Chapter Ten

THE STORM FINALLY BREAKS

'Since I see all the birds have flown, I do expect from you that you will send them unto me as soon as they return here.'

King Charles I, from the Speaker's chair in the House of Commons, 4 January 1642

Although the turmoil in Ireland came at a crucial point in the king's quarrel with parliament, on the surface at least many major matters of mutual discontent had been resolved and Charles's popularity with his people remained intact. The war with Scotland was over, the tax-raising powers of his personal rule had been ended and the worst of his counsellors had either been executed or hounded from public life. There was also a pressing need to put down the Irish rebellion – any popish threat against the state or body politic was bound to breed unity – and the king arrived back from his Scottish visit to be greeted by a welcome which Clarendon described as 'the greatest acclamation of joy that had been known on any occasion'. Thanks to the appointment of a Royalist Lord Mayor, Sir Richard Gurney, there was a triumphal entry when he arrived in London on 25 November 1641, his supporters spoke admiringly of the mutual affection that bound together the king and his people, the bells rang and the wine flowed. In return Charles promised the aldermen and merchants that he would 're-establish that flourishing trade which now is in some disorder among you'.

In other respects, though, the king was to find that in his absence nothing had changed, and when he addressed parliament on 2 December he was shaken out of any complacency that all was well in his English kingdom. Far from finding that his opponents had been placated by their reforms and the royal concessions, he discovered 'Jealousies, Fights and Alarms of dangerous designs and plots'.[1] Just as he had left Edinburgh convinced that he had won over his enemies, when he had not done so, he arrived back in his English capital to find that, far from settling matters with the Long Parliament, he still had a fight on his hands.

The cause of the unrest was a document known as the *Grand Remonstrance* which had been passed a month earlier while Charles was still in Scotland. Lengthy, prolix, strident and frequently confused, it was both a list of demands and a restatement of past grievances, more of a public manifesto than the petition it claimed to be. Pushed through by Pym and Hampden, and the result of earlier work by the parliamentary committees, it had been resurrected as a means of consolidating parliament's position at a time when its revolutionary fervour seemed to be waning. Its main intention was to assert the claims of parliament by firstly (and cleverly) listing the reforms already passed by the Long Parliament before proceeding to catalogue outstanding grievances which demanded attention in order to preserve 'the fundamental laws and principles of government, upon which the religion and justice of this kingdom are firmly established'.

Underpinning the *Grand Remonstrance* was the belief, held by Pym and his supporters, that there had been a conspiracy, 'a malignant and pernicious design' to subvert the religion of England, and that steps had to be taken to retrieve the position. With that in mind it urged the king to replace 'evil counsellors' – in other words, Catholics intent on furthering the Counter-Reformation – and their replacement with 'such persons . . . as your Parliament may have cause to confide in'. Episcopal votes should be abolished in parliament, discipline should be brought back into religious practice, the power of bishops curtailed and, with a nod in the direction of the Scots, a synod of British Protestant Church leaders should be formed. Members of parliament were also invited to add to the list of grievances, and many did so, the grave and as yet little-known representative for Cambridge calling for an investigation into abuses in the Commission of Sewers.

Dressed in a 'plain cloth suit, which seemed to have been made by
an ill country tailor', Oliver Cromwell was typical of the new breed who
made up Pym's main support in the Long Parliament – strong-willed,
intelligent and intent on reform.[2] He was born on 25 April 1599 in the
dying years of the Elizabethan age into a well-connected Huntingdon
family whose forebears included Thomas Cromwell, Henry VIII's
architect of the Protestant Reformation, and by his own account he
considered himself to be 'by birth a gentleman, living neither in any
considerable height, nor yet in obscurity'.[3] Neither poor nor rich,
Cromwell had been educated at the University of Cambridge, choosing
the recently opened Sidney Sussex College – considered to be a hotbed
of Puritan enthusiasm – but his father's death in 1617 cut short his
education. An early marriage, and a good one at that, followed three
years later. His bride was Elizabeth Bourchier, the daughter of a wealthy
City trader, and the couple settled down in Huntingdon, where
Cromwell was able to indulge his lifelong obsession with horses,
hunting and country pursuits. During the early years of Charles's rule
the Cromwells led ordinary solid lives of domestic tranquillity enriched
with the passing of the years by a growing family, and there they might
have remained but for Oliver's decision to enter politics.

In 1628 he was elected one of the members for Huntingdon, and
in the following spring he was one of those who refused to heed the
king's injunction to adjourn and witnessed the infamous incident
which led to the Speaker being forcibly held in his chair to allow the
debate to continue. It also led to the dissolution of parliament and to
the introduction of the Personal Rule, and both were destined to have
a lasting influence on the course of Cromwell's life. When he returned
to bucolic Huntingdon he was a changed man. First and foremost he
had witnessed power politics at work and had become aware of the
widespread opposition to popery and to the king's absolute rule. The
experience also made him aware of his connections and
responsibilities – John Hampden was a cousin – and this leaning
towards radicalism came at a time when he was questioning the
foundation of his own religious beliefs. He even considered the
possibility of emigrating to New England and joining the other
Puritan adventurers who were colonising the eastern seaboard of
North America with their mixture of fundamentalist faith and hard-
headed business acumen.

Emigration was an attractive proposition not least because many of his friends were involved with the New Providence Company and the lure of joining fellow Puritans in a great adventure suited the tenor of his religious inclinations. During the 1630s, that period of exaggerated calm when England seemed to be at peace with itself, Cromwell underwent a profound spiritual conversion which saw him achieving a state of personal grace in his relationship with God. Believing himself to have been reborn as one of the elect, those fortunate enough to feel God's favour working within them, Cromwell came to believe that salvation was a matter of the wrestling of the individual soul with God and that no earthly authority, however august, must be allowed to come between. It was an austere belief – it was meant to be – and, troubled by periodic bouts of debilitating melancholia, Cromwell embraced it with all the zeal of the true convert, writing to a cousin in a spirit of religious exaltation that this 'poor creature' had been saved:

> The lord accept me in His son, and give me to walk in the light, as He is the light. He it is that enlighteneth our blackness, our darkness. I dare not say, He hideth His face from me. He giveth me to see light in His light. One beam in a dark place hath exceeding much refreshment in it . Blessed be His Name for shining upon so dark a heart as mine! You know what my manner of life hath been. Oh, I have lived in and loved darkness and hated the light. I was a chief, the chief of sinners. This is true; I hated godliness, yet God had mercy on me. O the riches of His mercy![4]

The exact nature of those 'sins' remains a mystery, for there is nothing to suggest that Cromwell was more of a reprobate than any other young man, but before his election to a state of grace he must have believed that he was beyond God's love and compassion – otherwise he would not have written in such portentous terms about walking in darkness. That would explain the slightly hysterical note with which he described his conversion and the sense of providence which accompanied it: henceforth black would be black, white would be white, and compromise would be the work of the devil. It was to be a lasting influence. When he returned to parliament in 1640, this time as member for Cambridge, he was a different man, fired by an intensity of purpose which suited the times. So committed was he to driving through the *Grand Remonstrance* that when it was passed by the narrowest of margins – the dividing margin was only 11 votes – he famously told Lord Falkland, the member for Newport and a moderate, that if it had been rejected 'he would have sold all he had the next morning, and never seen England more; and he knew there were many other honest men of the same persuasion'.[5]

Throughout November the *Grand Remonstrance* had been picked over by the members clause by clause and as they did so divisions began to appear in their ranks. There were differences of opinion over how far parliament should go in accusing the episcopacy, a new sticking point was the propriety or otherwise of printing the *Grand Remonstrance* before it was shown to the king, and gradually a split became apparent between those who wanted to force Charles to accept change by extirpating popery, and those who sought compromise by adopting a more gradualist approach. Among the former were Pym, Hampden, Holles and Cromwell, while a grouping of what might be called constitutional Royalists including Hyde, Falkland, Lord Digby (son of the Earl of Bristol and a born intriguer whose advice to the king was not always the best), the poet Edmund Waller and Sir John Culpepper, a 'man of sharpness of parts and volubility of language' who was soon to be rewarded for his support by being appointed Charles's last Chancellor of the Exchequer.

Once the *Grand Remonstrance* had been passed by parliament it was forwarded to the king, who expressed some annoyance that it had already been published. Charles's reply was suitably admonitory: he denied that there were 'malignants' in his government, refused to accept that parliament should appoint his ministers and insisted that there was no need for reform of government or Church. As for the latter it was already reformed and in the king's view in no need of further tinkering:

> We are persuaded in our consciences that no church can be found upon the earth that professeth the true religion with more purity of doctrine than the church of England doth, nor where the government and discipline are jointly more beautiful and free from superstition, than as they are here established by law.[6]

To soften the blow Charles offered to raise an army of 10,000 soldiers to 'suppress this great insolency' of the rebellion in Ireland. Not unnaturally the overture was rejected and, as the crisis deepened, further confrontation between king and parliament became inevitable. Fired by the stories from Ireland of rumours of new plots by 'popish hell-hounds', the mood in London was becoming more belligerent and matters were not improved by the presence of 'reformadoes' – mercenary officers who claimed to support the king but spent most of their time lounging around London, drinking and causing trouble.

Against that troubled background both sides began jockeying for position and as Christmas approached attitudes began to harden. In a move which was bound to cause upset Charles dismissed the guard on the House of Commons and ended the commission of the Earl of Essex as Captain-General of the militia forces south of the Trent, a decision which heightened suspicions that the king was intent on a coup d'état. Matters came to a head on 23 December when Charles suddenly dismissed Sir William Balfour, an experienced Scots mercenary, from his post of Lieutenant of the Tower of London and replaced him with Colonel Thomas Lunsford, a reformado who had fought well at Newburn but had since been accused of murdering and eating children. While Charles had good cause to sack Balfour on account of his leanings towards parliament – he had already tried to bribe him to leave office, an offer the Scot rejected with disdain – the decision to replace him with Lunsford was utter madness. Here was a man with a dreadful reputation, a bullyboy and a troublemaker, yet the king was prepared to reward him with a position of power and in so doing to give ammunition to Pym, who saw in the appointment further evidence that there was a Catholic plot at the heart of the court. If Charles was looking for trouble he was not to be disappointed: there was an uproar inside and outside parliament and three days later, on Boxing Day, Lunsford was sacked and replaced by another professional soldier, Sir John Byron.

While the change of heart was welcomed, not least by the king's friends, the tension was not diminished by Lunsford's demotion. Far from being downcast he and his fellow reformadoes started swaggering around Westminster Hall threatening anyone who 'bawled against bishops' – those who were demonstrating against the presence of bishops in the House of Lords – and a scuffle broke out between the two groups. Threats were made, swords were drawn and a number of demonstrators were slightly wounded. It was only a minor incident but to Pym and his supporters it must have seemed that Lunsford had become a kind of royal bodyguard and the king's agent for suppressing free speech. Those fears would only have been stoked when Charles knighted Lunsford and gave a banquet for him and his friends.

Slowly the battle lines were being drawn and each side took up entrenched positions, both believing that the other was intent on making a pre-emptive strike. On 30 December twelve bishops combined to send a petition to the king remonstrating that the turbulence in Westminster made it impossible for them to sit in the Lords until the king had intervened to 'secure them from all affronts, indignities and dangers'. The protest only aggravated emotions and in a moment of high drama the Commons responded by impeaching the bishops for treason, a move that was bound to challenge the king's authority. While the motion was being debated the doors of the house were locked and Pym appealed to the Lord Mayor for the presence of the City of London's Trained Bands to guard Westminster because 'there was a plot for destroying the House of Commons'. There was also talk of adjourning to the Guildhall, but in seeking military assistance a step had been taken which altered the complexion of the quarrel.

The forces in question, the Trained Bands, were first raised as a part-time militia during Elizabeth's reign for the defence of the realm in the event of a Spanish invasion. Men fit for service aged from sixteen to sixty would be mustered during the summer months and divided into companies of 100-strong under the command of a local gentleman for drilling and weapon training. However they were not only far from popular but also not very efficient – when inspected by Sir John Norris, a professional soldier, 'he wondered that he could see no man in the kingdom afeared but himself'.[7] Only in London, where they numbered 6000 men, did they take their work seriously. Professionally drilled to use muskets and pikes, they were by far the best infantrymen in England – one company based in Cripplegate drilled every summer's morning at six o'clock and its captain, Henry Saunders, insisted on a high turnout at its musters. Used to being mocked as they carried out their drills, the volunteers were now the one force capable of restoring order in the capital, and in appealing to them for protection Pym could be construed as making a challenge to the king, not least because Charles was also relying on the Trained Bands to support him.

The year came to an end with further riots in Whitehall – scenes which made Charles fear for his family's safety – and with the Commons making fresh demands for forces to be raised to protect them under the command of the Earl of Essex, the one soldier whom they trusted. It is also probable that the king had been alarmed by the December debate on control of armed forces – an Impressment Bill was blocked in the Lords and there was also an abortive attempt to introduce a new militia bill which would have mobilised the militia under three unnamed generals. Things had come to a pretty pass if, as it seemed, parliament had war on its mind; as 1642 began Charles decided that he had to act against his opponents at Westminster.

During his visit to Edinburgh Charles had gathered sufficient intelligence (from Montrose and others) to know that Pym and his friends had encouraged a foreign power, the Scots, to invade England; there was ample evidence to suggest that the parliamentary reformers were behind the tumult in London and it was impossible to avoid the conclusion that they were responsible for alienating his subjects. As these transgressions amounted to treason the king believed that there was a case to be answered and accordingly ordered the Attorney-General, Sir Edward Herbert, to indict the five members thought to be most culpable – Pym, Hampden, Hesilrige, Holles and William Strode, the young member for Beeralston. For good measure the name of a Puritan peer, Lord Mandeville, son of the Earl of Manchester and a close associate of Pym, was added to the indictment. The charge was read out on 3 January, but the house declared that as this amounted to an infringement of privilege no action should be taken to apprehend the offending members.

If Charles is to be believed, the snub delivered by the members prompted him to go in person to the Commons the following day to effect the arrest before the quarrel descended into bloodshed. It is also possible that he was influenced by Henrietta Maria, who is supposed to have ordered him to take direct action and to 'pull these rogues out by the ears or never see my face again'. Fatefully Charles decided that he had to act and that there was no alternative available to him but to go the House of Commons in person to arrest his enemies, even if that meant infringing parliamentary privilege. Charles clearly knew what he was doing and he made sure that he had the necessary support. A message was sent to Sir Richard Gurney, the Lord Mayor, telling him to keep the Trained Bands away from Westminster; another was sent to the Inns of Court companies, whose members were mainly lawyers and students and therefore thought to be loyal to the Crown, ordering them to stand by. Then, gathering some 400 armed supporters – 'desperate soldiers, captains and commanders, papists, ill-affected persons, being men of no quality . . . panders and rogues' – Charles left Whitehall in his coach in the afternoon of 4 January 1642, bound for Westminster and a fatal confrontation. The moves had now been put in place to allow the playing out of one of the great set-piece scenes in English history.

Those indicted knew what was afoot, and no sooner had Charles and his party made their move than the conspirators (for so they seemed to the king) had made good their escape, slipping out of the building by a watergate where a boat took them to safe houses in the city. It was not a moment too soon, for the king was already in Westminster and ready to enter the House of Commons. Showing all his customary politeness, Charles entered the chamber accompanied by his brother-in-law, the Elector Palatine, removed his hat and gently asked the Speaker, William Lenthall, if he might borrow his chair. Looking round the assembled company to look for his enemies he offered a reproach which was greeted in silence:

> I must declare unto you here that albeit no king that ever was in England shall be more careful of your privileges . . . yet you must know that in cases of Treason, no person hath a privilege . . . since I see all the birds have flown, I do expect from you that you will send them unto me as soon as they return here. But I assure you, on the word of a king, I never did intend any force, but shall proceed against them in a legal and fair way.

Aware that the nest was empty, Charles invited Lenthall to tell him where the members were, only to receive the magisterial reply: 'May it pleasure your Majesty, I have neither eyes to see nor tongue to speak in this place but as the House is pleased to direct me, whose servant I am here.' With no other option but to retire as gracefully as possible, Charles replied, 'Well, well, 'tis no matter I think my eyes are as good as another's' and left the chamber with shouts of 'privilege' following him. Witnesses of the event said later that he seemed to be in a high passion, as well he might have been, having lost both the initiative and his regal dignity.[8]

In vain did Charles order the Channel ports to be closed to prevent the birds flying to the Continent; it mattered little that he proceeded to the Guildhall to order their arrest. The city was in uproar and, prompted by the wildest rumours, people either took to the streets to demonstrate against the king or started barricading their properties for an uncertain future. For the first time in living memory England's capital was gripped by the rumour of impending civil war, and as one witness remembered later, there seemed to be no end to the rumbling. This was Nehemiah Wallington, a Puritan tanner, whose commonplace book provides a lively, if frequently far-fetched, account of the war years:

> In the dead of night [6 January] there was great bouncing at every man's door to be up in their arms presently and to stand on their guard, for as we heard (as we lay in our beds) a great cry in the streets that there were horse and foot coming against the City. So the gates were shut and the cullises let down, and the chains put across the corners of our streets, and every man ready on his arms. And women and children did then arise, and fear and trembling entered on all.[9]

Faced by a breakdown in the civil power, parliament decided to act forcefully. On 7 January responsibility for control of the Trained Bands was removed from the Lord Mayor and brought under the control of a joint committee representing the aldermen and members of the Commons, a move which gave parliament protection and the nucleus of an army. Three days later command in the rank of Sergeant-Major-General was given to Philip Skippon, an experienced soldier with determined Puritan views who had served in the Dutch army and had a sure touch in dealing with the volunteers. The Trained Bands were organised into six regiments 1200 strong, each one known by the colour of its standard and each one representing a separate district of London, so that the men who trained together would also serve together. Their defection and the presence in the streets of enthusiastic Londoners supporting the parliamentary cause – Thames watermen, apprentices, students and the like – was enough to scare Charles into thinking that he had lost his capital. Lunsford offered to counter-attack but Charles would have none of it, as any Royalist intervention would have plunged the city into further anarchy. On the afternoon of 10 January he packed his family into a coach and left for Hampton Court, travelling through streets packed with jostling crowds whose shouts and jeers spoke only of revolution. That night, if the gossips were correct, the royal family was forced to sleep in one bed, so unprepared were their servants for the sudden flight.

The decision to bale out of London was a declaration. Charles had surrendered to parliament the focus of the administration and the law, the centre of business and finance, the heart of the country and its seat of power. As if to rub home the point that parliament was now the master, the five members came out of hiding the next day and were returned in triumph to Westminster escorted by the Trained Bands and other armed men, not just from London but also from Hampden's native Buckinghamshire. When the members finally entered the chamber their first act was to change the lock on the door through which Charles had entered before setting about their business. The symbolism was obvious but there was more to the moment than mere ritual. The five members had returned, parliament had made clear its distrust of the king, who had been forced to flee his capital for the safety of his residence upriver from Whitehall. Both sides felt imperilled, so much so that they could not bring themselves to be in the same city, let alone the same place, without armed protection. It was not yet outright war but the time for compromise was ebbing away: and there was no way out of the confrontation without one side or the other making unwarrantable concessions.

On 13 January Charles moved his little court to Windsor and began making preparations for Henrietta Maria to cross the Channel to seek help from likely supporters such as King Christian IV of Denmark, her husband's uncle, and Prince William of Orange. A month later she left from Dover with her daughter, having forced Charles to promise that he 'would never consent to an accommodation without my knowledge and through me' and taking with her the Crown jewels with which to raise money for her husband's cause. She proved to be as resilient in that role as she was in encouraging her husband's actions. In the United Provinces she succeeded in selling royal jewels and plate, raising £100,000 for purchasing arms – no mean feat as most Dutch merchants, being Protestant, favoured parliament. She also persuaded several professional soldiers to throw in their lot with the king, and from her exile she wrote constantly to Charles throughout the spring encouraging him to resist his enemies and remain constant in his resolution: 'I can never trust myself to those persons who would be your directors, nor to you, since you would have broken your promise to me.'[10] She alone in the royal camp wanted her husband to make a pre-emptive strike against parliament, to use force to retrieve his position, to fight or choose abdication.

The trouble was that Charles was not in any position to use military force to win back the initiative: his only attempt to do so had ended in farce when Lunsford made a half-hearted attempt to seize the arsenal at Kingston-on-Thames. The days were long past when, even if they were loyal to him, the aristocracy had sufficient military experience or could muster large numbers of soldiers. He lacked the funds to employ mercenaries, the position of the militia was unclear and in any case his advisers, most notably Hyde, were urging moderation and conciliation with parliament. The long years of peace, the legacy of the Elizabethan age, meant that most people were not minded to start fighting among themselves – a factor the king could not have mistaken as he continued his perambulations around southern England. On 7 February the royal family left Windsor for Dover and, having seen his wife depart for the Continent, Charles and his retinue left first for Canterbury and then for Cambridge. Wherever they went enthusiastic crowds greeted him warmly but there was also a sense of quiet desperation – many of his subjects urged him to return to London, otherwise the country would face ruin.

It was a curiously dislocated time. In London parliament went about its business and maintained contact with the king by correspondence, yet by leaving London without any warning Charles and his small court had given the impression that they had already departed the scene, a belief that was reinforced when inquisitive Londoners were seen walking freely around the royal apartments in Whitehall. Left to its own devices parliament continued to sit and to deliberate; as yet rebellion was neither on members' minds nor was it mentioned in debate, but having already resisted the king's assault on their privileges they were in not in any mood to compromise. When Culpepper raised a motion on 12 January asking that the king return to London this was sidestepped, as were other motions, on the grounds that there could be no accommodation until the five members were cleared of the charge of treason. In that sense their resistance was guided not so much by the king's breach of privilege, serious though it was, as by the 'ruffians' and 'evil counsellors' who had given him such bad advice. As for the Lords, throughout February there was a gradual and discreet exodus of Royalist members, some summoned by the king, others obeying their consciences.

With neither side prepared to give ground, a clash was inescapable, and it came in the shape of the Bishops' Exclusion Bill which removed the episcopacy from the House of Lords, and the Militia Bill which would transfer military command of the militia from the king to parliament. While Charles was prepared to accept the first piece of legislation he was certainly not prepared to hand over control of the militia and, mindful of Henrietta Maria's plea for defiance, he sent back the blunt message that he could 'by no means do it'. Stung by the refusal, parliament passed the bill on 3 March as an ordinance for safeguarding the realm; thereafter recruitment and management of the militia would be in the hands of the lords lieutenant of the counties, who were themselves appointed by parliament. A fortnight later they strengthened their grip on the armed forces when the Earl of Northumberland stood down from sea command of the navy and was replaced by his deputy, the Earl of Warwick, who was well known for his parliamentary sympathies and had been involved in the colonising of New England. Charles was outraged, for not only did he regard himself as the navy's patron, having personally ordered the rebuilding of the fleet, but he wanted to have his own man, Sir John Penington, in command. Parliament refused, Penington procrastinated when he received the king's orders to take the fleet to the Yorkshire coast, and as a result the navy remained under parliamentary control, a move which gave them command of the vital trading routes and the main ports.

Having refused to pass the Militia Bill, Charles made his next move, setting off for York up the Great North Road by way of Stamford, Newark and Doncaster. In all the journey took some three weeks and during its progress king and parliament remained in contact through a succession of 'declarations' aimed at finding some common ground on parliamentary, military and religious matters. Well-intentioned the correspondence might have been – each side was looking for concessions – but in stating and restating their position the declarations simply pushed the two sides further apart. When challenged at Newmarket with the first declaration which accused him of violating the law over the militia, Charles retorted angrily: 'You have asked that of me was never asked of any King.' By then he was already preparing for war. Ostensibly the journey to York had been made to provide him with an alternative capital in which he could deal with the Irish crisis, but he was also intent on seizing Hull with its arsenal and port through which the hoped-for arms from the Continent could be imported. He was also looking for support from the Scots, who had already dispatched Loudoun to York in an attempt to heal the breach between king and parliament.

This was not what Charles wanted to hear – not least because the inference of the Scottish message was that the king was to blame for the crisis – and Loudoun was sent back to Edinburgh with a message that while the king did not wish the Scots to meddle in English affairs he hoped that the Privy Council might condemn parliament's actions, 'that you will not be willing to see us suffer in honour or authority'. Although there was some sympathy for the king's plight and some dismay at the way events were unfolding in England, the Privy Council responded with an anodyne declaration of their hope that the quarrel would soon be solved. Also under discussion at the same meeting was a declaration from the English parliament on religious uniformity, a subject dear to the Covenanters' hearts, and this too influenced the Scots' response. As Baillie reminded them, the continuation of the Presbyterian reformation depended on the support of the English parliament, and its loss would be such a bitter blow, 'that all they [English parliament] has done or our parliament has done already, or whatever any parliament shall mean to do hereafter, is not worth a fig'.[11]

North of the border Charles's natural supporters included Airlie and Montrose, but for the moment he dared not allow either man to come to York for fear of offending the Covenanters. Instead, refusing to learn from past mistakes, he sent Hamilton north with a hare-brained scheme for Henrietta Maria to be invited to come to Scotland to mediate in the dispute. That mission also came to nothing, because the queen was considered to be the author of the king's misfortunes and a Catholic to boot.[12] Argyll, too, was contacted, as 'this is a time, wherein all my servants, that are noble and willing have occasion to show themselves . . . I cannot doubt of your readiness', but for all that Charles had flattered and rewarded this fairweather friend there was no response, and by the beginning of June all hope of Scottish support had collapsed, much to the relief of the English parliament. Hampden noted with satisfaction that the Scots had behaved 'resolutely'.

Ireland proved to be an equally unhappy hunting ground for support. Shortly after arriving in York Charles announced his intention of leading an army to 'chastise those wicked and detestable rebels (odious to God and all good men)', but it was far from clear if he would use Ormond's forces to defeat the Confederates or treat with the 'rebels' and make use of their forces. Fortunately nothing came of the plan, which was both foolish and dangerous as it suggested to Pym and his followers that Charles intended to use Irish military resources to recover his position. If Charles wanted help it would have to come from England.

Thanks to the generosity of the Earl of Glamorgan, whose son Lord Herbert was rewarded with the Order of the Garter, he was able to establish the semblance of a court in York, and to it came a number of peers including Bath, Bristol, Dorset, Newcastle, Richmond and Salisbury. From parliament in London came Culpepper, Falkland and Hyde, who was to emerge as Charles's principal political adviser. Appeals for money were met with donations of plate from the universities of Cambridge and Oxford, across the northern counties and Wales Charles made numerous appeals for men to join his cause, and the Earl of Lindsey, a tough veteran of the ill-fated Île de Rhé expedition, was appointed the Royalist army's commander-in-chief. A muster of Yorkshiremen on Heyworth Moor attracted 100,000 men, but many of them came to demonstrate against the Royalist cause, among them a young landowner from a military background called Sir Thomas Fairfax of Denton, who approached the king with a petition only to be haughtily swept aside.

Obtaining arms was also an imperative, and the best supply lay within the walls of Hull, where the weapons of Charles's northern army had been stored. Following parliament's demand for the arsenal to be transferred to London for use against the Irish rebels, Charles decided to enter the town himself and on 22 April sent his son James and the Elector Palatine to discover how the land lay and to pave the way for a royal visit. By then Hull had been garrisoned and its governor Sir John Hotham was under strict instructions not to allow any forces into the town. When Charles and a large military retinue arrived the following day Hotham stuck to his guns and refused the king admission. Left outside the walls in the rain, Charles had no option but to retire to nearby Beverley, where Hotham was declared a traitor. A second attempt to take Hull in July fared no better when a Royalist investment force was scattered by the defenders led by Sir John Meldrum, a Scots mercenary. On this occasion Hotham might have been minded to surrender the garrison, for he had in his hands the Royalist Lord Digby, who had won him round to support the king, but Meldrum stiffened his resolve and Charles was left to complain: 'Let all the world now judge who began this war.'

The war was also fought in words, with both sides issuing pamphlets and declarations justifying their position and actions and asking for support. Charles's supporters argued that the king, the person of the sovereign, was facing an unlawful challenge to his office and needed help to put the rebellion down; parliament responded that because the king, advised by evil counsellors, had taken the law into his own hands they had the responsibility of bringing him to his senses. 'The whole business of the matter,' explained Clarendon, 'was whether the King was above Parliament, or Parliament, in ruling, above the King.'[13] On 1 June parliament issued the Nineteen Propositions, which was more or less a demand for the king's unconditional surrender: the king would be required to give up the right to approve ministers and advisers and even the care and education of his own children; by accepting the Militia Ordinance he would abandon control of the armed forces; the Church would be reformed in accordance with parliament's wishes; Catholics would be excluded from the House of Lords and existing laws against them would be enforced.

Clearly Charles could not accept the demands. As his response put it when it was published on 18 June, if he approved the Nineteen Propositions: 'we should remain but the outside, but the picture, but the sign of a king'. Presciently he also added the thought that acceptance of parliament's wishes would breed 'eternal factions and dissension' and that the present and acceptable form of government would degenerate into 'a dark, equal chaos of confusion'. As for the religious demands, he insisted that the Church, needing no reformation, should be defended from Catholics and sectarians alike.[14] The issue of the Nineteen Propositions and the king's rejection of them meant that there was no way back: both sides had stated their positions and were not prepared to offer concessions; just as importantly, both sides believed that their actions were sufficiently justified to back them with force.

On 9 July 1642 parliament voted to raise an army of 10,000 volunteers, Pym having told them earlier that the confrontation was the fault of the king. Three days later command was given to Essex, whose orders were 'to rescue His Majesty's person, and the persons of the Prince and the Duke of York out of the hands of those desperate persons who were then about them'. Even at this late stage parliament clung to the formula that the king was only at fault in that he had fallen under bad advice and needed to be rescued – the very reason which had driven first the Scottish Covenanters and then the Irish Confederates to take up arms against his person.

As the summer wore on the tensions increased and in places the violence escalated. There was brawling in the streets of London between red-ribboned supporters of the king and anti-monarchists. In several county towns there was trouble when the local lords lieutenant tried to read Charles's Commission of Array – his riposte to the Militia Ordinance – and throughout England towns and counties started making their intentions clear. In Portsmouth, the garrison's governor, Sir George Goring, declared for the king, as did the University of Oxford, whose students formed Royalist trained bands. In Manchester, a Puritan stronghold, fighting between rival supporters led to the first English death of the conflict which was about to break out – Richard Percival, a local linen weaver. The weather was wet and with harvest approaching men from the countryside were loath to volunteer, but time was running out for them and soon they would be forced to choose, leaving more than one undecided soldier to echo Thomas Knyvett's anguished words to his wife: 'O sweetheart, I am now in a great straight what to do . . . I do fancy a little house by ourselves extremely well, where we may spend the remainder of our days in religious tranquil.'[15]

In the third week of August Charles ended the uncertainty by riding south to Nottingham with just under 4000 armed supporters to raise his standard on a wet and miserable English summer's day. The wars of three kingdoms were finally under way and, as the opposing sides faced an uncertain future, no one could say with any clarity how it would all end.

PART TWO

THE FIRST CIVIL WAR
1642–1647

Chapter One

FATHER AGAINST SON,
BROTHER AGAINST BROTHER

'Parents and children, brothers, kindred, I and dear friends have
the seeds of differences and divisions abundantly sowed in them.'

Harry Oxinden, letter from London to his cousin, January 1643

Nottingham was a statement of intent. When the king raised his
standard in the east midlands town on the evening of 22 August 1642
he was declaring war on his enemies in parliament, those traitors who
had set themselves up against royal authority and had therefore to be
shown the error of their ways. In the wet and the gloom the herald
making the proclamation stumbled over the words; Charles had made
last-minute amendments and the rain helped to smudge the result.*
Hyde later admitted that a 'general sadness covered the whole town',
for the launching of Charles's campaign was a low-key affair, partly as
a result of the weather and partly because no one was going to war
with a will. A few days earlier the king had been denied entrance to
Coventry, his progression through Newark and Leicester had met
with a lukewarm response and even in Nottingham, a comparatively
wealthy trading town, there was precious little enthusiasm for the

---

* On the wall of the General Hospital, on Standard Hill, at Nottingham, there is a tablet
which reads: 'On a mound about 60 yards to the rear of this tablet Charles I raised his
Standard, August 25th, 1642.'

royal cause and a good deal of disquiet about the cost of having his army quartered on the common.

Not that Charles commanded a huge force. With him were fewer than 2000 cavalrymen and a smaller number of Yorkshire infantrymen – the 'scum of the county' according to one observer – and the appeal for recruits, made ten days earlier, failed to encourage many to enlist. Nottingham had been chosen for the muster as much for its central position in the country as for any other reason, but that night there was a summer rainstorm and in the wind and the downpour the Royal Standard was blown down. Even the normally phlegmatic Astley, for whom war was war, was pessimistic, admitting 'that he could not give any assurance against his Majesty being taken out of his bed if the rebels should make a brisk attempt to that purpose'.

In fact the fear was far-fetched, for parliament too was trying to pull together, arm and equip an army of 10,000 men under the direction of its Committee for Defence. Command had already been entrusted to the Earl of Essex, the son of Queen Elizabeth's former favourite and another of those seventeenth-century soldiers who cut his teeth serving in the European wars. Cautious, loyal to his men and realistic – a prepared coffin accompanied him wherever he went – he was also smitten with melancholia and proved to be a lethargic commander. His gloomy outlook had not been helped by an unhappy love life: his first marriage to the flighty Frances Howard (daughter of the Earl of Sussex) had been annulled on the grounds of non-consummation due to his impotence, and his second wife Frances Powlett proved to be no more faithful to him. As for his military abilities, these might have been improved had he been forced to rise through merit, but having a huge personal fortune he never had to see a campaign through to its conclusion. Although he had fought in the Netherlands and at Cadiz under Buckingham his service had been fitful and his achievements limited. To balance that lack of experience he was well-liked and had Pym's support, both necessary requirements as parliament began its long march to create a professional army 'for the safety of the King's person and the defence of both Houses of Parliament'.

Most of the men under his command were from London, Surrey and Middlesex, and two weeks after the raising of the King's Standard

Essex led his army north towards Northampton, where it met up with volunteer contingents from the Midlands and East Anglia. Among the latter were a smart troop of horse, the forerunners of the Ironsides, which had been raised in Cambridge by Oliver Cromwell. As yet there was no cohesion to the army's structure and many of the regiments were simply groups of men who owed their allegiance and their day-to-day living to the wealth and standing of the colonels who had brought them into being. Hampden and Holles, both men of substance, raised regiments of foot, and among the nobility who had thrown in their lot with parliament were Henry Mordaunt, Earl of Peterborough; William Russell, Earl of Bedford; Edward Montagu, Viscount Mandeville (later Earl of Manchester); Henry Grey, Earl of Stamford; William Fiennes, Viscount Saye and Sele; and Robert Greville, Baron Brooke. Backing them up were soldiers of fortune who had taken parliament's shilling – experienced Scots in the shape of Balfour, Meldrum and Sir James Ramsey, a French artillery expert, Philibert Emmanuel de Bois, and a Croatian cavalry commander whose nom de guerre was Carlo Fantom.

When they all assembled in Northampton in the second week of September they were a rough-and-ready force whose parts were as yet much better than the whole. It would take time and the experience of battle to change them from a rabble into a disciplined force, for as the army swept out of London and headed north it plundered as it went, destroying anything that smacked of popery – glass and statues in churches – and making up their meagre rations by stealing from those luckless people whose lands they chanced to cross. 'Every day our soldiers by stealth do visit papist's and constrain from them both meat and money . . .' wrote a parliamentary officer, Sergeant Nehemiah Wharton, in a typical letter home, '. . . several of our soldiers, both horse and foot soldiers sallied out of the city [Coventry] unto the Lord Dunsmore's park, and brought from thence great store of venison, which is as good as ever I tasted, and ever since then they make it their daily practise so that venison is as common with us as beef with you'.[1]

In time the parliamentary army would come to be known as 'Roundheads', a term which managed to stick but is not entirely accurate. According to Lucy Hutchinson, the wife of a Nottinghamshire squire and one of the liveliest of the war's chroniclers, there had been a craze among the apprentice boys for cutting off their 'unloveliness of the love-locks', but 'that name of roundhead became the scornful term given to the whole Parliament army; whose Army indeed marched out so, but as if they had only been sent out till their hair was grown: two or three years after, any stranger that had seen them would have enquired the reason of that name'.[2] (Her own husband, Colonel John Hutchinson, who became the governor of Nottingham Castle had 'a fine thickset head of hair ... a great ornament to him'.) In fact there was little difference in the hairstyles of the two sides, the soldiers in both armies conforming to the custom of the day – growing their hair long and wearing facial hair of various styles and fashions. As for the Royalist 'Cavaliers', the term that stuck to the soldiers who followed Charles, it was simply a corruption of the Spanish 'caballeros' and was used by their opponents to mock the court's alleged allegiance to Continental Catholic ways.

Despite the ridicule, though, there were some leaders in Charles's army who were suited to the task in hand. To the Royalist side had come Prince Rupert of the Rhine, the Elector Palatine's twenty-three-year-old son who had already served as a cavalry commander in the Thirty Years War, having begun his military apprenticeship at the youthful age of fourteen. Recruited in the Netherlands by Henrietta Maria, Charles's nephew was clearly an asset in that he understood the art of cavalry warfare and had proved to be a courageous and dashing field commander, but he had a short fuse and was capable of causing great offence among his elders and betters, not least George Digby, with whom he promptly fell into a quarrel. Rupert was also headstrong and given to making rash moves, a failing that had led to him being taken prisoner by Imperial forces after leading a madcap cavalry charge at Vlemgo on the Weser in 1638. His aunt recognised his failings when she wrote to Charles commending his virtues but adding that he was 'not to be trusted to take a single step of his own head'. But Henrietta Maria was doing Rupert a disservice for, as he was to show, he had learned his lesson, was well capable of reading battles and understood the use of cavalry as a shock force to break enemy lines. Other factors also stood in his favour: his height, his good looks and his elegant clothes made him an unmistakable figure who seemed to lead a charmed life, all of which made him an attractive commander.

With him came a dog called 'Boy' (rumoured by parliamentarians to be his familiar), a clutch of regimental officers and his brother Prince Maurice of Nassau, another dashing commander who deserved the epithet 'cavalier'; but the presence of the two Palatine princes should not overshadow the part played by the other professional soldiers who had joined the king at Nottingham. While Charles enjoyed overall titular command as captain-general and the Earl of Newcastle was given command of the army of the north, there was a good leavening of professional soldiers. Two veterans of the German wars, Jacob Astley and Arthur Aston, were given command, respectively as Major-General of Foot and Colonel-General of Dragoons. Another veteran who rallied to the colours was Patrick Ruthven, the defender of Edinburgh Castle, who was ennobled as the Earl of Forth. Although a hard drinker – a vice he shared with another fine Royalist soldier, George Goring – he was experienced, battle-hardened and aware that battlefield discipline was the key to victory. With him came a further twenty-nine Scottish officers, all of whom had fought in Germany and all of whom would give backbone to the Royalist army. The last of their number, James King, now Lord Eythin, arrived the following year having finally been promised the pension that went with his title. Mercenary habits obviously died hard.

By the middle of September the king's army was beginning to take shape mainly through the issuing of Commissions of Array, a medieval instrument which allowed local landowners to raise forces for the king. Despite local opposition this proved to be a successful method of encouraging men to 'volunteer' – an element of impressment was always present – and within a few weeks of the raising of the standard the king's army had grown to 6000 infantrymen and 3500 cavalrymen (including dragoons used mainly for scouting). By contrast parliament relied on the Militia Ordinance which allowed lords-lieutenant to impress men and, while the measure had helped to swell Essex's army, many were the dregs of society who were as likely to desert as to fight and took every opportunity to loot and plunder from the local population. Few had any soldierly qualities and the majority were what Clarendon called 'the dirty people of no name' who had no particular wish to fight. In vain did well-meaning officers like Sergeant Wharton attempt to instil order and discipline, for even if they managed to do so they could not rely on fellow commanders being like-minded:

Certain gentlemen of the country informed me that Justice Edmonds, a man of good conversation, was plundered by the base blue coats and bereaved of his very beads, whereupon I immediately divided my men into three squadrons, surrounded them, and forced them to bring their pillage upon their own backs unto the house again: for which service I was welcomed with the best varieties in the house, and had given me a scarlet coat lined with plush, and several excellent books in folio of my own choosing; but returning, a troop of horse met me, pillaged me of all, and robbed me of my very sword, for which cause I told them I would either have my sword or die in the field, commanded my men to charge with bullet, and by divisions to fire upon them, which made them with shame return my sword, and it being towards night I returned to Northampton, threatening revenge upon the base troopers.[3]

The criminal violence was not all one-sided. At that stage of the war, in the months which saw the rival armies growing in strength and manoeuvring for position, Royalist units also indulged themselves in plundering the houses of parliamentarian supporters or people suspected of being of that persuasion. Rupert's cavalry troopers proved to be the worst offenders in that respect and, although there were no atrocities on the scale visited upon Germany, some of the veterans of the Thirty Years War clearly thought that warfare was an excuse for plundering houses and seizing other people's belongings. During the uneasy lull of the summer of 1642 several country homes were attacked by Royalist cavalry including the Earl of Stamford's at Groby near Leicester and George Marwood's at Nun Monckton close to York. A parliamentary pamphlet writer noted that the ruffians 'threatened Mrs Marwood and her servants with death to discover where her husband was and swore they would cut him in pieces before her face and called her Protestant whore and Puritan whore'. Other records were as bad as anything noted by Wharton. At Henley-on-Thames men of Sir John Byron's regiment were quartered at Fawley Court, the residence of Bulstrode Whitelocke, a lawyer and member of parliament. It mattered not that Byron had been entrusted by Charles with the safety of the Tower of London, when it came to looking after other people's property he was powerless to stop his 'brutish' soldiers from doing their worst. As Whitelocke wrote:

> They ate and drank up all that the house could afford; broke up all Trunks, chests and any goods, linen or household stuff that they could find. They cut the beds, let out the feathers and took away the curtains, covers of chairs and whatsoever they could lay their hands on they carried away or spoiled, did all that malice and rapine could provoke barbarous mercenaries to commit.[4]

As the war wore on officers in both armies used martial law to keep their armies under control. The parliamentary army became a byword for godliness and clean living, whereas the Royalist armies never quite lost a deserved reputation for profligacy. When a parliamentary officer boasted to his Royalist counterpart that his men were the better ordered he received the reply: 'Faith, thou sayest true; for in our army we have the sins of men (eating and drinking), but in yours you have those of devils – spiritual pride and rebellion.'[5] Even so, just as the use of the words Roundheads and Cavaliers is not always accurate, it would be wrong to characterise the differences between the two sides in the stark terms of joyless Puritans fighting funloving Catholic Royalists or ordinary Englishmen up in arms against the landed gentry and aristocracy. This was not a class war as such. Aristocrats served on both sides, the majority for Charles it is true, as did the landed gentry, who were more or less evenly divided and whose wealth, connections and ability to raise men made them vital to both sides in the opening months of the war. Some supported the king out of ingrained loyalty to the Crown and a long-held belief that rebellion against his person was wrong: 'I go with joy and comfort to venture a life in as good a cause and with as good a company as ever Englishmen did,' wrote the Cornish squire Sir Bevil Grenville as he prepared to take up arms against neighbours who supported parliament. 'And I do take God to witness, if I were to choose a death it would be no other but this.'[6] Religious faith could also guide a man: Sir William Campion of Sussex took refuge in prayer before deciding for the king:

I did not rashly or unadvisedly put myself upon this service, for it was daily in my prayers for two or three months together to God to direct me in the right way, and besides I had conference with diverse able and honest men for advice, who confirmed me in my judgement.[7]

Others made up their minds by deferring to ancient family ties of allegiance or because their feudal superiors had opted for that course. Religious faith was also a pointer. Many of the officers under Newcastle's command were Catholic, and in a declaration of 12 August Charles had made much of the fact that he was defending the established Church from harm at a time 'when such licence was given to Anabaptists, Brownists* and sectaries, while coachmen, feltmakers and such mechanic persons were allowed to preach, when such barbarous outrages and uproars, even in time of divine service and the administration of the blessed sacrament, were practised without control'.[8]

Matters were slightly more complicated for those who had thrown their weight behind parliament. A handful, such as the parliamentary diarist Sir Symonds D'Ewes, were driven by the belief that political and religious change was in the air and that it was morally right to rid the country of 'the wicked prelates and other like looser and corrupter sort of clergy of this kingdom who doubtless had a design by the assistance of the Jesuits and Papists here at home and in foreign parts to have extirpated all the power and purity of religion and to have overwhelmed us in ignorance, superstition and idolatry'.[9] Cromwell was probably correct when he said that 'religion was not the thing at first contested for' – the more extreme Puritans who believed devoutly in an extreme revision of Church government and a Catholic conspiracy directed by the pope were the Jacobins of 1642 – but most of Pym's supporters, including Cromwell, Hampden and William Strode, were in favour of continuing the reformation of the Church and detested Charles's adherence to Arminianism. For them and for others, religion and God's favour were part of the equation and, like

---

* Congregationalist followers of Robert Browne (1550?–1630), who believed in the principle that congregations are bound together and with God by a covenant which places them outside state or Church control.

Captain John Hodgson, most had pondered long and hard before making up their minds to oppose the settled order: 'When I put my hand to the Lord's work I did it not rashly, but had many an hour, day and night, to seek God to know my way'.[10] In the early days at least it was still comparatively easy for men like Hodgson to maintain the idea that they were fighting to free Charles from bad advisers who had broken the old bond of King, Lords and Commons, and 'For King and Parliament' was a slogan which counted for much.

Among many of the nobles with experience of the court there was mistrust and dislike of Charles – Essex felt both – but this did not always imply opposition to the role of the monarchy. Inevitably this lack of focus, allied to a belief that the situation had to be retrieved, led to much jockeying for position as minds were made up and then changed back again. Throughout the crisis Lord William Paget had been deeply involved with Pym in the moves to reform parliament, but the passing of the Militia Ordinance was a step too far and he had thrown in his lot with the king at York, explaining in 'an objectionable document' that he would not fight against the Crown:

> My ends were the common good, and while that was prosecuted, I was ready to lay down both my life and my fortune; but when I found a preparation of arms against the King under the shadow of loyalty, I rather resolved to obey a good conscience than particular ends, and am now on my way to his Majesty, where I will throw myself down at his feet, and die a loyal subject.[11]

Others had less noble aims and were destined to be less resolute. The undependable Yorkshire landowner Lord Savile declared for the king having been an early supporter of Pym, while the Earl of Holland, an intimate of the queen's court and brother of Warwick, threw in his lot with parliament. Both were destined to change their minds again, as did Hotham, the hapless governor of Hull who had famously refused entry to Charles on a wet summer's day. As for the Puritans of New England, they offered solid support to parliament and many fought in its army; only one leading personality, a Captain Jenyson of the Watertown militia, doubted the legality of taking up arms against the king, but he quickly changed his tune when his point of view was reported to the Governor of Virginia, John Winthrop.

There were also those who tried, vainly, to stay neutral and declared their allegiance unwillingly or under social or military duress, frequently changing their minds according to the situation in their locality. Summoned to join the king, Sir Edward Dering of Surrenden in Kent went 'willingly, but out of my own house and from my own country the most unwilling man that ever went . . . truth to confess, I did not then like one side or the other so well to wish to join myself with either. A third and composing third way was my wish and my prayer.'[12] To remain in the middle, though, was well-nigh impossible, for both parties had declared their intention to punish the other – supporters of Charles were condemned as 'delinquents' whose lands and fortunes would be sequestrated, while those who followed parliament were 'rebels' who faced death for treason. The wise old diplomat, Sir Thomas Roe, who had laid the foundations for Britain's links with Mogul India, came closest to the mark when he remarked of the situation: 'No neutrality is admitted, both parts resolve that those who are not with them are against them'.[13] Some counties also tried to keep the fighting out of their area by declaring neutrality, but their pleas were to no avail – Lucy Hutchinson noted shrewdly that 'every county has the civil war, more or less, within itself' – and soon a pattern of regional support began to emerge. For Charles the northern counties of Cumberland, Westmoreland and Northumberland were for him, as were North Wales, the counties which marched with the Welsh border and much of the south-west of England. For parliament London, Kent and East Anglia were strongholds of support, as were most of England's major towns, but within that pattern there were always exceptions. Much of Lancashire was Royalist but Manchester opted for parliament; Norfolk took time to come round to support parliament and Oxford, which later became Charles's headquarters, only did so because it was overawed by his forces. The pattern continued into families, with the result that they too were often torn apart by the conflicting arguments, with brothers fighting brothers and fathers taking up arms against sons.

In that late summer of 1642 the people of England were gradually coming to accept that they would have to take sides and that the choice would bring with it unwelcome consequences. The King's Standard-bearer, old Sir Edmund Verney, the Knight-Marshal and a landowner whose character was reputed to be 'one of the strictness of a Puritan, of the charity of a papist, of the civility of an Englishman', had struggled long and hard with his conscience, telling Hyde that he was conscience-bound to follow Charles – 'I have eaten his bread and served him near thirty years, and will not do so base a thing as forsake him' – but he had to live with the knowledge that although one son, Edmund, followed him, his eldest son, Ralph, had decided otherwise. Edmund wrote to Ralph:

> I beseech you consider that majesty is sacred; God sayeth, 'Touch not mine anointed.' Although I would willingly lose my right hand that you had gone the other way, yet I will never consent that this dispute shall make a quarrel between us. There be too many to fight with besides ourselves. I pray God grant a sudden and firm peace, that we may safely meet in person as well as affection. Though I am tooth and nail for the King's cause, and shall endure so to the death, whatever his fortune be; yet sweet brother, let not this my opinion – for it is guided by my conscience – nor any other report which you can hear of me cause a diffidence of my true love to you.[14]

He was not alone in seeing his family divided. Lucy Hutchinson's cousin was John Byron, and she counted Edward Hyde among her relations, but her husband John sided with parliament. One son of the Earl of Kingston sided with the king, the other for parliament, although Lucy Hutchinson noted tartly that the father was 'a man of vast estate and not less covetousness . . .[who] concealed himself'. Essex's sister Frances Devereux, who had been such a prop to him in the days of his marital misfortune, was married to one of Charles's principal supporters, the Marquis of Hertford, and there were even tensions in the Cromwell family. Oliver's cousin Henry Cromwell took out a party of horsemen to guard a Royalist convoy carrying plate and money to York, but found himself in a fight with another force led by Valentine Walton, his cousin's brother-in-law, much to the bemusement of the inhabitants of Cambridge. After all, this was the first fighting witnessed in England for over eighty years. As Bulstrode Whitelocke sadly told his wife that July, almost imperceptibly the country seemed to be sleepwalking into war:

It is strange to note how we have insensibly slid into the beginnings of a civil war, by one unexpected accident after another, as waves from the sea, which have brought us thus far, and scarce we know how, but from paper combats, by declarations, remonstrances, protestations, votes, messages, answers and replies, we are now come to the raising of forces.[15]

Throughout Britain reactions to the events of the summer of 1642 were mixed as people woke to the fact that life would never be the same again. In the Yorkshire port of Scarborough the Royalist governor, Sir Hugh Cholmley, spoke for many of his class when he admitted that what lay ahead filled him with unspeakable sorrow: 'I am forced to draw my sword, not only against my countrymen, but my dear friends and allies, some of which I know to be well affected in religion and lovers of their liberties.' Clarendon encapsulated that belief when he called the war 'unnatural', but against the heart-searching and the detestation felt by many the anticipation of the fighting to come unleashed all manner of half-hidden hatreds. There were clashes as lords lieutenant tried to stop the reading of Charles's Commissions of Array: in Leicester Lord Willoughby of Parham prevailed on the mayor not to read it only to have a rival landowner, Lord Henry Hastings (son of the Earl of Huntingdon). try to enforce its reading backed by a party of colliers. There were similar scuffles in other county towns and, while the disorder was confined to jostling and the exchange of insults, there was a worrying under-current of impending violence. Following threats on his life, one of the finest chroniclers of the war, Richard Baxter, a minister from Kidderminster, retired to Gloucester after trying to obey a parliamentary edict for demolishing 'all statues and images of any of the three persons in the blessed trinity, or the Virgin Mary, which should be found in churches, or on the crosses in churchyards' but his absence did nothing to calm the tempers of his mainly Royalist congregation:

When I came home I found the beggarly drunken rout in a very tumulating disposition, and the superiors that were for the King did animate them, and the people of the place who were accounted religious were called Roundheads and openly reviled and threatened as the king's enemies (who had never meddled in any cause against the King). Every drunken sot that met any of them in the streets would tell them, 'we shall take an order with the Puritans ere long'. And just as at their shows and wakes and stage-plays, when the drink and the spirit of riot did work together in their heads, and the crowd encouraged one another, so was it with them now. They were like tied mastiffs newly loosed, and fled in the face of all that was religious, yea, or civil, which came their way.[16]

Inevitably acts of iconoclasm were committed. The palace of the bishop of Ely was pillaged on the grounds that its incumbent was held to be 'one of the greatest papists in the kingdom' and in the chapel at Queen's College, Cambridge 'superstitious pictures' and other statues were removed or smashed under an ordinance to remove every 'Monument of Superstition and Idolatry'. All over England churches were attacked, and if found to contain 'popish' furniture such as communion rails, altars or 'idolatrous' images they were ransacked, much to the delight of those who formed the rabble. Priests were jostled and sent packing, again to general mirth, but in one horrific incident at Dorchester the Catholic chaplain to Lady Blanche Arundel was lynched as he tried to escape to France.

Most of the attacks were as much to do with an eruption of local bad feeling as with any religious extremism, but as the times were out of joint people allowed themselves to behave outwith the law. Riots spread from the eastern counties into the Midland towns of Coventry and Birmingham and continued northwards into Leeds and Bradford. Unemployment was the main reason but the mobs took their revenge on local landowners, either because they were Royalists or Catholics or both. All over England men locked their doors at night, hid precious belongings and kept their weapons by their sides. Trained Bands were posted to guard arsenals and bridges; in London parliament formed emergency committees and made arrangements to collect plate and money (repayable with 8% interest); in Worcester, held by one Puritan to be 'Sodom and [is] the very emblem of Gomorra, and doubtless worse'[17], priests were driven from their churches and replaced by army chaplains who demanded offerings for the cause.

Although there were to be pockets of the countryside where people did not know or understand what was happening, few could doubt that England was hovering on the brink of something unknowable and daunting. The mood spread into Scotland, where the General Assembly of the Church of Scotland was meeting in St Andrews with the Earl of Dunfermline as the king's commissioner. Against a background of concern that Royalist signatories to the Cumbernauld Band might stage a demonstration on behalf of the king, the Assembly considered rival declarations seeking Scottish support. From Charles came the promise that he had no other intention than to govern Scotland by its own laws 'and the kirks in them by their own canons and constitution', but the point was spoiled by his insistence on continuing royal supremacy over the latter, a concept which struck at the heart of the Covenanters' beliefs. The Scottish parliament, too, offered a settlement 'as shall be most agreeable to God's word' and held out the familiar bait of a stable union and uniformity of Church worship. Both declarations were heard out and both were answered with the sombre observation that the progress towards religious unity was proceeding at too slow a pace. That would be the price of Scottish support, but for the time being, for all that Charles had wooed them long and hard during his last visit to Edinburgh, the only offer from the Scots was to intervene as mediators in 'the unhappy quarrel'.[18]

As Montrose's biographers have pointed out, it was about this time that the marquis wrote the poem for which he is best remembered, 'To his mistress' (i.e. the nation or body politic), with its resounding sentiments about the impossibility of standing aside as the country descends into chaos:

> My dear and only Love, I pray
> This noble World of thee,
> Be govern'd by no other Sway
> But purest Monarchie.
> For if confusion have a part,
> Which vertuous Souls abhore,
> And hold a Synod in thy Heart,
> I'll never, thee more.

Like Alexander I will reign,
And I will reign alone,
My thoughts shall evermore disdain
A rival on my Throne.
He either fears his Fate too much,
Or his deserts are small,
That puts it not unto the Touch,
To win or lose it all.

In common with many others who decided to put their faith and trust in the king's cause, Montrose knew he might pay the ultimate price for confronting the fates which governed his life. Shortly after the king raised his standard Charles wrote to the Presbyterian cavalier thanking him for his unstinting loyalty: 'you are the one whom I have found most faithful and in whom I repose great trust'.[19]

Knowing that he could not remain long in Nottingham, Charles led his force westwards towards Worcestershire and Shropshire, where he had high hopes of finding support. So it proved. Men flocked over the border from Wales, the one region in Britain which was to be unstinting in providing manpower for the Royalist cause, and from as far afield as Bedfordshire. In Stafford he called them together to remind them that they were fighting against opponents who were traitors, and as crowds came out to greet him the king's spirits improved. He and his army were going to the wars to restore order and to punish treason; there could be no better cause. Peace had not been written off – urged by his advisers to be conciliatory he had conducted a flurry of exchanges with parliament at the end of August – but these had foundered because neither side was prepared to give up ground and negotiate. Now, with two armies on the move in the countryside to the north of Oxford, the first blows were about to be struck.

Chapter Two

First Shots: Edgehill

'We shortly expect a pitched battle, which, if the Cavaliers will but stand, will be very hot; for we are all much enraged against them for their barbarisms, and shall show them little mercy.'

Nehemiah Wharton, letter, September 1642

Essex's orders were quite plain: he was to 'rescue' Charles – as much from his evil counsellors as from himself – and then to bring him back to London. It was a wide-ranging commission and, being a taciturn man, he had not thought to ask for any amplification, nor did he proffer any tactical suggestions himself. As a soldier Essex realised that arrest was impossible without either defeating Charles's forces in a pitched battle and then dispersing them or attempting to overawe them into surrender. At the same time he had to prevent the Royalist army from making a sudden advance south to attack London. A precipitate move westwards could overstretch his lines of communication, while any unnecessary delay in making contact with the Royalists could allow them to sweep down the Thames valley towards London.

Other considerations crowded in to narrow his options. His army was large – it numbered 21,000 infantrymen in 18 regiments, 4200 cavalry in 61 troops of horse and dragoons – but it was only half-trained, if that. Morale was proving hard to maintain, a result of the lack of a working command structure and a general absence of purpose: the City regiments were becoming agitated both because they were nervous about moving too far from their home base and because they had not been paid. Mobility was also a problem. With him, at his insistence, Essex had brought an artillery train with 46 formidable pieces, but it was proving to be a mixed blessing as the narrow rutted roads hindered any rapid advance. Unseasonable wet weather did not help either. The roads were quickly cut up, the big cart horses hauling the guns frequently slithered to a standstill, and men had to bend their shoulders to the wheels to keep the artillery and barrage train moving – at any one time Essex's army would have stretched out over a five-mile section of road as it made its heavy way from Northampton towards Coventry. It might have helped matters if Essex had known his enemies' movements, but without an intelligence network, and not yet having created a reconnaissance arm, he was operating in the dark.

After the parliamentary army assembled at Northampton Essex moved it tentatively towards Coventry on 14 September before feinting west towards Worcester, where he would be able to block any advance made by the Royalist army. Charles, too, was balancing his options. From Nottingham the Royalist army had marched south-west to Stafford and then on to Shrewsbury, and as it progressed, so too had its numbers grown. Money started to come in – most people in this part of the south Midlands supported Charles's cause – but he still had to rely on getting the larger sums from wealthy supporters such as the Earl of Glamorgan. Some followed the Welsh earl's suit and gave unstintingly – despite sitting on the fence Kingston provided £5000 – while others such as the Earl of Worcester used gifts of up to £900,000 as a bargaining counter for future rewards and favours. It cost huge sums of money to keep an army in the field. Men had to be paid and clothed, equipment, ammunition and arms had to be supplied and resupplied and food and drink found and bought for the men and horses. This presented a massive logistical problem, and the scale of it can be seen in a basic unit such as a troop of horse of 70 men, which required 1.5 tons of bread every month as well as 13.5 tons of hay for the horses.[1] As neither side had planned for war, and as they were having to create the infrastructure for their armies on a day-to-day basis, there was clearly a need to bring the campaign to a speedy conclusion by winning an early victory. For

Essex that meant executing his commission from parliament and its Committee of Lords and Commons for the Safety of the Realm, which had been formed to direct the fighting; for Charles a decisive success in the field would break his opponents' resolve and leave London at his mercy.

The king was quite clear about his intentions. He was about to fight for his honour and dignity against a group of men who were traitors. Those who supported him warmed to that message, and in the valley of the River Severn he was welcomed and encouraged by the locals, so much so that he confided in his closest advisers that as right was on his side he would surely prevail. Around him he created a council of war whose key members were Culpepper, Digby, Falkland, Hyde, Rupert and Ruthven but, lacking a staff and any coherent chain of command, the system allowed Charles too much leeway, with the consequence that, in the opening months of the campaign, there was no sense of direction. Enthusiasm there was a-plenty and Rupert in particular busied himself with recruiting and training the Royalist horsemen, whom he found to be hardy riders and courageous in the field but totally lacking in military skills. As the Royalist army increased in strength the logical move would have been a pre-emptive strike on London but, undrilled and untrained, it was still an army without focus and with too few weapons, one observer in Worcester noting that many men were only equipped with pitchforks and primitive cudgels. As September wore on the two sides indulged in what might best be called shadow-boxing, with the Royalist forces taking shape in the upper reaches of the Severn valley while Essex manoeuvred ever closer to the north of the Cotswolds. So haphazard were the moves, that, sooner or later, they would have to come into contact with each other.

The chance came late on the afternoon of 23 September 1642 near the Worcestershire village of Powick, where the River Teme flows into the Severn: it was to be the first battle, or more precisely, skirmish, of the civil war in England. Having discovered that Essex was closing in on Worcester and its garrison (under the command of Sir John Byron), Charles ordered Rupert to take a force of around 1000 cavalry to protect a convoy which was carrying plate and other treasures towards the Royalist camp. As his men rested their horses at a place called Brickfield Meadow just to the north of the River Teme, Rupert received information that a large parliamentary force of horsemen and dragoons, commanded by Colonel John Brown, had crossed Powick Bridge and was moving towards him. Had Rupert withdrawn towards Worcester there would have been no shame, as he was not under orders to engage the enemy, but several factors gave him an advantage. Brown did not seem to know that a Royalist force was ahead of him and, after a night march, he was leading his exhausted men in a long line up a narrow country lane lined with thick hedges – the worst possible territory for mounted horsemen. Although Rupert could not have known it, his opponent's progress had also been compromised by the presence of three members of parliament under his command – Captains Edward Wingate and Nathaniel and John Fiennes – all of whom were preaching caution. Wingate in particular was keen to slow down the march to wait further orders from Essex, but Brown's second-in-command, Colonel Edwin Sandys, was anxious to reach Worcester and the force rode across Powick Bridge with a small number of horsemen riding ahead. As the noise of the parliamentary horsemen increased in volume, and knowing that many of his men had removed their armour, Rupert acted quickly. Drawing up his men in open order in Brickfield Meadow he waited for his opponents to walk into the trap.

Once baited, it was soon sprung. As the first troop of horse under Sandys's command emerged into the field they were met with a flurry of carbine fire from Rupert's dragoons. Caught by surprise and having no prior knowledge of the size or disposition of Rupert's force, the parliamentary troopers tried to return the fire, but it was too late. As they attempted to regroup the Royalist cavalry charged into the ranks, and there followed a short sharp action which saw Sandys's men being routed and driven back in confusion down the lane back towards Powick Bridge. Only Nathaniel Fiennes's men stood firm, waiting until the Royalists were almost on them, 'so that their horses' noses almost touched those of our first rank' before firing their weapons but, outnumbered and abandoned by most of their fellows, it was a lost cause. Even so, despite the mauling, that did not stop parliament from claiming the battle as a victory, as was made clear a day or so later by the publication of a pamphlet entitled *True and Happy Newes from Worcester*:

Upon Thursday last Prince Robert [*sic*] marched towards Worcester with his Army, being in number 500. Horse and not any Foot, and at his coming thither Mr Fines [*sic*] stood in opposition against him, where Prince Robert caused his men to discharge so fast, insomuch that there began a great skirmish between them, holding for the space of two hours: Prince Robert with his Forces began to retreat, and at that time the Prince lost 12 men, and Master Fines 5 men. The said Prince Robert is making of spoil, to the great hurt of the said City, and planting of Ordnance, and he has already spoiled and burnt some houses. This News was sent to the Honourable House of Commons upon the Saturday last, which signified that the Kings Majesty was in person at Worcester, and that the Earl of Essex is marching thither with 22000 men. Sent in a letter from the Honourable Mr Fines.[2]

Claiming of victories, regardless of the cost, was to be a feature of the war, as was the creation of local ballads regaling the prowess of the participants and often greatly embellished. Most were written from the Royalist point of view and in the case of the encounter in Brickfield Meadow the reporting was more accurate than the news issued in parliament's name:

> They fly, they fly, Prince Rupert cry'd,
> No sooner said, but away they hy'd;
> The force of his Armes they durst not abide,
> Which no body can deny.

While the fighting at Powick Bridge had not been a classic military action Rupert had shown verve and courage in taking advantage of his opponent's inability to manoeuvre, and the victory helped to underpin his reputation as a dashing cavalry commander: in Hyde's words the skirmish 'rendered the name of Prince Rupert very terrible'. It also produced the first military casualties of the war* with around 150 men, mainly parliamentarians lying dead in or around Brickfield Meadow.

---

* There had already been bloodshed. On 4 August, before Charles had raised his standard in Nottingham, a force led by Sir Ralph Hopton killed 27 parliamentarian troopers while recruiting near Shepton Mallet in Somerset. The action was known as Marshall's Elm.

Brown's force retired in disarray, unable to advance on Worcester, while Rupert withdrew north, having decided that the city was not worth defending. One other shibboleth was broken that September afternoon. Not only were Englishmen killing Englishmen for the first time in living memory, but the first bad blood was spilled. Men fleeing from the field were cut down and killed, and on reaching Worcester the parliamentary army found evidence, recorded by the ever watchful Nehemiah Wharton, that some of the wounded had also been 'stripped and stabbed and slashed . . . in a most barbarous manner'.[3]

The news of Rupert's success produced a tremendous fillip for the king's camp – Wharton reported that Rupert's men did 'boast wonderfully and swear most hellishly' – and raised hopes that the war might be ended before it had begun in earnest. A victory was a victory, however mean it might have been, and it would have helped the Royalists to erase the memory of the shortcomings outside Hull earlier in the summer when it seemed that every advantage lay with parliament. The defeat also discommoded the parliamentary side. By then serving as a chaplain in its ranks, Richard Baxter had been keen to see the fighting but only arrived in time to witness the rout:

> Though the enemy pursued them no further than the Bridge, yet fled they in grievous terror to Parshore, and the Earl of Essex's Life Guard lying there, took the Alarm that the Enemy was following them, and away they went. This Sight quickly told me the Vanity of Armies, and how little Confidence is to be placed in them.[4]

So great was Charles's pleasure when the news was brought to him in Chester that he knighted the messenger, Richard Crane, on the spot. Together with the steady stream of recruits it gave Charles the confidence to begin thinking of marching on London while the initiative was still his. Two possibilities were open to the king. Either he could engage Essex's force in battle in the vicinity of Worcester or he could give the parliamentarians the slip and march rapidly on London, leaving Essex to play catch-up.

The possibility of re-engaging the enemy was an attractive option and had Charles known of the panic which had accompanied Brown's retreat to Essex's main force at Pershore he might have been tempted. Against that, Essex had entered Worcester and garrisoned it with his larger army, and the general feeling in Charles's war council was that the ground around the city was not suitable for the kind of cavalry action which had routed the opposition. In any case only a few weeks remained before the onset of winter would put an end to the autumn campaigning season, and quick thinking was required if London was to be taken before then. That settled everything, and on 12 October the king's army set out from Shrewsbury towards London, moving first in a south-easterly direction to Bridgnorth and Kenilworth before heading towards Banbury. It was a week before Essex realised that his prey had slipped him.

What followed next was a game of cat and mouse with neither side being entirely sure of the other's movements. Map-making was an inexact art, and although John Speed had produced his series of county maps in 1611 under the title *The Theatre of the Empire in Great Britain*, much of the information was either inadequate or misleading, especially the delineation of heights. On both sides commanders relied on their ability to read the landscape, and in the early days at least this gave an advantage to the gentry and yeoman farmers in the Royalist army. The king's course took him along the Severn, and as the army moved through the autumn countryside more and more people flocked to his ranks, with the result that he had almost as many men under his command as Essex had.

Of the 15,000-strong army most were poorly equipped, some only having meagre farming tools at their disposal, but this was balanced by a sense that the advantage had passed to them. Moving at ten miles a day – unlike Essex the king only had 20 assorted cannon at his disposal – the straggling force reached the outskirts of Banbury on 22 October and parked itself over an area of roughly eight square miles, the intention being to take the town the following morning.

By this time Essex had been on the move for three days, but instead of trying to block Charles's route to London he had made ponderous progress while marching eastwards from Worcester. By then, too, the armies were almost in contact. Just as Charles's army was taking its ease outside Banbury Essex's men were trying to do the same thing a few miles to the north near the village of Kineton only four miles away from Edgecott, where Charles had established his quarters. Although both sides had made an attempt at scouting the countryside they did not make any contact until nightfall, when a small troop of

Rupert's cavalry accidentally blundered into a group of parliamentary soldiers at the village of Wormleighton and took them prisoner. The news came as an unwelcome surprise to Essex: instead of placing his army between Charles's army and London the Royalists had turned the tables on him.

A battle could not now be avoided. Charles had to win if he was to advance unmolested on London while Essex had to do his utmost to prevent that happening; meanwhile both sides were stymied by the fact that their forces were spread over a large area. Rupert's first thought was to mount a night attack on Kineton, but good sense prevailed and, having reconnoitred the area, he suggested making a stand on top of a steep ridge which overlooked Essex's headquarters. The king's nephew might not have been familiar with the English landscape but he was a sound judge of ground, and his chosen position was a good defensive escarpment. Known as Edgehill, it faced north-west, blocking the road to London, and the presence of the Royalist army on such a conspicuous escarpment was a direct challenge. By dawn on the following day, a Sunday, the first elements of Charles's army began moving on to the ridge and spreading themselves out for battle. First to arrive at dawn was Rupert with his cavalry to provide a screen while the infantry and artillery marched slowly into position on the open ground just below the top of the ridge. By the time they had assembled it was past midday and their presence had already become clear to Essex, who had been on his way to church when the news of the disposition was reported to him by 'a worthy divine'.

Now it was the opposition's turn to deploy, Essex taking his larger force on to the plain below the ridge to line up about two miles outside Kineton facing the Royalist army on their superior position. Under his command he had 14,900 men, the majority (12,000) infantry, and even though most of the guns had not yet arrived he enjoyed superior artillery firepower. Essex also knew what he was doing. His twelve regiments of foot were drawn up in three brigades, two being deployed forward in line under the command of Sir John Meldrum and Colonel Charles Essex, the second held further back and flanked by cavalry on both wings. The right was commanded by Sir William Balfour, Sir William Stapleton, a Yorkshire landowner, and Lord Feilding, whose father, the Earl of Denbigh, was fighting for the king, while the left was commanded by Sir James Ramsey with

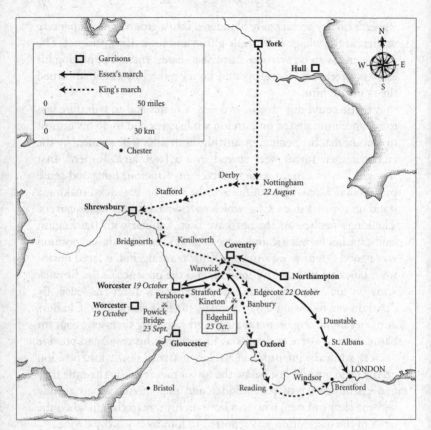

Garrisons
Essex's march
King's march

0   50 miles
0   30 km

York
Hull
Chester
Derby
Nottingham *22 August*
Stafford
Shrewsbury
Bridgnorth
Kenilworth
Coventry
Warwick
Northampton
Worcester *19 October*
Pershore
Stratford
Kineton
Edgecote *22 October*
Worcester *19 October*
Powick Bridge *23 Sept.*
Banbury
Edgehill *23 Oct.*
Dunstable
Gloucester
St. Albans
Oxford
LONDON
Bristol
Reading
Windsor
Brentford

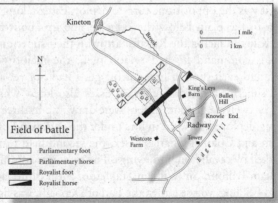

Kineton
Brook
0   1 mile
0   1 km
N
King's Leys Barn
Bullet Hill
Knowle End
Radway
Field of battle
Westcote Farm
Tower
Edge Hill

Parliamentary foot
Parliamentary horse
Royalist foot
Royalist horse

Holles's horse in reserve. Beyond them were smaller detachments of dragoons. At that stage, facing an army occupying higher ground, Essex had no reason to open the battle and might have been prepared to wait until reinforcements arrived to strengthen his position. After all, he had much to gain and nothing to lose by biding his time in his camp to the south-east of his army and awaiting developments.

He was not to know that matters were taking a turn for the worse in the Royalist army as cracks began to appear in its command structure. Nominally, the Lord General, the Earl of Lindsey, was in overall command and wanted to draw up the army in the Dutch fashion devised by Prince Maurice of Nassau – with the regiments in each of the five brigades being positioned two or three line abreast. This allowed greater flexibility in attack and defence, provided that the men could manoeuvre into new positions to make good gaps once battle was joined. Protected by cavalry on the flanks and reinforced from the rear it provided a tight fighting formation, the infantrymen in the middle equipped with the long 16-foot pike, the essential and much-feared weapon to blunt the force of any cavalry charge, and the musket, an inaccurate and potentially dangerous killing weapon for short-range use. However, the newly ennobled Earl of Forth (Patrick Ruthven), with his long years of European experience, wanted the Royalist infantry to line up in the Swedish wedge, with pikemen in the central block and musketeers in the wings, a relatively complicated system which demanded high standards of discipline if the firepower were to be effective.

By the time of Edgehill the performance of the musket had improved dramatically; it could pierce heavy armour at short range, but its use in battle demanded strict discipline. Musketeers had to be drilled carefully, not just to fire their cumbersome weapons in unison but also to maintain the regiment's safety. Each man carried kit which was highly combustible: in addition to the musket, and the firing pole on which to rest it in action, the musketeer was equipped with a bandoleer of powder bottles, a bullet pouch and a length of match-fuse dipped in saltpetre. Inevitably there were accidents in which men were blown up, and in at least one action there were heavy casualties when carelessness allowed ammunition wagons to ignite and explode. Even so, correctly drilled the musketeers could provide a heavy and penetrating field of fire, acting in conjunction with the pikemen who were there to defend the line from enemy cavalry. With that in mind the butts of most muskets were lined with steel for close-quarter clubbing.

As the overall commander Lindsey should have had the final word about the deployment, but as control of the actual battlefield fell to Forth, the field marshal, Charles agreed to the implementation of the Swedish wedge, not least because the Scot's plans had Rupert's enthusiastic support. This was too much for Lindsey, an old and experienced soldier, who angrily threw down his baton of office, saying that if he was not considered fit enough to lead the army he would rather 'die a colonel at the head of his regiment'. (He was destined to get his wish.)

Having assumed command, Forth drew up his army with three brigades of infantry in the middle, supported by two behind them and flanked by cavalry – Rupert, Maurice, Byron and the King's Life Guard on the right with the Earl of Caernarvon, Lords Wilmot, Grandison, Digby and Sir Arthur Aston on the left. Following the Swedish style, both sides had artillery and horsemen interspersed with the infantry forces, and in the early afternoon sun they made a brave sight, the infantry in a variety of solid-coloured coats, thick leather jerkins and the luckier ones with armour and quilt-lined metal helmets or 'pots'. On both sides the cavalrymen tended to be more flamboyantly dressed, some with velvet hats and embroidered coats and most wearing lucky keepsakes such as coloured scarves; all armed with swords and flintlock or matchlock pistols. Both of the commanding generals had won their spurs in the European wars, Essex in the Netherlands, Forth in Germany; now they were to bring internecine war to the gentle south Warwickshire countryside. 'Oh Lord, thou knowest how busy I must be this day,' prayed Sir Jacob Astley, the veteran of Lützen and a soldier who knew all too well what lay ahead. 'If I forget thee, do not thou forget me.'[5]

A fight was in the offing, but with Essex determined to stand his ground it fell to the Royalists to make the first move. At the council of war which led to Lindsey's sudden self-willed demotion it had been agreed that the king's army would have to take the initiative, attacking in the traditional style of the day, cavalry engaging cavalry on the flanks before attacking the centre. To do that they had to advance closer, and shortly after 1.30 p.m. the Royalist lines started advancing down from the ridge to the lower ground, stopping short of the opposition lines by about half a mile. As they did so there was a flurry of artillery fire from both sides, but it did little damage and was but a noisy prelude to the battle to come. For an hour or so nothing much happened, almost as if neither side was prepared to strike the first blow. Standards fluttered in the breeze, trumpets sounded above the occasional volley as officers encouraged their men. As reported by Sir Richard Bulstrode, who served in the Prince of Wales's regiment of horse, Rupert's words to the largely inexperienced cavalry were simple and direct: they were to charge hard at the opposition, firing off their pistols when they approached and following through with the sword. There was to be no 'caracolle' – wheeling in front of the enemy before discharging the weapon – as was the custom in Europe; just charge and use simple pace and strength to break the will of the other side:

> Just before we began our march, Prince Rupert passed from one wing to the other, giving positive orders to the horse, to march as close as was possible, keeping their ranks with sword in hand, to receive the enemy's shot, without firing either carbine or pistol, till we broke in amongst the enemy, and then to make use of our firearms as need should require, which order was punctually observed.[6]

The time was fast approaching when his words would be put into practice. Just after three o'clock, with the sun low in the sky, three ranks of Rupert's cavalry trotted down the slopes on the right, crossing the fields and the intersecting brook for all the world as if they were out for a gentle afternoon's hacking. With two hundred yards to go they broke into a canter which turned into a full-blooded charge as they approached Ramsey's lines, travelling at some forty miles an hour, as fast as a hunt in full cry after a fox. Very few of the parliamentary cavalrymen had experienced war before, and the sight of Rupert's horsemen bearing down on their static lines was too heavy a burden. As the Royalist cavalry swept in among them some fired off their pistols and turned while most simply fled, unnerved by the speed and aggression of the enemy charge. It was bad enough that they did so but, as they fled the field and hurried back towards Kineton, they left the infantry exposed and scores of musketeers in the

forward left brigade were cut down. Those who survived the first
charge scattered and ran, dismayed as much by the onslaught as by
the prospect of more carnage to come as Astley's Royalist infantry
began its advance, confident that they would be supported by the
returning cavalry. A contemporary report put the rout into stark
perspective:

> Whereupon our whole Army advanced in very good Order, the
> Ordnance of both sides playing very fast, but that of the Rebels
> began first. The Charge began between the 2 Wings of Horse; those
> of the Rebels not standing our Charge a quarter of an hour before
> they fled, our Men having the Execution of them for 3 Miles
> together, the Horse of both our Wings routing their Foot as well
> as their Horse; and 2 whole Regiments of their Foot were absolutely
> cut off, by those of their left Wing, besides those put into disorder
> by our Right.[7]

As the anonymous Royalist observer made clear, Rupert's successful
charge was replicated on the left as Wilmot's brigade rode headlong
into Feilding's parliamentarian horse, forcing them to scatter in panic.
Spectacular and daring though these offensives were, they did not do
much to help the cause of the Royalist army. Before the battle Rupert
had ordered his cavalrymen only to break the opposition's line, and
the speed and elan of the attack had done just that, but there was no
holding his men back. Their blood was up and instead of regrouping
to attack Essex's rear they continued the pursuit, harrying the fleeing
opposition horsemen as they fled towards Kineton. To make matters
worse, the second reserve line of Royalist cavalry, commanded by
Digby, Aston and Byron, joined in the attack. Obviously the sight of
the opposition fleeing before the Royalist horse was too great a
temptation, and contrary to Rupert's orders to support the infantry
attack the reserves joined in the affray, anxious to get some of the
glory.

Their impetuosity was to have serious implications for the outcome
of the battle. With only the centre holding – eight regiments of
infantry and two of horse – the parliamentary army was badly
exposed and vulnerable to attack by cavalry. Yet at the very moment
that the Royalist reserve should have been driving home its advantage

it was beyond the fields and hedges and riding pell-mell to the north-west to attack Essex's supply wagons. Among them were the King's Life Guard of Horse, Charles's personal bodyguard, who had begged to see action if only to prove that their smart uniforms were the equal of their military prowess. According to the evidence of Sir Philip Warwick, one of their officers, it was a bad move: 'contrary to all discipline of war, [both reserves pursuing the chase] left the King and his Foot so alone, that it gave Essex a title unto the victory of that day; which might have been his last day, if they had done their parts, and stood their ground':

> And it was the more strange, that the reserves would thus precipitately engage themselves, when they saw the King had given leave unto his own Volunteer-Guard of Noblemen and Gentlemen, who with their attendance made two such Troops, as that they consisted of about three hundred Horse: for a vanity had possessed that Troop, (upon a little provocation, or for a word of distaste the day before, or being called, The Troop of Show) to desire this honour of being engaged in the first charge; and I had the honour to be of the number, and to be one of the most inconsiderable Persons of it; and when we valued the estates of the whole troop, we reckoned there was 100000 £ per ann. in that Body, staked that day in that engagement against men of very disproportional quality.
>
> This was our first and great military misadventure; for Essex by his reserves of Horse falling on the King's Foot, pressed on them so hard, that had not some of our Horse returned in some season unto the relief of our foot, we had certainly lost the day, which all circumstances considered, we as certainly won.[8]

Some officers did their best to bring their men to their senses, most notably Sir Charles Lucas, a young veteran of the fighting in the Low Countries, who commanded Caernarvon's regiment, but at best only 200, or ten per cent of Rupert's force, managed to rein in their horses and regroup for further action. As happens so often in the course of a confused battle, Charles's difficulties turned out to be Essex's opportunity. When the infantry collided in the centre of the battlefield the way was open for the two reserve regiments of parliamentary horse to join the fight. Commanded by Balfour and Stapleton, they had avoided contact when Wilmot's men charged, and now they emerged from behind the hedges (near today's Battle Farm) to engage the advancing Royalist infantry and artillery just at the point when they seemed to hold the advantage.

This was the most violent stage of the battle. Although the cavalry actions had caused a number of casualties, the clash of the infantry was the real killing ground, with men grappling in hand-to-hand combat, slashing with swords and firing off their pistols at short range, inflicting wounds which, if they did not kill instantly, would probably do so later. Having smashed through the Royalist centre brigade Balfour's men rounded up the Royalist guns and cut their guide ropes to prevent them being dragged away. Stapleton's charge was partly repulsed on the left, but both regiments quickly regrouped to support the parliamentary infantry, now much encouraged and more than holding its own against their Royalist opponents who were on the back foot. Worse was to follow when the Lifeguard of Foot, responsible for guarding the Royal Standard, began to falter. In the fierce fighting around it old Sir Edmund Verney was killed, fighting to the last minute to save a flag which was the symbol of the king's honour. Also killed at this time was the Earl of Lindsey, dying at the head of his men in preference to leading the king's army. This was a key moment – the loss of the standard and of a senior commander could have dented morale – but as the flag was carried away a Royalist cavalry officer called John Smith* followed in hot pursuit and although wounded, he succeeded in bringing it back to the Royalist lines.

By then it was late afternoon and it was getting cold and damp. The soldiers on both sides, the majority experiencing battle for the first time, were exhausted by the shock of battle and unnerved by the experience of violence and sudden death. As Rupert's cavalry returned to the field in the dusk, the parliamentary army gave ground and began to retire. Even at that late moment a resolute cavalry charge might have saved the day by turning a retreat into a rout, but Falkland's suggestion was turned down, Wilmot arguing that, as the

* A devout Worcestershire Catholic, he was knighted for his services and, although he survived Edgehill, he was mortally wounded later in the war.

day was the king's, they might as well live to savour it. He was probably right. The men and horses were exhausted and in the gloaming neither side had any more stomach for fighting. By contemporary European standards Edgehill would have been a minor skirmish but, with 1500 lying dead or dying, the soldiers on both sides were drained by this first experience of battle.

> By this time it was grown so dark, that our Chief Commanders durst not Charge for fear of mistaking Friends for Foes (though it was certainly concluded by them all, that if we had had light enough, but to have given one Charge more, we had totally routed all their Army); whereupon both Armies retreated, ours in such Order, that we not only brought off our own Cannon, but 4 of the Rebels, we retiring to the Top of the Hill from whence we came; because of the advantage of the Place, and theirs to the Village where they had been quartered the Night before.[9]

Like the anonymous reporter both sides were left to count the cost. It was a bitterly cold night and no one had eaten since earlier in the day; apart from the brook which ran across the battlefield there was no water and men simply huddled down to take cover as best they could. 'No man nor horse got any meat that night and I had touched none since the Saturday before,' remembered Edmund Ludlow, an officer in Essex's lifeguard, 'neither could I find my servant who had my cloak, so that having nothing to keep me warm but a suit of iron [armour] I was obliged to walk about all night which proved very cold by reason of the sharp frost.' Even when food did arrive Ludlow was unable to eat, the cold and the aftershock of battle taking away any appetite.[10]

With only rudimentary medical services to hand – each regiment was supposed to have a surgeon and assistants – the badly wounded were simply left to die, if not from blood loss then from the sepsis and gangrene which followed. Throughout the night their moans could be heard, the misery made worse by the plague of local plunderers who swarmed on to the battlefield to rob the corpses and the dying, often dispatching the latter, indifferent to the suffering of the casualties on either side. Curiously, for death or survival on the battlefield is often governed by luck, two of those stripped of their clothes and robbed lived to fight another day. They were Sir Gervase Scrope, 'an old gentleman of great fortune in Lincolnshire', who was found naked by his son and with sixteen great wounds, and a man whom Edward Hyde called Bellingham, 'of ancient extraction in Sussex', who had sustained twenty wounds. According to the surgeons 'both these gentlemen owed their lives to the inhumanity of those who stripped them, and to the coldness of the nights, which stopped their blood better than all their skill and medicaments could have done, and that, if they had been brought off within any reasonable distance of time after their wounds, they had undoubtedly perished'.[11] Hyde's belief was confirmed by William Harvey, the physician who discovered the circulation of blood and who served in the king's army. Later Harvey told the diarist John Aubrey that Scrope owed his life to 'the cold clear weather, and a frost that night, which stanched his bleeding'. He also added the information that the old gentleman was obliged to haul a dead body on top of his in order to keep warm.[12]

The king fared only little better than the other survivors, taking what rest he could beside a fire lit in the lee of the ridge just below the village of Radway, not far away from the piles of bodies where Verney and the Lifeguard of Foot had fought their last battle. In fact, wearing his black velvet coat Charles had displayed no little courage throughout the day, at one point moving forward with his lifeguard when it seemed that Balfour might create damage in the centre. With him throughout the battle had been his two sons, Charles aged twelve and James aged nine, and it was during this phase of the battle that they were ordered to retire with Hyde to the top of the Edgehill ridge, leaving the younger prince to note that both sides continued 'to fire at one another even until night'.

Chapter Three

THE FAILURE TO TAKE LONDON

'Remember the cause is for God and the defence of yourselves, your wives and your children. Come, my honest, brave boys, pray heartily and God will bless us.'

Philip Skippon, order to the London Trained Bands,
13 November 1642

After a bitterly cold and damp night both sides woke to find themselves still facing one another across the field of broken bodies, but there was no fight left in either of them. By then Essex's army had been joined by Hampden's straggling infantry regiments, but most of his horse had scattered, some of the cavalrymen riding headlong through the night to London bringing with them a story of defeat and disaster. On the king's side an attempt was made to draw up the men into line of battle and Rupert sent out a cavalry troop to bring in seven abandoned artillery pieces from the front line, but there was never any intention of renewing the fight. At midday Essex's men began withdrawing towards Warwick to restore the supplies which had been lost to Rupert's cavalry at Kineton, and in due course the Royalist army retired too, returning to the billets they had occupied two days earlier. Both sides were discomfited further by local rumours which spoke of the battle being refought by spectral horsemen in the night sky against the ghastly background of the groans of the dying. So vivid and so widespread were these supernatural stories that Charles took the unusual step of asking for them to be investigated.

The first major battle of the war had been fought (in terms of lives lost Newburn and Powick had only been skirmishes), and although in strictly tactical terms it must be counted as a draw the advantage lay with Charles. Not only had Essex failed to defeat him but the road to London had not been blocked and morale in the king's army was high. Men who had not fought before had either taken part in the successful cavalry charge or had seen the opposition flee from the field, and even though there had been some hard pounding in the infantry clashes the king's men had not faltered. At the time it certainly seemed as if the battle had been won by the king, and that was the feeling of the first anonymous account of the fighting at Edgehill, written a few days later:

> The next day after the battle, the Earl of Essex finding his army extremely weakened and disheartened by the great blow they had received by his Majesty's forces, withdrew himself to Warwick Castle; and the same Night the remainder of his forces went also privately thither much distracted, whereof Prince Rupert having notice, the next morning pursued them, but they were all got into Warwick, or dispersed before he could overtake them; but his Highness took 25 wagons and carriages of the rebels, laden with ammunition, medicaments, and other baggage, whereof he brought away part, and fired the rest.
>
> This sudden returning back of the rebels to Warwick, is not only a sure argument of the weakness of their army, but has exceedingly disheartened all the country which adhered to them, and were before (upon a false rumour that the King's forces were defeated) ready to have risen and fallen upon his Majesty's forces.[1]

London, too, was thoroughly agitated by the news from Edgehill. The exaggerated reports suggested that the king was on his way to reclaim the capital, prorogue parliament and arrest the traitors named at Nottingham. The city's Trained Bands were called up and stood ready for action, armed ships were brought up the Thames to protect Westminster and hundreds of ordinary people flocked to the city's western approaches to help with the construction of earthwork defences. Those members of parliament who regretted the turn of events and wanted an end to the confrontation became restive. A 'peace faction' came into being under the leadership of Denzil Holles, and on 22 December a petition was presented to the House of Lords by a wide cross-section of London's community 'weighing the present wretched condition of this divided nation; and having just cause to fear the bitter and fatal consequences of a civil war already broken out among us even to the effusion of the abundance of blood in several parts of this kingdom'. At the other extreme those who believed that the war should continue agreed with Pym's suggestion to parliament that 'Scotch commanders' be recruited to strengthen Essex's army.

Had Charles acted quickly and marched on London he might have ended the war there and then, for although the capital was preparing its defences the presence of a large army on its outskirts would have inspired second thoughts about continuing a war which seemed to be spiralling out of control. From the north and from the West Country had come news of other Royalist successes. Forces under the overall command of the Marquis of Hertford had routed the parliamentary opposition at Marshall's Elm, Sherborne and Babylon Hill in Somerset and another army under Sir Ralph Hopton was threatening the port of Plymouth. At the other end of the country Newcastle had taken control of the city and port which bore his name and, using his own money and resources, was in the process of raising an army of 4000 men who came under the experienced command of the Scots mercenary Lieutenant-General James King (Lord Eythin). Opposing the Royalist forces was Ferdinando, Lord Fairfax, and his son Thomas, who received most of their backing from the Yorkshire clothing towns of the West Riding, but their cause was not helped by the presence of a number of subordinate commanders, including Hotham in Hull, who did not acknowledge Fairfax's commission from parliament. Only in Portsmouth, where Goring had been forced to surrender to Sir William Waller on 6 September, had there been a tangible parliamentary victory. Waller, a Devon squire, had thrown in his lot with the parliamentary army by raising a regiment of horse and emerged as one of its finest commanders.

Urged on by the Earl of Forth, and by Rupert who wanted to lead a flying column of cavalrymen to seize London, Charles had ample opportunity to strike a decisive blow, but the war was still too young for rash military action. Unnerved perhaps by the previous day's slaughter and prepared to listen to the voices of Digby and Falkland, who believed that the war could be brought to a negotiated peace, Charles turned his back on the idea of marching swiftly on London and in so doing lost his best chance of striking a major blow against his enemies in parliament. Instead his army moved towards Banbury, which fell without a fight on 26 October, before marching on to Oxford, 'the only city of England that he could say was entirely at his devotion', which would be his base and court-in-waiting for the next three years. There he was able to replenish his supplies – aided by the gift of plate from his friends in the university – and it was not until 6 November that his forces moved down the Thames valley to reach Reading. By then a quick victory was out of the question: the following day, having marched towards St Albans, the first elements of Essex's army had begun to arrive back in the capital.

Panic was mixed with resolution. Together with the Trained Bands Essex's men provided the capital with a garrison of 20,000 men; defiance was in the air but there was little stomach for a fight while there was the possibility of a truce. When the king reached Reading he received a delegation from the city asking for a 'cessation of arms', a request which Charles agreed to consider. At the same time parliament contacted the Scots, two of whose commissioners remained in London acting as go-betweens, renewing their request for support in their quarrel with the king and promising uniformity of religion by way of return. In the form of a declaration to the Scottish Privy Council and the General Assembly, the English parliament formally asked the Scots for help to suppress 'the common enemy of the Religion and Liberty of both nations'. Having been warned by Hamilton that the Scots might fall in with the appeal and that the 'two kingdoms will shit upon him in despite of what his servants can do', Charles sent Lanark north with a letter repudiating parliament's misrepresentation of events and claiming that his only wish was to preserve the Protestant religion and the liberties of England.[2] In the winter months ahead the battle to get Scottish support was to be fought with a good deal of skill and energy by both sides.

Back in Reading the peace talks were inconclusive. Charles was not averse to negotiating, but he was not minded to speak to traitors, and so a new delegation, headed by the Earls of Northumberland and Pembroke, was dispatched to enter into discussions with him. At the same time Charles was keen to regain the initiative, and on

11 November he moved his army forward to Colnbrook, where he ordered Rupert to take the town of Brentford as a prelude to the capture of London. The decision not only laid him open to charges of acting in bad faith but the subsequent action also provoked a good deal of hostility, due to the reckless behaviour of Rupert's cavalry troopers. When they rode in the following morning under the cover of mist from the river they were opposed by two regiments of parliamentary cavalry, one of which was commanded by Holles, the other by Lord Brooke. Many rode off at Rupert's approach but Holles's men in particular gave a good account of themselves and fought stoutly enough before being forced to retire. As they had done at Edgehill, Hampden's troopers appeared in the rear to give the parliamentary soldiers cover as they made their way out of the town.

Once again the Royalist cavalry had acted with energy and élan, forcing their opposition on to the back foot and harrying them as they tried to escape – a large number of Holles's men were drowned while trying to swim across the Thames to escape their pursuers. But just as they had done at Kineton, instead of consolidating their position Rupert's men started sacking the town in an orgy of theft and vandalism which was witnessed by many, including the Puritan tanner Wallington:

> Poor Brentford is made a miserable state for they [Rupert's men] have taken from the inhabitants all the linen, bedding, furniture, pewter, brass, pots, pans, bread, meal, in a word all that they have . . . they have taken from divers of the inhabitants some to the value of four hundred pounds . . some more . . . and from the poorer sort all that ever they had, leaving them not a bed to lie on, nor apparel, but what they have on their backs, nor a pair of sheets, nor a piece of bread, and what beer they drank not, they let run in their cellars.[3]

Stories like that terrified the population of London. While the writers engaged in some poetic licence – the sacking of Brentford was small beer by Continental standards and was replicated elsewhere later in the war – the reports brought home the ugly fact that civilians too would be caught up in the fighting. Exaggerated the reports might have been, but they provided a further spur for Londoners to defend their city, and there was no shortage of volunteers, many of them women, to help with the construction of the huge earthworks which were being thrown up to defend the capital – an activity later satirised by the Royalist poet Samuel Butler in his work *Hudibras*:

> From Ladies down to oyster wenches
> Laboured the pioneers in trenches
> Fallen to pickaxes and tools
> And helped the men to dig like Moles.[4]

The events at Brentford however acted as a catalyst. Here were no helpless victims to be robbed or raped but a citizens' army prepared to resist by digging and by taking their place in the front line. When Rupert's army pushed on towards London they were met at the village of Turnham Green, two miles to the east, by one of the most unusual armies ever to grace a battlefield. Its core was formed by Essex's army and the London Trained Bands but they had been reinforced by thousands of civilians, men and women, who stood side by side with the soldiers to defend the road into London. Here was a huge force, some 24,000 strong, united in its determination to hold the ground and prevent Charles from entering the English capital.

Having mustered on Chelsea Fields they had marched westwards out of the city on 13 November to deploy themselves in the area around Turnham Green. For the advancing Royalist army the opposition must have presented a mystifying though no doubt colourful sight, the different banners of the Trained Bands flying in the breeze, the mixture of soldierly uniforms with the clothes of the civilians. Citizens stood side by side with soldiers, many of whom had fought at Edgehill, while others were scattered in groups in the surrounding gardens and orchards, taking up their positions in the narrow lanes which bisected the flat landscape beside the Thames. In buildings and on the open ground they presented an unmovable object, a large mass of humanity standing impassively as the Royalist army lined up to the west.

They were prepared to fight too. Essex and Skippon rode from group to group giving them encouragement, the commander of the Trained Bands telling those assembled to pray devoutly and then to fight heartily, it being a Sunday. For Charles there was very little that his army could do. Outnumbered and short of supplies, they were not in the best physical condition for a fight – they would have seen the Turnham Green army being fed at lunchtime, always an unsettling sight for hungry soldiers – and the local conditions meant that they could not call on Rupert's cavalry. If they had fought the chances were that, regardless of who won, there would have been a high casualty list in the street fighting that would have followed, and Charles could not afford to alienate the country further by being seen to order the killing of so many ordinary people. In short, Turnham Green was a stand-off, with neither side wanting to make the first move.

By evening it was all over. Charles ordered his men to withdraw from their lines and slowly the huge citizens' army made its way back to London, no doubt well content that the city had been saved without bloodshed. No battle had been fought but it was a decisive moment in the campaign. The capital remained in the hands of parliament and with it the city's wealth, power and port. Charles had lost his best – and last – chance of retaking the capital and he was left with no other option but to retire westwards, first to Hounslow then by way of Hampton Court to Reading to take his army into winter quarters. He was still confident of victory, writing to Hamilton that he resolved to be 'a Glorious King or a patient martyr', but the initiative won at Edgehill had slipped away from him and with the campaigning season at an end his best hope lay in building up his own forces while trusting that the opposition might fall out over whether or not to pursue the war or attempt a negotiated peace.

Within his camp those contradictory aims led to indecision and muddle between his advisers and his military commanders, Sir Philip Warwick noting that 'neither of them stood in awe of him and so the consequences were fatal'.[5] On the one hand Digby and his supporters encouraged the king to continue the struggle, whatever the odds, while moderates such as Falkland and Hyde believed that there could be a workable peace settlement. Somewhere between the two Charles dithered, one part of him wanting to punish the traitors who had resisted the person of the king and plunged the country into chaos, the other hoping for the day when peace would return to the country. Perhaps too he was frightened of his wife. Henrietta Maria had told him before leaving for the Continent that there was to be no talk of compromise so long as there was a chance of defeating his enemies.

As Charles fell back on Oxford, Essex moved west to strengthen his position by taking Windsor and Henley-on-Thames and to threaten Reading, whose garrison was under the command of the veteran Aston, 'a man of rough nature [according to Clarendon] and so given to an immoderate love of money that he cared not by what unrighteous ways he exacted it'.[6] The move not only consolidated London's defences but by intimidating Reading it also gave Charles and his commanders a problem as they started quartering the Royalist army in Oxford, Abingdon and Wallingford with a protective screen of outposts based on Faringdon, Burford, Brill, Banbury, Woodstock, Enstone and Islip. In Oxford itself the university provided Charles with the basis for creating a new court and centre of administration. Christ Church became the king's residence as well as the seat of parliament (at least until 16 April 1644 when it was adjourned); the Privy Council met at Oriel College; Jesus, Pembroke and St John's Colleges were turned into living quarters for royal officers of state and higher-ranking soldiers, while other seats of learning took on a bellicose role. All Souls became the royal arsenal while New College was turned into a powder magazine. Few buildings were left untouched – the university had always supported the king, not so the town – and during that first winter of the war Oxford was gradually turned into an alternative English capital.

There were other signs of pseudo-normality. A mint was set up in New Inn Hall to create a new currency which included a crown piece, arrangements were made for collecting the king's taxes, and the first Royalist newspaper, *Mercurius Aulicus*, began to appear in January 1643 under the editorship of Sir John Berkenhead, a fellow of All Souls and one of the first professional journalists, who deployed a mixture of satire, squibs, caricature and half-truths in propagating the king's cause. Mockery was one of Berkenhead's most potent weapons, and he quickly discovered how crude parliamentary propaganda could be neutralised or, better still, made to look foolish. For example, when reports started coming out of the West Country telling of the rout of Sir Ralph Hopton's army in an ambush involving fire from heaven Berkenhead was quick to publish Sir John Denham's* spoof

---

* A Royalist poet and in the previous year the governor of Farnham Castle when it was captured by Waller.

lampooning not just the parliamentarians' gullibility but also the veracity of the story:

> Do you not know not a fortnight ago
> How they bragg'd of a Western Wonder
> When a hundred and ten slew five thousand men
> With the help of lightning and thunder?
> There Hopton was slain again and again
> Or else my author did lye
> With a new Thanksgiving for the dead who are living
> To God and His servant Chidleigh.[7]

Within a few weeks underground editions of the newspaper were being printed in London and its appearance inspired the publication of a parliamentarian rival, the *Mercurius Britanicus*, the creation of Captain Thomas Audley and later edited by the irascible Marchamont Nedham. Soon the rival editors were locked in a lengthy and frequently tedious journalistic war, each publication trying to outdo the other in scurrility and exchange of insults.

To add to the unreal feeling of the first winter of the war in England, Charles encouraged the mounting of masques and other entertainments designed to make some of his courtiers believe that little had changed in the daily round of their lives. Those with money continued to prosper but for others, such as Sir John Harrison, who had his estates in Hertfordshire sequestered by parliament, the move to Oxford was less agreeable. For him it meant giving up a large town house in London's Bishopsgate and taking his family, including his daughter, the diarist Lady Ann Fanshawe, to a residence which was clearly below their expectations:

> We, that had till that hour lived in great plenty and great order, found ourselves like fishes out of water, and the scene so changed, that we knew not at all how to act any part but obedience. From as good a house as any gentleman of England had, we came to a baker's house in an obscure street, and from rooms well furnished, to lie in a very bad bed in a garret, to one dish of meat, and that not the best ordered, no money, for we were as poor as Job, nor clothes more than a man or two brought in their cloak bags . . . for my

own part, I began to think we should all, like Abraham, live in tents
all the days of our lives.[8]

Ann, who married the diplomat Sir Richard Fanshawe, also mentions
that her residence in Oxford was also made miserable by the 'sad
spectacle of war' as soldiers marched out to fight to the beat of drum
and came back later war-torn and wounded.

Like many other cities Oxford had to come to terms with being a
garrison town and, although Charles did his utmost to restore a sense
of court life, it was difficult to avoid the constant noise of armies on
the move and the harsher realities of military life. Soldiers got into
fights in the taverns, where drunkenness was commonplace,
prostitution thrived and as the war dragged on the physical conditions
within the city deteriorated. Outbreaks of sickness and fevers, usually
typhus and smallpox, were difficult to contain in the overcrowded
city – 230 deaths were recorded in 1643 in the parish of St Mary
Magdalen. One of the most feared illnesses was a disease recorded as
'morbus campestris', which was blamed on the poor food available to
the ordinary people. Regular levies of taxation of the city and the
university added to Oxford's woes, but despite the hardships Charles
and his court lived as if they were still in residence at Whitehall and
not in a crowded and boisterous garrison town.

Restoring a semblance of normality, however artificial, was one
thing for the king, but coming to terms with the reality of the
situation was another and much more convoluted problem. First there
were the peace negotiations with parliament which occupied the rest
of winter and continued fitfully into the spring. Then there were the
plans for further campaigning, which required large-scale recruitment
and reinforcement if the future were to bring military success. The
first course of action meant entering into largely meaningless talks
with parliament – for in his heart of hearts Charles felt his position
and authority were being demeaned by speaking to such people – and
the second meant trying to encourage recruits to join his side, not just
in England but also in his other two kingdoms, Ireland and Scotland.
As far as the peace overtures were concerned, with the exception of the
growing peace faction around Holles, both sides regarded them with
a healthy cynicism, for neither was prepared to yield on the main
issues. Charles was not prepared to surrender an inch of his

sovereignty, arguing that his acceptance of parliament's demands would destroy the royal prerogative, while Pym and his party were equally determined to have most of the king's powers transferred to parliament.

Based largely on a greatly modified version of the Nineteen Articles, the talks between the king's party and the parliament's commissioners lasted from the beginning of February until the end of April, but they were destined never to find common ground: parliament continued to insist that power had to be removed from the episcopacy, while the king refused to budge from his support for the established Church and the Book of Common Prayer. In London while the two sides talked there had been a flurry of opposition to the war and a number of demonstrations caused by food and fuel shortages, but the outbursts were short-lived and with the coming of spring both sides were as far apart as ever.

While negotiating with the commissioners Charles was also engaged in correspondence with the Irish and the Scots. From the very outset of the troubles he had always entertained hopes of using Irish troops in his cause and had twice used intermediaries – first Antrim, then Strafford – to help him realise that aim, but the outbreak of hostilities in Ireland had confused matters. The Dublin government was split in its loyalties and, while Mountgarret's Catholic Confederates claimed to be acting on Charles's behalf, it was a fine decision whether or not to acknowledge their loyalty. Any public attempt to make contact would damage what was left of his relationship with the English parliament and would wreck any hope of continuing loyalty from the Dublin parliament, but that precarious state of affairs did not preclude using others to act on his behalf. In January, at the same time that Charles was opening talks with the parliamentary commissioners in Oxford he sent word to Ormond to try to arrange for a cease-fire in Ireland as a prelude to receiving Irish military aid. By April the request had become an order and it came at a crucial period in the fighting: Ormond had defeated Confederate forces at Old Ross and, despite shortage of food and delays in payment, Monro had restarted his sweeps and drives against the rebels in Ulster, burning the woods of the O'Neills of Clandeboy, a prominent local Catholic family. In so doing Monro's men added to their reputation for being more interested in plundering than restoring property, and there were consistent reports of Scots rounding up cattle in Antrim and shipping them back to Scotland.

Good politician that he was, Ormond was wary about entering into any agreement with the Confederates. The threat of using Irish troops in England had cost Strafford his head, and following the uprising of 1641 many English people entertained overblown fears about the rapacity and aggression of the Irish soldiery. Against that, Ormond disagreed strongly with the way in which the war against the Confederates was being waged under the direction of the Lord Justices who were ruling Ireland in the absence of a lord lieutenant. Under their direction reprisals against the civilian population were common-place and commanders like Coote gained dreadful reputations for their tactics of 'frightfulness'. Realising that this was counterproductive and aware of the king's plight,* Ormond entered into fruitful negotiations with Mountgarret, and as a result a Cessation of Arms was signed on 15 September. In return for the king's promise to consider repealing the penal laws and granting freedom of worship, the one-year armistice allowed the Confederates to retain the areas they had captured – about 90 per cent of Ireland. They also agreed to give the king £20,000 and a large number of cattle for his war effort, but the immediate effect of the truce was to allow Ormond to send troops across the Irish Sea to Wales and England. Although none were Irish Catholics, and some mutinied when they discovered that they were being forced to fight against parliament, the news that troops from Ireland were serving the king's cause merely added to fears that Charles was caught up in a Catholic conspiracy. For both sides it was a bad bargain: the troops did not significantly help Charles's war effort and during the subsequent negotiations in Oxford for a lasting treaty the Confederates were unable to persuade the king to make good his promises.

The Cessation of Arms also finally drew the Scots into the war, one result of the action being that Monro's army was left in Ulster, where they refused to acknowledge the truce and continued the campaign against the Catholic forces led by Owen Roe O'Neill. Throughout the winter months of 1642–43 both parliament and the king had been

---

* From Sir John Byron he had received the bald request: 'I see no reason why the King should not make any scruple of calling in the Irish, or the Turks if they would save him'.

wooing the Scots, who greeted the requests with their customary love of disputation. In January the Privy Council agreed to publish the king's letter of explanation, an action which attracted a petition from the Covenanters that any promises from the king were worthless. In turn this brought a further petition, the so-called Cross Petition, compiled by Hamilton and Traquair, which denounced the 'fearful and prodigious effects of a bloody and civil war' and trusted that the Crown would continue 'that happy union betwixt the two kingdoms which can never be conceived to be intended to weaken the head whereby it is knit together'.[9]

In the midst of the debate the Scots agreed to send five mediators led by Loudoun south to Oxford to try to bring king and parliament to their senses, but Charles would have none of it, telling the deputation on its arrival at the end of February that 'the differences between his majesty and the Houses of Parliament had not the least relation to peace between the two kingdoms'.[10] To counteract the inevitable hostility which would meet the rejection of the Scottish initiative Charles again sent Lanark north asking for support from the more moderate Covenanting leaders. His emissary was also ordered to use delaying tactics and to draw negotiations out as long as possible so that 'the first Breach should not come from his Party'. Considering the honours he had bestowed on his last visit Charles also hoped that there might be some displays of gratitude, but he reckoned that, even if none appeared, Lanark would be able to delay the debate long enough for the war to be over before the Scots decided whether or not to support parliament. As the debate rumbled on, to neither side's satisfaction, Charles felt confident enough to tell his friends that in his opinion no Scottish forces would ever dare to cross the border that year.

He was right in his timescale but wrong in guessing the outcome. Throughout the spring and summer of 1643 there was a good deal of conflicting intrigue in the Royalist camp. While Pym made it an act of religious and political duty to get the support of the Scots, Charles listened to the claims of his rival courtiers and hedged his bets. In February Montrose had journeyed south to confer with Newcastle and, while in northern England, he also met Henrietta Maria, newly arrived back from the Continent after raising funds and buying weapons for the Royalist cause. By that stage of the war Montrose was convinced that a separate civil war would break out in Scotland between the Covenanters and those loyal to Charles and that the king should act immediately to rally his supporters – 'all they lacked was the king's warrant, without which they would attempt nothing, with it there was nothing they would not attempt'. This was fighting talk and Henrietta Maria was prepared to listen, telling him that 'if his Majesty's servants would only agree among themselves, and not lose time, all the evil to be dreaded by that quarter [Scotland] may be prevented'.[11] She also held out the possibility of supplying him with arms from Denmark and praised the generosity of his offer, but Hamilton's arrival in York put paid to her enthusiasm for the creation of a separate Royalist army in Scotland. Not only was the support debatable, he counselled, but it would meet the powerful opposition of Argyll and, besides, any rebellion in Scotland would only bring Monro's army back from Ulster to crush it. For his pains in dissuading the king from these proposals Hamilton received a dukedom while Montrose was left to cool his heels, sure that he was right but unable to find anyone to listen to him.

In fact it was to be another kind of threat from Ireland which finally settled the issue of Scottish military support. In May the increasingly unstable Earl of Antrim was captured by Monro's men at Knockfergus in Ulster as he made his way back from York, and was found to be carrying letters which suggested that, in addition to fomenting a Royalist uprising, Charles was trying to induce Irish Catholic forces to invade Scotland on his behalf. At the end of 1643 the Western Isles were raided by one of Antrim's allies, Alexander MacDonald (sometimes MacDonnell), or to give him his Gaelic appellation Alasdair MacColla Chiotaich,* one of the greatest warriors of his day, a huge man whose feats included killing a cow single-handed, one hand holding it by the horns, the other wielding an axe. Although his latest expedition had more to do with avenging himself on the Campbells, the Irish threat provided evidence that, far from upholding the settlement of 1641, Charles was intent on supporting treacherous and damnable Catholic plots.

---

* His father was Colla Ciotach, or Colkitto, meaning 'ambidextrous', and the epithet is often and erroneously applied to him. The question of his nomenclature is addressed in the prologue to David Stevenson's *Alasdair MacColla and the Highland Problem in the 17th Century*. I have followed his usage of Alasdair MacColla.

When the English parliament renewed their request for military assistance in August they found a receptive audience from the Scottish Covenanters. The commissioners were led by Sir Henry Vane, who was under instruction to keep any religious agreement vaguely worded because the English parliament knew full well that, while it wanted a military alliance, the Scots were looking for a religious covenant which would bind the countries together in the Presbyterian cause. Somewhere between the two extremes, which were not compatible, both sides strove to find sufficient common ground for an agreement, the English being prepared to offer concessions on religious freedom and the Scots understanding only too well that a victory for the king might lead him to revoke the policies he had already offered them. Although some Scottish critics, such as John Spalding, thought it 'strange to see, how our army shall in the defence of the king, without his own consent, and under colour of religion, aid and assist the king's parliament of England now standing in arms against the king rebelliously' they were won over by the knowledge that the true religion would be defended:

> Now it was concluded by our Council and Estates to raise an army to go into England in defence of the good cause, the true reformed Protestant religion, rights of parliament, and liberties of England and Scotland, and to defend the king against all papists, prelates and malignant persons.[12]

The result was the Solemn League and Covenant which managed to be both a political and religious treaty and which came into being on 17 August 1643 – a mere ten days after the arrival of the English commissioners, an astonishingly short time considering the usual tenor of debate in Edinburgh.

Its intentions were summarised in six articles which promised to uphold the Protestant religion, to extirpate all relics of popery, to preserve the rights and liberties of the parliaments of both kingdoms, to arrest all incendiaries and false advisers to the king, to observe the Treaty of London and to lend full assistance to all signatories and not withdraw or fall into 'detestable indifference or neutrality'. In common with other declarations made by the king's opponents during the war, it also pledged 'to preserve the King's Majesty's person and authority', but the premise failed to placate Charles, who countered that the Scots' 'pride and tyranny' would encourage all true Englishmen to rise in his support. So, in return for a promise – left vaguely worded – 'for the reformation of religion according to the word of God and the example of the best reformed churches' parliament received a Scottish army which would number 20,000 at a cost of £30,000 a month. A treaty guaranteeing the arrangement was signed just over a week later on 26 August.

Given the factionalism which was endemic in Scotland, not every noble signed the new Covenant in the first instance, preferring to hedge their bets. Those living in England had their livings confiscated, and this move brought home to the others that the Covenanters would not tolerate any opposition; for the most part the Scottish nobility had signed up by the end of January 1643. Having decided that any resistance was doomed to failure Hamilton and Lanark fled to Oxford, where the former was imprisoned on charges of treason, a poor reward, but given his hopeless incompetence and over-confidence perhaps a just one in the circumstances. He would not be released until 1646, but his younger brother Lanark, having been stripped of all his offices, simply slipped back to Scotland, where prudence suggested that he throw in his lot with the Covenanters. Only Montrose and a handful of others remained true to the king's cause, pledging themselves in Oxford to support the king and oppose the Solemn League and Covenant, their words of defiance bringing a rebuke from Baillie that they had 'drawn up and passed a horrible Oath for holding us all as traitors':

We do hereby profess and declare that we esteem the said pretended Convention to be a presumptuous, illegal and traitorous meeting, as being designed to excite sedition and rebellion in that kingdom [Scotland]; and a most unjust invasion of this [England].[13]

The battle to win the support of the two Celtic kingdoms was finally over, with each side having gained some advantage from it in the form of support for their cause. (It could also be said that Charles's initiative to gain support from the Irish through the Cessation of Arms was balanced by parliament's resolution to sign the Solemn League and Covenant.) Of the two sides parliament had the better bargain, in that the Scots army fought as a unit on its behalf while the soldiers from Ireland were scattered throughout the king's army and had no identifiable separate identity. The events of the spring of 1643 marked a turning-point of no little significance, because they brought Scotland into the war and made events in Ireland ever more dependent on what was happening in England.

Chapter Four

HEARTS AND CITIES: THE WAR TO WIN THE CENTRE

'Alas poor England! How thou art distressed with War!'

Syon's Calamity or England's Misery
Hieroglyphically Delineated (1643)

As would happen later in the war, the attempts to find a peaceful solution were punctuated by further fighting and military manoeuvring. In the Thames valley Essex enjoyed numerical superiority over the Royalist army, but in the depths of winter he was not prepared to use his advantage and apart from a desultory raid on the king's garrison at Brill he was to all intents and purposes lying dormant until the spring. Both sides made fresh attempts to build up support and to create a coherent chain of command which took account of the territorial spread of the war. Training was also essential. The Royalist cavalry needed discipline and control while the infantry was still lacking the basic battlefield discipline which would enable men to face the shock of combat without breaking. The same applied to the parliamentary army, but with a different emphasis: while Essex's infantry had performed reasonably well at Edgehill the cavalry had not, a result of lack of experience and simple horsemanship – more men with experience of hunting rode in the king's army.

For Charles the over-arching need was still to take London, but for the time being, with Essex's army blocking his way and the city's defences being strengthened, that was impossible. Reinforcements were needed, but as these would take time to arrange and supply Charles had to organise his forces so that they could fight over a wide area and provide him with the means of attacking the capital. Separate commands were established in the north (Yorkshire, Lancashire and Northumberland) under Newcastle, and in the west (from Cornwall to Somerset and including the south coast counties) under Hertford, although Hopton emerged as his field commander. The strategy depended on Newcastle triumphing in Yorkshire and marching on London while the western army would reinforce the king's army in Oxford, having defeated parliamentary forces in the south-west. As for Charles, he had the command of what might be called the centre – that part of England which lies south of the River Trent but excludes the East Anglian counties, London and the south-east. As ever there were shifting loyalties within each area, but in this first phase of the war the main cockpit was in the middle England counties of Gloucester, Leicester, Oxford, Stafford, Northampton and Wiltshire which, together with neighbouring Shropshire, Hereford and Worcester, contained the main corridors to the north and west.

Much of this territory was the king's country – most of the influential land-owning families and corporations supported him – although there were substantial pockets of support for parliament, mainly in the larger towns. The counties of Bedford, Gloucester and Northampton were more or less solidly for parliament, while Leicester was evenly divided: the south including the city of Leicester had sided with parliament while the north was controlled for the king by Lord Huntingdon's younger son, Henry Hastings. However support did not always imply the offer of assistance. When John Hutchinson seized Nottingham Castle for parliament in January 1643 and laid plans to defend it he received only reluctant local support. Most of the townspeople supported parliament but they knew only too well that the creation of a garrison might attract Royalist retribution and they would then find themselves in the front line. Hutchinson's wife Lucy realised that this conflict of interests – the soldier's needs clashing with the civilian's concerns – weighed heavily on his mind:

> The attempting to preserve this place, in the midst of so many potent enemies, was a work of no small difficulty; and nothing but

an invincible courage, and a passionate zeal for the interest of God and his country, could have engaged Mr Hutchinson, who did not, through youthful inconsideration and improvidence, want a foresight of those dangers and travails he then undertook. He knew well enough that the town was more than half disaffected to the Parliament; that had they been all otherwise, they were not half enough to defend it against any unequal force; that they were far from the Parliament and their armies, and could not expect any timely relief or assistance from them; that he himself was the forlorn hope of those who were engaged with him, and had then the best stake among them; that the gentlemen who were on horseback, when they could no longer defend their country, might at least save their lives by a handsome retreat to the army; but that he must stand victorious, or fall, tying himself to an indefensible town.[1]

Leicester, too, was lukewarm about overtly supporting parliament, not because the people preferred the king's cause (most did not) but because they feared that a sizeable military presence would simply be a magnet for the king's army. If their side prevailed all might be well, but if a victorious Royalist force entered their town they knew only too well what fate awaited them.

In the weeks after Edgehill, with Essex deciding to adopt a cautious approach, the soldier who attracted the most attention was Sir William Waller, hereditary Chief Butler of England. Christened 'William the Conqueror' after his daring dash to capture Southsea Castle and take Portsmouth, he became a quick favourite with the people of London, who warmed to his exploits. Like many others he had seen service in Europe, fighting for Queen Elizabeth of Bohemia's hopeless cause in 1620, and he proved to be an able commander, described by contemporaries as a talented 'chooser and shifter of ground' and prepared to take chances when they were there to be taken. Aided by Meldrum he was a thorough professional, and he made little secret of the fact that he was serving parliament not for gain but to restore order, 'that God might have had his fear: the king his honour; the Houses of Parliament their privileges; the people of the Kingdom their liberties and properties; and nothing might have remained upon the score between us, but that debt which must be for ever paying and ever owing love'.[2] These were high-flown words, and a sense of style was part of Waller's capacity for leadership, but he also knew how to fight: following the fall of Portsmouth he successfully attacked Farnham Castle without the aid of artillery on 30 November, leading the attack sword in hand after exploding a petard underneath the main gate. A fortnight later he destroyed a Royalist force at Winchester.

Through his third wife Lady Anne Finch, the daughter of the Lord Keeper, he came into Pym's orbit and would probably have been marked for preference even before his pre-Christmas exploits in 1642 gave him military fame. As a reward he was made major-general of the first of the federated armies formed by parliament in 1643 – the Western Association Army formed by men from the counties of Worcester, Somerset, Gloucester, Wiltshire and Shropshire. Raised by Ordinances of Association these armies had specific instructions to 'associate themselves to protect the counties, raise horse and foot, money and plate, give battle, fight, and levy war, put to execution of death, and destroy all who should levy war against the parliament'. At the same time command of the Northern Army, operating mainly in Yorkshire, was given to Lord Fairfax, who proved to be a good handler of men and an inspiring leader. A Midlands Association was also formed, as was an Eastern Association, the latter proving in time to be the most durable and innovative of the parliamentary formations. Led first by Lord Grey of Groby, it drew its strength from the agricultural counties of East Anglia, and among its regimental commanders was the member of parliament for Cambridge who was described in official dispatches as 'our noble and active Colonel [Oliver] Cromwell'.

The encomium was not misplaced, for Cromwell was already emerging as an astute military commander who was revolutionising the selection of soldiers for the parliamentary cause. From the evidence of a conversation with his cousin John Hampden it is likely that he witnessed the latter stages of the fighting at Edgehill and was dismayed by the behaviour of the untutored parliamentary horse troopers:

Your troopers, said I, are most of them old decayed serving men and tapsters and such kind of fellows: and . . . their [Royalist]

troopers are gentlemen's son, younger sons, persons of quality. Do
you think that the spirits of such base and mean fellows will ever
be able to encounter gentlemen that have honour, courage and
resolution in them? You must get men of spirit . . . that is likely to
go on as far as gentlemen will go, or else I am sure you will be
beaten still.[3]

Understanding the worth of those gentlemanly qualities from the
example of his own background, Cromwell not only knew what he
was talking about but he was addressing a central problem about
recruiting which affected both sides. With no military tradition as
such, and lacking the experience of warfare, other than the brief and
half-hearted excursions in Europe, England was not a natural
recruiting ground and all too often men resented being taken far from
their homes to fight elsewhere. Even the professionally trained
London Trained Bands grew uneasy when marching out of the
capital. As yet unblooded in battle and backed by little military
theory, Cromwell realised that to overcome those defects he had to
select men personally who would be prepared not just to fight but to
persevere in the parliamentary cause. According to Bulstrode
Whitelocke, who observed the process, the soldiers recruited by
Cromwell were 'most of them freeholders and freeholders' sons who
upon a matter of conscience engaged in this quarrel'.[4] These were
men of middling rank, hard-working and reliable, who had been
'industrious and active in their former callings' and brought the best
aspects of their private and public lives to the soldier's trade. Cromwell
also made sure that those selected were sober and god-fearing.
Discipline was strict and according to one report in May 1643
swearing was punished by a twelve pence fine. In common with the
Scottish practice, a chaplain was also appointed to provide religious
guidance and sustenance. Richard Baxter of Kidderminster was
approached and, although he declined, he praised Cromwell's
imposition of strict discipline as a means of 'the avoidings of those
disorders, mutinies, plunderings and grievances of the country which
debased men in armies are commonly guilty of'.[5]
    It would take time and the experience of defeat for opposition to
Cromwell's ideology to be overcome – Manchester was not alone in
criticising Cromwell's selection of officers who were not 'gentlemen'

but 'common men, poor and of mean parentage' – and the campaign of 1643 would show how difficult it was for both sides to manage and organise their war efforts. Pay was not always forthcoming, there were problems with supply and resupply of rations, ammunition and equipment, and the existence of the independent commands meant there was no consistent chain of command. Only the Royalists, their captain-general being the king, had a coherent strategy, but even so the idea of a giant concentric pincer attack on London depended on too many imponderables – not just the defeat of the northern and western parliamentary armies but the capture of key garrisons such as Gloucester, Bristol and Hull.

In the early spring of 1643 the position of the Royalist army was dominated by the dormant presence of Essex's forces in the Thames valley and the far more serious threat posed by Waller to the west of them. While Essex was merely a block which prevented London from being attacked, the army of the Western Association was in the position of being able to cut off the Oxford garrison from a potentially plentiful supply of recruits from South Wales, where Lord Herbert was busily raising an army at a cost of £60,000 to his own purse. Although in need of discipline and weapons the Welsh levies proved to be the most loyal and steadfast of Charles's infantry troops. At Edgehill they had broken and were condemned as 'poor Welsh vermins', but they had gone on to play a leading role at Brentford and in combat were to prove themselves again and again as hard and reliable troops. Curiously parliament seemed to accept the king's hegemony in the principality and made little attempt to recruit there, perhaps because Sir William Brereton, a forceful enough commander, was driven out of town whenever he attempted to recruit in the March counties of present-day Clwyd. With good reason perhaps John Corbet, chaplain to the parliamentary governor of Gloucester, dismissed the place as 'blind Wales'.

However, they still had much to learn and Waller was their first tutor. On 24 March a force of 1600 Welsh infantry and cavalry drawn mainly from Monmouthshire made their way tentatively eastwards towards Oxford to join the king's army, but they got no further than a small town called Highnam on the west bank of the Severn close to Gloucester, a parliamentary stronghold. Confronted by troops ordered out to attack them by the town's military governor,

Lieutenant-Colonel Edward Massey, they decided to halt until Royalist reinforcements arrived to accompany them to Oxford. It was a bad mistake. Approaching them from the south was Waller's Western Association army, which showed brilliant improvisation to create a bridge made from boats (a modern Bailey bridge) ten miles to the south at Frampton and, once across the Severn, marched rapidly through the Forest of Dean to outflank the Welsh force. Surprised, outnumbered and demoralised by the sudden appearance of the enemy cavalry, they gave up without a fight and most went into captivity along with their arms and ammunition, leaving Waller master of the Severn valley and the approaches to Wales.

The news plunged the court into despair. Not only were the recruits badly needed to reinforce the king's army against the threat posed by Essex, but many, Hyde (as he then was) included, felt that Herbert had simply thrown away much-needed assets: 'if the money which was laid out in the raising, arming and paying that body of men, which never advanced the king's service in the least degree, had been brought into the King's receipt at Oxford, I am persuaded the war might have ended the next summer'.[6] Hyde was overstating the case, but he was giving voice to the concern felt at the king's lack of funds and shortages of manpower, which were to prove thorns in the Royalists' flesh throughout the war. Even at that early stage of the fighting Charles's army was short of ammunition and military equipment and it was numerically inferior to Essex's army.

However, in the immediate future there was some respite from the gloom caused by Highnam. To the north-west Stafford was saved from occupation by Brereton and Sir John Gell by a force led by the Earl of Northampton, who engaged the latter's men at Hopton Heath on 19 March before the two armies were able to unite. Both sides were evenly matched, but the battle was won by the Royalist artillery, which included a 29-pounder piece known as 'Roaring Meg' which made 'such a lane' through Gell's infantry that they were unable to close their ranks before Northampton's cavalry charged, a move which led to the capture of the parliamentary artillery. Although the charge was successful Northampton was unhorsed and killed by a halberd blow to his head while fighting on foot. A sour note was struck that night when Gell, a tough and uncompromising commander, refused to return Northampton's body and only offered to do so on condition that his cannons were returned. The Royalists refused, usable weapons being more important than a noble corpse. While the neighbouring and equally important town of Lichfield remained in uncouth parliamentary hands, a force under Gell having captured it on 4 March – its cathedral was denuded of 'popish trumperies', used as a stables and at one stage a calf was brought in for a mock christening at the font – the fact that Stafford was safe kept the route open to the Midlands for the arrival of Henrietta Maria and her convoy of money and munitions.

She had arrived back in England on 22 February, landing at Bridlington in Yorkshire, where her party met a hot reception from a parliamentary naval squadron. From her own account she behaved with remarkable coolness, telling her husband that 'the balls were whistling' about her and that as she took cover a sergeant was killed 'within twenty paces of me'. With her she brought an imposing array of weapons and ammunition to supply both Newcastle's and Charles's armies, but the latter's share could not be taken south until a safe corridor had been established. For the time being she went to live in a house by York Minster to rally support for her husband, meeting among other supporters the enthusiastic Montrose, whom she encouraged in his wish to create a rebellion in Scotland. It took another four months before she rejoined her husband, but she used the time to good effect, inspecting Newcastle's troops and writing constantly to Charles, reminding him of his promises to show 'firmness and constancy' and of the need to avoid the delays which had always 'ruined' him in the past. Clearly she knew her husband well.

The clearing of the obstacles which prevented the queen from reaching Oxford was left to Rupert, who had already scored the first military success of the year by capturing Cirencester on 2 February. The attack showed the king's nephew at his best, using surprise, speed and aggression to press home his advantage – while Wilmot mounted a diversion to the north, Rupert's force of infantry and cavalry stormed the town's main entrance. Fierce street-to-street fighting followed, 300 parliamentary soldiers were killed, 1200 were taken prisoner and, as had happened at Brentford and would happen elsewhere, the town was plundered. The same sequence was followed when Rupert took a force of 1200 cavalry and 700 infantry through

Chipping Norton and Stratford-on-Avon to Birmingham, 'an incurably Parliamentarian town' and supplier of sword blades to Essex's army. Despite stout resistance from the garrison and the local population, who jeered the 'devilish Cavaliers' as 'popish traitors', Rupert's troopers crushed the opposition on 3 April with two charges into the narrow streets and then set about punishing the town and its inhabitants. The story of the battle and its unhappy consequence was captured in a contemporary but not entirely reliable parliamentary report:

> Having thus possessed themselves of the town, they ran into every house cursing and damning, threatening and terrifying the poor women most terribly, setting naked swords and pistols to their breasts, they fell to plundering all the town before them, as well Malignants as others, picking purse and pockets, searching in holes and corners, tiles of houses, wells, pools, vaults, gardens and every other place they could suspect for money or goods, forcing people to deliver all the money they had.[7]

By laying waste to the town and setting fire to many of its houses, Rupert's force provided parliament with a propaganda coup which that tract and others did not fail to exploit. The news also terrified the merchants of Gloucester, who were rumoured to have offered payments to the Royalist forces to leave them alone if and when the city fell into their hands. Charles rebuked Rupert for his men's behaviour – the prince had in fact done his best to curb his men, knowing that plundering encouraged a breakdown in discipline – but the damage had been done: Birmingham had paid the price for supporting parliament and being seen to profit from it. There was another consequence which would soon typify the family nature of the fighting. During the action the old Earl of Denbigh was mortally wounded and his title fell to his son Lord Feilding, one of the commanders of the parliamentary horse at Edgehill.

Rupert's next target was Lichfield and its solidly guarded cathedral close. Being well supplied and surrounded by a deep moat, the garrison commander refused to surrender, his decision no doubt reinforced by the news from Birmingham. Lacking large artillery pieces Rupert could not breach the wall, and as he could not afford the time to starve the garrison into submission he had to find some other means of attacking the obstacle. Again his solution gives the lie to the belief that Rupert was only a madcap cavalry general. First he started draining the moat and then, using a good deal of ingenuity, he called up fifty miners from nearby Cannock Chase and set them to work tunnelling up to the walls of the close. Throughout the stand-off there were minor skirmishes during which prisoners were taken and the garrison caused great offence by hanging a Royalist soldier from the walls. Rupert was also being bombarded with letters from the king ordering him to return to Oxford to meet a new threat – Essex having wakened from his slumbers to move his army to threaten Reading – but the prince kept his nerve. On 20 April, having filled the tunnels with explosives, the besiegers discharged the mine, a breach appeared in the walls and following a brisk exchange of fire the garrison surrendered. It was the first time that gunpowder had been used in this way in England – originally mines were driven under the walls, propped up with wooden beams which were then burned, causing the fortifications to collapse into the subsequent hole – and on this occasion there were no reprisals, Rupert having taken to heart the king's admonition that he had to win hearts as well as cities. Five days later he reassembled with the Royalist army at Wallingford to help counter Essex's long-expected move.

Although Reading had stout defences, its garrison was weak, and the situation was made worse when its curmudgeonly commander Sir Arthur Aston was wounded in one of the first rounds of artillery fire, Essex's army having taken up position to the south of the town on the Berkshire side of the Thames. Command then fell to Colonel Richard Feilding, another of the Denbigh line, but he lacked Aston's stern resolution. Outside the town he could see Essex's main field army, and he was by no means sure that his anguished requests for help would be met by the king. Being concerned for the lives of his men, Feilding sued for a cease-fire and promised to surrender provided that he could take his men and baggage back to Oxford. No sooner had he done that than the Royalist forces led by the king and Rupert also appeared to the south, but Feilding would not break his truce and on 27 April he completed the terms of the surrender to Essex. For his pains he was condemned to death at a court-martial and was only saved by the intervention of Rupert, who sympathised with the predicament he had faced. Had Essex followed up his triumph with an attack on Oxford the Royalists would have been hard pressed to stop him but, as had happened at their last encounter, both armies marched away from each other, Essex to replenish his supplies and Charles to consider parliament's formulation for peace.

While Reading was falling, quite needlessly, into the possession of the parliamentary army Waller was discovering that he did not have everything going his way. Taking advantage of a local truce in the West Country (see next chapter) he decided to mount a foray into Wales which took him as far as Usk, but making no headway he decided to cut back to Chepstow on 6 April, his intention being to return to Gloucester. In front of him, coming down from the north and barring the way, was a force of 2000 Royalist infantry and cavalry led by Prince Maurice, Rupert's brother, and reinforced by a detachment from Oxford under the command of Colonel-General Lord Grandison. Having reached Tewkesbury, where they had taken a leaf out of Waller's book and crossed the Severn by way of a bridge of boats, the Royalists then fanned out into the Forest of Dean, hoping to cut off the Western Association army before it reached Gloucester. Spotting the danger Waller ordered his infantry, artillery and baggage train to cross the Severn at Aust and engaged Maurice's forces with his cavalry and dragoons near the village of Little Dean. It was no more than a confused skirmish and Waller's men were able to fight their way through to Gloucester, where there was a hurried conference to assess the situation: Waller would rest his forces in Gloucester while Massey's garrison would march on to Tewkesbury to seize it and smash Maurice's bridge.

This phase of the operation was completed successfully on 12 April – with Maurice still on the western bank of the Severn there was no opposition – and Waller brought up his cavalry later in the day to reinforce Massey's troops. His intention was to seize Upton Bridge to the north-west, thereby cutting off the Royalist force and preventing its return to Oxford, but he was too late. Maurice had crossed the river that same day and had drawn his men up in fighting order at the northern end of a sloping plain known as Ripple Field. When the two forces, both numbering 2000, clashed the following day Waller's run of success ended. Aware that he only had a small force of infantry – some 200 bluecoats from Massey's garrison – and could not deploy his artillery, Waller decided to withdraw from his superior position on Old Nan's Hill, and as he did so Maurice's cavalry attacked from the west. Trapped in the narrow lanes, Waller's men were stunned by the speed of the Royalist attack, and the line broke. In the pursuit which followed at least 80 were killed, some of them drowning as they attempted to ford the river at the nearby village of Uckinghall.

Although some soldiers in the parliamentary army fought well, most notably the infantry and the cavalry troopers of Hesilrige's regiment (known as 'Lobsters' on account of their heavy plate armour and lobster-tail helmets), it was still a defeat for William 'the Conqueror' and one which could have cost him dearly if his adversary had not been ordered to return to Oxford to join the operation to relieve the Royalist garrison in Reading. Like his brother, Maurice had deployed his cavalry well at Ripple Field: not only had he forced Waller, usually such a good reader of ground, to come down from Old Nan's Hill but he had attacked at precisely the right moment when the parliamentary force was at its most vulnerable. After the battle Waller went north to take Hereford before retiring to Gloucester to make his peace with Massey, who was not best pleased at the loss of his crack infantrymen.

Waller's next operation was an attempt to take Worcester at the end of May, but the city refused to surrender – the governor 'bad him be gone' – and an artillery barrage failed to persuade the inhabitants to change their minds, leaving Waller with no option but to retire once more to Gloucester. There was further discomfort for the parliamentary side on 18 June at Chalgrove, six miles to the south of Essex's new headquarters at Thame, the town to which the parliamentary army had moved a week earlier as a prelude to an attack on Oxford. Acting on intelligence that a supply train was approaching with funds to pay Essex's army, Rupert decided to mount an attack. (The information came from Sir John Hurry (or Urry), a Scottish mercenary who had deserted to the Roylists and would change sides again before the war was over.) Taking with him 1800 troopers, Rupert crossed the Thames at Chislehampton and began a daring night ride which took him right through the parliamentary army to reach the village of Chinnor at dawn. Following a brisk engagement with the local garrison the village was set alight but, realising he was in danger of being cut off from his line of retreat, Rupert began his withdrawal to Chislehampton, first sending on a detachment to secure the bridge. By this time he realised he would not find the convoy, which had been warned of his movements and had taken shelter, and by then Essex's men too had been alerted.

About two miles east of the river crossing, with Essex's men in hot pursuit, Rupert drew up his forces in a field at Chalgrove, putting his dragoons behind either side of the hedges lining the lane down to the bridge. The trap had been laid, but on seeing that the opposition's advance was dispersed Rupert made a headlong attack into its ranks with his Lifeguard while two other regiments of horse attacked the flanks. The result was confusion in the parliamentary force, which broke and scattered with Rupert's men pursuing them off the field. Over one hundred were taken prisoner and were marched back to Oxford as prisoners and half that number lay dead, cut down as they attempted to make their way back to Thame. Among the casualties was John Hampden, who was shot twice in the shoulder as he tried vainly to stop the rout. The wound turned gangrenous and he died six days later, on 24 June, at Essex's headquarters in Thame, his last words being a request to the Almighty to save the country. Not a professional soldier, he had raised his 'greencoat' regiment from his native county of Buckingham and had shown great courage in the field, twice appearing when all seemed lost – at Edgehill and Brentford – to put heart into men on the point of breaking and earning the praise of a soldier-poet called John Stiles:

> I have seen
> Him in the front of his Regiment-in-Green,
> When death about him did in ambush lie
> And whizzing shot, like showers of arrows, fly,
> Waving his conqu'ring steel, as if that he
> From Mars had got the sole monopoly
> Of never-failing courage.[8]

At Chalgrove Hampden's luck ran out, and one 'whizzing shot' ended the life of Pym's right-hand man and a politician-cum-soldier of no mean repute. His death was mourned on both sides, for although he had taken up arms against the king he was recognised as a moderating influence and was revered by many for his honesty and integrity.

Rupert's daring raid through Essex's lines was a major boost for the Royalist army. He and his men had ridden some forty miles in twenty-four hours, and although they had not captured the wagon train with its cargo of money they had inflicted casualties and taken prisoners. Other raids followed, including one led by Hurry, who attacked West Wycombe in Buckinghamshire. Although Essex held the strategic initiative he had no means of attacking Oxford; weakened by illness, desertion and lethargy, his forces were thoroughly demoralised. On the king's side the exact opposite was true. Rupert's raids and the steady stream of prisoners and booty entering Oxford provided a major fillip and the buoyancy was enhanced by the news that Henrietta Maria was on her way to join the king, bringing with her money and war matériel.

On 4 June she left York accompanied by 5000 men and moved south through the Midlands while Rupert rode out to meet her. Astonishingly, despite sightings of her force by spies under the control of Essex's Scoutmaster-General Sir Samuel Luke, she was not intercepted and there was little incident, other than at Burton-on-Trent, which was in the hands of the parliamentary army. According to *Mercurius Aulicus*, hardly an impartial reporter, the town was taken with little trouble and 'her Majesty's goodness and clemency was so exemplary, and like the royal self, that she forbade any violence to be offered to the town'. Luke heard otherwise and his report to parliament paints a somewhat different picture:

Some of her forces lately came to Burton upon Trent and fell upon the townsmen and drove 30 of them into the church who defended themselves bravely and killed many of the Cavaliers but at last were glad to demand quarter. But they refused to grant it but came in the night and cut all their throats, doing great spoil in the town, ravishing the women, forcing many of them to take to the river, where they drowned insomuch that above 20 were found and taken up dead this week, and they daily find more.[9]

It probably did happen as Luke recounted, for when the queen reached Oxford her little army brought with it a good deal of plunder. Before she arrived on 14 July she stayed one night at Stratford-on-Avon, where the local council paid £5 for cakes to be presented to her, and met her husband at Kineton, near to Edgehill. Her arrival was another cause for rejoicing. Bells were rung, crowds thronged the streets, the council paid for the approach road to be strewn with flowers to welcome her home, and Charles was elated to have her back at his side. The arms and money were much needed, and with a steady flow of recruits swelling his army's ranks his forces were now the equal of those commanded by Essex who, by contrast, seemed once more to have sunk into lethargy. Later in the summer the mood in the king's camp was enhanced by the news that Henrietta Maria was pregnant.

If the atmosphere in Oxford was tolerably light-hearted the same could not be said of London. The war in the north had cut off all supplies of coal, and although the weather had improved people were dispirited by paying higher taxes to fund the war when money was in short supply, and by the absence of good news from the war fronts. Visiting the city in May, the Scottish writer William Lithgow could not help noticing that although food was readily available, the spirits of the population were low:

> But it may be truly feared, that if these their general combustions draw to a winter leaguer, that both the city and kingdom shall smart for it: and why? Because both the armies, and also the petty armies in every county, do so sack and spoil the grounds, of horses, bestial, grass, corn and hay, and also pitifully plunder the people of moneys, victuals and domestic furniture, that the continuing of it in a short time shall ruin all.[10]

Pym, too, was nervous. He had lost in Hampden a good friend and supporter and the peace faction in parliament was growing restless, not just discontent with the lack of progress being made by the soldiers but actively questioning the wisdom of prolonging the fighting. The war taxes and forced loans were unpopular, and at one stage Pym was forced to imprison merchants who refused to pay them because they deemed them to be illegal. Demonstrations against the war became commonplace and there was a concerted effort to prevent war weariness from setting in: ministers used their sermons to whip up enthusiasm for the war and peace demonstrations were countered by others in favour of continuing the fighting. A feeble Royalist plot led by among others the poet Edmund Waller was quickly uncovered, and although its success would have depended on Charles's army capturing London – an unlikely eventuality in May 1643 – it provoked parliament to insist on a new oath of allegiance for all of its members. The news of the unrest in the English capital even reached Aberdeen, where Spalding noted that 'whole families, man, wife and children flew out of London for safety of their lives, some to one [part], some to another, and some for Scotland. Pitiful to behold!'[11]

The panic was caused as much by rumours of new plots as anything else, and as news of fresh setbacks reached the capital parliament came under pressure to replace the beleaguered Essex, who responded with the absurd suggestion that the issue should be decided by one last formal battle between the two armies. All the while Pym was becoming physically weaker, fighting his last great battle against cancer of the bowel. With the armies still fighting in the centre, west and north and with the Scots poised to join the fray at parliament's request, William Lithgow, then visiting London, was not far wrong in surmising that ahead lay a long and bitter journey before peace returned to the king's kingdoms.

Chapter Five

WESTERN WONDER:
THE WAR IN THE WEST COUNTRY

'Where is your King Jesus now?'

Royalist jeers following the fall of Bristol, 26 July 1643

Much of the concern whipped up in London was prompted by the news coming out of the western counties of Somerset, Dorset, Devon and Cornwall, which had seen some of the first fighting of the civil war in England. By the summer of 1643 William Waller had come a cropper in a pitched battle outside Devizes, the key city of Bristol had fallen to Rupert's forces and Gloucester was under threat. Exeter and Plymouth, both occupied by parliamentary garrisons, remained under siege but the West Country was more or less in Royalist hands. Most of the success was due to the king's exemplary field commander, Sir Ralph Hopton of Witham Priory in Somerset – the overall commander being the lethargic and bookish Marquis of Hertford. Like many other young men of his class, Hopton had spent time as a soldier in Europe, where he had been a brother-in-arms of William Waller in the service of Queen Elizabeth of Bohemia. They had become firm friends, and both had entered parliament, but now they were pitting their military wits against each other. A thoughtful man who believed that change should be gradual but not ignored, Hopton had supported the attainder of Strafford and assisted in the presentation of the Grand Remonstrance to the king, but when sides had to be taken in 1642 he concluded that his duty lay with Charles and he returned to Somerset to start raising forces for the Royalist cause.

Somerset was solidly Puritan and, despite his routing the smaller parliamentary forces during the late summer, lack of support forced Hopton to seek men further west. Initially he met with little success. An attempted muster at Bodmin attracted barely two hundred men, leaving him to complain that they treated it as 'a great fair'; and shortly after riding into Cornwall he was arraigned by the assizes in Truro for bringing armed men into the county. Hopton was acquitted immediately, but an important point had been made to him: support should not be taken for granted, especially when the harvest still had to be brought in. There were other problems. While Cornwall was a natural ally of the king and its trained bands offered him their loyalty, they were badly armed, had little training and the men made it clear that they did not wish to serve outside their county. Using what few troops he had at his disposal, Hopton began his campaign by occupying Launceston and using it as a base for raiding into neighbouring Devon, and in so doing training up his Cornish infantrymen to be a formidable fighting force. That the clannish Cornishmen were prepared to follow an outsider says much for Hopton's powers of leadership. However his options were stymied by the parliamentary commander opposing him – Colonel William Ruthin, a Scottish soldier of fortune and the military governor of Plymouth – who constantly harried him across the River Tamar, the boundary between the two counties.

Much of the action was disparate and disorganised, usually little more than running raids or skirmishes as each side tested the other's capabilities. There was also a lack of focus. In addition to raising and training his forces, Hopton had to take into account the investment of Plymouth and Exeter as well as dealing with the threat posed by Ruthin, who was shortly reinforced by forces led by the Earl of Stamford. Anxious not to lose command, Ruthin sought a decisive engagement with the Royalist forces in south-west Cornwall and at the beginning of January 1643 moved his army up to Liskeard to threaten Lostwithiel. It was a sensible move – Stamford was marching on Bodmin to the north – but Ruthin was unaware that the Royalist forces had received fresh supplies of weapons and money from three parliamentary ships which had been forced to take shelter in the port of Falmouth and had already declared for the king. Re-equipped with fresh weapons and with morale riding high, Hopton's army had marched to meet the threat posed by Ruthin. On 18 January they found themselves camped in the grounds of Lord Mohun's estate at Boconnoc, three miles to the east of Lostwithiel and within sight of the parliamentary army.

Next morning brought the first confrontation on an open piece of heathland called Braddock Down, with Ruthin's men deployed on 'a pretty rising ground' to the east and Hopton's drawn up on the western side. The area was dotted with trees and bushes and surrounded by hedged enclosures, and any advantage lay with Hopton, as the rising ground allowed him to conceal his numbers from Ruthin. Among the Royalist regimental commanders was the legendary Cornish squire Sir Bevil Grenville, a giant of a man, standing over six feet in height, most of whose men were his retainers or tenants, and before any fighting took place he made sure that they had said their prayers. Not that there was any undue haste to engage in battle: as they faced one another across the winter heath they were content to fire off desultory musket shots or, as Grenville put it when he wrote to his wife after the battle, 'we saluted each other with bullets'.

Although the sides were evenly balanced the Royalist army had fewer horsemen but more infantry. The action began when Mohun, a Cornish magnate, brought out two pieces from Boconnoc which were then concealed below the infantry, with the cavalry, as was normal, forming the wings. After two hours' stand-off the parliamentary force began a tentative advance only to be surprised by a salvo from the two guns. At that point the men of Cornwall countered, advancing rapidly over the open ground with Grenville to the fore, leading his men on foot, while Hopton's cavalry charged into the flanks. Ruthin's men managed to discharge one round but the weight of the attack was too much for them and they quickly broke. 'I had the van,' remembered Grenville, 'and so, after some prayers at the head of every division, I led my part away, who followed me with so great courage, both down hill, one hill, and up the other, that it struck great terror in them.'[1]

Stunned by the ferocity and determination of the Cornishmen's charge the parliamentary forces were soon in full retreat, and if Hopton had had more cavalrymen under his command Ruthin's losses would have been higher. As it was, the rout continued to Liskeard, where the Royalist forces took over one thousand prisoners and captured a good deal of booty including the opposition's artillery pieces, which Ruthin had rashly left behind. It was a well-won triumph. The Cornish infantrymen had shown courage and determination in pushing home the attack against a force which contained greater numbers of cavalry and Hopton had read the battlefield well, using surprise in the opening stages and timing the charge which broke Ruthin's line. As a commander Hopton had a reputation for being a strict disciplinarian – 'pay well, command well, hang well,' was his motto – but he also knew how to earn the trust of his men, making sure not only that were they well provided for but also that they understood the nature of their cause. Getting the additional supplies from the three parliamentary ships had been a bonus, but in winning his men's commitment the telling factor had been his forceful leadership at Braddock Down. Heartened by their success, the Royalist army moved out of Cornwall in pursuit of Ruthin and inflicted another defeat on him at Saltash three days later. More supplies fell into Hopton's hands and his opponent was obliged to escape back to Plymouth in a small open boat.

The way should now have been open for Hopton's army to concentrate on the siege of Plymouth. It was a tempting prize, as possession of the port would be an important factor in creating a Royalist navy, but lacking specialist equipment and personnel the task proved to be beyond their capabilities. As both sides regrouped, and Stamford's force headed back into Devon, there was another outbreak of skirmishing. Hopton had sent a column to harry Stamford's army but it was soon in trouble. Although it drove off a parliamentary force at Kingsbridge commanded by Major-General James Chudleigh, the twenty-five-year-old son of a Devon squire, it came to grief at Chagford in the early morning of 8 February. Ambushed by parliamentary musketeers the Royalist troopers were unable to regroup and in the confusion lost a number of men, including the young poet Sidney Godolphin, a close friend of Falkland and known generally as 'little Sid'. His last words were hardly memorable – 'Oh

God, I am hurt' – but he was widely mourned, not least by Hopton, who thought he was 'as perfect and as absolute a piece of virtue as the nation ever bred'. Even the gruff Grenville was moved to tell his wife that they had lost a gallant gentleman.

As happened so often in this topsy-turvy war, revenge for a battle lost – in this case Braddock Down – was not long in coming. Forced to deploy his men over a wide area, Hopton paid the price on 21 February when a parliamentary force under Chudleigh surprised two of his regiments near the village of Modbury as he was riding towards Plymouth. Commanded by Sir Nicholas Slanning and Colonel John Trevanion, both Cornish grandees, the Royalist units had been lulled into a false sense of security and were clearly not expecting to see any opposition in the area. After a short but sharp encounter on a hillside to the east of the village the Royalists were forced to retreat towards Plympton, leaving behind a hundred dead, about as many prisoners and five artillery pieces. To show their contempt Chudleigh's men set about vandalising the local St George's Church and its graveyard.

The following day the Cornishmen started retreating back towards their own county and, sensing a stalemate, Hopton agreed to a local truce with Stamford and Ruthin which would continue until 22 April. This cessation of hostilities, welcomed by both sides, allowed Stamford and Hopton to regroup and re-equip. It also freed the newly formed Western Association army to begin the process of tying up the Severn plain and the approaches to south Wales, but although that was a reasonably successful operation Waller informed his Devon colleagues that, while useful, such truces were not welcomed by him:

> I am still of the same opinion that besides the distaste given thereby to Parliament there can be nothing more destructive to the Kingdom and to your own county than these treaties. The Kingdom will lose by this neutrality that strength which might have been derived from your own county, and in this way, while this and that county shall sit down and think to save their own stakes, leaving the burden of the war upon a few shoulders, his Majesty will with the more ease subdue our party in the field, and that done (being Master of the field) march with ease through every corner of the Kingdom, and then all the privilege those poor counties shall obtain that sat down first will be to be devoured last.[2]

Waller was not far wrong. Hopton used the break to re-equip his forces while Stamford was reinforced with more men and artillery. No sooner had the truce ended than hostilities commenced a day later after Chudleigh led a strong parliamentary force of 2500 men to attack Launceston, where Hopton was dug in on nearby Beacon Hill. The Royalist commander's superior position and the rough ground protected him, but until Slanning and Trevanion arrived later in the day he was heavily outnumbered and had to withstand a determined parliamentary assault on the hill. Towards evening, feeling that the advantage had switched to his forces, Hopton ordered his men to charge in three columns, and once again the speed and aggression unnerved the parliamentary infantry, who were soon routed. Only the onset of night and a well-fought rearguard action commanded by Chudleigh saved them from worse damage.

Two days later, on 25 April, the young parliamentary general extracted a measure of revenge when he and a small number of cavalrymen ambushed Hopton's column on Sourton Down, on the fringe of Dartmoor near Okehampton, killing 60 men and causing an unwarranted amount of panic. Realising that his opponents had been unmanned by the unexpected assault, Chudleigh called up his infantry from Okehampton and, as a huge thunderstorm broke overhead, there was confused fighting over the rough ground during which neither side gained any tactical advantage. However, in that Hopton's force retreated in disorder as far as Bude on the Atlantic coast – one of his officers fled from the battlefield dressed in women's clothes – it may be counted as a victory for Chudleigh, the more so as dawn revealed the presence of large numbers of Royalist horses and supplies. In the confusion Hopton had also left behind all his papers, including orders from the king to march into Somerset to meet up with Maurice's field force. Not only did this give a military advantage to Stamford but this moral victory put fresh heart into the parliamentary army. It also prompted the untruthful boast of the 'western wonder', satirised by Denham, when 'a hundred and ten slew five thousand men with the help of lightning and thunder'.

The repercussions of the rout on Sourton Down showed Hopton at his best as a commander of men. Having lost his portmanteau he knew that his plans had been revealed to Stamford, who was busy at Torrington mustering a force of almost 6000 men with which to march westwards and stop the Royalists in their tracks. He also knew that he was outnumbered over two to one – his force numbered only 2400 infantry and 500 horse – and that if Stamford managed to link up with Chudleigh there would be little that he could do to stop the parliamentary advance into Cornwall. His one hope was to go on the offensive and march rapidly towards Stamford's army, which had taken up a strong defensive position at the top of a sloping hill just to the north of the village of Stratton. Marching down from Bodmin on 15 May, Hopton immediately recognised the danger and held a war council at which 'it was quickly resolved, notwithstanding the great visible disadvantage, that they must either force the enemies' camp, while their horse and dragoons were from them, or unavoidably perish'.[3]

The parliamentary army was dug in behind one of the ancient earthworks which dot the area – East Leigh Berrys lies to the east – and the hill itself was protected to the east by a steep wooded slope. However the slopes to the west, north and south were not so difficult that they would daunt determined men, and despite the setback on Sourton Down Hopton's Cornishmen still had the memories of Braddock Down and Launceston to sustain them. The battle would be won by hard pounding from the infantrymen, who would have to attack open ground, win it and dislodge their opponents. To do that Hopton decided to mount a central assault from the west led by Grenville while he and Mohun would attack from the south and two other columns under the command of Thomas Bassett and William Godolphin would complete the pincer from the north. If pressed home strongly enough Stamford's men would be trapped, and the precipitous eastern slope would put a difficult obstacle in the path of any exit route.

The battle began just after dawn, and although the Cornish infantry showed their traditional doggedness in attack the parliamentary positions remained intact. By mid-afternoon both sides were running out of ammunition, and with stalemate approaching, or at the very least a tactical withdrawal by the men of Cornwall, the battle was decided by a rash and unexplained sally by Chudleigh, who led out his men to attack the Royalist centre. There was some confusion when Grenville was injured but in attacking down the slope the parliamentary soldiers were soon cut off and surrounded. In the ensuing mêlée Chudleigh was captured. For Stamford this proved a double disaster: not only had the move failed but it left a gap in his defences which Hopton and Mohun were able to exploit. Within an hour their men had pushed into the parliamentary flank just shy of the summit and the battle was as good as over. Once again Stamford's men were forced to flee, leaving behind them a large quantity of booty including 13 artillery pieces, 70 barrels of gunpowder and large supplies of welcome provisions. Three hundred soldiers lay dead and a further 1700 were taken prisoner. It was a satisfying victory, well worth the consequent verse which Denham wrote for *Mercurius Aulicus*:

> But now on which side was this miracle try'd,
> I hope that at last we are even;
> For Sir Ralph and his knaves are risen from their graves
> To cudgel the clowns of Devon.

In fact the Battle of Stratton* was much more than an opportunity for the Royalist army to avenge itself after the night of thunder and lightning on Sourton Down. With Stamford having fled back to Exeter, Cornwall was once again in Royalist hands, and apart from Plymouth and Exeter Devon would soon follow as people saw which way the tide was running. An added bonus came from Chudleigh's decision to switch his allegiance following a lengthy discussion with Hopton and Grenville. Three weeks later he was joined by his father, another parliamentary commander, who declared: 'I have thrown myself at my Sovereign's feet, and embraced his gracious pardon.'[4] Better still, as far as Hopton was concerned, he received news from Oxford that Maurice and Hertford were marching westwards with 2500 men, including much-needed cavalry, to join up with him at Chard in Somerset – which they did on 4 June. With Stamford's men scattered, wounded or demoralised, the task of countering this new western army fell to Waller, who was fruitlessly engaged in attempting to force Worcester into surrender. As the Royalist army consolidated itself in Somerset, occupying the main towns of Taunton, Wells and

---

* Stamford lost the battle but his name lives on in the area: today the hill over which the battle was fought is known as Stamford Hill.

Bridgwater, the way was now open for the two veterans and friends of the Bohemian wars to fight it out on an English battlefield.

Waller's first move was to march his army south to Bath, which he entered towards the end of June to await the arrival of the Royalist forces from the north. As the two armies manoeuvred in the area around the city Hopton wrote to his old friend suggesting a truce to exchange captured men and to call a temporary halt to hostilities. Waller was much moved but his opposition to any cease-fire was absolute and on 16 June he replied to his 'noble friend' in terms which are not only moving but which spell out the central dilemma faced by men from similar backgrounds but fighting on opposite sides:

> The experience I have had of your worth, and the happiness I have enjoyed in your friendship, are wounding considerations when I look upon this present distance between us. Certainly my affections to you are so unchangeable that hostility itself cannot violate my friendship to your person, but I must be true to the cause wherein I serve. The old limitation usque ad aras* holds still and where my conscience is interested all other obligations are swallowed up. I should most gladly wait on you according to your desire, but that I look upon you as you are engaged in that party beyond a possibility of retreat and consequently incapable of being wrought upon by any persuasion. And I know the conference could never be so close between us, but that it would take wind and receive a construction to my dishonour. That great God, which is the searcher of my heart, knows with what a sad sense I go upon this service, and with what a perfect hatred I detest this war without an enemy, but I look upon it as opus domini [work of the lord], which is enough to silence all passions in me. The God of Peace in his good time send us peace, and in the meantime fit us to receive it; we are both upon the stage, and must act the parts assigned to us in this tragedy. Let us do it in a way of honour, and without personal animosities. Whatever the issue be, I shall never willingly relinquish the dear title of, Your most affectionate friend and faithful servant.[5]

---

* *amicus usque ad aras*. A friend even to the altar (of sacrifice); i.e., to the last extremity.

Three weeks later the two old friends were at each other's throats on a long steep-sided ridge to the north of Bath known as Lansdown Hill. Initially all the advantage lay with Waller, who had come out of the city on 4 July to meet the Royalist advance. On the high ground his men had thrown up breastworks of earth and stone to protect their musketeers and seven artillery pieces and this was flanked by woods which hid his cavalry and reserves. To Hopton it must have looked impregnable: early next morning the parliamentary army enjoyed the advantage of a superior position while his force was stretched out over a wide area to the north, or as one Royalist eye-witness, Lieutenant-Colonel Walter Slingsby, put it, 'thus fortified stood the fox gazing at us when our whole army was ranged in order of battle upon the large cornfield near Tughill'. A frontal attack being out of the question the two sides faced one another over the dead ground, Waller's men in their fortified position on Lansdown Hill, down from which they could fire their cannon, and Hopton's in the exposed fields below.

What followed next decided the course of the battle. After a two-hour stand-off Hopton decided that discretion was the better option and began to move his forces away from the hill towards the nearby village of Marshfield. For Waller the sight proved to be too much of a temptation and shortly after one o'clock he ordered the cavalry under Colonel Robert Burrell to charge down the hill, forsaking their position, while dragoons hidden from view behind the hedgerows also advanced in good order. Once in range of the rear of the Royalist cavalry they fired into its ranks, causing panic and confusion, and as the horses reared and bucked the line broke. This could have spelled disaster for the Royalist army but the Cornish infantrymen kept their nerve and refused to budge, firing their muskets into Burrell's horsemen and stopping the attack in its tracks.

Cornish blood was now up. Realising that his men were gaining a tactical advantage, Hopton gave the order to attack and amid fierce musket and cannon fire the Cornish infantry began to advance towards the hill with the cavalry in the centre. Moving on the flanks through the woods the infantry could take cover behind the walls and hedges which ran through the area, but the horsemen in the centre were forced to receive the brunt of the fierce parliamentary fire. By mid-afternoon the bulk of the infantry had reached the top and under Grenville's command had created a defensive line of pikemen and musketeers to meet the parliamentary cavalry's counter-attack. For Richard Atkyns, a troop commander, who was bringing up the Royalist reserves, this was the crux of the battle, an hour of close-quarter fighting which saw the tables being turned as Burrell's troopers failed in three separate charges to dislodge the men of Cornwall:

> As I went up the hill, which was very steep and hollow, I met several dead and wounded officers brought off, besides several running away, that I had much ado to get up by them. When I came to the top of the hill I saw Sir Bevil Grenville's stand of pikes, which certainly preserved our army from total rout with the loss of his most precious life. They stood as eaves of an house for steepness, but as unmovable as a rock. On which side of this stand of pikes our horse were, I could not discover, for the air was darkened by the smoke of the powder that for a quarter of an hour together (I dare say) there was no light seen, but what the fire of the volleys of shot gave; and 'twas the greatest storm that ever I saw, in which though I knew not whither to go, nor what to do, my horse had two or three musket bullets in immediately, which made him tremble under me at the rate, and I could hardly with spurs keep him from lying down; but he did me the service to carry me off to a led horse and then died.[6]

Horses were not the only casualties. Although the tightly knit ranks of pikemen had withstood the frantic charges of the opposition cavalry – tactics which had been developed by the Swiss in the fifteenth century – their triumph was blighted by the death of Bevil Grenville, who was axed in the head and died not long afterwards. His death was doubly poignant: not only did his fellow Cornishmen feel that they had lost a talismanic leader but before the outbreak of war Grenville's and Waller's family had been close friends. As he lay dying the battle gradually ground to a halt as the exhausted parliamentary survivors retreated south along the ridge to take up position behind a long wall. With Hopton's men now using the breastworks as their defences the two armies faced each other across a new divide, but darkness and combat exhaustion combined to prevent any further thought of fighting. Walter Slingsby noted that only the lights and occasional musket fire gave any indication of where they were positioned:

Thus stood the two armies taking breath looking upon each other, our cannon on both sides playing without ceasing till it was dark, legs and arms flying apace, the two armies being within musket shot. After it was dark there was great silence on both sides, at which time our right wing of shot got much nearer their army lodging themselves amongst the many little pits betwixt the wall and the wood from whence we galled them cruelly.

About 11 of the clock we received a very great volley of small shot but not mixed with cannon by which some of us judged that he was retreating and gave this at his expiring. But the general apprehension through our army was that the enemy had intention to try a push in the night for their ground, which they had so dishonourably lost. For we were then seated like a heavy stone upon the very brow of the hill, which with one lusty charge might well have been rolled to the bottom.[7]

Slingsby's fears, though logical, proved to be groundless. Around midnight Waller's army started withdrawing and made their way back to Bath, leaving behind them lighted matches in the wall to confuse the enemy about their real intentions. It had been a hard bruising day, and in that Hopton's men had cleared the parliamentary army from their position on Lansdown Hill they were left as the masters of the field. The battle had been won by Hopton, and Waller, usually so good at reading ground, had made basic tactical errors which had been fully exploited by the courage and dash of the Cornish infantrymen. It should have been a great victory and would have been had not disaster struck the following day. In an accident which was all too common at the time a lighted match was struck on an ammunition wagon (in this case by a parliamentary prisoner) causing it to explode and killing or wounding those in the vicinity. One of those hurt was Hopton, who had come up to inspect the prisoners. Richard Atkyns was on the scene just as the explosion occurred, but luckily for him he was 'three horse lengths' away:

It made a very great noise and darkened the air for a time, and the hurt men made lamentable screeches. As soon as the air was clear, I went to see what the matter was. There I found his Lordship [Hopton] miserably burnt, his horse singed like parched leather, and

Thomas Sheldon* (that was a horse's length further from the blast) complaining that the fire was got within his breeches, which I tore off as soon as I could, and from as long a flaxen head of hair as ever I saw, in the twinkling of an eye, his head was like a blackamoor. His horse was hurt and run away like mad, so that I put him upon my horse and got two troopers to hold him up on both sides and bring him to the headquarters, while I marched after the regiment.[8]

From Lansdown Hill Hopton was taken to nearby Marshfields, where his wounds were tended and his badly shocked men regrouped. Now it was the turn of the Royalist army to be on the receiving end and victory was rapidly turning into the possibility of defeat; their leader was badly wounded and shorn of cavalry they were left badly exposed. It was all very different in Waller's camp, which was being reinforced by the Bristol garrison. The sound of the explosion and the news of Hopton's injury came as a badly needed fillip. As the Royalist army moved east towards Chippenham and Devizes on 7 July their spirits were as low as their supplies. The Cornishmen were still grieving for their lost leader and Walter Slingsby could not help noticing that the country people of Wiltshire wanted to have nothing to do with them, 'so that we could get neither meal nor intelligence, two necessary things for an army'.[9]

Naturally Waller took full advantage of the Royalist plight and set out after them to force a decisive battle before Hopton could reach the safety of Devizes. It was a close-run chase: the Royalist army reached the town on the night of 9 July and Waller's army arrived early next morning to begin the siege, placing their artillery pieces on a high bluff to the east of the town. For Hopton this was the last straw. His army had almost run out of ammunition, the weather was wet (as it was most of that summer) and he was desperately short of cavalry. A war council was held chaired by Hopton, who was carried in on a stretcher and it was decided that the seriousness of the position required a desperate remedy. They would try to hold Devizes with the infantry while Maurice and Hertford took the remaining horsemen back to Oxford to get reinforcements. Against all the odds the break-out succeeded, riding fifty miles in one madcap night, but they

---

* Major Thomas Sheldon, an officer in Prince Maurice's regiment.

arrived only to find that Rupert had taken most of the Royalist cavalry into the Midlands to meet Henrietta Maria. However, Wilmot's brigade was already on the road, and to this was added Byron's men, giving the Royalists a bare 2000 cavalrymen when they made their rendezvous near Marlborough on 13 July.

Speed was of the essence. The Royalist horsemen set off immediately, even though some of them had ridden through the night, and by mid-morning they had reached a shallow valley to the north-east of Devizes where Waller's army had taken up position to the west. Bounded by two rolling hills, one of which, Roundway Down, gave its name to the battle, the open plain made a natural battlefield. It was also natural cavalry country, and Wilmot took full advantage of it. Attacking from the left with Byron on the right the Royalist horse charged Waller's flanks and the fighting quickly became a cavalryman's battle, with the parliamentary infantry in the centre unable to fire their muskets for fear of killing their own people. The fighting lasted little more than half an a hour and, although Waller's force contained Hesilrige's heavily armoured 'Lobsters', the speed and ferocity of the Royalist charge broke the opposition's lines. Terrified and out of control, many turned and fled to the west of the plain where there is a drop of some three hundred feet. Unable to rein up they clattered down the precipitous slope to meet a fate which is aptly described in the name given to the position after the battle – Bloody Ditch.

Those who survived fled, to leave the foot to meet the Cornish infantry now marching resolutely out from Devizes. At the same time Wilmot regrouped his cavalry to attack the unprotected and badly demoralised parliamentary infantry, who were soon overwhelmed. Six hundred were killed on Roundway Down, and over 1000 captured, along with their weapons and supplies. The Western Association army had been destroyed in less than two hours, leaving the Royalists with their most sweeping victory of the war. 'We must needs look upon this as the hand of our God, mightily against us for 'twas he only that made us fly,' wrote Captain Edward Harley, a parliamentary cavalry officer, after the battle. 'We had very much self-confidence, and I trust the Lord has only brought this upon us to make us look more to him, whom I am confident, when we are weakest, will show himself a glorious God over the enemies of his Truth.'[10] Within a fortnight events would show that Harley's God was not yet in a position to help.

Taking advantage of the destruction of Waller's army, Rupert set off with Hertford and 5500 men to join Hopton's army in the investment of the port of Bristol, England's second city. It was stoutly defended – the rivers Frome and Avon provided a natural boundary and the defences consisted of earthworks and ditches – but against those advantages the garrison had been weakened by the removal of 1200 men who had fought at Roundway Down and the governor Nathaniel Fiennes, a gloomy Puritan much given to prayer, did not enjoy the whole-hearted support of the city's merchants. A determined siege would probably have broken the inhabitants' resolve, but Rupert did not care to wait and at a war council on 25 July it was decided to storm the defences the following day, the main weight of the attack coming from the north and north-west while Maurice led the Cornish infantry from the south.

For the Royalists the day began badly. The Cornish infantry met determined opposition as they tried to scale the walls and in the hand-to-hand fighting lost Slanning and Trevanion, the two regimental commanders who had served Grenville so well. However, encouraged by Rupert, whose 'very name was half a conquest', the other Royalist forces fared better, and by mid-afternoon the outer earthworks had been breached and the inner defences were being fiercely contested. As the fighting continued in the narrow streets, casualties mounted on both sides and, running short of ammunition, Fiennes had no option but to surrender the city to Rupert. Faced by a determined attack and having too few men to defend his long perimeter defences the parliamentary governor was in an impossible position, and on his return to London did not deserve to be sentenced to death as a coward and a traitor. Happily Essex's intervention saved Fiennes's life, but even so, as he and his defeated men marched out of the city, they were treated to the indignity of being jeered and jostled by the Royalist soldiers. Just as bad, as Nehemiah Wallington noted with disgust from London, they marched out of the city knowing that Bristol was being left to the licentious behaviour of the ungodly men who were about to be quartered on its inhabitants:

This puts them to an intolerable charge, and the more, because divers of the Cavaliers will not be content to feed upon good beef, but must have mutton and veal, and chickens, with wine and tobacco each meal, and much ado to please them at all; causing, also, men, women and children to lie upon boards, while these Cavaliers possess their beds, which they fill with vermin. Besides, they fill the ears of the inhabitants with their blasphemous, filthy and wicked language, which no chaste ear, nor honest heart, can endure; yea, so desperately wicked are they, that those that billet them dare not perform any act of religion, neither to give thanks at meals, nor yet to pray, read or sing Psalms; but, instead thereof, they fill their houses with swearings and cursings, insomuch that they corrupt men's servants and children, that those who were formerly civil have now learned to curse and swear almost as bad as they.[11]

Of the two deprivations Wallington was in no two minds which was worse – the Royalists were also guilty of swearing on the Sabbath – but there is little doubt that the city of Bristol was not altogether unhappy at the outcome. Though courageous – he had proved that at Powick Bridge – Fiennes had been an unpopular governor. The Royalist presence brought the chance of opening up trade and as the city was the door to the West Country, most of which was in the king's hands, the time was ripe to change sides. Charles, too, benefited. Not only did he take possession of Fiennes's supplies and ammunition, including his war chest of £100,000, but eighteen merchant ships and four parliamentary warships came over to his cause to create the foundation of a Royalist navy. All that remained was to take Gloucester and open up the Severn valley and parliament's discomfort would be complete.

Fresh from his rout at Roundway Down, Waller had arrived back in London, where he promptly excused his leadership in the battle by blaming Essex for not coming to his assistance. The setback also incited demonstrations for peace balanced by fresh demands for a change in leadership and a more rigorous direction of the war. While it had been a good summer for the king – Bideford and Barnstaple fell to Maurice's Cornish army in August and Exeter followed on 4 September to complete his mastery of the west – the same could not be said for Pym and his colleagues.

Chapter Six

CHANGING FORTUNES:
THE WAR IN THE NORTH

'So let them now thy works plain see
Saying my little flock shall Conquerors be
And it was true Fairfax was then more great
But yet Newcastle made him sure retreat.'

Jane Cavendish, daughter of the Earl of Newcastle,
On the Thirtieth of June to God *(1643)*

It was not just in the west that Charles's fortunes were riding high.
That summer of 1643 also saw the fall of the key cities of Bradford and
Leeds and, although the port of Hull remained in parliament's hands,
a convincing victory at Adwalton Moor at the end of June had left
Yorkshire very much in the control of Newcastle's northern army.
While it was not enough to allow an advance to be made towards
London – Cromwell's presence in Lincolnshire blocked the way –
Newcastle still controlled the northern coalfields and had created an
army which showed itself well capable of beating Fairfax's
parliamentary forces. Newcastle had also had to fight hard to collect
allies to the king's cause, especially in Yorkshire, where support was
divided: just as Cornwall had been the key to gaining control of the
West Country so too did it fall to the great Royalist magnate to
impose himself on the northern counties.

A man in middle life when war broke out, William Cavendish, Earl
of Newcastle, immediately put his fortune at the king's service and
was perhaps the greatest aristocratic supporter of Charles's cause. A
nephew of the Earl of Devonshire, he entertained in regal style at his

seat, Welbeck, and in 1638 had been rewarded for his ostentatious loyalty to the Crown by being appointed governor to Charles I's children. In Clarendon's words, 'amorous in poetry and music' Newcastle had been a courtier to James I and during that time had developed a fine reputation as a patron of the arts. His clients included Van Dyck and he enjoyed the friendship of the philosopher Thomas Hobbes and the poet and dramatist Ben Jonson, who accompanied him on a walking tour of Scotland in 1617. Young Cavendish was also a man of action who was considered to be one of the finest horsemen of his day, his feats encouraging Jonson to write of him:

> When first, my Lord, I saw you back your horse,
> Provoke his mettle and command his force
> To all the uses of the field and race,
> Methought I read the ancient art of Thrace,
> And saw a Centaur past those tales of Greece,
> So seem'd your horse and you both of a piece![1]

This was not just flattery in return for a patron's interest: Newcastle might have appeared a wealthy and self-indulgent fop but he was also a good athlete made hard by country pursuits and an obsession with fencing. In January 1642 he had proved his abilities by riding sixty miles through the night in a vain attempt to persuade Sir John Hotham to declare Hull for the king, gaining admittance to the port by subterfuge 'in the quality of a private gentleman'. The mission failed, but with war approaching Charles had no hesitation in creating Newcastle the military governor of his four northernmost counties – Northumberland, Durham, Cumberland and Westmoreland – and granting him plenipotentiary powers. With typical energy Newcastle began raising an army and forming it into brigades and regiments, the task made easier by the size of his fortune and his belief that 'all men follow the purse'. The most notable of his units were the four regiments of Whitecoat foot soldiers, the famous 'Lambs', so-called on account of their pure woollen jackets, who were among the best infantry on either side. In fact only two regiments wore white, the others red and black, but the nickname stuck. His second wife Margaret left an attractive picture of the energy and drive which her husband brought to the task of raising an army from scratch. Money, connections and authority counted for much, but resolve and loyalty to Charles also prompted him 'rather to hazard all, than to neglect the commands of his sovereign':

> As soon as my lord came to Newcastle, in the first place he sent for all his tenants and friends in those parts, and presently raised a troop of horse consisting of 120, and a regiment of foot, and put them under command, and upon duty and exercise in the town of Newcastle. With this small beginning he took the government of that place upon him; where with the assistance of the townsmen, particularly the mayor and the rest of his brethren, within days he fortified the town, and raised men daily, and put a garrison into Tynemouth Castle, standing on the River Tyne, between Newcastle and the sea, to secure that port, and armed the soldiers as well as he could. Thus he stood upon his guard, and continued them upon duty; playing his weak game with much prudence, and giving the town and country very great satisfaction by his noble and honourable deportment.[2]

With the Scots mercenary Lord Eythin as the lieutenant-general in charge of the foot and the mercurial Goring commanding the horse, it was soon a formidable force, and Newcastle proved to be an able and energetic overall commander, his lack of experience in the field compensated for by his quiet authority and military demeanour. Clarendon noted that 'he liked the pomp and absolute authority of a general well and preserved the dignity of it to the full'. On the other hand Newcastle caused great offence in the parliamentary camp by appointing Catholics to command, but excused himself with the thought that, as Protestants had risen against the king while Catholics had not, he was honour-bound to use them to put down the rebellion. For his pains he was impeached, in absentia, by parliament.

Newcastle's principal opponent was Lord Fairfax, the commander of the parliamentary forces in Yorkshire, where there was a local agreement among opposing landowners not to commence hostilities. Fairfax's appointment in October 1642 ended the agreement, as did the bellicose behaviour of Sir John Hotham and his son in Hull, and Newcastle had no option but to listen to local Royalist appeals and march 8000 men into the county. Leeds and Wakefield were occupied and in the first encounter of the northern campaign – an inconclusive encounter at Tadcaster on 6 December 1642 – Fairfax was forced to withdraw to Selby. This allowed Newcastle to seize Tadcaster and in so doing to cut off Fairfax from his main source of support in the West Riding wool towns. A second force was sent south under Sir John Henderson, another experienced Scottish mercenary, to secure the town of Newark and its vital north–south crossing over the River Trent. The year ended with the Royalists having gained the upper hand and on 16 December Newcastle was duly thanked by the king for his efforts:

> The services I have received from you have been so eminent, and is likely to have so great an influence upon all my affairs, that I need not tell you that I shall never forget it, but always look upon you as a principal instrument in keeping the crown upon my head. This business of Yorkshire I account almost done.[3]

Not for the last time the king's optimism was misplaced. Yorkshire was very much unfinished business, and two people were to intrude on Newcastle's domain to make his life more difficult. The first was Henrietta Maria, arriving with her supplies from Europe, and the second was the generalship displayed by Sir Thomas Fairfax, Lord Fairfax's son, the so-called 'Rider on the White Horse'. (He was also known as 'Black Tom'.) Both, in their different ways, weighed heavily on Newcastle's command: the presence of the queen put an extra strain on his administration as he had to defend her presence and arrange for her convoy to be moved south, while the introduction of the younger Fairfax into the field provided him with a difficult opponent. The latter had already shown his mettle by retaking Bradford and on 23 January he interrupted the closed campaigning season by doing the same to Leeds, which fell after a two-hour battle. The seizure of both towns restored the links to the West Riding, and during the fighting young Fairfax had displayed the qualities which would make him such a great leader of men: an ability to read a battle, personal courage, even-handedness and an abiding concern for his soldiers' welfare. He also put his faith in God's help for the cause, writing after an encounter later that spring, 'I cannot but here acknowledge God's goodness to me this day.'

Shaken by the upset, Newcastle was obliged to retire into York and immediately set about reinforcing its defences in advance of the queen's arrival. Showing typical canniness he made the work self-sufficient by introducing compulsory civilian labour and putting up the local taxes to pay for the materials. The queen's arrival also proved to be an expensive burden – she reached the city on 8 March. Although Henrietta Maria delighted in riding on horseback among the soldiers and took an inordinate amount of pleasure in being styled the 'she-generalissima' her presence in the city was a distraction. As the queen she demanded due deference, and being an inveterate intriguer she used her residence as a smaller version of the court. Thus her presence tended to undermine Newcastle's position, not least because she insisted on attending his councils of war. That being said, she helped him to persuade Sir Hugh Cholmley to surrender Scarborough to the Royalist cause and worked equally hard, though ultimately unsuccessfully, to encourage the Hothams to take the same route.

Even when she left for Oxford at the beginning of June it was a mixed blessing. At a time when Newcastle was under pressure to move his entire northern army south to reinforce the king, he had to find troops for her escort, which was commanded by his young cousin Charles Cavendish. There was also still much business to be done before Yorkshire could be brought under Royalist control. At the end of February, shortly after the queen's arrival at Bridlington, the road south had been threatened when a parliamentary force, drawn from Lincolnshire, Derbyshire and Nottinghamshire and led by Colonel Thomas Ballard, attacked Newark. Over two days of fighting it succeeded in breaking into the town's fortifications on 28 February and only determined resistance by Henderson's garrison allowed the town to hold out. According to Lucy Hutchinson, who might be biased on account of her husband's presence, the Lincolnshire and Derbyshire men 'ran away' while the men of her own county were only forced to retreat through their commander's lack of effectiveness:

The lieutenant-colonel [Francis Pierrepoint, third son of the Earl of Kingston] in vain importuned Ballard to send them ammunition and relief, but could obtain neither, and so they were forced, unwillingly, to retreat, which they did in such good order, the men first, and then their captains, that they lost not a man coming off. The town was sallying upon them, but they discharged a drake [small cannon] and beat them back. The next day all the captains importuned Ballard that they might fall on again; so that the Nottingham forces returned with great dissatisfaction, though Ballard, to stop their mouths, gave them two pieces of ordnance.[4]

Earlier, and with much distaste, Lucy Hutchinson had noted that the defenders of Newark were mostly 'Irish papists' and that Sir John Henderson was probably one himself. No doubt her prejudice was fanned by the numbers of Catholics in Newcastle's army, but Henderson was a good commander whose worth was recognised with Ballard's dismissal and the appointment of the experienced Meldrum to replace him. Had Newark fallen Charles would have been cut off from the north and the expected supplies being brought by his wife.

With the coming of spring both sides were anxious to retrieve the advantage in Yorkshire. In an attempt to consolidate his position Fairfax decided to concentrate his forces at Leeds and he sent his son to the north on 30 March to cover him near Tadcaster. Thinking that this presaged a bigger attack on York itself, Newcastle sent out Goring with 1200 horse to investigate and he intercepted the parliamentary force on the open expanse of Bramham Moor to the south-west. Fairfax then ordered his infantry to retreat while he and his vastly inferior numbers of cavalry engaged Goring's force on the approaches to the moor. As the parliamentary force marched off, the skirmishes developed into a running battle on Seacroft Moor just outside Leeds. The exhausted infantrymen were no match for Goring's cavalry, who charged into their defenceless flanks. Not having enough pikemen, Fairfax was unable to form a defensive line, and his men were soon in trouble as the horsemen rode into their midst firing off their carbines and cutting down the rest with the sword. Although large numbers managed to get off the moor into the safety of Leeds, 200 men lay dead and four times that number were taken prisoner – 'the greatest losses' he had had to date, noted Fairfax after the fighting was over.

Revenge was not long in coming. Seven weeks later, on the night of 21 May 1643, Fairfax made a night attack on Wakefield with the intention of capturing some Royalist troops to exchange for those he had lost outside Leeds. Commanding the garrison was Goring, who was lying sick – whether from drink or illness is not clear – and although the Royalists had a numerical advantage Fairfax had the element of surprise. After 'a hot encounter' in the barricaded streets the town fell. As happens so often in this kind of confused fighting in built-up areas the margin between defeat and victory is not only slender but can hang on the outcome of bizarre incidents. At one point in the fighting Fairfax found himself trapped in a street full of Royalist troops; his capture would have been a terrible blow to his men's morale, but thinking quickly and having the benefit of two prisoners who kept their parole he managed to charge over a barricade and reach his own side:

> For, being advanced a good way, single before my men, having a [Royalist] colonel and lieutenant-colonel who had engaged themselves to be my prisoners only with me, and many of the enemy now between me and my men, I lighted upon a regiment of foot standing in the market-place. Being thus compassed and thinking what to do, I spied a lane which, I thought, would lead me back to my men again. At the end of this lane there was a corps de guard of the enemy's with fifteen or sixteen soldiers, who were just then quitting it with a sergeant leading them off whom we met. And seeing their officers, they came up to us taking no notice of me and asked them what they would have them do, for that they could keep the work no longer, the Roundheads (as they called them) came so fast upon them.
>
> The gentlemen who had passed their words to me to be my true prisoners said nothing. And, looking one upon another, I thought it not fit now to own them as prisoners, much less to bid the rest to render themselves to me. But, being well-mounted and seeing a place in the works where men used to go-over, I rushed from them and made my horse leap over the work. And, by a good providence got back to my men again . . . .[5]

Chivalry was still alive at that stage of the fighting, but for Fairfax the main consideration was the scale of his triumph when Wakefield eventually surrendered. This was 'more a miracle than a victory': 1500 Royalists fell into his hands, including Goring, who was sent to

London and later exchanged for a Scottish nobleman, the Earl of Lothian.* Goring's loss forced Newcastle to rely more heavily on the experienced but prudent Eythin, who was closer to him in age and who had already cautioned him not to attack Leeds in the aftermath of Seacroft Moor as such a move might 'cause the ruin of all the army, by too severe a slaughter'.

While attempting to impose himself on Yorkshire Newcastle was also taking steps to move his forces further south. Before leaving to escort the queen to Oxford Charles Cavendish had been involved in a series of raids further south, threatening Lincolnshire, which still had a significant number of Royalist supporters despite the fact that the county had sided largely with parliament. On 23 March, supported by Henderson and Colonel-General Henry Hastings, Cavendish captured Grantham and cut the road between York and London, a move that seemed to presage a full-scale invasion of the county. If so, the intention was made clearer when the Royalist force moved towards Boston, where they were engaged on Ancaster Heath by a smaller parliamentary force led by the younger Hotham and Lord Willoughby of Parham, a strict Puritan and the local commander for Lincolnshire. Having more cavalry at his disposal Cavendish ordered them to charge into the undefended parliamentary ranks and the fighting was soon over. Had Newcastle been able to uncouple his forces from Yorkshire to support his cousin, a move against London was a distinct possibility, but that was stymied by the continuing activity of the younger Fairfax and, in the south, by the arrival on the scene of forces led by Cromwell.

On 10 April, the day before the rout of Willoughby's force outside Boston, Cromwell had arrived in Huntingdon with five troops of horse and the promise of reinforcements drawn from the army of the Eastern Association. Although he was let down by its commander, the querulous Lord Grey of Groby, who argued that his first duty was the defence of Leicestershire, within a fortnight Cromwell had joined two other commanders, Sir Miles Hobart and Sir Anthony Irby, who were busily but fruitlessly besieging the village and old abbey of Croyland.

---

* William Kerr, Earl of Lothian, 'a bitter Covenanter and ever at the command of Argyll', had been sent to France to seek military support in December 1642. On his return he had been arrested by Charles and imprisoned in Bristol.

Ironically, the small Royalist garrison was led by one of Cromwell's cousins and it was proving a difficult position to take, mainly because the abbey was positioned on rising ground surrounded by marshland. It was not until 28 April that it fell following a brisk artillery bombardment.

Denied support from Grey, Cromwell and his fellow commanders joined up with the remnant of the forces defeated at Ancaster Heath and marched north, hoping to engage the Royalist army at Grantham. Having made their rendezvous at Sleaford on 9 May they entered Grantham two days later to find that the Royalist army had retired from the town but were obviously still in the area. In fact Cavendish had moved his force to the nearby port of Gainsborough, which had been captured by a Royalist raiding party from Newark earlier in the year and which was now the base for their operations in east Lincolnshire. Being unaware of their presence Cromwell and Willoughby left Grantham and set off towards Newark with the intention of attacking it. However, on 13 May their plans were thwarted. In the early morning Cavendish's cavalry routed three parliamentary troops who had been resting in the village of Belton, a skirmish which led to a more heated engagement on the open ground beside the River Witham south-east of Tolthorp. On this occasion, though, Cavendish did not attack but chose to stand his ground, probably because the hour was late and light was fading, and that decision gave the advantage to the opposition. Following the customary exchange of musket fire the parliamentary cavalry, led by Cromwell, charged into Royalist lines and in the ensuing fighting at least 100 of Cavendish's men were killed, with Cromwell claiming that 'we lost but two men at the most on our side'. He also left a highly coloured account of his first cavalry action which is the only description of the fighting at Belton and a reminder that winners usually have the benefit of writing history.

> So soon as we had the alarm, we drew out of our forces, consisting of about twelve troops, whereof some of them so poor and broken, that you shall seldom see worse. With this handful it pleased God to cast the scale. For after we had stood a little above musket-shot the one body from the other and the dragooners having fired on both sides for the space of half an hour or more, they not advancing

towards us, we agreed to charge them, and advancing the body after many shots on both sides, came on with our troops a pretty round trot, they standing firm to receive us; and our men charging fiercely upon them, by God's providence they were immediately routed, and ran all away, and we had the execution of them two or three miles.[6]

Although the victory was not as complete as Cromwell claimed – it was not followed by an attack on Newark, the purpose of the expedition – it did teach him two lessons. First, as he had already witnessed at Edgehill, a determined attack by cavalry could force the opposition to break and, secondly, triumph in the field brought further rewards. When the news reached London parliament voted him £3000 for the further support of his efforts. God might have given him 'a glorious victory over our enemies', as he wrote that evening to a friend in a mood of exultation, but in the short term temporal benefits were just as rewarding.

Cromwell's victory outside Belton was, of course, trumpeted by the parliamentary press; at that stage in the war when the Royalists seemed to have the upper hand any victory in the field was to be applauded, and that week's edition of *Special Passages* (a parliamentary newspaper) went out of its way to praise Cromwell's '2000 brave men, well disciplined'. Given the circumstances the encomium was fully deserved, but it has to be said, too, that those same men had shown a disquieting lack of control while quartered in Peterborough, where they had sacked the local cathedral. While some of the excesses were exaggerated in *Mercurius Aulicus*, the better to paint the parliamentary army in a bad light, there is little doubt that Cromwell's men did deface the cathedral by destroying outward signs of popery such as communion rails and crucifixes. They also damaged prayer books and organs as being contrary to their own religious observances and had quartered their horses in the cathedral. (The practice was also observed by Royalist forces, especially if the building had been used for military purposes.) Religious zeal was one reason for the depredations, a breakdown in discipline another, but the sorry truth is that in a country caught up in warfare soldiers on the move did indulge in iconoclasm and casual plundering, the diarist John Evelyn noting that as the times were out of joint 'it is impossible to avoid the doing of very unhandsome things in war'. It is also true, as Cromwell's biographer points out, that his later fame made him more of a target for censure (as did his relationship to Thomas Cromwell, the destroyer of monasteries) and that he was probably neither better nor worse than many other field commanders of the time.[7]

Having savoured his first triumph in command Cromwell remained in the area to build up his strength and for the time being the position in the Newark–Nottingham–Peterborough triangle remained in stalemate, allowing Newcastle to concentrate once again on ridding Yorkshire of the threat posed by Fairfax's forces, by then garrisoned in Bradford. Once again the weather had turned unseasonable, long days of wind and rain turned the countryside into a mire and made transportation of guns and wagons difficult. On this score Newcastle's army was doubly discommoded, as two of their artillery pieces, huge demi-cannon nicknamed Gog and Magog, quickly became bogged down and were only moved with great effort. However, Newcastle was intent on engaging Fairfax and began moving his forces westwards in an attempt to flush the parliamentary army out of the West Riding. On the way he captured Howley House, the residence of Lord Savile, which had been commandeered by a cousin, Sir John Savile, and although he would have been within his rights to have shown him no quarter – the parliamentary soldiers put up a fierce fight and there were casualties on both sides – Newcastle decided to pardon him, arguing that it was wrong to kill a man in cold blood.

By the evening of 29 June 1643 the Royalist army had reached a high ridge to the east of Bradford on Adwalton Moor. With 10,000 men under his command Newcastle outnumbered the opposition two to one, but that arithmetic was no barrier to Lord Fairfax's ambitions. After dawn the following day he took his army out of Bradford, which was not best suited to withstand a siege, and marched towards the moor. The result was a set-piece battle with the parliamentary army drawn up in line, Fairfax in the centre, Sir Thomas Fairfax on the right and Major-General John Gifford's foot soldiers, many of them untrained levies, on the left. It was a sensible move: part of the force was deployed on the hidden southerly slopes, making it difficult for Newcastle to gauge his opponent's strength, and the ground was not ideal for cavalry, broken up as it was by old coal-workings and rough hedges. The local topography helped to even up the odds but, as had been the case elsewhere in the fighting of the summer of 1643, the result hung on the Royalist cavalry's ability to break their opponents' lines.

With Goring absent, command of the horse passed to Colonel George Heron, but he was killed in one of the first charges. On the right the fighting was particularly ferocious. Sir Thomas Fairfax had dismounted his horsemen and they and the musketeers were able to use the cover to good effect to give what he called a 'hot welcome'. Although a second charge saw Heron's men get behind the opposition it was not enough to break the right flank, and in the close-quarters fighting Royalist casualties were high. The fighting on the left was equally determined, with Gifford's men holding out against a determined attack by the Royalist infantry. At this stage in the battle all was confusion: the two sides had battered each other's lines with artillery fire and cavalry charges but neither had gained any advantage. The firing continued across the hedgerows, and with the cavalry unable to operate Newcastle decided to launch his pikemen, including the famous 'Lambs', against what he perceived to be Gifford's weaker flank. Led by Colonel Posthumous Kirton, 'a wild and desperate man', these shock troops 'broke into the very rage of battle, and with so much violence, fell upon the right wing of those rebels that those . . . turned their backs'. A sense of confusion giving way to elation comes out in the description which Newcastle gave to his second wife Margaret and which she was able to capture in her biography written later in life:

> At last the pikes of my lord's army having had no employment all the day, were drawn against the enemy's left wing, and particularly those of my lord's own regiment [the Lambs], which were all stout and valiant men, who fell so furiously upon the enemy, that they forsook their hedges, and fell to their heels. At which very instant my lord caused a shot or two to be made by his cannon against the body of the enemy's horse, drawn up within cannon shot, which took so good effect, that it disordered the enemy's troops. My lord's horse got over the hedge, not in a body (for that they could not), but dispersed two on a breast; and as soon as some considerable number was gotten over, and drawn up, they charged the enemy

and routed them. In an instant there was a strange change of fortune, and the field totally won by my lord, notwithstanding he had quitted 7000 men to conduct Her Majesty, besides a good train of artillery, which in such a conjuncture would have weakened Caesar's army.[8]

The charge settled the issue for Newcastle. Shaken by the unexpected Royalist advance, Gifford's flank broke, and as they began to flee the battlefield the Royalist artillery placed some intensive fire into Lord Fairfax's lines in the centre. Seeing their chance the cavalry renewed their efforts. Fairfax's army was as good as beaten and his part of the parliamentary army was soon in full retreat towards Leeds. Only his son held firm on the right, but as he became aware of the chaos further up the hill he was left with no option but to withdraw in an orderly fashion towards Halifax. For Newcastle it had been a crushing victory: he had taken 1400 prisoners as well as supplies and guns, 500 parliamentary soldiers failed to march off alive from Adwalton Moor, and to all intents and purposes the Fairfaxes had lost the West Riding.

Of the two, Sir Thomas had left the field in better shape – he had been dismayed by the breaking of Gifford's flank and had not been given any warning of his father's sudden retreat – and he was determined to try to hold Bradford, even though by his own account it was an 'untenable place'. By next day he had reached the town, having driven his men through the night, but any chance of defending the Yorkshire wool town was always going to be a forlorn hope. Newcastle's army with its superior artillery was outside the town on the high ground and although Fairfax tried to offset the advantage by placing two light cannon on the church tower, protected by woolpacks, they quickly became a prime target. By 2 July, a Sunday, all resistance had come to an end, leaving Fairfax with no option but to start negotiations for a general surrender. Later that night he and a small force of cavalry broke out of the town, leaving it open to Newcastle's men. The inhabitants expected a bloodbath: before escaping himself, a young apprentice called Joseph Lister described his fellow citizens' worst fears:

But oh! what a night and morning was that in which Bradford was taken! What weeping and wringing of hands! None expected to live any longer than till the enemies came into the town, the Earl of Newcastle having charged his men to kill all, man, woman and child, in the town, and to give them all Bradford quarter, for the brave Earl of Newport's sake.* However, God so ordered it, that before the town was taken, the Earl gave a different order, that quarter should be given to all the townsmen . . .

Some desperate fellows wounded several persons, that died of their wounds afterwards; but I think not more than half a score were slain; and that was a wonder, considering what hatred and rage they came with against us. But we were all beholden to God, who tied their hands and saved our lives.[9]

Among those saved was Thomas Fairfax's wife, Anne, the daughter of Sir Horace Vere, but having treated her 'with all civility and respect' Newcastle returned her to Hull, using his own coach. Lister was right to be surprised by the Royalist army's forbearance, but given Newcastle's unwillingness to indulge in revenge killings he was wrong to give the credit to the Almighty.

Matters fared no better for the parliamentary commanders in Leeds. No sooner had Lord Fairfax reached the town than it was seized by prisoners who had broken out of captivity and, having seized weapons from the town's magazine, were able to hold on until Newcastle arrived to relieve them. By the middle of the month Yorkshire was in Royalist hands and Fairfax father and son were left embattled in the fortress at Hull, which was soon under siege by Eythin. This was what Newcastle had set out to achieve but the securing of the county did not yet allow him to consider moving on towards London. In common with the Cornishmen his northern army did not relish the idea of campaigning so far away from home, and Newcastle himself was uncomfortably aware that his position would never be completely safe while Hull remained in parliamentary hands. With its seaward approaches the port was easily supplied and with its secure inner and outer lines of defences it acted as a bastion for the two Fairfaxes while they set about rebuilding their forces. Their arrival also coincided with the arrest of Sir John Hotham and his son,

---

* Mountjoy Blunt, Earl of Newport, had been sacked as Newcastle's second-in-command and later sided with parliament.

who had finally and fatally decided to turn coat and support the Royalist cause. They were held by sailors from the parliamentary ship *Hercules* under the command of Captain Moyer and were eventually sent to London, where they were tried and executed two years later. Old Sir John had been arrested by his cousin, a parliamentary officer, with words that exemplified the divisive anguish of the war: 'Sir John, you are my kinsman, and one I have much honoured, but I must now waive all that, and arrest you as a traitor to the kingdom.'[10]

Only one cloud blotted the horizon. While trying to recapture Gainsborough (taken by Willoughby on 20 July), Newcastle's daring young cousin Charles Cavendish was killed, hacked to death by Captain-Lieutenant Thomas Berry after being knocked from his horse in what his opponent, Cromwell, called a 'quagmire'. The battle was a further step in the seemingly inexorable rise of the Huntingdon commander. Accompanied by the Scots mercenary John Meldrum with men from Lincolnshire, Nottingham and Northampton, Cromwell's force was advancing to Willoughby's aid when they collided with Cavendish's men near the village of Lea outside Gainsborough on 28 July. Although the Royalist force had a tactical advantage, having occupied the only high ground in the area, just east of Gainsborough, the Lincolnshire infantry advanced to within musketshot of their opponents. This was the cue for Cavendish to unleash his cavalry, but as he did so Cromwell's horse, kept in reserve, counter-attacked with great resolve. In Cromwell's words, 'I pressing on forced them down a hill, having good execution of them, and below the hill, drove the General [Cavendish] with some of his soldiers into a quagmire':

> We came up horse to horse, where we disputed it with our swords and pistols, a pretty time, all keeping close order, so that one could not break the other. At last they a little shrinking, our men perceiving, pressed in upon them, and immediately routed this whole body, some flying on one side, others on the other of the enemy's reserve; and our men pursuing them, had chase and execution about five or six miles.[11]

It was a well-won orderly battle in which Cromwell had used timing and intelligence to launch his cavalry at a time when the opposition was overstretched, and by killing Cavendish he had the bonus of removing one of Newcastle's most able commanders. Not that it was decisive: in the aftermath Cromwell and Meldrum were forced to retreat when Newcastle's main army arrived and Gainsborough was forced to surrender on 31 July.

The action also marked the end of further fighting in the north that summer. Cromwell retired to Huntingdon, where he threw himself into the much-needed task of raising further men for the parliamentary cause, offering his famous phrase, that he 'would rather have a plain russet-coated captain that knows what he fights for and loves what he knows than what you call a gentleman and little else. I honour a gentleman that is so indeed'.[12] That summer saw his military ambitions being further rewarded: he was appointed governor of the Isle of Ely and promoted as one of the Earl of Manchester's colonels in the army of the Eastern Association. As for Newcastle, having failed to force Nottingham to surrender – the governor John Hutchinson 'scorned to yield on any terms to a papistical army led by an atheistical general' – he moved his forces north to concentrate on the weighty matter of Hull.[13]

Chapter Seven

STALEMATE

'God give a sudden stop to this issue of English blood.'

Sir Ralph Hopton to Sir William Waller, 16 December 1643

As the summer of 1643 drew to a close all the advantages appeared to lie with the king. In the north, west and centre his forces had inflicted defeats on the parliamentary army which, while not decisive, had lowered morale and reduced its fighting strength. Soldiers who find themselves all too often on the losing side easily become dispirited, especially if they begin to lose faith in their commanders; and with the exception of Cromwell, Fairfax and Waller, the parliamentary leadership had not excelled. Key points such as Oxford, Bristol, Newcastle and the West Riding were in Royalist hands and, following Newcastle's success in Yorkshire and Lincolnshire, the East Anglian counties with their agricultural wealth were under threat: if they fell into Charles's hands the way would also be open to attack London from the north. Parliament's supremacy at sea was also being diluted by the creation of an embryonic Royalist navy, the first ships being those captured after the fall of Bristol and the money to operate them coming from local merchants. This proved to be a boon during the autumn, when they were used to transport men and supplies from Ireland to north Wales. Better still, they were able to carry out their duties unhindered by any opposition. Warwick, the parliamentary naval commander, was facing mutiny among his fleet as a result of severe underfunding and was rarely in a position to order his ships to put to sea for convoy duties.

There was also continuing unrest in parliament, where Pym's declining genius was finding it ever more difficult to control those who wanted a negotiated peace. He also had to keep his more bellicose colleagues in check, and when the fiery member for Berkshire, Henry Marten, made the outrageous suggestion 'that it were better one family [Charles's] should be destroyed than many' Pym had him expelled from the Commons and imprisoned in the Tower of London. This was undoubtedly parliament's lowest point, but at that time of adversity, when the only hope of help lay with the Scots and Henry Vane the Younger's negotiations in Edinburgh, the first steps were taken to produce the army which would retrieve the parliamentary position – the new Army of the Eastern Association under the command of the Earl of Manchester, formerly the Lord Mandeville whom the king had attempted to impeach. On 10 August a parliamentary committee was formed to empower the Eastern Association, which was based at Norwich, to raise 20,000 men 'in constant pay' to protect the East Anglian frontier and 'from time to time [to] send out scouts to discover how and in what manner any enemy approacheth near the frontiers'.

Although Manchester was not a trained soldier he possessed energy and commitment to the cause, and he was a sound administrator who believed in treating his men fairly and well. Not that raising an army was an easy matter. Men rallied to its ranks as much through coercion as through any enthusiasm for the war, but it proved difficult to keep them. Pay was often not forthcoming, arms and equipment were lacking and the whole enterprise was marked by inefficiency on a grand scale. Throughout the summer and well into the winter Cromwell's letters ring to his frustration with the system. In one he points out that he had been forced to pay for boots out of his own pocket; another warns that his men would lose their patience if they did not receive pay and equipment and a postscript agonises about the end-result of these shortcomings: 'The force will fail if some help not. Weak counsels and weak actings undo all. Send at once or come or all will be lost, if God help not. Remember who tells you'.[1] On the credit side, he had teamed up with Henry Ireton, a driven man and a good soldier, who was to become Cromwell's second-in-command and later, a son-in-law.

If the balance was tipped in Charles's direction that did not mean that everything was going his way. While he held the upper hand in the north and the west two obstacles prevented him from achieving his ambition of combining his forces for an attack on London. These were the strategically important fortified towns of Gloucester and Hull, and both needed to be taken before further thought could be given to the wider picture. Gloucester controlled the upper Severn valley with its lucrative wool trade while Hull and its protected port was the key to Yorkshire. As long as they both remained uncaptured the surrounding area could hardly be secured and, in Hull's case, as Newcastle's forces were raised and funded locally it had to be taken before campaigns elsewhere were considered. Charles also realised that the fall of both places would be a tremendous fillip to his cause and a further blow to parliament's dented morale.

With that in mind and buoyed up by the fall of Bristol he set about besieging Gloucester on 10 August, hoping for a quick and efficient result, his optimism being underpinned by the possibility that its governor, Edward Massey, might be willing to change sides and surrender the city. However, when summoned, the young and imperturbable Massey held firm, a bold decision given that he had only 1500 men under his command and the local defences were no stronger than Bristol's.* This should have been the signal for Rupert to repeat the tactics which he had used so successfully in July, but when Charles declined to storm Gloucester in order to avoid heavy casualties the task was entrusted to the Earl of Forth. Although Forth's hands were tied by the king's orders not to risk men's lives it has to be said that the old Scots commander's tactics were unsuited to a speedy resolution. Following skirmishes in the suburbs, during which Massey's defenders fought with great courage, the siege settled down to a familiar pattern of attrition.

---

* Massey had commanded the Earl of Stamford's Bluecoats. There is evidence to suggest that he sent a message to the king declaring his willingness to surrender if the king appeared with a superior force, but it is not clear if he meant what he said or was trying to gain time to allow a relief force to arrive.

Artillery was brought up to fire 'great shot against the walls', sappers started building a mine under the east gate, and a protective siege engine was built which would provide cover for the musketeers. It was all in vain. The atrocious summer weather hampered Forth's plans and rain filled the mines with water, preventing them from being fired. At the same time Massey ordered several successful counter-attacks against Royalist positions, a countermine was constructed, but best of all, according to his chaplain John Corbet, the parliamentary commander had the happy knack of inspiring confidence and raising morale. Amid the roar of the Royalist cannon and the terror of the heavy mortar bombs which fell in the streets, he seemed to be everywhere, leading by example and keeping everyone busy while reassuring them that help would soon be on its way:

> The sadness of the times did not cloud the countenance of the people. They beheld their fortunes with a clear brow, and were deliberate and cheerful in the endeavours of safety. No great complainings were heard in our streets; no discontent seized on the soldiers, at other times prone to mutiny; men of suspected fidelity did not fail in action; every valuable person was active in his own place. The usual outcries of women were not then heard, the weakness of whose sex was not overcome by the terrible engines of war. And our becalmed spirits did implore divine assistance without confusion. The Governor personally performed, ready at every turning of affairs, and gracing the business with speech and gesture. Upon the least intimation of diffidence he pretended rational hopes of success, adding withal that our late yielding could not mollify the King's army; and if in the close we must needs be lost, no surer means of safety than by the utmost gallantry to constrain honourable conditions.[2]

However, surrender was never a consideration and Massey's optimism was not misplaced. Encouraged by the news of Gloucester's resistance parliament ordered Essex to march to its aid with 15,000 men. On Hounslow Heath on 24 August he reviewed his forces, which had been reinforced with five regiments of London Trained Bands, and left the next day for the west, marching in a wide sweep north of Oxford by way of Brackley, Stow-on-the-Wold and Cheltenham. Due to the wet weather progress was slow, and Essex's force was further hampered by a severe storm when they reached Prestbury Hill on 5 September. By then within sight of Gloucester, which lay ten miles away, Essex ordered his artillerymen to fire off their guns as an encouragement to Massey's garrison. The gesture was much needed, for they were down to their last reserves, but the sound of gunfire also alerted Charles to the danger, and not wanting to be trapped between two forces he ordered the siege to be lifted and took his army south-east to Painswick. Three days later Essex led his troops into Gloucester, his mission successfully accomplished; Massey's heroic stand, which had lasted almost four weeks, had saved the city for parliament.

Although the king was upset by the failure to take Gloucester, Essex's move presented him with a fresh opportunity to bring the war to a successful conclusion. If he could place his forces between Essex's army and its return route to London he would be able to force a battle which, if successful, would destroy the main parliamentary army and with it the crack regiments of Trained Bands. Essex seemed to be aware of the danger, too. A week after securing Gloucester he moved his depleted army north along the west bank of the Severn towards Tewkesbury, giving the impression that he was about to return to London by the same northerly route. Then he stopped at the river crossing and began building a bridge of boats almost as if he was about to move towards Hereford and from there invade Wales. It was a good ruse but Charles and his council were not taken in by it. Instead, they countered it by moving their army north-east, first towards Sudeley Castle and then to Pershore to block the road back to London through Warwick. Essex had to think quickly: having strengthened Massey's garrison his army was smaller, his men were tired and he was unwilling to face a fixed battle that might do to him what Hopton had done to Waller at Roundway Down. In short, he knew only too well that another heavy defeat would leave parliament without a reliable field army.

As the game of hide and seek continued, heavy rain made life difficult for the soldiers in both armies. It was a moment which demanded bold action, and Essex supplied it on the evening of 15 September when he took his chance by marching his army rapidly south-east towards the Chilterns and the southern route back to London through Swindon and Reading. Cirencester was reached the next day and after a brief fight it fell, its supplies and ammunition

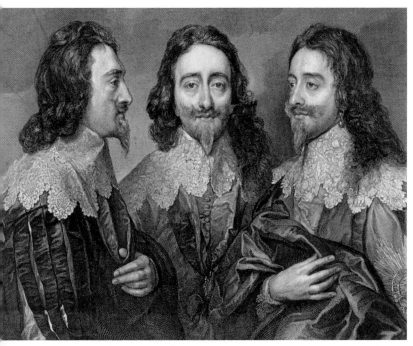

Charles I captured in triplicate by Van Dyck, one of the many artists who enjoyed royal patronage in the halcyon days of the King's reign. *(Mary Evans Picture Library)*

Headstrong and passionate, Queen Henrietta Maria supported her husband by stiffening his resolve and raising funds for the Royalist cause. *(Mary Evans Picture Library)*

A bitter critic of the Crown, John Pym was one of the five members of parliament whom Charles I tried to arrest in 1642. *(Mary Evans Picture Library)*

Archbishop William Laud: his imposition of the Prayer Book on Scotland triggered the first fighting of the civil wars. *(Mary Evans Picture Library)*

Presbyterian cavalier: James Graham, Marquis of Montrose, won Scotland for the Royalist cause. *(Mary Evans Picture Library)*

His support for the Crown cost him dear: Thomas Wentworth, Earl of Strafford, was executed when Charles I abandoned him in 1641. *(Mary Evans Picture Library)*

One of the many Scottish veterans of the Thirty Years War, Alexander Leslie commanded the parliamentary army at Marston Moor. *(Mary Evans Picture Library)*

Lord Lieutenant of Ireland, James Butler, Earl of Ormond, the commander of the Royalist forces in Ireland. *(Mary Evans Picture Library)*

Weak and indecisive, the Duke of Hamilton excited mistrust amongst his fellow Scots and proved to be an inept military commander. *(Mary Evans Picture Library)*

Ranald MacDonnell, Earl of Antrim, the focus for rallying Royalist support in Ireland and Scotland. *(National Portrait Gallery)*

'I see that the birds are flown': Charles I's ham-fisted attempt to arrest the five members of parliament. *(Mary Evans Picture Library)*

Raising the royal standard: Charles I began his military campaign in Nottingham on a wet and windy August morning. *(Mary Evans Picture Library)*

Commander of the Royalist cavalry forces, Prince Rupert, Count Palatine, proved to be a dashing and resourceful battlefield general.
(Mary Evans Picture Library)

ather against son, brother against brother: the Battle of Edgehill opened the fighting n England and left neither side with any advantage. *(Private Collection/Bridgeman Art Library)*

Cruel cavaliers on the rampage: propaganda was widely used by both sides throughout the war. *(Mary Evans Picture Library)*

In Oxford, his court-in-exile during the winter of 1644–45, Charles I rejected repeated parliamentary calls for a peace treaty. *(Mary Evans Picture Library)*

Oliver Cromwell, 'our chief of men', the main architect of the parliamentary revolution. Elected Lord Protector in 1653. *(Mary Evans Picture Library)*

Parliament won back the north of England at the Battle of Marston Moor: 'an absolute victory obtained by God's blessing'. *(Harris Museum and Art Gallery, Preston, Lancashire, UK/Bridgeman Art Library)*

Sir Thomas Fairfax, the commander of the New Model Army, was the war's outstanding tactician but took no part in Charles I's trial. *(Private Collection/Bridgeman Art Library)*

The parliamentary victory at the Battle of Naseby, fought on 14 June 1645, effectively ended the first phase of the civil wars. *(Private Collection/Bridgeman Art Library)* being much welcomed by the parliamentary soldiers who had been on the march for almost a month. That good fortune was counter-balanced when Rupert discovered that Essex had escaped and he set off in pursuit with the Royalist cavalry, taking a parallel route some ten miles to the north, his intention being to force Essex into a fixed battle. The opportunity came on the morning of 18 September when his force collided with Essex's army at Aldbourne Chase, five miles north-west of Hungerford. Although outnumbered three to one the Royalist cavalry pressed home their attack and caused enough damage for Essex to delay his march towards Newbury, where he was hoping to find fresh supplies and shelter for his weary army. Taking advantage of the confusion Rupert regrouped his cavalry and rode them into Newbury, a move which cut the road to London and made a battle inevitable.

Once again Rupert had shown his value to his uncle's cause, first by marauding Essex's army and forcing it to halt, and then by out-manoeuvring it to cut off its retreat. The action also allowed the Royalist army to spend a reasonably comfortable night under cover, well supplied with food and drink, while Essex's men had to bivouac in the cold and the rain. It also provided them with the best ground on the plateau south of Newbury and the River Kennet where the two armies drew up in line to face each other on the morning of 20 September. However, either by bad judgement or carelessness a spur of high ground to the north, known as Round Hill, had not been secured and this 'most gross and absurd' error allowed it to be occupied by a small force of artillery, infantry and cavalry commanded by Sir Philip Skippon. This obliged Sir Nicholas Byron to try to clear the position with a force made up of infantry and cavalry while Rupert attacked from the left across Wash Common. Both sides were evenly matched, with around 14,000 in both armies, but thanks to the terrain with its hedges and enclosures the course of the battle was muddled and confusing, even for those who fought in it.

Artillery fire did most of the damage and accounted for most of the 3500 casualties, Henry Foster, a sergeant in the Red regiment of the Trained Bands noting that the 'execution' was 'somewhat dreadful when men's bowels and brains flew in our faces':

They began their battery against us with their great guns, above half an hour before we could get any of our guns up to us. Our gunners dealt very ill with us, delaying to come up to us. Our noble Colonel Tucker fired one piece of ordnance against the enemy, and aiming to give fire the second time was shot in the head with a cannon bullet from the enemy. The Blue regiment of the trained bands stood upon our right wing, and behaved themselves most gallantly. Two regiments of the king's horse which stood upon their right flank afar off, came fiercely upon them and charged them two or three times but were beat back with their musketeers, who gave them a most desperate charge and made them fly.[3]

The steady fire and resolute behaviour of the Trained Bands' musketeers and pikemen meant that Round Hill remained in Skippon's hands, and Byron's failure to dislodge them negated any success enjoyed by Rupert in the centre. It was a seesaw kind of battle, with action rolling along a broad front, but neither side was in a position to exploit any temporary advantage. With men being able to regroup in the narrow lanes and take up new positions stalemate was inevitable and as darkness fell the fighting simply petered out. On the Royalist side there had been notable casualties including the Earl of Caernarvon and Lord Sunderland, but the saddest loss was the unforced death of Lord Falkland, the increasingly unhappy secretary of state who decided to ride as a private trooper in Byron's brigade, having 'in the morning of the battle called for a clean shirt, saying that if he were slain they should not find his body in foul linen'. Some of his friends then dissuaded him from venturing himself as having no call to it, being no military officer. But he replied that he was weary of the times, and 'foresaw much misery to his own country, and did believe he should be out of it before night'.[4] He got his wish, being cut down in a bullet-shower while pushing his horse through a gap in the hedges on Round Hill. With his good sense and his calm demeanour Falkland's loss to the king's cause was as great a misfortune as that sustained by parliament with the death of Hampden at Chalgrove Field three months earlier.* In his place as secretary came the feline and ill-starred Lord Digby.

---

* Showing no little malice, John Aubrey claimed that Falkland's death was not due to lofty ideals but was caused by the death of his mistress and his remorse at failing to persuade Charles to continue the siege of Gloucester.

That night Charles held a council of war. Although some of the cavalry commanders wanted to hold the position until the next day, a move which would have forced Essex to renew his attack, the low supplies of shot and powder decided the issue. Convinced that his army could not withstand another day's fighting Charles ordered his men to move off the field and to make their way north back to Oxford. The next morning Essex woke to find Wash Common empty and the way to London open; all that discomfited his army was a brief action near Aldermaston where his rearguard was attacked by Royalist cavalry, but for Charles any chance of settling the war in 1643 had disappeared. In purely military terms Newbury was just as much a draw as Edgehill had been, but with one important difference. Whereas Charles took an advantage from that first battle which could have been exploited, he lost it at Newbury. Had he defeated Essex and destroyed his army, parliament would have been forced to negotiate a peace. London would have been open to attack and, with the army of the Eastern Association still being constructed, there would have been little stomach for further fighting. But Charles had shown himself to be indecisive, refusing to take risks and allowing his field commanders to be lackadaisical in their positioning of the army before the battle. Essex on the other hand had been bold and resolute when those virtues were needed and had shown flair: he fully deserved the rapturous welcome which greeted him and his army (including Sergeant Henry Foster) when they marched back into the capital at the end of the month:

> The Lord Mayor together with the aldermen of the City met us at Temple-bar and entertained us joyfully, many thousands bidding us welcome home and blessing God for our safe return. Thus God that called us forth to do his work brought us through many straits, delivered us from the rage and insolence of our adversaries, made them turn their backs with shame, giving us victory, and causing us to return home joyfully.[5]

Essex's army had not only relieved Gloucester but had made sure that the Royalist army was not in any position to threaten London. Its return also coincided with better news from the north, where the Fairfaxes had confounded all Newcastle's efforts to lay siege to Hull by cutting the River Humber's dikes and flooding the surrounding countryside. At the same time Cromwell had managed to get into the city to confer with the defenders, and in so doing he began his long and fruitful association with 'Black Tom' Fairfax. It proved to be a profitable meeting for the parliamentary cause. Both were able to break out with 25 troops of cavalry on 20 September to cross into Lincolnshire and make contact with Manchester's Eastern Association army, which was advancing on Boston to threaten the Royalist position at Newark.

While his opponents were mustering Newcastle ordered Henderson to pull together a force of 3000 cavalry and dragoons to secure the key Norman keep at Bolingbroke which stood fifteen miles to the north of Boston. As a result of this move the two armies met on 11 October on open ground near the small village of Winceby three miles south of the castle. Warned of Henderson's approach by Fairfax, whose cavalry had acted as advance scouts, Manchester drew up his men on the southern ridge with his and Cromwell's regiments at the front and Fairfax's men in the rear, acting as a reserve. Following brisk skirmishing between the rival dragoons Cromwell brought up his cavalry but took no further part in the action after his horse was shot from beneath him. It could have been worse: in the mêlée which followed his assailant, Sir Ingram Hopton, was cut down by another trooper before he could do further damage.

A predictably confused clash followed as the Royalist cavalry joined the battle from the north, and the fighting might have petered out if Fairfax had not intervened. Showing a good deal of skill and ability to read the battle he took the reserve along the ridge to the eastern flank and ordered them to charge directly into the Royalist line, leading from the front and encouraging his men to 'fall on'. Surprised by the suddenness and ferocity of the attack, the Royalist cavalry broke and started to retreat as best they could towards the south-west. Their undisciplined disorder was their undoing. In the narrow lanes lined by high hedges they became trapped and Fairfax's men took a heavy toll. The name of the place tells its own story: Slash Hollow. As Rupert's men had done at Edgehill, Fairfax's cavalry pursued the fleeing remnants for several miles, driving home their advantage and helping to bring Lincolnshire into parliamentary hands.

As a result of the action at Winceby the Royalists abandoned

Gainsborough and Lincoln, and that same day Meldrum ended the siege of Hull by leading an early morning sortie against Newcastle's force which resulted in the capture of several artillery pieces, including Gog and Magog. With Lincolnshire secured by Manchester and Hull still in parliamentary hands, any hope that Newcastle had of moving on London had disappeared, and the year ended with the only threat to the capital coming from a newly formed force led by Ralph Hopton, whose wounds had healed and who had been ennobled as Lord Hopton of Stratton.

Following a meeting in Oriel College, Oxford on 29 September Hopton was directed to secure Dorset, Wiltshire and Hampshire 'and so point forward as far as he could go towards London', but the men under his command turned out to be undistinguished and poorly trained, many of them being the reinforcements which Ormond had arranged to be sent across from Ireland. Opposing them was a new force drawn from Kent, Sussex, Surrey and Hampshire, strengthened by three regiments of Trained Bands and commanded by Waller, who was anxious to put behind him his drubbing at Roundway Down. He did not have long to wait. Despite the appalling winter weather, and following a desultory siege of the Royalist stronghold of Basing House, a heavily fortified pile in Hampshire belonging to the Marquis of Winchester, the two armies clashed at Alton on 13 December, a bitterly cold winter's day. The recently established Royalist garrison in the town under the command of Lord Crawford was surprised by Waller's men, who had taken a circuitous route to avoid detection. On their approach Crawford's cavalry broke out of Alton, leaving behind the Royalist foot, who were forced to withdraw into St Laurence's Church. Fighting with the desperation of doomed men, they put up a determined resistance: according to Elias Archer, an officer in one of the Trained Bands regiments, the defenders in the church neither asked for quarter nor gave it until they could see that all was lost, 'except some desperate villains which refused quarter':

> By this time the church-yard was full of our men, laying about them stoutly, with halberts, swords and musket-stocks, while some threw hand-grenades in the church windows, others attempting to enter the church being led on by Major Shambrooke, (a man whose worth and valour envy cannot stain) who in the entrance

received a shot in the thigh (whereof he is very ill). Nevertheless our men vigorously entered and slew Colonel Bowles [Richard Bolle, the Royalist infantry commander], their chief commander at the present, who not long before swore, 'God damn his soul if he did not run his sword through the heart of him which first called for quarter'.[6]

When Bolle fell resistance began to crumble, but not before eighty Royalists had been killed, a number of corpses being found behind a hastily erected breastwork of dead horses in the church itself. Ten times that figure became prisoners, leaving Waller well satisfied with the day's work. He then attempted to capitalise on his success by laying siege to the West Sussex castle of Arundel, but it did not fall until early in the following year, 6 January 1644, when the onset of ferocious winter conditions made any further campaigning impossible. A vivid account of the siege, and with it a grim picture of the horrors of civil strife, was written many years later by Lady Mary Springate* for her American Quaker grandson. Although heavily pregnant she defied the winter roads and had hurried down from London to be with her husband Sir William, who had fallen ill with typhus fever during the action:

When we came to Arundel we met with a most dismal sight: the town being depopulated, all the windows broken with the great guns, and the soldiers making stables of all the shops and lower rooms; and there being no light in the town but what came in from the stables, we passed through the town towards his [Springate's] quarters. Within a quarter of a mile of the house the horses were at a stand, and we could not understand the reason of it, so we sent our guide down to the house for a candle and lantern and to come to our assistance. Upon which the report came to my husband, who told them they were mistaken, he knew I could not come I was so near my time. But they affirming that it was so, he commanded them to sit him up in his bed, 'that I may see her'.[7]

---

* Her daughter Gulielma married the Quaker William Penn (1644–1718), the founder of the state of Pennsylvania.

Two days later her husband was dead, aged only twenty-three, and his body was buried in his native Sussex.

As the war progressed scenes like those were to become distressingly familiar throughout the three kingdoms. Viciousness, too, was creeping in. In Cheshire on St Stephen's Day a parliamentary force boxed up in the tower of St Bartoline's Church in Barthomley in Cheshire refused to surrender and was massacred after a fire was lit to flush them out. The Royalist commander Sir John Byron claimed that by killing the enemy he was simply carrying out his military duty: 'I put them all to the sword, which I find to be the best way to proceed with these kind of people, for mercy to them is cruelty'.[8] The message got through to his opponent, Sir William Brereton: unnerved, the parliamentary commander quickly lost his grip on the county by the end of the year, and the only garrison remaining to him was Nantwich, in which he found himself besieged until Sir Thomas Fairfax came to his relief on 25 January 1644.

The arrival of the soldiers from Ireland in the autumn of 1643 also raised temperatures: on 24 October 1644 parliament passed an ordinance forbidding the grant of quarter to 'any Irishman or papist born in Ireland' taken prisoner in England, and among the first victims were 70 soldiers who were thrown into the sea when their ship was captured off the Pembrokeshire coast by a parliamentary warship. The ruling was later rescinded, but not before many parliamentary commanders had made full use of its powers and continued to do so throughout the war. Brereton and Fairfax were guilty of allowing Irishmen to be executed and Cromwell infamously concluded that hanging Irish soldiers was 'a righteous judgement of God upon these barbarous wretches'. That the official practice was curtailed owed much to the example of Prince Rupert.[9] Following the parliamentary army's capture of Shrewsbury in February 1645 Colonel Thomas Mytton executed a dozen Irish Catholic officers in the Royalist garrison; by way of retaliation Rupert hanged the same number of English Protestant prisoners on crab-apple trees, having made the protest to Essex that he had always shown quarter to prisoners, whatever their nationalities or religions.*

---

* The number would have been thirteen, but one of those chosen, Philip Littleton, saw his old master Sir Vincent Corbett ride by. On his intercession Rupert agreed to save Philip's life 'on condition he would never bear arms against the king'.

By this time John Pym was dead, having succumbed to cancer on 8 December 1643. While his death had come as little surprise – he had been in obvious pain for weeks – it did leave a void in parliament. He had been the driving force behind the Grand Remonstrance and the architect behind the grievances against the Crown. As such he can be counted as a true revolutionary because he started the process which curbed the power of the Crown and helped to lay the basis for parliamentary democracy. Articulate, energetic and a nimble debater, he took the lead in a largely inexperienced House of Commons and helped it to keep its nerve during the dismantlement of Royal absolutism. A terminal illness carried him off but his death was certainly hastened by the unyielding effort which he put into his work and his death was much mourned. Such was the respect in which he was held that parliament agreed to pay off the debts he had accrued as a result of neglecting his private business interests in England and New England.

In the vacuum which followed, Sir Henry Vane (the younger), the leader of the war party and the broker of the agreement with the Scots, emerged as the leading politician in the Commons. A rigid Puritan who Clarendon thought had 'somewhat in him of extraordinary', he enjoyed the support of Hesilrige and Cromwell's cousin, the Solicitor-General Oliver St John, one of the key supporters of the Attainder which led to Strafford's execution. By then, too, Scottish support had been assured and an army of 18,000 foot, 3000 horse, 600 dragoons and 120 artillery pieces was mustering on the border in preparation for the invasion of England. Led by Lord Leven – Sandy Hamilton was once again the commander of the artillery while David Leslie (another soldier of fortune but no relation of Alexander, being the grandson of Robert Stewart, Earl of Orkney, Mary Queen of Scots's half-brother) was Master-General of the Horse – the force was disciplined and well-equipped, each regiment had its own minister (some had half a dozen), prayers were held in the morning and evening and the death sentence was mandatory for rape, pillage and murder. All the regiments were tightly-knit and cohesive units whose recruits usually came from the same locality. One, the Stirlingshire Foot, raised by Lord Livingston and commanded by Lieutenant-Colonel Andrew Bruce (another German veteran), was raised from presbyteries in Stirling and Dumbarton; another, the

Tweeddale Foot, raised by the Earl of Buccleuch and commanded by Lieutenant-Colonel Walter Scott, was raised solely from the presbytery of Selkirk. All had been commanded to 'live together as friends and brethren' and any lack of training was more than balanced by their religious certainty and the memory of the earlier successes during the Bishops' Wars. By the third week of January the first elements of this blue-bonneted psalm-singing army had crossed the border into England at Kelso and Berwick, marching easily over the frozen River Tweed, its aim to tackle the city of Newcastle and bring the fighting in England to a speedy conclusion.

The last elements of the deal had been signed on 25 September 1643 when parliament ratified the Solemn League and Covenant and a Committee of Both Kingdoms was established to direct the war. Composed of seven peers, fourteen members of parliament and four Scottish commissioners led by Lord Maitland, it replaced the cumbersome Committee of Safety to emerge as a military executive which enjoyed the sole direction of the war without the necessity of referring its plans to the Commons or the Lords. It was not the only change introduced to secure the support of the Scots: in pursuit of the aim to introduce a Presbyterian Church government an Assembly of Divines from both countries met at Westminster Abbey. Among the Scottish members were five ministers, one of whom was Robert Baillie, and three elders, including Archibald Johnston of Wariston, all of whom were pleasantly surprised by their English colleagues' enthusiasm. 'They harangue long and very learnedly,' wrote Baillie to his cousin. 'They study the questions well before hand, and prepare their speeches; but withal the men are exceeding prompt, and well spoken. I do marvel at the very accurate and extemporaneous replies that many of them usually do make.'[10] Relief at Scots support was one reason for the optimism; a desire to show unity at a difficult time another, but the Westminster Assembly's cohesion could not last, for the very good reason that the English parliament had no intention of imposing the Scottish Presbyterian system on their own people. Within six months Baillie had changed his tune and was complaining about English verbosity and prolixity, informing his cousin that 'this is an irresolute, divided and dangerously-humoured people: we long much to see them settled, and our nation honestly rid of them.'[11]

But during that first winter of cooperation unity was the

watchword. Despite ending the year on a high note parliament's military fortunes were precarious and the atmosphere in London remained gloomy and full of foreboding. All amusements were cancelled and there was a general air of exhaustion. Even in the king's camp at Oxford the mood was tense: 1643 had been a year when the king could have won the war, now he was left trying to keep his armies in the field while a new threat came from the north. 'The country is in a most pitiful condition; no corner of it free from the evils of a cruel war,' wrote Baillie in one of his first letters home as he recalled a different London before the war. 'Every shire, every city, many families, divided in this quarrel; much blood and universal spoil made by both where they prevail.'[12]

Chapter Eight

KEEP YOUR POWDER DRY:
MARSTON MOOR

'Swounds, do you run? Follow me!'

Prince Rupert, order to fleeing Royalist cavalry troopers,
Battle of Marston, 2 July 1644

Once Leven's Scottish army had crossed the border into Northumberland it made slow progress. The severe winter conditions stood against them: heavy snow and floods blocked the roads and, being the largest army in the field, it was not always easy to keep everyone fully provisioned and content. Much was expected of it, and even though contemporary critics scoffed at the expedition for being 'raw, untrained and undisciplined', its size and Leven's reputation as a fighting soldier made it a formidable force. Besides, having been schooled in the great wars of movement in Europe he knew all about the art of manoeuvre and the need to keep his army fed, supplied and in good order before they were brought to battle. With them went Argyll and Sir William Armyne, representing the Committee of Both Kingdoms charged with the direction of the war, and by the second week of January a London news-sheet, the *Parliamentary Scout*, was reporting enthusiastically that Newcastle would soon fall and that 'we may here fall to rigging up old and new ships to fetch in coals, which by that time they [the Scots] get thither, no doubt there will be coals ready to get in; therefore let those who have wood sell good pennyworths, lest they repent it.'[1]

The confidence was misplaced. Although the local Royalist commander, Sir Thomas Glemham, was taken by surprise as news of the Scottish move filtered through to his forward headquarters at Alnwick, he was able to fall back through Northumberland to Newcastle, having first destroyed the bridge over the River Aln. By 28 January 1644 Leven had established a base at Morpeth, but he still had to wait for the arrival of his rearguard and his heavy siege guns which had been sent by sea to Blyth before he could consider any attack on Newcastle. Heavy rain and a sudden thaw also delayed him, and by the time Leven appeared before the city on 3 February Newcastle and Eythin had arrived with 5000 reinforcements. Not that Leven knew of this move: the first inkling came when the mayor responded to Argyll's invitation to surrender with the testy thought that 'his Majesty's General being at this instant in the Town we conceive all the Power of Government to be in him'.[2]

As well as taking command Newcastle had seized the initiative by setting fire to the suburbs in the north and south-east to deprive Leven's men of shelter, and by sinking ships in the mouth of the Tyne he prevented the parliamentary navy from offering support or bringing in supplies by sea. He also sent out aggressive cavalry patrols to harry the Scots' lines of communication and to destroy local supplies in the Tynemouth area. Unable to respond until he had his big guns, Leven threw his men round the city and commenced building a bridge of boats across the Tyne. Under the circumstances he could do little else, but the lack of action irked more forceful officers such as Sir James Turner, who had managed to escape from Ulster to find not only inactivity but dangerous inactivity:

> They had but a little narrow bridge to pass in their going and coming, and if 2000 had fallen stoutly out of the town on them, they had killed and taken them every man, for retire they could not. Argyll hearing this was my opinion, which was seconded by others asked Dear Sandy [Hamilton], Sir James Lumsden and myself, what was best to be done. We were unanimous that false alarms should be given about the whole town, to divert the enemy from sallying too strong upon Stewart [Colonel William Stewart, Galloway Foot, responsible for guarding the bridge], for the town's outer guards of horse had certified them within his approach. I was

sent with this message to the General [Leven], whom I found going
to supper. When I returned I was ashamed to relate the answer of
that old Captain; which was he feared the brightness of the night
(for it was moonshine) would discover the burning matches to
those on the walls.[3]

Turner's wording makes it clear that he had not forgiven Leven for
his unwillingness to help the Scots army in Ulster during the previous
summer, but the old general was not just temporising; he had other
ideas. Under orders to clear the north of England, he did not want to
be tied up in a lengthy siege of Newcastle and on 22 February, leaving
behind a force of investment, he marched the bulk of his army west
along the banks of the Tyne before crossing the river and heading
south towards Sunderland. The move did not take Newcastle himself
by surprise: he had already warned the king that the Scots were
'raising the whole country of Northumberland, which is totally lost,
all turned to them, so that they daily increase their army, and are now
striving to pass part of it over the river, so to environ us on every side,
and cut off all provision from us'.[4] Realising that his only hope was
to force a battle, Newcastle followed suit by leaving a small force to
guard the city while he set off in pursuit of the Scottish host.

The next few weeks saw both sides playing a ponderous game of
bluff, facing one another over a landscape of 'unpassable ditches and
hedges', neither side willing to offer battle until the odds were fully
stacked in their favour. Both, especially the Scottish commander, have
been criticised for not engaging with each other, but given the terrain,
the weather and the circumstances it is difficult to see how they could
have done otherwise. Newcastle used the delaying tactics because his
army was smaller, Leven because he was unsure of his lines of
communication and supply routes, but on 24 and 25 March both
sides had to engage when they clashed at Hilton outside Sunderland.
Forced to withdraw from their position on Bedwich Hill, the Scots
used their artillery to good effect to drive off the opposition's cavalry,
forcing Newcastle's men to withdraw to Durham.

At the battle, serving their king, were two Scots whose presence in
snow-covered Northumberland was a reminder that decisions to
support one side or the other could be based on romance, not to say
eccentricity. The first was Captain Frances Dalziel, bastard daughter

of the Earl of Carnwath, the commander of a troop of horsemen who rode under the banner of a black flag sporting a naked figure hanging from a gibbet. The second was Montrose, in command of an ill-assorted unit of 200 troopers mounted on 'lean ill-appointed horse' which had been given to him by Newcastle and which formed the basis of a fledgling Scottish Royalist army. Now enjoying the king's favour as his Lieutenant-Governor of Scotland and its Captain-General, Montrose had finally convinced Charles that he should receive a commission to support his cause north of the border. Together with Antrim, who had also joined the court at Oxford, a plot had been hatched whereby the Ulster magnate would invade the west of Scotland while the newly appointed marquis would raise forces as best he could in the borders and the north-east of Scotland. Come the beginning of April they would rise for the king. Antrim had already shown his worth outside Sunderland: it was Montrose who had persuaded Newcastle to make the sally against the Scots which could have been decisive had it been pressed home with greater aggression. Montrose remained in the area after the battle and, after fruitlessly trying to raise forces in the south-west of Scotland, returned in May to command the forces besieging Morpeth. (All too typically, its commander Lieutenant-Colonel James Somerville was a kinsman of his.)

The Scots claimed that 'the Lord was pleased to give [them] the victory', Newcastle told the king that it was at best an honourable retreat, but already matters were looking bleak for the Royalist commander. In addition to coping with Leven, whose army would be better placed for action come the spring, there was worrying news from Yorkshire, where the Fairfaxes had successfully attacked Selby and defeated its commander Sir John Belasyse, taking 3000 prisoners into the bargain. Not only was this a signal disaster to the Royalist cause in the north but the road south had been cut and York was left unprotected.

In despair at the turn of events and fearing that his position at court was at risk, Newcastle offered the king his resignation but this was refused, Charles replying that if Newcastle or Eythin left his service his cause was as good as lost. 'Remember,' he told him, 'all courage is not in fighting; constancy in a good cause being the chief, and the despising of slanderous tongues and pens being not the least ingredient.' Heartened by the support, Newcastle rushed south with 6000 infantry and 5000 cavalry and was able to enter York on 16 April. Behind him came Leven, anxious to meet up with the Fairfaxes and to begin the siege of York which would mark the next and perhaps the decisive stage in the campaign, for if the city fell all Royalist hopes of holding the north of England would be shattered. Charles realised as much when he told Rupert that 'if York be lost I shall esteem my crown little less'.[5]

The two parliamentary armies, Leven's and the Fairfaxes', met at Wetherby on 18 April 1644 and four days later they were outside the walls of York to begin a siege which would last until the middle of the summer. With its three miles of stout ramparts York was a well-protected city whose defences stymied the parliamentary commanders' best attempts to breach them – not only did the besieging army lack the means to attack it but they did not have the numbers to complete the encirclement at the northern extremities. Windmills and farms in the surrounding area were destroyed, a mine was dug under St Mary's Tower and desultory attacks were made on the city's outworks, but Leven and his English colleagues knew that to gain a decisive advantage they needed more men, and that meant waiting for Manchester's Eastern Association army, which was still in Lincolnshire and anxious not to move until that area had been secured.

The defending army also needed to be reinforced. Although Newcastle had reduced his garrison by ordering his cavalry to break out under the command of Sir Charles Lucas, a move which freed them for service elsewhere and removed the need to provide fodder for the horses, he was outnumbered four to one and his supplies were dwindling. Shortly after arriving in the city he told the king that although he had introduced strict rationing he could only hold out for two months at best. His main hope lay in Rupert, who had just taken a hastily improvised force to relieve Newark, which was being besieged by a parliamentary army under Meldrum's command. Recently appointed Captain-General of Cheshire, Lancashire, Worcestershire and Shropshire, Rupert's commission was to restore order in the north-west, but on 7 and 12 March he received urgent messages from the king ordering him to move as quickly as possible to help Sir Richard Byron, who had succeeded Henderson as Newark's governor. If the town fell into parliamentary hands it would block the road to the north and make it doubly difficult to relieve York. Before Rupert could pay heed to Newcastle's warning – 'please to come hither and that very soon too' – he had to save Newark, and this he did on 21 March with a decisiveness and speed which left Meldrum's poorly disciplined force in tatters.

This was one of the most breath-taking victories of Rupert's military career, an operation which demonstrated not only speed and decisiveness but also good judgement and no little cunning. The sides were evenly matched and Meldrum was an experienced commander, but what separated them was Rupert's leadership. First he took his improvised force at speed across country, averaging eighteen miles a day and giving his opponent little chance to retaliate or guess his intentions. Then, having arrived at Bingham within ten miles of Newark, he embarked on a night march with a small advanced guard to prevent Meldrum from retreating until his main force arrived. Rupert's troopers arrived just before dawn on 21 March to find the parliamentary army drawn up in its siege position to the south of the town close to a fortified building known as the Spittal. Fearing that they might attempt to move off and avoid a battle, Rupert decided on an immediate attack even though his force of cavalrymen numbered little more than 500.

It proved to be the crucial moment of the battle. From their superior position on a bluff known as Beacon Hill the Royalist cavalry charged headlong into their opponents and plunged deep into their ranks. The collision scattered the parliamentary horse and caused tremendous confusion, with the Lincolnshire Horse retreating in disarray, although two regiments launched a counter-attack which almost cost Rupert his life – a parliamentary trooper managed to grab him, only to have his hand sliced off by a Royalist officer, Sir William Neale. By the time the bulk of the Royalist force arrived the battle had been decided. Byron had led out a relieving operation from the town which prevented Meldrum from escaping to the north and, hemmed in between the town and the Royalist army, 'the poor old gentleman' had no option but to sue for terms. He had not been helped by some of the units under his command fleeing or refusing to obey orders, and although he was allowed to march his army away from Newark with their colours and personal arms intact, the Scots commander was mortified by the scale of the defeat, which Clarendon believed to be one of Rupert's finest achievements:

> His highness resolved to try what he could for Newark, and undertook it before he was ready for it, and thereby performed it. For the enemy who had always excellent intelligence, was so confident that the prince had not a strength to attempt that work, that he was within six miles of them before they believed he thought of them.[6]

Anxious to start creating an army to march north, Rupert withdrew to Shrewsbury, but before he could start work he received a summons from the king to join him and his war council in Oxford. After the crushing victory at Newark the Royalists had been thrown into confusion by an equally striking defeat at Cheriton in Hampshire, where Waller out-thought and outfought an army commanded by Hopton and Forth. The prize was Winchester, and following two weeks of sparring the armies eventually met on open ground to the east of Cheriton village, with Hopton's men on the edge of a depression to the north while Waller attacked towards the woods from the south. Hard close-quarters fighting followed as the two sides clashed and a mixture of musket and artillery fire eventually checked the parliamentary advance. If Hopton had been able to follow Forth's advice to stay on the defensive he might have won the day but, unexpectedly and unaccountably, 'with more youthful courage than soldier-like discretion', a Royalist regiment on the right started moving into the depression between the two lines. For Hesilrige's 'Lobsters' this was too tempting a target, and when they charged into the isolated and unprotected infantry they made short work of them: within minutes most had been killed or captured.

With the battle facing stalemate, the unanticipated action encouraged the cavalry on the left, commanded by the experienced Sir William Balfour, to join the fray by attacking Hopton's foot soldiers. Led by Colonel Walter Slingsby the infantry responded to the assault in determined fashion, 'keeping their ground in a close body, not firing till within two pikes length [32 feet], and then three ranks at a time, after turning the butt end of their muskets, charging the pikes, and standing close, preserved themselves, and slew many of the enemy'.[7] Others fared less well. On the right Forth ordered the cavalry to attack, but its impetus was checked by artillery fire and the determined resistance of the parliamentary horse. This put pressure on Hopton in the centre, but his attempts to counter-attack fizzled out and he was left with little option but to retire as best he could, leaving Waller with what Balfour called 'a great victory over our enemies beyond all expectation'. Not only had the previous year's defeats been avenged but the Royalist cause in the Thames valley had been badly dented.

Cheriton also changed the complexion of the war for both sides. Although Essex counselled gloomily that by itself the victory was meaningless – 'Newark is not taken, Lincolnshire is lost; Gloucester is unsupplied and the last week there was but a step between us and death and – what is worse – slavery' – the news provided a boost for the parliamentary cause, and as is usually the case in times of optimism, encouraged recruiting.[8] In contrast the Royalist camp was aghast at the turn of events and the secretary of the king's council of war, Sir Edward Walker, caught the mood when he observed that the defeat 'necessitated his Majesty to alter the scheme of his affairs and in the place of an offensive to make a defensive war'. An emergency council of war was held on 25 April to discuss how to deal with the strategic situation facing the various Royalist armies. Rupert proved to be the dominant military personality, Clarendon noting acidly that, while Hopton displayed his customary integrity, Forth feigned deafness and 'with the long custom of immoderate drinking, dozed in his understanding which had never been quick and vigorous'.[9]

After much noisy debate, occasioned by the conflicting opinions of Digby, Wilmot and Culpepper, it was agreed that Hopton's men should be absorbed into the king's Oxford army, that Rupert should take a force north to assist Newcastle at York, that the queen, now heavily pregnant, should be removed to Exeter and that Maurice should be given additional help for his investment of the Dorset port of Lyme. On 6 May, the day that Manchester finally took Lincoln, thereby allowing the Eastern Association army to move north to York, Rupert arrived back in Shrewsbury to raise his own force. First he had to settle Lancashire, both to gain control of the port of Liverpool and to impose his uncle's authority on the county. Wisely, he sidestepped the heavily defended parliamentary town of Manchester – now under

Meldrum's command – but he did impose his stamp on neighbouring Bolton – known as the 'Geneva of the north' – which was sacked on 28 May. The routine seizure of the town was blighted by violence and the slaughter of large numbers of the defenders after they had captured one of Rupert's officers and hanged him as an Irish papist traitor. In the frenzied aftermath of the battle little quarter was given and anything up to 1000 parliamentary soldiers and civilians were killed in one of the war's worst massacres.

In Bolton Rupert was joined by the 5000 cavalry who had escaped from York and were now under the command of the recently released George Goring. A week later they laid siege to Liverpool, and after some stiff resistance it too received the Bolton treatment, Adam Martindale, a scholar-soldier in the garrison, reporting that even though quarter was offered 'Rupert's men, upon their first entrance, did (notwithstanding these terms) slay almost all they met with, to the number of three hundred and sixty and, among other, divers of their own friends, and some artificers that never bore arms in their lives, yea, one poor blind man; yet the first that I met with offered me quarter before I asked'.[10] Suddenly the war was getting nastier.

Nevertheless from a purely military point of view Lancashire had been secured for the king, and the port of Liverpool was in Royalist hands, leaving Rupert free to consolidate his forces for the push to York. But just as he was rejoicing in his good fortune a distressing letter arrived from the king in Oxford bringing news of disaster, largely unforced. With Rupert away the council of war overturned his defensive policies and had withdrawn the garrisons from Reading and Abingdon to begin an offensive in the west. Suddenly the defensive ring around Oxford was exposed, and the vacuum was quickly exploited by Waller and Essex, whose armies, lying respectively at Bagshot and Henley-on-Thames, were able to move quickly up the Thames to threaten Oxford, forcing Charles to retreat to Worcester. Confessing that it had been wrong to ignore Rupert's advice, Charles then proceeded to give his nephew a set of orders which were both contradictory and confusing:

> If York be lost I shall esteem my crown little less; unless supported by your sudden march to me; and a miraculous conquest in the South, before the effects of the Northern power can be found here.

But if York be relieved, and you beat the rebels' army of both kingdoms, which are before it; then (but otherwise not) I may possibly make a shift upon the defensive to spin out time until you come to assist me. Wherefore I command you, by the duty and affection that I know you bear me, that all new enterprises laid aside, you immediately march according to your first intention, with all your force to the relief of York. But if that be either lost, or have freed themselves from the besiegers, or that for want of powder, you cannot undertake that work, that you immediately march with your whole strength, directly to Worcester, to assist me and my army; without which, or your having relieved York by the beating the Scots, all the successes you can afterwards have must infallibly be useless unto me.[11]

Deciding on balance that he had no option but to march north to the relief of York before returning 'immediately' to Worcester, Rupert began moving his army, now almost 14,000 strong, north towards Preston and then into the Ribble valley across the Pennines, arriving at Skipton on 26 June. What he did not know and what was still hidden from the king when he wrote the letter on 14 June was that the position in the Thames valley had already changed due to Essex's inability to work with Waller. A week earlier they had met at Chipping Norton and agreed to part company. Waller would continue the pursuit of the king while Essex would march south-west to the relief of Lyme, where Maurice was being kept at bay by the stout defence offered by the town's commander, Robert Blake, who would later add to his laurels by becoming England's greatest fighting sailor since Drake.

In vain did the Committee for Both Kingdoms order Essex to return; he was determined 'to reduce the West' and believed that he had the army to do it. Having raised the siege of Lyme on 14 June he marched his army further west into Cornwall, leaving Waller to deal with a king who could not believe his good fortune at this sudden turn of events. Not that the danger was over. Waller showed his mettle by marching rapidly on Evesham and forcing Charles to retire north to Bewdley, a move which seemed to indicate that he was trying to link up with Rupert's forces. Waller thought as much and the consequences worried him. He had already informed his parliamentary masters that Charles's army was 'mouldered away and to a very small proportion, and I think it lessens every day': given the circumstances it would not be a surprise if the king joined forces with his nephew and returned with a huge army to crush first him and then Essex. Acting on that hunch Waller sent his cavalry ahead of him to stop the king should that be his aim; at the same time he called a meeting of local magnates at Stourbridge in an attempt to increase the size of his army to meet the threat.

Waller was right in thinking that Charles was looking for reinforcements but wrong in guessing that they would come from Rupert. Only two days were spent in Bewdley, and by 15 June Charles was back in Worcester and preparing to march back by way of Broadway and Stow-on-the-Wold in the general direction of Oxford, where he hoped to be resupplied and reinforced by the local garrison. This done, he marched north-eastwards to Buckingham, which he reached on 18 June. By then Waller realised the nature of the game and told parliament that, as soon as he had received news of Charles's move, 'I rose, and leaving my foot to march gently after with two regiments of horse to cover them, I advanced, with the rest of my horse and dragoons after me, to Evesham.' On the way he collected more recruits and, following a convoluted perambulation through the English countryside, the two armies eventually came within sight of each other on a sunny afternoon to the south-west of Banbury.

What followed on 29 June was a curious imitation of a battle. Waller occupied the high ground on Crouch Hill to the west of the River Cherwell while the Royalist army was strung out in a long line to the east and moving slowly northwards towards Daventry past the village of Cropredy. Thinking to outmarch him, Waller followed suit, and while this was happening he took advantage of a gap which had opened up in the line of march. Seeing his chance he sent a strong force to hold the river crossing at Cropredy Bridge and another to a ford to the south at a position called Slat Mill, his aim being to halt the Royalist advance and destroy the rearguard. Four hours of fierce but desultory fighting followed; by mid-afternoon the attacks had petered out and following a brisk artillery duel the battle was over. For two more days the two armies glowered at one another from their positions across the Cherwell before deciding what to do next. Without any real hope of success Charles tried to persuade Waller to

come over to his side. He also took time to admonish one of the more
notable prisoners, Colonel James Wemyss, a Scot and one of the great
gunners of his generation, whom he had appointed master-gunner in
1638 only to see him side with parliament.

News that a parliamentary force was heading in his direction forced
Charles to break off the engagement on Monday 1 July and to march
back over the Cotswold Hills to Evesham to consider his next move.
Tactically the battle had been a draw, with any advantage going to the
Royalists, who captured Wemyss and fourteen of his guns, but the real
loser was Waller. The troops who had joined him along the way began
deserting him – one reason why he could only watch while the
Royalist army retreated – and most shamefully of all his London
regiments mutinied or, as he put it, 'come to their old song of "Home!
Home!"' Three weeks later Waller was back in London, dispirited and
knowing that the heart of his army was broken. 'My lords,' he told the
Committee of Both Kingdoms, 'I write these particulars to let you
know that an army compounded of these men will never go through
with your service, and till you have an army merely your own, that
you may command, it is in a manner impossible to do anything of
importance.' Just as bad had been the behaviour of the men under the
command of Major-General Richard Browne, who had been sent to
assist him. They, too, mutinied and might have killed their
commander had he not allowed them to plunder a nearby Royalist
house near Henley. Waller's ire was predictable: 'Such men are only
fit for a gallows and hell hereafter.'[12]

None of these events was known to Rupert when he arrived at
Knaresborough ten miles to the west of York on 30 June 1644. His
movements had been of considerable interest and concern to the three
parliamentary generals outside York – Manchester had joined Fairfax
and Leven on 3 June to complete the encirclement to the north of the
city. The speed of Rupert's advance had taken them by surprise and,
bearing in mind Meldrum's fate at Newark, they decided not to risk
a confrontation outside the city walls. Also, being unsure of the size
of the Royalist army and still waiting for Meldrum and the Earl of
Denbigh to reinforce them, they decided to lift the siege on 1 July and
to move their field army to a defensive position west of the city near
Long Marston. This forced Rupert to make a sweeping detour of
twenty-two miles to approach the city from the north, for he realised

that he could not engage the parliamentary army without the support of Newcastle's garrison troops. York was duly relieved that same night and Rupert gave immediate thought to engaging the opposition as quickly as possible.

Three imperatives guided his decision. He was under the king's orders to achieve an early result at York, he was already outnumbered and knew that the opposition was about to be reinforced, and with the parliamentary army drawn up to meet a threat from the west he hoped to compensate for his numerical inferiority by attacking them unawares. Against that, his men had just endured a bruising march and Newcastle's men were not prepared for battle – on being relieved many had run out of the city to ransack the trenches while others refused to fight until they had been paid. Newcastle also counselled that a delay might allow the parliamentary generals to fall out among themselves, but that was a long shot: that same evening they were already redeploying their army by moving south towards Tadcaster to bar any move Rupert might make in that direction. Hearing that, Rupert sent out scouts who came across the leading elements of the parliamentary army – Scottish infantry – on a wide expanse of moorland known as Marston Moor. By dawn the area was filling up with troops as Rupert's men and the parliamentary army moved into position, the latter having abandoned their march south. The last to arrive was the York garrison, Newcastle having made clear his opposition to the battle, as did Eythin, who taunted Rupert that his impetuosity had cost lives before: 'Sir, your forwardness lost us the day in Germany [Siege of Lemgo, 1638] where yourself was taken prisoner.'

He also criticised Rupert's deployment for the battle, arguing that it looked well on paper 'but there is no such thing in the field'.[13] This was a slur, as Rupert had had most of the day to draw up his 18,000 men in Swedish style, with musketeers and cavalry formed in squadrons, his own horse on the right with Lords Byron and Molyneaux commanding the first and second lines, the infantry in three lines in the centre and Goring commanding the horse on the left, he taking the first line, Lucas the second. Opposing them to the south, at a distance of only 400 yards, the parliamentary army was drawn up with Cromwell's horse on the left and Sir Thomas Fairfax's horse on the right, both supported by Scots horse troopers. In the

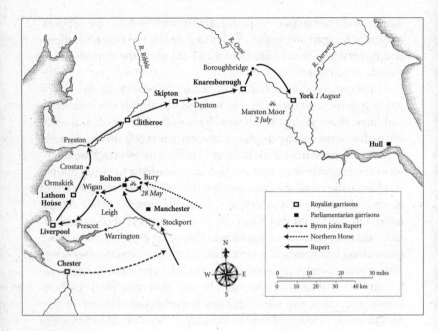

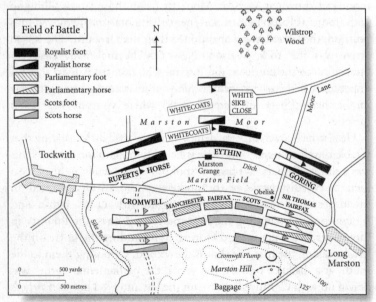

centre in six brigades were the infantry regiments – Manchester's on the left (commanded by Major-General Laurence Crawford), Fairfax's in the centre and the Scots on the right under the command of Lieutenant-General William Baillie. The second line of infantry was composed of men from Manchester's and Leven's forces and there were further Scots in reserve. Numbering 28,000 and under Leven's overall command, the parliamentary army had a numerical advantage, but on the open expanse of moorland Rupert had the benefit of a ditch running in front of his line which acted as an obstacle to cavalry and in which he placed musketeers. By then it was almost evening and the late hour and a flurry of rain showers almost persuaded Rupert that there would be no fighting that day. From his opponent's ranks he could hear the Scots singing metrical psalms. He retired to the rear to eat his supper, Newcastle repaired to his coach to smoke his pipe and their men began to relax. Fighting could wait for another day.

But it was not to be. Leven had noted the loosened discipline in his opponent's ranks and shortly after half past seven he ordered his men to attack at a 'running march' just as a thunderstorm broke. Matters went best for them on the left, where Cromwell's horse, backed by Leslie's Scots troopers, and Crawford's infantry drove back Rupert's right flank in less than an hour, pushing it to the east and causing Byron's cavalry to break in disarray. For Cromwell's scoutmaster the troopers' discipline was 'the bravest sight in the world', but his pleasure was short-lived when Rupert led a counter-charge which had to be checked by Leslie's men:

> Cromwell's own division had a hard pull of it, for they were charged by Rupert's bravest men both in front and flank. They stood at the sword's point a pretty while, hacking one another; but at last (it so pleased God) he broke through them, scattering them before him like a little dust. At the same instant the rest of our horse of that wing had wholly broken all Prince Rupert's horse on their right wing, and were in chase of them beyond their left wing.[14]

During the fighting Cromwell was wounded by a slash to his neck and was forced to retire to have it treated, but Leslie's intervention steadied his men and soon the Royalist cavalry were 'flying along by Wilstrop Wood [to the north of the moor] as fast and as thick as could be'.

Things were going less well on the right, where Fairfax's charge had ended in disaster. Finding their progress checked by broken ground and clumps of bushes they came under musket fire from Goring's men and suffered such heavy casualties that they were soon in flight, with only Lord Eglinton's lightly armed Scottish horse holding their ground. When Lucas's second line charged it caused further panic, and in the confusion many of the infantry on the right were put to flight. The hysteria spread to the high command: believing that the day was lost, both Leven and Lord Fairfax decided that discretion was the better part of valour and having failed to rally their men joined them in undignified retreat. Writing to Ormond after the battle Sir Arthur Trevor left a vivid description of an army in disordered retreat:

In the fire, smoke and confusion of that day, the runaways on both sides were so many, so breathless, so speechless, and so full of fears, that I should not have taken them for men; both armies being mingled, both horse and foot; no side keeping their own posts.

In this horrible distraction did I coast the country; here meeting with a shoal of Scots crying out 'Weys us, we are all undone'; and so full of lamentation and mourning, as if their day of doom had overtaken, and from which they knew not whither to fly: and anon I met with a ragged troop reduced to four and a Cornet; by and by with a little foot officer without hat, band, sword, or indeed anything but feet and so much tongue as would serve to enquire the way to the next garrisons, which (to say the truth) were well filled with the stragglers on both sides within a few hours, though they lay distant from the place of the fight 20 or 30 miles.[15]

Not all the Scots behaved badly. Two regiments of pikemen (Lindsay's and Maitland's) stood their ground and repulsed successive charges, taking Lucas prisoner into the bargain, but it was not enough to win the day. In the centre most of the Royalist foot was still intact and Goring's cavalry, busy raiding the baggage train, remained a potent force. It was then that the parliamentary horse showed their mettle and the benefit of their training. In the twilight Fairfax had managed to link up with Cromwell and from the east, below Wilstrop Wood, they fell on Goring's horse, who were now forced to 'fight again for that victory which they thought had been already got'. It was a lost cause. In place of the men who had scattered before their first charge the Royalist cavalry found themselves fighting the disciplined horse troopers of the Eastern Association army and Leslie's Scots, both of whom 'performed their duty with such resolution and courage, as they utterly routed the enemy's army and chased them into the gates of York, as many as could escape; and all this performed before 12 o'clock in the night, the moon with her light helping something of the darkness of the season'.[16]

With the field cleared of cavalry the way was open for Cromwell and Leslie to deal with the remaining Royalist foot in the centre, composed mainly of Newcastle's infantry penned in at White Sike Close, where they were still vainly trying to engage their opponents. Defending their own ground and knowing that the battle was lost, they chose to die where they stood rather than surrender, and under the light of a harvest moon they paid the butcher's bill. The last to die were Newcastle's 'Lambs', their white coats, according to one observer, becoming their winding sheets. Few who saw the slaughter ever forgot it. James Somerville, a Scottish colonel and the erstwhile defender of Morpeth, was among their number:

Neither met they [Cromwell and Leslie] with any great resistance, until they came to the Marquis of Newcastle's battalion of white coats who first peppering them soundly with their shot, when they came to charge stoutly bore them up with their pike, that they could not enter to break them. Here the parliament horse of that wing received the greatest loss, and a stop for time to their hoped-for victory, and that only by the stout resistance of this gallant battalion, which consisted near of four thousand foot, until at length a Scots regiment of dragoons, commanded by Colonel Frizell [Colonel Hugh Fraser of Kynneries], with other two, was brought to open them upon some hand, which at length they did; when all their ammunition was spent, having refused quarters, every man fell in the same order and rank wherein he had fought.[17]

Only thirty men survived the slaughter. Perhaps it was a glorious end – they were men of the north defending their own country – but it was also unnecessary. Not only had quarter been offered, which would have allowed them to fight another day, but it robbed Charles's forces of its best infantry at a time when disciplined foot soldiers were at a premium. Four thousand Royalist soldiers died on Marston Moor in a battle which lasted just over two hours; half that number were parliamentary casualties. It was the bloodiest encounter of the civil war to date and it dealt a tremendous blow to Charles's influence in the north. York was again under threat of siege – as the stragglers made their way back they found the gates shut against them – and large amounts of supplies and arms had fallen into the hands of the parliamentary forces which were still encamped on the moor. Resistance was still possible, but shocked by the carnage and dismayed by their defeat the Royalist leadership had a collective loss of nerve.

Newcastle and Eythin were the last to leave the field, and they met up with Rupert, who had been forced to hide in a bean field after the rout of his cavalry. It cannot have been a happy conference, each commander blaming the other, and it led to the collapse of the northern command structure. Two days later Rupert and Goring took their forces back into Lancashire, taking with them Montrose's small army, the former to secure the north-west, the latter to return to Scotland accompanied by two companions to raise the king's standard 'for the defence and maintenance of the true Protestant religion, his Majesty's just and sacred authority, the fundamental laws and privileges of parliaments, the peace and freedom of the oppressed and thralled subject'.

A different fate awaited Newcastle. Fearing the 'laughter of the court', or more likely the king's censure for his slowness in deploying his forces, he resigned his commission and retired to Scarborough, where he took ship to Hamburg to begin an exile in Paris which lasted until the Restoration in 1660. With him, albeit in another ship, went Eythin and other senior officers from his army. Having spent a huge part of his personal fortune in supporting the king's cause, Newcastle was played out, and in his wife's words, 'he had nothing left in his power to do his Majesty any further service in that kind', but his departure meant that the north was virtually lost to the king. It also allowed the parliamentary forces to disperse: Leven to take the Scots north to complete the investment of Newcastle, Cromwell and Manchester back to Lincolnshire, while the Fairfaxes remained in Yorkshire, where Pontefract and Scarborough remained in Royalist control. As for York, it surrendered on 16 July. The garrison was permitted to march out with the full honours of war.

For the parliamentary army Marston Moor was a triumph. It proved the worth of the Eastern Association horse, soon to be called 'Ironsides' after Rupert's professional evaluation of them; Thomas Fairfax was confirmed as an outstanding commander and the foot regiments had behaved well under their Scottish commanders, Crawford, Baillie and Lumsden. Leven's decision to engage proved to be decisive because it is clear that neither Rupert nor Newcastle were expecting an attack so late in the day, and although the Scot can be faulted for his panicky retreat, in the smoke and confusion of the fighting, he believed that the collapse of his right signalled the defeat of his entire force. Later, when he was being forced to defend his reputation, Cromwell would claim that next to God he himself was the architect of victory, but that was stretching a point. By instilling discipline in his troopers he was able to make two decisive charges, each time supported by Leslie, but the fact that Marston Moor saw a battle at all was due entirely to Rupert's decision to engage in one. To the end of his life he kept close to him the king's ambiguous but fateful command that York had to be relieved and the enemy defeated. One further sadness awaited Rupert: among the casualties on the field of battle was his white poodle 'Boy', throughout the earlier fighting a loyal and constant companion.

Chapter Nine

THE PITY OF WAR

'It was easy to begin the war, but no man knew where it would end.'

The Earl of Manchester, following the Battle of Marston Moor, 2 July 1644

If Marston Moor was, in Cromwell's words, 'an absolute victory obtained by God's blessing', its bloody nature also proved that Englishmen and Scotsmen were prepared to fight and kill each other to the bitter end. At one point during the slaughter of Newcastle's 'Lambs' Sir Thomas Fairfax was seen trying to stop his troopers' swords, crying out that they were slashing Englishmen, but an amnesty having been refused no quarter was given. This was now war to the knife. Others died equally horrible deaths, hacked down as they fled from the field, and many more died from the kind of horrific wound endured by Gabriel Ludlow of Hesilrige's regiment, 'with his belly broken and bowels torn, his hip-bone broken, all the shivers and the bullet lodged in it'. In close-quarters fighting where damage was done by musketball or sword-slash there was nothing glamorous in the aftermath of the seventeenth-century battlefield, as dying men called for help which would never be forthcoming. Those who survived also faced the possibility of death from the scavengers who haunted the battlefield in the aftermath of the fighting, robbing the dead and killing off those who resisted. On the day after the battle a woman was seen vainly seeking her husband's body: this was Lady Towneley, whose husband was a Royalist cavalry colonel. Coming across her among the scene of carnage, Cromwell was so moved that he ordered one of his troopers to act as her escort, a kindness which she never forgot.[1]

However, while Marston Moor was a well-won battle it was not decisive and the army which won it quickly dispersed. As it did so, growing differences of opinion opened up between Cromwell and Manchester over the need to prosecute the war with greater determination, and the first sounds were heard of the Scots' disapproval of Cromwell's growing ambition, Baillie noting that it seemed 'that Cromwell alone, with his unspeakably valorous regiments, had done all that service'.[2] Although the Committee for Both Kingdoms exhorted its field commanders 'to lay aside all disputes of their rights and privileges, and to join heartily in the present service', Cromwell remained unhappy. He had not welcomed the alliance with the Scots, thought little of their military ability, and while he had signed the Solemn League and Covenant, he was opposed to the introduction of Presbyterian Church government. Small wonder that he had grown to dislike Laurence Crawford, Manchester's Scottish major-general and a strict fundamentalist, who was not only twelve years his junior but had superior military experience, having been a professional soldier in Europe all his working life. Equally indicative of Cromwell's thinking was the selection of 'godly' and 'plain' men to his regiments, among them soldiers who were 'Independents' inclined to political liberty and religious nonconformity. This had already led him to quarrel with Crawford, who had sacked Lieutenant-Colonel Henry Warner for refusing to sign the Solemn League and Covenant, and before the year was out similar disagreements would lead him into a long and acrimonious quarrel with Manchester.

The unease in the parliamentary camp was fuelled by news of a fresh setback which undid all the good work created on Marston Moor – the crushing defeat of Essex's army at Lostwithiel near Fowey in Cornwall on 2 September 1644. This came as a result of the parliamentary commander's imprudent rush into the West Country, leaving Waller to engage Charles's forces, his aim being to wrest Cornwall from the king's control and, with any luck, to capture

Henrietta Maria before she left the country. In both hopes he was to be confounded: by the time Essex arrived the queen had managed to escape from Falmouth on a Dutch ship. Although Essex managed to raise Maurice's siege of Lyme – a signal success – no sooner had he done the same for Plymouth and crossed the Tamar on 26 July than Charles, accompanied by Hopton and Maurice, was in hot pursuit with 16,000 men. Far from seizing the initiative Essex was in danger of overstretching his lines of communication and getting cut off in the West Country, but still he pressed on, trusting that his display of force would encourage the people of Cornwall to change sides. It was a faint hope. By the time he reached Bodmin on 28 July Charles was only twenty miles behind him at Launceston, and Essex reported to parliament that only a 'few gentlemen' had thrown in their lot with him. Under the circumstances his main hope lay with Warwick's warships in the Channel.

Throughout the siege of Lyme parliamentary ships had provided hope and sustenance to Robert Blake's garrison. They were not the deciding factor but, as had been the case during the siege of Hull the previous autumn, their presence and the supplies they brought with them had given much needed hope to the hard-pressed town. Now Essex hoped that Warwick's ships would follow his army down the Channel as he moved on Dartmouth and the Cornish ports, which were in Royalist hands. Once these had been regained and Cornwall had been secured it might then be possible to think about recovering the key port of Bristol, such was the growing strength of the parliamentary navy in the Irish Sea and Bristol Channel. First of all, though, the naval and land forces had to act in tandem, and their failure to do so led to Essex losing his earlier advantage.

Two problems beset him. First, he had to leave garrisons at the places he had relieved and to cover his lines of communications; secondly, his supplies began to run low and he was refused help by the local population. If he could hold out until Waller arrived to threaten the king's rear all would be well, but this balancing act depended on holding the port of Fowey until Warwick's ships arrived and, unknown to him, these had been delayed by contrary winds. Undecided about what to do next and unclear about the general strategic situation – he was not to know that Waller could only afford to send a weak force of 2000 under the command of the Scottish general John Middleton – Essex took the option of defending Fowey by placing his main field army at Lostwithiel, which covered the estuary of the River Fowey. It was an all-or-nothing solution because if defeated in a pitched battle his army would be cut off and destroyed; their only hope was to hold out until the navy arrived.

Against him he faced an army that outnumbered his three-to-one and would soon be joined by Sir Richard Grenville's force, which had been besieging Plymouth. Charles had the upper hand, but even at that crucial stage of the campaign when he needed a decisive victory to keep control of Cornwall he was suddenly faced by a crisis in his command structure. Lord Wilmot, who was becoming increasingly unhappy about his lack of preferment, began to have second thoughts about the good sense of prosecuting the war and voiced his opinion that it might be better to find an accommodation with parliament. Unfortunately for the king's Master of Horse, he did not attempt to hide his views and, worse, communicated them to Essex. In itself this was not treasonable, for Charles himself was in correspondence with the parliamentary commander in an attempt to persuade him to combine with him to bring about a 'happy settlement', an offer which Essex politely declined as it needed parliamentary approval. What settled Wilmot's fate was his suggestion that the two men unite to find a solution by ridding the king of the councils of Digby and Rupert, the two men thought by parliament to be the most culpable of his 'evil advisers'.

The plot was betrayed by Digby, no friend, and Wilmot was arrested while riding at the head of his men on 8 August and sent back in disgrace to Exeter, from where he went into exile in France. He was replaced by the ubiquitous Goring, but the manner of his dismissal caused great offence in the Royalist cavalry. Wilmot might have been, as Clarendon claimed, a hard drinker who was 'proud and ambitious and incapable of being contented', but he was popular and he had good reason to feel that his leadership at Roundway Down and Cropredy Bridge had been overlooked by the king. Still, the consequences were not all bad: the capable Goring was given a new command and the Royalist army also lost the services of Wilmot's friend, the hopeless general of artillery Lord Percy. His replacement was the more than capable Hopton.

At any other time the incident might have been unsettling, but such was the momentum of the Royalist army in the west and so high were the odds stacked in its favour that it proved to be little more than a hiccup. By the time Grenville's force arrived from Bodmin three days later, Essex had been effectively surrounded. In an attempt to cover his position he had placed the main body of his infantry in Fowey while another large force was placed on Beacon Hill to the east of Lostwithiel and at the derelict Restormel Castle to the north. From his headquarters at Boconnoc House – used by Hopton for the same purpose before Braddock Down – Charles responded by securing the eastern bank of the Fowey estuary at Polruan and Bodinnock before attacking the position on Beacon Hill on 21 August. This his army accomplished with skill and discipline, marching along a broad front, four miles long, while Grenville's men attacked Restormel Castle. By nightfall the position had been secured and the Royalist army was looking down into Lostwithiel.

With this move Essex's army was now trapped, and Charles completed the process by sending cavalry under Goring and Sir Thomas Bassett to secure St Blazey to the west, a deployment which also prevented supplies from being shipped in through the small port of Par. Surrender seemed to be the only option for Essex. There was no sign of Warwick's fleet and even if it arrived it would be attacked by the Royalist positions at Polruan; on land Middleton's relief force had only managed to get as far as Sherborne. Essex's only hope was to attempt a breakout and to exploit the fact that Charles's forces were stretched out over a fifteen-mile front. The weather, too, was helping neither side, the earlier sunshine having given way to heavy rain and unseasonable sea-mists.

The deadlock was broken on 30 August when two deserters arrived at Boconnoc with the news that Essex's cavalry were to break out that night and attempt to escape eastwards while his infantry retreated into Fowey. Steps were taken to defend the route the parliamentary horse would take, but it was in vain. At three o'clock in the morning, when spirits are usually at their lowest, 2000 horses and men under the command of Sir William Balfour dashed out of Lostwithiel and clattered up the road to Liskeard. By dawn they were at Saltash and all but 100 escaped back into Devon, where they were able to link up with Middleton. While this was an embarrassment to the Royalists it spurred Charles into action, and at seven o'clock in the morning he ordered his men to move into Lostwithiel as Essex's men began the retreat south in some disorder, the road being 'extreme foul with excessive rain'. A running battle followed, with Essex's army being pushed down towards Fowey, where they took up a new position at nightfall around a circular double-ramparted earthwork fortress known as Castle Dore. With no cavalry to support them the infantrymen were tired and demoralised, and although their commander, Sir Philip Skippon, wanted to continue fighting the end was drawing near. That night Essex decided to cut and run, escaping in a fishing boat which took him to Plymouth. He excused his flight with the thought that he was too important a commander to fall into enemy hands: 'I thought it fit to look to myself, it being a greater terror to me to be a slave to their contempts than a thousand deaths.'[3]

That night it rained heavily – a further blow to morale – and by morning Skippon's cause was hopeless. He called for terms and the next day, 2 September, his army marched out of Fowey with their personal weapons to begin the long trail back to Southampton and Portsmouth, arriving later in the month a broken and depleted force. For the king it had been a personal triumph. Not only was Lostwithiel a resounding victory which went some way to avenge the defeat at Marston Moor – Essex called it 'the greatest blow we have ever suffered' – but the king had displayed great powers of leadership by keeping his army under control along a wide front and moving it astutely into the attack. He erred on the side of magnanimity by allowing Skippon's men to march away with their arms and their colours, but this was balanced by the behaviour of his own men as the defeated parliamentary army began its long march back to London. Among those watching them was Richard Symonds of the king's Life Guard of Horse:

They all, except here and there an officer, (and seriously I saw not above three or four that looked like a gentleman) were stricken with such dismal fear, that as soon as their colour of the regiment was passed (for every ensign had a horse and rode on him and was so suffered) the rout of soldiers of that regiment was pressed all of a heap like sheep, though not so innocent. So dirty and so dejected as was rare to see. None of them, except some few of their officers, that did look any of us in the face. Our foot would flout at them and bid them remember Reading, Greenland House (where others that did no condition with them took them away all prisoners), and many other places, and then would pull their swords, etc away, for all our officers still slashed at them.

The rebels told us as they passed that our officers and gentlemen carried themselves honourably, but they were hard dealt withal by the common soldiers.[4]

Several of those officers had their coats and hats stripped from them and others were 'abused, reviled, scorned, torn, kicked' as they marched past the jeering Royalist ranks in the steady downpour. It was an undignified and sullen end to the battle, which underlined the divisions caused by the war. At one point two brothers in Charles's army saw a third brother in the parliamentary ranks and had to be restrained from pulling him out and putting him to the sword

Two days later Charles moved his army back to Tavistock, but his progress was slow. On 11 September he summoned the governor of Plymouth to surrender, and when this was refused he left Grenville to begin again the task of besieging the port while he moved to Sherborne. His intentions were unclear but they caused alarm in the parliamentary camp. Terrified that the king intended to march on London, parliament ordered Waller to move his army into Dorset while Manchester took his Eastern Association army, albeit tardily, towards Reading. In fact Charles had fairly limited objectives. He wanted to capitalise on his victory but the presence of the two parliamentary armies posed a threat he could not ignore. In order to secure his position at Oxford he had to relieve three key positions at Basing House, Donnington Castle and Banbury and he had to secure the routes into Wales. To meet those needs Rupert, by then back in Bristol, was ordered to take the offensive into Gloucestershire in the hope that this might draw Waller's army, and if this failed he was to meet up with the king's main army at Marlborough. Although suffering from exhaustion and depression Rupert rallied to the task and quickly raised a force comprising Welsh infantrymen, the remnants of Newcastle's army and the Northern Horse, an elite cavalry corps of 'gentlemen of quality' commanded by Sir Marmaduke Langdale, a Yorkshireman whose sepulchral appearance had earned him the name of 'The Ghost'. Assembling the force proved to be a lengthy business, and by the time it was on the move the king had been drawn into battle, for a second time, at Newbury.

Encouraged by the news that Goring had successfully dislodged Waller's cavalry from Andover, Charles hoped to push on to relieve Basing House, which had been besieged by a parliamentary force since July. However, Waller's retreat and Manchester's advance blocked the way, and a confrontation became inevitable when the armies moved into position around Newbury in the fourth week of October. It was a difficult position for the king: he had a smaller army and was unsure if Rupert would arrive in time to support him but, even so, he was by no means unable to offer battle. By then the parliamentary armies had been strengthened by the arrival of the remnants of Essex's army, sufficiently recovered from their long march and under Skippon's command,* but their command structure was woefully inadequate. No one was in overall control, the direction of the operations being vested in a council which was answerable to the Committee of Both Kingdoms. It also helped the Royalist cause that Charles's army had taken up a dominating position to the north of Newbury: to the right was the town and the River Kennet, while his left was protected by the walls and guns of Donnington Castle.

Faced by the obstacle, which soon became apparent to their scouts, the war council met on 26 October and agreed that the Royalist army would have to be outflanked and attacked from the rear while the main force mounted a frontal assault. The plan was probably devised by Waller, and its final form was assisted by the information given by the turncoat Sir John Hurry, who had turned traitor once more, bringing with him an accurate picture of the disposition of the king's army. That night Waller took the flanking force, made up of Essex's infantry and Cromwell's horse and amounting to some 13,000 men, north on a long circular march which brought them on to Wickham Heath behind the Royalist army by the following afternoon. At this point the plan began to go awry. As the march progressed Waller's men came under fire from Donnington Castle, and in an attempt to relieve the pressure Manchester ordered his foot to begin a feinting attack which resulted in some hard fighting along the line. It was a

---

* Diplomatically perhaps, Essex had caught a cold and remained behind at Reading.

well-meant gesture, but as the success of the move depended on both sides attacking simultaneously it achieved little other than to alert the Royalist army to the danger facing them. Fortunately for them, though, the parliamentary plan was already unravelling. Waller finally got into position in the middle of the afternoon and began an attack which broke the Royalist left, but Manchester dithered and it was not until dusk that his men were ordered to move.

At one point in the skirmishing the king came close to being captured or killed as Maurice's horse broke and fled and he was saved only by the timely intervention of his Life Guard of Horse. There was some hard fighting on the left sector which centred on the village of Speen, but the advantage won by Waller's infantry was not exploited by Cromwell's horse, who were slow to intervene and played no particular role in the battle. By nightfall the fighting had died down, and if there was no decisive result at least Charles's army of 9000 had put up a good defence against a superior enemy attacking on two fronts. Sensing that his men were unlikely to repeat their efforts the following day, Charles ordered them to retreat towards Wallingford and Oxford. A belated attempt was made at pursuit and Sir John Boys, the governor of Donnington Castle, was summoned to surrender, but the second Battle of Newbury was over and it was one which the much larger and fresher parliamentary army should have won.

A chance to regain the initiative came within the next fortnight when Charles brought 15,000 men to raise the siege of Donnington Castle and retrieve the artillery train which he had placed in Boys's care. A brief and undignified confrontation followed on 9 November at Speenhamland, near the castle, but Manchester was resolved not to fight, not least because he was outnumbered and Rupert's cavalry forces were in the vicinity. There was some desultory skirmishing and an exchange of fire – Symonds saw that 'a musket bullet in volley shot the king's horse in the foot as he stood before his own regiment in arms' – but little else, and as the light faded Charles's army rode off, as if in triumph, colours flying, drums beating and 'trumpets prattling their marches'.[5] Ten days later the siege of Banbury was lifted and on 23 November the king was able to take his army back into winter quarters in Oxford. And so, after the shock of losing the north at Marston Moor, the year drew to a close on a reasonably high note with the west, south-west and Wales secured. Rupert had been newly installed as lieutenant-general of the king's armies in place of Forth, who had been injured at Newbury and was considered too querulous and ancient for the struggle which lay ahead; as a reward he was appointed to an English earldom (Brentford), an unusual honour for a Scot.

If hearts were high in the king's camp no such harmony reigned on the opposite side. On the contrary, at a meeting of senior commanders held on 10 November the extent of the schism within had become perfectly clear when Manchester pointed out the uselessness of further action against the king. 'Gentlemen, I beseech you let's consider what we do,' he counselled. 'The King cares not how oft he fights, but it concerns us to be wary, for in fighting we venture all to nothing. If we fight 100 times and beat him 99 he will be King still, but if he beats us but once, or the last time, we shall be hanged, we shall lose our estates, and our posterities be undone.' This was the voice of a man sick of war, who wanted to negotiate a peace settlement before Charles attracted military assistance from France or elsewhere in Europe. Manchester was not alone in harbouring defeatist thoughts, but his words brought a hasty rebuke from Cromwell, by now the most pugnacious and determined of the parliamentary commanders. 'My Lord,' he replied, 'if this be so, why did we take up arms at first? This is against fighting ever hereafter. If so, let us make peace, be it never so base.'[6]

It was not the end of the matter. The row rumbled on over the winter in parliament and the ensuing debate paved the way for the creation of a national professional armed force called the New Model Army. It began when Hesilrige addressed the House of Commons, still dressed dramatically in military clothes, to give the first account of the events at Newbury and Donnington, and to extol 'the gallantry and conduct of all the commanders and the valour of the soldiers'. While this was not in doubt members wanted a more objective view of the fighting and why it had not proved possible to pursue the king. After Waller and Cromwell added their explanations later in the month the disagreement between the latter and Manchester became public and increasingly unpleasant. Addressing the house on 25 November, Cromwell finally released the bitterness he felt towards the commander of the Eastern Association army when he said that 'the said Earl hath always been indisposed and backward to engagements, and the ending of the war by the sword, and always for such a Peace as a thorough victory would be a disadvantage to – and hath declared this by principles express to that purpose, and by a continued series of carriage and actions answerable'. Manchester responded with a detailed reply drafted for him by Crawford, but the quarrel was rapidly escalating beyond the two men into a wider sphere in which Manchester represented the 'Presbyterians' (moderate, in favour of unified Church government, pro-peace) and Cromwell the 'Independents' (radical, in favour of freedom of worship, pro-war). In private Manchester accused his rival of filling his regiments with Anabaptists and sectaries, a breed of people who would do away with titles and privileges and were potential regicides.[7]

To make matters worse, this view was being shared increasingly by the Scottish commissioners in London, who believed that Cromwell was under the sway of 'these wild and enormous people' and that as a result the Solemn League and Covenant was under threat. They hoped that Cromwell might have made a noose for himself by aiding the creation of an army full of independents intent on 'dissolving the union of the nations, of abolishing the House of Lords, of dividing the House of Commons' and shared with Essex the view that their joint enemy was a dangerous incendiary who should be impeached. Privately, Cromwell responded by saying that he would rather fight the Scots than accept their religious principles and in so saying he expressed a view which was gaining increasing currency – that the Scottish demands were not worth the weight of their military support. Even the mild-mannered Baillie could see how events were turning against his people when he wrote home presciently explaining his fear that 'the Independents are resolute to give in their reasons against us, and that shall be the beginning of an open schism: likely after that, we shall be forced to deal with them as open enemies'.[8] That day was still far off, but the quarrel needed a solution, and parliament found it by setting up a committee to examine the charges.

Cromwell's next move showed the measure of the man as a politician of stature who was in control of his own destiny. Speaking to the House of Commons on 9 December, and using words which his biographer found 'reminiscent of Mark Antony after the death of Caesar',[9] Cromwell raised the matter from an argument about personalities and methods to one of principle upon whose outcome the future of England depended:

> It is now a time to speak, or forever hold the tongue. The important occasion now is no less than to save a nation out of a bleeding, nay, almost dying condition, which the long continuance of this war hath already brought it into; so that without a more speedy, vigorous and effectual prosecution of the war – casting off all lingering proceedings like soldiers of fortune beyond sea, to spin out a war – we shall make the kingdom weary of us, and hate the name of a Parliament.
>
> For what do the enemy say? Nay, what do many say that were friends at the beginning of the Parliament? Even this, that the members of both Houses have got great places and commands, and the sword, into their hands; and, what by interest in the Parliament, what by power in the Army, will perpetually continue themselves in grandeur, and not permit the war speedily to end, lest their own power should determine with it. This I speak here to our own faces is but what others do utter abroad behind our backs. I am far from reflecting on any. I know the worth of those commanders, members of both Houses, who are yet in power: but if I may speak my conscience without reflection on any, I do conceive if the Army be not put into another method and the war more vigorously prosecuted, the people can bear the war no longer, and will enforce you to a dishonourable peace.[10]

As well as being no mean orator, Cromwell also emerged as a first-rate parliamentary tactician. Obviously briefed beforehand, Zouch Tate, the chairman of the committee investigating the quarrel, moved that 'during the time of this war no member of either House shall have or execute any office or command, military or civil, granted or conferred by both or either of the Houses'. This was seconded by Sir Henry Vane and the result was the Self-Denying Ordinance which came into force the following year in a slightly amended form. The House of Lords was sceptical and demanded modifications but the basic precept of the ordinance remained intact. At one stroke the command structure of the parliamentary forces had been changed by preventing members of parliament or members of the House of Lords from holding military positions, a decision that removed Essex and Manchester from their commands but not, as we shall see, Cromwell.

In Oxford Charles took some comfort from the reports of parliament's squabbles, but before the year was out his mood was cheered further by the news coming out of Scotland. Leven had captured Newcastle on 22 October, but in his northern kingdom the king had found a new champion in Montrose, who had won a succession of stunning victories over his king's enemies. At a time when the war was becoming more savage – the executions of Irish prisoners and the butcher's bill at Marston Moor – the story of Montrose's exploits also offered a hint of high romance, of a hero risking everything against the odds in the cause of the king. With his bold moves – starting an adventure with 'two followers, four sorry horses, little money and no baggage' – everything about Montrose was shrouded in glorious mystique. He was a son of the Kirk yet he hated religious fanaticism; he was no friend to the divine right of kings, yet he raised an army to fight for the king. He was a Lowland aristocrat yet he earned the loyalty and the respect of his Highland and Irish army. He has also been fortunate with his biographers, not least John Buchan, himself a Presbyterian cavalier full of contradictions – in the dedication to his biography Buchan saw his brother William as his hero while he apostrophised himself as his polar opposite:

> With Bruce we crouched in bracken shade.
> With Douglas charged the Paynim foes;
> And oft in moorland noons I played
> Colkitto to your grave Montrose.

The reality of Montrose's experiences, though, was somewhat at odds with Buchan's romantic view of his hero: the reality was that Montrose fought a savage low-intensity war against the Covenanting opposition. In the fighting old scores were paid off, property was wilfully destroyed, quarter rarely given, and in one incident he condoned the killing of civilians, but his daring and his focused courage single out Montrose as a great visionary leader. He had arrived back in Scotland in the days after Marston Moor to find Huntly in hiding, and with his absence any hope of support had evaporated. A lesser man might have given up, but shortly after his arrival at a kinsman's house in Strathearn Montrose received the welcome news that support from Ireland was on its way in the shape of 2000 Irishmen loyal to Antrim and commanded by Alasdair MacColla, who had landed in Mull at the end of June 1644 and had raised a Highland army from the ranks of clans opposed to Campbell. Not every clan chief was impressed – many were Protestant and the Irish were disliked – but by the time Alasdair MacColla had made contact with Montrose he had attracted the support of the Macphersons, the MacDonalds of Keppoch, and the Farquharsons.

The great adventure began on Truidh Hill near Blair Atholl, where Montrose raised his standard 'for the defence and maintenance of the true Protestant religion, his Majesty's just and sacred authority, the fundamental laws and privileges of Parliaments, the peace and freedom of the oppressed and thralled subject'. Wearing trews and a bonnet he cut a romantic figure; he had squared his conscience and decided that while he had signed the Covenant six years earlier his allegiance now lay with the king and the maintenance of the settled order. His conduct certainly impressed the men of Atholl – Stewarts and Robertsons – who having opposed Alasdair MacColla's army now threw in their lot with it. With a force of just under 3000 men they set off south, marching to Castle Menzies before heading east towards Perth, which was defended by a Covenanting army commanded by Lord Elcho and consisting of men from Fife, Perthshire and Angus.

They met on open ground at Tibbermore (or Tippermuir) in the rich agricultural plain of Strathearn to the west of Perth on 1 September, a hot Sunday, their lines drawn up across the valley, Montrose deploying his men in a long line, only three deep. Before the battle ministers led Elcho's men in prayer as their flags fluttered in what little breeze existed – one banner left little room for compromise, it read 'Jesus and no quarter'. But the Highlanders and Irish were equally determined and after facing a volley of cannon fire they began advancing, gathering speed as they charged up to the opposition lines before firing off their weapons and then plunging in with the sword and the dirk. Some men, unarmed, picked up stones and threw them at the astonished parliamentary levies, who quickly lost their nerve and broke. After the subsequent mêlée and chase 1300 men lay dead, some 800 were captured and large numbers of weapons and supplies were plundered. The rout was total and that evening Montrose accepted the surrender of Perth, a key city which commanded the routes into the Highlands and the north-east.

A first victory always gives an army confidence, but the next step was fraught with problems. In the aftermath of the battle several clansmen left for home carrying their booty with them – a perennial problem with Highlanders – but it was essential to keep up the momentum, not least because news arrived that Argyll was hurrying towards the city with a large army from the west. On 4 September the Royalist army marched out of Perth heading towards the key towns in the east and north-east. Dundee was summoned to surrender but refused – its harbour allowed it to be supplied from the sea and it was well protected – leaving Montrose and Alasdair MacColla little option but to march on to Aberdeen, no stranger to strife. On their way through Angus they were joined by the Earl of Airlie and other local gentry and they arrived outside the north-eastern city on 12 September.

Since Montrose had last visited Aberdeen it had been brought under firm Covenanting control and it had been heavily defended in the expectation that it would be the next Royalist target. Leadership of the local forces was in the hands of the Lord Balfour of Burleigh and Major Arthur Forbes, a professional soldier. The next morning, 13 September, Montrose summoned the magistrates to surrender 'and give up your town in the behalf of his Majesty' but the provost politely declined as he contested that the city and its inhabitants 'have been ever known to be most loyal and dutiful subjects to his Majesty'. Following the parley, during which much drink was taken, the envoys made their way back, but as they did so one of the local militiamen shot the drummer-boy in cold blood, an action at which Montrose 'grew mad and became furious and impatient . . . charging his men to kill and pardon no one'.[11] Having broken the rules of war, Aberdeen would pay the full penalty as Montrose brought his army from their positions at Garthdee towards Justice Mills, the open land on the western approaches on the north bank of the Howburn.*

---

* The land, close to the city centre, has been completely built over, although some of the contemporary names are remembered in the names of the modern streets.

The Covenanting army had the advantage of height, being lined up on a crest of rising ground, and they possessed more horse and superior artillery, but they lacked leadership and with it the élan of a general will to win, Patrick Gordon of Ruthven, a witness, observing that 'the [Covenanting] horsemen, being almost composed of lords, barons and gentlemen of quality, were all divided in several opinions, for want of a head, whose opinion and order they ought to have followed'.[12] That lack of cohesion proved to be their undoing. Following an exchange of volleys and cavalry charges, one led by William Forbes of Craigievar which came unstuck when the Irish allowed the horsemen through only to fall on them from behind and an ill-advised attempt by Balfour of Burleigh to outflank the Royalist force, the Irish and Highland regiments dropped their pikes and muskets and swept up the slope, swords and dirks in hand. For the opposing infantry, many untried and most terrified, the charge was too ferocious to resist and within minutes they were in full flight. Some of the militia units retreated in good order and tried to resist but in the city's narrow streets there was no hiding place as the Irish caterans and Highlanders fell on them 'hewing and cutting down all manner of man they could overtake within the town, upon the streets, or in their houses'.

Black Friday (doubly unlucky: it was 13 September), which saw the sack of Aberdeen, was one of the worst atrocities of the fighting in Scotland and it left a stain on the honour of 'gentle Montrose', but his men's blood was up and they had been promised due reward for their victory. Four years earlier Montrose had intervened to prevent Aberdeen from being burned down, but now it felt the full force of a revenge attack which shocked even those, like John Spalding, who were well disposed to the king's cause:

The Irish continued Friday, Saturday, Sunday, Monday. Some women they pressed to deflower and other some they took perforce to serve them in the camp. It is lamentable to hear how the Irish who had gotten the spoil of the town did abuse the same. The men they killed they would not suffer to be buried, but tore them of their clothes, then left their naked bodies above the ground. The wife dared not cry nor weep at her husband's slaughter before her eyes, nor the mother for the son, nor daughter for father; which, if they were heard, then they were presently slain also.[13]

Aberdeen was a bad business. The burgh records concluded that 'eight score' citizens had been killed (160, but it was probably more, Spalding noting that most had been killed in the 'flight, falling back to the town'), women were raped and houses and businesses looted. Before pulling his army out of the city Montrose caused a proclamation to be read claiming he had only come to Aberdeen to restore its people to obedience to the king but he could not afford to dally either to savour his victory or to secure the city. Once more Argyll's army was on his tail, having reached Brechin to the south on 16 September, when he was joined by forces led by other Covenanting magnates including the Earl Marischal, Forbes, Fraser and Crichton.

From Aberdeen Montrose and Alasdair MacColla moved into Speyside and then back over the hills to Atholl, burning crops and rounding up cattle and horses as they went. Behind them came Argyll, who laid waste to the lands around Huntly and the Braes of Gicht as well as in Deeside, all Gordon lands, but the Covenanting leader had no desire at this stage to force a confrontation. The closest the two armies came to a battle was at the end of October when Montrose was back in the north-east, after Alasdair MacColla had left for the MacDonald lands of the west to find fresh recruits. On 28 October there was a brief skirmish near Fyvie Castle on the River Ythan after lackadaisical intelligence almost allowed Argyll to get the better of the Royalist force by making a determined push towards Fyvie. Montrose retrieved his position by rapidly deploying his men on a strong site on the high ground above the Park Burn and its marshy ground where they were well placed to withstand the Covenanters' assaults. Fighting continued over two days, but with neither side able to establish an advantage they both withdrew and a general truce was declared. With winter drawing in, Argyll took his army back into Strathbogie while Montrose and his men marched over the hills back to Blair Castle in Atholl.

While the first part of his campaign had ended in stalemate, the victory at Tibbermore and the sacking of Aberdeen had made Montrose's and Alasdair MacColla's reputations. To their supporters they were totemic leaders who brought victory (and loot) to the Royalist cause; to the Covenanters they were blood-thirsty villains and the devil incarnate – Montrose already had a price on his head, £20,000 dead or alive. Together the two men had forged a useful military partnership, Montrose with his inspiring leadership and ability to read a battle and Alasdair MacColla with his strength and courage, which every man admired and wanted to emulate. The best was still to come, but as Robert Baillie noted at the time, their names were on everyone's lips and few in Scotland had not heard of their exploits, of that 'strange coursing . . . thrice round about from Spey to Atholl, wherein Argyll and Lothian's soldiers were tired out; the country harassed by both, and no less by friends than foes, did nothing for their own defence'.[14]

Chapter Ten

SMILE OUT TO GOD IN PRAISES: NASEBY

'A useful lesson to British kings never to exceed the bounds of their just prerogative, and to British subjects never to swerve from the allegiance due to their legitimate monarchs.'

Obelisk erected by the Lord and Lady of the Manor of Naseby, on the Market Harborough Road, 1832

If the army led by Montrose and Alasdair MacColla was a lightly armed guerrilla force, well-suited to a fast-moving campaign, the 'new modelled' army envisaged by Cromwell was a completely different outfit, a professional and disciplined regular force, well paid and well equipped, under the control of an independent commander-in-chief. Following the introduction of the Self-Denying Ordinance – the Lords did not agree to it until April 1645 but its spirit was observed from the outset – parliament busied itself with its implications at the beginning of 1645. Based on the forces led by Essex, Manchester and Waller, it would consist of ten regiments of horse each numbering 600 men, twelve foot regiments each numbering 1200 men and a regiment of 1000 dragoons, but it would take time before these numbers were achieved.* On 21 January command was given to Sir Thomas Fairfax, an obvious choice on account of his military

---

* The armies of the Northern Association and the Western Association remained in being, command of them being given, respectively, to Sydenham Poyntz, who had served in the imperial forces in Germany, and to Gloucester's governor Edward Massey.

distinction and because he was not a member of parliament. Skippon became major-general in charge of the foot but the post of lieutenant-general of horse, a post for which Cromwell was obviously suited, was left open. In keeping with the enthusiasm for modernisation it was also agreed that the infantrymen should wear a uniform coat of red.

The reforms put an end to the military careers of Cromwell's two bugbears, Essex and Manchester, and ended his quarrel with the latter, but his own position was anomalous. He had been one of the prime movers for the creation of a unified professional force (Waller, too, had advocated such a move) and he believed in the principle that members of parliament should not have military commands, yet he had emerged as one of the few parliamentary leaders to show flair as a soldier. He was also a leading figure in parliament during that busy winter. In addition to laying the foundations for the creation of a professional army other matters also demanded attention. Following pressure from the peace party and the Scots commissioners there was a further round of talks with the king's representatives at Uxbridge, but as the terms offered were harsher than anything discussed before – Charles would have been obliged to sign the Solemn League and Covenant and permit the establishment of a Presbyterian Church government – the process came to nothing. While Charles agreed that something should be done to stop the people of Britain 'fighting like beasts' he treated the negotiations with contempt; all thought of any settlement on parliament's terms having evaporated, Charles told his wife that 'the unreasonable stubbornness of the rebels' made any solution impossible. For Cromwell's part he does not seem to have been too displeased when the talks finally ended on 24 February. Only the Scots were aggrieved: their hopes of creating a national Church were fast receding with what seemed to them to be the inexorable growth of the power of Cromwell, the Independents and the 'unhappy and unamendable prolixity' of the Assembly of Divines. As Baillie noted with growing dismay, his English colleagues were 'an irresolute, divided and dangerously-humoured people' who only wanted 'a lame Erastian presbytery'.[1] Not even the execution in January of the Scots' old enemy, the long-imprisoned Archbishop Laud, could convince them that they were getting a good bargain from their relationship with London; in their view things could only get worse. As the New Model Army came into being, the opportunity was already being taken to get rid of many of the Scottish professional soldiers, most notably Crawford, who were replaced by Independents and transferred to the forces in the regions. (Crawford, Cromwell's bête noire, was killed during the siege of Hereford in August 1645.)

In the short term, though, despite the military reforms which would take time to become effective, parliament still needed Leven's army and were impatient to see it marching back into England for the campaigning season which was about to reopen. Ironically, the renewal of hostilities would also provide Cromwell with the means of bypassing the Self-Denying Ordinance and retaining his field command. Whether or not that had always been his intention is open to doubt. Such was the sincerity of his support for the measure that it is unlikely that he was being disingenuous in making the call while hoping privately to be excluded from its terms. His supporters might have prayed that he would not be lost to the army, but his re-appointment as a field commander came about as a result of the renewal of fighting and the happy coincidence that by the time the ordinance became law he was already in the field.*

Parliament's alarm was caused by Goring, who took a force through the southern counties to Farnham at the beginning of February, a move which threatened Portsmouth and, more importantly, raised fears that he might attack London. Once again Waller was called on to command the parliamentary forces, and Cromwell and his Eastern Association horse were put under his command, the Committee for Both Kingdoms enjoining all officers 'to give all ready obedience to such directions, orders and commands as you receive from him [Waller], for performance of which obedience they will require a strict account'. It was a temporary measure but the times were desperate and there was unrest in the ranks of the parliamentary army – there had been mutinies at Henley and Leatherhead in regiments opposed to being transferred from Essex's command. Lack of pay was also to blame for the outbreak of rebelliousness which even affected Cromwell's Ironsides.

---

* Sir William Brereton and Sir Thomas Middleton also retained their military commissions and their seats in the House of Commons.

A frustrating bout of shadow-boxing followed as the two forces marched and counter-marched through the southern counties, at various points threatening Weymouth, Taunton, Salisbury and Melcombe but never engaging in anything more dangerous than brief skirmishes. After the Self-Denying Ordinance became law on 3 April Waller returned to London to resign his commission for the last time and to leave history with a good impression of his ambitious second-in-command:

> He at this time had never shown extraordinary parts, nor do I think that he did himself believe that he had them; for although he was blunt he did not bear himself with any pride or disdain. As an officer he was obedient, and did never dispute my orders nor argue upon them.[2]

For the object of that report there was to be a different future. While Waller was forced to lay down his sword Cromwell's commission was kept in being to allow him to command his regiments of horse for fresh service in the Midlands as part of an operation to prevent the king from breaking out from Oxford.

The threat was real enough, even though the war was slowly slipping out of the king's hands. On 22 February he had lost Shrewsbury when a parliamentary force surprised Sir Michael Ernle's garrison and infamously executed thirteen Irish officers. The capture of the town closed the link between Oxford and the north-west, and the Royalist position in the surrounding area was also taxed by the emergence of 'Clubmen', societies of local farmers and peasants who combined to protect themselves 'against all murders, rapines, plunders, robberies or violence which shall be offered by the soldier or any oppressor whatsoever'. Although neutral, they caused the Royalist forces a good deal of trouble in Shropshire, Worcestershire and Herefordshire in the spring of 1645, at a time when the king was trying to impose his authority on a region which according to one Royalist witness, Henry Townshend, was becoming thoroughly disenchanted with the turmoil of war. Particularly detested was the habit of 'free quarter' practised by Royalist troops, mainly the cavalry:

That the County is fallen into such want and extremity through the number and oppression of the Horse lying upon free quarter that the people are necessitated (their Hay being spent) to feed their horses with corn while their children are ready to starve for want of bread.

Their exacting of free quarter, and extorting sums of money for the time of their absence from their quarters, mingled with threats of firing their Houses, their persons with death, and their goods with pillaging.

Their barbarous seizing men's persons, and compelling them to ransom themselves with very great sums of money to their undoing; and disabling them to assist his Majesty, and that without any order, or warrant; as (for instance) Mr Foley, the two Mrs Turvey and many others.[3]

Townshend ended his litany of horror stories with the thought that it was small wonder that those oppressed 'do not stick to say that they can find more justice, and more money, in the Enemy's quarters than in the King's'. There is ample evidence that parliamentary soldiers had been equally injurious with 'insolencies, oppressions and cruelties' but in the early days of the movement the Clubmen were an irritating diversion for Royalist forces. Rupert certainly thought so: he was not above executing their leaders if he found them over-troublesome.

The south-west was also being vexatious. A separate administration, or court, had been established at Bristol led nominally by the fourteen-year-old Prince of Wales and guided by Hyde, Culpepper and Hopton. It gave the young man a role and in so doing reduced the possibility of father and son being captured together in the event of a serious defeat; but it achieved little, other than to rid Charles of the counsels of Hyde, who was beginning to oppose Digby's notion that the war had to be fought to the bitter end. One of its objectives was to bring some coherence to the Royalist commanders' military activities in the south-west, but this proved a lost cause as the main personalities – Grenville besieging Plymouth and Sir John Berkeley at Exeter – did not take kindly to interference and were acting as independent warlords. Unlike his brother Bevil, Richard Grenville was a hot-headed authoritarian who had been imprisoning and executing personal enemies, including a solicitor who had acted for his estranged wife in a land settlement case. He refused to take orders from Goring, his military superior and yet another Royalist commander whose reputation was being sullied by the 'horrid outrages and barbarities' committed by his men.

Faced by this intransigence and hampered by a chronic lack of infantry, Rupert was only able to proffer a modest plan of action. Realising that he had to increase the area of Royalist influence if he were to attract new recruits, he was in favour of consolidating the counties in Royalist control and using them as a basis for expansion. This meant securing Ludlow and the Welsh Marches and linking up with his brother, who was engaged against Brereton at Chester. The strategic concept was relatively simple – to combine with the Oxford army and march north to defeat the Scots and regain control of the north – but first the Royalists would have to relieve Chester and move into Lancashire and Yorkshire to find new support. In pursuit of this plan Langdale had taken the Northern Horse to lift the siege of Pontefract, which they did on 1 March, killing 300 of the opposition in the process. Langdale's daring raid badly discomfited the Committee for Both Kingdoms, forcing them to send an urgent message to Leven to bring his army out of its winter quarters in Northumberland south into Yorkshire. Further funds were promised on 18 March but the Scottish Estates, alarmed by Montrose's run of success (see next chapter), were unwilling to send their men south while 'Irish rebels and malignants' were causing so much trouble in their own country. In response to the committee's request for military assistance Leven sent four regiments under David Leslie to help Brereton in the north-west, but as he also had to supply troops to deal with Montrose he informed the committee that he was unwilling to move into Yorkshire, lest his absence tempt Charles to try to link up with his Scottish and Irish allies.

Rupert was in favour of moving north, Digby less so, and as a result the king dithered and delayed, partly because Cromwell was operating in the Oxford area, rounding up draft horses for the New Model Army. He had also enjoyed some military success which confirmed his stature as an astute commander. On 24 April he routed a force led by Northampton and that night summoned Bletchington House, which was commanded by Colonel Francis Windebank. Although Cromwell's demand was bluster – without artillery he was powerless and the house was strongly fortified – Windebank chose to surrender because he did not want to subject his young wife to the horrors of war. For his pains Windebank was court-martialled and executed on his return to Oxford, despite the fact that Rupert interceded on his behalf. One other factor intruded. The delay in the Royalist camp was also caused by uncertainty about what the New Model Army would do once it came into being at the end of April. It was easy to satirise it as the New Noddle Army, but would it provide a realistic threat?

The answer came when Fairfax marched it out of Windsor on 30 April 1645 and headed west towards Blandford, his orders being to lift the siege of Taunton. This put Charles and his advisers in a quandary. While they did not want to lose possession of the town they also scented opportunities in the north. Goring argued persuasively in favour of pursuing Fairfax and defeating his fledgling army in the West Country, but Rupert stuck to the original plan of heading north, believing that a victory in the west would not be of much value as the king controlled the area. He also doubted Grenville's military capacity, but his overwhelming argument rested on the increasingly desperate need to win back the northern English counties with their potential support for the cause. An added bonus would be that any Royalist move north would force parliament to rethink the deployment of its own forces, thereby returning the initiative to Charles. Unhappily, when the Royalist war council met on 7 May its members could only agree to compromise: Goring would take 3000 men to attack Fairfax, leaving the king with 8600 to engage the Scots.

By then the New Model Army had reached Blandford, with Cromwell's troopers covering it to the north, and while there Fairfax received an urgent letter from the Committee of Both Kingdoms informing him of the king's movements. Rightly fearing that Charles would break out and move north, gathering support as he went, they ordered Fairfax to detach one brigade to relieve Taunton, where Blake, the hero of Lyme, was hard-pressed, while the bulk of the army headed towards Oxford to seek battle with the Royalists. A siege was a serious military gamble: not only was Oxford well defended but Fairfax had to wait for his artillery train to arrive from London. An investment began on 19 May but vigorous counter-attacking by the garrison made it a lost cause and the attempt was abandoned early the following month. By then Charles and his army were already on the move north, having taken cognisance of the advice given by George

Wharton, the court astrologer, who counselled the king that his reading of the heavens 'do generally render his Majesty and his whole army unexpectedly victorious and successful in all designs' in what he called 'the battle of all for all'. (His parliamentary rival William Lilly thought otherwise: he prophesied that 'God is on our side; the constellations of heaven after a while will totally appear for the Parliament, and cast terror, horror, amazement, and frights on all those damned-blades now in arms against us.')[4]

To begin with the signs were propitious and favoured Wharton's judgement. Reaching Market Drayton on 22 May, Charles heard that Brereton had lifted his siege of Chester and from Scotland came news of a further triumph by Montrose and the subsequent withdrawal into Westmoreland of Leven's depleted army. The news was countered by a setback at Evesham, which fell to a force led by Massey – a serious loss because it cut communications between Oxford and Worcester – but Charles was sufficiently encouraged to continue the offensive. Acting on Rupert's advice it was decided to attack Leicester first, both to reduce an important parliamentary garrison and to relieve pressure on Oxford.[5]

The Royalist army arrived outside the city on 29 May and Rupert summoned the small garrison commanded by Colonel Sir Robert Pye to surrender. When this offer was refused the Royalist artillery 'began to play' on the southern walls and four hours later they had been breached sufficiently to allow the infantry to start their assault as night began to fall. The street fighting continued until dawn. Most of it was a bloody hand-to-hand business in which quarter was rarely given and the garrison continued to resist long after they had any hope of beating off the invaders. This undoubtedly prompted the worst excesses: men who have been fired up by combat and have seen their friends die are not usually given to displays of forgiveness come the cease-fire. According to one contemporary report Pye's soldiers surrendered and asked for quarter only to be killed in cold blood, women were raped and houses plundered. In one incident witnessed by Richard Symonds Royalist soldiers 'hanged Master Raynor, an honest religious gentleman and one Mr Sawer in cold blood'. Around 700 soldiers and civilians lost their lives during and after the battle; among them were 200 Scots who surrendered only to be rounded up and massacred.[6]

As Lucy Hutchinson related it, the loss of Leicester 'was a great affliction and terror to all the neighbouring garrisons and counties' but other than that it did not confer any immediate military advantage on Charles's army. There were of course consequences. Shocked by the news of the sacking, the Committee of Both Kingdoms ordered Fairfax to abandon the siege of Oxford on 5 June and to march north in the expectation that Charles would now move on East Anglia. Four days later he was ordered to bring the Royalists to battle, and just as significantly, Cromwell was confirmed in his position of Lieutenant-General of Horse, the commission lasting in the first place for three months. At the same time Leven was begged to march southwards 'with all possible expedition', a request he honoured, and but for the lack of draft horses the Scottish army would have reached the Midlands before it did on 22 June.

Charles, too, was looking for reinforcement and an urgent request had been sent to Goring to return from the West Country, but he refused, being too enamoured of his independent command and the prospects it offered him. This rebuff not only robbed the king of much-needed cavalry, but Goring's letter of refusal fell into Fairfax's hands, giving him accurate intelligence of the forces at Charles's disposal. The New Model Army had also evolved a better system of reconnaissance and on 12 June their scoutmaster Leonard Watson was able to report that Charles's forces were encamped on Burrow Hill, south of Daventry, and that the king was busily engaged 'a-hunting' deer in nearby Fawsley Park. Even at that late stage and despite Goring's absence Charles remained sanguine about his chances, writing to his wife that he was more optimistic than he had ever been before in the war. Like much else that happened in Charles's career, his cheerfulness was hopelessly misplaced. Far from being the toy army which many of his officers painted it, Fairfax's force was 14,000 strong and its best regiments were based on the Eastern Association units which had wreaked so much damage at Marston Moor. Against that, if Clarendon's figure is accurate and the numbers were probably higher, he could only produce 3300 foot and 4100 horse,* a total which gave his opponents a two-to-one superiority.

---

* In *The Civil Wars of England* John Kenyon argues that the figures should be reversed, which would mean that 'Fairfax now had twice as many cavalry as Charles and 40 per cent more infantry.' (pp. 142–143)

Even before any fighting began the Royalists were in a weak position: their one hope was to withdraw north back towards Leicester to seek reinforcements either from Wales, where Sir Charles Gerrard was recruiting, or from Goring's returning cavalry force. Executed sooner the move might have worked, but already there was dissent in the Royalist camp and on 11 June the army had only withdrawn a few miles to the north, as far as Market Harborough. Burned by his experiences the previous summer, Rupert favoured a further withdrawal but was overruled by Charles, who heeded Digby's advice that a retreat would be bad for morale and that as the New Model Army was close at hand – only a matter of miles away at Kislingbury – the time had come to test it in the field. In fact Fairfax's men were already on their heels – a Royalist patrol was surprised by the opposition while eating supper in an inn in the village of Naseby, some five miles to the south. Now a battle could not be avoided.

Having decided to stand and fight, a position had to be chosen, and in the early hours of 14 June, at Rupert's prompting, the Royalist forces began deploying along a high ridge to the south which ran from the village of East Farndon to Great Oxenden. It was a good position, but as Rupert looked across the broad expanse of undulating heath he was uncomfortably aware that a low ridge obscured his view of the New Model Army who were deploying below Naseby ridge to the south. Scouts were sent forward to determine what was happening, but being either lazy or timorous, they came back with the unlikely report that there was no sign of the rebel army. Showing no little impatience, Rupert rode off with his Lifeguard to do the job himself, but what he saw made the picture no clearer – parties of horsemen seeming to be riding away from Naseby ridge. This was the vanguard of Fairfax's army manoeuvring into position, with Fairfax and Cromwell trying to get a feel for the best place to do battle with the Royalists. Believing that Rupert would not take the initiative by attacking, Fairfax thought it better to occupy the lower ground, but with his eye for detail Cromwell pointed out the marshy waterlogged fields which would then lie between them and their opponents – hardly cavalry country. 'Let us, I beseech you,' he exclaimed, 'draw back to yonder hill, which will encourage the enemy to charge us, which they cannot do without absolute ruin.'[7]

His advice was taken and the New Model Army lined up on the

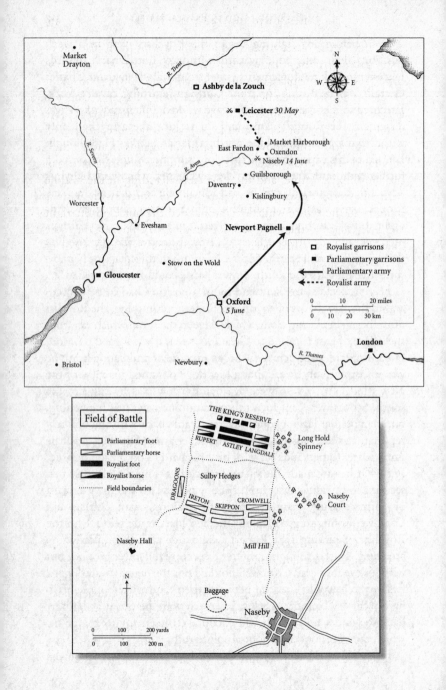

Market Drayton

R. Trent

Ashby de la Zouch

⚔ **Leicester** *30 May*

Market Harborough
East Fardon • • Oxendon
⚔ Naseby *14 June*

R. Avon
• Guilsborough
Daventry •
• Kislingbury

Worcester •

• Evesham

R. Severn

Newport Pagnell ■

• Stow on the Wold

Gloucester ■

☐ **Oxford**
5 June

London ■

R. Thames

• Bristol   Newbury •

☐	Royalist garrisons
■	Parliamentary garrisons
←	Parliamentary army
⤎	Royalist army

0   10   20 miles
0   10   20   30 km

Field of Battle

▱	Parliamentary foot
▱	Parliamentary horse
▰	Royalist foot
▰	Royalist horse
⋯	Field boundaries

THE KING'S RESERVE

RUPERT ASTLEY LANGDALE

Long Hold
Spinney

Sulby Hedges

DRAGOONS

IRETON SKIPPON CROMWELL

Naseby
Court

Naseby Hall

Mill Hill

N

Baggage

Naseby

0   100   200 yards
0   100   200 m

other side of the Naseby ridge, a ploy which kept them just out of sight of the Royalist army which Rupert had ordered to deploy on Dust Hill, a sloping piece of ground which swept down to the moor giving his horse an open field for attack. Cromwell's suggestion was a good one in other respects – many of the men in Fairfax's force were seeing action for the first time and might have been unnerved as the Royalist army moved into position, drums beating, their colours blowing in the breeze, the armour of the cavalry glinting in the morning sunshine, and the king himself riding in the middle with his sword drawn. Rupert deployed his forces with Astley's infantry in the centre while he commanded the horse on the right and Langdale's Northern Horse stood on the left. Opposing them the New Model Army had been drawn up under Skippon's word of command, the foot in five regiments in the front line with a second line of three, the cavalry on the right commanded by Cromwell, the left under the direction of Henry Ireton, newly appointed Commissary-General. To Ireton's left, along the Sulby hedges, were hidden Colonel John Okey's dragoons, their task to enfilade the Royalist horse when they attacked.

Morale on both sides was good. The Royalists' confidence was high after Leicester and they made an imposing sight on Dust Hill. Fairfax's men were also equal to the task, well equipped (though hungry) and positive that they had the better leaders. Cromwell himself was in no doubt of the outcome. Watching the Royalist forces line up in all their panoply of power he put his trust in the God who had so carefully overseen his every move:

> When I saw the enemy draw up and march in gallant order towards us, and we a company of poor ignorant men, to seek how to order our battle . . . I could not riding alone about my business but smile out to God in praises, in assurance of victory, because God would, by things that are not, bring to naught things that are.[8]

He did not have long to wait to test his beliefs. At about ten o'clock in the morning Rupert's horse charged towards Ireton's position while Astley's infantry moved forward to fire into the opposition's lines, the king with the reserve in the centre. Although the first charge was checked, Rupert's second line led by the Earl of Northampton punched their way through Ireton's flank, which was quickly in disarray. As happened at Edgehill the troopers swept on towards the baggage train in the rear and once again Rupert was hard-pushed to rally them again for further action. Meanwhile, having fired off their muskets, the infantry in the centre were fully engaged with their pikes and swords and as Sir Edward Walker, secretary of the Royalist war council, recorded the battle, against the odds Astley's men were gaining the upper hand:

> Presently our forces advanced up the hill, the rebels only discharging five [artillery] pieces at them, but overshot them, and so did their musketeers. The foot on either side hardly saw each other until they were within carbine shot, and so only made one volley; ours falling in with sword and butt end of muskets did notable execution; so much as I saw their colours fall and their foot in great disorder. And had our left wing but at this time done half so well as either the foot or the right wing, we had got in a few minutes a glorious victory.[9]

It was not be, for all that some elements in Skippon's lines were already casting down their weapons and running back into the rear lines. Everything now hung on Langdale's brigade, which collided with Cromwell's front lines of horse on the slopes of the hill and, outnumbered, were soon checked after 'firing at very close range' and pulling out their swords for close-quarters combat. The Northern Horse did not lack courage but they did not possess numbers and were soon in disarray and making their way to the rear. It was at this stage in the battle that Cromwell showed grace under pressure. A hot-blooded pursuit would have been understandable; instead he drew his men into four formations and in disciplined order drove the remnants of Langdale's regiments from the battlefield before reassembling them for a decisive attack on the Royalist foot. More than anything else their calmness and discipline decided the battle.

As Cromwell's troopers moved steadily forward they passed the Royalists' reserve led by the king with his Lifeguard in attendance. Never short of courage, Charles made to attack them, and would have done so had not the Earl of Carnwath been riding next to him. Swearing a great Scots oath – this was the Scottish nobleman whose tomboy daughter had led a troop of cavalry alongside Montrose in Newcastle's army the previous year – Carnwath pulled the king's bridle to the right, checking the impulse but giving the impression that those around him should retire. Some in the vicinity accepted the invitation and fled in panic, breaking the centre of the reserve and taking them from the field at the very moment they were needed to support the foot. This was the critical moment of the battle. At the same time that Astley needed support he was left isolated and a prey not just to Cromwell's troopers but also to Okey's dragoons, who had left the cover of the hedges and were busily employed attacking the Royalist right. Suddenly matters looked very ominous for the hard-pressed infantry, who saw that they were being surrounded and that no support would be offered by their own cavalry, which had either been driven off or was scattered in the rear areas of Fairfax's lines. By the time Rupert had managed to rally them the battle was as good as over. Fairfax had realigned his men into 'a second good battalia at the latter end of the day', his formations replicating the order in which they started the battle, and Astley's men were already asking for quarter. Soon men were in flight down the lanes to the north with Cromwell's troopers in hot pursuit, cutting and slashing as they went, remaining true to their orders not to dismount for plunder. For the Royalist Symonds this 'dismal Saturday' was almost over, but for men like Joshua Sprigge, Fairfax's chaplain, it had only just begun:

> Our horse had the chase of them [Royalists] from that place, within two miles of Leicester (being the space of fourteen miles), took many prisoners, and had the execution of them all that way. The number of the slain we had not a certain account of, by reason of the prosecution of our victory, and speedy advance to the reducing of Leicester. The prisoners taken in the field were about five thousand, whereof six were colonels, eight lieutenant-colonels, eighteen majors, seventy captains, eighty lieutenants, eighty ensigns, two hundred other inferior officers, besides the King's footmen and household servants, the rest common soldiers, four thousand five hundred. The enemy lost very gallant men, and indeed their foot, commanded by the Lord Astley, were not wanting in courage.[10]

By nightfall, having passed through Leicester, Charles had escaped to Ashby-de-la-Zouch, where he was joined by Rupert and Maurice before making their way to Hereford on 19 June, having completed the 120-mile journey in five anxious days. From there the king went into Wales to stay with the Earl of Worcester at Raglan where, according to Walker, 'as if the genius of the place had conspired with our fates, we were there all lulled to sleep with sports and entertainments; as if no crown had been at stake, or in any danger to be lost.'[11] Behind him he left a trail of death and the virtual destruction of his field army. Although the casualties were lower than at Marston Moor – a result of the smaller numbers and the refusal of the infantry to martyr themselves as the Lambs had done – around 1000 men had been killed, compared to one-fifth of that number in Fairfax's army. Many of the casualties were killed in the pursuit from the field, despite the fact that quarter had been requested. Those who survived, some 4500 according to Joshua Sprigge, were rounded up by Colonel Nathaniel Fiennes's men (who had served in Cromwell's second line) and marched to London, where they and their captured standards were paraded through the streets in a mock recreation of a Roman triumph.

That was not the only reminder of a more barbaric past. Not content with killing men as they tried to escape from the battlefield, some of Fairfax's men indulged in a dreadful act of brutality when they caught up with the Royalist wagon train behind the lines. Among the camp followers who accompanied the armies of the time were large numbers of women. Some were soldiers' wives or partners; others were described by a contemporary chronicler as 'whores and camp-sluts that attended that wicked army'. About one hundred of them could not speak much English and were accounted to be Irish and therefore tarred with the same brush as their fellow Catholics, who had slaughtered Protestants without mercy four years earlier. In fact, because there was a large number of Welsh infantrymen in the king's army, they were probably Welsh, but that mattered not: their nationality and their failure to speak the language of their aggressors were enough to condemn them. The fact that they were thought to be loathsome prostitutes did not help, but that was a secondary reason. Others, those who could speak English but who were still held to be whores, were promptly disfigured by having their faces slashed or their noses slit, presumably pour encourager les autres. Neither Cromwell nor Fairfax responded to the atrocity, which was widely reported without comment in the parliamentary press.

Not only lives were lost. In addition to surrendering large amounts of ordnance and ammunition, supplies and 'the rich plunder of Leicester', the parliamentary army also retrieved the king's letter books and cabinet letters, which contained all his correspondence from the previous two years. This proved to be a dreadful loss, for not only did the letters supply parliament with an accurate account of the king's affairs during the campaign, especially the correspondence with his wife, but they also revealed the extent of his attempts to find reinforcements from elsewhere, most notably from Ormond in Ireland and from the Duke of Lorraine in France. Suddenly here was evidence of the king's duplicitous behaviour, which members of parliament had long suspected – that he was prepared to hire Catholic mercenaries to come to fight in Britain in return for money and royal favours. If that were so, it made the struggle worthwhile, to rescue the country from a popish plot, and when the correspondence was published under the title of *The King's Cabinet Opened* its appearance was a great boost to the parliamentary cause.

For the king, though, it was a great embarrassment, and Hyde denounced the action as 'barbarous', but the truth could not be gainsaid; Charles had done everything possible to find support from outside England. Through his own efforts he persisted in his belief that Ireland was a potential reservoir of troops ready and willing to fight on his behalf provided that they were given sufficient encouragement. In pursuit of that aim Ormond had been kept under pressure to deal with the Confederates, who responded by saying that they would only support the king if he, Ormond, joined forces with them to expel the Scots from Ulster. Not only was such an outcome most unlikely but by corresponding with Catholic leaders Charles was only confirming suspicions that he was intent on imposing their religion in Britain. Charles's cause was not helped when his correspondence with Ormond revealed an offer to repeal Poynings's Law and other legislation injurious to Catholics in return for the supply of 10,000 troops.

Two other initiatives conspired to put the king in a bad light. At the end of the previous year Inchiquin, the leading Protestant magnate in Munster, had turned coat and declared for parliament, who supplied him with arms and men to hold the ports of Kinsale and Cork. This was a blow to Charles – with the Scots in the north it gave his enemies a larger measure of control in Ireland – but he had already responded by appointing the Earl of Glamorgan, a leading Catholic whose wealth did not compensate for his lack of common sense, to go to Ireland and 'to conclude a peace with the Irish [Confederates] whatever it cost'. Not the most capable of diplomats, Glamorgan set to work with a will in Dublin, planning to raise an army of 10,000 men and making wild promises which thoroughly alarmed Ormond.*

Similar and equally rash offers had been made in Paris, where Henrietta Maria presided over a small exiled court and used her influence to try to persuade her family – her brother Louis XIII had died in 1643 – to supply arms and men for Charles's cause. At the time Cardinal Mazarin virtually controlled France (Louis XIV was only seven years old), and while he did not want to see his country follow England's example, whereby the Crown's independent powers were curtailed by parliament, he was not prepared to sanction the dispatch of an expedition to save a king whose cause was faltering. Like other European leaders Mazarin was not unhappy to see England torn apart and unable to involve itself in European affairs at a time when France had gained the initiative over the Habsburgs in the Thirty Years War following Duke of Enghien, the young Condé's annihilation of the imperial forces at Rocroi in May 1643. (Another factor was the Congress of Westphalia, aimed at ending the conflict, which had come into being the previous year.) Mazarin's one positive suggestion was positively dangerous – that Henrietta Maria should approach the disgraced Duke of Lorraine, who commanded an undisciplined mercenary army in the imperial service. He accepted the invitation to bring his 'pack of wolves' across to England but, fortunately, nothing came of the matter after transport ships could not be found.

Undeterred, Henrietta Maria turned to France's allies the Netherlands and Sweden, offering the former a marriage alliance through the Prince of Wales and ceding Shetland and Orkney to the

---

* Glamorgan took his time getting to Dublin. He set out in January 1645 but was shipwrecked and did not arrive until midsummer.

latter. She also made an appeal to the pope, but Innocent X's only response was to send a nuncio to Ireland charged with the impossible responsibility of achieving the restoration of Catholicism with Charles's connivance. This was Giovanni Battista Rinuccini, the archbishop of Fermo, a hard-line militant who proceeded to immerse himself in Ireland's tortuous affairs and was destined to cause a good deal of trouble during his embassy, which lasted until 1649.

In the short term Charles's best hope lay in linking up with Montrose, whose succession of victories in Scotland encouraged the king to think of moving north once more, but he only got as far as Doncaster on 11 August when his way was blocked by Leslie's Scottish cavalry. In any case the attempt was wishful thinking, for the rest of the summer only brought news of fresh disasters. Following his victory at Naseby Fairfax had retaken Leicester before marching into the West Country to destroy Goring and raise the siege of Taunton. They met at Langport on 10 July, where the New Model Army's self-belief and discipline won them a battle which they could easily have lost. When Bridgwater fell later in the month all resistance in Somerset came to an end, although it would not be until the following year that Hopton surrendered Devon and Cornwall. To add to Charles's woes Leven had brought the Scottish army deep into England, and by 30 June had begun the investment of Hereford, where the Scots were forced to seek free quartering from the local population. The sight of these ferocious-looking and strangely dressed foreigners caused alarm in the neighbourhood, as did their behaviour. 'Their voracity was almost proverbial,' remembered one witness years later.

For all that events were conspiring against the king, he maintained a determined cheerfulness of demeanour and refused to allow any displays of melancholy within his court. When Rupert suggested that peace negotiations were the only sensible conclusion the king offered the dignified reply that while 'there is no probability but of my ruin' he would not give up the cause because 'God will not suffer rebels to prosper, or His cause to be overthrown; and whatever personal punishment it shall please him to inflict upon me must not make me repine, much less to give over this quarrel'.[12] Montrose's exploits continued to cheer him, fresh blood might yet be found in Wales and Ireland, and it was still possible that Naseby, 'the unfortunate loss of a most hopeful battle', might be countered by divisions within the enemy's ranks. The latter hope was a fond one but it was not without basis. There were Presbyterians to be found, above all the Scots ever-ready to be disgruntled, who were secretly dismayed by the victory as they saw in it the steady ascendancy of Cromwell and the Independents. When they read Cromwell's dispatch to the Speaker their suspicions were confirmed. The last paragraph was deleted but it was soon published, and in it could be heard the first echoes of his growing belief that the war was not just about opposition to the king, it was also about freedom of religious conscience:

> Honest men served you faithfully in this action. Sir, they are trusty; I beseech you in the name of God not to discourage them. I wish this action may beget thankfulness and humility in all that are concerned in it. He that ventures his life for the liberty of his country, I wish he trust God for the liberty of his conscience, and you for the liberty he fights for.[13]

Typically, and in common with other parliamentary commanders, Cromwell thanked God for his support and for securing the victory which was the beginning of the end of Charles's cause. The reality was that Naseby had been lost for the king by a succession of circumstances – Goring's absence, Rupert's wild leadership and the superiority of the New Model Army – and having been defeated it would be a well-nigh impossible task to retrieve his position in England. Now Scotland was to be Charles's last and best chance of survival.

Chapter Eleven

MONTROSE'S ANNUS MIRABILIS

'Were you familiar with the Goirtean Odhar? Well it was manured, not by the dung of sheep or goats, but by the blood of Campbells after it had congealed.'

Iain Lom, 'The Battle of Inverlochy', 2 February 1645

While Leven's army was parked outside Hereford in an increasingly ineffective siege the first steps were being taken by some members of the Scots nobility – their number included Lothian – to make contact with the king through the Earl of Callendar's nephew, Sir William Fleming, who was staying with Charles at Raglan. On hearing of the move Leven tried to put a stop to the meeting, sticking to the soldier's line that he would not be a party to politicking and that if they wanted to continue the dialogue they should 'follow the straight and public way, applying yourself to the parliaments or Committees of Both Kingdoms'. Leven had obviously learned as much about politics as warfare in Germany, but despite his entreaties a meeting was held in secret on 5 August 1645, when Fleming was able to tell his fellow Scots that the king was minded 'to bring the matter to an honourable treaty' with them. Nothing was promised but the first steps had been taken in the long dance which would see the Scots change their tune in an attempt to keep their religious demands sacrosanct.

The change of heart was not unpredictable. To the more suspicious in Leven's army and the Estates in Edinburgh, it seemed that parliament had broken the terms of the Covenant, that everything was being done to benefit Fairfax at Leven's expense and that this turnabout was due to the growing influence of Cromwell and the Independents. The dissatisfaction was mutual: many English members of parliament felt that they had a bad bargain, that apart from Marston Moor and the capture of Newcastle the Scots had been over-cautious and of little use in the field. Now, at Hereford, they were being equally querulous and, just as bad, making a nuisance of themselves in the surrounding countryside. 'They have lost all affection here,' wrote Sir Robert Honeywood to Henry Vane on 9 September, 'and will do more unless their armies engage more truly for the future, and their counsels and ours be more united, whereby they may gain the hearts of the people again, which are not lost, but in suspense.'[1]

In the short term the bad feeling was patched up by a meeting of the English and Scottish commissioners, the former agreeing to make more supplies available while the latter repledged their obligations 'by Covenant, Treaty and joint declaration of both kingdoms never to lay down arms till the peace of both be settled', and Leven moved his Scots north and east to begin the siege of Newark. Disheartened by the turn of events, the old soldier offered to resign his commission, but this was refused by the Estates. A further reason for his distress had been the steady trickle of worried news from Scotland reporting Montrose's string of military successes and asking him for reinforcements. This placed him in a quandary: his masters, the Estates, were frantically trying to raise fresh forces to put down the rebellion which had flared in their backyard, yet Montrose's victories had encouraged Charles to think of moving north to link up with him. To counter that threat and in response to a request from the English parliament Leven had already detached David Leslie with a force of eight regiments of horse, one of dragoons and 500 musketeers, a move which weakened his army in England, as most of the men were veterans of Marston Moor.

Whereas 1645 had offered nothing but setbacks to the royal cause in England, everything had gone its way north of the border, where Montrose and his lieutenant, Alasdair MacColla Ciotaich, were enjoying a year of miraculous victories. The two men had joined forces again at Blair Atholl at the end of November 1644 after Alasdair

MacColla had traversed the lands of Arisaig, Morar and Moidart trying to drum up support which was slow in coming. Those who did rise to his call were traditional enemies of Clan Campbell – MacDonalds from Keppoch, Glengarry and Glen Coe, Camerons from Lochaber – but, by the standards of the day, they were lightly armed with muskets, swords, axes and even bows and arrows. Nonetheless they were battle-hardened and hardy mountain-men, and they needed to be because Alasdair MacColla had devised a daring plan of campaign which worried even the optimistic Montrose. Basically, he called for a hard-hitting attack into the Campbell lands, to get supplies, to strike at the heart of the power exercised by MacCailein Mor (the Marquis of Argyll), and in so doing to allow his men to gain a measure of revenge over their reviled enemies. If that did not happen, argued Alasdair MacColla, his Highlanders would simply return home on the grounds that their efforts counted for nothing unless 'they crushed the Campbells, devastated Argyll with fire and sword, and administered a terrible and telling chastisement to this hideous receptacle of bandits, plunderers, incendiaries and cut throats'.[2]

Bold words, but Montrose knew the execution would be a test of the men's endurance. Even in summer the high mountain ranges and inaccessible glens of Argyll's homeland presented a challenge – not only were they difficult to traverse but they gave an advantage to the defenders – and in midwinter with the snow on the peaks the going would be many times harder. Even so, Montrose could see the sense of the argument: no one would expect an attack (least of all Argyll, who took comfort in the old Campbell boast, 'it's a far cry to Loch Awe'), it would win them much-needed supplies and it would strike terror into the hearts of the opposition. Montrose was enough of a romantic to be persuaded and at the beginning of December his army began its march westwards through Breadalbane and Glenorchy to the head of Loch Awe and then on to Inverary. Most were Highlanders, but with him went the Earl of Airlie and his son Thomas Ogilvy and a clutch of Gordons enraged by Argyll's razing of their lands in the north-east. Luck was on their side. The winter was milder than usual, the Campbells were slow to react, local guides helped them through the mountain passes and within a fortnight they were in Argyll's heartland.

What followed was a mixture of military necessity and tribal revenge. Houses were burned down, cattle were rounded up and any man with the name of Campbell was put to the sword. From Loch Awe-side the army moved north into Lorn and Lochaber, killing and plundering, and by the end of January they had progressed up the Great Glen as far as Kilcumin (later Fort Augustus), where Montrose produced a new Covenant binding them, Highlander and Lowlander alike, to 'stand to the maintenance of the power and authority of our sacred and native sovereign, contrary to this present perverse and infamous faction of desperate rebels now in fury against him'.[3] While at Kilcumin he received news that Argyll was to the south of him intent on revenge; at the same time, further up the Great Glen lay a Covenanting army raised by Mackenzie of Seaforth. Fortuitously, tradition has it that the bringer of these tidings was the bard of Keppoch, Iain Lom, whose writings both illuminated and praised in extravagant terms the next stage of Montrose's and Alasdair MacColla's campaign. Shortly before the opening encounter Alasdair MacColla asked the poet if he would take part in it, only to receive the reply that he would watch what happened and then tell the story. That would be enough.

Trapped between the two armies, Montrose decided that his best option was to attack the army closer to him – Argyll's to the south. It was a good decision. One regiment of foot consisted of Lowlanders, veterans of the fighting in England but unfamiliar with the local territory, and although Montrose was not to know it his rival had dislocated his shoulder and had retired to Inverlochy, where he prudently boarded his galley anchored in Loch Linnhe. Command of his forces was given to his kinsman Sir Duncan Campbell of Auchinbreck, a professional soldier, who lined up his forces on the flat ground to the south-west of Inverlochy Castle, clearly expecting the attack to come from the Great Glen. Montrose and Alasdair MacColla had other ideas. On 31 January 1645, outnumbered two-to-one, they led their 1500 men on an extraordinary flanking march across the roadless snow-covered mountains of the western Monadliath, keeping to the high ground by way of the Corrieyairack Pass until they crossed Glen Roy and Glen Spean to come down on Inverlochy on a bitter moonlit night on 1 February. They had marched thirty miles in under thirty-six hours over some of Scotland's wildest terrain – an astonishing achievement. Cold, hungry, footsore – even Ogilvy's horse had followed the march – the small force could have wavered, but two factors stood in their favour: inspired leadership and an absolute hatred of the Campbells. Their opponents' disposition between the castle and the shore also helped – the clansmen in the centre with Campbells and the Lowland foot on both flanks.

As day broke the Royalist army advanced as it had done at Tippermuir, on a broad front with Alasdair MacColla on the right, the Irishman Magnus O'Cahan on the left, and Montrose in the centre, and once again it was the speed and ferocity of their charge that won the day. Although Auchinbreck's men put up determined resistance there was no coherent organisation in the defensive lines, and once men started running away others followed suit, anxious to avoid certain death. Few managed even that. Over half their number were slaughtered, either on the field of battle or in the immediate surroundings; those who tried to reach the safety of the castle were cut off by Ogilvy's horse and massacred. Only the Lowland foot received quarter, but to be called Campbell was to accept the death sentence: Auchinbreck was given the choice of being 'lengthened or shortened', that is hanged or beheaded, and replied in Gaelic that the alternatives gave no room for choice.* Alasdair MacColla decided for him, a single blow decapitating his opponent or, if another version is to be believed, messily slicing his head above his ears. Watching the events from the hill above the field, Iain Lom was true to his word and left a carefully phrased but vividly expressed description of the battle:

> On the day they thought all would go well
> the heroes chased them over frozen ground;
> many a great sallow-skinned sloucher
> lay on the surface of Ach an Todhair.
>
> Those who climbed the Mound of the Watch
> could see newly-lopped paws ill-salted,
> the film of death on their lifeless eyes,
> after the slashing they had from sword-blades.[4]

Inverlochy broke Argyll's power in the west Highlands, leaving MacCaileain Mor little choice but to escape in his galley and flee back

---

* Dha dhiu gun aon roghainn – 'two evil alternatives that give no room for choice', Cowan, *Montrose*, 185.

to Edinburgh having witnessed the massacre of his clansmen. It also added to a belief that Montrose was invincible, his winter march over the mountains being cited as evidence, and that no soldier could withstand the ferocity of the charge mounted by Alasdair MacColla's Highlanders and Irish caterans. Even their deadly enemies, the Covenanting leadership, were nonplussed: they saw in Montrose and Alasdair MacColla God's hand at work, chastising the people of Scotland for their pride and lack of godliness and, as Baillie reminded them, 'there is no strength of refuge on earth against the Lord'. The success also attracted others, more worldly perhaps, to join the cause, and it prompted Montrose to write to Charles warning him off any talk of peace (this was the time of the Uxbridge talks) and promising to come to his aid with a 'brave army' to crush the rebels:

> Only give me leave, after I have reduced this country to your Majesty's obedience, and conquered from Dan to Beersheba, to say to your Majesty then, as David's General did to his master, 'Come thou thyself, lest this country be called by my name'. For in all my actions I aim only at your Majesty's honour and interest, as becomes one that is to his last breath, your Majesty's most humble, most faithful and most obedient Subject and Servant.[5]

Taking the remote west Highlands was one matter, but Montrose knew that he had to enlarge his power base, and that meant marching again into the north-east to rouse the support of the Gordons – a march of over a hundred miles. His route took him up the south side of Loch Ness, over Strathnairn, into Moray and on to Elgin, which became a temporary headquarters while he tried to rally support and his men harried the property of those whose help was not forthcoming. The great houses of Ballindalloch, Brodie, Culbin and Redhall were destroyed, as was the Earl Marischal's 'pleasant park of Fetteresso . . . utterly spoiled, plundered and undone'. Montrose's greatest catch was Huntly's son George, Lord Gordon, who was to become a friend and intimate, but his example did not encourage many others of his class. Despite intensive recruiting and merciless punishment of recalcitrants Montrose was not receiving the support he might have deserved, and all the while another Covenanter army was being assembled under the leadership of one of Leven's commanders, Sir William Baillie, veteran of Germany and Marston Moor. Under his command, in charge of the horse, was none other than Sir John Hurry, 'a tall stately fellow' who had started his career on the side of parliament before giving Rupert the vital information which enabled him to win Chalgrove (for which deed he was knighted) and then changing sides after the disaster at Marston Moor. His morality aside, he was a capable soldier.

As news of Inverlochy began to trickle back to Edinburgh a worried meeting of the Estates ordered William Baillie northwards to engage Montrose, who had moved his army in the direction of the Mearns, the fertile coastal littoral which connects the north-east with the central lowlands. The two armies met at the end of March on opposite banks of the River Isla near Coupar Angus, where Montrose chivalrously offered his opponent free passage of the river to allow a pitched battle, but Baillie was not to be drawn and chose to retire. Montrose was now intent on joining forces with the king, but his route south over the Tay was blocked by his opponent and he was forced into a tortuous game of hide-and-seek. This did not suit his Highlanders, who preferred battle and looting to tedious line-marching and manoeuvring. With summer approaching many began to desert, leaving Montrose and Alasdair MacColla with barely 3000 men. An attempt was made to take Dundee on 5 April but a combination of drink-induced lack of discipline on the Highlanders' part and the arrival of Hurry's horse led to a quick and, given the circumstances, surprisingly well-ordered retreat into the hills of the north-east, where Montrose all but disappeared from sight.

In fact, once again, he was trying to gain new recruits. Lord Gordon went back to Strathbogie to rally his people, Alasdair MacColla to the lands of Mar, while Montrose traversed most of Perthshire, all the while hoping that Charles would make good a promise to provide him with a force of 500 cavalry. At the same time Baillie covered the routes south in case of any breakout towards Edinburgh while Hurry moved into the north-east to harry the Gordons. This succession of moves and counter-moves led to the next battle between Montrose and the Covenanters.

The campaign began in the third week of April when Montrose received intelligence of Hurry's intentions and decided immediately to move north to help Gordon. At that time he was at Balquhidder in the Trossachs but, nothing daunted, Montrose set out on another of his swift cross-country marches, his route taking him through Atholl, across the Braes of Angus, over the footpaths of the eastern Grampians and on to Deeside. As the crow flies the distance was around 150 miles but the route proved hard going, taking him across the barren roof of eastern Scotland to threaten Aberdeen. From there he moved through Strathbogie towards Elgin while Hurry fell back on Inverness to be reinforced by levies recruited by local Covenanting landowners. Hurry was no fool: he hoped to lure Montrose into hostile territory while Baillie marched his army up from Dunkeld through the 'pleasant country' of Atholl, burning and plundering as they went. His plan was to create a force which would outnumber and destroy Montrose's Highlanders.

On 8 May Montrose's army made camp on the western slopes of a north–south ridge near the village of Auldearn just to the east of Nairn. Below lay undulating rough ground giving way to bogs and a rise now known as Deadman's Wood. It was a good position, but Hurry hoped to surprise his enemy with a rapid night march and fall on them at dawn. However, the weather being damp and misty, he was forced to allow his musketeers to fire their weapons to clear them of damp powder, and inevitably the noise of the discharge betrayed their movements. With little time to spare before the expected attack Montrose evolved a hastily improvised plan which would compensate for his unpreparedness and his numerical inferiority – some 2000 against Hurry's 4000. In effect a phantom army was created. Alasdair MacColla held the centre just to the west of Auldearn with his Highlanders and Gordons while, behind him, his right and left flanks were protected by horse commanded by Gordon and Lord Aboyne, his brother, who had joined the Royalist force at Balquhidder. To the opposing side this would look like the main bulk of Montrose's army, and to complete the ruse the royal standard was raised just to the rear, as if to form a command point. Meanwhile, out of sight, in a hollow to the rear, Montrose positioned the bulk of his force including the Gordons' horse;* the trap had been baited and to spring it, as Hurry's

---

* Some historians, notably Gardiner, have argued that Montrose positioned his force on the left flank. The contemporary accounts of the battle are ambiguous but given the shortage of time between Hurry's arrival and the need to mount a defence it seems unlikely that Montrose had the luxury of much forward planning.

men approached, a party of musketeers in Alasdair MacColla's lines opened up with a brisk rate of fire.

The plan was to lure them into the open ground before hitting the flanks, but its success depended on the Highlanders' steadiness and ability to absorb pressure in a static defensive action, tactics for which they were not best suited. So it proved. As Hurry's men made their way over the mire through the morning mist the MacDonalds noticed that Campbells were in the front line under the command of Sir Mungo Campbell of Lawers. This was an insult to their name and, goaded into action, Alasdair MacColla's force began breaking ranks, charging recklessly into the oncoming regiments and beginning a long and bitterly contested battle in the soggy ground in the centre. Seeing the confusion Montrose ordered Gordon and Aboyne to attack Hurry's flanks. At the same time the hidden infantry joined the affray in the centre and their impetus shattered Hurry's ranks. The battlefield became a killing ground in which Hurry's army was annihilated: 2000 lay dead and many more were slaughtered on the road to Inverness while Montrose suffered only 200 casualties, most of them Irish or Highlanders. As had become the norm in this fast-running guerrilla war, prisoners were not taken and quarter was rarely given or, indeed, requested. Among those who lived to fight another day was Hurry himself, who was among the last to leave Auldearn, but the experience obviously marked him as he promptly switched his allegiance once more to throw in his lot with Montrose.

By any standards Auldearn was a worthy if fortunate victory, hastily organised by Montrose and mercilessly executed by the soldiers under his command.[6] In its aftermath all the credit was given to Montrose, but the towering figure was Alasdair MacColla, who showed great leadership qualities in rallying the foot and providing an example by fighting in their midst as the two lines collided – 'a wonderful feat of arms for his fellows to imitate'. However the battle was not decisive. Hard on the Royalists' heels was William Baillie's army, reinforced by two regiments of horse, and Montrose knew that he had to destroy it before he could move south into central Scotland. It would be no easy matter: he had to recoup his strength and once again Alasdair MacColla retired to the west to get reinforcements. This left Montrose and Baillie to play a complicated game of military chess over the Mearns, the Braes of Angus and the lands of Mar, neither man wanting to commit his forces to battle until they were ready, yet anxious not to lose contact. In Strathdon, near the town of Keith, they almost came to blows, but Baillie refused the offer of a pitched battle as the ground was not to his liking. All the while both commanders were weighing the odds and each believed that the advantage was falling their way. Montrose had been encouraged by the numbers of recruits which had joined him after Auldearn – for the first time his army was not numerically smaller than their opponents – while Baillie, under pressure from the Estates to engage the enemy, had taken heart from Alasdair MacColla's absence.

The two armies eventually met on the south side of the boggy mass of the River Don on 2 July near the small settlement of Alford, twenty miles inland from Aberdeen. Montrose had cleverly placed his army on rising ground to the south-west, known as Gallows Hill and covering the Suie road, but once again displaying his tendency to be unpredictable he positioned the bulk on the reverse slope, leaving the rearguard on the ridge. To Baillie, advancing from the north towards the river crossing at Boat of Forbes, they looked like an insignificant force in retreat and their disposition offered all manner of temptations. To his eye the opposition seemed to be moving away from a favourable position and the lie of the land offered the possibility of using his horse to outflank them on the left. This was exactly what Montrose wanted – to draw his enemy on to ground of his choosing, the bog with the river to the rear – and Baillie did not disoblige him. Montrose waited until the bulk of Baillie's horse was over the river before ordering his army to take up their positions on the ridge, ready for battle – his Highlanders and Irishmen in the centre under the command of Angus MacDonald of Glengarry, with Gordon's horse on the right and Aboyne's on the left.

Everything in Baillie's long experience would have told him to avoid battle on such unpromising ground, but now he was committed, not just by the river to his back which made a hasty retreat difficult but also by the bellicose exhortations of Lord Balcarres, a committed Covenanter who commanded the horse. With no other option available but to fight, he drew up his army on the boggy ground with his cavalry on the left. Less than half a mile separated the two sides and in the uneasy summer morning heat both watched and waited for the word of command. As had happened so often in this fast-moving campaign, the fighting started as if by accident. Behind Baillie's army could be seen large numbers of cattle, their movement creating a dust cloud, and knowing them to be rustled beasts from their own lands the Gordon horse attacked downhill to engage their Covenanter opponents 'at close quarters, fighting hand to hand so stubbornly that none could advance a foot or a nail's breadth but over the body of his foe, while retreat was impossible, so great was the crush of men pressing on behind'.[7] So tightly were the men engaged that muskets were quickly discarded in favour of the sword and whatever else came to hand.

Aboyne's attack on the left did equal damage, smashing into the unprotected right flank with the foot in support. It was not just men who died: horses had their bellies ripped open or were hamstrung by Irish dirks. Later Baillie insisted that his infantry 'behaved themselves as became them' but they could not withstand the charge of the clansmen and in a few minutes they were overcome. So confused was the mêlée, as men struggled and fought with each other hand-to-hand, that regimental commanders could often not tell friend from foe. In the confusion Lord Gordon was felled by a shot to the neck, leaving an anonymous balladeer to conjecture that it might have come from his own side:

> There came a ball shot frae the west,
> That shot him in the back;
> Although he was our enemy,
> We grieved for his wrack.
>
> I canna say 'twas his own men,
> But yet it came that way;
> In Scotland there was not a match,
> To that man where he lay.[8]

His loss was a bitter blow, all the more so as it was the Gordons who had won the day, and as news of his death trickled back through their lines Montrose's men took their revenge. The Gordons offered no quarter, chasing the fleeing Covenanters over a wide area and hunting them down with efficient brutality. One site tells its own sorry story, Blaudy Faulds – bloody enclosure – near the village of

Tough. About one thousand men were killed in the space of less than an hour and the vast majority were Covenanters. Within the space of a month Montrose had destroyed the two main Covenanting armies, and although Baillie had escaped to the south, where his offer of resignation was refused by the Estates, the Royalist cause in Scotland was now seemingly unstoppable – but only if Montrose could get sufficient men and supplies.

Alasdair MacColla brought the former – 3000 Highlanders and islanders, including men of Clan Ranald and Macleans of Duart – but not the latter, which led to more raids of the farming stock of Angus and the Mearns. Baillie, too, was being reinforced by men from Fife, the borders and the south-west, and by the end of July he had around 6000 men under his command. Crucially, some 800 of these were cavalry, giving him an advantage over Montrose of ten to one – at least until Aboyne and Airlie returned with reinforcements. Until that happened Montrose's position was insecure, and he was lucky to avoid engagement with the opposition when he moved his army south towards Methven Woods near Perth. He had to fall back north on Dunkeld, but that was the last move which Baillie forced him to make. There he was joined by fresh cavalry forces drawn from the Gordons and Ogilvys which provided him with the capacity to engage the Covenanting army for what he hoped would be the decisive battle of the campaign.

Once again Montrose was able to choose the place where it would be fought – at Kilsyth in the Campsie Fells, midway between the Forth and Clyde, where the Lowlands meet the Highlands. He had moved his army there to prevent reinforcements from Glasgow and the south-west reaching the Covenanting army and also to force Baillie to follow him. On 14 August Montrose drew up his men on rough rising ground facing to the west between two streams, with some cottages and farm buildings in front of him which he prudently occupied. The next day, having pursued Montrose from the south through Bridge of Earn, Stirling and Denny, Baillie drew up his forces to the east on an equally secure piece of rising ground. However, the general's own position was not as assured: he was accompanied by an advisory committee of divines and notables who included Argyll, Balfour of Burleigh and Balcarres, who were intent on gaining revenge and who offered a stream of contradictory advice, all to Baillie's disadvantage. Unfortunately for the Covenanting cause they held the majority and, although Baillie counselled that they should not engage immediately, he was overruled. The net result was an order to move to the north to outflank Montrose, presumably to cut off his means of escape, but it also meant marching the men in front of their enemy, a hazardous enterprise at any time but doubly dangerous on hilly ground. Baillie protested but he was forced to carry out their orders: thus was the battle won and lost, leaving 'bodies like clothes a-bleaching' on the surrounding hillsides.

Not long after the move began the two sides clashed near the cottages, the Covenanters not realising that they were occupied and the Highlanders, led by Ewan MacLean of Treshnish, taking full advantage of the fact. The fighting wasted a good deal of shot and effort for little advantage and it attracted the support of Alasdair MacColla's clansmen, a move which cut Baillie's army in two. At the same time Aboyne's horse had attacked on the left in support of their kinsmen, the Gordon foot, and although they were in danger of being cut off Montrose read the situation well. Turning to the Earl of Airlie he said that his 'veteran courage' made him the only commander capable of retrieving the situation. The Ogilvy horse were equal to the challenge and their intervention, charging up the slope, changed the balance of the battle. Despite Baillie's exhortations and his orders to his reserves to hold firm the Covenanting army started to break and scatter as best they could towards Falkirk. Few made it. The fleeing Covenanters were cut down and massacred, this time in their thousands, the carnage made worse by the Highlanders' desire for revenge: news had reached them of the massacre of their women camp followers at Methven a few weeks earlier. Very few of the 6000 who began the battle on that hot summer's day lived to see it end. The last Covenanter army had been destroyed utterly, leaving Montrose the master of Scotland.

Yet, tragically for him, at the very point when he had fulfilled his promise to Charles, power was already slipping out of his hands. One problem was his Highland army: fast-moving on the march and aggressive in the attack, it was unsuited to the next stage of consolidating its victory. For the Scots and the Irish Gaels war was an end in itself, an opportunity to gain plunder and to take revenge on their age-old enemies, the Campbells. Denied the chance to sack the rich city of Glasgow to the south, they sulked when it became apparent that Montrose was intent on winning hearts and minds as well as battles. When he entered the city two days later he was greeted with acclaim by its citizens, who were relieved that a strict code of military discipline had been installed to prevent outrages like those afflicted on Aberdeen. Prevention being as good as cure, Montrose moved his headquarters to Kirkton of Bothwell and set about the king's business. A meeting of parliament was called for 20 October (it would meet in Glasgow as Edinburgh had been visited by the plague), up and down the land Royalist prisoners were released from captivity, Edinburgh surrendered, as did its port of Leith, Alasdair MacColla set off with his forces to subdue Ayrshire and the wavering aristocracy flocked to Montrose's fold. These included the Marquis of Douglas and the Earl of Annandale, but many more were eldest sons sent by fathers who wanted to be seen to support Montrose but understood the sense of hedging their bets. For a short season it appeared as if Charles had reclaimed Scotland, that, as the poet Drummond of Hawthornden expressed it, a 'golden age' had returned and anarchy had been quelled.

It was all mirage. In name Montrose was the king's Lieutenant-Governor in Scotland, but his writ did not run far and the support of the Lowland population was not whole hearted. The Church still wielded enormous power and this in turn bred anxiety about Montrose's reliance on the wild Highlanders and uncivilised Catholic Irish who, according to one contemporary, were 'too cruel; for it was everywhere observed they did ordinarily kill all they could be master of, without any notion of pity or any consideration of humanity; nay it seemed to them there was no distinction between a man and a beast; for they killed men ordinarily with no more feeling of compassion and with the same neglect that they kill a hen or capon for their supper; and they were also without all shame, most brutishly given to uncleanness and flighty lust'.[9] However, the Gaels were also homesick, uneasy about being so far away from their clan lands and anxious to return to their families in the mountains and along the western seaboard. By late summer most were on the move north, anxious to be gone yet promising to return come the spring. It would not be the last time in Scotland's history that the Highlanders' refusal to travel forth of Scotland would lead to the failure of a military enterprise.

After being knighted Alasdair MacColla also left to ravage southern Argyll, and on 4 September 1645 Montrose left for the eastern borders in pursuit of an alliance with Home, Roxburgh and Traquair, all powerful local magnates. He left behind 500 of his Irish caterans under O'Cahan's command, but the two leaders and comrades-in-arms would never meet again. A further blow was inflicted by Aboyne, who withdrew his support and the services of his men. Angered at being passed over as General of Horse – the appointment had gone to the Earl of Crawford – he, too, was uneasy about leaving his family's lands unprotected. It must have been a bitter blow to Montrose, but blind optimism and self-belief made him continue, even though he must have known that retreat back into the Highlands would have been the safer option; he held to the view that his quest had not ended but was only just beginning. Hoping that Charles would soon link up with him and that the leading nobility of the Scottish Borders would provide large numbers of men, he led his much depleted army south towards the Gala Water, where he found that no support would be forthcoming. Fortuitously for them, but tragically for Montrose, Home and Roxburgh had already allowed themselves to be arrested, a move which made it appear that they supported the king's cause but were prevented from doing so by the intervention of the Covenanter leadership. With everything going wrong, Montrose went south again to Jedburgh, where he received the first intelligence that David Leslie was to the north with a powerful force of 4000 horse and 2000 infantry. As he had done at Fyvie, Montrose now trusted to luck and his instincts, instead of employing scouts. Unaware that Leslie had struck rapidly south from Tranent towards the borders – an overnight march of thirty miles following the Gala Water – he made his camp at Philiphaugh, two miles outside Selkirk, on low-lying ground where the waters of the Yarrow and Ettrick meet.

On the night of 12 September discipline was lax and the men were stood down and relaxed. When the attack came in the following morning out of a mist-filled dawn no one was ready for it. Some defences had been built in the haughs and the Irish foot put up stout resistance against Leslie's troopers but they were badly outnumbered and lacked both firepower and the support of an effective cavalry screen. The fighting was all over in less than an hour. Some manag to escape, including Montrose, who was persuaded not to sell his life cheaply but to live to fight another day – with him went Douglas, Airlie and Crawford – but a different fate awaited those who survived the battle. Loyal officers such as O'Cahan and Nathaniel Gordon, whose dash and élan had served Montrose so well at Auldearn and Alford, were tried and executed as traitors and, despite being granted quarter by Leslie, the surviving Irish foot were simply put to the sword on the orders of the accompanying ministers, their reasoning being that the offer had only been made to their officer, Adjutant Stewart, and not to them. Once they had dispatched the soldiers, again in the name of the Lord of Hosts, the Covenanters set about slaughtering the camp followers – 300 women, children and cookboys – for no other reason than that they were idolatrous papists and as such fully deserved to be purged by the forces of the righteous. The work went merrily on, said one minister, or, as the balladmaker put it, the winners had every justification to extirpate those who had taken up arms against the accepted order:

> Now let us a' for Lesly [*sic*] pray,
> And his brave company,
> For they hae vanquished great Montrose,
> Our cruel enemy.[10]

During the winter and into the following summer Montrose remained at large in Scotland, still hopeful of raising support in the Highlands, but the year of victories was over, crushed at Philiphaugh when he simply ran out of luck and support. With his defeat Charles lost all hope of using his northern kingdom to rescue his cause in England. Now, if he wanted support from the Scots he would have to look to the same people who had been fighting to defeat his loyal lieutenant-governor.

Chapter Twelve

THINGS FALL APART

'I resolve, by the grace of God, never to yield up the church to the government of Papists, Presbyterians or Independents, nor to injure my successors by lessening the crown of that ecclesiastical power which my predecessors left me.'

King Charles I, manifesto issued at Huntingdon, 24 August 1645

Philiphaugh was not just the end of Charles's hopes in Scotland, it also presaged his defeat in England. By the time the news reached him he had received even more grievous information: that Bristol had fallen to parliament and to make matters worse – if that were possible – Rupert had surrendered it without putting up much of a fight. When the siege began in the middle of August Rupert had assured his uncle that he could hold out against Fairfax at least until Christmas, and Charles had taken him at his word, leaving him to his own devices while he himself marched north to try to link up with Montrose. Rupert had good cause for optimism. Fresh supplies of food had been brought into the city from south Wales, there were ample stocks of lead for making ammunition, and although his garrison was small – only 800 horse and 700 foot – they were experienced soldiers with good officers. He had also enjoyed a number of successes in the field outside Bristol, sending out cavalry sorties to harass the New Model Army and to burn positions before they could be occupied but, for all his energy and commitment, the tide was turning against the Royalist garrison. Against him Fairfax had 12,000 men in his army – more than twice as many as Rupert had when he besieged the city two years earlier – and the parliamentary general also had the advantage of a force led by Massey which could be deployed as a screen to prevent any counter-attack from Goring in Devon. By 24 August Bristol was completely cut off, and although Rupert hoped that Fairfax would hesitate before mounting a full-scale assault the future looked bleak.

Perhaps, in his quieter moments, Rupert was already close to losing heart. In the days after Naseby Charles had talked about reinforcing Bristol and using it as his headquarters, but the fall of nearby Bridgwater had changed all that. While Rupert could understand his uncle's reasoning about his policy in the west – the port was strategically important for communication with the Royalists in the south-west – he could not fathom why Charles was so keen to make for Scotland in the aftermath of the crushing defeat at Naseby. Being Rupert he put his thoughts to paper in a letter written to the Duke of Richmond on 24 July. Having poured cold water on the Montrose expedition plan he went on to doubt the probability of Irish recruits arriving, but his main point was to question the wisdom of continuing the war. Coming from his Captain-General and the man who had his complete confidence the letter could not have made happy reading for Charles:

> If I were desired to deliver my opinion what other ways the king should take, this should be my opinion which your Lordship may declare to the King. His Majesty hath now no way left to preserve his posterity, kingdom and nobility, but by a treaty. I believe it is a more prudent way to retain something than to lose all.[1]

The letter obviously hurt the king but he responded to this brutal piece of military realism with an equally forthright letter which made it absolutely clear that the fight continued, that he could not give it up without losing honour and dignity and that there could be no surrender, whatever the odds stacked against him. The way would be hard and long, privations lay ahead, but it would all be worthwhile if the king's cause and God's interests were defended:

> Now as for your opinion of my business and your counsel thereupon, if I had any other quarrel but the defence of my

religion, crown and friends, you had full reason for your advice. For
I confess that speaking as a mere soldier or statesman, I must say
there is no probability but of my ruin; yet as a Christian I must tell
you that God will not suffer rebels and traitors to prosper, nor this
course to be overthrown: and whatever personal punishment it
shall please him to inflict on me, must not make me repine let
alone give over this quarrel . . .[2]

It was a remarkably prescient letter which tells us much about the
king's singular sense of purpose. Reality had crept in to tell him that
victory was unlikely, yet he would not yield to the rebels, putting all
his trust in his religious faith and in a higher mystical belief that,
because right was on his side, justice would eventually prevail. In the
meantime his temporal plans demanded attention: he would clear the
rebels from Herefordshire, Goring would bring his army up from the
West Country, both would march on Bristol and their combined
might would defeat Fairfax and Cromwell. With Montrose carrying
all before him in Scotland the tide would turn and the year would end
well. There was to be no more talk of negotiation or defeat.

Three weeks later – the letter was written on 3 August 1645 – Bristol
was in dire straits. The New Model Army had surrounded it, plague
had broken out inside the city walls and Fairfax had written the first
summons asking for surrender. Even though the official summons was
followed by a personal letter in which Fairfax outlined his views on
the conflict, Rupert would not countenance surrender. At a council
of war three options were considered – a break-out, the defence of the
inner fortifications, an all-out do-or-die defence in the hope that the
initial assault would be repulsed and that winter would come to their
aid. Of these three it was agreed to adopt the third in the hope that
the resulting siege would be called off. From a military point of view
and given the lack of numbers it was a sensible decision, but Rupert
and his council knew that casualties would be high. After the rejection
of a further entreaty from Fairfax and Cromwell addressed to the
citizens of Bristol and offering them safe quarter should they
surrender it was only a matter of time before parliamentary patience
ran out. When it did, in the early hours of 10 September, the resulting
battle was short, sharp and effective. The defences on the
Gloucestershire side of the city soon fell, allowing the supporting

regiments to enter the city, and despite the sharp resistance Fairfax's
men were inside the inner defences by dawn. In one defensive fort,
Prior's Hill, Rupert's men refused to lay down their arms and were
offered no quarter.

Seeing that further resistance was futile and realising that a huge
casualty list was in the offing Rupert decided to sue for terms. He
could have held out in the inner city for longer but this would have
led to the total destruction of Bristol and the loss of civilian lives. As
a soldier Rupert was obliged to fight on but, had he done so, it would
have been at a terrible price. A trumpeter sounded the cease-fire and
under the circumstances honourable terms were agreed – Rupert and
his men were allowed to march out with their weapons and colours
and to return under escort to Oxford. For the Royalists the defeat of
their commander-in-chief was a shattering blow (though not to their
military strength, as the force was allowed to fight again). For
Cromwell it was a victory justified by God 'for the terror of evil-
doers', but, apart from the military or religious considerations some
good came from it. First, Bristol was spared and, secondly, Rupert's
reputation was enhanced, though not in the way he might have
expected. The officer escorting him back to Oxford had felt the full
fury of the Royalist cavalry charge at Naseby and, having been
wounded, entertained little love for Rupert. During the march he got
to know him and liked what he saw – a fellow military man on the
other side of the divide who had acted honourably to save a city – and
friendship of a sort was struck.

Unfortunately Charles did not share that parliamentary officer's
opinion. Just as parliament had punished Nathaniel Fiennes for losing
Bristol, so too did the king vent his fury on his favourite nephew. This
was little short of treason, the promise to keep Bristol for four months
had been worthless, the news had left Charles so distraught that he
had no choice but to strip Rupert of his command. On 14 September
the letter of dismissal was written and signed:

> Though the loss of Bristol be a great blow to me, yet your
> surrendering it as you did, is of so much affliction to me that it
> makes me forget not only the consideration of that place, but is
> likewise the greatest trial to my constancy that has befallen me; for
> what is to be done after one who is so near me both in blood and

friendship submits himself to so mean an action? (I give it the easiest term). Such – I have so much to say that I will say no more of it: only lest rashness of judgement be laid to my charge, I must remember you your letter of the 12 August, whereby you assured me you would keep Bristol for four months. Did you keep it four days? . . . My conclusion is to desire you to seek your subsistence, (until it pleases God to determine my condition), somewhere beyond the seas, to which end I send you herewith a pass; and I pray to God to make you sensible of your present condition, and give you means to redeem what you have lost; for I shall have no greater joy in a victory, than a just occasion without blushing to assure you of my being

Your loving uncle and most faithful friend.

Charles R[3]

As a prince of the royal blood and the king's nephew Rupert had enjoyed a privileged position which his own military ability had reinforced, and his fall from grace was bound to be all the harder. By the same token, as Charles had excused many of his wilder actions and had made much of him at court, the disappointment and anger were bound to be more pronounced. The recent memory of the letter Rupert had written about the 'prudent way' must also have rankled: Charles was not given to defeatism and Rupert's talk of a treaty had angered him, not least because it came from a close and trusted relation. When the breach came it was bitter, leaving the king to regret the instant collapse of his cherished plan to combine with Goring and Rupert to smash Fairfax and Cromwell once and for all. Malign influence was also at work: the king was under the sway of Digby, who was delighted to see the fall of his main opponent at court. Rumours abounded in the king's entourage that Rupert was in contact with parliament to save his skin and that he intended to open negotiations for replacing the House of Stewart with the House of Palatine. As evidence, Digby pointed to the fact that Rupert's brother Charles Louis, the Elector Palatine, was in London hoping to act as a peacemaker and in so doing advance his own claims to the throne. Rumour had it that he had been awarded a pension of £8000 and that the 'betrayal' of Bristol was a halfway house to winning parliament's confidence. It was all nonsense but, in an edgily declining court, it was believed, so much so that the king also dismissed the governor of Oxford, William Legge, on account of his close friendship with his nephew. For his pains Digby was appointed lieutenant-general of the Royalist forces in the north.

What followed was equally galling – the failure to make any headway in getting to Scotland – and following the news of Montrose's collapse Charles was left with a declining number of options. Digby counselled that the generals in the west, Grenville and Goring, would still come good but this was wishful thinking – the first was intent on feathering his own nest through a reign of terror and, by most accounts, the latter was in a state of perpetual inebriation. The king also put much faith in the arrival of Glamorgan's Irishmen, but as this would entail the retention of Chester (then under Byron's command) the port became the next venue on the king's itinerary. The Royalist force arrived on 23 September to find it under partial siege by forces led by Colonel Michael Jones, who had only managed to make any headway on the eastern side. Thinking to outflank him Charles took his Lifeguard into the city, crossing the bridge over the Dee, while Langdale took the remains of his Northern Horse to an open piece of ground to the south-east called Rowton Heath, the intention being to attack Jones's investing army from the rear and pin it against Chester's fortifications.

The plan might have worked but for the unknown presence of a large force of parliamentary horse led by the indomitable Sydenham Poyntz which was in hot pursuit. By the following day it had arrived within sight of Langdale's force, and its appearance put the old cavalry commander in a dreadful predicament: with Poyntz behind him he could not fall on Jones, and a first attempt at driving off his new tormentor failed. The stalemate was broken when Jones dispatched a force to join Poyntz to give him a numerical advantage while the king ordered out a sortie of cavalry led by the recently ennobled Earl of Lichfield (Lord Bernard Stuart, the Duke of Richmond's younger brother) and Lord Charles Gerard, who had done much to rally his cause in Wales. It was a bold move, but the day ended in disaster when the parliamentary cavalry routed Langdale's horse on Rowton Heath. As the men fled, most towards Chester, they were pursued and a furious scrimmage developed beneath the city walls as Lichfield's and Gerard's horse became hopelessly entangled with the remnants of

Langdale's force and the pursuing parliamentarian troopers. In the
mêlée it became impossible to tell friend from foe and the Royalist
forces were quickly destroyed under the eyes of the defenders on the
city walls, including Charles himself, who had a grandstand view from
his position in the Phoenix Tower on the north-east side of the city.
As Sir Henry Slingsby, an ardent Royalist, noted, the horrors of war
and the reality of his own weakened position were at last affecting the
king, leaving him only with stoic acceptance of his plight:

> Here I do wonder at the admirable temper of the king, whose
> constancy was such that no perils never so unavoidable could move
> him to astonishment. But that still he set the same face and settled
> countenance upon what adverse fortune soever befell him; and
> neither was exalted in prosperity nor dejected in adversity; which
> was the more admirable in him, seeing that he had no other to have
> recourse unto for council and assistance, but must bear the whole
> burden upon his shoulders, when as the general of an army, if it be
> destroyed, has recourse to those that employed him, which will
> somewhat ease his heart's grief and supply the loss by new levies.
> And by this accident I never found him moved at all though the
> loss was so much greater by my Lord of Lichfield's death, his
> kinsman, and whom he loved so dearly.[4]

More heart's grief lay ahead, but Charles's immediate concern was
to clear out of Chester before Poyntz attacked again. The defeat
ended all hope of his reaching Scotland – when he reached Denbigh
on 28 September he received the news of Philiphaugh – but he still
had high hopes that Goring might be able to join up with him for
a decisive tilt against Fairfax. With that in mind he divided his
forces, sending Digby and Langdale north towards Scotland with
the remnants of the Northern Horse, while he set out to seek refuge
in Newark.

Increasingly the atmosphere in his camp was a mixture of frenzied
optimism and pure fantasy. Before leaving his king Digby wrote a
wild letter to Ormond full of half-truths and downright lies, praising
Rowton Heath as a victory and claiming that Montrose and Crawford
had routed Leslie in Westmoreland; all fabrications, but no one was
deceived. A hint of reality returned when Rupert arrived at Newark

with Maurice and a hundred unruly supporting horsemen on 16 October. On his way from Oxford he had escaped being killed when a musket misfired during a clash with parliamentary soldiers and his blood was up. Hearing of his approach Charles tried to prevent him from entering the town, but Rupert had not ridden so far and encountered so many dangers to be denied. He demanded the soldier's prerogative of a court martial and was grudgingly granted one. It absolved him of blame for surrendering Bristol but chided him for not holding out longer and unsurprisingly the compromise verdict failed to cool tempers. Still fearing that his nephew was intent on gaining power for himself, Charles decided to sack Sir Richard Willis as governor of Newark for no other reason than he was too friendly with Rupert. If the decision was meant to cause offence it succeeded. Rupert and his supporters burst into the king's presence and made angry demands which bordered on mutiny. The next day, 28 October, Rupert, Maurice and Willis, together with 200 supporters, left the king's service, taking with them passes to travel abroad – it would take another eight months before they were able to do so.

That noisy interlude only served to underline how untenable was the king's position. In the first week of November he returned to Oxford, where the stream of bad news became a torrent. From Yorkshire came the intelligence that the Northern Horse had been routed at Sherburn-in-Elmet on 15 October. It was an unnecessary defeat for this once-proud unit, which was made up of 'officers, gentlemen of quality and their attendants', most of whom regarded war as a slightly more serious extension of their hunting pursuits. Before going into action their commander, Marmaduke Langdale, had reminded them of their responsibilities and their high reputation in words that were increasingly out of kilter with the times:

> Gentlemen, you are all gallant men, and have done bravely, but there are some that seek to scandalise your gallantry for the loss of Naseby field. But I hope you will redeem your reputation, and still maintain that gallant report which you ever had. I am sure you have done such business as never has been done in any war with such a number.[5]

If ringing phrases won battles the Northern Horse should have been triumphant, but what could have been a victory became a disaster. Having ridden into the town the advance guard successfully engaged a smaller parliamentary unit and put it to flight, but those following up became confused. Thinking that the cavalry racing out of Sherburn-in-Elmet were their own men, they panicked and galloped away. The survivors fled over the Pennines and made their way through Cumberland with the intention of getting to Scotland. That, too, was not to be. Nine days later the last remnants of the Northern Horse were destroyed on the treacherous sands outside Carlisle by a superior force of Scottish cavalry commanded by Sir John Brown. Langdale and Digby managed to escape by boat to the Isle of Man before moving on to Dublin, but that defeat finally ended Royalist resistance in the north and left Charles without any coherent cavalry force.

About this time Basing House fell to Cromwell. Known to its defender, the Marquis of Winchester, as Loyalty House, or Old Loyalty – every window was inscribed 'Aimez Loyauté' – it had held out for the king since the beginning of the war and had become a talisman for the Royalist cause. Heavily defended, it had defied Waller's guns, but in the autumn of 1645, with the war almost at an end, Cromwell had access to sufficient heavy artillery pieces, and the draught-horses to pull them, to make short work of the building. A summons to surrender was ignored, Winchester replying that he would keep Cromwell's letter as evidence of his rebellion, and then the guns set about their business on 13 October. Two days later they had done their work and Cromwell's men rushed into the defences, running amuck as they shot and stabbed, killing without discrimination and grabbing whatever came to hand. All this was done with Cromwell's blessing, although, being the commander, he stayed well away from the actual sacking.

Around one hundred people were put to the sword, among them a number of Jesuit priests and a young girl who tried to protect her clergyman father, Dr Griffith. Also found dead was the body of a man accounted to be nine feet high as well as 'some officers of quality'. Winchester survived, as did the architect Inigo Jones, who had been asked to help plan the house's defences but found a different fate awaiting him. For his pains the creator of King Charles's Banqueting

Hall at Whitehall was stripped of his clothes and had the indignity of walking away naked covered only by a blanket.

Hatred of papism was one reason for the atrocity – Basing House was a shelter for Catholics and Winchester was one of England's leading Catholic noblemen – and greed was another. According to Hugh Peters, Cromwell's chaplain, the house was 'fit to make an emperor's court' and while idolatrous images were destroyed large amounts of furnishing and clothing were ransacked to be sold in London. The God-fearing Peters left a vivid description of the day's work:

> The plunder of the soldiers continued until Tuesday night. One soldier had 120 pieces in gold for his share, others plate, others jewels. Amongst the rest, one got three bags of silver, which (he not being able to keep his own counsel) grew to be common pillage amongst the rest, and the fellow had one half crown left for himself at last. Also the soldiers took wheat to the country people, which they held up at good rates for a while, but afterwards the market fell, and there was some abatements for haste. After that they sold the household stuff, whereof there was a good store; and the country loaded away many carts, and continued a good while fetching out all manner of household stuff, till they had fetched out the stools, chairs, and other lumber which they sold to the country by piecemeal. In these great houses there was not one iron bar left in all the windows (save only what was in the fire) before night. And the last work of all was the lead, and by Thursday morning they had hardly left one gutter about the house.[6]

Then, having carried away everything worth selling, they pulled down the house, as much for strategic considerations as an example to others. Only the adjoining tithe barn remained intact. As for Winchester he was carted off to the Tower of London and his two sons were ordered to be brought up as Protestants. Before going he was subjected to a religious grilling by Hugh Peters which ended with Winchester's noble thought that if the king had 'no more ground in England than Basing' he would still do it all again.

Though not as perfervid in his beliefs as, say, Wariston, Peters was a formidable presence in the New Model Army. Together with

Richard Baxter he was one of its leading ministers and he brought to his task the crossing of the Bible with the sword – not for nothing was he nicknamed 'the Reverend Dragoon'. Like many other Independents of his ilk he had become convinced of his sinfulness at an early age and his life had been spent trying to assuage it and to find peace with his God. After leaving Cambridge he entered the Church but his alienation from Laud's doctrines forced him to emigrate and for the latter part of the 1630s he had been minister at Salem in New England, where he balanced his bellicosity towards the Pequod Indians with a sense of righteousness blessed by God's grace. On returning to England to throw in his lot with the parliamentary cause he showed the same spirit – he hated the royal family and some measure of his missionary zeal can be seen in his report to the House of Commons on the sacking of Basing House:

> We see who are his Majesty's dear friends, and trusty, and well-beloved cousins, and counsellors; the marquis [Winchester] being the pope's devoted vassal.
> And thus the Lord was pleased in a few hours to show us, what mortal seed all earthly glory grow upon, and how just and righteous the ways of God are, who takes sinners in their own snares, and lifteth up the heads of his despised people . . .[7]

For the king's cause everything now depended on the remaining forces in the West Country which came under the nominal control of the Prince of Wales and his council in Truro, but here, too, time was running out. Before the year ended Goring had made his excuses and left for exile in France, the command of his forces eventually passing to Hopton, who came out of retirement to rally an army which Clarendon dismissed as 'being only terrible in plunder, and resolute in running away'. Loyal soldier that he was, Hopton told the prince that he would accept the position even though he knew he would forfeit his honour – 'since his Highness thought it necessary to command him, he was ready to obey him with the loss of his honour'.[8] The Royalist army was in disarray, with the Prince of Wales being forced to arrest Grenville after he refused to obey orders. Against the New Model Army, with Fairfax in the ascendant, it stood no chance.

The end was not long in coming. Dartmouth had fallen on 19 January 1646 after a short night attack and 1500 Cornishmen fell into Fairfax's hands. All were well-treated and were given the choice of returning to their homes or joining the New Model Army, the parliamentary commander believing that nothing was lost by showing clemency to former enemies. Exeter was the next target, but as hard winter weather began to set in Fairfax wanted an early end to the campaign, and that meant beating Hopton, who had decided to make a stand at Torrington. Leaving a brigade to continue the investment of Exeter Fairfax took his army north into the valley of the River Torridge to attack the small market town on its position high above the river. After marching through atrocious weather conditions the attack went in shortly after midnight on 17 February, the flashpoint being a firefight between the defenders and dragoons sent forward by Cromwell to reconnoitre the Royalist defences. Although Hopton had planned his defences as best he could, throwing up barricades and blocking the narrow streets, his opponents had the advantage of weight of numbers and within two hours' close-quarters fighting 'at push of pike' it was all over. Those who could, fled; those who could not, surrendered, and the casualties would have been smaller than 200 had not the Royalist magazine suddenly exploded killing the same amount over again, most of them parliamentary prisoners in the church. As the timber, stones and lead showered down there were some lucky escapes, most notably Fairfax, who was spared injury, as he wrote afterwards, through 'God's great mercy'. Undeterred he continued the pursuit into Cornwall: Launceston fell, then Bodmin, and on 2 March Royalist resistance came to an end when the Prince of Wales retreated to Pendennis Castle to sail for the Scilly Isles.

Four days later Fairfax offered terms to the defeated Royalist commander, who accepted them on 12 March, having concluded that Cornwall had done as much as it could for the king's cause and that therefore the war in the west was over. The next day the two generals dined together, two veterans of thirty-one months of almost non-stop fighting, and in common with many opponents they found that they had much in common. Fairfax was inclined to be generous and gave his pass to Hopton, telling him that he was:

. . . one, whom (for personal worth and many virtues, but especially for your care of, and moderation towards the country) we honour and esteem above any other of your party, whose error (supposing you more swayed with Principles of Honour and Conscience than others) we most pity, and whose happiness (so far as consistent with the public welfare) we should delight in more than in your least suffering.[9]

The Royalist officers were offered similar terms, another tribute to Fairfax's belief that the wounds caused by the war could only be healed by refusing to pay off old scores. Having made the surrender Hopton went into exile, as did Richard Grenville, although for different reasons – he feared that Fairfax would not be minded to treat him so well and that he had 'no reason to expect the least degree of leniency'. Given his savage behaviour in the West Country he was probably right. Hopton died in Bruges in 1652, Grenville six years later.

By the time of their surrender Chester had finally fallen to Brereton's besieging army and Hereford, too, was captured and its cathedral stripped of its ornamentation. With the king now marooned in Oxford, all that remained was a steadily reducing number of garrisons and fortified houses which had been under siege for so long that they had been transformed from strategic nuisances into important symbols of resistance. Some had already fallen – most notably Scarborough Castle, which was forced to surrender after its supplies ran out in July 1645. Its governor, the turncoat Sir Hugh Cholmley, was allowed to go into exile. Violence accompanied the end of others – Shelford House in Nottinghamshire remained in Royalist hands under the command of Sir Philip Stanhope, who refused several summons to surrender. When it fell to Poyntz's forces in November the Royalist garrison was offered no mercy. According to one account they 'chose rather to die in their obstinance than ask for quarter, upon which their desperate pertinacy (there being about 180 of them in the house) most of them suffered the edge of the sword'.[10] Many more were simply destroyed to prevent them falling into enemy hands – Ashby Castle in Leicestershire, Bridgnorth Castle in Shropshire and, fatally for Charles, Woodstock House, a strategic outpost which guarded the approaches to Oxford. All fell with the autumn leaves and with them went Charles's hopes.

Resistance was also crumbling in Scotland. Having escaped into the Highlands Montrose failed to make contact either with Alasdair MacColla, who was busily ravaging the Campbells' lands, or with Huntly, who continued to refuse to make any common cause with him. He led some desultory raids which proved to be a nuisance to Middleton, the new Covenanting army commander (David Leslie having returned to England), but they achieved nothing. Even Huntly refused to meet him, riding away from Strathbogie when he approached. Only Alasdair MacColla continued his run of success, beating a force of Campbells at Lagganmore in Glen Euchar and laying siege to several strongholds but, having embarked on a tribal war, these actions were of little use to the king. In the months following the end of the Cessation, stalemate had also visited the fighting in Ireland: having been given the command of the English and Scots armies in Ulster Monro had driven Ormond's forces out of Lord Chichester's town of Belfast in May 1644, but once the Estates brought back most of his Scottish army to counter the threat posed by Montrose he had been unable to capitalise on his success by taking Dundalk and Newry.

Now only one field army was left to the Royalist cause – 3000 men of Hereford and Monmouth under the command of Lord Astley at Worcester. In one last desperate bid against the odds the old veteran of Gustavus Adolphus's wars was ordered to fight his way into Oxford to reinforce the garrison for one last stand until the fantasy replacements arrived from Scotland, Ireland, France or, indeed, all three countries. Astley was a good soldier, well versed in the art of manoeuvre, but he was outnumbered and outgunned and his defeat was inevitable. To reach Oxford he had to pass the powerful garrisons at Gloucester and Evesham, and although he managed to get halfway to his destination his army was overcome near Stow-on-the-Wold, north of Cirencester, on 21 March. Some of the horse escaped to complete the journey but the bulk of the infantry, mostly Welsh levies, simply surrendered. Together with his cavalry commander, Sir Charles Lucas, Astley was taken prisoner and interred in Warwick Castle, but before he was led away from his last battlefield he told his captors that as far as he was concerned the war was over: 'You have done your work, boys, and may go play, unless you will fall out among yourselves'. Another officer, Sir William Dugdale, was equally succinct and fatalistic: this had been 'the last encounter' that 'the Royalists were able to make with those insolent Rebels'.[11] As it would turn out both men were wrong in their forecast of events, but one truth was inescapable: by the spring of 1646 Charles had simply run out of options and had no more territory under his control to offer any determined resistance. Shorn of an army to command, he was king now only in name.

Chapter Thirteen

CONFEDERATES FOR THE KING

'I am as little obliged to the Irish as I can be to any nation, for all this year they have only fed me with vain hope, looking upon my daily ruin.'

King Charles I to Queen Henrietta Maria, 8 February 1646

For all that he was forced to spend the winter of 1645–46 observing the collapse of his power, Charles remained remarkably resilient and continued to demonstrate that mixture of fatalism and optimism which had led him so far and for so long. He had not wavered in his belief that he would never sacrifice the Church for political gain or do anything which would weaken the authority of his Crown, and he expected the same of his closest supporters in Oxford. Defeatism was banned, and although he no longer had access to Digby's breezy enthusiasm that matters would improve he tried to retain a sense of normality. While this was good for morale in a city which was reaching the end of its tether, the king's mood flew in the face of reality. The news that did enter Oxford was universally bad, and as each day passed so were all hopes of outside intervention dashed. A lesser man might have given way to despondency – any thought of going into exile was immediately and unhesitatingly dismissed – but Charles never lost sight of the prospect that his friends or relations might rally to him with the reinforcements and money on which he was gambling his future.

Ireland was his main buttress and he placed great faith in Glamorgan's and Ormond's ability to broker a deal which would give him access to Irish soldiers. After the defeat at Naseby Charles had confided in Ormond that the turn of events had reduced him 'from a very prosperous position to so low an ebb as to be a perfect trial of all men's integrities to me', and that he was looking to his friends for support.[1] Clearly that meant finding reinforcements, but Ormond was undecided how to act – the best of his forces had already been sent to England – and he was wary of any dealings with the Confederates who remained the best source for producing large numbers of troops. He also had to deal with Glamorgan, who had been given the king's commission in April 1644 to do just that – negotiate with the Confederates. This placed Ormond in a dreadful quandary and, believing that his authority had been weakened, he had offered his resignation to Charles in November, only to have it refused.

Ormond was the king's Lord Lieutenant and the proxy ruler in Ireland who had to cope with the Confederates, yet when the gadfly Glamorgan arrived in his bailiwick there was another servant of the king's operating behind his back in an ambassadorial role. That much was made clear to him in a letter the king had written on 27 December 1644. While it was couched in ambiguous terms, Ormond could have had little doubt that Glamorgan was not visiting family as his cover suggested (he was married to Lady Margaret O'Brien, daughter of the Earl of Thormond) but was in Ireland on the king's business:

I have thought good to use the power I have, both in his affection and duty to engage him in all possible ways to further the peace there [Ireland]; which he hath promised to so. Wherefore (as you find occasion) you may confidently use and trust him in this, or any other thing he shall propound to you for my service; there being none in whose honesty and zeal to my person and crown I have more confidence.[2]

A warning note was sounded in a coded postscript – 'His [Glamorgan's] honesty and affection to my service will not deceive you: but I will not answer to his judgement' – but the king was playing a dangerous game. If the mission went wrong the failure would not only undermine Ormond's authority but would give proof positive to the English parliament that Charles was intent on making a compact with the hated forces of Catholicism. In keeping with the ethos of the court there was also an element of favouritism in the promotion of Glamorgan. His father, the Marquis of Worcester, was one of Charles's greatest financial patrons and the family seat of Raglan Castle had been used as a retreat in the uneasy days following Naseby. The family was also solidly Catholic but, as Clarendon argued, their religion mattered not if they gave so much unstinting support to the Crown:

> The Lord Herbert [Earl of Glamorgan] was a man of more than ordinary affection and reverence to the person of the King, and one who he was sure would neither deceive or betray him. For his religion, it might work upon himself but could not disquiet other men. For though he was a Papist he was not like to make others so.[3]

That background and Glamorgan's enthusiasm for the cause of recruiting Irish troops made him an ideal candidate for the commission but, unwisely, the king's instructions carried an additional clause that Glamorgan should supersede the Lord Lieutenant in the event of his incapacity, either through illness, death or misconduct. In other words, as indicated in a letter of 12 March 1645, when Glamorgan entered into discussions with the Confederates' Supreme Council or any other body which might be useful he would be acting on the king's behalf:

> So great is the confidence we repose in you, as that whatsoever you shall perform, as warranted under our signature, pocket signet, or private mark, or even by word of mouth, without further ceremony, we do, on the word of a king and a Christian, promise to make good to all intents and purposes, as effectually as if your authority from us had been under the great seal of England, with this advantage, that we shall esteem ourself the more obliged to you for your gallantry in not standing upon such nice terms to do us service, which we shall, God willing, reward. And although you exceed what law can warrant, or any powers of ours reach unto, as

not knowing what you have need of, yet it being for our service, we oblige ourself, not only to give you our pardon, but to maintain the same with all our might and power; and though either by accident, or by any other occasion, you shall deem it necessary to deposit any of our warrants, and so want them at your return, and to supply anything wherein they shall be found defective, it not being convenient for us at this time to dispute upon them; for of what we have here set down you may rest confident, if there be faith and trust in men. Proceed, therefore, cheerfully, speedily, and boldly, and for your so doing this shall be your sufficient warrant.[4]

Stated in such sweeping terms the commission gave Glamorgan ample powers to take all necessary steps to achieve the aim of raising a new army (which he himself would command), even if that meant entering into a treaty which did not meet with Ormond's approval. It was a recipe for disaster. As everything in Ormond's background stood against making any deals with the Confederates – on that score he enjoyed the support of his own, mainly Protestant, council in Dublin – Glamorgan could not have hoped to win over the Lord Lieutenant, yet in the early summer of 1645, after a long and tortuous journey, he arrived in Ireland fully intending to deal with a group of Catholic Irishmen whom most Englishmen condemned as rebels.

No sooner had Glamorgan arrived in Dublin than he set off to Kilkenny and entered into discussions with the Confederate Supreme Council. He made swift progress, but this was not a surprise, as he was offering them a good deal. Within three weeks, on 25 August, he had concluded a treaty which, by the extreme nature of its terms, was bound to be disagreeable to Ormond and to cause great offence to Protestants in general. In return for the provision of 10,000 armed soldiers to fight on the king's behalf in England (the costs to be born by Catholic grandees in Europe), Glamorgan made the following promises: complete tolerance for all Irish Catholics, exemption from jurisdiction of the Protestant clergy and the restoration of all Catholic Church lands. Furthermore, Glamorgan gave an undertaking that in time the treaty would be ratified by parliament and that Charles would honour all its clauses.

These were far-reaching concessions and ones which would alarm even moderate Protestants, for they appeared to align the Crown with

Catholic interests and the forces of the Counter-Reformation. Glamorgan hoped to keep the terms secret, but given the open nature of the discussions and the number of participants involved that was a forlorn hope. Within weeks it was common knowledge in London that the king was trying to raise troops in Ireland, and the rumours were given added weight when it became known that the pope had sent a nuncio to the Confederation in the shape of the cultivated and austere Archbishop Rinuccini. Coming on top of the embassies already sent to Kilkenny by France and Spain, the appearance of the pope's suave representative in November only served to confirm fears that the king was about to enter into an unholy alliance with the Irish Catholics.

Rinuccini was a commanding personality whose mission was simply stated – the restoration of the Catholic Church in Ireland with Charles's connivance. The nuncio's task might have had missionary intentions, but given the situation in Ireland it quickly assumed temporal overtones. Together with his authoritative personality this made the archbishop a formidable adversary; he was able to overawe the members of the Supreme Council who, being devout Catholics, respected him as the pope's emissary, and he soon found that Glamorgan was susceptible to his influence. At his first meeting Rinuccini discerned that Charles's representative was equally keen to secure a treaty – but for quite different reasons – and he worked on him obliquely.

From the outset Rinuccini made it clear that the secret treaty was worthless unless Glamorgan could guarantee each and every clause in the king's name. Having planted doubts in a man who was never really sure of his abilities, he proceeded to rack up the pressure by introducing a new set of concessions including the extreme (and unrealisable) demands that the next Lord Lieutenant be a Catholic and that Catholic bishops be allowed to sit in parliament. The pay-off was that 3000 troops would be made available immediately and could be transferred to Chester without further ado. For Glamorgan it was a glittering prize. The king's cause would receive a massive boost, Chester would be saved at a time when the Royalist war effort was in danger of collapse, and he, Glamorgan, would be the sole author of the rescue. With no other cards to play Glamorgan agreed to the new treaty, leaving Rinuccini to report to the Vatican on

28 November : 'I have induced the Earl of Glamorgan to promise me all the conditions which Your Eminence will see in the enclosed papers signed by him.' That same day Glamorgan wrote to Ormond telling him that he had obtained the necessary 'propositions for peace' and the deal was signed three weeks later on 20 December.[5]

Glamorgan's reasons for acting in this wild and unconsidered way were rooted in the desperate situation facing the Royalist party. He knew how critical it was to get military support from Ireland and he believed that Charles's commission gave him the authority to agree to new terms, however immoderate. By keeping the treaty secret he hoped to have it changed or even rescinded later, for he must have known that its contents would never gain royal or parliamentary approval. All that mattered to him at that juncture was getting the troops; this persuaded him to sign a treaty secure in the knowledge that the king's support for his actions was unconditional. One other factor convinced him which arose from Rinuccini's persuasiveness: he had been made to believe that the nuncio was not just serious about re-establishing the Catholic Church in Ireland but wanted to use that as a first step towards supporting Charles and defeating parliament.

All might have been well, the treaty might have remained secret, the troops might have assembled and even set sail, but for the run of bad luck which seemed to afflict Charles's cause in Ireland. For a start, keeping the details confidential was a lost cause. Copies of the first Glamorgan treaty had been printed and distributed to leading clerics and its details were a matter of common gossip. Then, the country being in a lawless state with three armies still in the field, it was inevitable perhaps that the papers would fall into the wrong hands. And so it proved. While the negotiations were still fresh Malachi O'Queely, archbishop of Tuam and president of the Connacht council, was ambushed by a patrol of Scots troopers while making his way from Kilkenny to Sligo. During the fighting he was killed, but that was the least of the Confederates' misfortunes. O'Queely's baggage was ransacked, and among his papers was found a copy of the offending first treaty. Realising its importance the commanding officer sent it to Monro's headquarters in Belfast and then it made its way to parliament in London. Though not as compromising as the Rinuccini version, the treaty still offered concessions which were anathema to Protestants. When the terms were read out in parliament on 16 January 1646 they caused fresh outrage for, as Robert Baillie reported to his colleague Robert Ramsay, here was proof (if it were needed after the revelations at Naseby) that the king was intent on forging an alliance with the Irish Catholics. There could be no more heinous sin:

> What troubles us most is Ireland. The Pope this half year has had a nuncio there. Both the Spanish and French Kings have had their residents at Kilkenny. We had a rumour of it before, but this night the copies of the writs from the English commissioners in Ireland have been read in the committee of both kingdoms, and tomorrow are to be reported to the Houses, wherein the King gives ample commission to the Earl of Glamorgan to give full liberty to his loyal Catholic subjects of Ireland of their religion, restores to them all the church-lands in Ireland, recalls all the laws against Popery there. We fear that this shall undo the King for ever; that no repentance shall ever obtain a pardon of this act; if it be true, from his Parliaments.[6]

Parliament's main concern was that the treaty was only the tip of the iceberg, that the supply of Irish troops was part of a pan-European Catholic conspiracy which would see an Irish army land at Chester while Alasdair MacColla would sweep into the Scottish Lowlands to secure it in advance of attacking the north of England, and a large French army would cross the English Channel and invade the southern counties. Baillie was shocked by the disclosure, as well he might have been, for it came at the same time when the king was negotiating with the Scots about reaching a settlement with them.

Like a boy whose guilty secret has been uncovered, Charles immediately set about distancing himself from Glamorgan. Two weeks later he wrote to parliament stating that Glamorgan had acted without his permission and that he was unaware that the negotiations were taking place; while his emissary had acted unwisely it had never been his intention to do any harm. By that stage of the war the king's protestations had a hollow ring and were simply discounted. He almost managed to retrieve some lost dignity when Ormond ordered Glamorgan to be arrested and charged with treason on 26 December, the Lord Lieutenant's resolve having been stiffened by Digby's unexpected arrival in Dublin, following his escape from the north of England.

What followed next was pure theatre. Digby and Ormond combined to make the treason charges stick, but their actions seem to have been inspired more by the need to maintain a sense of decorum than to exert any real pressure on the hapless Glamorgan. When asked under whose orders he was acting Glamorgan responded that not only had he always done everything with Ormond's full knowledge and consent but that he carried the king's commission as outlined in the letter of 12 March. Throughout the proceedings, Glamorgan protested his innocence, writing to his wife that 'this cloud will soon be dissipated by the sunshine of the King, my master' and that he would soon be released. All the evidence points to a whitewash. Digby advised Glamorgan that the king would deny everything and warned that the revelations would be his ruin because they showed Charles to be duplicitous and a secret friend of Rome, and the matter was soon dropped. On 22 January Glamorgan was released from arrest, ironically at the very moment when Charles was trying to prove his innocence to the English parliament. Within a week the treaty was repudiated and Ormond was assured by the king: 'on the word of a Christian, I never intended that Glamorgan should treat anything without your approbation, much less without your knowledge'.[7] As for his punishment, that, too, was to be put to one side for the time being:

Albeit I have no just cause, for the clearing of my honour, to command (as I have done) to prosecute Glamorgan in a legal way; yet I will have you suspend the execution of any sentence against him until you inform me fully of all the proceedings. For, I believe, it was his misguided zeal, more than malice, which brought this great misfortune on him and on us all.[8]

In other words, it would be better for all concerned if the episode was written off as simple misadventure. Charles said as much when he wrote to Glamorgan on 3 February claiming that in one way and another both men had been traduced:

Glamorgan, I must clearly tell you, both you and I have been abused in this business; for you have been drawn to consent to conditions much beyond your instructions and your treaty has been revealed to the world. If you had advised with my Lord Lieutenant (as you promised me), all this had been helped. But we must look forward. Wherein in a word I have commended as much favour to be shown unto you as may possibly stand with my service or safety; and if you will yet trust my advice (which I have commended Digby to give you freely), I will bring you so off, that you may still be useful to me: and I shall be able to recompense you for your affection.[9]

As ever, Charles found personal friendships hard to break, even though, as in Glamorgan's case, he was putting them to a severe test by bending the truth and believing only what he wanted to believe. Then, as the truth finally came out, he tried to put a different gloss on events by disclaiming any part in them. His actions were to no avail because parliament chose not to believe his excuses; as Baillie pointed out, the king's late repentance counted for nothing, and even the loyal Digby was moved to admit that the secret negotiations seemed to prove to the king's enemies that Charles was a closet Catholic.

It was not the end of the affair. After his release Glamorgan was confronted by Rinuccini, who produced a new draft treaty signed by Henrietta Maria and the pope which had been brokered by an intermediary in Rome, Sir Kenelm Digby. It offered even more advantageous terms, but without the king's ratification it was quite worthless. Even so, that did not deter Glamorgan, who had not yet received the news of Charles's repudiation and was still keen to convince Rinuccini of his sincerity. Clutching at straws, he persuaded the nuncio that he would be able to secure the king's agreement provided that 6000 troops were made available to him to cross over from Waterford into south Wales. He even tried to bring Ormond into the plot, writing to him on 8 February that 'the expectancy of a more advantageous peace wrought by her Majesty soon wipes out the clandestine hopes of my endeavours to serve the nation'.

His last-ditch efforts were helped by the Supreme Council, which was becoming nervous lest the king's demise in England and Scotland would encourage parliament to send a combined army to attack them in Ireland. To shore up the imminent collapse of royal power they agreed in mid-February to dispatch a force of 2000 men under Antrim to cross over to Scotland to distract the Covenanters. At the same time they made arrangements for 6000 soldiers to assemble in Waterford for service in England, provided that Glamorgan could find the transport. His hopes buoyant once more, Glamorgan wrote to Culpepper advising him that at long last his goals had been achieved – 'having overpast many rubs and difficulties, the long-expected work is at last encompassed' – but it was not to be. For all that Glamorgan received the commission of lord-general from the Confederates, his writ did not run far enough to order sufficient ships and without access to his family funds he lacked the capacity to hire them. When news of Chester's fall and the king's repudiation reached Ireland at the beginning of March the decision was taken to cancel the expedition and to use the forces against Inchiquin in Munster. Antrim's expedition went ahead: he landed in Argyll in May and was met with acclaim, but the end of the war in England scuppered any hopes of his linking up with Alasdair MacColla for a lengthy campaign against the Covenanters. Antrim went with Rinuccini's blessing – the nuncio was the author of a fantastic religious morality tract called *Il Cappuccino Scozzese* ('The Scottish Capuchin') – but he was more intent on restoring the Irish branch of his family on Scotland's western seaboard than on furthering the king's cause.

With Glamorgan's authority permanently damaged by the withdrawal of Charles's patronage, Ormond acted swiftly in the summer of 1646 to get an accommodation with the Old English faction which would produce a compromise peace with the Confederation. This would be an 'open' treaty which offered political but not religious concessions to the Catholics in return for military support, Ormond having persuaded them that their best hope lay not with a victorious parliament but with a restored king. Known as the 'Ormond Peace', it promised to enact the Graces and to provide a parliament untrammelled by Poynings's Law, but the terms were out of kilter with the times. Ormond was not to know that, while he was negotiating with the Old English moderates led by his brother-in-law Lord Muskerry, the king was about to enter into a new agreement with the Scots. He had also underestimated Rinuccini's influence at Kilkenny. Working on those who opposed the plan, mainly clerics and the dispossessed Old Irish, the nuncio mounted a coup at the end of August and took over interim command of the Supreme Council. Those who supported the deal were arrested, threatened with excommunication and sidelined from the new administration which was formed under Rinuccini's direction.

This left Ormond in a sorry state. He owed his position as Lord Lieutenant to the king, but given the state of affairs in England it was a worthless office. Far from forging a lasting peace with the Confederates he had seen them come under the sway – and pay – of the pope's representative, who had shown his true colours by making it clear that his true purpose was the restoration of Catholicism in Ireland and not the restoration of Charles to the British throne. Matters were not improved for him by a string of military successes enjoyed by Owen Roe O'Neill, who had decided to throw in his lot with Rinuccini. Having retired to Connacht to rebuild his army he captured a number of parliamentary strongholds before falling on Monro's Ulster army at Benburb in County Tyrone on 5 June. This was the biggest setpiece battle of the Confederate stage of the war, and it was the only occasion when Irish forces won a decisive victory in the field. Both sides were evenly matched in numbers but the ground did not suit Monro's men: forced up against the Blackwater river on a narrow plain his pikemen had difficulty deploying and were unable to rely on the support of reserve lines. Watching the action was O'Neill's Franciscan chaplain, Father O'Mellan, who revelled in the 'bloody rout', seeing it as a vindication of his commander's exhortation to his men to remember that they were fighting against heretics who had driven out their chieftains, robbed their land and oppressed their religion:

> The retreat developed into a demoralised rout. It was then that the Irish let loose their battle-cry. At times in the lead, at times in their midst, the general was encouraging and inciting his men. The slaughter continued until the final disappearance of the long last ray of sunlight made further pursuit impossible. Numbers of the enemy were drowned in the Blackwater and in the lake of Knocknacloy.[10]

O'Mellan's description is a reminder that warfare on the Celtic fringes was not at all modern or progressive: it was a brutal and bloodthirsty business in which quarter was rarely offered. In the resulting shambles, by the priest's reckoning 3548 men were slaughtered, most of them Scots. Already weakened by withdrawals to Scotland and by the unwillingness of English units to serve under Monro's command – one regiment of horse led by Sir Theophilus Jones had to be threatened with being disarmed before they sullenly fell in with the Scots – the Covenanter army was virtually wiped out as a fighting unit. Ironically, Benburb was the kind of battle for which this veteran of Breitenfeld and the German wars had been trained, and given better troops he might have performed better. But being a professional (that is, a mercenary) Monro blamed his men's sinfulness and refused to be suitably chastened – either by the scale of the defeat or by the loss of his wig on the field:

> The Lord of Hosts had a controversy with us to rub shame on our faces, as on other armies, till once we shall be humbled, for a greater confidence did I never see in any army that was amongst us, and we behoved to taste of bitterness as well as others of both nations; but praised be God, being now humbled before God, we increase in courage and resolution.[11]

Monro was later imprisoned in the Tower of London, but he found some consolation by marrying the widow of Lord Montgomery of Ards (who had served under him at Benburb) and settling in Ulster. The victory at Benburb should have encouraged O'Neill (another professional) to press ahead and clear Ulster of parliamentary forces, but instead he took his army south to Kilkenny to lend his support to Rinuccini.

Later that summer he was in action again when his army was ordered to capture Dublin to break the power of Ormond and his council. The campaign started well enough with the capture of Roscommon, but disagreements between O'Neill and his great rival Thomas Preston, commander of the Leinster forces, led to an inconclusive siege which petered out in November with the arrival of winter, leaving Ormond still in control of the Irish capital and free to open negotiations with parliament. The year which had begun with Charles trying to get support from the Irish Catholics ended with him in league with the Scots while the Confederates on whom he had counted so much were hopelessly divided by internal dissension. As for Glamorgan, his hopes crushed, he joined the growing number of Charles's supporters in exile in France, where they spent their time optimistically trying to encourage the leading European Catholics to rally to their lost king's cause.

Chapter Fourteen

The Beginning of the End

'Thou piece of clay, where thou sittest, think of thy Death,
Resurrection, Judgement, Eternity.'

Rev. Andrew Cant, sermon preached before King Charles I
at Newcastle, 5 July 1646

As matters became ever more desperate in Oxford Charles still hoped
that he might be able to turn to other means of extricating himself
from his predicament. While Glamorgan and Ormond had been
dealing with the Confederates in Ireland the king had been making
overtures to parliament, but his requests for free passes for his
representatives had been refused, ending any hope of a negotiated
peace and leaving Charles to complain that 'nothing will satisfy them
[parliament] but the ruin, not only of us, our Posterity, and friends,
but even monarchy itself'. With those avenues blocked he decided to
turn once again to the Scots, whom he knew to be war-weary and
increasingly suspicious of the intentions of the English
parliamentarians. The ground had been laid the previous autumn
when Sir William Fleming had made contact with Leven's camp
outside Hereford; now that the Scottish army was involved in an
acrimonious and half-hearted siege of Newark the efforts to engage
the Scots were renewed and carried through with good deal of gusto.

The deciding factor was the arrival in London of Jean de
Montereul, a young diplomat sent by Mazarin in August 1645 to act

on France's behalf with the Scottish commissioners. As France had always enjoyed close political connections with Scotland, Mazarin hoped that his ambassador would encourage a détente between the Scots and the king which would not only check parliament but keep the country sufficiently weak and divided to be unable to meddle in European affairs. In his initial discussions with the Scots Montereul found that he was knocking at an open door, telling Mazarin shortly after his arrival that the Scots wanted peace both to preserve their honour and 'in view of their interests, which have more influence on these people, since while the war lasts they cannot obtain payment of what is owing to them by the English, and it is probable they will have still greater difficulty in obtaining it if the Parliament remain victorious, since it is true that benefits conferred by States are easily forgotten, and very often repaid by insults; thus everything tends to induce the Scots to come to terms, to which the unfortunate state in which they are situated in their own country may still further contribute, and the apprehension they have lest the English may get the better of them, and improve the condition of this country at their expense'.[1] It was a fair assessment: the Scots were tiring of the war because their religious aims were not being achieved and the cost of keeping an army in the field was slowly bankrupting them. They were also aware that the Solemn League and Covenant was unpopular in England – it had not been universally signed – and, as Baillie told Robert Ramsay on 16 January, the growing power of the Independents, especially in the army, meant that the prospect of any accommodation with the king had finally disappeared:

> The King being brought to so low a condition, has been sending these weeks bygone message upon message, for a Treaty of peace. It's true, the leading party of the Parliament seems much to fear and be averse from all peace for the time, as prejudicial to their private designs; yet our affairs in Scotland, yea the state of the land also, calls for peace on any equitable terms: which has made our Commissioners have many long and unpleasant debates upon the answers to the King's messages, while they laboured to eschew that which some endeavoured, the impossibility of any further dealing with the King: yet we did ever at last agree in good terms.[2]

Against that background the Scots commissioners in London started playing a double game – assuring their English allies that they would 'never lay down arms till the peace of both [kingdoms] be settled' yet continuing their conversations with Montereul.

At the beginning of January 1646 the French diplomat travelled to Oxford to represent the Scottish position to the king. Before leaving he had listened to Loudoun's complaints about the English parliament's ingratitude towards the Scottish war effort and their tardiness in paying arrears, but he also knew that the Scots would not entertain any accommodation with the king unless he agreed to their long-cherished hope of establishing Presbyterian Church government in all parts of his three kingdoms. This advice he passed on to the king, adding that while the Scots 'only wished to preserve him' they would not shift on the matter of religious governance. Once again this proved to be a sticking point, but as Charles was still exercising several options, including the Irish link, and had no urgent need to decide one way or the other, he told Montereul that he had no particular objection to Presbyterianism but he would never allow it to become the established Church – 'he would rather lose his crown than his soul'.

To this the commissioners replied that they were prepared to treat the king with 'all honour and respect' but Charles could not expect help from them unless he signed the Covenant either before or upon his arrival at the Scottish camp. Realising that the Scots' insistence on this point would end any hope of a settlement between the two parties, Montereul returned to London and on 16 March won from them a concession that they would offer Charles the protection of Leven's army provided that he would remit the ecclesiastical question to the parliaments of Scotland and England. However, by that stage Charles still had high hopes of Ireland and had even spoken of returning to London to reclaim his authority by playing off the rival factions in parliament. He even thought it might be possible to find an accommodation with the Independents, but any hope of returning to his capital ended on 1 April when parliament made it clear that his presence would not be welcomed.

With that door closed and with the Glamorgan treaty exposed and discredited, the king had no option but to throw in his lot with the Scots. Two days later Montereul left Oxford for Leven's camp outside

Newark, taking with him the terms which Charles had agreed should form the basis of his new alliance. In return for their protection and support 'in the procuring of a happy and well-grounded peace . . . and in the recovery of his Majesty's rights' Charles would be prepared to take instruction in the Presbyterian religion and 'to strive to content them in anything that shall not be against my conscience'.[3] To Montereul these were the best terms Charles could hope to find and he was convinced that the Scots would agree to them, but the Scots prevaricated, leaving Charles to rage that they were 'abominable relapsed knaves' and that he would go into exile rather than make further concessions. In desperation he wrote to Fairfax offering to surrender, 'if only he might be assured to live and continue as king still'. This was passed to Cromwell, who announced its contents to parliament, but the plea was ignored. With the New Model Army rapidly encroaching on Oxford and time running out, Charles had to make a decision and act on it. At three o'clock in the morning of 27 April a party of three men slipped out of Oxford on horseback, crossed Magdalen Bridge and headed south towards Dorchester and Henley. Two were obviously gentlemen – the king's chaplain Michael Hudson and a close friend John Ashburnham – while the third who rode behind with the baggage was heavily disguised as a servant. This was Charles, taking his leave of his last court and about to put his fate in the hands of the same Scots who had been the original author of all his recent misfortunes.

Having made his escape Charles then prevaricated, hoping against hope that emissaries would arrive from London to welcome him back, but it was all wishful thinking. He rode as close to the capital as Harrow-on-the-Hill, then turned north towards Cambridge, reaching Downham on 30 April to take up lodgings in the Swan Inn. By then Hudson had been sent to Montereul in the hope of getting better terms, but the French emissary could only produce a vague promise that the Scots would take the king into their protection and treat him honourably and would not force him to any act which troubled his conscience. Realising that the offer would not be improved, Charles set off for Newark and arrived in the Scottish camp outside the town on 5 May, having met up with Montereul at Southwell. Somewhat untruthfully, Leven wrote immediately to the Committee of Both Kingdoms assuring them that the king's arrival

was 'a Matter of much Astonishment' and that he had been put under
arrest in David Leslie's headquarters. More to the point, he advised
them that the king's first action had been to demand the surrender of
Newark from its governor Lord Belasyse. The letter also advised them
that the king's disguise had created 'much amazement to see into how
low a condition his Majesty was brought'.[4] Among the officers present
in the camp was James Turner, who might have served in Charles's
army had he caught a ship to England instead of to Scotland. Hard-
bitten mercenary though he was, he was still shocked by his fellow
countrymen's brusque treatment of their king:

There did E[arl] Lothian, as president of the Committee, to his
eternal reproach, imperiously require his Majesty (before he had
either drunk, refreshed or reposed himself), to command my Lord
Bellasis [sic] to deliver up Newark to the Parliament's forces, to sign
the Covenant, to order the establishment of Presbyterian
government in England and Ireland, and to command James
Graham (for so he called Great Montrose), to lay down arms; all
which the King stoutly refused, telling him that he who had made
him an Earl had made James Graham a Marquis. Barbarously used
he was, strong guards put upon him, sentinels at all his windows.[5]

Nonetheless the Scots had a powerful pawn in their hands. They
hoped that Charles would become a Covenanted King and that
through him they would reach an agreement with parliament which
would bring to fruition the policy of the Solemn League and
Covenant. To secure their prize properly Leven's army withdrew to
Newcastle, taking the king with them, and arrived in the city on 13
May. During the journey strict orders had been given to all officers 'to
forbear to have any dealing, or entertain any correspondence, or have
any company upon the march, or in any of the quarters, with any
person formerly in service against the Parliament of England', a
proclamation which left the king in little doubt that he was less a
guest and more of a prisoner of his Scottish hosts.

That impression was reinforced when he reached Sir James
Meldrum's garrison in Newcastle. No one of any authority was
present to greet him as he rode into the town accompanied by 300
horse, the *Weekly Intelligencer* reporting that 'neither Drum, nor

Trumpet, nor Guns, nor Bells, nor shouts of people were heard, but brought in more like a prisoner than a King'. The only voice that was raised came from a lone supporter who shouted a welcome, but Leven put a stop to any further gestures by issuing a proclamation which prevented 'known Papists or Delinquents' having access to him.[6] Charles was lodged in New House, which was also used by Leven and Lumsden, but restrictions were placed on his movements and it was even reported that watchmen had been placed at all entrances to monitor 'what persons came in or out'. His torments were increased when a succession of Scots divines arrived to begin his religious education on the weighty subject of Presbyterianism, the intention being to encourage him to sign the National Covenant. The first was Alexander Henderson, one of its authors, who debated with him the respective virtues of episcopalianism and Presbyterianism, but Charles was not to be moved. The divine's death in the middle of August ended that part of the process but others arrived to preach, threaten, cajole and, when the occasion demanded, tearfully implore the king to 'hearken to counsel' and accept the Covenant. Small wonder that Charles wrote to Henrietta Maria complaining of the 'barbarous usage' which was his daily lot in Newcastle.

It was a race against time. The Scots had to convert the king to maintain their advantage, and in their way of thinking Charles's future rested in his own hands: if he was to continue receiving their protection then he had to accept the Presbyterianism form of Church government. As stated by Argyll it was not their intention to destroy the monarchy but to reform it, and when the Scottish grandee came to address the subject in the House of Lords at the end of June he implied that Scotland was acting not only in its own interests but in those of England as well:

> Therefore let us hold fast that union which is so happily established betwixt us; and let nothing make us again two, who are so many ways one – all of one language, in one island, all under one king, one in religion, yea one in covenant; so that in effect we differ in nothing but in the name (as brethren do) which I wish were also removed, that we might be one if the two kingdoms think fit; for I dare say, not the greatest kingdom in the Earth can prejudice both so much as one of them may do the other.[7]

Argyll's speech was a powerful call for the maintenance of the union, and it was much needed, for as Baillie pointed out from London the Independents, especially those in the army, were now becoming distinctly hostile to their ally:

We thought the King his coming to us, would have quickly settled all [he wrote to William Spang on 26 June]; but yet the danger is great. This people is very jealous, and the Sectarian party, intending only for private ends to continue the war, entertain their humour – 'Let the Scots doe and say what they can, yet certainly they cannot be honest: they have a design, with the King and foreign nations, to betray and ruin England; therefore let us be rid of them with diligence: if they will not immediately be gone, let us drive them home with our armies.' To these foolish and most mad counsels, the King's unhappiness does daily contribute.[8]

In fact the news of Charles's arrival at the Scots' camp at Newark had been greeted with consternation in London, forcing a vote in the Commons that 'this kingdom has no further use of the continuing of the Scots army within the Kingdom of England', but while the king was in the hands of an ostensible ally there was little practical to be done. Besides, the war still had to be concluded, and that depended on the king ordering his supporters to halt all resistance. On 19 May Charles sent an address to his English parliament asking for a peaceful settlement; at the same time he wrote to Montrose to disband his remaining Highland forces, to pass on the order to Huntly, Airlie, Crawford and Ogilvie and to go into exile. The marquis received the letter on 2 June and three months later he took a ship to Norway, having taken his farewell of his remaining soldiers at Rattray, near Blairgowrie in Perthshire. By then Sir Thomas Glemham, the governor of Oxford, had surrendered to Fairfax on 20 June and the last remaining outposts were following suit, the last to fall being Harlech Castle in Wales on 15 March 1647. Only in Kintyre did Alasdair MacColla sit it out, defying the wishes of both king and parliament.

However, despite their anger, the English parliament had to co-operate with the Scots to forge a peace settlement with the king. The result was the Newcastle Propositions, a set of conditions drawn up by the English parliament with the Scottish commissioners, which outlined the terms which Charles would have to accept for 'a safe and well grounded peace'. These were agreed on 25 June, and on 13 July a deputation of six commissioners led by the Earl of Pembroke set out for Newcastle and arrived ten days later to be met with as little ceremony from the Scots as had been accorded to Charles two months earlier. The demands they carried were those of a party who knew that the initiative had passed to them: the king would be required to sanction the Covenant and become a Presbyterian, he would be obliged to surrender control of the militia for twenty years, bishops were to be abolished and a common religion established in England and Scotland, and over sixty of the king's main supporters were to be exempted from pardon. Before the demands were made Charles had stated that he was not prepared to make any concessions, but when the commissioners, accompanied by Argyll and Loudoun, met him on 24 July he softened his tone, claiming that there could be no 'speedy answer because this business is of high concernment' – and indeed it was, as the Newcastle Propositions affected the way he would govern his two kingdoms in the years to come.

Something of the old Charles returned when he asked Pembroke if his commission allowed him to negotiate, to be told that the deputation only had power to present the propositions to him and to receive his answer within ten days. 'Saving the honour of the business,' replied the king, 'an honest trumpeter might have done as much.' In fact Charles was in a delicate position. He was in no position to reject the propositions outright, but to accept them undiluted would be to compromise his position, his religion and his relationship to his people. To stall would also put him in a bad light, as it would appear that he did not want peace, yet he was anxious not to agree to anything which might jeopardise the royal prerogative. When the ten days allowed by the commissioners came to an end Charles tried to buy additional time by offering to come to London under safe conduct so that the questions could be debated at length, an offer which Pembroke said he 'thought fit not to send because we know not whether the House will be pleased to take notice of it'.

On 2 August Pembroke and his party returned to London and although Argyll said that the Scots and English commissioners 'parted in love' a rift was growing between the two allies and the Scots were becoming increasingly resentful. They had entered the war to achieve the aim of imposing a uniform Church government on the two kingdoms, but this the king refused to concede, and now they had reason to believe that the aim would not be supported wholeheartedly by the English parliament. 'The King's answer has broken our heart,' wrote Baillie on 4 August. 'We see nothing but a sea of new more horrible confusions. We are afraid of the hardness of God's decree against that mad man, and against all kingdoms. We look above all to God; for below is full of darkness.' A fortnight later his gloom and his fears increased as he came to the conclusion that the 'king's madness' would lead to the demise of the Crown and the triumph of the Independents and 'schismatics'.[9] In vain did one of the accompanying ministers, the Reverend Cant, preach on the example of Amasiah,* 'who willingly offered himself unto the Lord' in the land of Judah. Charles refused to budge on the propositions, telling the Scottish commissioners, now joined by Hamilton, that he refused to yield and would not be 'fiercely assaulted from Scotland'.

As the terms of the Solemn League and Covenant were becoming increasingly untenable and were unlikely ever to be achieved, the Scots commissioners informed the English parliament on 12 August that they were prepared to withdraw their army from the north of England on condition that they were paid £1.8 million, the money still outstanding to them. Their allies were outraged by the size of the demand as almost one-third of the sum consisted of the free quarter they had already received, and a process of haggling brought the sum down to £400,000, to be paid in two equal instalments, the money being found from a new loan and from the profits from the sale of Royalist properties. During the discussions which took place throughout September and October the king's position was also discussed, and although the Scots made a case for being consulted on what happened next they were told bluntly that while Charles remained on English soil it was the English parliament's responsibility to deal with the matter. As Montereul told Mazarin, the Scots were left in a difficult position: practically bankrupt and aware that Charles would never agree to their demands, they had little option but to end the alliance and seek reparations, yet their patriotism and pride were offended by being treated as junior partners:

---

* One of the captains who supported Jehoshaphat, II Chronicles: 17:16.

What embarrasses most the Scots is to see themselves burdened
with the person of the king, which they can neither deliver up to
the English, nor put into prison without perjury and infamy, and
are not able to preserve without danger and without drawing down
upon them all the armies at present in England.[10]

What Montereul forbore to say, but what was none the less true, was
that, had the Scots decided to support the king, Leven's forces would
have been no match for the New Model Army.

Charles, too, seemed to understand the way matters were going,
and not for the first time began thinking about escape. France seemed
to be the best destination, but on 16 September he wrote to his
daughter Princess Mary to ask her husband, William of Orange, to
send a warship to the Tyne. Nominally it was to allow him to send
messages to Henrietta Maria, but when the 34-gun vessel arrived at
the beginning of November the Dutch captain asked permission to
stay in the roads of the Tyne to have the ship's hull careened. Its arrival
prompted rumours that other Dutch vessels were on their way and
that the king was hatching an escape plan, and so it proved. While
naval reinforcements did not materialise Charles did make a half-
hearted attempt at escape over the Christmas period, the idea being
that the ship would leave Newcastle and pick him up at Hartlepool.
The Dutch captain was summoned, money changed hands but a
combination of maladroit planning and lack of wind put paid to the
venture. Once the plot was discovered on 26 December Leven
doubled the guard on Charles, who found that his only remaining
solace was being allowed to play golf at Shielfield under the eye of
men he came to regard as his jailers. All further hope of escape was
scuppered with the arrival in the new year of three parliamentary
warships, the *Leopard*, the *Constant Warwick* and the *Greyhound*.

The episode was concluded on 23 January 1647 when Pembroke
and the English commissioners returned to Newcastle to inform the
king that they were under instruction to conduct him into their
custody. Charles then turned to the Scots commissioners to ask if they
would be prepared to take him to Scotland, only to receive the reply
that they 'may not now be put to give any answer'. With no other
avenues open to him Charles agreed on 28 January to be taken into
what amounted to protective custody at Holdenby (or Holmby)

House in Northamptonshire, a royal mansion built by Sir Christopher Hatton and acquired by James I in 1607. By then the first Scottish units had started withdrawing from Yorkshire and the first chests of parliamentary cash had started arriving in Newcastle. Two days later Skippon arrived with his first regiments to take over the northern garrison and the last elements of the Scottish army of the Solemn League and Covenant paraded in the town before marching north to be disbanded. Leven ordered them to ensure a 'friendly and brotherly parting' but the people of Newcastle, mainly women, would have none of it, running after them, shouting abuse and throwing stones at them. It is not clear if they were demonstrating their support for the king or their relief at the departure of an invading army, but the Scottish action soon attracted the Judas jibe that 'traitor Scot sold his king for a groat'. As ever, Montereul was more pragmatic, telling Mazarin that while he could not forecast 'what will be the result of the bargain that the English have just concluded with the Scots, it seems to me that they have not separated very satisfied with each other'.[11]

On its arrival back home the Scottish army started disbanding on the orders of the Estates, who decided to keep in being a smaller force of seven regiments of foot, 1200 horse and 200 dragoons to restore order in the west Highlands and the north-east. The homecoming was muted, for many of the ordinary soldiers in the Newcastle garrison had enjoyed 'warm quarter' and were observed to go away unwillingly; many were equally loath to go on further active service in what became known as Scotland's New Model Army but which was described by Baillie as 'very small and ill-provided'. Despite those shortcomings, though, there was still work to be done in mopping up the remaining Royalist resistance in the west of Scotland. Following a heavy defeat by David Leslie's regiments at Rhunahaorine in Kintyre in the last week of May, Alasdair MacColla retired to Ireland, never to return. A few days later the Covenanting victory was besmirched by the massacre of the garrison occupying Dunaverty Castle. Called on to surrender, the commander, Archibald MacDonald of Sanda, refused and his refutation of the offer sealed his men's fate. Leslie was minded to let the MacDonalds go back to their homes but his chaplain John Nevoy wanted the Lord's work to be done and so 300 men were massacred, only a handful being spared on condition that they went into exile. Among the officers involved in the slaughter was

James Turner, who had seen his fair share of atrocities in Germany but did not deny that 'here was cruelty enough; for to kill men in cold blood, when they have submitted to mercy, has no generosity in it at all'.[12] By the end of the summer the Hebridean islands of Gigha, Jura and Mull had all been pacified by Middleton's and Leslie's forces, and the last act was played out in November when Huntly fell into the hands of the Covenanting forces.

While this was happening in the west of Scotland Charles was enjoying a somewhat different turn of fortune. He was still a prisoner but he was treated better than he had been by the Scots, being shown deference as king and having a good table and the servants to make life agreeable. During the ride south through the bitter winter weather he had been touched by the cheering crowds which had lined some parts of the road, and even Fairfax, who had escorted him into Nottingham, had shown respect by kissing his hand and asking his opinion of events in Ireland. Only in the matter of religion was he still circumscribed by parliament's decision to appoint two Presbyterian chaplains to his household and to refuse him access to Anglican rites, but there were other diversions. Playing bowls became a passion, he visited Cambridge and was entertained at neighbouring great houses. Although under guard – the garrison commander at Holdenby was Richard Browne, one of the parliamentary commanders at Cropredy Bridge – his life was hardly arduous. He even felt moved to make an offer to parliament over the Newcastle Propositions. On 20 May he agreed to cede control of the militia for ten years and would become a Presbyterian for a trial run of three years but only if parliament allowed him to come to London to state his case. The proposal was rejected not just because the concessions were too late but also because parliament was caught up in a new struggle with the New Model Army over what to do with it now that the fighting had come to an end.

A Presbyterian faction led by Waller, Holles and Sir Philip Stapleton wanted to come to terms with the king through the Newcastle Propositions and impose their form of Church government on the kingdoms. Foolishly, for they had misunderstood the mood of the army and its growing radical leadership, they also took a unilateral decision in March to disband the infantry regiments of the New Model Army without payment of arrears and to reduce all senior officers, bar Fairfax, to the rank of colonel. All that would be left would be a small force of horse and 10,000 foot to act as garrison troops in 45 towns; at the same time a volunteer force of 12,500 would be raised to restore order in Ireland, where the situation was getting out of control. On 20 February Ormond had abandoned his attempts to reach an accommodation with the Confederates and resigned his post as Lord Lieutenant, leaving the problem in parliament's hands. The obvious solution was to close down the New Model Army and send it to Ireland in a different form.

To try to reform the army was a bad move, because most men had not been paid for at least three months and were unlikely to accept being disbanded without receiving those arrears. They had won the war for the parliamentary cause and they wanted their just reward. Fairfax's regiment alone was owed over a year's pay. They were further irritated by a decision not to be offered a general indemnity for acts committed during different periods of the fighting when troops had often taken the law into their own hands. Fearing civil suits for compensation for looting, taking quarters without payment and assaults on the civilian community, the soldiers wanted a measure of protection, but this had been refused. Lack of finance was a principal reason – the arrears amounted to £300,000, a huge sum, and the country's economy had been disrupted by the war – but there was also the traditional dislike of a standing peacetime army and a widespread desire to demilitarise the country for its own protection. The policy quickly backfired: in place of the expected return to normality as soldiers were demobilised, the decision led to fresh confrontation with men who were more than ready to stand up for their rights.

The position was complicated further by the presence of Independents and other radicals in the middle ranks, men who believed that the triumph over the king presaged a new age of equality and the creation of a new Godly society in which wealth and privilege had to be eliminated and God's elect rewarded. Richard Baxter had caught the mood when he visited the army shortly after Naseby and found 'a new face of things which intimated their intention to subvert both church and state'. He thought that the war had been fought to save the king from delinquents and that the Covenant engaged 'both papists and schismatics', but instead he encountered a growing belief that many soldiers wanted to use the victory to create a more egalitarian society.

Even Cromwell had become a stranger, bidding him only a cold welcome and refusing to address him other than was necessary:

> I perceived that they took the King for a tyrant and an enemy, and really intended to master him, or to ruin him; and that they thought if they might fight against him, they might kill or conquer him; and if they might conquer, they were never more to trust him further than he was in their power; and that they thought it folly to irritate him either by wars or contradictions in Parliament, if so be they must needs take him for their King and trust him with their lives when they had thus displeased him. They said: 'What were the lords of England but William the Conqueror's colonels? or the barons but his majors? or the knights but his captains?' They plainly showed me, that they thought God's providence would cast the true religion and the kingdom upon them as conquerors.[13]

Although the point at issue was payment of money owed to the army and as yet had little to do with radical politics, the presence of the Independents reinforced the notion that the army was rapidly becoming a law unto itself and might even take the law into its own hands. To protect the army's interests, first the cavalry and then the infantry regiments began organising their own committees of 'agitators' (agents or shop stewards) to demand their rights and large numbers of officers joined their number. Strike action followed (see following chapter) and instead of the expected post-war settlement, which would have seen the return of the settled order, the country hovered on the brink of a new confrontation between the moderates in parliament and the radicals in the army. In an attempt to defuse the situation, on 27 April parliament offered to pay six weeks' arrears, but it was too late. A month earlier the House of Commons had passed a motion condemning a strike at Saffron Walden and had warned the soldiers that any further disruption would lead to them being 'proceeded against as enemies of the state', a threat which made them doubly aggrieved as it seemed to question their loyalty. As Cromwell told Fairfax, the Commons were creating a stick for their own backs; the Presbyterians and moderates were 'men who have so much malice against the army as besots them'.[14]

Chapter Fifteen

THE LEVELLERS AND THE PUTNEY DEBATES

'I think that the poorest he that is in England has a life to live as the greatest he.'

Colonel Thomas Rainsborough, giving evidence at the Church of St Mary the Virgin, Putney, 29 October 1647

The crisis in the army in the spring and summer of 1647 came at the worst possible time for parliament. Money was tight, the harvests were bad, trade had been disrupted and a settlement had still to be reached with the king. In Ireland Ormond had surrendered his powers to parliament and had left for France on 19 June, having given the keys of Dublin and the other principal towns to Colonel Michael Jones, who had arrived earlier in the month with a parliamentary army of 2000 men. Trained in the law, Jones had fought for the Royalist cause but changed sides at the time of the Cessation and, on arriving in Ireland, his first task was the imposition of local taxes to pay for the war. This was no easy matter with the country so impoverished – even Dublin failed to find the requested weekly rate of £433 – but Jones enjoyed more success in the field by marching into County Meath to inflict a devastating defeat on Preston's Leinster army at Dungan's Hill near Trim on 8 August. Up to 4000 men were killed during and after the battle – among them were 400 Highlanders who had followed Alasdair MacColla to Ireland – but despite that setback and another in Munster, where Inchiquin defeated a force under Lord Taaffe,* the military power of the Confederates had not been broken. O'Neill's Ulster army was still intact and Archbishop Rinuccini still held sway in Kilkenny: if Ireland were to be brought to heel Jones would need more money and more troops, but first parliament would have to come to terms with its disaffected army.

The soldiers' unrest came as a shock to the army leadership in London and even radicals such as Cromwell were taken aback. When parliament sent commissioners to Saffron Walden on 21 March to explain that the purpose of the reforms was to raise eleven New Model Army regiments for service in Ireland they were shouted down with demands for payment of arrears and the granting of a general indemnity for their actions during the recent war. With feelings running high the men produced a petition outlining their demands, and to the commissioners' alarm it became clear that they had the support of influential officers such as Fairfax, Ireton, Edward Whalley, Robert Hammond and Thomas Pride. The proposals were hardly revolutionary – past services had to be rewarded before future duties were undertaken – but the Presbyterian faction in parliament under Holles had little sympathy for them and seemed intent on further confrontation by pushing ahead with the formation of the new Irish army. Without consulting the army parliament gave overall command to Skippon, while Massey, formerly governor of Gloucester, was appointed lieutenant-general of horse.

The red rag had been shown, and the bull reacted a few weeks later when a new parliamentary delegation returned to Saffron Walden on 15 April. Two hundred officers had gathered in the local church in no mood to compromise. Asked if they would serve in Ireland they stalled and replied that they would only go if they were allowed to serve under their wartime commanders – 'Fairfax and Cromwell and we all go!' they cried.† Privately, Fairfax said that he could well understand their fury, not least because they had been threatened as traitors, 'before any proof made that there were any that did retard the

---

* The Battle of Knocknanuss, fought on 13 November 1647, also saw the death of Alasdair MacColla, 'basely stabbed in the back' after surrendering.

† Pay and promotion were offered as inducements, but out of an army 21,000 strong fewer than 2000 took them.

service', and he refused outright to denounce them. A fresh petition and appeal was produced and signed; it was at this point that the regiments began organising their strike with the appointment of agitators to speak on their behalf against those members of parliament who 'like foxes lurk in their dens, and cannot be dealt withal, though discovered, being protected by those who are entrusted with the government of the kingdom'.

Fairfax and Cromwell sympathised with their men's plight but found themselves in a difficult position, so much so that the former took himself off to London with what seemed to be a diplomatic breakdown in health while the latter gave serious thought to taking his regiments off to serve the Elector Palatine in his attempts to regain his property in Germany. (The Thirty Years War was drawing to a close and the Elector was anxious to recover his territory.) By the middle of May both men were forced to become involved again when Fairfax was ordered to return to his post and Cromwell was asked to head a fresh delegation which included Ireton, Skippon and Charles Fleetwood, who had been one of Manchester's regimental commanders and was now a leading Independent member of parliament. They took with them to Saffron Walden a promise to increase the payment of arrears by two weeks, but once again the meeting came to nothing and ten days later, on 25 May, parliament took the rash step of announcing the disbanding of the army, with the exception of the garrison troops and those who had already volunteered for Ireland. The cutbacks would begin on 1 June and the first unit to go would be Fairfax's own regiment.

If parliament hoped that the army would be cowed by the announcement they were badly mistaken. A general muster was called and the regiments assembled at Newmarket in Suffolk with the object of showing their strength before making fresh demands to parliament. On top of their claims for arrears and the granting of an indemnity they now insisted on the removal from the parliamentary records of the comment that they were enemies of the state and the punishment of the eleven members who had produced it. Above all, in a declaration published on 14 June they made it abundantly clear that they wanted their rights to be protected and their past services recognised:

We are not merely mercenary soldiers, brought together by the
hopes of pay and the fortunes of wars; the peace of our country, our
freedom from tyranny, the preservation of due liberty, the
administration of judgement and justice, the free course of the laws
of the land, the preservation of the King, the privilege of
Parliament, and the liberty of the subject, were the main things
which brought us together.[1]

The mood was revolutionary and the split with parliament in
danger of widening to such an extent that a military coup seemed
inevitable. If that happened Cromwell and Fairfax would be forced to
take sides for, although they had managed to retain their neutrality by
agreeing with their men's demands while urging moderation, they
could not remain on the fence if the army took the initiative. For
Cromwell, a leading member of parliament and a successful wartime
commander, the position was untenable: his support for the army
would eventually bring him into conflict with his parliamentary
colleagues and his credit with the troops would soon run out if he
failed to support their claims. That conflict of interests produced the
defining moment in his career. Long regarded as a natural leader, a
general whom the soldiers trusted, Cromwell now had to choose
which direction he would follow. He could throw in his lot with
parliament, but that would mean supporting the moves to disband
the army which, if successful, would remove his power base. Or he
could support the army, crush its radical elements, which he
distrusted, and heal the rift with parliament.

As he pondered his next move a succession of events helped him to
make up his mind. Back in London he received the intelligence that
steps were being taken by the Presbyterian faction to take the king
into their custody and to call on the protection of the Scottish army.
Cromwell's own freedom was also at risk, as his enemies in the House
of Commons believed that, not only was he the sole author of the
army's unrest, but he had done nothing to keep it in check. With
London becoming an increasingly unruly place – there had been riots
and the local militia had been placed under parliamentary control –
Cromwell met with officers and associates loyal to him, including
Hugh Peters, and it was from these meetings at his house in Drury
Lane, over 'small beer and bread and butter', that the momentous

decision was taken to secure the king's person. The move had been suggested by the regimental agitators who rightly recognised that Charles was an important bargaining chip, or, as Fairfax put it, 'the Golden Ball cast between the two parties', but there is little doubt that Cromwell was privy to the plot. So imposing was his authority within the army that nothing of that importance could have been agreed without his connivance; at the same time the agitators knew that they needed his imprimatur before they acted. Cromwell being ambitious, it is also probable that he covered his back by telling the conspirators that while he approved of the initiative he would disown them if their plot backfired.

The instrument for the mission was George Joyce, a tailor in civilian life but in the summer of 1647 a cornet in the New Model Army and before that a trooper who had served under Cromwell in the army of the Eastern Association. Despite his modest rank he had the reputation of being a radical firebrand – Fairfax called him an 'Arch-Agitator' – and he must have enjoyed some authority among his peers, for he was given command of 500 men drawn from four different regiments to carry out his task. At the end of May he took them to Oxford to secure the arsenal, then he rode on to Holdenby and arrived late at night on 2 June to find Richard Browne's garrison unwilling to let the men enter. As the argument grew hotter – Browne, a major-general and a parliamentary commissioner, was clearly suspicious of so momentous a mission being commanded by a junior officer and was not in the habit of taking orders from a subordinate – the king was alerted and having been told what was afoot agreed to meet Joyce, who entered his chamber fully armed. Behaving with considerable personal courage, Charles confronted his unexpected visitor and asked him what he wanted. To take the king into protective custody for his own good, came the cornet's reply, adding for good measure a promise that the king would not be obliged to undertake anything which was against his conscience. Faced with little alternative, Charles agreed on condition (which was granted) that he was allowed to bring his servants with him. Later, Joyce told John Rushworth, Fairfax's secretary, what happened next.

At dawn the next day, Charles walked out of Holdenby to find Joyce waiting for him with his fully armed troopers lined up behind him – an impressive and thought-provoking sight. However, Charles was not overawed. Once again he quizzed Joyce about his reasons for taking him away and pushed him hard on his authority for so doing. Rattled, but anxious to be on the move, Joyce replied that he was acting to prevent the outbreak of another civil war and to foil a plot against the Crown. As to the commission he carried he had already said enough; it was time to go.

'I pray you, Mr Joyce, deal ingenuously with me,' continued the king, 'and tell me what commission you have.'

'Here is my commission.'

'Where?'

'Behind,' replied Joyce, pointing to his troopers.

'It is as fair a commission and as well written as I have seen a commission written in my life: a company of handsome proper gentlemen as I have seen in a great while. But if I should refuse to go with you, I hope you will not force me? I am your King and you ought not to lay violent hands upon your King, for I acknowledge none here to be above me but God.'[2]

Those last words should have horrified a man of Joyce's persuasion, but he calmly riposted that his men were simply trying to take the king with them and meant him no harm. First Oxford and then Cambridge were suggested as the destination, but the king demurred and offered Newmarket, not knowing, of course, that Fairfax and his army had already mustered there. Before leaving for the first halt, Hinchingbrooke House near Huntingdon, Joyce wrote an excited letter to Cromwell, or failing him Hesilrige or Fleetwood: 'We have secured the King . . . you must hasten an answer to us, and let us know what we shall do. We are resolved to obey no orders but the General's [Cromwell's]; we shall follow the Commissioner's [Browne's] directions while we are here, if just in our Eyes . . . we shall not rest night nor day till we hear from you.'[3]

The letter suggests two things: that Joyce was under orders which were either made by Cromwell or at least known to him, and that little thought had been given to securing the king and his party. When Joyce rode south with his prize his only plan was to get the king into the army's hands as quickly as possible. The following night saw them at Childerley Hall, Sir John Cutt's modest Tudor mansion, where Charles finally received Fairfax and Cromwell on 7 June, the former kissing his hand while the latter simply bowed his head.

The news of the king's capture caused a sensation when it became known in London, but it settled Cromwell's mind. Now his place was with the army; this was providence, it was as if God had spoken to him directly. He rode north to Newmarket to join Fairfax and to find the army in a dangerous mood, its stated intention being to punish parliament and to obtain freedom of religious conscience for all its ranks. Having tried to remain neutral and to broker a solution, Cromwell now found himself the leader of the army in all but name – true to his soldierly instincts the apolitical Fairfax remained the supreme military commander, but the catalyst was now Cromwell. In his memoirs the diplomat Sir John Berkeley recognised the drift and understood perfectly well that Cromwell had crossed a Rubicon of sorts:

> After Cromwell quitted Parliament his chief dependence was on the Army, which he endeavoured by all means to keep in unity, and if he could not bring it to his sense, he, rather than suffer any division in it, went over himself and carried his friends with him into that way which the Army did choose.[4]

When Cromwell arrived at Newmarket an Army Council was established by a Solemn Engagement to provide direction and coherence to the forthcoming campaign. Consisting of the generals plus two commissioned officers and two rankers from each regiment, it was a soviet before its time and it gave much-needed unity and a sense of direction to a revolt which could so easily have become aimless or reduced itself to mere violence. A Humble Representation was then produced which bound the men in common cause, swearing never to give up the fight until all their demands had been met. This was followed by the declaration of 14 June which demanded the impeachment of the eleven members, the dissolution of parliament itself and the right 'to assert and vindicate the just power, and Rights of this Kingdom in Parliament for those common ends premised, against all arbitrary power, violence and oppression and against all particular parties, or interests whatsoever'. Within the space of three months the army had moved from being an organisation on strike for pay and privileges to being a revolutionary movement more representative of the people than parliament. All the while it was moving further south to threaten London, taking the king and reaching Uxbridge in the middle of the month. With the northern army also in revolt, having mutinied and imprisoned its commander, Sydenham Poyntz, parliament was suddenly facing the prospect of an armed revolt against its authority.

In desperation parliament started making concessions – on 3 June it offered to pay arrears and to expunge the slur from the records – but it was too little too late, and by the time the month ended it found itself having to negotiate with the army as if it were a hostile party and not an instrument under its control. On 29 June an end to the impasse seemed to have been reached when the eleven members withdrew voluntarily and parliament agreed 'that they do own this Army as their Army, and will make provision for their maintenance'. As a result Fairfax started withdrawing his regiments from the immediate vicinity of London, but this was just a tactical move; the generals still had to restore order within the army and part of that settlement meant reaching an understanding with the king. With the crisis delicately balanced, Cromwell still held to the view that Charles was central to the solution and that the restoration of his crown was a necessary ingredient if order were to be restored in England, telling Sir John Berkeley that 'no man could enjoy their lives without the King had his rights'.[5]

This honeymoon period between Charles and the leading Independent army officers raised hopes that there might be a speedy conclusion to the civil war. So smoothly did the talks go that Cromwell was moved to tell Berkeley that he thought Charles to be 'the uprightest and most conscientious man of his three kingdoms', a belief founded more on the easy familiarity of the king's personality than on any solid psychological evidence. At the time Charles was being treated as if his rights as a monarch were not in dispute: he was quartered in some style in his father's hunting lodge in the town, he was allowed to hunt and indulge in other sports and maintained a small court which allowed him to entertain local supporters. Those privileges remained intact when he was moved further south on 24 June to Caversham, where he was reunited with two of his children, James and Elizabeth, at the Greyhound Inn in Maidstone, a scene so touching that even the generals were moved to tears. Had he been a less driven man Cromwell might have fallen under the royal spell –

according to Berkeley's evidence he was for ever telling him that it was never his intention 'to introduce a popular government against the King' – but throughout the negotiations for a settlement he managed to keep a sensible distance, a wise precaution. Cromwell was not to know and slow to realise that all this time Charles was prevaricating, courting other Independents while talking to the Presbyterians and keeping open his lines of communication to the Scots through the Earl of Lauderdale.

However, the negotiations did not please everyone. Among those who were wary of any dealings with the king and who distrusted the Independents' overtures was a remarkable group of radical freethinkers who opposed the monarchy, resented religious establishments of any kind and held that a parliament derived its rights from the people and not from any other source. Known by their enemies as 'Levellers', they represented the growing dissatisfaction with the existing order and a new concern with natural human rights and the rights of freedom. Their polices included a limited franchise, the abolition of the episcopacy and the reformation of parliament to make it the instrument of the people's wishes. Or, as one of their leaders William Walwyn put it: 'parliamentary authority is a power entrusted by the people (that chose them) for their good safety and freedom; and therefore a Parliament cannot justly do anything to make the people less safe or less free than they found them.'[6] With their fundamentalist beliefs and sacred regard for natural freedoms it is tempting to see the Levellers as proto-socialists, not least because they preached a greater degree of social equality and a form of libertarian republicanism, but their policies also advocated a free market economy, the importance of individualism and a taxation based on income. As such they appealed to the smaller traders, farmers and skilled artisans, many of whom were parliamentary cavalry troopers (or, as the Levellers saw it, citizens in uniform). Lucy Hutchinson admired them, calling them 'men of just and sober principles', but she also acknowledged that their 'honest declarations' made them 'hated by all the designing self-interested men of both factions [Independents and Presbyterians]'.[7] By the summer of 1647 they were a growing force in the New Model Army, a recognisable group, strident, well organised, vocal and, as far as Cromwell was concerned, likely to cause trouble.

They also were blessed with independent-minded leaders. In addition to William Walwyn and Richard Overton – who articulated his beliefs in the simple statement, 'by natural birth, all men are equal and alike born to the like propriety and freedom' – the outstanding leader was John Lilburne, 'Free Born John', who had been born into a wealthy Durham family in 1615 and who served in the army of the Eastern Association, becoming a lieutenant-colonel, before the imposition of the Solemn League and Covenant forced his resignation. On leaving the army he continued to publish pamphlets critical of the government, one of which, *A Remonstrance of Many Thousand Citizens*, attacked the Earl of Manchester. It also led to his imprisonment in July 1646 – typically, Lilburne had refused to acknowledge the authority of the House of Lords to try him. With the growing radicalism of the army it was inevitable that the Levellers would soon form a coherent group within its ranks, the third faction after the Presbyterians and the Independents, and they were instantly recognisable by the touches of sea-green material they wore in their uniforms.

It was inescapable too that sooner or later they would clash with the Independents over the treatment of the king, and the flashpoint was provided by a new attempt to reach an accommodation with the Crown. Known as the Heads of the Proposals, it had been drawn up by Henry Ireton, now Cromwell's son-in-law, at the end of July. At all levels it was an honourable compromise: the royal family was to be restored, parliament was to have biennial sessions, a new Council of State would be created in place of the Privy Council, the militia would come under parliament's control and, although bishops would be abolished, there would be no imposition of the Covenant. Berkeley, now a key negotiator, advised that the terms were so moderate that they should be accepted – 'never was a Crown so near lost so cheaply recovered' – but Charles would have none of it, arrogantly brushing aside the proposals with the vainglorious comment that nothing could be done without his compliance: 'You fall to ruin if I do not sustain you.' At the back of his mind was the old hope that the longer the talks continued the deeper would become the split between the Independents in the army and the Presbyterian elements in London and Scotland, and that as a result he could only prosper from it. Writing to his cousin William Spang, Robert Baillie, the Scots divine, could only see trouble ahead, a rudderless England crashing towards the rocks:

> These matters of England are so extremely desperate, that now twice they have made me sick; except God rise, all is gone there. The imprudence and cowardice of the better part of the City [of London] and parliament, which was triple or sextuple the greater, has permitted a company of silly rascals [the army], which calls themselves no more than fourteen thousand, horse and foot, to make themselves masters of the king, and parliament, and City, and by them of all England; so that now that disgraced parliament is but a committee to act all at their pleasure, and the City is ready to fright the parliament, at every first or second boast from the army. No human hope remains but in the king's unparalleled wilfulness, and the army's unmeasurable pride.[8]

The storm foreseen by Baillie broke on 21 July when London was hit by a week of riots inspired by the widespread dismay of having to pay the costs of a standing army. War weariness had settled in: the working people of London demanded a return to normality, and even though most had supported parliament during the fighting they now wanted a peace to be brokered, even if that meant a settlement with the king. Apprentices assembled at the Guildhall and a Solemn Engagement demanding the king's restoration was signed amid the swearing of bloodthirsty oaths that opponents would have their guts pinned to their ears and such like. Then, in an echo of the events that had brought Charles's personal rule to an end, the House of Commons was invaded and the Speaker was held in his chair until he agreed to the rioters' demands to surrender control of the militia. Fearing for their safety eight peers and fifty-seven Independent members fled west out of London to seek the protection of the army, which was now camped on Hounslow Heath. Among them was the Speaker, William Lenthall, and the Earl of Manchester, who decided that his Presbyterian principles would not protect him from the mob.

It was at this stage that Charles, encouraged by the rioting, rejected the Heads of the Proposals and in so doing helped to pass the advantage to the Independents. Backed by the presence of the Speaker, Fairfax was now free to enter the city to restore order and effectively to seize power. On 6 August 1647 Cromwell led the main body of the army into London, the men wearing sprigs of laurel in their hats as if celebrating a victory. Fairfax was installed as Constable of the Tower and to all intents and purposes the capital was put under military control. Prudently, the eleven members decided to flee to the Continent – among their number were Waller and Massey, two battle-hardened commanders who had served the parliamentary cause so loyally during the recent fighting.

With London under military control, Charles was brought to Hampton Court, where Cromwell and Ireton renewed their efforts to get him to agree to the Heads of the Proposals. If he had accepted them then, at the end of July, or even if he had agreed that they formed a basis for further discussion, the army might have taken him back into London with them. Had they done so there is little doubt that he would have been restored there and then, but Charles was still engaged in his favourite ploy of watching and waiting and hoping that his opponents would fall out among themselves. Although he continued to listen to Cromwell and Ireton and to debate the matter with them, he was doing little more than casting around. In vain did Cromwell threaten the king with the imposition of the much harsher Newcastle Propositions if he did not accept the more lenient offer.

On a practical level Charles's tactics were not altogether illogical. From his friends at court – for so Hampton Court had become – he knew all about the uneven tenor of the times, through Lauderdale he maintained contact with Scottish friends, notably Hamilton, and he still entertained hopes of a settlement with the Presbyterians. If he banked on further unrest within the army then he was also not disappointed. On 18 October five of the more radical regimental agitators, all Levellers, presented Fairfax with a new manifesto called *The Case of the Army Truly Stated*, which called for the dissolution of parliament and the introduction of a new constitution granting suffrage to 'all the free born'. It also pointed out that the demands of the declaration of 14 June had not been met and asked why the generals were engaging with the 'unworthy crown' instead of heeding their soldiers' grievances. Although no one in the high command, least of all Cromwell, had a good word to say for the Levellers, whom they regarded as subversive agitators, the new paper had to be addressed if further disruption were to be avoided. Fairfax believed

that the time had come to bring the issue into the open and so began the celebrated Putney Debates.

Held in the Church of St Mary the Virgin in Putney, they opened on 28 October 1647, and although the debate came to nothing in that no concrete decisions were taken, it did produce a vivid picture of the aspirations of contemporary political thinkers who were reaching towards the concept of universal manhood suffrage, men like Thomas Rainsborough (or Rainborow), who had raised a regiment for Manchester composed largely of New Englanders, his sister being the wife of the governor of Massachusetts. An inveterate intriguer and a committed Puritan, he provided the most succinct articulation of the Leveller position when he addressed the General Council of the Army on the first day of the debates. In response to the discussion led by Ireton about who should be included in the franchise, Rainsborough replied:

> I think that the poorest he that is in England has a life to live as the greatest he; and therefore, truly, sir, I think it's clear that every man that is to live under a government ought first by his own consent to put himself under that government; and I do think that the poorest man in England is not at all bound in a strict sense to that government that he has not had a voice to put himself under.[9]

These were stirring words, their implication greatly in advance of their times, and they were made in response to the publication of an even more radical document entitled *An Agreement of the People for a Firm and Present Peace* which became the main focus of the debate. Far more outspoken than any other paper produced for consideration by the army, this called for biennial elections to a new parliament which would rule without assent of the House of Lords and the king, the creation of electoral districts with equal numbers of inhabitants, religious freedom and the abolition of conscription. It was the work of John Wildman, a fanatical young lawyer, and its demands were equally extreme (for the day at least): in place of the traditional notion that the right to vote should be equated with a property qualification there would be a new electoral system which Wildman summarised as, 'Every person in England has as clear a right to elect his representative as the greatest person in England.' To Ireton this sounded suspiciously like the introduction of universal manhood suffrage without property qualifications, and in his view it was nothing less than a call to anarchy. Like Rainsborough he spoke at length and with great passion in trying to counter a theory which he believed would only lead to further unnecessary confrontation:

> If the principle upon which you [Rainsborough] make this alteration, or the ground upon which you press that we should make this alteration, do destroy all kind of property or whatsoever a man has by human constitution, I cannot consent to it. The Law of God does not give me property, nor the law of nature, but property is of human constitution. I have a property and this I shall enjoy. Constitution founds property. If either the thing itself that you press or the consequences of that you press do destroy property, though I shall acquiesce in having no property, yet I cannot give my hand to it because it is a thing evil in itself and scandalous to the world, and I desire that this army may be free from both.[10]

Ireton understood the revolutionary nature of the proposal – that, were it to be accepted by the army, it would have to be forced on the country, thereby instigating a new round of fighting – and he argued forcefully and cogently against it. Being a man of property himself he was in a parlous position, for it could appear that he was protecting vested interests; and being a high-ranking officer in the army he could sympathise with the voices of colleagues such as Captain Edward Sexby, who argued that the soldiers of the New Model Army were merely mercenaries unless they had 'a right to the kingdom', that is, they enjoyed the vote. It could not have been an easy matter for the diligent and idealistic Ireton to listen to the arguments of the rank and file who had supported the war against the king and who now believed that they should be rewarded with the right to take part in national affairs. He entertained a visceral dislike for them and thought their ideas hopelessly idealistic, but if the Levellers and the other soldiers had fought and suffered to bring in a new order, then logic was on their side.

The presence of Cromwell in the chair turned out to be the decisive factor. He sided with his son-in-law and also upheld the view that it would be wrong to introduce a constitutional change which

envisaged the abolition of king and parliament, yet to maintain unity
he had to appear even-handed. As a moderator he proved that he had
a sure touch, counselling against 'hot' arguments and allowing both
sides to have their say, a process that was helped by his prolix style
and his line of argumentation, which few could follow. After some
long-winded discussion which went on all day on 30 October he
managed to have the debates put forward by 48 hours, to 1
November, when discussion of Wildman's paper was adjourned to
allow further debate on how to treat with the king. The subsequent
discussions lasted the whole week, and it was a long and acrimonious
business which gave every impression of being incapable of
resolution. On the one hand Cromwell and Ireton wanted to preserve
a negotiated settlement which included the Crown, while a growing
groundswell of opinion wanted to break off all negotiations with the
king and perhaps even punish him. Amid growing rancour the chair
was given to Fairfax, who cut through the arguments and brokered
an agreement which ended the debate for the time being and laid
preparations to re-assemble with the rest of the army at a muster later
in the month.

Fairfax's resolution underlined his authority within the army. If the
debates had been allowed to continue, with Ireton and Rainsborough
wrangling fruitlessly over the interpretation of what constituted a
property right, they would have given power to the extremists, one of
whom, Major Thomas Harrison, had already called Charles 'a man of
blood' and urged his prosecution at a meeting of the Army Council
on 11 November. With others accusing the king of being 'him that
intended our bondage and brought cruel war upon us' there was a
possibility that the army would be suborned by extremists and its
power divided. This Fairfax understood full well: for most soldiers the
issue was more about pay and conditions than gaining the vote and
their general was determined to see them rewarded. At the same time
the army had to be disciplined and its morale restored: that meant
acting firmly and decisively against the threat posed by the Levellers.

Fairfax's plan was simple but effective, and it stymied the Levellers'
intention of using the muster to rally the army behind them the better
to press the claims contained in the Agreement. Instead of ordering
a general muster he gave notice that there would be a rendezvous in
three separate places on 15, 17 and 18 November. He also issued a

riposte to the claims made by the Levellers and made it clear that he demanded the obedience and duty of every soldier in the New Model Army, offering in return a speedy resolution on arrears of pay and a promise to work for free elections for all who had served in the recent war. This was language which soldiers understood, and when the crunch came they supported 'Black Tom'. The first rendezvous at Cockbush Field near Ware in Hertfordshire was an edgy affair with political tensions running just below the surface. Seven regiments had been ordered to muster, but on the day they were joined by two others, commanded by Thomas Harrison and Robert Lilburne (Freeborn John's elder brother), and they marched on to the field wearing Leveller favours in their uniforms. Initially their provocative behaviour was supported by two officers, Colonel William Ayres and Major Thomas Scott, who were 'observed insinuating diverse seditious principles unto the soldiers', but as John Rushworth recorded, his master was in no mood to temporise. Feeling that the mood might turn ugly if Ayres and Scott continued to stir up trouble, Fairfax acted quickly and decisively by arresting both men and moving to nip the trouble in the bud:

> Some inferior persons were likewise committed for dispersing factious papers, as the Agreement of the People etc among the private soldiers, and finding those people who pretend most for the freedom of the people, had dispersed divers of those papers among Colonel Lilburne's regiment of foot, the most mutinous regiment in the army, strict command was given for them, to tear them, and cast them away, which was done; and the Captain-Lieutenant [William] Bray, who was the only officer above a lieutenant left among them, the rest being driven away by the mutinous soldiers, and one them wounded, was taken from the head of that regiment, and committed to custody; it being alleged, that he had led the soldiers to that rendezvous, contrary to orders. And afterwards, a council of war being called in the field, divers mutineers, for example sake, were drawn forth, three of them were tried and condemned to death, and one of them [Richard Arnold] whose turn it fell to by lot, was shot to death at the head of the regiment, and others are in hold to be tried.[11]

It was rough and ready justice and it was meant to be. Fairfax understood the mood, and realising that he had to puncture it he acted decisively: in addition to the punishments recorded by Rushworth copies of the *Agreement of the People* were torn up and Leveller favours were ripped off uniforms. Seeing the public disgrace of the two Leveller regiments, and no doubt intimidated by the execution of the man whose fate was decided by lot, the others protested their innocence and reaffirmed their loyalty, shouting as they marched off the field, 'The King and Sir Thomas!' When the next two musters took place they passed off without incident and for the time being the army was loyal, and reconciliation replaced confrontation. There would be no widespread mutiny and the Army Council agreed that there would be no further attempts to negotiate with the king. It was a sensible solution which effectively sidelined the Levellers and put the revolt in its proper context. Those battle-hardened men were not mutinous by nature and most had excellent combat records but, freed from the need to fight, their minds had quickly turned to the equally pressing needs of peacetime and their own futures

At Ware the army's unity was cemented and the influence of the Levellers was curbed. It was a timeous solution, because Cromwell and Fairfax had just received the extraordinary news that the king had gone missing – the information was probably also known to the men – and with him their main bargaining counter had disappeared. Four days earlier, Charles had disappeared into thin air at Hampton Court and no one, not even his guardian Colonel Edward Whalley, knew where he had gone. All that was left in his room were two letters, one thanking his custodians for their care and the other explaining that he needed the freedom to consider his options: 'Let me be heard with Freedom, Honour and Safety, and I shall instantly break through the clouds of retirement, and show myself ready to be Pater Patriae.'[12]

Chapter Sixteen

THE KING'S ENGAGEMENT

'From devils and Kings, Good Lord deliver me. It's now high time, up and doing, I desire any government rather than that of the King.'

Thomas Wroth MP, speech in the House of Commons,
3 January 1648

The main reason for the king's flight was that he feared for his life. The Levellers' revolt and the rumblings about prosecution had unsettled him and he was uncertain of the army's willingness to protect him. It is probable, too, that he had tired of the endless negotiations with Cromwell and Ireton and wanted to escape from the problem, just as he had done when he had abandoned London almost six years earlier. Claustrophobia was also a factor: while it had been agreeable to follow outdoor pursuits during the summer and to entertain guests, he was increasingly confined inside and kept under heavy guard as the days grew shorter and the weather worsened. He seems to have made up his mind to escape on 3 November 1647, when he confided his plans to William Legge, who had held out for so long in Oxford, the place of the king's last escape, and who had been allowed to remain with him at Hampton Court. Through him he contacted Ashburnham and Berkeley, who met at Thames Ditton on 7 November to hatch a suitable plot, but – all too typically as far as the king's affairs were concerned – there was an immediate difference of opinion about how best to execute the escape. Berkeley was all for making for the West Country, where there was still a vestige of Royalist support and a number of friendly ports, should escape to the Continent be necessary; whereas Ashburnham counselled the bolder plan that Charles should stay in England to make one last effort to recover his throne.

At some stage in the proceedings a compromise was reached whereby Charles would take himself to the Isle of Wight, whose new governor, Colonel Robert Hammond, was thought to be friendly to the Royalist cause, having already announced his suspicions of the Levellers. According to Ashburnham, whom he had met in London before taking up the post, Hammond had said that 'he was going down to his government because he found the army was resolved to break all promises with the King; and that he would have nothing to do with such perfidious action'.[1] Whether or not Charles agreed to the plan is open to doubt, as both courtiers' accounts differ on the subject, but the king was in no mood at tarry at Hampton Court. During the evening of 11 November he took advantage of his habit of retiring early to write letters to slip out of his quarters and make good his escape. On the opposite side of the Thames Ashburnham and Berkeley were waiting with horses and the small party rode off, accompanied by a number of servants, leaving an astonished Whalley to discover the flight after it was too late to apprehend them. The king and his followers made their way south through the Forest of Windsor to Southampton, where they took stock. It was at this point that Charles finally rejected Berkeley's plea to cross over to France and fell in with Ashburnham's alternative of taking a boat to the Isle of Wight.

While the king stayed at the Earl of Southampton's house at Titchfield the two courtiers travelled ahead of him across the Solent to sound out Hammond at his headquarters at Carisbrooke Castle, which had been reinforced to counter the threat of invasion by France. Hammond was a young but experienced army officer; his public criticism of the Levellers showed that he did not lack courage, but when Ashburnham and Berkeley arrived with their news he was unmanned, uttering only: 'Gentlemen, you have undone me.' Slightly mollified by the promise that his honour would not be compromised, the colonel agreed to treat the king with honour and the three men crossed over to the mainland to meet Charles at Titchfield. Then it was the king's turn to say that he was 'undone', for the arrival of the parliamentary commander meant that he had little option but to put himself under his protection. Somewhat meekly, and aware that the possibility of escape to France had ebbed away, Charles agreed to go to Carisbrooke Castle where he would accept Hammond's offer of protection.

Like many other impulsive decisions taken by Charles it was one which he quickly came to regret. His mood lifted when he received a warm welcome in the island's capital, Newport, and he was allowed to receive visitors in the chambers provided for him, but to all intents and purposes he had exchanged Hampton Court and Whalley for Carisbrooke and Hammond. That much was made clear by the latter when he summoned a group of local gentlemen to meet the king in Newport the following day. Among them was Sir John Oglander, a Royalist who had been imprisoned in London but had been granted parole. Later he recorded what was said:

> Gentlemen [said Hammond], I believe it was as strange to you as to me to hear of his Majesty's coming into this Island. He informs me necessity brought him hither and there were a sort of people near Hampton Court, from whence he came, that had voted and were resolved to murder him, or words to that effect, and therefore so privately he was forced to come away and so to thrust himself on this Island, hoping to be secure here. And now, gentlemen, seeing he is come amongst us, it is all our duties to preserve his person and to prevent all comings over into our Island. I have already stopped all passages into our Island except three, Ryde, Cowes and Yarmouth, and at them have appointed guards. Now I must desire you all to preserve peace and unity in this Island as much as you can.[2]

Hammond ended his speech by telling the assembled company that he had 'sent an express to Parliament' giving them information about the king's whereabouts. The news was announced to the House of Commons by Cromwell, who had a family interest in the matter, Hammond being married to the daughter of his cousin John Hampden, and he assured the members that his kinsman would do his duty honestly and diligently. To those present Cromwell seemed to be possessed of an 'unusual gaiety', as well he might have been.

After thinking that the king had slipped out of his hands, he now found Charles back in captivity and sufficiently isolated to keep him away from the influence of the Levellers and the Scots. So carefree did Cromwell seem that rumours started that he had engineered the whole episode by giving the idea to Ashburnham and Berkeley, both of whom he knew well, and then by putting pressure on Hammond to fall in with the plan once it was revealed to him. A letter written by him to Hammond warning of death plots, which was shown to Charles, had also been cited as evidence that Cromwell wanted to influence events by stirring the king into action. However the conspiracy theory does not take into account the haphazard nature of the escape, the last-minute decision to choose Carisbrooke and the possibility that, having engineered the flight, Charles could just as easily have fled to France had Berkeley's advice been heeded. Although Cromwell's complicity is an attractive possibility, one which would reinforce his growing understanding of the demands of realpolitik, it is alas pure conjecture.

In any case Cromwell still had the army on his mind, for although matters seemed to have been settled in the field at Ware there was still much to play for in parliament, where Rainsborough and others exerted influence and talked darkly of impeachment. Once again Cromwell was caught between two extremes. His mind told him that the continuation of a reformed monarchy lay at the heart of any settlement – that had been his position throughout the struggle – yet he had also been touched by the feelings expressed at Putney. (The softening did not apply to the army: like Fairfax he was relentless about imposing high standards of discipline.) Somewhere in the middle his attitudes began to shift. On 19 November he spoke warmly in the House of Commons about the need to give its soldiers greater political influence; then a week later he spoke out against Charles at a meeting of the Army Council. He was even alleged to have said, 'that, if we cannot bring the Army to our sense, we must go to theirs, a schism being evidently destructive'.[3] That threat of a split must have been a powerful factor in Cromwell's thinking, for without the army's backing his political influence would wane. It is also possible that he had received intelligence from Carisbrooke that Charles was in discussions with the Scots, and an attractive story exists that he and Ireton, disguised as troopers, managed to intercept a letter from

Charles to Henrietta Maria giving full details of the negotiations.[4]
Certainly as November drew to a close Cromwell's actions show that
long-submerged doubts about the king's sincerity started coming to
the surface.

Whatever the origins of Cromwell's gradual change of heart, the
mood in parliament was already turning against the king. The war
had ended eighteen months earlier, yet a settlement was no closer and
the main stumbling block was Charles, who had simply stonewalled
when the different proposals were put to him. The House of
Commons' frustration was shown when it ignored a letter from
Charles, dated 17 November, asking for a resumption of the talks and
offering a number of concessions including the promise to become a
Presbyterian for three years, to give up control of the militia and to
grant free pardons. Charles sent a reminder three weeks later but it
was also received in silence. Instead parliament responded by passing
the Four Bills, proposals which were as draconian as the Newcastle
Propositions and as such signalled parliament's refusal to tolerate the
king's unwillingness to reach a settlement. The bills' main points were:
the militia to be kept out of royal control for twenty years; episcopacy
to be abolished; funds to be made available to pay the New Model
Army; parliament to meet at its own discretion; all honours awarded
since 1642 to be annulled and leading Royalists to be put on trial.

As the proposals were not presented as a basis for negotiation but
as a piece of legislation requiring royal assent, they were taken to
Carisbrooke by a delegation led by the Earl of Denbigh. Charles was
given four days to consider the matter, but when the deadline expired
on 28 December he refused to put his signature to the bills, as to do
so would mean surrendering his authority and giving power to an
omnipotent parliament. As he haughtily told the delegation, at that
stage in his career he was not minded to 'divest himself of all
sovereignty'. Denbigh had served as an ambassador under Charles and
was versed in the arts of diplomacy, but harsh words were spoken as
the unsatisfactory encounter drew to a close. A fresh breach was
inevitable and tempers on both sides were beginning to get hotter. In
deciding to stall, Charles was no doubt influenced by the most recent
Army Council debate, which had been held at Windsor a week earlier
and which had included a call for him to be tried for his life as a
criminal. The same meeting had also agreed that Thomas

Rainsborough should be rewarded by being appointed vice-admiral – another sign that the Levellers had not yet been levelled.

On receiving the king's latest rejection parliament passed the Vote of No Addresses on 3 January 1648, legislation which not only broke off all negotiations with the king but made it a treasonable offence for anyone to attempt to make contact with him. The debate was notable not just for the decision to break with the king but for Cromwell's public change of heart. Charles was no longer the trustworthy gentleman, as he had thought the previous summer, but had become a 'dissembler' whose word was not to be trusted and whose heart had hardened. Instead of negotiating with such a person parliament should consider the men who had won the war for them – the army – and should 'suffer not misery to fall upon them' lest they take matters into their own hands 'as nature dictates to them'. This volte-face was compounded at the end of Cromwell's speech when he put his hand on his sword as he proposed that the king should be omitted from all future negotiations. That same day he wrote to Hammond warning him to be on his guard and to search out any 'juggling' by the king or his courtiers. As yet Cromwell was not in favour of disestablishing the monarchy – his argument was with Charles, not the Crown – but following the Vote of No Addresses there was a noticeable hardening of his attitude towards the nature of monarchy. While the Vote of No Addresses was being passed on 11 February Cromwell's speech was observed to be unusually invective against 'monarchical government'; he also supported the move to bring the Committee of Safety back into being.

There were those who suspected that Cromwell's change of heart was driven by ambition and that he was intent on seizing power for himself. John Hutchinson was of that number, his wife recording that when Cromwell had visited Nottingham it was not difficult to understand the belief held by the Levellers who 'first began to discover the ambition of Lieutenant-General Cromwell and his idolators, and to suspect and dislike it'. Being a straightforward man who brooked no dissembling, Hutchinson was completely honest when Cromwell asked him what the Levellers in the army really thought of him:

> The colonel, who was the freest man in the world from concealing
> truth from his friend, not only told him what others thought of

him, but what he himself conceived; and how much it would darken all his glories, if he should become a slave of his own ambition. Cromwell made mighty professions of a sincere heart to him, but it is certain that for this and suchlike plain dealing with him, he dreaded the colonel, and made it his business to keep him out of the army; but the colonel desiring command, not to serve himself but his country, would not use that art he detested in others, to procure himself any advantage.[5]

As Lucy Hutchinson so shrewdly discerned, on one level Cromwell was ambitious. His dual career as soldier and politician had allowed him to emerge as a commanding figure, and he would not have been human had he not wanted to impose his beliefs on a wider public. No political leader who ever lived would have wanted less, and Cromwell was never behindhand in coming forward when he wanted to cement his interests. He might have prayed long and hard and he might have believed that his star was guided by God's Providence but he was also well capable of engineering his own destiny. That restless ambition made him enemies, but he was also a shrewd judge of events: at the very moment when he was turning away from the king he had good reason for so doing. Just as he feared, Charles was indeed guilty of 'juggling'. On the day that he had received the Four Bills, which he never had any intention of signing, Charles had entered into a new and explosive agreement with the Scots of his northern kingdom.

Known as the Engagement, it offered much better terms than those produced by parliament, which were virtually the Newcastle Propositions rehashed. In return for military assistance to rid England of the burden of the New Model Army, a prerequisite before any future discussions with the Long Parliament in which the Scots would be included, Charles promised to accept state Presbyterianism for a trial period of three years and agreed to work harder for a closer union between the two countries. Equally to the point as far as the Scots were concerned, the king pledged to do his utmost to suppress 'the opinions and practices of Anti-trinitarians, Anabaptists, Antinomians, Arminians, Familists, Brownists, Separatists, Independents, Libertines and Seekers, and generally for suppressing all blasphemy, heresy, schism, and all such scandalous doctrines and practices as are contrary to the light of nature or to the known principles of Christianity, whether concerning faith, worship, or conversation: or to the power of Godliness, or which may be destructive to order and government or to the peace of the Church and nation'.[6] Clearly the Scots had not forgotten that the terms of the Solemn League and Covenant had not been honoured, and now they wanted a measure of revenge. For all that the Engagement smacked of double-dealing, the king was within his rights to throw in his lot with the Scots. Not only had the English parliament become a very different body from the one which had been elected in 1641 but its actions were being controlled by the army with its unconstitutional council.

As for the Scots, they were incensed at being sidelined from the negotiations with the king and could now clearly see that they had made a bad bargain at Newcastle by allowing Charles to fall into the hands of the English army. Instead of holding the whip-hand their power had evaporated and the religious revolution of the National Covenant was endangered. They too were keen to get the best bargain they could, even if that meant sending an army south to 'endeavour that there may be a free and full Parliament in England, and that his Majesty may be with them in honour, safety and freedom, and that a speedy period be set to this present Parliament, and that the said army shall be on the march before the said peaceable message and Declaration be delivered to the House'. Once signed the Engagement was placed in a lead casket and buried in a secret place in the grounds of Carisbrooke Castle.

In fact it was to take somewhat longer to raise an army capable of taking on England's professional parliamentary force which, despite the process of disbandment, was still in being and still capable of offering a determined response to any military invasion. Even so the Scots took heart from the schism between the army and parliament, which they hoped would grow wider once hostilities began. They also reckoned on the support of English and Irish Presbyterians equally loyal to the king who had become disillusioned by the army's growing strength and its capacity to influence political matters in England. The Scottish commissioners, Lanark, Lauderdale and Loudoun, had been in contact with Charles since October, when he had been quartered at Hampton Court – at one point they arrived with a posse of armed horsemen and urged him, fruitlessly, to escape with them to Berwick – and as allies they had been allowed to visit him at

Carisbrooke. While doing so they and Traquair had played a long game, offering concessions and buying fresh advantage whenever the king appeared to be weakening, above all working on the shared dismay at the changes that had taken place in English politics. Greater union with England was also an aim: once the fighting had come to an end there would be freedom of trade between two kingdoms and the king undertook to employ 'a considerable and competent number of Scotsmen' as privy councillors and to spend more time in his northern kingdom.[7]

Charles's refusal to sign the Four Bills and the growing suspicions about the Scots changed the mood dramatically. Hammond was ordered to strengthen the guard at Carisbrooke to prevent Charles from escaping – Legge, Ashburnham and Berkeley were dismissed and Charles received a new secretary in Sir Thomas Herbert, whose *Memoirs* produced a vivid picture of the king's last days in office – while in London there was renewed talk about impeaching or deposing the king in favour of one of his sons.* Having passed the Vote of No Addresses parliament dissolved the Committee of Both Kingdoms, which removed the need for any further collaboration with the Scots and replaced it with the Committee of Derby House. At the beginning of January the Scottish commissioners also left London and returned north to try to convince their fellow countrymen that they had done the right thing in pledging to support the king.

The hardening mood in parliament was matched within the city by a sudden outbreak of anxiety about the power wielded by the Independents and the effect it had on the lives of ordinary people. Amid great dismay the Christmas celebrations of 1647 had been curtailed, shops had been ordered to remain open for business and all public celebrations had been banned. Soldiers were deployed to pull down street decorations while in a sign of defiance some churches deliberately mounted extravagant displays of greenery and services were held from the Book of Common Prayer. There was also unrest outside the capital, particularly in Ipswich and Canterbury, where there was a riot after a football match played in the streets got out of

---

* James, Duke of York, put a stop to the speculation that he might be preferred to his older brother by escaping to France dressed as a girl.

control, forcing the mayor and magistrates to flee. A contemporary newspaper report claimed that 'the counties are full of discontent' and while the unrest had been occasioned by the puritanical attempt to ban Christmas festivities it was also accompanied by the cry to restore the king.

While these riots were prompted more by the curtailment of enjoyment than any tangible support for Charles they did nothing to calm nerves already unsettled by the rift between the army and parliament. Soldiers were back on the streets of London, sparking fears of fresh military intervention, and they were needed when there were disturbances on 27 March, the anniversary of Charles's accession to the throne. Some idea of how fraught the atmosphere had become can be seen in the case of Captain Burley, a misguided army officer who, on hearing that Charles was being kept prisoner at Carisbrooke, marched on the castle beating a drum and followed by a motley crowd of women and children. There was no threat to public security or to the king's safety but Burley was put on trial at Winchester on 22 January 1648 and executed as a traitor. It was an absurd and cruel sentence for a man who was more confused than culpable; and it was also an unwelcome sign of the temper of the times.

Throughout the early part of 1648 there is a distinct sense that the main protagonists were waiting on events. Under close protection at Carisbrooke Charles plotted fruitlessly and foolishly to escape while hoping that the Engagement would bear fruit and restore his fortunes. So close was Hammond's watch that there was little chance that any of the escape plans would have succeeded – these included sawing through bars, various disguises and bribing guards – but in truth Charles was relatively comfortable. He had time to read, to write endless letters to his wife and friends, to play bowls, and there are even hints of a romantic dalliance with a younger woman whom he called 'sweet Jane Whorwood'. Cromwell, too, was biding his time. Disaffection in the army was not yet a thing of the past – even Fairfax's lifeguard regiment mutinied and had to be disbanded – but on 9 January the General Council of the Army brought its existence to an end itself and voted to support the parliament in reaching a political settlement. Lilburne and other radicals accused Cromwell of 'fresh trinkettings' with the king, that is, negotiating in return for political and financial reward, but that was very far removed from the truth. At Putney Cromwell had stressed the importance of reconciliation and, as for the benefits of a republic, he told Edmund Ludlow, a member of parliament who was no friend of the king, that although he believed it was feasible he was not convinced it was desirable.[8]

As for the Scots the ball was firmly in their court, and they still had everything to play for if they wanted to retrieve their position. Once back in Edinburgh the Scottish commissions began the lengthy process of persuading their fellow countrymen that the Engagement with the king offered the best solution to Scotland's needs and that it was the best hope of preserving the Covenant. However, there was a sticking point: unlike the Solemn League and Covenant the new agreement was not supported by the Scottish parliament and it did not have the all-important approval of the General Assembly of the Church of Scotland. Robert Baillie summed up the position in a letter written to Spang while the commissioners were still negotiating with Charles:

> The present sense of many is this: If the King and the army agree, we must be quiet and look to God; if they agree not, and the King be willing to ratify our Covenant, we are all as one man to restore him to all his rights, or die by the way: if he continue resolute to reject our Covenant, and only give in some parts of the matter of it, many here will be for him, even in these terms, but diverse of the best and wisest are irresolute, and wait till God give more light.[9]

Having sworn to maintain the Covenant it would be difficult for 'diverse of the best and wisest' to support the compromise agreement hatched by Hamilton, the chief architect, and February was to see the beginning of a lengthy political and religious struggle in Edinburgh to have the Engagement adopted as an article of Scottish policy.

To make that task more difficult the English parliament had dispatched its own commissioners to Edinburgh in an attempt to persuade the Scots to turn their backs on the agreement they suspected Charles had entered into – the Engagement was not made public until 25 February – but they found few takers. When the Scottish parliament was convened on 18 March Argyll was no longer in his usual position of being able to dominate events and found that

Hamilton enjoyed a large majority – of the fifty noblemen fewer than ten supported him, among them his old allies Eglinton and Balmerino. Only the Church supported Argyll, but it too found itself in a quandary. For the better part of the previous year it had approved the idea of using the Scottish army to attack England and to rid parliament of Independents and sectaries, but Church leaders were not prepared to support an agreement with Charles which might imperil the Covenant. No sooner had the English commissioners arrived than ministers used their pulpits to attack the concept of the Engagement and to speak with one voice against Hamilton – one minister prophesied the destruction of his line should the treaty be approved – but any relief the Englishmen might have felt on hearing these words was quickly abnegated. After Hamilton's doom had been forecast the same minister turned on the English commissioners, reproaching them as 'traitors and perjurers'. Not that those listening to him would have been surprised by the outburst: one of the English commissioners was Stephen Marshall,* a friend of Pym who had preached the necessity of war in February 1642, taking his text from Judges 5: 23, where the people of Meroz are cursed for refusing to help Barak and Deborah in the deliverance of Israel: 'Curse ye Meroz, said the Angel of the Lord, curse ye bitterly the inhabitants thereof; because they came not to the help of the Lord, to the help of the Lord against the mighty.'

Those who supported Hamilton became known as Engagers, and although they were in the ascendant a tortuous path had to be followed before Scotland threw in its lot with a king whose rule they had opposed for the past decade. Throughout the spring the parliament and the General Assembly sat in Edinburgh to discuss the proposals, and it was a long and wearisome business. Basically, the Kirk's commissioners were against the Engagement because Scotland would be sucked into a war with the English parliament and its army for no appreciable gain to the aims of the National Covenant. The two sides were only separated by a matter of yards – they were sitting in the Parliament Building and the High Church of St Giles – and conferred only by exchange of documents, but their points of view

* Montereul was less taken with Marshall's standing, calling him 'preacher marshall, a man of small knowledge and scanty eloquence'.

were unlikely to be reconciled. On 30 March the assembly produced a paper which made it clear that war was out of the question until the religious question had been settled, but this only provoked parliament into issuing a provocative statement to its English counterpart demanding that the Covenant be taken throughout England, Presbyterianism introduced and all 'heresies and schism' extirpated.

The deadlock was not broken until 20 April, when the parliament produced a new declaration making demands which would be totally unacceptable south of the border. These began with the charge that the English parliament had broken the terms of the Solemn League and Covenant and demanded uniformity of religion throughout the three kingdoms, the release of the king, and the total disbandment of the 'sectarian' New Model Army. Unless this happened, warned the Scots, 'we have resolved to put the Kingdom presently in a posture of defence as it was *in Anno 1643*.' The die was now cast. A week later the army began to mobilise while at the same time the General Assembly issued its last word on the subject, declaring the Engagement to be 'unlawful' and offering the hope that their fellow countrymen would 'keep themselves from being ensnared and carried alongst in any course contrary to the Covenant'. As ever it was Baillie who offered the most sensible gloss: while Scotland had a just cause to oppose the 'Sectarian army in England', the removal of the Independents would be accompanied by the return of an unreformed king and 'the yoke of tyranny in the state, of popery and prelacy in the church'. There was also no guarantee that the English, having broken the Solemn League and Covenant, would keep any promises, and Baillie was by no means certain that victory was guaranteed:

> We may draw in upon Scotland so much of the Sectarian army as will overrun our plain country, and in a short time infect our Church with the leaven of their doctrine, and change our estate. When wise men will not be pleased to go on in a way of reason, to void apparent dangers, occasion is given to fear their designs, and of driving them on for some purposes of their own.[11]

Having lived in London for three years and seen the power of Fairfax's army Baillie was right to be cautious. His fears were quickly borne out, for Leven's old army was no longer in being and it proved difficult to raise a new one. David Leslie was offered the post of lieutenant-general of horse, but he refused and it was given to John Middleton. William Baillie, the former parliamentary general, was dragged out of retirement and given command of the foot, while overall command went to Hamilton, hardly an inspiring choice given his almost total lack of military experience. One contemporary said that, while Hamilton might have been the wisest man in the kingdom and 'the greatest statesman' and 'deepest politician', he was defective in one important respect: 'that he had never practised the art military'. Just as bad, his second-in-command was the Earl of Callendar, who was not only an indifferent soldier (despite his experiences in Germany) but thought himself superior to anyone else in the army. It also proved difficult to raise the 30,000 men demanded by parliament: ministers throughout the country had preached against the enterprise and in many country areas, notably the south-west, young men were loath to disobey an injunction of that order. Another bad summer and the threat of poor harvests also persuaded them to stay at home. The only professional troops were 2000 foot and 1200 horse under the command of Sir George Monro, Robert's nephew, whom Hamilton rapidly recalled from service in Ulster. Lauderdale had also been scheming with the commander of the parliamentary navy, Sir William Batten, who was keen to see a settlement with the king and was wary of the Independents, but a plan to transfer the fleet to Scottish control came to nothing. From a purely military point of view the Engagers' enterprise appeared to be doomed before it even began.

In 1640 Scotland had provided the trigger for the first civil war by taking its army south in support of religious demands which were being opposed by the Crown. Eight years later a second civil war was to be started by another army marching the same route but this time intent on easing England out of the grip of the Independents in the army and freeing the king. One other factor decided the issue for the Scots Royalists. From their agents in Paris they knew that Mazarin was still being tempted by Henrietta Maria's requests for French military support, but to gain that and to benefit from the 'Auld Alliance' with their age-old allies they would have to show their mettle first. The point was made by Montereul in discussion with Leven, who railed against the French failure to support Charles. 'I replied to all this in the most obliging but the most general terms I could think of,' the French ambassador reported to Mazarin, 'which was all the more easy for me as he had given me the reply himself, that the other governments and the English being dissatisfied wanted to see what the Scots would do for their king before doing anything for them'.[12] Not for the first time Scots would be going to war against their southern neighbours without any real hope of bringing the action to a successful conclusion.

PART THREE

THE SECOND AND THIRD CIVIL WARS 1648–1651

Chapter One

WALES RISES FOR THE KING

'I do prefer by far
An unjust peace before the justest war.'

*Rowland Watkyns, Vicar of Llanfrynach, 'The Common People',
from* Poems without Fictions *(1662)*

In the second volume of his *History of the English-Speaking Peoples* Sir Winston Churchill provides a concise, 'short and simple' synopsis of the Second Civil War: 'King, Lords and Commons, landlords and merchants, the City and the countryside, bishops and presbyters, the Scottish army, the Welsh people, and the English Fleet, all now turned against the New Model Army. The Army beat the lot.' As an exact piece of historical analysis it can hardly be bettered but its pithiness does not tell the whole story. All of the elements listed by Churchill were involved, directly or indirectly, but the Second Civil War* was not just a record of Fairfax and Cromwell sweeping all before them: had there been a greater coordination of effort on the part of the Royalists in England, Scotland and Wales the conflict would not have been rolled up as quickly as it was. The Scottish Engagers' failure to raise a capable army, the rash of unconnected revolts in Wales, Yorkshire, Kent and East Anglia and a loss of nerve by naval mutineers

---

* It was the second round of the civil war in England, but the fighting in 1648 was the third phase of the conflict which had begun in Scotland in 1639–40.

in the Downs, the safe anchorage between the Kent coast and the Goodwin Sands in the approaches to the Thames estuary, all combined to make the next stage of the conflict a hopeless cause for the king and a just and God-fearing undertaking for the parliamentary faction.

The complexion of the war changed too. Whereas the fighting between 1642 and 1645 had been relatively civilised in that rules of engagement were respected and quarter was offered and accepted (except of course on the wilder Celtic fringes where defeated enemies could expect no mercy), the fighting in 1648 was marked by a new savagery. War weariness was one reason, the people of England had had their fill of battles and killing, but the overpowering emotion was revenge, and this was frequently taken in full measure by the parliamentary army. They had triumphed in 1645 only to see fighting break out again and they were determined to punish those who were vaingloriously tempting God's providence by plunging the country into disorder. Soldiers went to war promising to deal once and for all with the malignants who had broken the peace; not least of these was King Charles I, now considered by many to be the sole author of all the country's misfortunes. At the end of a lengthy prayer meeting held at Windsor in April, parliamentary officers, Cromwell included, vowed 'if ever the Lord brought [them] back in peace, to call Charles Stuart, that Man of Blood, to an account for the blood he had shed, and the mischief he had done to his utmost against the Lord's cause and people in these poor nations'.[1] Fearing that their own shortcomings had perhaps also been to blame for the fall from grace, the convocation also manufactured a fair degree of self-loathing, with the prayers directed at man's 'many iniquities', but the general mood was one of determined vengeance. This time round they would finish the business and there would be no quarter for the miscreants who had preferred the shedding of blood to negotiated settlement and change.

One example of frightfulness will stand for many. At Woodcroft Hall in Lincolnshire Michael Hudson and a small number of companions held out against the opposition until they were forced on to the roof by parliamentary troopers. They asked for quarter but it was refused. Instead they were thrown into the moat below, but somehow Hudson managed to save himself by holding on to some projecting stones or a drainage spout. His pleas for mercy were ignored; instead his fingers were slashed and he was allowed to fall into the waters below. But that was not the end of his torment. His bleeding body was fished out of the water and before he was finally executed his tongue was cut out. Hudson had fought for the Royalist cause at Edgehill and was the king's chaplain who had accompanied Charles on his dramatic escape from Oxford in April 1646.

The revolt in support of the king began in south Wales during the last week of March 1648 when Colonel John Poyer, governor of Pembroke, galvanised a rebellion among discontented soldiers under his command. Non-payment of arrears and the order to disband regiments at Cardiff, Swansea, Carmarthen and Pembroke provided the spark for the rebellion, but it was fanned by a good deal of mistrust about the Independent faction in the army and this was briskly translated into support for the king. A parliamentary officer from a humble background, Poyer had distinguished himself during the first round of fighting, emerging as a tough battlefield soldier, and he showed equal courage and determination in refusing to hand over his garrison when the parliamentary adjutant-general, Colonel Fleming, demanded access to Pembroke Castle. Encouraged by the support of other Welsh troops under the command of Colonel Rowland Laugharne, who also objected to being disbanded, Poyer's men rode out of Pembroke and scattered the parliamentary force. Perhaps drink gave Poyer courage – according to Whitelocke he was 'a man of two dispositions every day . . . in the morning sober and penitent, in the evening drunk and full of plots'[2] – but he was obviously a bold soldier whose qualities of leadership turned a local disturbance in one corner of south Wales into a widespread revolt.

Within days Poyer had been joined by Laugharne, the son of a local landowner who had once served as a page to Essex, and by Rees (sometimes Rice) Powell, another parliamentary colonel who had changed sides. The Norman fortress at Tenby was secured and the unfortunate Fleming was attacked and surrounded by forces loyal to Poyer at Llandeilo. Over a hundred parliamentary soldiers surrendered, but there were casualties – the adjutant-general's body was found in the town's church with a bullet in his head, the result, many thought, of Fleming's despair and shame, which led him to take his own life. When the news of the revolt reached London there was consternation.

Pembrokeshire had been under parliamentary control since the beginning of the war, despite frequent successful Royalist raids which had seen fortresses like Kidwelly and Picton changing hands several times. Poyer was thought to be a loyal and responsible commander who had pacified the area in 1645 and Fleming was a popular and well-respected senior parliamentary officer.

Now the area was a place of rebellion, Poyer was condemned as 'a shameful Apostate' and Fairfax acted swiftly by sending reinforcements led by Colonel Thomas Horton, who also took with him promises of cash payments and indemnities to bring the rebels back on side. Coming on top of another rash of rioting in London at the beginning of April when apprentice boys had marched on the city with cries of 'Now for King Charles', it was clear that support for the Royalist cause was re-emerging and had to be crushed before it got out of control. The unrest in the capital was put down by troopers led by Cromwell and Fairfax, but they failed to address the rioters' grievances. Many of the marchers came from Kent and Surrey, and while their main grievance was an unwillingness to contribute to the costs of maintaining the army it was clear that they also brought with them broad, if unfocused, support for the king. Similar riots for similar reasons took place in several East Anglian towns, especially where regiments had been garrisoned. Those taking part wanted the soldiers to go back to their homes and to have the country returned to the halcyon days of peace. Another spur to radical action had come from the new and unwelcome Puritan tendency to act against traditional festivities such as Christmas – in London soldiers patrolled the streets and were permitted to enter houses suspected of cooking celebratory food – and to put a stop to displays of public enjoyment.

Colonel Horton soon found that it would be no easy matter to pacify south Wales, and as April wore on, the battle lines became more firmly drawn: Chepstow Castle was taken under Royalist control by Sir Nicholas Kemeys and on 9 April Poyer mustered 4000 men of Pembroke on Colby Moor, the scene of an earlier battle (1 August 1645) when Laugharne had routed a Royalist force. They wore blue and white ribbons in their caps with the motto 'We long to see our King' and, as Horton reported to parliament, their revolt was being supported by most of the local population, who were equally infuriated by having to pay higher taxes to keep an unwanted army in their area:

> The more is the pity, some of those parts are miserably bent to oppose the Parliament and the Army, as appears by this: for as the Parliament forces march forward they make away and carry with them their wives, their children, and drive away their cattle, with what goods they have or can get together, and flee into the woods and into the mountains, leaving their houses empty. Many of the smiths are also gone, they themselves having cut down their bellows before they went; for they being a spiteful mischievous people, have in many places spoiled and carried away what they conceive may be of use to our forces; and in some places there is neither a horse-shoe to be had, nor a place to make it, if one would give 40s. to have a horse shod. Therefore, some extraordinary and unusual course must be taken to end this trouble and bring down the stomachs of these little-less-than-barbarous people.[3]

In an attempt to persuade the local people that their support was mistaken Horton arranged for an address to be published explaining the reasons for his action, but the ploy cut little ice – the leaflets were written in English and could not be understood by the mainly Welsh-speaking community. By way of reply Poyer and Powell issued their own declaration, showing that they had moved from their original position of opposition to military cutbacks towards support not just for the king but also for a return to the status quo:

> That we will use our best endeavours to bring the King to a personal treaty with his Parliament in freedom, honour and safety: to the End that Just prerogative of the King, Privileges of Parliament, Laws of the Land, Liberties of the People may be maintained and preserved in their proper bounds *and the Protestant religion, as it now stands established by the Law of the land, restored throughout the kingdom with such regard to tender consciences as shall be allowed by the Act of Parliament.*[4]

From Pembroke they had made contact with the king at Carisbrooke, and although no replies had been received – Charles recorded his 'dislike' of their action – the two Welsh commanders clearly believed that they had captured the spirit of the times by contesting the rule of the army. Poyer also held high hopes of support from Inchiquin in Ireland. Earlier in the month the Munster magnate had changed sides and declared for the king, a result of self-interest and the machinations of Ormond, who had sent an emissary to Ireland to rally support for the king. Having proved his loyalty to the parliamentary cause by slaughtering large numbers of Catholics – the most recent massacre being the destruction of Lord Taaffe's army at Knocknanuss – Inchiquin had reverted to the Royalist side at a time when Ormond was trying to harness support for Charles among the Old Irish nobility. In all his dealings Inchiquin was thoroughly disreputable and self-interested, and Poyer's hopes of support were based as much on wishful thinking as on the Irishman's tenuous family links with Pembroke.

By the end of the month the revolt had spread into Brecon, Radnor and Monmouth and a force of some 8000 Royalists led by Laugharne was making its way eastwards to threaten Cardiff. If that city fell south Wales would be lost and the only hope of retaking it would depend on continuing possession of the great harbour at Milford Haven which had remained resolutely in parliamentary hands. With Horton making little headway the task of pacifying Wales was given to Cromwell, who set out for Gloucester on 3 May, taking with him many of the men who had fought under him in the great days of 1644 and 1645 when victory at Naseby seemed to have made further fighting unnecessary. Two years had passed since they had last been in action and Cromwell was acutely aware of the need to rebuild esprit de corps and to reinforce the sense of divine mission which accompanied their march into the West Country. At Gloucester, scene of the memorable siege and Massey's heroics, he stopped to address his regiments, telling them that:

> He had often times ventured his life with them and they with him, against the common enemy of this kingdom . . . and therefore desired them to arm themselves with the same resolution as formerly and to go on with the same courage, faithfulness and fidelity, as sundry times they had done, and upon several desperate attempts and engagements . . . for his part he protested to live and die with them.[5]

It was nobly spoken, and even if the exact words were recorded and perhaps polished later they had the desired effect on Cromwell's men, who responded with loud cheers of support. Not that the rebels had any reason to feel downcast: when the news reached Wales that Cromwell was approaching, Poyer told his men that he would 'give him [Cromwell] a field and show him fair play, and that he would be the first man to charge against the Ironsides; saying that if he had a back of steel and breast of iron he durst and would encounter him.'[6]

For all the warlike rhetoric, Cromwell and his parliamentary forces did not face any easy task. The rebellion in Wales had to be subdued, an attack from Scotland was inevitable and there were outbreaks of pro-Royalist agitation in the Kent towns of Sittingbourne, Faversham, Rochester, Sandwich, Dartford and Deptford. Men loyal to the king were taking up arms and by the end of May had formed themselves into an army 10,000-strong which set out to claim the south-east of England for Charles. To meet the threats, Fairfax divided his forces, sending Cromwell to Wales while another force of four regiments (three foot, including Lilburne's and Harrison's, and one horse) was sent north to Yorkshire under the command of Major-General John Lambert, the commissary-general and a young radical free-thinker whose 'subtle and working brain' had been much admired by Bulstrode Whitelocke. Skippon would remain in command of the depleted London garrison while Fairfax dealt with the threat from Kent. Having disbanded several regiments the New Model Army was dangerously overstretched to deal with a campaign on three fronts – in the north, the south-east and in south Wales, where the first pitched battle of this phase of the war was about to be fought – but, though depleted, the parliamentary soldiers were not only more experienced but better led.

Faced by the threat posed by Laugharne's force, Horton brought three regiments of foot and one of horse down from Brecon into the south Glamorgan coastal littoral. Lacking sound intelligence he did not know that his opponent's army was made up mainly of poorly equipped countrymen who had little or no military training; all he knew was that from a purely military point of view this numerically superior force had to be countered and quickly destroyed. The opportunity came on the morning of 8 May, when the two armies met near the village of St Fagans by the River Ely, to the west of

Cardiff. The battle was fought over small fields intersected with hedgerows and, as happened so often during that long wet summer, the ground was heavy from the relentless rain, conditions which made life difficult for Horton's horse. In the first stages of the battle neither side could gain any advantage, with the infantry in the centre contesting each foot of ground, but eventually the experience of the professional parliamentary soldiers told and Laugharne's men were forced to scatter in disarray. Many managed to escape, but in the narrow lanes of the surrounding countryside and at the fiercely contested bridge over the Nant Dowlais stream several hundred Royalists were slaughtered. The exact numbers were not recorded, but according to local tradition the waters of the Ely ran red.

Horton's victory at St Fagans broke the Royalist field army, which was no longer able to offer a tangible threat, leaving Laugharne and its remnants to hurry back westwards to the safety of Pembroke. By acting quickly and decisively Horton had virtually stopped the rebellion in its tracks, and he was within his rights to send a dispatch to Speaker Lenthall claiming that it had been a hard-won victory:

> And that God's mercy may be the more magnified in this late happy success over our enemies, I think it is now seasonable to make known unto you the straits we were in, and difficulties which encompassed us about; we having a potent enemy lying within two miles upon much advantage of ground, before us the high mountains, close to us on the right hand, the sea, near unto us on the left Chepstow taken and Monmouthshire beginning to rise in our rear, besides our great want of provisions and long and hard duty, all which seemed to threaten our sudden ruin. That God should please in this condition so to own us, as to make a way for us through the midst of our enemies, and to scatter them every way is a mercy not to be forgotten, especially those who have more immediately tasted of it.[7]

Like many of the colonels in the New Model Army, Horton was a straightforward soldier who, in Cromwell's words, 'knew what they fought for and loved what they knew'. Loyal to his cause, God-fearing, tough-minded yet fair to his men, he was typical of that breed of fighting man who was forced to learn his trade as he went along,

yet like Cromwell he was always careful to ascribe his success to divine
intervention. Men of that kind in the parliamentary army were not
just 'saints' but inspired, modest and intelligent leaders who quickly
mastered modern tactics and seem genuinely to have enjoyed being
soldiers. Discipline, too, was at a premium and in keeping with the
tenor of that year Horton understood the worth of example. After the
fighting was over, four officers from Laugharne's army were taken on
board the parliamentary warship *Admiral Crowther* and court-
martialled for treason. One was shot and three were hanged.

Two days later Cromwell and his regiments arrived at Monmouth
and the town of Chepstow was retaken. Lacking artillery, Cromwell
was unable to besiege the castle and decided to push on westwards,
leaving behind a small investing force under the command of a
Colonel Ewer. Already the wind had been taken out of the Royalist
sails. The defeat at St Fagans had encouraged most fair-weather rebels
to return home and only Pembroke (Laugharne and Poyer) and Tenby
were still under Royalist control. The latter had defied all of Horton's
attempts to break the siege, but the arrival of the warships
Bonadventure and *Expedition* made life increasingly difficult for the
garrison, which not only had to endure daily naval artillery fire but
was also running out of food and water. However, Cromwell decided
not to delay but pushed on to Pembroke and on 24 May parked his
regiments outside the castle's stout medieval walls while he waited for
artillery to be brought up to him by sea from Gloucester to Milford
Haven. Once again the parliamentary navy's control of the Irish Sea
and Bristol Channel was a factor in supporting land operations and
an indication of its importance to the war effort.

There was a further delay when the guns were used to lift the siege
at Chepstow and while he waited Cromwell found himself bogged
down on the hills to the south-east. Attempts to attack the walls came
to nothing, as the siege ladders were too short and Cromwell was
forced into the position – unusual for him – of having to watch and
wait and, as Hugh Peters put it, to rely on providence. 'We have
wanted bread, lain in cold fields, constant rain, our guns sunk in the
sea and recovered,' wrote Cromwell's chaplain. 'We had a desperate
enemy and few friends but a mighty God.'[8] Inside the castle, food was
beginning to run out, and there was a rash of desertions, but as
Pembroke enjoyed its own water supply Poyer's men were still in a

reasonably strong position. And as Cromwell told parliament, not only did they still enjoy the support of the local countryside but they had become 'a very desperate enemy who, being put out of all hope of mercy, are resolved to endure the utmost extremity':

> The country, since we sat down before this place, have made two or three insurrections, and are ready to do it every day, so that looking to them, and disposing of our horse to that end, and to get us in provisions, without which we should starve, this country, being so miserably exhausted and so poor, and we having no money to buy victuals. Indeed, whatever may be thought, it is a mercy we have been able to keep our men together in the midst of such necessity, the sustenance of the foot being but bread and water.[9]

Eventually the heavy guns arrived on 1 July and following a brisk bombardment Cromwell summoned Poyer to surrender, threatening him, his soldiers and others in the town with 'misery and ruin' unless they complied. Realising that further resistance was pointless, Poyer and Laugharne surrendered on 11 July and threw themselves on parliament's mercy. On the whole Cromwell was minded to show clemency to all except those whom he considered to be the authors of all the troubles. The leaders – Laugharne, Poyer and Powell (Tenby had fallen on 31 May) – were sent to London for trial, eighteen senior commanders were sent into exile, a further two hundred were dispatched overseas to help colonise the island of Barbados,* and Haverfordwest Castle was partially destroyed to prevent it being used again. As for the rest of the insurrectionists, the men who had first risen in revolt for payment of arrears and who had thrown in their lot with the king, they were disbanded and sent home, just as they were going to be earlier in the year.

A different fate awaited their leaders, who were treated as traitors and turncoats. The following year the three principals were put on trial for their lives, and all were found guilty and sentenced to death, even though only one paid the ultimate penalty. At Fairfax's insistence

---

* The first settlers had arrived on the uninhabited Caribbean island in 1627 as part of a venture organised by the Anglo-Dutch financier Sir William Courteen.

lots were drawn, with a child making the blind selection in a macabre ceremony. Laugharne and Powell were handed papers which read 'life given by God' while the unfortunate Poyer's paper was blank. Showing what Clarendon called 'singular courage' and dignity he faced a firing squad in the Piazza at Covent Garden early in the morning on 25 April 1649. His accomplices were sent into exile. Although Laugharne eventually returned to live in England, becoming a member of parliament after the Restoration, his estates had been forfeited – Horton was the beneficiary – and he never received the royal pension which he felt was due to him.

All three men were equally culpable in that they had changed sides – turncoats could not expect lenient treatment, especially in a civil war – and they had been bound together in common cause in support of the king. They were all Pembroke men: Poyer had committed the county to parliament in 1642 and had been responsible for defending it against the threat of invasion from Ireland; Powell had fought in Ormond's army until 1643, when he returned to help his friends in his native county, eventually becoming governor of Tenby; Laugharne was the most experienced, having served in the Low Countries, and had led the parliamentary army which crushed the Royalists at Colby Moor. But there were differences. Laugharne and Powell were members of the county's landed gentry, whereas Poyer, a merchant, was considered something of an upstart. When their revolt began they felt strongly enough about the lack of consideration given to their men to resist openly the disbandment of the regiments under their control. When this turned into a revolt in favour of the king – Laugharne became involved when he took offence at his commission for Pembroke being awarded to Horton – it was more of a knee-jerk reaction than any planned effort to restore Charles to the throne.

It was not the end of the matter in Wales, either. Late May saw a small uprising in Caernarvon led by a local man, Sir John Owen of Clennau, but his 'barbarous and unChristianlike usage' was quickly put down at Bangor. More serious was the uprising in Anglesey which followed hard on the heels of the fall of Pembroke, but it quickly fell victim to local jealousies and squabbles. Command of the forces should have been given to Lord Byron, who arrived in the island early in July, but the local magnates preferred Richard Bulkeley of Baron Hill, who came from an old-established Anglesey family. He was eventually defeated at Red Hill on 1 October after the parliamentary commanders, Thomas Mytton and his brother-in-law Sir Thomas Myddleton, took their forces by boat across the Menai Strait from Conwy and marched them towards Beaumaris Castle. Like many of the other unsuccessful Welsh leaders Bulkeley went into exile.

Ironically, most of the issues which had triggered the fighting in England, Ireland and Scotland were irrelevant in Wales, where there was little interest in Puritanism or in the congregationalist demands of the Independents. Nor did the landed gentry share the constitutional concerns of their opposite numbers in England. Loyalty to the Crown was also more widespread and accounted for the support given to prominent Royalists in the north such as Owen and William Salisbury, both of whom caused endless trouble to Sir William Brereton's parliamentary forces. Most of Wales remained defiantly Royalist between 1642 and 1645, and it was one of the period's many confusions that Pembroke plumped for parliament and that the most successful of the Welsh parliamentary commanders were Laugharne and Poyer. With naval support they subdued south-west Wales and made it impossible for Charles to remain at Raglan, his bolt-hole following the battle of Naseby. Three years later one was in exile and the other was facing the musketeers of the army in which he had once given loyal service.

The pacification of Wales was not just important for putting down Royalist sentiment in the country; it was also essential for parliament's longer-term plans to deal with the troubles in Ireland, Milford Haven being the main port for transporting men and supplies and for conducting naval operations against Irish privateers. While its army was engaged in countering the threat from Scotland and the unrest in Kent and East Anglia, parliament could not afford to invade Ireland, but the delay did not help the Confederates. Following the failure of the Glamorgan mission its ranks had become hopelessly factionalised, split between those who supported Rinuccini's hard-line approach (mostly clerics and Old Irish landowners of Gaelic descent) and a peace party which broadly favoured the Royalist cause in return for religious tolerance. As a result of the succession of military defeats in 1647 the Confederates reconsidered their options and decided that it was impossible to continue the war against parliament without outside support. Meeting at Kilkenny in November their general assembly debated two possibilities: they could persuade Charles to ally himself with their cause in return for religious concessions, or they could turn to France or Spain for military assistance and in return Ireland would become a protectorate of either country, with or without Charles as its ruler.

This latter suggestion was given careful consideration in Paris and Madrid, as it would keep Ireland in the Catholic fold and discomfit England, but in the end the peace faction was able to persuade the assembly that their best hope lay with the House of Stewart. At the end of the year fresh approaches were made to Henrietta Maria's court in exile and it was decided that the focus of the Royalist cause would be the Prince of Wales, Ormond would return to Ireland as Lord Lieutenant to unite the different factions, and the Confederates would enter into an alliance with the Scottish Engagers. It was an ambitious plan, but local rivalries and jealousies put paid to any idea that a united force would immediately cross over to England and Scotland to take on and defeat the parliamentary revolution.

The proposal also caused further trouble in Ireland. Outraged by this development, Rinuccini excommunicated all those who had turned to Ormond, and before long the nuncio would leave Ireland for ever, infuriated by its squabbles and intrigues. The situation was thoroughly confusing. In his support Charles could count on Ormond's coalition of Royalists and Confederates and O'Neill's Ulster Catholics, while parliament looked to its forces in Ulster under the command of George Monck and Michael Jones's field army in Leinster. For parliament it was just as well that this not unexpected torpor had settled over Irish affairs: the revolt in Wales had been overcome relatively easily and the lines of communication to Milford Haven restored, but there was plenty of trouble afoot in England and Scotland, where Royalist hopes still flickered.

Chapter Two

A SUMMER OF DISCONTENT

'Never was the fair face of such a faithful County turned of a
sudden to so much deformity and ugliness.'

*Sir Anthony Welden, writing from Swanscombe in Kent
to the Derby House Committee, May 1648*

For the English Royalists any new revolt would only bear fruit if they
managed to free the king from captivity at Carisbrooke, and several plots
were hatched by, among others, his servant Sir Henry Firebrace, who had
been permitted to continue in royal service. All failed, some of them
farcically so (stones thrown at windows, partially filed bars camouflaged
with wax and a variety of false wigs and peasant costumes), and by the
end of April 1648 Hammond removed Charles to more secure quarters
on the north side of the castle, where he remained for the rest of the
summer. Had the king managed to flee and make his way to London
there is no saying what would have happened, such was the force of
popular opinion in his favour, but the lack of any concerted action by the
English Royalists meant that the uprisings in England during the spring
and early summer of 1648 were little more than a series of confused and
unrelated incidents. As for Charles, he certainly knew what was afoot and
he placed great hopes on the Scots being able to use their military strength
to assist the efforts of those loyal to him in England, but there is no
evidence that he had any direct involvement in the rash of uprisings which
took place in south Wales and south-east England during this period.

In the first instances the English revolt was little more than a series of local riots directed against parliament's unwillingness to disband the army. Throughout April there were outbreaks of rioting in Norwich and Bury St Edmunds, and the counties of Essex and Suffolk sent petitions to London asking for the restoration of normality and a negotiated settlement with the king. Inevitably the Trained Bands were called out to quell the disturbances, and just as inevitably many ordinary people were killed or injured and property damaged in the subsequent scuffles. In Norwich, for example, ammunition was accidentally exploded, killing forty innocent bystanders and damaging the church of St Peter Mancroft. All these commotions were easily quelled by parliament's security forces, but the fervour shown for the king was unwelcome evidence that Charles, the 'man of blood', still attracted considerable support.

Locked away in Carisbrooke Charles posed little immediate threat, but his presence there acted as a reminder that the king was still a potent force, perhaps more effective than he had been since the war began. While he was not surrounded by advisers, as he had been in the past, he was free to keep in touch with his wife and proved a generous correspondent, writing regularly and promiscuously about his affairs without giving much thought to security. That meant that his dealings with the Scots were common knowledge, a failing that only added to a belief within the army and parliament that they were dealing with a man whom they could not wholly trust. Charles continued much as before, refusing to concede that his position was grave and placing great faith in the ability of outside agencies to come to his help, be they Scots Covenanters, English Presbyterians or Irish Catholics. In that respect his wife's role in France was still important. With the Thirty Years War on the verge of closure, Henrietta Maria never gave up her hopes of a French military intervention, and she had the support, too, of her eldest son, the Prince of Wales, now a sprightly eighteen-year-old based in Jersey and anxious to involve himself in his father's cause.

Clearly the problem posed by the Crown had to be addressed, and the outbursts of trouble-making were accompanied by debates in parliament on the constitutional settlement and, pressingly, on how to deal with the king. Parliament was still bent on compromise if one could be found, and in pursuit of finding one it was agreed to suspend the Vote of No Addresses so that contact could be retained with the king at Carisbrooke. Steps were also taken to silence a resurgence of Leveller activity. Encouraged by the reconciliation effected by Cromwell in January a group of agitators met at St Albans to promote a new petition demanding equal rates of taxation, the abolition of excise duty and the creation of a fresh franchise, 'that therefore the birth-right of all English men be forthwith restored to all which are not, or shall not be legally disenfranchised for some criminal cause, or are not under 21 years of age, or servants, or beggars; and we humbly offer, that every county may have its equal proportion of representers'.[1] The high command was alarmed by the gathering, and on the same day that parliament was meeting to reinforce its adherence to monarchical government, an army Council of War summoned the St Albans Levellers to Windsor, where they were roundly reprimanded.

Not everyone was enamoured of these moves to treat with Charles; they seemed to smack of indecision and an unwillingness to address the central problem of the quarrel, namely the position of the Crown. Henry Marten's republican voice was heard again in parliament at the end of March proposing that the House of Commons should 'go through stitch with their work, and to take order about deposing the King', a move which was supported by Ludlow, now emerging as another leading republican. There was also continuing distrust of Cromwell and a fear that he might be tempted by offers of preferment to find a solution which would see the king returned to power and an accommodation found with the Presbyterian faction at the expense of the Independents and Levellers. John Hutchinson, ever suspicious of Cromwell's motives, returned to London, where 'he found the Presbyterian party so prevalent there, that the victories obtained by the army displeased them; and they had grown so hot in the zeal of their faction, that they from thenceforth resolved and endeavoured to close with the common enemy, that they might thereby encompass the destruction of their Independent brethren'. With him he took his family, not just because he valued their support but because his house in Nottingham was being repaired after the depredations it had suffered, it being 'so ruined by the war that he could no longer live in it, till it was either repaired or newly built.'[2]

All fears about concessions evaporated on 1 May when news reached London about the violence in south Wales and the repulse of Fleming's expedition. With Scotland on a war footing hostilities were obviously about to break out again; political considerations had to be put to one side and the army had to take charge once more 'to go out and fight against those potent enemies, which that year in all places appeared against us'. It was at this stage that Fairfax showed his mettle. Now Lord Fairfax of Cameron, following the death of his father earlier in the year, he rose to the occasion not only by demonstrating his powers of leadership but by refusing to panic. Those attributes were needed, too, for no sooner had he dispatched Cromwell to Wales and Lambert to the north of England than Kent went on a pro-Royalist rampage on 11 May. The immediate cause was an attempt by the officious parliamentary commissioner Sir Anthony Weldon to punish merrymakers who had played football in the streets of Canterbury the previous Christmas. Brought to trial for creating 'a tumult' – windows and heads had been broken, the local jail liberated and there had been fighting in the streets – the case was thrown out amid scenes of wild celebration which quickly sparked off demonstrations in the county's main towns.

While these outbreaks were an embarrassment to Weldon and through him to the Derby House Committee, there was a more serious intent behind them. A petition had been drawn up demanding a settlement between king and parliament, the disbandment of the army, government by established laws, and reform of taxation. Around 20,000 people signed it, ministers preached in its favour at Sunday services, praising the 'blood of the martyrs of Kent', and it was supported by a committee of Kent Royalists who included prominent landowners such as Sir Thomas Peyton of Knowlton Court, Sir Richard Hardres and his brother-in-law Sir Thomas Godfrey of Heppington. There was also a plan to create forces to protect local interests, but it quickly came unstuck on the question of command and control. None of the local gentry was powerful enough to win support throughout the county and there was considerable resentment from the moderates about the interference of Royalists from outside Kent who were dismissed as interfering 'foreigners'. The arrival of the Earl of Norwich,* recently returned from exile and

---

* He had negotiated the marriage with Henrietta Maria and remained one of her closest advisers in exile. His son was Lord George Goring, the wayward Royalist cavalry commander.

backed by Henrietta Maria, changed all that. Greatly respected as a nobleman of 'frolic and pleasant humour' (according to Clarendon), Norwich had been the Master of the Queen's Horse and, although he lacked military experience, he quickly proved himself 'most apt to reconcile factions'. Over 10,000 men of Kent rose for Norwich on 21 May on the moorland outside Maidstone and under his uncertain direction started marching on Blackheath and the capital.

Again, the news caused consternation in London, and not just because parliament had good historical reasons to fear Kentish tempers – in the fourteenth and fifteenth centuries Kent had been the cockpit for similar revolts against authority led by Wat Tyler and Jack Cade which lived on in the folk memory. The county was also on London's doorstep, but against that there were no reasons to think that Kent was anything less than loyal. It had escaped the fighting which had disfigured other parts of England during the civil war. Now it turned its face against parliament and a large body of men was marching on the capital at a time when many of the best New Model Army soldiers were dealing with conflict in Wales and the threat of invasion from Scotland. All that was left to Fairfax were a number of depleted regiments numbering 6000 men – 'our small body' he called them – and the Lord-General was by no means certain that they would be enough to contain the threat. On 27 May he moved them from the city on to Hounslow Heath before marching east towards Blackheath, which he reached three days later. There Fairfax took the surrender of a thousand poorly armed civilians who suddenly decided that they were not soldiers at all but simple petitioners with not a thought of violence on their minds.

The experience cheered Fairfax, but from an intelligence report written by one of his colonels two days later the opposition's intentions suddenly seemed alarming. While there had been further desertions among the men of Kent who had answered the initial call but had no real intention of going into battle against the professionals of the New Model Army, Colonel Barkstead, one of Fairfax's regimental officers, reported new rumours that the Royalist ranks were being swelled by experienced reinforcements in advance of an invasion:

The enemy still continues at Dartford. They give themselves to be 10,000 but the countrymen lessen every day. Very many officers

and soldiers that have formerly served the King come in hourly to them. The discourse among them is that if the country will not stand to them they will immediately possess themselves of all the castles and strongholds, and thereby secure landing for the Irish, French or Danes, of whose coming they fondly flatter themselves and the malignant part of the county. These countrymen that are come home do extremely cry out against the gentlemen that did engage them, looking upon themselves as utterly undone, which is the only cause of their coming home, hoping thus to keep their necks out of the halter.[3]

Apart from the news of the desertions this was not encouraging (the rumours had in fact been exaggerated), but worse followed on 27 May when information arrived from the Downs that six ships of the parliamentary navy had mutinied and declared for the king. Among them was the flagship *Constant Reformation*, whose crew had prevented the new vice-admiral, Thomas Rainsborough, from returning after visiting the coastal defences ashore. The trouble had been long fermenting. Rainsborough was not popular; his appointment as vice-admiral had been blocked by the Lords and was only pushed through at the beginning of the year because of the need to have a responsible fleet to block any attempt to rescue the king from the Isle of Wight. While the navy had been loyal to parliament throughout the conflict, the seamen's allegiance had been tested by Rainsborough's appointment. Not only was his predecessor Sir William Batten a popular figure but the new commander was a well-known radical. (This was not a recommendation: unlike the army there was never any support for the Independents within the fleet.) Rainsborough had also created new fears by delaying the appointment of captains – a sign, many thought, that he was investigating the political affiliations of his senior officers.

No sooner had the unrest flared in Kent than Peter Potts, the Admiralty Commissioner in Chatham, started counselling that the trouble could spread to the fleet, but his warning came too late. Deal, Walmer and Sandwich were occupied by mutineers, Dover was besieged and Rainsborough was sent ashore to lick his wounds and to send a string of alarmed messages to London, forecasting fresh outbreaks of mutiny in Portsmouth and Harwich. To limit the damage parliament decided to recall the Earl of Warwick, who had surrendered his post as Lord High Admiral after the Self-Denying Ordinance had been passed, and he immediately set off for the Downs to try to reason with the mutineers. The fleet would have preferred to have Batten returned, but he was now under suspicion of dealing with the Scots and the Royalists in France. In an earlier incident he had already incurred the wrath of parliament by allowing six of the eleven members impeached by the army to cross the Channel when they fled into exile in August 1647. As they carried passes from Speaker Lenthall, Batten felt that he had no jurisdiction to stop them, but his decision was greatly resented by the army and led directly to his resignation a month later.

Warwick was liked and respected but he failed to understand his seamen's suspicions about parliament's intentions, and after a heated parley on 30 May the Lord High Admiral was forced to return to London with the mutineers still in command of the Downs. His next move was more successful: on 4 June he arrived in Portsmouth and persuaded the crews not to join the mutiny but to continue their allegiance to parliament. It was a key moment, for had the Portsmouth ships mutinied the Harwich squadron would have followed suit, parliament would have lost command of the Channel and Mazarin might have been persuaded that the moment had arrived to lend Charles military support. As it was, the trouble was still far from over: with only one part of the navy settled and with the mutineers left to their own devices every effort had to be made to crush the Kentish rebellion before it spread into the neighbouring counties. Although his forces were over-extended, Fairfax did just that.

His immediate objectives were twofold – to raise the siege at Dover and to deal with the main body of the Royalists at Maidstone, Rochester and Gravesend, the latter having been occupied by a garrison consisting of Kentish men commanded by 'fifteen knights and many commanders of the king's army'. A small force under Colonel Gibbons was dispatched to march through the Weald to the Channel coast while Fairfax advanced along the south bank of the Thames towards Gravesend and Rochester. Finding the latter town heavily defended he moved over the North Downs through their heavily wooded lanes by way of Meopham to threaten the main body of Norwich's army. At Malling, which he reached on 1 June, he turned east and by crossing the Medway at East Farleigh was able to drive a wedge between the two opposition camps at Aylesford and Maidstone.

As had happened earlier in the war, the battle was decided by poor scouting. The first that Norwich knew about his opponents' movements came in the early evening when his dragoons collided with Fairfax's advance party on Penenden Heath, sparking off a running battle which left Maidstone exposed. The order was given to storm the town – garrisoned by two regiments under the command of Sir William Brockman and Sir John Mayney – and as Fairfax later reported there followed 'four or five hours' hot service' as both sides fought from one position to the next in Maidstone's narrow streets, one contemporary report claiming that the ground was won not so much in terms of feet but 'by inches'. For all that they were fighting a tough army of veterans the Royalists gave a good account of themselves, and it was not until midnight with a thunderstorm raging overhead that Fairfax was in total command of the Kentish capital. Those who surrendered, some 1300, were granted quarter and told to return to their homes. Suddenly war was not an adventure but a bloody and comfortless undertaking; the farmers among them remembered their neglected fields sodden by the unseasonable weather, and with the harvest still to be brought in set off for home.

As for the rest of the army, some drifted off into exile, others rode north to join the garrison at Rochester, while a rump of 3000 followed Norwich in a mad decision to march on London. What they were trying to achieve is open to doubt – Norwich must have hoped to gain the support of those Londoners who had rioted in support of the king a month earlier, but he still had to face Skippon's trained bands. Fairfax was evidently not overly concerned by the move, as he only dispatched one regiment in pursuit under the command of Colonel Edward Whalley. His confidence was justified. When Norwich arrived at Blackheath on 3 June he found the city gates closed against him, a setback which encouraged a large number of desertions, his men fading away into Surrey and conveniently losing their weapons as they did so. Like the Cornishmen who reached the River Tamar and refused to go any further, the men of Kent were not prepared to cross the county boundary. The rump, a party of around 500, crossed the Thames, some by boat, others on horseback, and settled down in

Stratford and Bow with no clear idea of what to do next. Although their move cut off the eastern approaches to the capital, Whalley had reached Mile End by the following day, leaving Norwich in a desperate position, as by then it was clear that no one in London was willing to support him. His best hope lay in Essex, where the local Royalists had staged an uprising at Chelmsford led by Sir Charles Lucas and supported by Lords Capel and Loughborough and by two other professional soldiers, Sir George Lisle and Sir Bernard Gascoigne; but that good news was balanced by parliament passing an ordinance of indemnity on 5 June offering a pardon to the men of Essex provided that they did not help Norwich's cause.

Clearly the small Kentish force could not stay near London, and on 7 June Norwich rode to Chelmsford to meet Lucas, a cantankerous but dashing Royalist cavalry commander whose family estates lay nearby and whose word was influential enough to persuade most of the local population to ignore the parliamentary indemnity. (Those who insisted on standing up for their rights were simply arrested.) The two men decided to combine their forces at Brentwood two days later and to head north into Suffolk and Norfolk, where there were promises of further Royalist support, leaving the pursuing Whalley to report to Fairfax that the opposition was 'like a snowball, increasing'. However, the growth was matched by an iciness in the command structure. Ostensibly Norwich was in command but Lucas, a veteran of Marston Moor, was a crusty martinet who did not like having his ideas countermanded. He also had nothing to lose, having broken the parole he had been given following his capture at Stow-on-the-Wold in 1646; when he suggested that the army should stop to recruit in his home town of Colchester no one was prepared to gainsay him.

Behind them Fairfax was coming up, one leg racked by gout but determined to close with the Royalists, while ahead of him at Coggeshall lay another parliamentary force under another Essex landowner, Sir Thomas Honeywood. Sensing the danger, Lucas took his force on a north-westerly feint past Braintree and then eastwards to Halstead, which allowed them to move into Colchester on 13 June, just ahead of the parliamentary forces. Fairfax hoped to repeat the tactics which had taken Maidstone, but Lucas's infantry in the centre put up a determined resistance. The close-quarters fighting outside the southern walls of the city was as ferocious as anything else seen in the war, with one difference – it was accompanied by a savagery which brooked no quarter, the parliamentary soldiers attacking 'like mad men killing and slaying them [Royalists] in a terrible manner, even in the cannon mouths'. The slaughter continued into the night until a sally by Royalist cavalry scattered the opposition infantry and all bar one hundred of Lucas's men managed to reach the safety of the city walls.[4]

A siege then began, an operation which was not to Fairfax's liking but one which he conducted with his usual brisk efficiency. Lacking sufficient heavy equipment to break down the walls, he circumvallated the city with a chain of defences linked by ten small forts and captured Mersea Island to the south to prevent supplies being brought in from the sea by way of the River Colne. The action was punctuated by occasional sallies which led to nothing but caused a string of casualties, the defenders set fire to the suburbs and there was the usual exchange of fire which encouraged both sides to make claims that illegal methods were being used. The Royalists were supposed to be using soft-headed or poisoned bullets while Fairfax was accused of inhumanity when he cut the water supply and melted down the lead pipes for ammunition. Both sides suffered, too, from the appalling summer weather, with rain falling most days, turning the surrounding countryside into 'a continual flood'. Food, too, became scarce, and by the middle of July Lucas's garrison was forced to eat horse and dog meat, hardly a recommendation for the civilians to hold out. Before the Royalists entered the town the local population and its leading figures had been opposed to the continued existence of the New Model Army, branding them as 'heretics and schismatics' unworthy of support, but, as a contemporary report revealed, finding themselves worse off under Lucas, they 'longed for the deliverance by the hands of those whom they so despised before'.[5] And there was no escape, either. When a party of women crept out of the city they were rounded up by parliamentary troopers, stripped and sent back again to exist in a kind of no-man's-land outside the walls until they were readmitted.

Inside the town Lucas ruled with a rod of iron, refusing to listen to grumbles and ignoring several summons to surrender – Clarendon said that his 'rough and proud nature made him during the time of their being in Colchester more intolerable than the siege or any fortune that threatened them'.[6] Having backed himself into a corner he was determined to hold out as long as he could in the hope that events elsewhere would come to his assistance. Although he had been discommoded by the fall of Pembroke, which freed Cromwell's army for action elsewhere, that same week also brought reports that Hamilton's Scottish army was on the march and would soon be sweeping through England. There was also fresh hope from Surrey, where the Earl of Holland, once more in the king's service, and the young Duke of Buckingham had raised the royal standard at Kingston-on-Thames on 4 July and were about to march on London. And from the fleet came the most sensational news of all. Nine ships in the Downs had taken advantage of the collapse of the revolt in Kent to sail for Holland, where they were joined by the Prince of Wales and Batten.

For the members of the Derby House Committee sitting in London at the beginning of July 1648 the situation seemed extremely grave, and as happens in time of emergency, rumours were believed and the threat posed by the Royalists appeared to be much greater than it really was. On 4 July a petition was presented to both houses of parliament demanding that the king be allowed to return to the capital to resume negotiations. To this the Lords agreed but the Commons insisted that before any offer could be made the king would have to accept their conditions about instituting Presbyterianism and surrendering control of the militia. There is little doubt that Royalist sentiments prevailed in most parts of what are today the Home Counties, but it was by no means certain that they would be translated into action. Potential supporters hedged their bets and waited to see how the military situation unravelled that summer – the Scots would have to defeat the parliamentary army, Colchester would have to hold out and Holland would have to rally sufficient support to capture London.

Of the three outcomes the latter venture was doomed before it began. Despite the support of Buckingham and his younger brother Lord Francis Villiers and the presence of Jan Dalbier, a Dutch soldier of fortune, Holland's enterprise failed to rouse more than 500 supporters to join the Royalist cause. As an attempt on London was out of the question Holland decided, somewhat half-heartedly it must be said, to take Reigate Castle but, finding the way blocked by a regiment led by Sir Michael Livesey, a tough parliamentary commander, the Royalists retreated through Surrey. On Surbiton Common there was a brief skirmish which saw the Royalist horse being badly mauled and during which young Villiers was killed. His death, like Sidney Godolphin's at Chagford earlier in the war, was much lamented by the romantics, he being youthful, high-spirited, gallant and possessing what Clarendon called 'rare beauty and comeliness of person'.

In fact Villiers's Royalist rearguard fought with great courage, but their gallantry was not enough. Holland's support started melting away and the remaining 200 men wandered aimlessly north, passing through Harrow to St Neots, where they rested on the evening of 9 July. Tired, rudderless and dispirited, they were quickly overcome by the parliamentary force which had been following behind them. Holland was captured and sent to London, Dalbier was swiftly dispatched and only Buckingham managed to escape. The revolt's failure came at the worst possible time, as the Scots were slowly crossing the border into England and were counting on a diversion in the south which would tie down parliamentary forces and weaken Fairfax's ability to respond to the Royalist challenge. In Kent, too, the revolt was as good as over; already parliamentary agents could see that the rebellion had been more of a disunited local disturbance than a planned uprising. The remaining threat was the mutiny in the fleet which had raised the spectre of a foreign power – France or the Netherlands – taking advantage of the situation, but reports from the county suggested that there would be no local support, should foreign forces land in support of the king:

> They resolved to adhere to their late principles and to stand for the defence of the liberties of their unconquered nation, and have declared their joint resolution to oppose all forces whatsoever that shall endeavour to make an inroad within the bowels of this county, to disturb the peace thereof, being resolved to display their banners in opposition to the ban of the new-raised Royalists.[7]

Now only Colchester provided a check, but by the beginning of August the effects of famine had become a daily reality and the disheartened civilian population was putting increased pressure on

Norwich and Lucas to surrender. Being desperate men they refused – there were later reports, probably untrue but believed at the time, that they told the weeping women to eat their children – and they also took no notice of Fairfax's summons, which would have allowed the ordinary soldiers to return to their homes unharmed. Though courageous, their resistance only hardened Fairfax's determination to punish them as miscreants who had brought nothing but misfortune on the heads of innocents. The parliamentary commander also knew that he held all the aces – by the time that negotiations for the capitulation of Colchester began on 27 August the Scots had been defeated and Fairfax was able to issue harsh terms of submission which, under the circumstances, were understandable, 'that they be rendered or do render themselves to the Lord General or whom he may appoint without assurance of quarter, so as the Lord General may be free to put some immediately to the sword if he see cause; although his Excellency intends, chiefly and for the generality of those under that condition, to surrender them to the mercy of Parliament, and of the mercy of the Parliament and General there has been large experience.'[8]

In other words, the punishment of those who surrendered would be reduced to a lottery, and so it turned out. Immediately after entering the town Fairfax's war council met on 28 August to decide the fate of the leading opposition leaders. Norwich and Capel, being members of the nobility, were sent to London to be 'proceeded upon by the power of civil justice', but the three Royalist soldiers, Lucas, Lisle and Gascoigne, were sentenced to death, the executions to take place that evening. They were shot in the castle yard, Lucas being executed first and showing defiance to the end. As he was led forward he turned to Ireton and asked him on what grounds he was being punished. As a rebel who had committed high treason, replied the parliamentary commander whom many believed to have argued most forcefully for the death sentence. Lucas showed commendable grace as he met his end, and his riposte carried considerable weight when he argued that he was fighting as a soldier in the service of a lawful king: 'I do plead before you all the laws of this kingdom. I have fought with a commission from those that were my sovereign's, and from that commission I must justify my action.'

Lisle was next to die. After protesting that he wished only to see the king, his master, on the throne again, he asked the firing squad to step a little closer so that they might kill him cleanly. Told by one of the squad that they were unlikely to miss him Lisle replied: 'Friends, I have been nearer you when you have missed me.'[9] When it came to Gascoigne's turn to prepare himself he was unexpectedly reprieved, as he was a Tuscan soldier – Bernardo Guasconi fighting under a nom-de-guerre. That gesture of mercy notwithstanding, the executions produced a stain on the 1648 campaign and left Fairfax open to the charge of committing an atrocity. Both Lisle and Lucas carried a royal commission and in their minds they were fighting on the king's behalf to put down an illegal rebellion. Once they had become prisoners they felt that they should have been granted honourable terms and not condemned to death without trial. There is also the question mark over the terms of the surrender which, though straightforward, breached earlier agreements about the granting of quarter after a fair fight.

Against that, as Fairfax reported to Lenthall, the three men had to be punished 'for some satisfaction to military justice, and in part of avenge for the innocent blood they have caused to be spilt, and the trouble, damage, and mischief they have brought upon the town'.[10] He also argued that Lucas deserved his fate, having broken the parole that had been given after he was released in 1646. While there is some logic to his reasoning, the overwhelming emotion at the fall of Colchester was the need for immediate revenge. Having seen England plunged into violence once more, and the people of the town forced to endure two months of hardship and suffering, Fairfax and Ireton were in no mood to be charitable. The Royalist commanders might have been fighting a good fight but they were also serving a king whose duplicity had been revealed by the Scots' invasion at a time when he was still trying to deal with parliament. For that Lisle and Lucas had to die, as would Capel a year later. As for the garrison soldiers, they too faced an uncertain future. Although Fairfax promised that it was his intention for them 'to go free', many were sent to Bristol to be sold into slavery in the West Indies while others were forced into exile in Europe, on condition that they joined the army of the Venetian Republic.

All that remained of Royalist resistance was the fleet of eleven warships which returned to the Downs in the middle of July under the command of the Prince of Wales, determined to force an engagement with Warwick, but that bold gesture also came to nothing. Lacking any clear strategy the fleet stayed close to the Thames estuary, stopping merchant shipping but refusing to make any positive move to engage the parliamentary fleet. An attack on London was mooted but the prince prevaricated, fearing (not without reason) that a defeat would take him into captivity. That lack of momentum damaged the crews' morale. This curious episode ended at the end of August as both fleets manoeuvred in the shallow waters off Shoeburyness, neither side being willing to begin an engagement. A storm on 30 August eventually separated the fleets and the arrival of the Portsmouth squadron settled the issue. Unwilling to fight a night action, the prince decided to take his ships back to the safety of Dutch waters, even though there were grounds for thinking that the loyalty of Warwick's crews would have been tested by a battle. With his ships went the last of the Royalist hopes: a week later Sandown Castle surrendered to Warwick and the Welsh and English stages of the conflict known as the second civil war were almost at an end.

Chapter Three

NOTHING BUT THE HAND OF GOD: PRESTON

'It is Scotland, and Scotland only, can save the King and England. All others have their rise from the expectation of Scotland.'

The Earl of Lauderdale to Lady Carlisle, 19 July 1648

By the time that the summer bushfire rebellion had been extinguished in England and Wales, the threat posed by the Scots had also been crushed. Hamilton had hoped to raise 30,000 soldiers for his invasion of England, but the figure was impossibly optimistic and by late spring it became clear that the menfolk of Scotland were not prepared to join him in what many Church ministers had denounced as a wicked enterprise. Even his Lanarkshire tenants refused the call and, elsewhere, in Ayrshire and the south-west, areas which were quickly becoming the main Covenanting centres in Scotland, men fled to Ulster or deep into the hills of Galloway rather than be rounded up for service. Glasgow, too, failed to respond and, after the magistrates refused to cooperate with Hamilton's conscription order, Sir James Turner, back in action again, took squadrons of troopers into the city and quartered them on the unwilling inhabitants. This proved not only to be 'not very difficult', but it produced 'an argument strong enough, in two or three nights time, to make the hardest headed Covenanter in the town to forsake the Kirk and to side with Parliament'.[1] The neighbouring town of Paisley was the next to receive this effective treatment, but elsewhere in the west of Scotland unwilling recruits proved to be not just recalcitrant but violent with it.

The worst incident occurred at Mauchline Muir in Ayrshire in the second week of June, when a mob of anti-Engager Covenanters gathered to proclaim their refusal to serve in any new war to restore the monarchy. Earlier they had assembled on Loudoun Hill outside the town of Kilmarnock; prayer meetings were held and the gathering began to attract other protesters, including groups of armed horsemen from the surrounding countryside. As the situation started to deteriorate Callendar and Middleton moved troops into the area to suppress the danger, and this inevitably led to violence. With the mood turning ugly Middleton rode forward with 600 horse to break up the meeting, but he had misjudged the size, strength and feeling of the Covenanters' gathering. A call to disperse was ignored, and when his troopers moved on to the moor they were blocked by the opposition horse, which outnumbered them two to one. Only the arrival of reinforcements led by Callendar prevented a disaster, and as they approached the Covenanters chose discretion, quickly dispersing into the surrounding countryside. A full-scale battle had been avoided, but in the brief frenzy of skirmishing there were casualties: among the wounded on the Royalist side was Sir John Hurry, who was last seen fighting for Montrose, having deserted William Baillie after Auldearn. Now he was back in action, serving the same parliamentary general who was now engaged in the cause of restoring the king.

The rout on Mauchline Muir was both a minor irritant and a solid reminder of the opposition facing the Engagers, and it created doubts in the Royalist army's high command. Lanark, Hamilton's brother, argued that the trouble in Ayrshire and the south-west should be put down before England was invaded, otherwise a civil war would break out once the Engager army had crossed the border. In Edinburgh Robert Baillie had noted as much, writing of the 'great animosity' of the people towards the enterprise and fearing that 'so soon as our army shall be intangled with the English, many of our people will rise on their backs'.[2] He had just returned to Edinburgh for the summer's General Assembly, which showed its colours by passing a Declaration against the Engagement, censuring parliament, proclaiming the move unlawful, criticising ministers who had not preached against it and drawing up a list of 'the chief insolencies committed by the soldiers'. This was hardly the voice of a people acting in common purpose, and Lanark was right in believing that the invasion of England could be sufficiently unpopular to spark a different kind of conflict at home.

His ever-confident brother thought otherwise, and Hamilton's optimism was shared by Lauderdale, who argued that the invasion of England had to be mounted quickly to coincide with planned local risings in the north and to take advantage of Holland's attempt to rally Royalist support in the south. The troublemakers among the anti-Engagers could be dealt with once the king had been returned to the throne and the Cromwell faction defeated. As long as the dissidents were contained in the south-west they did not pose a danger, and Hamilton remained supremely optimistic that a large Scottish army could be raised and that its superior numbers and prowess would be no match for an English army which appeared to be hopelessly divided. His thinking was pure fantasy. Not only had he failed to comprehend the bitterness and anger created by the outbreak of the latest round of internecine fighting, but he did not realise the strength of his fellow countrymen's antipathy to the Engagement. As the family's historian later explained, the Scots were not interested in risking their lives for a cause which seemed to be both wrong-headed and politically dubious:

> The regiments were not full, many of them scarce exceeded half their number, and not a fifth man could handle a pike. The horse men were the best mounted ever Scotland set out, yet most of the troopers were raw and undisciplined. They had no artillery – not so much as a field piece – very little ammunition, and very few horses to carry it; for want of which the Duke stayed often in the rear of the whole army till the countrymen brought in horses and then conveyed it with his own guard of horse.[3]

There were also problems in getting George Monro's force across from Ulster. He hoped to bring 3000 men to support the Engagers, but the parliamentary navy's command of the sea made it a risky process. At least 300 were returned to the province after their transports were intercepted by government frigates, and the senior officers had to resort to using small fishing craft for nocturnal crossings over the North Channel to Galloway. Even that ruse did not help matters, as the men arrived in piecemeal numbers and were usually refused support from the local population, and even attacked. Eventually 1500 foot and 400 horse made their way into Scotland, but once there, divisions in the Engagers' command structure and petty jealousies among the leading personalities meant that these battle-hardened troops made little or no contribution to the forthcoming campaign.

The trouble was that Hamilton was running out of time and events south of the border were already forcing the issue. Lambert's Yorkshire force had been reinforced by a regiment each of foot and horse and he could also call on other forces in north Wales and Newcastle. Because Fairfax believed that the Scots would invade by the traditional eastern route Yorkshire had been chosen as the base for Lambert's operations, and when Berwick was seized by Sir Marmaduke Langdale on 28 April the parliamentary deployment seemed to make sense. However that was only a prelude to another Royalist commander, Sir Philip Musgrave, taking over control of Carlisle and asking the old commander of the Northern Horse to join up with him. Langdale moved quickly on to the offensive and by the end of May a Royalist force of some 3000 had been assembled in Cumberland and Westmoreland, the plan being to march south to link up with forces commanded by Colonels Morris and Paulden, who had captured the key west Yorkshire town of Pontefract.

To counter the threat Lambert acted decisively, taking his forces north-west at the end of April and forcing Langdale to surrender Penrith and Brougham Castle and to move back into the safety of Carlisle. With his headquarters at Appleby Lambert was in a good position to block any move south through Lancashire or Yorkshire, and his confidence was high. Under him were men who had fought at Marston Moor and Naseby, and the majority of these were Independents for whom the fresh outbreak of violence was an affront to their beliefs and their dignity. In contrast, Langdale's men were a shadow of that once great fighting formation the Northern Horse and they were operating at a greater disadvantage: having made their move at Berwick and Carlisle they needed the assistance of the Engager army if they were to make any impression against the superior parliamentary forces. In the sense that Langdale forced the Scots to do something, his uprising was bold but tactically naive.

Hamilton and Lauderdale realised that they had to make a move, and the predicament facing the north of England Royalists provided an emotional spur for them to act sooner rather than later. If the Carlisle garrison were to fall it would deny the Scots the assistance of Langdale's cavalry regiments, English troops would be on the border and the attack on England would either face immediate resistance or the invading army would be attacked from the rear by Lambert's regiments. Against that, as Turner pointed out in his memoirs, time was running out for the creation of a fully equipped and fully manned army:

> To march to his [Langdale's] relief, were to leave half of our forces in Scotland unlevied, and one enemy behind our hand, ourselves in a very bad condition, without money, meal, artillery, or ammunition; to suffer him to perish was against honour, conscience, and the reason both of state and war. It would have given our enemies occasion to insult; would have brought the Duke's honour (rudely enough dealt with by some before) to an everlasting loss, and would have given such just apprehensions of jealousies to the Royalists in England, that never one of them would have joined with us.[4]

Hamilton might not have possessed all the military prerequisites but he knew all about honour and reputation. On 4 July, against his brother's advice but with Lauderdale's support, the Engager army mustered in Annandale in the Scottish West March, a rich fertile strath which down the years had been the scene of much bitter cross-border fighting – an internecine battle between the Johnstones and the Maxwells in 1593 resulted in 700 deaths, the worst clan battle in Scotland's history – but fifty-five years later, on a wet summer's morning, only 10,500 answered Hamilton's call to arms. Most were inexperienced and badly led, the army lacked sufficient supplies, weapons and ammunition, but if it could meet up with the English Royalists and Monro's Ulster force it would be bigger than anything Lambert could offer. Also, not all of its regiments were poor specimens. Although Carnegie's Foot consisted mainly of a motley crew of Dundonian tailors and bonnet-makers who had been hurriedly enlisted through a quota system, others were commanded by experienced leaders who had seen action in the earlier fighting, among whom could be counted Lords Montgomery and Yester. Had they been led by the shrewd and hard-headed David Leslie the story of their invasion might have turned out rather differently.

To begin with Hamilton displayed some urgency. Five days later he was in Carlisle, forcing Lambert's men to withdraw, but Langdale's uprising caused him to use the unfamiliar western route into England and, while that would allow him to attack Manchester, it would also bring him into the orbit of Cromwell and the parliamentary forces around Gloucester. Any success would depend on his moving swiftly and deliberately south to take advantage of the three-way split in Fairfax's army and to encourage other Royalist support to come out into the open. But already cracks were appearing in the command structure. Callendar could not hide his contempt for Hamilton, who in turn showed no stomach for questioning his subordinate's line of thinking. Worse, Hamilton tended to agree with every proposal made to him, as if it were his own idea.

The weather was vile, too, 1648 being one of the worst summers on record, with Oglander claiming that 'the heavens were offended with us for our offence committed to one another for, from Mayday till the 15th of September we had scarce three dry days together'. As a result food was expensive and in short supply. Lacking their own supplies and as *Mercurius Britannicus* had it, 'bringing their lice and their Presbytery among us', the Scots were forced to forage and live off the land, a move which Leven had avoided eight years earlier and one which inevitably alienated the local population who, as Oglander noted, only had bad harvests ahead of them:

Men made an ill shift with their wheat. When a dry day came, they would reap and carry it presently into their barns, although they mowed it wet. I believe most was mowed so wet that much of it will grow in the barn, and I am confident wheat and barley will bear such a price as was never known in England. His Majesty asked me whether that weather was usual in our island. I told him that in this 40 years I never knew the like before.[5]

Oglander was writing from the Isle of Wight, but the rain also fell just as heavily in Cumberland, and when Hamilton's army eventually set out for the south six days after it had arrived in Carlisle its progress was slow and painful. On 14 July it straggled into Penrith, where it stopped for three days to regroup and to send scavenging parties into the surrounding countryside, but by then the delays were costing Hamilton's army not only time but the destruction of what military advantage it once possessed. By then Pembroke had fallen, freeing Cromwell to march rapidly north to join Lambert, and although his force of 3000 foot and 1200 horse was exhausted after its efforts in Wales they attracted further numbers on their way through Derbyshire and Nottinghamshire. Hamilton could not have known Cromwell's exact movements but he must have realised that the delays would kill off any hopes that the English Royalists would join the fight against the parliamentary army. The longer the Scottish commander procrastinated, the greater chance Lambert had of reinforcing his small army with Cromwell's Ironsides and of seeing the odds swing his way. The hesitation continued at Kirby Thorne, where the Scots waited a full fortnight for George Monro's reinforcements to arrive at Kendal, Turner noting wearily that not only were the recruits 'raw and undisciplined' but the wet weather played havoc with the practice-firing of their muskets.

It was not the end of the Scots' difficulties. Even when the Ulster units did arrive they were hardly made welcome: Callendar refused to accept Monro as an equal while the Ulster veteran was unwilling to put himself under his or William Baillie's command. A more able commander would have ironed out those difficulties but, unable to keep his subordinates in order, Hamilton could find no other solution to the impasse than to order Monro to remain at Kendal with Musgrave's regiment and another commanded by Sir Thomas Tyldesley until the artillery train being organised by his brother arrived from Scotland. Having risked their lives in dangerous night crossings, these experienced and battle-hardened soldiers from Ulster were to be no better than garrison troops while inexperienced men marched further south into England. Two men were to blame for this absurd state of affairs – Monro with his arrogant refusal to serve under other commanders and Callendar with his autocratic personality – and the decision to omit the Ulster soldiers from the next stage was one of the worst taken by Hamilton in this ill-starred campaign.

Only one thing stood in the duke's favour. By taking his time and moving at a snail's pace he made life difficult for Lambert, who was trying to read his opponent's intentions. The niggardly rate of the advance did not suggest an attack down the west coast, but it could not be ruled out, as Lancashire was Royalist territory which could provide recruits and supplies. On the other hand Hamilton could be preparing to change direction to Newcastle or to move his men over the Pennines towards Yorkshire and the east coast route to London. As the young general's orders were to delay the Scots as long as possible he hedged his bets by moving a small garrison to Appleby while placing the bulk of his force at Barnard Castle to cover the Stainmore Pass route into West Yorkshire. With only 5000 men under his command he had to use his forces with care and the situation was made more precarious for him when the Appleby troops were forced to surrender to the advancing Scots on 31 July.

By then the invading army had almost reached Hornby Castle near Lancaster, which had been seized by the Earl of Derby in the early stages of the first civil war, and it was there, on 9 August, that Hamilton finally had to decide which strategy to adopt. Typically, for there was no reason why matters should run smoothly at this late stage, there was another round of dissent when the commanders sat down to discuss their plans. Baillie, the infantryman, wanted to continue down through Lancashire and to take Manchester while Middleton and Turner were all for crossing the Pennines into the open heathland of Yorkshire, good cavalry country. Turner recorded:

When my opinion was asked, I was for Yorkshire, and for this reason only, that I understood Lancashire was a close country, full of ditches and hedges, which was a great advantage the English would have over our raw and undisciplined musketeers; the Parliament's army consisting of experienced and well trained soldiers and excellent firemen; on the other hand, Yorkshire being a more open country, and full of heaths, where we might make use of our horse, and come sooner to push of pike. My Lord Duke was for Lancashire way, and it seemed he had hopes that some forces would join him in his march that way. I have indeed heard him say, that he thought Manchester his own if he came near it. Whatever the matter was, I never saw him tenacious in any thing during the time of his command but that.[6]

In the end the decision was taken by Hamilton to continue moving south into Lancashire, where there was a good chance that they would be joined by parties of Royalists from north Wales under the command of Lord Byron. By then it probably mattered not which route was taken, as Cromwell was only four days' march from joining up with Lambert, who had been sufficiently alarmed by the sighting of Langdale's cavalry patrols to take the precaution of withdrawing towards Richmond. It had taken Cromwell a fortnight to get his men that far north, a distance of some 280 miles, while the unwieldy Scots had come a bare hundred miles in twice that time. As the commander of the northern forces Lambert should by rights have exercised overall command, but it was unthinkable that leadership should not pass to the older and more experienced Cromwell, who had in any case taken the opportunity of writing to the Derby House Committee to have it confirmed that he would be the overall commander-in-chief – his first independent command in what one officer called 'a fine smart army, fit for action'.

Having made their decision the Scottish army started trundling south through Lancashire, but its movements were by no means coherent and little attempt was made to keep the stragglers moving. Langdale's horse provided a cavalry screen to the east, where he received the first intelligence that Cromwell was in the area (foolishly he dismissed the news as idle gossip), while the main force headed south on a broad front in the general direction of Preston and the River Ribble. It was at this point that things started going seriously wrong in Hamilton's army. In an attempt to keep his soldiers supplied he ordered Middleton to take the cavalry ahead to Wigan, a move which brought in some forage at the expense of further alienating the local population, but it also separated the main body of the horse from the long lines of infantry which were closing on Preston.

Once again reconnaissance on both sides was poor. For all that the Scottish army was spread out over a large area Cromwell had no clear indication of its movements and was forced to act on his own reading of how the situation might develop. The sensible plan was to march on Preston while keeping to the south bank of the Ribble to block Hamilton's route. Either the Scots would have to cross the river before joining battle or they would be forced to find another route to the east. But Cromwell had other ideas. He believed that the better option would be to keep to the same north bank on which the Scots were deployed and force the issue there. Either there would be a battle which he hoped would be decisive in his favour or he would deny the Scots any hope of retreating north. As he told Speaker Lenthall after the battle, there was only one issue at stake: 'It was thought that to engage the enemy to fight was our business.' Monro, too, was a factor. Hamilton was clearly expecting his imminent arrival but Cromwell was not to know that, far from marching south, Monro was sticking to his orders and awaiting the arrival of the artillery in Kirby Lonsdale. The plan having been agreed, Cromwell's regiments marched along the Ribble as far as Stonyhurst Park,* where they camped for the night: they were now seven miles from Hamilton's army at Preston and only Langdale's small force of 3000 foot and 600 cavalry, blissfully unaware of the danger, stood between them.

At dawn the following day Hamilton ordered Baillie to start driving the infantry across the river. Clearly he did not believe the rumours that Cromwell was in the vicinity or he had found a new sense of urgency, but no sooner had the men started crossing Preston bridge than news came from Langdale that he was under attack by Cromwell's Ironsides on Ribbleton Moor and that this was no probing sortie but a full-scale assault by a large force of infantry and cavalry. The nature of the fighting was dictated by the landscape – small fields surrounded by high hedges and dissected by narrow lanes – and soon a hard close-quarters battle was being fought, with musketeers using the hedges for cover while the pikemen closed on each other. For John Hodgson, a Cromwellian infantry officer, this was the epitome of war:

---

* Now a Jesuit boarding school which contains the table on which Cromwell is supposed to have slept on the eve of battle.

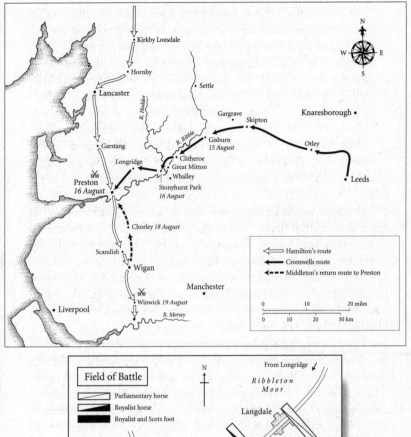

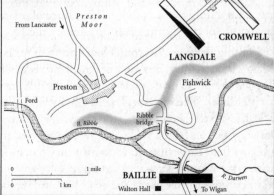

They were drawn up very formidably. One Major Poundall and myself commanded the forlorn of foot [a picked body of men detached to the front to begin the attack]; and being drawn up by the moor side (that scattering we had being not half the number we should have been), the general comes to us, and commands to march. We not having half our men come up, desired a little patience; he gives out the word, 'March!' and so we drew over a little common, where our horse was drawn up, and came to a ditch, and the enemy let fly at us (a company of Langdale's men that was newly raised). They shot at the skies, which did so encourage our men, that they were willing to venture upon any attempt . . .[7]

Langdale's predicament threw the Scots into confusion. First Hamilton ordered Baillie to stop the army's advance over the bridge so that they could go to Langdale's aid, but this was immediately countermanded after Callendar interrupted with a different piece of advice. The Scottish infantry had been shorn of its cavalry, Middleton having not yet returned from Wigan, and it would be suicide to face Cromwell without the support of the horse. As had become the norm, Hamilton did not disagree, taking the decision, even though he knew that he was leaving Langdale's Englishmen to an uncertain fate at the hands of their fellow countrymen. Their only hope would be to fight their way back to Preston, cross the river and rejoin the Scottish army. The ignominious decision was only partially remedied by Hamilton's own courage in leading a party of lancers to the fighting on Ribbleton Moor, but his confused thinking and willingness to sacrifice his own men were beyond excuse.

After four hours of fighting against superior numbers Langdale's men started falling back on Preston. Their commander managed to reach Baillie's headquarters, but most of the infantry were forced to surrender, while the horse made their way north as best they could to join up with Monro. Their retreat allowed Cromwell's regiments to fall on the Scots, who retreated towards the Darwen, a tributary of the Ribble. Only nightfall and the steadily pouring rain stopped the death toll being higher than the estimated 1000 men they had lost.

Hamilton's army was still separated from its cavalry arm, and with Cromwell's men now to the north the road back to Scotland was blocked. A hurried council of war produced the usual disagreements:

Baillie and Turner wanted to make a stand but Callendar, the author of most of their misfortunes, advised that a night march on Wigan would allow them to meet up with Middleton and face Cromwell with a stronger force. In vain did the experienced Turner urge that it was a recipe for disaster to march an exhausted army through the night without transport, Callendar had the last word. Musketeers were ordered to take only enough powder for their flasks while the rest would be blown up with a long fuse to disguise their intentions. Shorn of most of their kit, the dispirited men started out for Wigan, taking the route through Standish. They were not to know that further to the east Middleton was bringing up his cavalry through Chorley, neither side being aware of the other's presence. To complete the farce the long fuse was extinguished in the rain and large supplies of much-needed powder fell into parliamentary hands.

In any case the next stage of the battle was already as good as lost: Hamilton had barely left when Cromwell realised that the Royalist army was on the march, and he acted quickly and decisively to counter the move. Dividing his forces he put 4000 men in Preston to defend it from an expected attack by Monro's force while two regiments of cavalry, led by Colonel Francis Thornhaugh, set off in pursuit of the Scots. In the early morning of 18 August they collided with Middleton's horse and both sides took heavy casualties, among whom were Thornhaugh, a favourite of Cromwell's, and Sir John Hurry, who was wounded and taken prisoner. At the same time Baillie's foot were drawn up on Standish Moor to the north of Wigan, and to the advancing parliamentary army it appeared as if they were about to make a stand, but without dry powder and soaked to the skin the Scots had no stomach for further fighting. Instead they withdrew first to Wigan and then on to Warrington, where they hoped to be reinforced by Byron's Welshmen. Their flight was to no avail. Not only were they outnumbered, they were also tired, hungry and far from home. All they had left was their pride and their fighting spirit, and they needed both when Cromwell's men fell on them at Winwick to the north of Warrington. Both sides fought with equal ferocity and determination, the Scots because there was nothing left for them but to fight to the last and the Ironsides because they were savagely keen to bring the war to an end. Pike pushed against pike for a good three hours before the remnants of Hamilton's army of invasion broke and fled the field. Many were killed by the outraged local population as they made their way into Warrington to begin the hopeless task of defending the bridge. Ten thousand men were taken prisoner after Baillie sued for terms, but not before he begged his men to shoot him rather than face the disgrace. The battle is remembered for Cromwell's telling phrase that the victory was 'nothing but the hand of God', but he also left a more prosaic description for the edification of parliament:

> We held them in some dispute till our army came up, they maintaining the pass with great resolution for many hours; ours and theirs coming to push of pike and very close charges, and forced us give ground; but our men, by the blessing of God, quickly recovered it, and charging very hard upon them, beat them, from their standing, where we killed about a thousand, and took (as we believe) about two-thousand prisoners.[8]

In fact the numbers were higher, as was his computation of the size of the opposition (he told parliament 21,000), but the defeat of the Engagers' army was total. Those who escaped from the killing fields of Winwick did not fare much better than those taken prisoner. The cavalry fled south, led by Hamilton and taking with them Callendar, Langdale and Turner. There were bitter recriminations on the way, Callendar and Hamilton 'each blaming the other for the misfortune', and after they reached Uttoxeter in Staffordshire the men refused to go any further. True to type, Callendar took himself off, eventually reached London and escaped to the sanctuary of the Netherlands. Langdale followed his example but only reached Nottingham, where he fell into parliamentary hands, only to escape later, unbelievably, given his height and age, dressed as a milkmaid. Middleton, too, was captured and sent to prison in Newcastle, from which he also escaped, but the luckless Hamilton was forced to capitulate to Lambert, who had been ordered by Cromwell to pursue and capture the Royalist horse. Put on trial for treason under his English title, the Earl of Cambridge, he was executed the following spring in the company of the equally hapless Earl of Holland and Lord Capel.

Just as the General Assembly had warned when the venture began – on 12 July they condemned Hamilton as a traitor to the Covenant and declared the Engagement to be 'sinful' – the treaty with Charles was a disaster for Scotland, and there was more trouble in the offing. Those who had been watching and waiting to see the outcome of the Engagement put their opposition to it into practice. As the news from Preston trickled back to Scotland there was a new uprising in the south-west as anti-Engager Covenanters threw out the remaining cavalry troops which had been quartered on them. Most of the insurgents were poorly armed religious extremists, but they captured the mood of that section of Scottish society who opposed the Engagement and they attracted to their cause several noblemen, including Eglinton and Leven. Their revolt spread into the central belt and once they had assembled in sufficient numbers they marched on Edinburgh. This became known as the 'Whiggamore Raid', the term coming from the Scots word 'whig', to spur on a horse,* and it marked the final collapse of the Engagement.

Edinburgh opened its gates to the insurgents in the first week of September, Leven secured the castle and David Leslie announced that he was siding with Argyll, who was making preparations to return to the capital from his self-imposed exile in Inverary. Loudoun also threw his hat into the ring, a tactful move as the power of the Campbells was once more in the ascendant. The Estates, now led by Lanark, were forced to flee to Stirling, where they received the protection of Monro's Ulster forces, fresh from their escape from the north of England. A new civil war seemed inevitable. Monro and Lanark believed that their remaining Engager forces had the edge over the opposition: a collection of poorly equipped Whiggamores, Argyll's Campbell clansmen, and the retinues of Eglinton, Cassilis and other Lowland noblemen. In purely military terms they were probably right – Argyll's clansmen were repulsed outside Stirling on 12 September – but they had not reckoned on Cromwell, who had brought his Ironsides up to the Scottish border and was demanding the return of Berwick and Carlisle. If not, what he could not achieve by persuasion would be gained by force.

---

* According to Bishop Burnet the insurgents used the word 'whiggam' to encourage their horses. At first only fundamentalist Covenanters were known as Whigs, but by 1689 it was applied to the 'Petitioners' who supported the exclusion from the succession of James, Duke of York.

In fact Cromwell's demands were reasonably moderate and couched in language which the Covenanters understood. A letter of 18 September to Loudoun, recently appointed Chancellor of the new administration, reflected more on what they had in common than on any fundamental differences: 'the late dispensation, in giving so happy success against your and our enemies in our victories, may be the foundation of the union of the people of God in love and unity'.[9] It was not strictly true, as Cromwell was still vitally opposed to the Presbyterianism which the Covenanters demanded, but the cordial messages struck the right note and both sides were prepared to concede that they were the Godly party and for the time being could act in union. For their part the Estates saw that resistance was pointless and on 26 September conceded their power to Argyll and ordered Monro and his men to return to Ulster. The first decision was implemented but the second was frustrated by events in Ireland, where the growing parliamentary forces in Ulster under General George Monck had surprised Robert Monro and recaptured the Scottish strongholds in Belfast, Coleraine and Carrickfergus. Old Monro was sent to London as a prisoner while his nephew George was forced into exile in the Netherlands. Monck, an experienced professional soldier on the Royalist side, had been a prisoner in the Tower of London until 1646 when he took the Covenant and was sent to Ireland to support Jones in his efforts against the armies of the Confederation.

With peace in the air Cromwell took his army into Scotland and on 4 October entered Edinburgh, where he lodged in the Canongate and enjoyed the dubious honour of dining with Argyll and Wariston. They may or may not have discussed the future fate of the king – no record exists apart from Turner's second-hand comment that 'they agreed with him in my Lady Home's house in the Canongate, that there was a necessity to take away the King's life – but it was hardly a meeting of true minds.* As Gardiner so neatly put it, 'the head of the English party of toleration could hardly long remain on good terms with the head of the Scottish party of intolerance', and so it would prove, but between

---

* While welcoming the downfall of the Engagers, Robert Baillie reminded his cousin William Spang that the 'cursed army of Sectaries' was still in being.

them Cromwell and Argyll cobbled together a deal which kept the alliance together without achieving any longer-term aims. All Engager military units were to be disbanded and by an Acts of Classes those who had supported the Engagement (and, earlier, Montrose) were to be disqualified from holding public office for a period of years which would be decided by their complicity in the attack on England. The Church, too, was purged: over a hundred ministers lost their livings for failing to condemn the Engagement and lay patronage of ministers was abolished – henceforth they would be chosen by local church sessions. Argyll and Wariston re-emerged as the dominant personalities and the Kirk Party, as it was known, was in the ascendant.[10]

Although Cromwell failed to recognise the fact that these men still held to the Solemn League and Covenant and still prayed for the divine day when Presbyterianism would be triumphant, he was well pleased with the settlement and rode south three days later, leaving Lambert in Scotland with two regiments to support the new regime. From Edinburgh he made his way to Durham, where he began preparations for laying siege to Pontefract Castle, the last remaining Royalist stronghold which was still holding out and would continue to do so until March the following year. Its reduction was essential but as Cromwell told parliament 'the place is very well known to be one of the strongest inland garrisons in the kingdom; well watered; situated upon a rock in every part of it, and therefore very difficult to mine'. From inside its walls its defenders had also terrorised the surrounding countryside, causing outrage by sending out four soldiers to murder Thomas Rainsborough, the hero of Putney and the villain of the Downs, at his house in Doncaster. Although Cromwell kept in touch with his friends in parliament during the operations which he described as his 'waiting posture', he did not return to London until 6 December, by which time the army was once more in control of parliament.

Chapter Four

PRIDE'S PURGE

'Let us look into providences, surely they mean somewhat. They
hang so together, have been so constant, so clear and unclouded.'

Oliver Cromwell to Colonel Robert Hammond,
6 November 1648

Far from helping the king, the failure of the Royalist military
operations in 1648 convinced many of the army's leaders that there
could never be any satisfactory agreement with Charles. The Royalists
had broken the peace and plunged the country into another vicious
war and the king himself had displayed bad faith by using a Scottish
army to protect his interests and to overturn the victory of 1645; if
further outrages were to be prevented, then the issue of the king had
to be settled. More moderate members in the House of Commons
also scented this new mood and began to fear that the army might
take the matter into its own hands and encourage the introduction of
unwelcome reforms. That fear spurred them to resume negotiations
with the king, but – as Turner saw it – and having witnessed events
from the outset he was no mean judge – the defeat at Preston and the
severity with which the army had responded to the uprisings marked
the beginning of the end of the king's cause:

It is a true saying, 'Man proposes', and 'God disposes'; neither is it
in the power, or within the reach of the wit of weak man, to project

a business with so much caution, or prosecute it with so much industry, prudence or courage, but it may be blasted from Heaven, and rendered unsuccessful by these contingencies which can neither be foreseen nor prevented. The truth of this we found in this unhappy expedition. What was intended for the king's relief and restoration, posted him to his grave.[1]

At the time Turner was being held a prisoner in Hull, where his soldierly bearing had won him a number of privileges, and he wrote that passage with the benefit of hindsight, but he was not far wrong in saying that once the Scots had invaded England and been defeated the king's life hung in the balance. One of two extremes would decide the issue. On the one hand there were the moderates, mainly Presbyterians, who looked for limited political, constitutional and religious reforms and who had no quarrel with the king's person. On the other hand stood the Independents, still a minority, for whom the recent war had been fought for quite different aims, namely the radical reconstruction of Church and state and the dawning of a new age of godliness. For them Charles stood in the way of introducing wider-ranging social and religious reforms. Both parties were wary of the other's motives. The moderates feared that the Independents, backed by the army, would create a democratic revolution which would change for the worse England's social and political fabric, while for their part the Independents could see little point in entering into a personal treaty with the king. Somewhere in the middle ground, outside politics in the English shires, there was a general yearning for peace and the return of a settled social order: Nathaniel Fiennes caught the mood with his comment in the late summer of 1648 that most people were tired of civil strife and wanted 'a safe, well-grounded peace'.

Against that background, on 1 September, parliament appointed fifteen commissioners to enter into a new round of negotiations with the king. Both parliamentary factions were represented, although the moderates were in the majority, and in a spirit of reconciliation it was also decided to include Scots advisers, even though parliament had condemned them as 'enemies to this kingdom'. At first it was thought that the talks should take place in London but, fearing an outbreak of public support for the king, it was agreed to hold them in the town hall of Newport on the Isle of Wight. Basically, the points at issue were those which had been rehearsed earlier at Hampton Court and, surprisingly, in the early stages the talks proceeded at a goodly pace. Charles was allowed to sit under a canopy of state backed by his closest advisers, including the earls of Richmond and Southampton, and to the delegates he seemed relaxed and regal in his demeanour, almost as if he were back in the early days of his personal rule. Both delegations faced each other across a large table, and the debate was conducted in a way to be known later as 'proximity talks', both parties being free to discuss sensitive points in the privacy of adjoining rooms.

After the talks opened on 18 September agreement was quickly reached on the need for the king to drop all wartime declarations once the treaty had been agreed and to admit that parliament had been forced to wage war in its 'just and lawful defence'. It was a bitter, though necessary, physick for the king, but worse was to follow when the matter of religion was raised. Once again it proved to be the principal stumbling block. On 25 September the commissioners reiterated their demand for the abolition of the prayer book and episcopacy and for the introduction of Presbyterianism in their place, and once again Charles prevaricated. The debate continued into October, with Charles only making the modest concession that he was prepared to accept Presbyterianism for three years, an offer which parliament was not prepared to accept, on the grounds that the king would be free to change his mind once the period of grace had ended. Sir John Evelyn, an Independent, spoke for both factions in the House of Commons when he said: 'The army and well-affected abroad would think very strangely that the King should be at liberty, and no further security given for their liberties than his bare word, and, therefore, I humbly conceive that if the King's offers were so large as we desire, yet in no case ought we to yield that he should come hither till they were passed into acts.'[2]

On the political front matters went more smoothly. Charles agreed to surrender control of the militia for twenty years and to subject the selection of ministers to parliamentary approval. He also conceded to parliament the right of governance of Ireland and in return was granted a compromise on the punishment of the 'delinquents' who had supported him; but on episcopacy he was obdurate. For all that two of the commissioners, Holles and Harbottle Grimston, went down on bended knee to entreat Charles to yield as much as possible lest the army intervene, the king gave no ground. On the signing of the Covenant which formed part of the proposals to introduce Presbyterianism he merely said that Scottish interests would have to be taken into account, and on the episcopalian question he insisted that bishops should remain in office after the period of Presbyterian Church government had been introduced but only with the 'counsel and assistance of Presbyters'. As he had shown while fencing with the Scottish divines in Newcastle in 1646, Charles argued his case forcefully and intelligently, delighting in the debate with the divines who accompanied the parliamentary commissioners.

When dealing in public for high stakes Charles was in his element, and the Earl of Salisbury noted that 'the king is wonderfully improved' – but the issues involved in the debate were too dear to his heart to allow the concessions to be made without hurting his conscience. Even though he sensed that he had to make them to keep the army at bay, both for his sake and parliament's, he was not unaware of the sacrifice both to himself and his high office. In his desperation his mind turned once again to escape. Newport offered greater opportunities than the confines of Carisbrooke and he had hopes that his host in Newport, William Hopkins, would produce a plan which might enable him to slip away. Considering the concessions he had made, which were far more comprehensive than anything he had been prepared to yield at Newcastle or Hampton Court, Charles was all too aware that he was giving up his authority for little more than his own salvation. As he told Hopkins in a letter written on the evening after the militia concession (9 October) he had to escape if only to salve his conscience:

I pray you rightly to understand my condition, which I confess, yesternight I did not fully enough explain, through want of time. It is this: notwithstanding my too great concessions already made, I know that, unless I shall make yet others which will directly make me no King, I shall be at best but a perpetual prisoner. Besides – if this were not, of which I am too sure – the adhering to the Church – from which I cannot depart, no, not in show – will do the same: and, to deal freely with you, the great concession I made this day – the Church, militia, and Ireland – was made merely in order to my escape, of which I had not hope, I would not have done; for then I could have returned to my strait prison without reluctancy; but now, I confess, it would break my heart, having done that which only an escape can justify. To be short, if I stay for a demonstration of their further wickedness, it will be too late to seek a remedy; for my only hope is that now they believe I dare deny them nothing, and so be less careful of their guards.[3]

It was a fair diagnosis. His position was being gradually eroded and power was ebbing away from him. If the terms of the personal treaty were accepted he would be little more than a creature of parliament, a puppet ruler like the Doge of Venice. Just as intolerable, by making the concessions he had disavowed the divine authority of his position, and in so doing had committed the 'greatest sin' of his life. The only way out of that moral maze was the escape to France which should have been attempted when he first broke out of Hampton Court the previous year. However, despite Hopkins's best efforts any chance of fleeing had long gone – during the negotiations Newport had become an armed camp – and as winter began to take a grip on the land Charles remained as much a prisoner as he had ever been. He still clung to hopes that help might arrive from an outside source – from Henrietta Maria in France, from the Prince of Wales's fleet in Helvoetsluys or from Ormond in Ireland – but neither his wife nor his son could marshal the necessary forces and his correspondence with Ormond, which was common knowledge, only betrayed his duplicitous nature. At the very time that Charles was conceding the governance of Ireland to parliament he was busily telling his lord lieutenant: 'though you will hear that this treaty is near, or at least most likely to be concluded, yet believe it not; but pursue the way you are in [an alliance with the Confederates] with all possible speed'.[4]

When the period allowed for debate expired on 6 November it was extended for a further fortnight, and then for another four days, but although an agreement of sorts was patched up on 27 November events elsewhere were conspiring to kill off the personal treaty. From the very beginning of the negotiations the army and its more radical supporters in parliament had been suspicious of any attempt to reach an accord with the man they held to be responsible for the recent turmoil. Increasingly seen as a focus for anti-monarchist sentiment,

Ludlow had led the way early in September when he told Fairfax that the army would have to involve itself in politics 'to prevent the ruin of themselves and the nation'. Ireton, too, was keen to use the army to protect the revolution and if necessary to arrest Charles. Described by Burnet as having 'the principles and temper of a Cassius in him', Cromwell's son-in-law had come to the conclusion that the negotiations in Newport had to be ended as a prelude to Charles's arrest but, as was the case with Ludlow, his request for military intervention was studiously ignored by Fairfax. Demonstrating commendable caution, 'Black Tom' stayed put with his soldiers in St Albans, insisting that their chief grievance was the absence of pay.

And yet the reckoning could not be postponed much longer. On 11 September the Levellers had published a new document, the *Humble Petitions of Well-Affected Persons*, which called for the immediate implementation of the *Agreement of the People*. It attracted 40,000 signatures and its agenda was thoroughly radical – it included a call for annual elections, religious toleration, the banning of conscription, equality before the law and trial by jury, the abolition of imprisonment for debt and the freeing of trade from monopoly restrictions. It was a persuasive document and its timing was shrewd. In the aftermath of the Putney Debates the Leveller leadership had been sidelined, a position they had been forced to accept during the summer campaigns, but in the uncertain atmosphere created by the Newport negotiations they clearly believed that the time had come to restate their case and to take the opportunity of 'making this a truly happy and wholly Free Nation'. The petition was rejected by parliament, but this only led to fresh rioting during which new and persistent calls were heard for the abolition of the monarchy.

During and after the Putney confrontation Ireton had made no secret of his opposition to the Levellers' philosophy of 'natural rights', which he believed would destroy the 'most original, the most civil constitution of this kingdom, and which is above all, the constitution by which I have any property'. Now he was not sure that he could further his political aims without their support and thought that the time might have come for an alliance, albeit temporary, with them. Unable to prompt Fairfax into action he took himself off to Windsor, where he rapidly produced a new set of propositions contained in a document entitled *Remonstrance of the*

Army. Described by Whitelocke as 'the beginning of the design against the King's person', this was the first attempt to articulate a manifesto for a post-monarchical Britain.

Its message was hard-line and radical and its vocabulary suitably severe. In the opening passages Charles's record during the recent conflict was rehearsed, as was the support of those 'delinquents' who had aided and abetted him. Above all, the king stood condemned of causing 'all the bloodshed in these intestine wars', and unless this guilt was acknowledged there was the fresh danger that parliament might decide to 're-inthrone' him as a result of the Newport talks. To prevent that the *Remonstrance* concluded with a demand that Charles be brought to justice and the monarchy abolished; and furthermore, the current parliament should be annulled and a new House of Commons elected on a revised electoral system. For a country which had been ruled by the checks and balances provided by monarch and parliament, England found itself on the verge of becoming a republic, forced on it by the will of a small number of army officers.

Ireton was bound by moral chains to that cause but he also understood how precarious was his position. Parliament might yet reach an accord with the king, London might be reclaimed by Royalist supporters, and the old order restored. It was all possible; Charles only had to yield to Presbyterianism, a Treaty of Newport would come into being and the immediate crisis would be resolved. To prevent that, Ireton had to find allies, and his first port of call was the army's headquarters in St Albans, where the Council of Officers met on 7 November to spend four days debating the *Remonstrance of the Army*. This time there was no repetition of the high democracy of Putney when debate was open to rank and file. Only officers attended, but a majority voiced doubts about purging parliament and arresting the king – Fairfax led the way with his disapproval of any move which was 'tending to overthrow the government of the kingdom', and that proved to be the majority verdict. Although the northern regiments voiced their support for the *Remonstrance*, at the end of the conference the Council remained undecided, much to Ireton's dismay.

Fearing that he might be outflanked, Ireton did what politicians have always done when they want to push through unpopular legislation: he entered into a coalition with his opponents, namely the Levellers. When the St Albans conference came to an end he, Hugh

Peters and Colonel Thomas Harrison met with Leveller leaders at the Nag's Head Tavern in the Strand to discuss and agree additional and more extreme modifications to the *Remonstrance*. In this revised form parliament would dissolve itself and a new body would be elected incorporating many of the Levellers' recommendations from their *Agreement of the People*. It is doubtful if Ireton would have activated these proposals – he was against any radical reform of the franchise – but the Nag's Head meeting gave him the political support he needed and its findings would put further pressure on the army. A new constitutional settlement was now inevitable: as Cromwell's secretary Richard Spavin noted in a letter to his friend William Clarke, the old order was changing and giving way to something new and much more demanding:

> I verily think God will break that great idol the Parliament, and that old job-trot form of government of King, Lords, and Commons. It is no matter how nor by whom, sure I am it cannot be worse if honest men have the managing of it – and no matter whether they be great or no . . . the Lord is about a great work, and such as will stumble many mean-principled men, and such as I think but few great ones shall be honoured withal.[5]

In its new form the *Remonstrance* was an extraordinary document in that it demanded the annulment and reform of an elected parliament and called for legal steps to be taken against the king, who would not be replaced 'upon the election of, and as upon trust from the people, by such their representatives, nor without disclaiming and disavowing all pretence to a negative voice against the determinations of the said representatives or Commons in Parliament'. In place of rule by the king abetted by council, this revolutionary document proposed its abolition and a radical extension of the franchise – all of which matched the demands of the Levellers. While the proposals were being finalised the Council of Officers sent their own terms to the king outlining the conditions he would have to accept in exchange for the army returning him and his family 'to a condition of safety, honour and freedom in this nation, without diminution to their personal rights, or farther limitation to the exercise of the regal power'.[6] As the new paper simply repeated demands for a permanent constitutional settlement which would have limited the Crown's authority while retaining an element of power for the army, Charles rejected the offer, a decision which left Fairfax and his officers with no option but to accept Ireton's *Remonstrance*. With some abruptness it was sent to parliament on 20 November together with a demand for immediate payment of arrears.

Revolution was now in the air, and the balance of power had suddenly switched to Ireton and the army. Even at that late stage parliament still hoped to retrieve its position by forcing the king to accept enough of their conditions to secure a personal treaty – one of their commissioners, John Crewe, wrote despairingly on 6 November asking for 'a satisfactory answer to the King's propositions' – but they too were running out of time and options. Fatally, they postponed consideration of the *Remonstrance* for a week in the hope of getting better news from Newport, and two days later Fairfax ordered the army to move its headquarters from St Albans to Windsor to bring it within striking distance of London. On 26 November Peters conducted a lengthy prayer meeting – it lasted eight hours – 'to direct them [Council of Officers] in the great business now at hand', and while the soldiers sought comfort and a sign from their God, matters were moving inexorably to the endgame suggested by a Leveller slogan of the day:

> The Treaty's now affected, all's agreed;
> Draw, draw for Freedom, or we're slaves indeed.

Faced by agreeing to a document which would have voted them out of existence the House of Commons did its best to put off the evil hour. When the extended period for negotiation came to an end on 27 November, the day when their commissioners finally left the Isle of Wight, they postponed the debate for another four days, a move which sealed the king's fate. While Fairfax distrusted the main thrust of the *Remonstrance* the latest move at Westminster was evidence that parliament meant to continue its negotiations for a treaty, come what may. As he also knew that Charles was intent on a last-minute escape it was essential to bring the king into the army's custody. The only obstacle was Colonel Hammond, who was about to discover the truth behind his frightened comment to Berkeley and Ashburnham that by bringing the king to him on the Isle of Wight they had undone him. The first intimation had come earlier in the month in a letter urging on him the necessity to secure Charles from escape; the second came in an order from Fairfax commanding him to return to army headquarters to allow another officer, Colonel Isaac Ewer, to take his place. A man of scrupulous morals, Hammond replied that, as his orders had come originally from parliament, he was honour-bound to carry them out and could not be countermanded by the army. However, as an army officer his loyalty was also to Fairfax and the high command; struggling with his conscience to find a way to satisfy both parties he decided to cross over to Windsor for further consultation, leaving his command in the charge of his deputy officers, who were enjoined to prevent the king's removal unless the order came from parliament.

It was to no avail. On 1 December Fairfax ordered that the king be removed from Newport and taken under close guard with Herbert across the Solent to the grim surroundings of Hurst Castle, a sixteenth-century fortress or blockhouse guarding the seaward approaches. The following day the army moved on London and quickly occupied it, taking key points and installing Fairfax's headquarters in Whitehall; as a military coup it was economically executed and the result highly effective. While troops watched the streets parliament met for an all-night session on 5 December during which they denounced the king's removal as being illegal, but their influence had now all but disappeared. Those who still held out hopes of an agreement with the king were considered to be guilty of trying to restore him and his authority, while as Lucy Hutchinson reported, 'on the other side, it so frightened all the honest people, that it made them as violent in their zeal to pull down, as the others were in their madness to restore, this kingly idol':

> Colonel Hutchinson was that night among them, and being convinced in his conscience that both the cause, and all those who with an upright honest heart asserted and maintained it [concessions to the king], were betrayed and sold for nothing, he told them that the king, after having been exasperated, vanquished and captivated, would be restored by that power which was inconsistent with the liberty of the people, who, for all their blood, treasure and misery,

would reap no fruit, but a confirmation of their bondage. It had been a thousand times better never to have struck one stroke in the quarrel, than, after victory, to yield up a righteous cause; whereby they should not only betray the interest of their country and the trust reposed in them, and those zealous friends who had engaged to the death for them, but be false to the covenant of their God, which was to extirpate prelacy, not to lease it.[7]

On the following day the coup entered its second and decisive stage when Ireton decided to purge parliament of all those members who opposed the *Remonstrance*. His chosen instrument was Colonel Thomas Pride, said to have once been a brewer's drayman and one of the new men in the army – officers who held their rank not on account of social background but from their ability. Most were from a lower class than Ireton and Cromwell – Ewer had been a domestic servant – and in their presence in positions of power the radical and democratising aims of the *Remonstrance* were made manifest.

Acting on Ireton's orders, but without Fairfax's knowledge, Pride took his soldiers to the House of Commons early in the morning of 6 December and took up position by the lobby. Accompanied by Lord Grey of Groby, an enthusiastic anti-monarchist who was asked to identify those who opposed the army, Pride's task was simple – to block entrance to those who had voted for the treaty with the king. It was a crude but effective move. Around 140 members were refused admission and turned away; of these 41 were arrested and secured first in a basement room nicknamed 'Hell' and then in various taverns in the Strand, leaving a 'rump' of 156 members, all of whom were considered to be malleable. When the members asked by whose authority the soldiers had acted – the king's name had not been mentioned – Peters, who was present, replied: 'By the power of the sword.'

Fairfax was reported to be furious about the action but he was powerless to do anything about it. The rump of members also tried to secure the release of those imprisoned, and succeeded in freeing two, Nathaniel Fiennes and Sir Benjamin Rudyerd, both of whom had flirted with the pro-treaty faction, but it was not until a few days later that the rest were eventually sent home on parole. As Peters had so rightly put it, the 'rump' parliament was no longer responsible to the people but to the might of the army. That much became clear in the ensuing days when up to 80 members refused to attend and a much slimmed down House of Commons was forced to push through legislation to revoke the repeal of the Vote of No Addresses and to annul all the votes made in favour of accepting the treaty with the king. Those who remained did so for many reasons – self-vindication, personal fear or a blinkered vision of duty. Whitelocke, soon to make a prudent departure to the country, neatly expressed the dilemma facing him and his fellow unpurged members:

Many of these, upon debate and advice of friends, and considerations that they were chosen by their country to serve for them in this parliament, and that the violence was not offered to these, but to other members, whereof these were not made the judge, nor was it left in their power to desert the parliament and their trust, while they might have liberty to continue in that service. Their reasons persuaded many to continue.[8]

Events were now moving quickly. In rapid succession a number of moderate members and former army officers were detained and jailed without trial on the charge of treasonably cooperating with the Scots – these included Browne, Clotworthy, Massey (who managed to escape) and Waller, all of whom had served parliament with distinction in the fighting between 1642 and 1645. 'Seized upon by the Army as I was going to discharge my duty in the House of Commons,' noted the latter, 'and contrary to privilege of Parliament made a prisoner in the Queen's Court. From thence carried ignominiously to a place under the Exchequer called Hell, and the next day to the King's Head in the Strand; after singled out, as a sheep to the slaughter, and removed to St James's.'[9] Waller spent the next three years under lock and key, as did Browne, who was imprisoned in Wales, where he claimed he was treated worse than any Royalist.

Thus did the Long Parliament enter its most ignominious phase – 'this fag-end, this veritable Rump of a Parliament with corrupt maggots in it', as one contemporary described it, thereby giving it its alternative name. Its immediate purpose was to establish a means of trying Charles as a war criminal, and this it did with a will, passing an ordinance on 1 January 1649 establishing a High Court of Justice before which the king would be tried for betraying the compact he had with his people, the justification for the move being that 'by the fundamental laws of this kingdom, it is treason in the King of England for the time being to levy war against the Parliament and kingdom of England'. It was a high-risk strategy, for it was by no means certain that those who plotted against the king's person had the total support of the country, but at a time when military might was the deciding factor the Rump Parliament was in an unassailable position. Nonetheless, for all that a military coup had taken place and for all that the army held sway there were still doubts about the legality of what had taken place.

Within the Army Council, which was engaged in framing a new *Agreement of the People*, there was much heart-searching about the godliness or sinfulness of their actions, and their culpability should they be wrong. So full of self-doubt was the atmosphere – balanced to a certain extent by a mood of self-justification – that the uncertainty permitted an extraordinary intervention which smacked more of quackery than any religious intent. Towards the end of December an approach was made by Elizabeth Pool, a young woman variously described as a 'virgin' or 'a monstrous witch', who had experienced visions which seemed to suggest that the army was right to try the king, that she had witnessed 'a woman crooked, weak, sick and imperfect in body' (England) who would be cured by 'a man who is a member of the army'. Here was the divine intervention which many had been seeking, the message coming from a devout young woman: 'The divine will calls me to believe, and you to act.' Later she would change her tune and her mumbo-jumbo would be directed against those who demanded the king's death, but it is an indication of the tensions of that midwinter season that battle-hardened and devout men who had fought at Naseby were prepared to heed the superstitious ramblings of an unknown woman.[10]

By then Cromwell had returned to London from the siege of Pontefract – his critics claimed, unkindly and foolishly, that he had tutored Elizabeth Pool – and his presence was to be a deciding factor in the events that followed. He arrived back on Fairfax's orders shortly after Pride's Purge, telling Ludlow that while he had known nothing of it, 'since it was done he was glad of it, and would endeavour to maintain it'.[11] His absence in his 'waiting posture' in the north had been to his advantage, as he had not been asked to show his hand too early and had been allowed the luxury of awaiting the outcome of what he held as 'providences' – waiting on events and God's will before acting. Cynics argued that this is a shorthand for the application of fate to excuse or explain the need for action, but Cromwell would have none of it, telling parliament that 'feigned necessities, imaginary necessities, are the greatest cozenage that men can put upon the providence of God'. There he was speaking as a Puritan who believed absolutely in predestination, the Protestant belief in the existence of an elect whose actions are justified as part of God's covenant with man on condition of repentance and obedience. To be one of the elect was to have entered into a concordat in which God's providence was ever-present and all-consuming, and Cromwell understood its force and solemnity, seeing in it, as he told Hammond in November, 'some glorious and high meaning'.

If providence guided events then Cromwell was equally sure that he had to respond accordingly, and once back in London he quickly entered the debate on the king's future. To begin with he hoped that some means might be found to offer a compromise which would yet save the king's life but, as the month wore on and Charles rejected yet another overture from the army, he began to change his tune. God had cast this providence on them, he told parliament, and they must act accordingly. By the time the year ended he was more forthright. 'I tell you we will cut off his head with the crown on it,' he urged in a memorably bloodthirsty phrase. As with many key moments in his life Cromwell deliberated long and hard before making up his mind, but once a decision had been reached he displayed limpet-like qualities in remaining true to his own mind.[12]

As for Charles, he too was on the move. On 19 December he was taken from Hurst Castle back to Windsor, where conditions were more to his liking and where he was guarded by Thomas Harrison, who made no secret of his desire to have the king executed. Charles sensed this and asked the colonel if he meant to murder him, only to receive the reply that the king must face the law, which was 'equally obliging to great and small'. During the journey Charles thought again of escape, but as that would mean breaking his parole he continued to Windsor, ironically the very place where the army had agreed to punish that 'man of blood', Charles Stewart. There he was treated with some solemnity and allowed to pray in the chapel of St George, although to his regret he was unable to keep Christmas with customary 'pies and plum porridge'. On 19 January 1649 he was ushered into the royal coach and taken under Harrison's escort to St James's in London, now being used as a state prison.

Before leaving Hurst Charles had admitted to his son that he feared that the worst was about to happen: 'the corn is in the ground; we expect the harvest'. The season had finally arrived.

Chapter Five

THAT MEMORABLE SCENE

> 'He nothing common did or mean
> Upon that memorable scene,
>   But with his keener eye
>   The axe's edge did try;
> Nor called the gods, with vulgar spite,
> To vindicate his helpless right;
>   But bowed his comely head
>   Down, as upon a bed.'

> *Andrew Marvell, 'An Horatian Ode upon*
> *Cromwell's Return from Ireland', 1650*

The British were no strangers to regicide. William Rufus was killed in mysterious circumstances while hunting in the New Forest in 1100; his brother and successor Henry was the probable culprit. More recently Henry VI had died of 'pure displeasure and melancholy' in the Tower of London in 1471 – another way of saying that he was murdered, in his case by the Duke of Gloucester – and Richard III himself was the last English king to die on a battlefield (Bosworth, 1485).

The Scots, too, were not averse to killing their kings and, likewise, tribal enmities were often the cause. James I was murdered by conspirators in the Dominican Priory in Perth in 1437, and his grandson James III 'happinit to be slane' in a lowly cottage following his defeat by rebels at the Battle of Sauchieburn in 1488. James IV was the last Scottish king to die in battle (Flodden, 1513) but the closest parallel with Charles's predicament in 1649 was the case of Mary Queen of Scots, who was forced to abdicate twenty years before being executed in 1587 on the charge of plotting against her cousin Elizabeth.

Before signing the warrant Queen Elizabeth suffered agonies of conscience over the execution, but there was considerable support for her action, as the Scottish queen was a focus for Catholic discontent and she had already been implicated in a number of plots against the English Crown. Parliament in particular abhorred 'this most wicked and filthy woman'; and after Mary's execution at Fotheringhay Castle in Yorkshire the people of London celebrated in the streets. Even so, Mary was tried and condemned by a tribunal which had no right to sit in judgement over her. In keeping with contemporary legal practice she was not allowed a counsel to defend her and no witnesses were permitted to speak on her behalf, but the main complaint about her trial lay in its illegality – she was the ruler of another country, Scotland, and could hardly be tried for treason under English law. Logically, she should have been tried by her peers, but that was disallowed. In the end Mary provided the legality for her own trial before appointed commissioners by agreeing to appear before it, and in so doing she created the image of herself as a deeply wronged martyr. The nobility of her bearing and the quiet sincerity of her pleading lived on longer than any doubts about the English tribunal's right to actually put her to death, and the events created a lasting historical motif – the saintly doomed queen betrayed by her malevolent cousin.

As it had been with Mary, so it was with the grandson she would never see. Once the ordinance appointing the High Court of Justice had been established it was passed to the House of Lords, where it met its first opposition, the Earl of Northumberland declaring that its basic premise was wrong:

Not one in twenty of the people in England are yet satisfied whether the king did levy war against the Houses first, or the Houses first against him; and, besides, if the King did levy war first, we have no law extant that can be produced to make it treason in him to do; and, for us, my Lords, to declare treason by an Ordinance when the matter of fact is not yet proved, nor any law to bring to judge it by, seems very unreasonable.[1]

Just as there had been doubts about the legality of trying a monarch in Mary's case, so did the same arguments re-emerge in the House of Lords some sixty-two years later, and the ordinance was duly rejected. Under normal circumstances the Commons could not have proceeded further, but the times were out of joint and a streak of ruthlessness appeared in public affairs; on 4 January, using language that presaged the birth of the United States of America a century later, the Rump passed three further resolutions stating the legality of its position: 'That the people are, under God, the original of all just power: that the Commons of England, in Parliament assembled, being chosen by and representing the people, have the supreme power in this nation; that whatsoever is enacted or declared for law by the Commons in Parliament assembled, hath the force of law, and all the people of this nation are concluded thereby, although the consent and concurrence of King or House of Peers be not had thereunto.'[2] The resolution showed England what politics would be like without a king and without the checks and balances provided by the upper house.* Two days later, on 6 January, the ordinance became law as an act of parliament and the way was open to begin the legal proceedings against the king.

The resolution allowed for the appointment of officials 'for the hearing, trying and adjudging the said Charles Stuart', and these consisted of 135 commissioners who would act as judge and jury. Of those named only 68 appeared on the first day of the trial which opened in Westminster Hall on 20 January. Most of the army's commanders absented themselves, among them Skippon, Lambert and Fairfax, whose wife famously appeared in his stead to answer his summons with the stinging rebuke, 'He has more wit than to be here.' Ireton was there, as were Cromwell and Ludlow, but the tribunal lacked recognised legal minds, and that absence gave its proceedings more of the flavour of a show trial than any acknowledged legal assembly. To conduct the prosecution parliament had appointed four nonentities, most of England's senior judiciary including the Chief

---

* The Scots also denounced the trial when their parliament opened on 4 January. The complaint was repeated by Lothian and his fellow Scottish commissioners in London, who protested against any 'harm, injury or violence' being done to 'his Majesty's person'. Their plea was ignored.

Justice and the Attorney-General having washed their hands of the matter. The only one with any competence was John Cook, a well-travelled Gray's Inn barrister who happened to be a teetotaller and a committed social reformer ahead of his times – among other innovations he favoured the creation of a free health service. He was accompanied by John Ashe, the Attorney-General Anthony Steele, who defected at the last minute, and Isaac Dorislaus, a noted Dutch jurist and friend of Cromwell whose presence was thought to lend a sense of academic credibility to the occasion.

The Lord President or presiding judge was John Bradshaw, another barrister and judge of the Sheriff Courts, who found himself promoted beyond his experience and abilities. Born at Stockport in Cheshire in 1602 he had a reputation for being short-tempered and long-winded, but as a committed republican he was not unwilling to take his chance when it was offered to him. He had few doubts about the rightness of his behaviour but he must have had qualms about what he was doing, because underneath his robes he wore armour and, equally prudently, his beaver hat was lined with steel. Later, Milton was to say of Bradshaw that he was greater than 'all former Tyrannicides in the precise degree in which it is more manly, just and majestic, than to kill him Misjudged',[3] but that was a supporter speaking. Although Bradshaw was a good jurist he was pompous and slow-witted, as he showed when he failed to provide any satisfactory answer to Charles's charges that the court had no authority to try him. Like many others involved in the process of trying the king, he comforted himself with the thought that he was simply doing his duty to the country, its people and the God they worshipped.

Before the proceedings opened, the final arrangements for the trial were made in Westminster Hall, the seat of the English legal system. It was a massive building, begun under William Rufus in 1097, some 300 feet long and 100 feet high, the roof being notable for its huge hammered roof beams carved out of native oak. The edifice was home to a number of courts – the Court of Common Pleas, the King's Bench, Chancery and Court of Exchequer, all of which were constructed of movable partitions – and to try the king a new structure had been put in place. At the north end of the hall a stage had been built to seat Bradshaw, with his fellow judges placed behind him in three serried ranks. Two clerks sat at a table to take notes and the dock itself had a red velvet chair and a small table on which pen and paper had been placed. In an attempt at dignity a screen had been built behind the dock to conceal the king from the crowd behind, but this good intention was compromised by the construction of grandstands which contained seats for the wealthy and the curious to watch the unfolding drama.[4]

If the killing of kings had a precedent in English history then the great hall at Westminster had also witnessed its share of stirring moments. Two kings had lost their crowns within its walls, Edward II in 1327 and Richard II in 1399, and countless others had been condemned to death as villains or traitors. Sir William Wallace, patriot to the Scots, outlaw to the English, had been given the awful sentence of being hanged, drawn and quartered in 1305 after leading a guerrilla war against King Edward I; the saintly Thomas More was convicted of treason and executed in 1535, having resigned as Lord Chancellor on grounds of conscience three years earlier; and in more recent times the hall had been the place of trial for Charles's nemesis, the Earl of Strafford. Now it was to be the scene of another momentous event in the nation's history, one which would never be repeated, and as if to reinforce the fact that the court was in essence a military one, captured Royalist standards had been hung on display.

To this contrived place of justice Charles came on the morning of 20 January 1649, his escort being made up of halberdiers under the command of one Colonel Thornton. Earlier he had been moved under heavy guard by boat from St James's to the Whitehall Steps and from there by barge to the Westminster house of the antiquarian Sir Robert Cotton before being summoned into the great hall; the army was taking no chances of demonstrations in the king's favour. Charles had dressed carefully for the part, being clothed in black, the badge of the Order of the Star of the Garter prominent on his cloak and the bejewelled St George hanging from his neck on the order's blue ribbon. He cut an impressively regal figure, not least to the commissioners who nervously watched his arrival from the windows of the Painted Court. Among them was Cromwell, who was rumoured to have gone pale before reminding his fellow judges that the king's first question would be directed at the court's authority to try him and that they must have an answer. The silence was broken by the irrepressible republican Henry Marten, who boldly stated that it was being done 'in the name of the Commons in Parliament assembled and all the good people of England'.[5] Once again the regicides persuaded themselves that they were not a murderous minority acting on their own behalf but a group of righteous men acting for the greater common good. It was to be their only justification.

Charles's bearing was also noted by those who witnessed his entrance. He failed to remove his hat, as if to defy the court's legality, gazed firmly in the judges' direction and scornfully glanced round the crowded hall before taking his seat. Then Cook rose to read the charges against the king, namely that he had 'attempted to erect an unlimited and tyrannical power to rule according to his will, and, in pursuance of this design, had levied war against the present Parliament, and the people therein represented'. In a vain attempt to interrupt his tormentor Charles started banging his cane on the floor, only to see the silver tip fall off. It was an electrifying moment, one which no one present ever forgot. Cook stopped speaking as Charles looked helplessly around him, waiting for a servant to retrieve the tip just as he would have done on any other day of his reign. Suddenly he was alone and vulnerable, and with no one there to do his bidding Charles had to look to himself and pick up the tip. That done Cook continued with his task, recording that evidence would show that at several battles the king had been seen in arms and that he had been the instigator of the resumption of the fighting in 1648. This was enough to condemn him as 'a tyrant, traitor, murderer, and a public and implacable enemy of the Commonwealth of England'.[6]

On being hailed thus Charles let out a contemptuous laugh; then Bradshaw asked him how he pleaded before 'the Commons assembled in Parliament and the good people of England'. Charles had never been a confident speaker, but the intensity of the trial seemed to inspire him. He responded to Bradshaw's request with the statement that he would not answer the charge until he had been informed by what legal authority he was being tried. After all he had been arrested without charge and brought forcibly to London. Not without irony, he insisted that he was still their lawful king.

It was a credible challenge and it clearly irked Bradshaw: Charles, he explained, had been put on trial 'in the name of the people of England, of which you were elected king'. That was a mistake, Charles was not an elected king, and he responded by reminding the court of the hereditary principle and by claiming that he was more representative of his people 'than any here that come to be my pretended judges'. Although Bradshaw tried to deflect him, Charles was in full song, ending his protest with the declaration: 'Let me see a legal authority warranted by the Word of God, the Scriptures, or warranted by the constitution of the Kingdom and I will answer'. This was the response Cromwell had feared, and as no answer was forthcoming Bradshaw adjourned the court, while some members of the public called out 'Justice! Justice!' and others 'God save the King!' Two days later the court reassembled, only for the scene to be repeated: not only did Charles decline to plead but he continued to question the court's legality, telling Bradshaw that he refused to cooperate with a body which he held to be illegal:

It is not my case alone; it is the freedom and liberty of the people of England; and do you pretend what you will, I stand more for their liberties; for if power without law may make laws, may alter the fundamental laws of the kingdom, I do not know what subject he is in England that can be sure of his life, or anything he calls his own.[7]

To this Bradshaw responded that the court had the sanction of the House of Commons, only for Charles to claim that there was no precedent for that body being 'a Court of Judicature'. With Charles refusing to make any plea, Cook's charges were read again and on that stalemate the day's proceedings came to an end. The charade continued the following day, with Charles repeating his claim that he stood for the liberties of the people of England and Bradshaw telling the clerks to record the king's guilt by default. Faced by this impasse Bradshaw then adjourned the court to meet in private session in the adjoining Painted Hall. Meanwhile Charles was removed to Cotton's house, where he spent time with Bishop Juxon, who had asked to be his chaplain when the two men met earlier at St James's, the Bishop of London having been detained at the time of Pride's purging of parliament.

What followed next is difficult to piece together, for the session was held in camera, but the main activity seems to have centred on putting steel into those who were wavering. There were fears that Fairfax might use the army to intervene. Unlikely though this was – Fairfax certainly opposed the trial, but he would have refused to do anything which would have stirred up a new civil war involving the army – London was agog with rumours about the trial's legality and what might be done to stop Cromwell and his friends. A group of Presbyterian clergy had challenged the proceedings and the Scottish commissioners made the last of three bitter denunciations on 22 January, their ire being stirred as much by residual loyalty to their native-born king as by fear of what the future would hold after he had gone. As the members of the High Court of Justice continued talking in the Painted Hall, its energies were being directed towards only one goal: the condemnation and execution of the king.

The next day, 25 January, there was a return to a semblance of judicial procedure when 33 witnesses were produced to give evidence of the king's military crimes. He had been seen raising the standard at Nottingham and others had observed him in arms or giving orders at just about every battle from Edgehill to Naseby. All this was solemnly noted as evidence that Charles had levied war against his people, but the truth was that the court had already made its decision, or at least its more forceful members – Cromwell, Grey of Groby, Ireton, Harrison – had made it for them. As the gathering of evidence continued they were simply looking forward to the moment when they could proceed with the authorised execution of the king. That evening those commissioners present, only 46 of them, agreed that 'the court will proceed to sentence against Charles Stuart, King of England; that the condemnation of the King shall be for tyrant, traitor and murderer; that this condemnation shall extend to death'. From being tried as a traitor before a court which carried no authority, Charles would now face judicial execution by an executive body without any opportunity of pleading his case. The king was about to be put to death.

Showing his usual determination – once he had made up his mind he was never less than resolute – Cromwell was one of the chief movers, meeting objections with the argument that the king had broken his contract with the people and had to face the death sentence, and pushing aside lingering doubts about the legality of the court's actions. God's work was being done, he insisted, and they were the chosen instruments. All that remained was the need to find a larger quorum, and the next day 62 commissioners finally agreed the appropriate sentence, namely that Charles, 'as a tyrant, traitor, murderer and public enemy to the good of this nation, shall be put to death by the severing of his head from his body'.[8] Among the names on the warrant were those of Cromwell, Ireton, Pride, Harrison and Ewer, all soldiers who had fought in the recent war, and it seems that, having made up their minds, they consented to signing it with a good will.

Later, some tried to extenuate their actions by claiming that they had been coerced. One regicide, Sir Richard Ingoldsby, said that Cromwell had forced him to sign by marching him across the room and holding his hand; another, Thomas Waite, excused himself by saying that he had been tricked; but this was rewriting history after the event in an attempt to excuse themselves. Later they might have felt guilty about their actions, but the mood in Westminster that January was one of divine retribution and the need to right a wrong. After signing there were reports that some of the commissioners, Cromwell included, had inked one another's faces in the manner of boisterous schoolchildren, almost as if they had to find an outlet for what they had just done. Lucy Hutchinson was probably closer to the mark when she said that there was no coercion and 'that all men herein were left to their free liberty of acting, neither persuaded nor compelled; and as there were some nominated in the commission who never sat, and others who sat at first, but durst not hold on, so all the rest might have declined if they would'.[9] She was a good witness – among the signatures was her husband John's.

Having come to a conclusion the court reconvened in Westminster Hall after lunch to complete the terrible business. The crowd was large and expectant, Bradshaw was dressed in scarlet robes, a black hat on his head, and his guards were tense and strained. Realising that once sentence was passed he would forfeit his right to address the court, Charles took the initiative and asked to be heard. To this Bradshaw responded that he had been 'brought before the court to make answer to a charge of treason and other high crimes exhibited against him in the name of the people of England', but he was interrupted by a fresh disturbance in the public gallery. A masked woman's voice shouted out that it was a lie, that not a quarter of the people of England supported the trial and 'Oliver Cromwell is a traitor'. Once more it was thought to be the adventurous Lady Fairfax who made the interruption, and as the security guards raised their muskets she had to be escorted from the court.

After the uproar died down Bradshaw agreed that the king could address the court provided that he did not 'offer any debate'. Charles kept his word and made a moving and reasonable request for his case to be heard in front of the Commons and the Lords, an appeal which found some takers in the ranks behind Bradshaw. One commissioner, John Downes, member for Arundel, was sufficiently moved to support this right, asking of his fellow judges 'Have we hearts of stone?' and though he was hissed down by a furious Cromwell there was a brief adjournment to allow the point to be debated in a neighbouring room which housed the Inner Court of Wards.

Downes's intervention was to no avail. Cromwell persuaded the gathering that they were dealing with 'the hardest-hearted man that lives upon the earth' and the court reassembled to allow Bradshaw to sum up before the sentence of death was passed. Once more Charles tried to make himself heard but the trial was over and he was hustled out of the hall under escort and taken to Whitehall, where Juxon and Thomas Herbert, a secretary appointed by parliament, attended him. The following day he was taken to St James's Palace, the move designed so that he would not be troubled by the sound of workmen constructing the scaffold that was taking shape outside Inigo Jones's Banqueting Hall with its wondrous ceiling painting by Rubens completed in 1634 to celebrate the union of England with Scotland. It was a last piece of kindness: the court had already given orders to three officers, Colonel Francis Hacker, Colonel Huncks and Lieutenant-Colonel Phayre, that the king would die on Tuesday 30 January, a bare forty-eight hours later.

During his remaining time in this life Charles prepared himself as best he could and, as he had done so often before, he took comfort in the doctrines of the Church of England, the cause which he had supported for so long and so selflessly. Juxon, an uncomplicated and gentle man, administered to his spiritual needs, which centred on prayer, communion and the scriptures, taking his texts from the prayer book, that 'fatal book' (as he called it) which had been the cause of so many of his recent troubles. If there was a strong sense of fatalism in his sadly emasculated court it was balanced by Charles's serenity and religious faith as he made his own preparations to face the unknown. Some were practical. On the Monday he burned his papers and his cipher books and divided his remaining jewels among his retainers and his two youngest children. He had already received a last letter from the Prince of Wales from The Hague, where he had been attempting to encourage the Dutch to intervene on his behalf,* but the most poignant moment came when he said his farewells to Princess Elizabeth and Prince Henry, both of whom had been held in custody since 1645.

He had not seen them for fifteen months and they were bewildered and scared – the princess was thirteen and a weakly child, Henry only ten. To his daughter he said that she must learn to forgive those who were about to put him to death, that he was about to die 'a Glorious death . . . for the laws and liberties of this land and for maintaining the true Protestant religion' and that following his martyrdom (for so it seemed to him) 'the Lord should settle his throne on his son, and that we shall all be happier than we could have expected to have been had he lived'. Not unnaturally these words had a dreadful effect on the girl, for she suddenly understood what was about to happen and she burst into tears, saying that she would never forget. Nor did she, penning a description of the day's harrowing events that very evening. His words to the young Duke of Gloucester were no less comforting:

Sweetheart, now they will cut off thy father's head; mark, child, what I say: they will cut off my head and perhaps make thee a king; but, mark what I say: you must not be a king so long as your brothers Charles and James do live; for they will cut off your brothers' heads when they can catch them, and cut off thy head too at the last, and therefore I charge you do not be made a king by them.[10]

Solemn the statement might have been, but Charles's words were sincerely meant. He was keenly aware that on his death his eldest son would succeed him immediately and that parliament might then

---

* There were claims that the Prince of Wales sent the generals a blank sheet of paper with his signature inviting them to name their conditions, but although it exists in the Bodleian Library, Oxford, it is not believed to be authentic.

create Henry as a puppet ruler, thereby sowing the seeds of a future dynastic struggle. He was not to know that parliament was already wrestling with that conundrum and had prepared an act forbidding the proclamation of any successor, a move which would effectively abolish the monarchy. Nonetheless, he was relieved and heartened by Henry's sturdy reply that he would 'sooner be torn in pieces' before allowing himself to be made king. The pathetic scene ended in tears and last hugs, the royal retainers and the guards being equally affected by it.

On his last night Charles took communion and retired to bed, telling Herbert to prepare his clothes for the important business of the following day. He rose early and put on clean clothes, taking care to wear two shirts so that he might not shiver on the scaffold and give his enemies the chance to gloat that he was frightened. 'I fear not death,' he told his secretary. 'Death is not terrible to me: I bless my God I am prepared.' The next hours were spent in prayer with Juxon, who took morning service, taking his text from St Matthew 27 which relates Christ's Passion: 'When the morning was come, all the chief priests and elders of the people took counsel against Jesus to put him to death.' It was not a deliberate choice, just the Prayer Book's text for the day, but it was a prescient one, for shortly after Juxon had finished his ministrations the aptly named Colonel Hacker arrived to escort Charles on his final journey to the scaffold.

It took them across St James's Park, the route lined with heavily armed soldiers, to Whitehall, where Charles rested for a while in his old bedroom and fortified himself with a small loaf of bread and a glass of wine. At that point a tearful Herbert asked to be excused the last terrible sight and Charles, accompanied by Juxon, went through the Banqueting Hall towards the black-draped scaffold which jutted out into the street from the central window. Iron staples had been driven into its floor lest the king should refuse execution and have to be forcibly restrained, and as a consequence the block was low, a detail which Charles noted. With him were Juxon and Hacker and the two executioners, who were heavily disguised with masks and false beards; before him in the street was a vast multitude of the curious who had come to see their king being put to death. Permitted to make a last speech – the traditional perquisite of anyone facing execution – Charles found this to be impossible, such was the crush of soldiers between him and the crowd, but his last words were heard by Juxon and Hacker and recorded by a secretary.

Protesting his innocence and claiming that his submission did not signify guilt, Charles went to his death unrepentant, telling his people that he desired only their liberty and freedom. Then, in a telling comment which summed up why he and parliament had gone to war, he reminded them that 'liberty and freedom consists in having government, those laws by which their lives and their goods might be most their own. It is not their having a share in the government; that is nothing appertaining unto them. A subject and a sovereign are clean different things; and, therefore, until you do that – I mean that you put the people in that liberty – they will never enjoy themselves.' There was a final protest about military rule before Juxon prompted him to make his final submission: 'I die a Christian according to the Profession of the Church of England, I have a good cause and a gracious God.' Having said his last words he made his final preparations, donning a white nightcap and asking Juxon to tuck his hair into it to give the executioner a clear view of his neck – perhaps he had been told of the botched execution of Mary Queen of Scots, when the first blow glanced off her head and it took a second strike to decapitate her. His last words to Hacker were: 'Take care they do not put me in pain.'

In keeping with the style of execution of the day Charles lay prone, face down with his head on the block, and had indicated that he would raise his arms as if in crucifixion as a sign to the executioner to strike. His last words and actions were recorded for posterity by John Rushworth, who was part of the silent reproachful crowd:

Dr Juxon: 'There is but one stage more. This stage is turbulent and troublesome. It is a short one. But you may consider it, it will soon carry you a very great way. It will carry you from earth to heaven, and there you shall find your great joy the prize. You haste to a crown of glory.'

King: 'I go from a corruptible to an incorruptible crown, where no disturbance can be.'

Dr Juxon: 'You are exchanged from a temporal to an eternal crown, a good exchange.'

Then the king took off his cloak and his George [Order of the

Garter], giving his George to Dr Juxon, saying, 'Remember!' (it is thought for the Prince), and some other small ceremonies passed. After a while the King, stooping down, laid his neck upon the block; and after a little pause, stretching forth his hands, the executioner at one blow severed his head.[11]

A single strike cut off the king's head cleanly, and as the axe hit home a deep groan rose from the crowd, a terrible sound which one witness had never heard before and hoped never to hear again. It was shortly after two o'clock on a bitterly cold winter's afternoon, and for the first time in recorded history England was without a king or a lawful successor.

The last rites were carried out by the executioner, who held up Charles's head with the traditional words: 'Behold the head of a traitor!' Then the soldiers began clearing the streets while the king's remains were removed from the scaffold and placed in a velvet-lined coffin which was taken back into Whitehall. There the head was sewn back on again and the body embalmed for burial just over a week later in the royal vault at St George's Chapel, Windsor. Juxon took the service and the king's coffin was carried by the earls of Richmond, Hertford, Lindsey and Southampton, but there was one further indignity when the bishop was prevented from using the Prayer Book. As the snow fell – white, the colour of innocence – Charles went to his last resting place in silence.

The king was dead, there was no doubt about that, but it was another matter if the regicide had any basis in law, natural or otherwise. There is a traditional story, recorded by the antiquarian Joseph Spence, that while the king's body lay at rest on the night of the execution Cromwell visited it incognito but was observed by the Earl of Southampton. The story was passed down to the eighteenth-century poet Alexander Pope, and if it is true the figure gazed at the coffin before uttering the words, 'Cruel necessity!'[12] Even if it is not true it deserves to be, for those words sum up the motives which drove the regicides. Having waged war against the absolute rule and having decided on a form of government which ruled out Charles and his family, the only way forward was the elimination of a king who had been irresolute, deceitful and bad for the country. As Cromwell regarded the position, it was indeed necessity, or God's providence, that Charles had to die, however cruel the means. Hugh Peters had claimed as much when he preached in St James's on the eve of the execution, taking his text from Isaiah chapter 14, on the restoration of Israel and the destruction of Babylon: 'The Lord hath broken the staff of the wicked, and the sceptre of the rulers.'

In other words no other solution was possible, and if the trial and its outcome smacked of judicial murder the process was done not just to appease the men in power but for the benefit and future prosperity of the people of England. Besides, the regicides felt that God himself had spoken to them by granting them the victories in the field which showed that right was on their side and that the king's style of rule stood condemned. In that sense the recent war had not just been about winning but defeating evil and wrong-headedness which was itself an affront to God. According to Lucy Hutchinson, and she was not alone in harbouring these thoughts, killing the king had not been an act of fanaticism but an act of grace which permitted no other outcome:

> The gentlemen that were appointed his judges, and divers others, saw in him [Charles] a disposition so bent on the ruin of all that opposed him, and of all the righteous and just things they had contended for, that it was upon the consciences of many of them, that if they did not execute justice upon him, God would require at their hands all the blood and desolation which should ensue by their suffering him to escape, when God had brought him into their hands.[13]

Later, after the Restoration, Lucy's husband John was condemned as a regicide, but neither she nor he retreated from the view that Charles's death was right and inevitable and that those who engineered it were in the right. As for the person of the king, there was widespread relief that the business had been completed and in a country ravaged by war, its economy in tatters and its infrastructure in need of repair and investment, many people hoped that the future would only bring better things. That did not mean a lack of regret for the king's death. A commonly expressed sentiment had it that Charles was by no means the worst ruler England had ever had, and that he was simply unfortunate and misguided. In time that sentiment embraced the idea that Charles was a martyr who had met his end with dignity and grace, a true Christian who died to extirpate the sins of his people. The belief gained momentum when the *Eikon Basilike* ('The King's Image'), *The Pourtraicture of His Sacred Majestie in His Solitudes and Sufferings*, was published immediately after Charles's death. Popularly supposed to have been the king's creation, it was in fact the work of Dr John Gauden, later bishop of Worcester, and it quickly went through forty-seven editions, its popularity ensured by the portrayal of the king as a divine martyr.

The book's success and his own enshrinement would have pleased Charles, for in some respects the manner of his death cancelled most of the debts outstanding against him. Compared to those monarchs who had gone before him he had not been a particularly evil man. Unscrupulous, duplicitous, authoritarian and wrong-headed: all these vices can be laid at his feet, for he was very much a product of his background and upbringing, and in that respect he was more misguided than culpable. He attempted to force unwelcome religious doctrines on his people, he refused to pay any heed to the cravings of those who wanted change and who regarded the war as a means of achieving a more tolerant and democratic style of government. To the very end he clung to his belief in the absolute monarchy. Even on the scaffold he reminded his opponents that having a share in government was not their right. To Charles, during a life which had already required him to give ground to his opponents, that would have been a compromise too many.

Chapter Six

THE CREATION OF A COMMONWEALTH

'Freedom is the man that will turn the world upside down, therefore no wonder he hath enemies.'

Gerrard Winstanley, A Watch-Word to the City of London (1649)

Executing the king was only one step in reforming the governance of his English kingdom; the next stage was making sure that the new administration worked. The chosen means was the Commonwealth,* which had come into being on 4 January 1649, three weeks before the king's execution, when the Rump Parliament decreed that they, representing the people, could make laws without the concurrence of the king and the upper house. The body reassembled on 1 February and its first act was to confirm that those members who had voted for a treaty with Charles should be excluded until such time that they relented and changed their minds. Their next move was the much more radical step of voting for the abolition of the 'useless and dangerous' House of Lords; on 7 February they approved a motion 'that the office of a king in this nation, and to have the power thereof in any single person, is unnecessary, burdensome, and dangerous to the

---

* Originally a term signifying the public good, its meaning had become the body politic, or a state in which the people have an interest. By 1618 it was used to describe a republic or 'free state', and that meaning was applied to the period following Charles's execution.

liberty, safety and public interests of the people of this nation, and therefore ought to be abolished'. The acts authorising these changes were passed on 17 and 19 March respectively, and as they passed on to the statute books those who hoped for radical political change must have taken comfort from language which spoke optimistically of 'a most happy way [. . .] for this nation (if God see it good) to return to its just and ancient right, of being governed by its own representatives'.[1] In that hope the reformers were to be confounded, but no one could doubt that there had been a revolution in English politics.

In little more than a week after the king had been executed, a small and unrepresentative group of people made a far-reaching change to the way in which their country would be governed henceforth. Behind them stood the army, still a potent force and, despite Fairfax's unease, still the means of allowing the Rump Parliament to impose its authority on the country. The security provided by the army and the absence of any opposition gave the members of the new administration a free hand, and they moved quickly to fill the void. Even the symbolism of statehood underwent a rapid transformation. A new Great Seal was produced, one side showing the House of Commons at work with the inscription 'In the first year of freedom, by God's blessing restored, 1648'; the other showing a map of England neatly cut off along the border with Scotland and a map of Ireland with both coats of arms. Other seals of office were replaced with all acknowledgements to the king removed – the king's arms were removed from the mace and the royal badge of office was stripped from the liveries of all parliamentary servants. At the Exchange the king's statue was taken away and in its place appeared the inscription, *Exit tyrannus, Regum ultimus.* The coinage too was replaced and a new series of coins appeared bearing the arms of England and Ireland with the inscriptions 'The Commonwealth of England' and 'God with Us'. Even warships had to be rechristened, the first to be built in 1649 being launched with the name *President.* As one contemporary newspaper put it, 'old England now is grown perfectly new, and we in another world'.

Necessity was the main driving force. With the abolition of the monarchy and the House of Lords many administrative and legal institutions had also disappeared – the Privy Council, the Exchequer, the Admiralty, the Star Chamber, and with them important posts such as the Lord Chancellor, the Chancellor of the Exchequer and various secretaries of state. All that was left was the truncated House of Commons whose Speaker, William Lenthall, had become, perforce, the highest dignitary in the land, but that was not enough: as demanded by the *Remonstrance of the Army* parliament was supposed to dissolve itself to enable a permanent political settlement to be agreed.

Clearly this state of affairs could not continue, otherwise the business of the country would grind to a halt. The chosen instrument for change was the Council of State, an executive body consisting of 41 members or councillors, all of whom would be chosen by parliament to settle 'the government of this nation for the future in the way of a republic without a King or House of Lords'. In turn the council would govern through a series of standing committees which looked after foreign affairs, the armed forces and Ireland, and it would be re-elected annually. Among its first members were Cromwell, Skippon and Fairfax and from the peerage Denbigh and Salisbury. At the same time the judiciary was reformed; the king's name was removed from all oath-taking and from the names of courts such as the King's Bench Court, which became the Upper Bench. For those Royalists still under arrest and awaiting trial a new High Court of Justice was instituted and under its auspices, Hamilton, Holland and Capel were sentenced to death, the executions being carried out by beheading on 9 March outside Westminster Hall.

The following day Bradshaw was nominated president of the Council of State, but already the new body was facing a challenge from those who thought that they had just exchanged one kind of dictatorship for another. The Leveller faction within the army was deeply suspicious of the changes. To them the Council of State was a puppet of the army and they complained that the revolutionary proposals of the *Agreement of the People* had been ignored. Far from introducing a new electoral process the army leaders had simply coerced parliament into establishing a new and undemocratic executive authority which would continue the status quo under another guise. Having been lulled into supporting the regicides at the time of the purging of parliament the Leveller leaders now found that they been duped. Their anger was fuelled, too, by the plans to raise an army to intervene in Ireland, where Ormond was consolidating Royalist support: having fought a long war, and still waiting for arrears of pay, many soldiers were horrified at the prospect of being forced to take part in a new campaign. The disaffection found its voice in a new remonstrance, *England's New Chains Discovered*, penned by John Lilburne, which appeared on 26 February and which called for the immediate dissolution of the Council of State, the abolition of the current parliament and the election of a new body with free and fair elections. With its tart reminder that it was wrong 'for one and the same persons to be continued long in the highest commands of a military Power' – a dig at Cromwell – *England's New Chains Discovered* was a product of the revolutionary spirit which still existed in the army and a reminder from the Levellers that their *Agreement of the People* had been so callously forgotten.

Lilburne's message swept through the disaffected ranks of the army and three days later, on 1 March, it became the basis of a petition which criticised the establishment of the new order and called for measures to defend the liberties of the people. Fearing a fresh outbreak of unrest the Army Council had the eight petitioners arrested and brought to court martial at Newmarket for attempting to foment mutiny. Five were found guilty and cashiered, the sentence being carried out by breaking their swords over their heads after they had been paraded before their regiments, symbolically riding backwards in ignominy, their faces turned towards the horses' tails. Far from cowing the rebels, though, the sentences merely encouraged them. Having been expelled from the army they had no reason to remain loyal to their former leaders, and once back in London they produced another and more audacious complaint entitled *The Hunting of the Foxes from Newmarket and Triploe Heaths to Whitehall by Five Beagles late of the Army*. The work of Richard Overton, the pamphleteer, this listed the men's complaints and grievances before launching into a bitter denunciation of Cromwell and Ireton and 'their conclave of officers':

> First if you do but remember, the king to his death stood upon this principle, that he was accountable to none but God; that he was above the parliament, and above the people. And now to whom will these be accountable? To none on earth. And are they not above the parliament? They have even a negative voice thereover: formerly the Commons could pass nothing without the concurrence of the Lords, now they dare pass nothing without the

concurrence of the conclave of officers: we were before ruled by king, Lords and Commons; now by a general, a court martial, and House of Commons: and we pray you what is the difference? . . . we have not the change of a kingdom to a commonwealth; we are only under the old cheat, the transmutation of names, but with the addition of new tyrannies to the old: for the casting out of one unclean spirit they have brought with them in his stead seven other unclean spirits, more wicked than the former, and they have entered in, and dwell there; and the last state of this commonwealth is worse than the first.[2]

A further allegation was that Cromwell was 'aspiring . . . towards a new regality'. The charge came at the worst possible time for him. On 23 March the Army Council commissioned Cromwell to take command of the forces which were being raised for service in Ireland. Understandably flattered by the approach and keen to test his military abilities against a people whom he disliked for their 'barbarism', Cromwell was aware of the dangers. While he wanted to see God's will executed he knew that any expedition would stand or fall on the quality and quantity of troops available to him, and he was by no means certain that the money could be found to pay for them, especially at a time of economic uncertainty. Now there was the added problem of restlessness within the army's rank and file, and this would have to be weeded out, not least because some Leveller literature supported 'the cause of the Irish natives in seeking their just freedoms'. Added to the possibility that his enemies might use his absence to undermine his position the last thing Cromwell needed was the presence of mutinous soldiers under his command. A week later, on 30 March, the House of Commons approved his appointment and the first steps were taken to choose the regiments which he would command. The means was by lottery, with a child drawing papers out of a hat, those marked 'Ireland' being selected,* those blank being

---

* The English forces numbered 8000 foot, 3000 horse and 1200 dragoons and among the regiments drawn from the hat were Ireton's, Lambert's, Adrian Scrope's and Thomas Horton's (horse); Ewer's, Cook's, Hewson's and Deane's (foot); and five troops of dragoons commanded by Major Abbot and Captains Mercer, Garland, Fulcher and Bolton. Cromwell's, Phayre's and Robert Venables's regiments had already been designated.

excused, but that indifferent method did nothing to still the voices of the protesters who could see their freedoms being eroded.

On 24 March John Lilburne published another document, *The Second Part of England's New Chains*, which demanded the dissolution of the House of Commons and the election of another parliament. So seditious was the paper thought to be that this time Lilburne was arrested, along with Overton and two others. Brought before the Council of State he was asked to explain himself and his actions. This Lilburne did with great spirit and energy, and he also took the opportunity to claim that his life was in danger if he remained in army custody. Ludlow and others were minded to allow the four Levellers to be freed on bail but they lost the motion by one vote and, urged on by Cromwell's warning words, Lilburne and his colleagues were committed to the Tower:

> I tell you, sir [said Cromwell addressing Bradshaw as president of the Council of State], you have no other way to deal with these men but to break them or they will break you; yea, and bring all the guilt of the blood and treasure shed and spent in this kingdom upon your heads and shoulders, and frustrate and make void all that work that, with so many years' industry, toil, and pains, you have done, and so render you to all rational men in the world as the most contemptiblest generation of silly, low-spirited men in the earth to be broken and routed by such a despicable, contemptible generation of men as they are, and therefore, sir, I tell you again, you are necessitated to break them.[3]

Lilburne was not tried until later in the year, when to universal joy he and his accomplices were acquitted, but that was not enough to still his supporters' anger and disgust. A series of petitions was raised and presented to the Council of State throughout April and there was further unrest within the army, exacerbated by the impending transfer of regiments to Ireland. On 17 April 300 men of Hewson's regiment threw down their arms rather than serve in Ireland. They were promptly dismissed and replaced by men drafted from other regiments, but a week later Whalley's regiment mutinied in Bishopsgate in support of the Levellers and refused orders to leave London. As they were not a formation designated for Ireland this was considered to be a more serious disturbance, and Cromwell and Fairfax had to intervene personally to restore order. At the subsequent court martial of the fifteen ringleaders five were sentenced to death. Although the sentence was only carried out on one of them – Robert Lockyer, a known agitator who faced the firing squad in front of St Paul's Cathedral ten days later – there was a furious outcry and thousands of demonstrators attended his funeral. Tellingly, they wore sea-green ribbons in honour of Thomas Rainsborough, who had been murdered the previous year and whom they regarded as their political father-figure.

Once again a mutiny had been quelled, but the root causes of the resentment had not been cured and as Cromwell feared, the canker lived on. To him this was an assault not just on the new administration but also on the fabric of law and order within the country which, if not checked, would lead to anarchy. This authoritarian posture might seem strange in one of the leading regicides, but Cromwell was no mere rebel interested in breaking down one form of government and replacing it with another. He respected too many of the values, such as the property qualification, which the Levellers wanted to dismiss and he had no interest whatsoever in liberalising the suffrage. In his view those who espoused such radical ideas were dangerous and irrational men who were intent on destroying the fruits of the recent civil war. Only political expediency had encouraged him to join with them the previous November; now that the crisis of the king's trial and execution had passed he was determined to bring the Levellers to heel.

It did not take long for the trouble to reappear. At the beginning of May the men of Scrope's and Ireton's regiments mutinied at Salisbury and declared that they were not prepared to go to fight in Ireland. Lack of pay was one reason, but they were also impelled by what had happened to Lilburne, and many of them made public statements that they would take no part in any military action against a people, the Irish, whose liberties were under threat. Other formations followed suit, notably Colonel Reynolds's regiment, which joined the mutiny at Banbury and found a leader in Captain William 'King' Thompson, an activist who had already been dismissed from the army following a drunken brawl. Reynolds was able to bring the situation under control but Thompson made off with his supporters to try to join the other mutineers at Salisbury. As many of the regiments of the New Model Army were quartered in the vicinity there was a danger that the mutinies might spread. This is what Cromwell dreaded. Men who had fought alongside one another at Naseby and Preston would find themselves on opposite sides, and in the turmoil of another war the Royalist faction aided by the Scots or the Irish (or both) would take advantage of the chaos.

It was a defining moment and Cromwell rose to the challenge. As the trouble spread, Thompson took his mutineers to the north while the Salisbury garrison made preparations to meet the expected riposte. If they could combine the mutineers would pose a considerable threat and others might join their cause. For Cromwell and Fairfax there were two issues at stake: they had to put down the rebellion and at the same time they had to keep the other troops loyal, especially those who would be marching against their erstwhile brothers-in-arms. Two regiments of horse and three of foot were chosen from the London garrison but, instead of sending them south-west without further ado, they were paraded in Hyde Park, a gesture which made it clear to them that they were protecting the people of England whose eyes would be on them. When Cromwell addressed them he showed considerable delicacy by eschewing the vocabulary of retaliation and adopting words which spoke of the need to protect their freedoms and to punish those 'delinquents' who threatened the peace of the land. He also promised them that their arrears of pay would be met, and he was as good as his word, having managed to find funds worth £10,000 which had been earmarked for the navy.

Four days later the regiments reached Andover, where Cromwell again harangued his men, telling them that he was determined to restore law and order, and as he had done before the Welsh campaign in the previous year he resolved to live and die with them. Not wishing to cause further bloodshed Fairfax sent a message to the mutineers that he meant them no harm and that they should enter into talks to resolve the situation. By then the men were desperate and knew that they had to attract other regiments, notably Harrison's in Berkshire, and their movements meant that Fairfax had to pursue them as they made their way through Newbridge and Bampton towards Burford. There they were surprised during a night attack on 13 May directed by Fairfax, who had driven his forces forward with great speed and determination, covering forty-five miles before nightfall. Cromwell was entrusted with the actual assault and the brief skirmish between determined troopers and the dispirited outnumbered mutineers was soon over. A handful were killed when shots were exchanged in the dark and the rest, some four hundred men, were locked up for the night in the Church of St John the Baptist.

At first light the following day a court martial was convened and following the mutineers' admission of guilt they were all condemned to death. In the event three ringleaders were executed – Cornet James Thompson, whose brother had managed to escape, and two corporals, Perkins and Church – while a fourth, Cornet Henry Denne, was reprieved at the last minute. To rub home their guilt the surviving mutineers were forced to watch the executions from the church roof. Later, they had to listen to a lengthy speech on godliness preached by Cromwell, but at least they had escaped the terror of the firing squad, and as a contemporary account makes clear it was a dreadful moment:

This day Cornet [James] Thompson was brought into the churchyard (the place of execution). Death was a great terror to him, as unto most. Some say he had hopes of a pardon, and therefore delivered something reflecting upon the legality of his engagement, and the just hand of God; but if he had, they failed him. Corporal Perkins was the next; the place of death, and the sight of his executioners, was so far from altering his countenance, or daunting his spirit, that he seemed to smile upon both, and account it a great mercy that he was to die for this quarrel, and casting his eyes up to His Father and afterwards to his fellow prisoners (who stood upon the church leads to see the execution) set his back against the wall, and bid the executioners shoot; and so died as gallantly, as he lived religiously. After him Master John Church was brought to the stake, he was as much supported by God, in this great agony, as the latter; for after he pulled off his doublet, he stretched out his arms, and bid the soldiers do their duties, looking them in the face, till they gave fire upon him, without the least kind of fear or terror. Thus was death, the end of his present joy, and beginning of his future eternal felicity.[4]

The remaining men were then released, and in the mopping-up operations which followed 'King' Thompson was killed on 17 May in an ambush near Wellingborough. The mutiny was over and the Levellers had finally been levelled. In the weeks that followed known agitators were weeded out and dismissed but, more importantly, further funds were found from parliament to pay the army, which was now costing a £100,000 a month to maintain. By the summer a credible strike force had been raised for service in Ireland.

Inevitably, the unrest spawned other quasi-revolutionary movements, the most prominent being the Fifth Monarchists and the Diggers or True Levellers, the latter being a splinter group whose members believed in communal land ownership. At their most harmless they went on to common land to cultivate it, but when organised under the leadership of William Everard and Gerrard Winstanley, both visionaries and avid pamphleteers, they posed an obvious threat to freeholders and landowners, thereby undermining the whole principle of property ownership. The Diggers' first organised land-grab came at St George's Hill at Walton-on-Thames near Windsor in April, but even though the would-be settlers were dispersed by troops and their leaders taken to London they refused to be cowed. Interviewed by Fairfax on 19 April the Digger leaders kept their hats on their heads, explaining that the general was 'but their fellow creature', and made insolent demands for the right to claim land as their own. But that was not all. Within a week Winstanley, a cloth trader from Wigan, published a further pamphlet attacking land ownership and urging ordinary people to take matters into their own hands:

> Break in pieces quickly the band of particular property, disown this oppressing murder, oppression and thievery of buying and selling of land, owning of landlords and paying of rents, and give free consent to make the earth a common treasury, without grumbling; that the younger brethren may live comfortably upon earth, as well as the elder, that all men may enjoy the benefit of their creation.[5]

Sentiments of that kind were revolutionary in England – 'true freedom lies in the free enjoyment of the earth' – and it would be many years before they gained a popular currency, but in 1649 the visionary ideals of the Diggers failed to find sufficient takers to turn the movement into a serious political threat. The Diggers' 'colony' near Windsor was cleared away by the security forces, with many local freeholders turning out to help chase them away. A similar fate awaited the Diggers the following year when they attempted to found a 'free colony' at Cobham which was quickly cleared, as were a number of other colonies in Kent, Buckinghamshire and Northamptonshire, and the utopian communist fancies preached by Everard and Winstanley – 'the poorest man hath as true a title to the land as the richest man' – gradually faded into history.

More serious and longer-lasting was the appearance of the Fifth Monarchists, a millenarian group who believed that the Kingdom of Jesus Christ and his saints was at hand, that it would last a thousand years, and that this would take over from the four kingdoms of the ancient world (Assyrian, Persian, Greek and Roman) as had been prophesied in Daniel 2: 44: 'And in the days of these kings shall the God of heaven set up a kingdom, which shall never be destroyed: and the kingdom shall be left to other people, but it shall break in pieces and consume all these kingdoms, and it shall stand for ever.' The Fifth Monarchy Men, as the creed's followers were known, thought that the emergence of the fifth kingdom was at hand, as early as 1656, and that its harbinger was the execution of Charles I. Ahead of that date it was their duty to create assemblies of righteous believers and latter-day saints 'to determine all things by the Word, as that law which God will exalt alone and make honourable'. The movement was particularly strong in Norfolk, and in time it attracted sufficient numbers all over England to become a recognisable and influential political grouping. With their absolute insistence on the elect as the only people capable of governing the country, the Fifth Monarchists attracted their share of religious fanatics, but their leadership included sincere and level-headed soldiers such as Harrison, Henry Danvers and Robert Overton, a leading parliamentarian and kinsman of the Leveller pamphleteer. With a strong following in the army, the Fifth Monarchy Men were soon to emerge as one of the leading opposition groups to Cromwell.

In the aftermath of the king's execution, with its iconoclasm, political uncertainty and a widespread belief that change was not only inevitable but also desirable, Cromwell was concerned lest the

Royalists take advantage of the situation. For the time being those fears were in fact groundless. Shocked by the execution of the king, those who had supported Charles had sunk into apathy, bewildered and appalled by what had happened. Writing in *Mercurius Pragmaticus* shortly before the trial began, Marchamont Nedham expressed their incredulity that an anointed king was to face trial at all. Now that the worst had happened his questions remained unanswered:

> What court shall their King be tried in? Who shall be his Peers? Who shall give sentence? What eyes dare be so impious to behold the execution? What Arm be outstretched to give the stroke against the Lord's Anointed, and shall not wither like that of Jeroboam, when he lifted it against an anointed prophet?[6]

Most affected by the news was Charles's eldest son, the Prince of Wales. Although the Commonwealth government sealed the Channel ports in an attempt to stop the news reaching Continental Europe, or at least to slow it down, it took only five days for the first newspaper reports to comment on the events in London. Still trying to rally military support in the Netherlands, the young prince did not receive the official notification of his father's execution until 5 February. Eleven days later he was proclaimed king in the Channel Island of Jersey which had been his base in the previous year. It was a noble and quixotic gesture, but if he were to make a concerted attempt to regain his father's throne he had to look to his kingdoms to the north.

As things stood at the beginning of 1649 England was a lost cause for the Royalists. The execution had taken its toll by leaving supporters dispirited and frightened; grown men were said to have fainted in horror on hearing the news and as Clarendon put it, remaining Royalists in England were 'broken and subdued'. Some went into exile in Europe, a few, inspired by Henry Norwood, a Worcestershire squire, 'did fly from their native country, as from a place infected with the plague' and emigrated to Virginia, which for a while became a centre of Royalist support in the American colonies. Those who remained were excluded from public life unless they swore a new oath to be 'true and faithful' to the Commonwealth. In country houses men might meet in a spirit of defiance to make drunken loyal toasts or to talk clandestinely about raising a new army to restore the monarchy, but in the summer of 1649 the reality was that the Royalist cause in England was as dead and buried as its lost king.

In London the new regime had cemented its authority, parliament had been purged and only in Yorkshire were Royalist troops still in action – at Pontefract Castle, the last Royalist stronghold, which did not surrender until 22 March. Six months later the garrison commander, Colonel John Morris, was executed, as was his second-in-command, Michael Blackburne: it was one of the last acts of retribution of what had become known as 'Cromwell's New Slaughter-House'.[7] Elsewhere the country had succumbed to lethargy; the signs of war were still evident in many parts of the countryside where fighting had taken place, taxes had to be raised for the army and for the forthcoming invasion of Ireland, and any enthusiasm for the changes was tempered by a general war-weariness and a feeling that the fledgling government had yet to prove itself. Under those circumstances Prince Charles could not expect any help from his English subjects. That left Scotland and Ireland, but in both countries support would be tempered by the opposing religious beliefs of Presbyterianism (the National Covenant) and Catholicism (the Confederation of Kilkenny).

In fact the first tangible sign came from Edinburgh where, on the very day that the young prince learned of his father's fate, the Lord Lyon King of Armes had proclaimed him Charles II, King of Great Britain, France and Ireland, at the Mercat Cross, although this was tempered by an accompanying Act of Parliament which suspended the granting of the title until the new king had signed the Solemn League and Covenant. Flattering though that support was, Charles and his advisers still thought that their best hope lay in Ireland, where Ormond had entered into a new agreement with the Confederates on 17 January. Basically, this was a reprise of earlier understandings which offered concessions on freedom of religious practice and an unfettered parliament in return for men and military muscle. The force delivered into his hands numbered 15,000 men and 500 horse which, together with Inchiquin's army, would provide a challenge to the parliamentary forces in Ulster and Leinster. With Dublin in their hands the way would be open for an invasion of England, and with that plan in mind Ormond had written to the young prince inviting him to cross over to Ireland to rally support for his cause. Further optimism came in February when Prince Rupert arrived off Kinsale with a small force of eight warships; this was enough to convince the new administration that the subjugation of Ireland had to be undertaken to prevent it becoming a power base for Royalist sympathies.

Wisely the Prince of Wales did not react to Ormond's invitation and as the summer progressed it became clear that the plans for Cromwell's invasion of Ireland had put paid to any immediate help from that source. That left Europe, but apart from a flurry of letters of sympathy from the electors of the German states the response to requests for help was muted. Europe's royal families might have been shocked by the events in England and appalled by what had happened to one of their number but, exhausted by the Thirty Years War, they were not prepared to offer any support, military or otherwise. France proved to be particularly unhelpful, although Henrietta Maria continued to hope that the Duke of Lorraine would make good his numerous promises to raise an army of invasion. Besides, the country was facing its own internal problems with the Fronde, a struggle between Mazarin and the parlement of Paris over taxation for the war effort, which had erupted in the summer of 1648. With insurrection in the air – the parlement was supported by a number of disaffected nobles and by some provincial leaders – Mazarin was sufficiently alarmed by events to threaten to use the army to blockade the capital. Denounced by the parlement as a 'disturber of the public peace, enemy of the king and his state', Mazarin was convinced that he might be sacrificed as Strafford had been and that the future of the monarchy was at stake. In March 1649 a truce was patched up, only for unrest to break out again three years later, but it too faltered, due to the lack of any unified opposition. Later, once the unrest of 1648 and 1652 was sufficiently far away, it became known as the Fronde, after a Parisian street game with strings (frondes), as though by giving it a safe name its importance was diminished. At the time however Mazarin had looked across the Channel and seen Pride's Purge leading to the subjugation of parliament and the elimination of the king, and he was by no means certain that the actions would not be replicated in France.

There was one further point of connection. During the Fronde there was a sudden outbreak of pamphleteering, the first of its kind in French history. Some 5000 pamphlets were published airing grievances about taxation, the war and the fact that France was being guided by two outsiders, Mazarin, an Italian, and the regent, Anne of Austria, who were lovers and thought to be secretly married. It was not on the same scale as the industry in England but the appearance of these political pamphlets had the same undermining effect that they had in England in the days following Charles's execution. Radicals like Lilburne and Winstanley and others were prolific producers of pamphlets, many of which contained eloquent pleas for more democracy and the desirability of a greater equality of land and possessions. Others were anonymous, but no less influential for that, the most important being *Tyranipocrit Discovered*, which was published in Rotterdam, and *Light Shining in Buckinghamshire*, which was produced by a local group of Levellers and contained a clarion call for greater equality – 'All men being alike privileged by birth, so all men were to enjoy the creatures alike without property one more than the others'.[8]

What with the proliferation of the various cults and the influence they enjoyed within the army, the Council of State decided that a counterblast was necessary and the task fell to John Milton, one of the best-known poets of his age and a pamphleteer who had already caused controversy on account of his attacks on episcopacy and his forthright views on religious, civil and domestic liberties. In February 1649 he published *The Tenure of Kings and Magistrates*, which put forward the argument that 'no man who knows aught can be so stupid to deny that all men naturally were born free' and as such had a right to depose of a monarch; as a result he was appointed Secretary to Foreign Tongues, working directly to the new administration. Awarded a stipend and an office, he moved into Whitehall, where he set about supporting the Council of State's policies and attacking anyone who was critical of them. One of his first tasks was to counter the arguments expounded by the *Eikon Basilike*, and this he did in *Eikonoklastes* ('Image-Breaker'), a withering attack on the king's fancies, which though painstakingly argued failed to achieve any widespread popularity. Whereas the *Eikon Basilike* went through 47 editions, Milton's counter-attack only managed to be published in two editions.

Nonetheless the new government's appointment of Milton as a

propagandist for the cause was a masterstroke, not least because he shared many subversive ideas with the Levellers, believed in a more equitable division of property and disliked all established churches and their associated ceremonies. At the same time his intellectual qualifications were beyond reproach. His early poetry had been written in the 1630s – *On the Morning of Christ's Nativity*, *L'Allegro*, *Il Penseroso*, *Lycidas* – and by the time of the civil war he had emerged as one of the great English prose stylists, writing a series of pamphlets on subjects ranging from Church governance (*The Reason of Church Government*, 1642), the need for divorce in incompatible marriages (*The Doctrine and Discipline of Divorce*, 1643) and above all his peerless defence of freedom of expression in *Areopagitica* (1644):

> I deny not, but that it is of greatest concernment in the Church and Commonwealth, to have a vigilant eye how books demean themselves as well as men; and thereafter to confine, imprison, and do sharpest justice on them as malefactors. For books are not absolutely dead things, but do contain a potency of life in them to be as active as that soul was whose progeny they are; nay, they do preserve as in a vial the purest efficacy and extraction of that living intellect that bred them. I know they are as lively, and as vigorously productive, as those fabulous dragon's teeth; and being sown up and down, may chance to spring up armed men. And yet, on the other hand, unless wariness be used, as good almost kill a man as kill a good book. Who kills a man kills a reasonable creature, God's image; but he who destroys a good book, kills reason itself, kills the image of God, as it were in the eye. Many a man lives a burden to the earth; but a good book is the precious life-blood of a master spirit, embalmed and treasured up on purpose to a life beyond life.

Milton was almost blind when he accepted the commission, but there was no accompanying failing of his intellect or vigour. Next in line he mounted an energetic defence against the findings of the French scholar Salmasius (Claude de Saumaise), who had been commissioned by Charles II to produce *Defensio Regia*, attacking the regicides and exonerating his father. This appeared in England late in 1649, and Milton responded two years later with *Pro Populo Anglicano Defensio*, a curious mixture of high learning and personal invective, which was considered to be so scurrilous that the French authorities in Paris ordered it to be burned in public. In England, though, it was deservedly popular: Salmasius was considered to be Europe's greatest scholar, but by general consent Milton had out-thought him by proving that Charles had not been assassinated but had been rightly executed to fulfil the will of the people. As a result the relatively unknown Milton won plaudits throughout Europe and the literary triumph helped to cement his reputation as a radical and unorthodox thinker who never wavered from his belief that 'to take away from the people the right of choosing a government takes away all liberty'.

Chapter Seven

THESE BARBAROUS WRETCHES: DROGHEDA AND WEXFORD

'He who could take Drogheda, could take hell.'

Sir Phelim O'Neill, on hearing of the fall of
Drogheda, September 1649

It had taken time to recruit the force which would invade Ireland and subjugate it to the Commonwealth's will. The need to find the money to finance the expedition and the opposition of the Levellers had combined to forestall the raising and provision of the army, and it was not until the early summer of 1649 that Cromwell could turn his thoughts to an operation which was as much about defeating the rebellious Irish and ending the threat of invasion as it was about striking a blow against Catholicism. With him as his chaplain he took John Owen, a fiery preacher who shared his master's view that the coming campaign had about it the sense of a divine mission. Cromwell's dislike of the Irish and his contempt for Catholicism and all its rites were well known: both were to play a part in the way he conducted his operations in the country whose internal situation was predictably confused.

Ormond and his Confederate allies had used the delay to take advantage of the weakness of the Commonwealth army under the command of Michael Jones which was defending Dublin. By the third week in June Ormond's army was to the north of the city and he was not without hope of reducing it, Inchiquin had taken Drogheda, which commanded the road to Ulster, and he had summoned the Presbyterian Scots to rally to Charles's cause. Elsewhere the situation was less easy to read. To the north Monck commanded Commonwealth troops at Dundalk, Carlingford and Carrickfergus and opposing him was the rump of the Scottish Presbyterian army and Owen Roe O'Neill's Ulster Catholic force, both of which were potential Royalist allies. However, the latter was in an isolated position, as he had opposed Ormond's alliance with Inchiquin and the expected support from the nuncio, Cardinal Rinuccini, had failed to materialise. That left him little option but to enter into a secret agreement with Monck in April which allowed both armies to cease hostilities for three months, a move to the liking of both commanders. It was that kind of muddle which Cromwell was determined to stamp out: the time had come to end the perennial threat of invasion from Ireland and to remove from the Royalist cause a potential ally in the shape of a contentious Irish army.

When Cromwell set out from London in the late afternoon of 11 July he flew above his coach a white standard, the colour of peace, and his escort consisted of eighty officers, the flower of the New Model Army. He left with the prayers of three ministers ringing in his ears; once again he was being called upon to do God's work and surely the Almighty's providence would aid his hand. It had taken the better part of the past half year to prepare his force and to find the funds to maintain it, but at last retribution was on its way. Ireland was about to feel Cromwell's firm hand and if the sketch writer of *The Moderate Intelligencer* is to be believed, resistance was futile in the face of such overwhelming force and authority:

> He went forth in that state and equipage as the like hath hardly been seen, himself in a coach with six gallant Flanders mares whitish grey; divers coaches accompanying him, and very many great officers of the army; his lifeguard consisting of eighty gallant men, the meanest whereof was a commander or Esquire in stately habit, with trumpets sounding almost to the shaking of Charing Cross, had it now been standing.* Of his lifeguard are many

---

* Charing Cross was raised by King Edward I to mark the spot where the coffin of his wife Eleanor stopped for the last time on its way from Harby, Nottinghamshire, to burial in Westminster. It was destroyed by Puritan iconoclasts early in 1647.

Colonels; and, believe me, its [sic] such a guard as is hardly to be paralleled in the world. And now have at you my Lord Ormonde! You will have men of gallantry to encounter, whom to overcome will be honour sufficient and to be beaten by them will be no great blemish. If you say 'Caesar or nothing' they say 'a republic or nothing'.[1]

The implication was that Ireland was fortunate in the extreme to be graced by such a man as Cromwell and that Ormond should shiver in his shoes at his approach. The Royalist leader did nothing of the sort, although he did make the pertinent remark to Charles that he feared Cromwell's money more than he did his face – before leaving England Cromwell had managed to suborn Lord Broghill, son of the Earl of Cork, and a prominent Royalist soldier who would play a prominent part in the forthcoming campaign.

Cromwell went to Ireland with clearly defined gubernatorial powers. His military rank made him commander-in-chief of the English expeditionary force – Fairfax retained the title of Lord General – and added to that he was Lord Lieutenant of Ireland, charged with the authority to bring the country under civilian control once the fighting was over. For that, too, there was a plan: Ireland would be 'replanted with many noble families of this nation, and of the Protestant religion'; having beaten the Catholic rebels, the newly pacified country would be put in the hands of good English Protestant stock and a purged Ireland would emerge from its barbarous priest-ridden chaos.[2] That sense of divine mission underpinned Cromwell's campaign in Ireland: having defeated Ormond and his allies he would bring Ireland into the fold of the Commonwealth and a brave new country would emerge. In short it was a righteous cause and one that had God's blessing.

Revenge was also on the agenda. Later in the campaign Cromwell would talk about the need 'to ask an account of the innocent blood that hath been shed' during the insurrection of 1641, still regarded as unfinished business, and to rub home that point he reminded his soldiers before leaving England that they were latter-day Israelites about to crush the wicked and to retrieve the lost land of Canaan. Just as England had been cured by killing the king, so too would Ireland have to face a similar physic.

From London Cromwell's entourage moved to Bristol and then on to his old stamping ground in south Wales before crossing over to Dublin from Milford Haven. Before embarking he received the splendid news that Michael Jones had managed to break out of his defensive lines in Dublin and had inflicted a substantial defeat on Ormond's forces at Rathmines on 2 August. To Cromwell, this was God's hand at work; following the 'astonishing mercy' which had seen Jones's little army, only 4000 in number, defeat a force almost five times as strong, he was marching with destiny once more. Not only was Jones's victory a good omen before the onset of this latest crusade but it allowed Cromwell's fleet to sail directly into the Irish capital and to start its operations almost straight away. On 13 and 14 August the invasion force set sail – 12,000 soldiers, their horses and equipment on board 130 sailing ships.

No sooner had Cromwell arrived and recovered from the sea-sickness which plagued his brief voyage than he set to work with a will. A proclamation was issued reassuring the Irish that his army would not demand free quarter and that there would be no pillaging of the countryside. Instead they would pay for everything they needed and any officer or soldier found guilty of breaking that rule would be punished. This was winning hearts and minds, and it worked. While Cromwell had little love for Irish Catholics and lost no opportunity to berate the inhuman atrocities that had been committed by them in 1641 – if all the allegations were true – he could see no point in alienating the ordinary people and, of course, he was keen to retain the loyalty and affection of the English settlers. As he told the Irish in one of his first public pronouncements, he wanted to return their country to a state of grace:

That as God had brought him thither in safety, so he doubted not but, by his divine providence, to restore them all to their just liberty and property; and that all those whose heart's affections were real for the carrying on of the great work against the barbarous and blood-thirsty Irish, and the rest of their adherents and confederates, for the propagating of the Gospel of Christ, the establishing of truth and peace and restoring that bleeding nation to its former happiness and tranquillity, should find favour and protection from the Parliament of England and receive such endowments and gratuities, as should be answerable to their merits.[3]

Cromwell's comments were well-received; he was after all preaching to the converted, most of Dublin's Catholics having already been expelled by Jones during the siege, and he was constantly at pains to reinforce the idea that he was pacifying Ireland, not merely conquering it. However his primary aim was to defeat Ormond's Royalist forces, and his first target was Drogheda, or Tredagh as it was known to the English, a prosperous town at the mouth of the River Boyne, some thirty miles north of Dublin, albeit along a long and winding road. Captured by Inchiquin's forces on 18 July it was under the command of the veteran Royalist commander Sir Arthur Aston, last seen five years earlier at Reading, and its capture was the key to any advance into Ulster. On 10 September Cromwell arrived outside its walls and in time-honoured fashion flew a white flag and summoned Aston to surrender, adding that 'if this be refused, you will have no cause to blame me.' Predictably the offer was rejected, the white flag was lowered and replaced by the blood-red one of war, and the operation to reduce Drogheda began.

The situation facing Cromwell was this. Realising that Ireland's independence as a Catholic state had been compromised, O'Neill, now a sick man, decided to put aside his doubts about the policy of concession being pursued by the Confederates, ended his truce with Monck and threw in his lot with Ormond. This gave the Irish magnate a conglomerate force of Old English, Old Irish Catholics and Protestant Royalists united in their support for the Stewart cause. At their first council of war at Drogheda on 27 August the commanders decided that their best chance was to hold the seemingly impregnable city and to waste Cromwell's resources by tying him down in a lengthy siege. There was nothing wrong with their thinking. Cromwell's lines of communication and resupply were long, it was late summer, and if the city held out Cromwell's army could find itself still outside its walls when the winter wet season arrived. And even if the city did eventually collapse it would be a hard fight and Cromwell's depleted army would be in no position to fight a second battle with troops held in reserve by Ormond. Against that, they clearly did not know that Cromwell's hearts-and-minds initiative had given him much needed local support in the way of supplies, and they were perhaps unaware that Cromwell had brought with him a modern artillery train which contained siege guns which had not been seen before in Ireland.

The uneven road to Drogheda forced Cromwell to send his big guns by sea while his foot and horse regiments took the overland route and arrived to the south of the city on 3 September. They set up camp on rising ground, which became known later as Cromwell's Mount, and awaited the arrival of the field pieces which would decide the issue – eleven mortars and siege-guns, two of them eight-bore, and twelve field guns, all manned by experienced gunners. Ahead of them their objective presented a well-defined prospect. Drogheda had been a walled town since Norman times, and although it was split by the Boyne both the southern and northern half-circles of the defensive walls were solid and impressive. In some places the wall was at least six feet thick and it was in good repair throughout its circumference; behind it wooden drawbridges linked the two halves, but they would not be a factor until, or unless, the outer defences had been breached. With no other bridges over the river, Cromwell had no option but to attack the city from his immediate line of march, even though it presented an awkward target with the land falling away in front of the walls.

For all that the walls provided a solid means of defence, Aston was not in the strongest position for a commander about to face a better-armed and better-equipped besieging army. Ormond had promised him all the men and 'full proportion of ammunition' that would be needed to withstand a lengthy siege, but even before the action began Aston was complaining about the paucity of the supplies of powder. His own artillery was sparse, consisting as it did of a number of small-bore pieces which were mere pea-shooters compared to the big guns operated by Cromwell's army. As for the garrison, it numbered three-thousand, but Ormond hoped that two valiant soldiers, 'Colonel Hunger and Major Sickness', would soon be marching to their assistance by infiltrating the besieging army. There was, too, the threat posed by Ormond's field army to the north, especially if it could be reinforced by O'Neill's forces, which were still in camp at Ballykelly near Derry in Ulster.

On the day before the siege opened confidence remained high, one Royalist officer, Sir Edmund Verney, telling Ormond that the 'men are all in heart and courage, having still had good success in our sallies, and we do little fear what the enemy can presently do against us'.[4] They were brave words, and typical of a family which had given such loyal service to the Crown – Edmund's father was the Royal Standard-Bearer who had fallen at Edgehill – but the reality was rather different, as the sallies on Cromwell's lines had only resulted in heavy casualties and a further weakening of Aston's garrison. One attack saw 200 men falling into captivity for no tactical advantage. Aston had one other cross to bear: his grandmother Lady Wilmot and a number of other women, also relatives, had made contact with the parliamentary army and had let it know that they wanted to surrender to Cromwell. Aston solved the problem by expelling her from Drogheda, having first received Ormond's permission 'to turn her and her malignant family out of town, for though she be my grandmother, I shall make powder of her, else she play me such foul play'.[5] For a commander about to undergo trial by siege it was hardly the best of portents.

From the rising ground to the south Cromwell's guns came into play shortly after the refusal to heed the summons. The firing continued all day, the gunners taking their bead from the south-eastern corner tower of the walls and the steeple of St Mary's Church which stood behind it. Under the relentless barrage breaches began to appear in the walls both at the tower and by the main southern gate into the town. Night brought respite and a chance to repair the damage, but after the firing recommenced the next day, 11 September, Cromwell thought that the first assault could begin. Three regiments of foot, the forlorn hope, were chosen for the task. Although their first assault was repulsed in the breach with one of the colonels being killed, a second and more determined attack, in which Cromwell was involved, succeeded in breaking the defences, and according to Whitelocke, who based his account on his son James's experience, 'God abated the courage of the enemy; they fled before us till we gained the town and they all agreed in the not giving of quarter.'[6]

Once inside the town the battle was as good as won. Cromwell's battle-hardened troops were too strong for Aston's garrison and they made short work of securing it. Their task was aided by the failure to raise the drawbridge across the Boyne, an omission which is all the more inexplicable given that Aston was expecting Ormond's army to come to his rescue. What followed next was inevitable. As Cromwell's men swept into the town, to use his words from his report to the Speaker, 'they put to the sword about two thousand men'. Over the years this massacre has been used to exemplify English frightfulness and to demonise Cromwell in the eyes of the nationalist community. Later, descriptions of the fighting during the siege were carefully collected and disseminated by the Irish clergy; they had a wide currency and for the most part, they were believed as evidence of English Cromwellian atrocities. The following story, based on anecdotal information, is typical of the genre:

> The city being captured by the heretics, the blood of the Catholics was mercilessly shed in the streets, and in the dwelling-houses, and in the open fields; to none was mercy shown, not to the women, nor to the aged, nor to the young. The property of the citizens became the prey of the parliamentary troops; everything in our residence was plundered; the library, the sacred chalices, of which there were many of great value, as well as all the furniture, sacred and profane, were destroyed. On the following day, when the soldiers were searching through the ruins of the city, they discovered one of our fathers, named John Bathe [Taaffe], with his brother, a secular priest: suspecting that they were religious, they examined them, and finding that they were priests, and one of them, moreover, a Jesuit, they led them off in triumph, and accompanied by a tumultuous crowd, conducted them to the market-place, and there, as if they were at length extinguishing the Catholic religion and our society, they tied them both to stakes fixed in the ground, and pierced their bodies with shot till they expired.[7]

It did not take long for the stories to be magnified in such a way that it was not just the garrison which was slaughtered but vast numbers of civilians. The most colourful of these emanated from Thomas Wood's infamous memoirs, the memories of a soldier whom his colonel thought to be too fond of 'buffooning'. When they were published in 1663 by his brother Anthony Wood, an Oxford historian, they quickly became accepted as gospel, both because they were shocking and because they put Cromwell in a bad light. One episode in particular attracted a huge readership, and in time it came to represent all that was atrocious about the English soldiers' behaviour when they took Drogheda. After regaling his audience with the information that Aston 'had his brains beat out, and his body hacked and chopped to pieces', Wood presented a lurid picture of the fate awaiting those civilians who tried to hide. Children were used as shields as the soldiers advanced and in the vaults of a church they came across 'the flower and choicest of the women of the town':

> One of these a most handsome virgin and arrayed in costly and gorgeous apparel, kneeled down to Thomas Wood with tears and prayers to save her life; and being stricken with a profound pity, he took her under his arm, went with her out of the church, with intention to put her over the works and to let her shift for herself; but then a soldier perceiving his intentions, ran his sword through her belly or fundament; whereupon Mr Wood seeing her gasping, took away her money, jewels &c., and flung her over the works.[8]

If true, this was a despicable atrocity, but apart from Wood himself there is no evidence that such an incident took place, and Gardiner tartly observed in his own account two centuries later that he had refused to use the story as Wood was 'just the sort of man . . . to invent a story to shock his mother and his steady, antiquarian brother'.[9] Although the massacre of innocents at Drogheda entered Irish nationalist mythology, more measured research conducted by the historian Tom Reilly concluded that 'not only was there no outright slaughter of the defenceless inhabitants, but we now find that there is absolutely no evidence to substantiate the stories of the massacre of even one unarmed person on the streets of Drogheda'.[10]

Even so, the city was no place for faint hearts on the 11th and 12th of September 1649. The garrison was put to the sword, and there is more than Cromwell's account to justify the claim. Perhaps as many as 3000 lost their lives, and among their number were Catholic priests who may or may not have been combatants. To a modern sensibility the number of casualties signifies a massacre; that the decision was taken to do them to death is enough to mark Drogheda as an atrocity in a war in which quarter had usually been freely given. Some of the stories of the final moments of the survivors have a hideous ring. Soldiers who had taken refuge in the steeple of St Peter's Church perished horribly when the church was set alight, Cromwell noting that one man was heard shouting: 'God damn me, God confound me, I burn, I burn.' Among the last to die were Aston and his staff, who were cut down in a fortified position known as Millmount on the south bank of the river. The cantankerous old Royalist met an awful end, having his wooden leg chopped off because his killers believed, wrongly, that he had hidden gold pieces inside it.

All this makes savage reading and, although Tom Reilly has proved that many of the eye-witness accounts of military deaths were themselves exaggerated, being written some years after the event, there is little doubt that Drogheda experienced a massacre of its garrison once its walls had been breached. Again this sounds appalling even to a world which has witnessed far worse atrocities in the centuries which followed Drogheda, but there was a reason for the dispatch of the survivors: they did not just die in an isolated incident which was an exception and not the rule. When Cromwell appeared outside the city walls and demanded its surrender Aston knew that by refusing the offer he was condemning his men to death in the event that they were defeated in battle. According to the rules of war, as both commanders understood them, once a summons had been refused the attackers were under no obligation to offer quarter after the walls had been breached. This has additional edge if the defenders had been resolute in their efforts: in the heat of the moment as the attackers broke in and saw their fellow soldiers being cut down they were unlikely to offer the hand of friendship to their assailants. It is a predicament born of battle itself. All too often fighting soldiers who defend to the last minute and then try to surrender find themselves being dispatched with the words 'Too late!' ringing in their ears.

Unfortunately, as also happens in the heat of battle, there were misunderstandings which added to the battle's reputation for grisliness and allow it to be mentioned in the same breath as some of the horrors of the Thirty Years War. In some instances Commonwealth officers did offer quarter, perhaps out of pity for their opponents or, more likely, to save their own men's lives in unnecessary fighting, but were then forced to obey Cromwell's order of 'no quarter'. Several reports speak of prisoners being killed after they had surrendered, and these incidents probably did take place. For Cromwell's soldiers this was their first experience of warfare in Ireland, and many would have believed that they were fighting an inferior species of savage Catholics who had already taken thousands of lives in similar fashion in 1641. Cromwell himself reported that the destruction of St Peter's was justified, 'the last Lord's Day before the storm, the Protestants were thrust out of the great church called St Peter's and they [the Catholics] had public mass there', and his main report to Lenthall on 17 September makes no bones about the justice of his actions:

> I am persuaded that this is a righteous judgement of God upon these barbarous wretches who have imbrued their hands in so much innocent blood, and that it will tend to prevent the effusion of blood for the future, which are the satisfactory grounds to such actions, which otherwise cannot but work remorse and regret.[11]

All this was regrettable but there is little doubt that hatred of Catholicism and dislike of the Irish helped to form Cromwell's decision to destroy an enemy force which had been described as the flower of Ormond's army. Even though many of the defenders were English Royalists – Verney was among the casualties – that was not the point. They were fighting for the Royalist cause, and beyond that for the wider purposes of the Catholic Church. If Cromwell wanted to send a message to others that a similar fate awaited them, the lesson was not lost. On hearing of Aston's defeat the Royalist garrisons at Dundalk and Trim fled, leaving Ormond to lament that it was impossible for anyone to imagine 'how great the terror is that those successes and the power of the rebels had struck into their people'. With the campaign far from over and with autumn approaching, the ability to instil 'terror' in Catholic minds would be a powerful disincentive – Cromwell recognised it as such when he reported back to London in October that his best chance of success lay in hitting the enemy 'whiles the fear of God is upon them'.

By then he had crushed Ormond's forces for a second time. His next target, by no means obvious, was the strategically important port of Wexford in the south-east, with its links to Continental Europe – Wexford had for long been a source of annoyance, as its harbour played host to a number of successful privateers – and Cromwell hoped to use it for winter quarters. Already the weather was worsening. With the onset of heavy autumn rain it was not easy getting the large Commonwealth army south through the hilly countryside of Wicklow, and when the first units arrived at the beginning of October they found the town 'drowned in rain and dew'. Dysentery had set in and the one saving grace was that the accompanying naval and transport ships were able to enter the port of Rosslare on 2 October after the small garrison had run away on the approach of Cromwell's army. Cromwell established his headquarters on a rocky outcrop to the south, known today as Cromwell's Fort.

Inside Wexford itself there was an equal level of agitation and dismay. The leading citizens and the local council were minded to capitulate both because they were unwilling to undergo a siege and also because they had no particular love for Ormond and his faction. However, the military governor, Colonel David Sinnott, was determined to resist, and when Cromwell's summons arrived on 3 October he played for time by asking to consider the matter with his civilian colleagues. Over the next forty-eight hours there was a bizarre exchange of letters as Cromwell pushed ahead with his preparations for the siege while Sinnott awaited the appearance of 1500 reinforcements led by Ormond's Lord Lieutenant of Horse, Lord Castlehaven. Their arrival on 5 October strengthened Sinnott's garrison but he was forced to concede command to Castlehaven, his superior officer, and this merely spun out the correspondence. To add to the confusion Ormond arrived to the north and was able to ferry 500 more men into the town and to order the evacuation of all non-combatant civilians.

That was the final straw. Eight days after arriving Cromwell ordered his artillery to open fire on the town, aiming first for the castle which lay at the southern edge of the defences – Wexford faced the sea and was protected on the landward side by a high and reasonably thick wall. The bombardment forced Sinnott to ask for a recommencement of the negotiations, but his demands were so extreme – preservation of the Catholic faith, the safe evacuation of the garrison and the payment of an indemnity – that Cromwell would have been within his rights to have brushed them aside. Instead he sent a reply refusing to 'answer with some disdain' and offered instead quarter for the garrison and a promise that 'no violence shall be offered to their goods and that I shall protect their town from plunder'. Even at that late stage Cromwell was prepared to show mercy, but all hopes of a happy conclusion were dashed by a bizarre act in which the commander of Wexford Castle, Captain James Stafford, took advantage of the lull caused by the negotiations to surrender to Cromwell. Either he had lost heart or been suborned – the evidence is not clear – but he believed that there was no point in resisting the powerful English army. His decision opened the floodgates. Later he would bear the mark of traitor and a contemporary account described him as 'a vain, idle young man and nothing practised in the art of military'.

Without further ado, and certainly not from Cromwell's order – he was still penning his reply to Sinnott – the castle was occupied and its guns were turned on the disbelieving defenders, who started to flee in panic from the walls. This was the cue for the Commonwealth soldiers to storm into the city, and in his report Cromwell told Lenthall that from that point onwards Wexford's fate was settled:

> And when they were come into the market-place, the enemy making stiff resistance, our forces brake them, and then put all to the sword that came in their way. Two boatfuls of the enemy attempting to escape, being overpressed with numbers sank, whereby were drowned near three hundred of them. I believe, in all, there was lost of the enemy not many less than two thousand; and I believe not twenty of yours killed from first to last in the siege.[12]

Less than an hour later the city was in English hands and the bulk of its garrison was dead, slaughtered in the streets by more powerful and aggressive opponents or drowned trying to escape north across the River Slaney. Atrocities were committed aplenty too. All priests were slaughtered without quarter, as were civilians found bearing arms, and, as Cromwell admitted, others were drowned trying to escape the slaughter. As had happened at Drogheda the English soldiers had been given their head, and they needed no second invitation to slaughter the Irish or to extirpate this nest of pirates. That so few of their own number were killed speaks volumes for their own professionalism, hardened by eight years of warfare, and the ineptitude of the Royalist defenders, most of whom were novices. Cromwell was not slow in excusing their actions: this was God's hand at work, the people of Wexford being made to pay for the cruelties they had formerly meted out to Protestants in 1641, and he remained unabashed by the slaughter, telling Lenthall that it had been 'a righteous judgement'. His one regret was that in destroying the town his soldiers had made it unfit for winter quarters: 'I could have wished for their own good, and the good of the garrison, they had been more moderate.' Still, there was always a bright side. Peters thought that Wexford was 'a fine spot for some Godly congregation, where house and land wait for inhabitants and occupiers. I wish they would come.'[13]

From a military point of view Cromwell had achieved his objective. Wexford had been removed as a possible entrepot for Royalist support from France. Now that it was in Commonwealth hands it could also be used as a port of entry for the next wave of colonisers and settlers. Above all, Cromwell was determined to smash the Royalist cause in Ireland and to prevent the country being used as a launching-pad for an invasion in support of the Prince of Wales. The Protestant interest had to be preserved and Catholicism brought under control. In that respect the siege of Wexford and its murderous outcome was another stage in the subordination of Ireland to English interests, but in common with the previous engagement at Drogheda, it soon became synonymous with Cromwellian brutality. In time both actions attracted concomitant myths of barbaric behaviour – Thomas Wood's slaughter of virgins in Drogheda and the widely reported vision of a sorrowful woman in the skies above Wexford – and the idea of English frightfulness became deeply embedded in the Irish consciousness, never to be forgotten.*

With Wexford destroyed Cromwell left a small contingent behind to guard it and took the rest of his army westwards towards Munster. His first obstacle was the town of Ross on the River Barrow, which was guarded by a small garrison of 1500 soldiers. Summoned to surrender, the governor, Sir Lucas Taaffe, prevaricated, hoping to buy time as Sinnott had done. Once again Cromwell insisted that his aim was to prevent further 'effusion of blood' and in the subsequent exchange of letters he promised that the garrison would be allowed to surrender with honour and that the inhabitants would be 'permitted to live peaceably, free from the injury and violence of the soldiers'. On one point only was he obdurate. When Taaffe insisted that his people be granted 'liberty of conscience' Cromwell replied that if by that term Taaffe meant freedom of worship, then that would be denied:

---

* The site of the massacre in Wexford is marked by a plaque in the present-day Bull Ring and in the nearby Franciscan church.

For that which you mention concerning liberty of conscience, I meddle not with any man's conscience [he wrote on 19 October]. But if by liberty of conscience you mean the liberty to exercise the Mass, I judge it best to use plain dealing, and to let you know where the Parliament of England have power, that you will not be allowed of.[14]

This was straight talking. To modern ears it smacks of intolerance but Cromwell was simply stating the contemporary position. Celebrating mass was banned in England, and as Cromwell saw his duty as conquering Ireland, then he would certainly make no exceptions in Ross or elsewhere. Whereas a person had a right to be a Catholic and to worship God in their own way they could not take part in an illegal and, in Cromwell's mind, a superstitious and heretical religious ceremony. Taaffe took the hint and surrendered the town that same day.

In the aftermath of the siege Cromwell consolidated his position, but with the approach of winter his army was racked by dysentery and fever and he himself fell victim to the illness. Waterford and Duncannon both remained intact, despite the best efforts of Ireton and Jones, and there was a danger that his army might become bogged down and fall a prey to the Royalist army which was gathering strength in Kilkenny. But elsewhere things were going well for the Commonwealth cause. On 16 October the English Protestant faction in Cork captured the city and expelled the Irish Catholic garrison and large numbers of Inchiquin's army began deserting. Other towns in Munster followed suit in the days that followed – Youghal, Capperquin, Mallow – and the insurrection was fanned by Broghill's presence along with the backing of troops under Phayre's command. From the north came more encouraging news: Owen Roe O'Neill died in Cavan on 6 November after a debilitating illness and with his passing the Ulster Catholics had lost not only a capable military commander but a talismanic leader who was still being lamented two centuries later by nationalist poets such as Thomas Davis, a Munsterman and perfervid nationalist who is better remembered for editing *The Nation* newspaper than for his bombastic verse:

We thought you would not die – we were sure you would not go,
And leave us in our inmost need to Cromwell's cruel blow,
Sheep without a shepherd, when the snow shuts out the sky –
Oh, Why did you leave us, Owen? Why did you die![15]

The New Model Army also lost one of its heroes to illness. On 10 December, as Cromwell took his men into winter quarters in the coastal town of Youghal, he reported to Lenthall that he had lost Michael Jones, 'his noble friend and companion in labours' whose victory at Rathmines earlier in the year had made the expedition possible.* It was a hard winter and his men were weakened by the same illness which carried off Jones; so great was their suffering that Cromwell reported that the army was 'fitter for an hospital than the field'. Were it not for God's support and the failure of the Irish to unite against it the Commonwealth army would have been in dire straits. That temporal manifestation mattered for, although Cromwell's army was weakened and overstretched, Ormond did little to force the issue, even though he had almost 7000 men at his disposal and the potential to raise more. With the English in control of most of the land between Cork and Belfast, and with more troops bound to cross over to Ireland in the new year, Ormond's hopes of raising Ireland for the Prince of Wales were at an end.

---

* Rumour had it that both men had been poisoned: O'Neill by having his boots impregnated (his limbs had been incapacitated by what seems to have been osteomyelitis); Jones at Cromwell's jealous hand and not the 'pestilent and contagious fever' reported to Lenthall.

Chapter Eight

THE CURSE OF CROMWELL

'We come to break the power of a company of lawless rebels who, having cast off the authority of England, live as enemies to human society.'

Oliver Cromwell, declaration to the Irish clergy, 14 January 1650

With Ireland in the grip of winter and the Commonwealth forces quartered across southern Munster, the next stage of the war was dominated by a propaganda battle. At the beginning of December 1649 the Irish clergy met at the ancient monastic settlement of Clonmacnoise to attempt to unite the various factions against the English invaders and give a sense of purpose to Irish resistance. Their means of persuasion was a declaration to the people of Ireland warning them that Cromwell came not as a liberator but as a destroyer of their religion and a plunderer of their property, and that no one should be deceived by his promises of safeguarding individual liberties:

And consequently, we beseech the gentry and inhabitants, for God's glory and their own safety, to the uttermost of their power to contribute with patience to the support of the war against that enemy, in hope that by the blessing of God they may be rescued by the threatened evils, and in time be permitted to serve God in their native country and enjoy their estates and the fruits of their labours, free from such heavy levies or any other such taxes as they bear at present; admonishing also those that are enlisted of the army to prosecute constantly, according to each man's charge, the trust reposed in them, the opposition of the common enemy in so just a war as is that they have undertaken for the religion, King and country, as they expect the blessing of God to fall on their actions.[1]

This call to wage what was in effect a holy war on behalf of their king and the Catholic faith was followed by a second declaration on 13 December expressing the clergy's 'detestation against all such divisions between either provinces or families, or between English and Old Irish, or any of the English or Scots adhering to his Majesty', and both were printed for wider distribution. This unexpected intervention did little to bring about the unity the Church was seeking – it can hardly have appealed to the Confederation's Protestant supporters – but it did allow Cromwell to answer in kind and in so doing to make clear his opinions about Ireland, its Catholic faith and its relationship with England. With time on his hands he produced a lengthy and frequently intemperate response which was aimed at the 'undeceiving of deluded and seduced people: which may be satisfactory to all who do not shut wilfully their eyes against the light'.

He began by attacking the Catholic Church in general and then he launched into a radical rewriting of Irish history, accusing the clergy of breaking the union with England and in 1641 of provoking 'the most unheard-of and most barbarous massacre, without respect of sex or age, that ever the sun beheld'. This was Cromwell the Puritan in full flow, his hatred of the unreformed practices of Catholicism made manifest and his missionary intentions laid bare – 'You are part of the anti-Christ, whose Kingdom the Scripture so expressly should be laid in blood; yea in the blood of the Saints.' It was a ferocious document, written with passion, restrained anger and grim self-justification, and to modern minds it is little short of a declaration against the Catholic faith and all who practised it. Not unnaturally perhaps it shows Cromwell in the stern and unforgiving light of the avenging angel, but read as it would have been read in 1650 it is little more than a retailing of contemporary English Puritan attitudes towards the Irish and the Catholic Church in general. It also justifies the practice of plantation, which, according to Cromwell, would cost the

Exchequer six million pounds, a hefty price for preserving liberties and one which every Irish person should consider before they made up their minds about whether or not they should take part in the rebellion against the Commonwealth.

However, there is more than unthinking vituperation in Cromwell's comments. While his ire is directed against the clergy and against those who had taken up arms for the king and therefore deserved to be punished, he was willing to excuse those who 'have not been actors in this rebellion'. They would not suffer either by being mistreated or by having their property confiscated but 'as for those who, not withstanding all this, persist and continue in arms, they must expect what the providence of God (in that which is falsely called the chance of war) will cast upon them'. For those miscreants there would be no mercy:

> We are come to ask an account of the innocent blood that hath been shed; and to endeavour to bring them to an account (by the blessing and presence of the Almighty, in whom alone is our hope and strength), who by appearing in arms seek to justify the same. We are come to break the power of a company of lawless rebels, who having cast off the authority of England, live as enemies to human society, whose principles (the world hath experience of) are, to destroy and subjugate all men not complying with them. We (by the assistance of God) to hold forth and maintain the lustre and glory of English liberty in a nation where we have an undoubted right to it; – wherein the people of Ireland (if they listen to such seducers as you are) may equally participate in all benefits, to use liberty and fortune equally with Englishmen if they keep out of arms.[1]

Clearly Cromwell hoped that his warnings would be heeded and that the Irish would resolve to end their rebellion peaceably. If they did, he counselled, there would be forgiveness, but if not they must expect their deserts. No doubt he meant well – Cromwell had shown before that he preferred to give opponents the opportunity of climbing down and avoiding violence – but his words were unlikely to douse the pride of the nationalists. To them the message was uncompromising: end all resistance, give up the religion which started the rebellion, withdraw support for the Crown and then conform to English practices.

Cromwell reopened the campaign on 29 January 1650, his intention being to occupy the counties of Kilkenny and Tipperary, the heartland of the Confederation, and to capture the main Royalist garrisons within them. By then he had received fresh supplies from England and his army had largely recovered from the sickness which had weakened it earlier in the winter. This logistical support was crucial to his men's well-being: the arrival of pay, the ready supply of food and fresh clothes raised morale, as did the presence of reinforcements. Having spent the worst part of the winter in tolerable comfort, Cromwell's army was ready for action, and the opening moves met with swift success. In quick succession the towns of Fethard, Cashel and Cahir were all summoned and all fell with little trouble, mainly because the terms offered were surprisingly generous. The garrison troops were allowed to march out with 'colours flying, matches lighted' and the townspeople were offered firm guarantees about their safety. One reason for the lenience might have been Cromwell's liking for the local countryside. This was horse-breeding country, and one local tradition has it that he stood on the rising ground near Fethard and declared that it was a country worth fighting for.[2]

Cromwell's priority was to capture the town of Kilkenny. Not only was this the nominal capital of the Confederation but it was central to Ormond's power, its well fortified castle a reflection of the Butler family's wealth and authority in the area. It was a prize worth capturing and, encouraged by the possibility that a Confederate officer, one Captain Tickell, would betray the town in return for a hefty bribe, Cromwell had high hopes that he could take it without a fight. However, duplicity was not required. When he arrived outside the town on 23 March he found that not only had Tickell's ruse been discovered and the man hanged but that the governor, Sir Walter Butler, was disposed to negotiate. Five days later the town fell. Once again the Irish garrison was permitted to leave with full honours and the civilian population was left unmolested. It was a good outcome to the first stage of Cromwell's campaign of 1650, but already his days in Ireland were numbered. No sooner had he taken Kilkenny than the Council of State informed him that he would shortly be recalled to

England to deal with the new threat posed by an impending rapprochement between the Prince of Wales and the Scots.

The execution of King Charles I had effectively ended the union of the crowns of England and Scotland. The relationship had lasted for forty-six years but, with the creation of the Commonwealth, England had become a republic, leaving the Scottish parliament with every right to declare Charles II as their new king. No sooner had the news of the old king's execution arrived in Edinburgh on 5 February than Prince Charles had been proclaimed 'King of Great Britain, France and Ireland', his father having been done to death 'by the traitorous parliament and army (all honest men being formerly removed)'. Even though the new English administration had announced that death was the penalty for anyone who attempted to give sustenance to the succession of the Stewart line, the Scots were not impressed. On the contrary, they were much aggrieved by what had happened at Whitehall. Their commissioners in London had done their best to halt the execution of the king and the Committee of Estates had sent a final appeal to Fairfax on 29 January urging him to take into consideration Scotland's 'advice and consent' and to reflect on 'the honour of Scotland' before taking such a decisive step. This might seem a strange response from a country which had exchanged the king for a financial payment in 1647, a transaction which had the Judas touch and lost them many friends, but there was logic both to the Scots' dismay over the execution and their subsequent proclamation of the new king.

The decision had nothing to do with the Engagers' attempts to help Charles I in the previous year. They had been discredited, their surviving leaders, Lauderdale and Lanark, had gone into exile and the new Argyllist parliament had lost little time in stamping its moral and political authority on the country by passing the Act of Classes which not only condemned the Engagement but excluded its supporters from public life until they offered full repentance. Malignants were the main target, but also included in this catch-all extirpation of wickedness were sinners 'given to uncleanness, bribery, swearing, drunkenness or deceiving', witches, dissemblers and fornicators and all those who neglected their worship on the Lord's Day. Backed by a Church in the ascendant, Argyll's new Scotland was intent on purging the country of all religious and political failings, even if that meant introducing a kind of police state in which defaulters would be punished by 'scurging, nailing of lugs [ears] ... and boring of tongues'. The purge of the body politic extended to the Church: ministers thought to be too liberal on the question of episcopacy were ejected and lay patronage of ministers was abolished with their appointment being given over to local kirk sessions. Even the army was purged with an edict being passed by the Church's General Assembly which put soldiers under 'church discipline' and made it impossible for any man to volunteer unless he was 'faithful in the Covenant'. In this born-again country of the godly, only the elect could hope for preference while those who had supported the Engagement stood condemned as being 'most sinful and unlawful'.[3]

This was more extreme than Pride's purging of the English Long Parliament: by passing the Act of Classes the Kirk Party kept the Solemn League and Covenant at the forefront of their policies and sent a reminder to their English neighbours that they too were still party to it. There was a price to be paid for this absolutism. By punishing the Engagers the Kirk Party was still thinking in terms of Anglo-Scottish unity and of the possibility of a Presbyterian Church settlement, but now they faced a dreadful conundrum. Their Presbyterian allies in the English parliament had been ousted and the 'cursed sectaries' in their place had engineered the execution of the king without any consultation. Not only was this a breach of diplomatic courtesy which enraged the prickly Scots, but the action itself was deeply insulting. However much the Scots might have disliked Charles I for his arrogance and double-dealing, he was their anointed monarch, and, as a people, the Scots had always respected the king's person. Now that Charles I had been executed at the insistence of English republicans – Independents and sectaries whom the Scots had never trusted – the Church turned its displeasure on those responsible. Within a week of proclaiming Charles II king, the Scottish parliament put the country 'in a posture of defence' and waited for the English attack which they believed was inevitable. Robert Baillie was in Edinburgh for those momentous events and could not help but voice his concern that the king's death was a signal that matters would get only worse: 'One Act of our lamentable Tragedy being ended, we are entering again upon the scene.'[4]

In fact the Council of State had no intention of interfering in

Scottish affairs at that moment; it had its own problems dealing with the Levellers and other sects and by the summer it was too preoccupied with the need to quell the Irish troubles. Cromwell had put the matter in perspective when he outlined his priorities to the General Council of Officers on 23 March 1650:

> I had rather be overrun with a Cavalierish interest than a Scotch interest; I had rather be overrun with a Scotch interest, than an Irish interest; and I think of all this is the most dangerous; and, if they shall be able to carry on their work, they will make this the most miserable people in the earth for all the world knows their barbarism, not of any religion almost any of them, but, in a manner, as bad as Papists, and truly it is thus far that the quarrel is brought to this State that we can hardly return into that tyranny that formerly we were under the yoke of . . . but we must at the same time be subject to the kingdom of Scotland and the kingdom of Ireland for the bringing in of the King. Now it should awaken all Englishmen who perhaps are willing enough he should have come in upon an accommodation; but now he must come from Ireland or Scotland.[5]

It was a soldier's response: first deal with the Irish, who appeared to be capable of launching an invasion against England (the old and constant fear), then tackle the Scots, whose army had been destroyed at Preston in the previous year and would be hard pushed to regroup quickly. Although the Scots had made contact with the Prince of Wales the greater threat appeared to come from Ireland and Ormond's combined Confederate forces. Now that they had been dealt a body blow with the fall of their main garrisons and the death of O'Neill the situation had eased, and the Council of State was right to think of bringing home its most able commander to deal with the Scots. Cromwell was a loyal soldier of the Commonwealth and was ready to do his duty, but he would not have been the man he was had he not wanted to finish his task in Ireland by reducing the remaining Royalist strongholds of Clonmel, Galway, Waterford and Limerick.

Elsewhere things were going his way. In Kerry Broghill had mopped up most of the opposition – he captured the bishop of Ross in Macroom, County Cork, and hanged him a few days later outside the castle of Carrigadrohid after its governor refused his summons – and in the north the Ulster army had made the surprising choice of Emer Macmahon, Bishop of Clogher, as its commander in succession to Owen Roe O'Neill. This left Ormond without any serious military experience, and this weakness was exacerbated by reports that many of the Protestants in Inchiquin's regiments were anxious to stop fighting for the Royalist cause. In an attempt to retrieve his position Ormond had summoned the leading prelates to meet him in Limerick on 9 March, but far from helping him to rally support they proposed the formation of a new council to direct the war, a move which would have tied his hands even more firmly. As he was a Protestant his options were limited and he could do little other than object: 'Trust me, they will not, and trust them, I cannot.'

The capture of Kilkenny and the difficulties within the Royalist camp gave Cromwell breathing space, and he used it to begin the negotiations for a truce with Inchiquin's disgruntled soldiers. By the end of April it had been agreed that free passes would be given to those who wanted them, provided that they left Ireland or moved into the areas governed by the Commonwealth. Many took advantage of the offer, including Inchiquin himself, who went into exile in France, where he found himself the object of Irish émigré suspicions on account of his support for parliament between 1644 and 1647; but when Ormond was offered a similar deal he angrily rejected it. It was a brave but quixotic decision: shorn of troops and surrounded by an increasingly hostile party, Ormond was isolated and in his heart of hearts must have known that the Royalist cause in Ireland was as good as dead.

Cromwell also understood his opponent's predicament but he wanted to avoid a conclusion which left Ireland undefeated but with sufficient potential to continue waging a long and messy guerrilla war against English forces. To do the job properly he had to turn his attention to the remaining garrisons, beginning with Clonmel, an attractive walled Norman town to the north of the River Suir and within sight of the imposing heights of Slievenamon. Its governor was no less impressive – Hugh Dubh ('Black Hugh') O'Neill, a nephew of Owen Roe, and an experienced soldier who had fought sufficiently long in the Spanish Netherlands to be well versed in the art of siege warfare. Under him he had 1500 men from the northern counties of

Cavan and Tyrone, and a hundred of those were cavalrymen whom he planned to use as skirmishers outside the defences. He also had the support of the townspeople, an important consideration, as neither the soldiers nor the civilians were in any mood to surrender. When Cromwell arrived to the north of the town with his big siege guns on 27 April and sent the customary summons, Black Hugh refused and prepared for a lengthy siege.

Cromwell's tactics were dictated by the terrain. To the south Clonmel was covered by the river, and the ground on both sides, to east and west, was too marshy for use by soldiers. That left the high ground to the north, Gallows Hill, and it was there that he positioned his artillery, which enjoyed such an elevation that the shells could be lobbed into the town. For O'Neill it was not a promising situation, but he had tough and determined troops and the town's walls were thick and compact. He was also prepared to take the initiative by sending out raiding parties to harry the enemy camp. While these were never more than pin-prick raids they had an annoyance factor and kept morale high at a time when the town was running short of food. In those early stages of the siege O'Neill was confident that he could hold out long enough to tie up the English army and give Ormond time to bring down the Ulster Catholic army for a decisive engagement in the field.

However, even if the Ulstermen had possessed a better commander than the Bishop of Clogher they were unlikely to march so far south, even to lend assistance to an O'Neill, a kinsman of their lost leader. All that was left for the garrison was Black Hugh's guile and their own courage and forbearance. Both would be needed. As the days went by the power of the English artillery began to take effect and by 17 May the breach in the walls was considered to be large enough for a first assault. As he had shown at Basing House five years earlier, Cromwell disliked this kind of action because it was expensive in terms of his men's lives and denied him the chance of surprise. Being blunt instruments, sieges were also difficult to read, and much depended on the willingness of the attackers to press home the assault if the opposition refused to yield any ground. Against a determined commander who was prepared to be active in defence, a siege conducted by superior numbers was by no means a foregone conclusion. So it proved at Clonmel.

Unknown to Cromwell, O'Neill had used the night before the attack to strengthen his inner defences behind the breach in the main wall. Using whatever material was to hand – mostly earth, stones and timber from the shelled houses – he constructed a semi-circular fortification with a ditch in front of it and two hidden cannon at its apex. His men took up position all around it, some hidden in the overlooking houses, others behind the rapidly constructed battlements. The idea was to draw the attacking force through the breach into the enclosed area, which would quickly become a killing ground – the cannon would fire chain-shot at waist height, a sure means of stopping a charge, especially if the line of retreat became blocked. There was never any risk that Cromwell would not attack, and after a psalm-singing session the assault began at dawn the following day. As a contemporary account reveals (it was written some years later) the English soldiers fell into O'Neill's carefully sprung trap:

About eight o' clock in the morning in the month of May and the English entered without any opposition; and but few were to be seen in the town till they so entered; and the lane [created by the breach in the wall] was crammed full of horsemen armed with helmets, back breast swords, musquetoons and pistols. On which those in the front seeing themselves in a pound, and could not make their way further, cried out, 'Halt! Halt!' On which those entering behind at the breach thought by those words that they were all running away, and cried out 'Advance! Advance!' as fast as those before them, till that pound or lane was full and could hold no more.[6]

With Cromwell's men trapped and confused, O'Neill gave the order to counter-attack, and as the shots poured into the packed compound the Commonwealth soldiers had no chance. Cut down by musket fire and by the scything chain-shot of the cannon, they died where they stood, often horribly so, and within an hour the slaughter was over. A thousand men of the seemingly unbeatable New Model Army lay dead and the town was still intact. A furious and bewildered Cromwell arrived outside the North Gate to encourage his men forward into what he assumed would be a battle in the streets only to find that his entire assault force had been defeated. A second assault was ordered and courageously pressed home, but no advantage was gained. By nightfall Cromwell was forced to order his men to retire and the post-battle report to London was one of the most curt he ever had cause to write:

Yesterday we stormed Clonmel, to which work both officers and soldiers did as much and more than could be expected. We had with our guns made a breach in their works, where after a hot fight we gave back a while; but presently charged up to the same ground again. But the enemy had made themselves exceeding strong, by doubling works and transverse, which were worse to enter than the breach; when we came up to it they had cross-works, and were strongly flanked from the houses from within their works, the enemy defended themselves against us that day, until towards evening our men all the while keeping up close to their breach; and many on both sides were slain.[7]

In fact the deaths on both sides are difficult to compute, as there is a paucity of first-hand accounts of the battle. (Reilly asserts that the above description was hardly written in Cromwell's style, and given the scale of the defeat he would not have wanted to dwell on the subject, as he had done so fulsomely after more successful engagements.) It is possible that the New Model Army lost at least 2000 men from death or from the effects of wounds – this was a close-quarters battle in which men received shot from close range or were stabbed by pike and were unable to retaliate. As for the Royalist deaths, they too are unknown but must have amounted to several hundred, and would have been more had O'Neill decided to continue his resistance. However, running low on ammunition and knowing that he could not repeat the tactics which had stood him so well, he took his men out of Clonmel that night and made his way to Waterford, leaving the mayor to sue for surrender. The following day Cromwell was furious to discover that O'Neill had gone, for his army was included in the terms, but he kept his word and his soldiers stayed their hand, an unusual gesture given the casualties they had suffered at the hands of the Irish Royalists. Some accounts claim that two Dominican priests and 'not a few women' were put to the sword, but these owe more to later myth-making than to any contemporary reality.

In any audit of war Clonmel was a military setback for a commander who remained unbeaten throughout the fighting in the three kingdoms but, despite the setback and the feelings of disappointment it must have engendered, it was not a defeat. Cromwell had seen a large number of his men killed, and for a soldier who was careful of risking lives that was a heavy blow. Even so, the fall of Clonmel effectively ended Royalist opposition in Ireland. Henceforth it would be impossible for Ormond to raise an army of invasion, for not only had his forces been decisively beaten by the New Model Army but his own support was in disarray. With the benefit of historical hindsight the Irish threat was always negligible – a shortage of military skill and an absence of funding were two reasons, English military superiority another – but the memory of Strafford's offer to Charles I was still potent. And in any case, in many English minds, the uprising of 1641 was still unfinished business: Catholic Ireland had to be punished for its depredations and the massacre of innocent Protestants.

Seen in that unforgiving light, Cromwell's expedition was successful. By using superior military strength he crushed the Irish Royalists and took away all hope from the Prince of Wales that he could count on an Irish army to come to his aid in England. He had also subjugated Ireland to such an extent that the planting policy could proceed without local opposition – with Ireton now taking over command, the slow grinding down of the remaining opposition would continue apace. At any rate Cromwell was satisfied. He had accomplished most of what he had set out to achieve and had only been in the country for just over nine months, a good return on the outlay of time and effort. After securing Clonmel he went south to Youghal, and from there, on 29 May, took ship for England. His arrival in London was the signal for huge celebrations. People lined the streets to cheer him and Speaker Lenthall welcomed him home with the sonorous words: 'This day [4 June] Cromwell, the Parliamentary victorious general and Lord lieutenant of Ireland, took his seat in the House, give thanks in an eloquent oration for his great and powerful services unto the Parliament and Commonwealth, setting forth the great providence of God in those great and strange works which God had wrought by him as instrument.'[8]

Ahead lay the task of subjugating Scotland and closing it down as a reservoir of support for the Royalist cause. That would need more funds – the Irish venture had cost £3.5 million – and a new army, but there were few doubts that if the last of the three kingdoms was to be brought under the control of the Commonwealth, then the man to do it was Cromwell. Behind him in Ireland he left a country where the war would carry on for another three years, but for the Confederates and their allies it was already a lost cause. On 21 June 1650 the Bishop of Clogher's Ulster army was destroyed at Scarriffhollis outside Letterkenny in Donegal. Two thousand men were killed and those commanders who survived the battle were quickly executed. There was little cheer elsewhere. By the end of the summer a chain of garrisons and fortified towns had surrendered – Carlow on 24 July, Waterford on 6 August and Charlemont on 14 August – and Ormond himself was under siege. Limerick refused to be protected by him; the town chose instead the erstwhile governor of Clonmel, Hugh Dubh O'Neill, and on 12 August a convocation of prelates decided to annul Ormond's authority, preferring instead to put their faith in God, who 'for His own name's sake will deliver us'. By then the Prince of Wales, too, was on the point of cutting him off, leaving Ormond with little option but to prepare to go into exile. Behind, in the rank of Lord Deputy, he left Lord Clanricard, who was at least a Catholic, but all that he had to his name were the garrisons in the fortified towns of Athlone, Galway and Limerick.

Inevitably, the manner of Cromwell's victory cast a long shadow over the country's history. He had come as an invader and his army had demonstrated a ferocity which had been mostly absent from the fighting in England. (Less so in Scotland, where the Royalist Montrose had waged war without quarter and had been indifferent to civilian suffering.) The sieges at Drogheda and Wexford were bloody affairs, and even though it now appears that the mass murders of unarmed civilians did not take place, there was still a combined butcher's bill of five thousand souls in both towns – a sum that can only be compared with the casualties at the two set-piece battles of Marston Moor and Naseby. No matter that Cromwell insisted that he preferred to summon towns by persuasion and wanted to preserve civilian life, he failed to control his men in both sieges and the result was a heavy loss of life. If the 'curse of Cromwell' lived on for many generations thereafter and is still not without resonance today, then

Cromwell only has himself to blame. His disdain for the Irish and his contempt for the Catholic faith made him an unyielding opponent and he pushed home his military superiority with a zealousness which far excelled the strength of the opposition. Only in England was his victory lauded: a day of thanksgiving was declared and the partisan *Mercurius Politicus* was moved to claim that Cromwell was 'one of the wisest and most accomplished of leaders, among the present and past generation'.

Chapter Nine

PRINCE OF WALES, KING OF SCOTLAND

'If God would send him among us, without some of his present counsellors, I think he might make, by God's blessing, as good a King as Britain saw these hundred years.'

Robert Baillie, letter to William Spang, after meeting the Prince of Wales, 30 March 1649

Cromwell's string of victories having put paid to Ormond's hopes of uniting Ireland behind the Royalist cause, Prince Charles's best hope for support lay in his other Celtic kingdom, Scotland. But just as Ireland had been so hopelessly divided, so was Scotland in one of its all too familiar fractious states. In essence the political strong man there was Argyll, who had re-emerged following the crushing of the Engager army at Preston, but the intervening period had seen a diminution of his authority. The Kirk Party remained inviolate, its strength enhanced by the purging of the Royalists, and the authoritative Committee of Estates was under the firm guidance of Loudoun. In arranging the post-Preston settlement with Cromwell's backing Argyll hoped that his power would be cemented by the old parliamentary alliance and its anchor, the Solemn League and Covenant, but he failed to see that his ally, Cromwell, drew his support from the New Model Army and not from the English parliament. And in forging a union between Church and state he also neglected the disciplined authority of the theocratic Covenanters whose fanatical excesses had infuriated the nobles and landed gentry.

That lack of support and the antagonism of the fundamentalist Church eroded Argyll's standing within the country and forced him into rethinking his attitude towards the Crown. Ostensibly the Commonwealth should have been an ally and Scotland should have followed its republican leanings, but support for the king, even among the clergy, was strong and Argyll could not ignore it. Here his musings were helped by the return of Lanark and Lauderdale, who had returned briefly to Scotland, having renounced the Engagement. Both promised not to disturb the peace – the latter was soon to succeed his brother as the Duke of Hamilton – and, having repented, they were given leave to travel to The Hague on 27 January 1649. Once there, they were in a good position to make representations to the young king, and there is little doubt that they became part of a broader effort to encourage Charles II to accept the Scottish crown in return for the imposition of the Covenant in all three kingdoms and the establishment of a Presbyterian form of Church government as promised by the Solemn League and Covenant. To make these representations, commissioners were chosen from the parliament and the Church, the leading personalities being Baillie and the Earl of Cassilis.

The commissioners arrived in The Hague on Easter Monday, 27 March, and the following day had their first meeting with the king. The first impressions were favourable. Having presented Charles with bound copies of the Covenant and the Westminster text, Baillie was much taken with the young man's grave demeanour and an absence of dissembling, both virtues which had been lacking in his haughty and reserved father:

> He is one of the most gentle, innocent, well-inclined Princes, so far as yet appears, that lives in the world; a trim person, and of a manly carriage; understands pretty well; speaks not much. Would God he were among us.[1]

In addition to their religious demands the Scottish commissioners brought with them a further ultimatum, that the new king should remove from his court a 'cursed man whose scandalous carriage, pernicious counsels and contagious company cannot fail to dishonour and pollute all places of his familiar access and to provoke the anger of the most high God against the same.'[2] This wretch, 'the most bloody murderer of our nation', was the Marquis of Montrose, who had arrived in The Hague from Brussels, only to hear the report of his old patron's execution, news which caused him first to faint and then to utter words of defiance: 'We must die, die with our gracious king. May the God of life and death be my witness, that henceforth life on earth will be bitterness and mourning.' Montrose's sudden appearance unsettled Lauderdale, who refused to be in the same room as him, such was his dislike of Montrose's savage behaviour as a military commander. Having gone into exile at the end of his year of miraculous victories and spent the time travelling around Europe, Montrose had made contact with the Prince of Wales's court through Prince Rupert and had immediately offered to do everything in his power to advance the Royalist cause. So impassioned was Montrose that the news of the king's death temporarily unmanned him. He took to his room for two days and emerged with barbarous and vengeful lines which gave vent to his feelings of personal outrage:

> Great God and Just, could I but rate
> My grief to Thy too Rigid Fate!
> I'd weep the World in such a Strain,
> As it would once deluge again:
> But since Thy loud-tongu'd Blood demands Supplies,
> More from Briareus Hands, than Argus Eyes,
> I'll tune Thy Elegies to Trumpet sounds,
> And write Thy epitaph in Blood and Wounds!

It would have taken a more dispassionate man than the Prince of Wales to ignore such a cry from the heart, and Montrose was duly rewarded on 22 February 1649 by being granted the commission of Lieutenant-Governor and Captain-General of the Royalist forces in Scotland. While this was music to his ears it immediately caused friction among his fellow countrymen who were trying to gain the attention of the sorely-pressed prince. To them the presence of the bellicose marquis was a distraction at a time when they were trying to convince Charles that his best hope for a restoration of the Crown lay in Scotland and the Covenant. At the time Charles was hoping to hear encouraging reports from Ireland and was minded to hedge his bets, not least because news had already reached him of a Royalist uprising in the north of Scotland. Started by Thomas Mackenzie of Pluscardine (Seaforth's brother) and supported by Sir Thomas Urquhart of Cromarty, its initial aim was self-protection – the gentlemen in question had been required to sign an oath of allegiance to the new government – but it quickly became a more general uprising. At the end of February Inverness was seized, while in Atholl there was another uprising led by Lord Ogilvy and Thomas Middleton, two Engager commanders who had escaped from their imprisonment in England.

Faced by trouble on two fronts, David Leslie sent a small force into Perthshire to prevent Ogilvy and Middleton joining up with the northern revolt while he marched north towards Inverness. His presence decided the issue in the short term – the Atholl uprising ended as quickly as it began while Mackenzie took his small force of 700 men into the wilds of Ross and Cromarty. The main victim of the unrest was the hapless Marquis of Huntly, head of the Clan Gordon, who had never been able to decide the level of his support for Charles I. Suspicious of Montrose, so much so that he refused him military support when it was most needed, dithering and obstinate in taking advice, he had been taken prisoner in November 1647 after leading a feeble revolt in the north-east. On 22 March, to meet the Church's growing demand for punishment of those suspected of malignancy, he was executed in Edinburgh, a move which encouraged his successor, Lord Lewis Gordon, Montrose's old supporter, to throw in his lot with the northern rebellion.

In April a combined force of Mackenzies, Mackays and Gordons, numbering about 1000 men, marched south out of Ross into Badenoch with the intention of raiding the north-east. With Leslie in the south all that stood between them were three troops of horse and a picket of musketeers commanded by Colonel Gilbert Ker and Lieutenant-Colonel Archibald Strachan, which had been placed in the north earlier in the year. Everything pointed to a Royalist success – they had the element of surprise, weight of numbers and seasoned commanders in Gordon and Middleton – but they allowed themselves to be surprised by Ker's small force of 100 cavalry troopers while encamped near Balvenie in the Spey valley on 8 May. The entire force was captured and Royalist support crumbled as quickly as it had begun. There were no reprisals but the easy victory had the unfortunate consequence of persuading Church leaders that their purges had had the desired effect, that small numbers of righteous, God-fearing men could overcome the malevolence of malignants and sectaries. If there were any doubters, and in the charged atmosphere of a country under clerical sway, they would have kept their silence, then there was the force of biblical example in Gideon's 300 who crushed the Midianites: 'This is nothing else save the sword of Gideon, the son of Joash, a man of Israel: for into his hand hath God delivered Midian and all the host.' (Judges 7: 14).

The news of the uprising also gave weight to Montrose's presence at The Hague by encouraging hopes that he might lead a new rebellion in Scotland and fulfil his promise to avenge the king in 'blood and wounds'. By early summer he had been given a further commission to act in Charles's name to raise funds and find weapons and men to invade Scotland. It was not a hopeless cause – in the aftermath of the Thirty Years War Europe was awash with unemployed mercenaries, and there was sympathy in most courts for the Stewart cause – but it was stymied by Charles's inability to come to any firm decision about his future. Unlike his father, who played off the different factions and made promises which he had no intention of keeping, the Prince of Wales lived up to Baillie's expectations by listening to his supplicants. While hoping that Ormond would provide the best hope of restitution in Ireland and while giving Montrose grounds for optimism, he continued to treat the Scottish commissioners with all due respect. He also took advice from Lauderdale and Hamilton (as Lanark had now become, following his brother's execution), both of whom favoured a compromise agreement with Argyll and the Kirk Party.

However, to have done that would mean accepting the Solemn League and Covenant, and Charles was well aware of the dangers of entering into an agreement which had an adverse bearing on his English subjects. In his ear too was the siren voice of Montrose reminding him that he had no need to treat with the Scottish commissioners as he was a hereditary king who was not obliged to accept conditions. For a month he stalled, but pressed by requests for a written response he delivered his reply on 19 May. It was not encouraging: while he was prepared to accept the Covenant and

Presbyterian doctrine in Scotland he could not make any similar declaration for England and Ireland, as it was not in his power to act 'without the advice of my respective Parliaments of these two Kingdoms'. While not unexpected, his response gave 'great grief' to the ever hopeful Baillie and the Scottish negotiating team had no option but to leave The Hague immediately to report back to Church and parliament.[3]

It was not the end of Baillie's troubles; no sooner had he returned to Edinburgh than he found himself under a cloud when the General Assembly met in July. With the fundamentalists in the ascendancy he was thought to be too 'inclined to malignancy' for his own good and was much criticised for testifying on behalf of a number of ministers who had been expelled to suffer the penance of living 'soberly, righteously and godly' existences outside the Church until they had fully repented. One of them, William Colville of Edinburgh, had only been accused of failing to criticise the Engagement, but that sin of omission was enough to condemn him. Even William Strang, the devout principal of Glasgow University was under suspicion of malignancy.* Although Baillie lent his ready support to both men, at the end of the Assembly he went back to Glasgow to preach at the Tron Kirk, wisely keeping out of Church affairs until the witch-hunt was over.

His enforced sequestration lasted less than a year, for he was too experienced a negotiator to be kept out of public affairs for long. At the meeting of the Commission of the General Assembly in February 1651 the main item on the agenda was a letter from Charles stating his 'readiness to condescend to all their just and reasonable demands', a concession which had to be put to the test by a committee to which Baillie was readily appointed. Although he was not selected as one of the commissioners sent back to the Netherlands to negotiate with Charles, his advice was sought in interpreting the king's offer, which on the surface at least appeared to be a capitulation to Scottish demands. In fact it was no such thing, but it offered enough for negotiations to reopen: Charles agreed to sign the Covenant and to abide by the terms of the Solemn League and Covenant, but only as

---

* 'By great study and violence' Strang was forced to resign in April 1650 and Baillie refused an offer to take his place: 'God guided my hand to be resolute'.

it referred to 'the Kingdom of Scotland'. But it was a start, and Argyll agreed that new talks should take place with the uncrowned king in the Dutch town of Breda.

That the Scots should have changed their tune owed everything to the remarkable brand of pragmatism which Argyll brought to politics. During the summer he had fought off an English proposal, backed by Wariston and others, to enter into a treaty of friendship with the Commonwealth, a decision which would have made Scotland, effectively, a republic. With Loudoun's support Argyll argued that they were bound to back Charles not just because he was the legal king but because his throne had been usurped by a 'prevailing party of Sectaries, who have broken the Covenant, and despised the Oath of God, corrupted the truth, subverted the fundamental Government by King and Parliament'. The Church, too, was indignant, not least because it wanted to impose the Covenant on all three kingdoms and to create its blessed society of saints purged from the vileness of 'adultery, fornication, incest, bigamy and other uncleanness and filthiness'. Argyll was keeping clear water between himself and the Kirk leaders, but their support for the anointment of the Prince of Wales was a powerful factor in keeping open his contact with Charles as summer passed into winter.[4]

By then, the beginning of 1650, Charles had moved his court to Jersey, as his residence in the Netherlands was proving a provocation to the English – their ambassador Dr Dorislaus, a regicide and therefore a strange choice, had already been murdered – and the exiled court's presence interfered with Dutch neutrality. During that time Charles had seen his hopes of Irish support dashed by Cromwell's subjugation of the country, and he had heard nothing from Montrose to suggest that he had won sufficient support for an invasion of Scotland. Faced by the pressing necessity to win back the crown he had no option but to turn once again to the Scots Covenanters. His means of communication was George Winram of Liberton, a moderate and an associate of Argyll, who had arrived in Jersey the previous autumn on a mission sanctioned by Argyll to persuade the king to come back to the negotiating table. Initially Winram thought his task was hopeless, but as winter began he saw Charles's hopes evaporating and he was confident that the Scots' 'just demands' would have to be met sooner rather than later:

His [Charles's] case is very deplorable, being in prison where he is [so the Scots considered Jersey], surrounded by his enemies, not able to live anywhere else in the world unless he would come to Scotland by giving them satisfaction to his just demands; yet his pernicious and devilish council will suffer him to starve before they will suffer him to take the League and Covenant. I am persuaded no rational man can think he will come that length at last; but if he could once be extricate from his wicked council, there might be hope.[5]

Winram's letter was written in mid-November, by which time there was no doubting the news of Cromwell's successes at Drogheda and Wexford, leaving the Prince of Wales with little other option but to enter into 'a treaty on honourable terms' with the Covenanters. Even so, Charles was too much of a Stewart to place all his hopes in the one enterprise: at the same time that he was maintaining contact with Argyll's party in the hope of reaching 'a full and happy agreement' he was encouraging Montrose to capitalise on the earlier risings and demonstrations inside Scotland, entreating him to 'go on vigorously, and with your wonted courage and care . . . and not be startled with any reports you may hear'.[6] Not that the marquis needed any encouragement; his passionate support for the king was born as much out of loyalty and a sense of duty as a restless need to prove himself – Burnet was not alone in thinking that Montrose lived his life as a high romance. To the marquis the matter was clear-cut: it was his duty to serve the king by raising an army in Scotland while Charles spun out the negotiations with the Covenanters.

He had some useful allies from the past to help him. Old Patrick Ruthven, the Earl of Brentford, had been sent to Sweden to try to raise men, money and munitions. Colonel John Cochrane, one of the players in the Incident, was on a similar mission in north Germany, in Madrid the Earl of Crawford was attempting to negotiate a loan from the Spanish court, and Montrose himself had spent most of the summer of 1649 attempting to drum up support in northern Europe. It could have been a dispiriting time, but such was the strength of Montrose's resolve (or the power of his optimism) that he felt obliged to announce his cause in Copenhagen in July, calling on all loyal Scottish Royalists 'by all ties sacred and civil . . . to join with me in this pious and honourable engagement'. His plan was to invade Scotland from the north, beginning in Orkney, to cross to the mainland to pursue those who had refused his call to arms and to 'kill them as vagabonds, rogues and regicides'. The declaration made it clear that the people of Scotland had until 5 November to make up their minds.

Unfortunately, for all the bold words, Montrose had very little real support. In Sweden Lord Eythin, last seen at York, was supposed to be raising an army of mercenaries. In Scotland Montrose looked to the Gordons and Ogilvy and the backing of clansmen in Atholl and Badenoch, and there was a wild rumour that Middleton was on the point of persuading Leslie's cavalry force to change sides. From Germany Sir James Turner offered to help and sent money, but by the end of the summer all that Montrose had at his disposal was one elderly ship and some 200 men in arms. Knowing that something had to be done if his campaign were to emerge from the shadows, Montrose sent this small force to Kirkwall, the main town in Orkney, under the command of the elderly George Hay, Earl of Kinnoul. Then he set off for Gothenburg on one last quest for support.

It was a dispiriting time, made worse by hard winter weather. Even though he received funds and much moral support from an exiled Scots merchant related to the MacLeans of Duart, by the year's end all he had was a small force of 600 mercenaries and a limited supply of weapons. An advance guard left on 14 January and a month later Montrose followed on board the frigate *Herderinnan*, leaving behind Eythin to organise the second wave. With the party was one old ally who had seen more than his fair share of fighting and who had been Montrose's opponent at Auldearn – Sir John Hurry, one of the war's most battle-scarred mercenary soldiers, who had switched sides more times than he cared to remember. Montrose's ship flew a white standard depicting a lion about to leap from one rock to another and the motto 'Nil Medium': for a man who was always at the point where extremes met, nothing further needed to be added.

The frigate reached Orkney in the third week of March, and on arrival Montrose found that his position was bordering on chaos. The sudden death of Kinnoul meant that local levies had not been mustered or trained, and from the Scottish mainland there was no comforting news that the promised support would materialise. He knew he could count on those who had taken part in Pluscardine's uprising, but as for the others it seemed to be a case of wait and see. If he enjoyed some early successes and gave notice that a second year of miracles was in the offing the Royalist magnates would rally to his standard; if not, he must have recognised that he would be on his own. His mood was not lightened by a letter from Charles informing him that he had agreed to talks in Breda. With it came the reward of the Order of the Garter, but that honour and the words of reassurance could not disguise the fact that Charles was backing two horses. While discussing a settlement with the Argyll party he was encouraging Montrose to take up arms against them:

> We require and authorise you therefore to proceed vigorously and effectually in your undertaking; and to act in all things in order to it, as you shall judge most necessary for the support thereof and for service in that way; wherein we doubt not, but our loyal and well affected subjects of Scotland will effectually join with you, and by that addition of strength either dispose those that are otherwise minded to make reasonable demands, to us in the Treaty [Breda], or be able to force them to end it by arms, in case of their obstinate refusal.[7]

In his last letter to his sovereign Montrose sent a diplomatic reply thanking Charles for the honour and confirming his loyalty, but at that juncture he must have known that his military intervention would do nothing to stop his patron rushing into the arms of the Covenanters.

At Breda, which he reached on 16 March, Charles was doing precisely that. With Ireland lost and the outcome of Montrose's expedition uncertain he had little option but to treat with the Scots and try to negotiate the best available bargain. It would not be easy, for the new commissioners were unyielding in their demands. Although there were moderates in their number, and although Charles enjoyed the support of his privy councillors – Hamilton, Newcastle and Buckingham – the Scots wanted their full pound of flesh. First and foremost he was required to sign the Covenants and to impose their conditions on all three kingdoms; furthermore all members of his household would have to embrace Presbyterianism. As for the Scottish parliament, he was to confirm all acts passed since 1641 and for his own part he was to annul all recent commissions and treaties, a move which would have led him to disown Ormond's treaty with the Confederates and Montrose's expedition in the north of Scotland.*

Charles was aghast at the demands, which were harsher than any other visited by the Scots on his family. In vain did he argue that he was in no position to impose Presbyterianism in England and Ireland without the authority of the respective parliaments; the more extreme commissioners, headed by Cassilis, were adamant. Two weeks later Charles's brother-in-law, William, Prince of Orange, intervened in the talks with the proposal that Charles accept the Covenants and their conditions in Scotland only, but it was to no avail, and there followed a period of stalemate while the royal party considered the options. There was little leeway. If Charles was to regain the crown for the Stewarts his only means of support were the Scots, a point which had already been made by other European courts when they had been asked to contribute to his cause. That was the overriding consideration and the Scots commissioners sensed it: as Winram had so astutely noted, Charles was in a 'deplorable' position and only the Scots could extricate him from it. As for their ambitions, the royal signature on the Covenants would be but another and perhaps decisive step towards the creation of a Presbyterian kingdom purged of popish practices and other sectarian malignancies.

During the shadow-boxing which took place in Breda both sides seemed to recognise that there was an element of bad faith in their negotiations. They were also playing for high stakes, and in the end it was the Scots who held all the aces. On 17 April Charles capitulated, agreeing to sign an Oath of the Covenant and to all matters appertaining to Scotland but holding out on the imposition of Presbyterianism in England and refusing to annul the Irish treaty. He also asked for a reconciliation with the Engagers and the restitution of their rights, but this request gave further offence to the commissioners, who would only signify that the matter could be considered further once the king was in Scotland. To all intents the Scots had been given all that they had requested, and in return

---

* To rub salt into the wound Montrose was referred to simply as the 'rebel James Graham'.

Charles received their support in his campaign to restore the monarchy. On 29 April the commissioners assented on condition that the Irish question be reconsidered in due course and the Treaty of Breda was signed two days later. Everyone seemed satisfied but to Alexander Jaffray, one of the more extremist commissioners, it was a bad business for both sides. In his diary that night he noted that common sense had been supplanted by the demands of realpolitik, a state of affairs which was good for no one.

> We did both sinfully entangle and engage the nation ourselves and that poor, young Prince to whom we were sent, making him sign and swear a Covenant which we knew from clear and demonstrable reasons that he hated in his heart.[8]

By signing the treaty Charles had cut Montrose adrift and left him to his fate. A letter was sent on 3 May ordering him to surrender and disband his forces, but it never reached him. Showing the mixture of energy, determination and raw courage that was his hallmark, Montrose had pushed ahead with his plans as best he could. On 9 April he ordered Hurry to cross over the Pentland Firth to Caithness and to make his way to the Ord of Caithness at the end of the east coast littoral. Having done that Montrose and the main force crossed over to John O' Groats and marched to nearby Thurso, where the Royalist mission was declared. It quickly became clear that local support would be scant and, keen to maintain the momentum, Montrose led his men south towards the Ord, then on towards the bulk of Dunrobin Castle, home to the Sutherlands, which was immune to assault. From there he moved inland up the valley of the River Fleet towards the town of Lairg, where he waited for reinforcements from Sutherland, but only one local laird, Alexander Sinclair of Brims, heeded the call. With no reason to tarry in the hills Montrose took his force south, and on 27 April they were near Carbisdale on the south side of the Kyle of Sutherland, a stretch of slow-moving water where the rivers Oykell and Shin combine to flow into the Dornoch Firth.

As he expected little opposition – there had been reports only of a small troop of horse in the vicinity – Montrose had sent out no scouting patrols, a familiar failing. Unknown to him a small but potent force of cavalry was closing in. Numbering 300 troopers and led by the same Colonel Strachan who had triumphed at Balvenie the previous year, it had been summoned from Inverness to make contact with Montrose's army before Leslie's main field force arrived from Brechin, where it had mustered two days earlier. An uncompromising and ruthless soldier who had fought against the Engager army in 1648, Strachan was in no doubt that with God's help he would crush the rebel Montrose, no matter that the odds seemed to be stacked against him.

While Montrose outnumbered his opponent three to one, most of his soldiers were farming and fishing lads who had never witnessed the terror of a charge of dragoons or heard the crack of musket fire. Montrose had done his utmost to give his men a tactical advantage by deploying them in a narrow glen where the Culrain Burn runs into the kyle (a narrow channel) and the heights of Creag a' Choineachan rose behind them, but they did not survive the first charge, scattering in confusion after the initial assault. Luck as well as good judgement had been on Strachan's side. He had arrived in the area from the south-east and was concerned about pushing ahead too quickly, as the following day was a Sunday and, being the man he was, he would not order his men into action on the Sabbath. However, he possessed a good scoutmaster in Alexander Monro, who knew the country well, his son-in-law being Neil Macleod of Assynt who lived nearby. Taking advantage of the concealment offered by a gully in the approaches to the Culrain Burn Monro decided to keep the main force hidden while a troop of horse made themselves visible to Montrose. The ruse worked, and by the time that the Royalist army saw the advancing cavalry it was too late to offer much resistance. The forty horse at their disposal were quickly destroyed and the infantry on the slopes of Creag a' Choineachan broke and scattered as soon as Strachan's troopers collided with them. Four hundred were killed in under two hours of fighting, many of them drowning as they tried to cross the kyle.

Montrose was wounded but managed to flee from the battlefield to make his way west into Assynt. There he threw himself on the mercy of Neil Macleod of Ardvreck, whom he perceived to be friendly, being a supporter of Seaforth, but times had changed and Ardvreck had changed his allegiance to Sutherland, who was close to Argyll and a prominent Covenanter. He was not honour-bound to show any mercy to Montrose and neither did he. On 4 May he handed the marquis over to a government officer, Major-General Holborn, and accepted the reward of £20,000 which had been offered for the capture of Montrose in 1644. He also attracted the obloquy of those Highland Royalists who believed that he had betrayed a guest, and Iain Lom, ever faithful to the victor of Inverlochy, castigated him as the 'stripped branch of the perjured apple-tree without fruit or honour or comeliness'. It was a sorry but not unexpected outcome for a man who had given such unstinting and simple-minded loyalty to the House of Stewart and had been double-crossed by way of return. The sorry truth was that Montrose lacked any tangible support either in the immediate vicinity or in the rest of Scotland, his army consisted mainly of a bare 1600 men, untried Orcadians, and his chances of reinforcement were slim.

Montrose was taken south to Edinburgh in a sad peregrination to Beauly where he was joined by some 200 prisoners including the battle-scarred Hurry. From there they continued east to Inverness, Montrose mounted on 'a little shelty horse' (a Shetland pony) without a saddle and with ropes for stirrups, and from there the route took them through the lands of the north, past Nairn and into Garioch and Strathdon, territory which he knew well. Skirting Aberdeen, hardly a welcome port of call, they continued through the Mearns to Dundee, where a ship waited to take the prisoners to Leith. They landed there on 18 May and Montrose was taken immediately to the Tolbooth prison in Edinburgh, where on the following day, the Sabbath, he endured trial by sermon, the visiting ministers accusing him of the sins of pride and causing death and destruction. Little did they know that a greater sinner stood in their midst. The captain of the guard was Major Thomas Weir, who had seen service in Ulster and who was considered to be a fine upstanding citizen. In his case it was all a sham: twenty years later he would meet a similarly dreadful end, being burned at the stake after confessing to crimes of sorcery, bestiality and incest with his sister Jean.

Montrose's brief, though no doubt tedious stay in the Tolbooth was only a prelude to the legal proceedings he faced the following day in Parliament House. With dignified grace he pleaded that he was acting in the name of the king and that there could be no more honourable grounds but, despite his pleading, there could only be one sentence.

Read by Wariston, it was a terrible fate: Montrose was to be hanged for three hours by the Mercat Cross, then his body was to be cut down, the head cut off and displayed at the Tolbooth, followed by the amputation of the legs and arms, which would be dispatched for display on the town gates of Stirling, Glasgow, Perth and Aberdeen. Whatever remained would be interred on the common ground of the Burgh Muir.

Montrose had seen death many times before, and as a tough guerrilla fighter had visited it on thousands of his fellow countrymen, but this was a traitor's death, and he faced his own with remarkable equanimity. Like the sovereign he served so loyally he was transfigured by the moment, walking to the scaffold the following morning, according to one witness, dressed like a bridegroom:

> He was convoyed out by the baillies out of the jail, clothed in a scarlet cloak richly ornamented with golden lace. He stepped along the streets with so great state, and there appeared in his countenance so much beauty, majesty, and gravity, as amazed the beholders; and many of his enemies did acknowledge him to be the bravest subject in all the world, and in him a gallantry that braced all the crowd, more becoming a monarch than a mean peer; and in this posture he stepped up the scaffold, where, all his friends all wellwillers were debarred from coming near, they caused a young boy to sit upon the scaffold, by him designed for that purpose who wrote his last speech in brachography [shorthand].[9]

Before being dispatched from the monstrous gibbet which stood thirty feet high, Montrose said a prayer for himself, the ministers having refused that duty, forgave his executioners and handed them the traditional pieces of gold. Then, with copies of his declarations hung round his neck* he climbed the ladder and was launched into eternity. His captors were as good as their word. Three hours later he was cut down and the grisly butchery begun, in fulfilment of the last lines he ever wrote:

---

* To these was added a copy of George Wishart's *De Rebus*, an adulatory contemporary biography.

Let them bestow on ev'ry airt a limb;
Open all my veins, that I may swim
To Thee my Saviour, in that crimson lake;
Then place my pur-boil'd head upon a stake;
Scatter my ashes, throw them in the air;
Lord (since Thou know'st where all these atoms are)
I'm hopeful, once Thou'lt recollect my dust,
And confident Thou'lt raise me with the just.

The manner of his death cancelled many of Montrose's shortcomings – his impetuosity allied to a vainglorious nature, his cruel excesses in warfare and his bloodthirstiness – and in time he came to be recognised as a martyr in the Royalist cause. The feeling was heightened by the fact that he was betrayed by the young Prince of Wales and left to his fate in the interests of finding a political solution to the business of restoring the Stewarts to the throne. Cutting him loose in that cavalier way was akin to signing his servant's death warrant, and in the strictly moral sense Charles was unworthy of Montrose. At the time, though, Charles had no other option, and he would soon show the same degree of cynicism by signing the Oath of the Covenant while refusing to heed its message other than as a means to the real end of retrieving his position.

Chapter Ten

A SIGNAL MERCY: DUNBAR

'I profess they run!'

Oliver Cromwell, watching the rout of the Scottish army
outside Dunbar, 3 September 1650

In the aftermath of Montrose's grisly execution the other captured insurgents also received their punishment. The mercenaries were given passes to return to their homes, but apart from a handful of Orcadians who were also freed, most were sold into slavery or into the service of the French army. No mercy awaited Montrose's principal lieutenants, who were either beheaded or hanged according to their station. Among them was Sir John Hurry; having turned his head so often that he could scarcely have known which way it faced, he finally lost it in Edinburgh on 29 May. The most that can be said of him is that he always strove to give his best service to whoever was paying him at the time and that he died in a hopeless cause; the worst opinion is that he could never decide which side to back and paid for that failing with his life.

Having disposed of James Graham, as Montrose was always styled by his enemies, the Scottish parliament turned to the matter of their newly covenanted king. On 2 June Charles left the Netherlands for Scotland on board the Dutch ship *Skidam*, taking with him a retinue which included Hamilton and Lauderdale as well as the Duke of

Buckingham (George Villiers, the son of his father's erstwhile favourite) and two Anglican chaplains. He departed under a cloud. On the day that Montrose had been executed parliament tightened its grip on the conditions agreed at Breda. Charles was obliged to take the oaths immediately, he was to condemn Ormond's treaty and his plea for the rehabilitation of the leading Engagers was ignored. This meant that Charles was to be held in thrall to the Scottish Committee of Estates and that he was to be denied the advice of the men he was bringing with him to Scotland, all against his will and his own religious and political inclinations. As one contemporary broadsheet put it, the prince had been 'safely caught in the springe [trap] of the kirk'.

For Charles it was an unhappy voyage, and as it turned out his personal discomfiture was exacerbated both by contrary winds and the threat of pursuit by Commonwealth warships and by the constant interrogation of his pious fellow travellers. Although he continued to fight his corner by arguing that he could not agree to conditions without the consent of the English parliament, the Scottish commissioners were adamant that if he wanted their support it had to be all or nothing. When the conditions drove the Scottish squadron to take shelter off Helgoland north-west of Bremerhaven Charles was finally beaten down. He signed the conditions without further ado and agreed to take the oaths, thereby binding himself to the Presbyterian cause, swearing 'in the presence of Almighty God, the searcher of all my hearts' to accept the Covenants and to observe the practice and customs of the Church of Scotland both for himself and his family 'and shall never make opposition to any of these, nor endeavour any alteration therein'.[1] It was a solemn oath, taken before God and man, and while it was not taken lightly it was taken under duress and in pursuit of Charles's own ambitions. The Kirk believed that in its newly Covenanted king it had a convert to the cause, or at least one whose conversion would be tempered in the stricter Presbyterian climes of Scotland; but for Charles it was but a matter of expediency. With nothing else in prospect he had to take each day as it came.

On 23 June the ships reached their final destination in Spey Bay in the Moray Firth, where Charles took his oath before being rowed ashore through the early summer mist to his new kingdom. He was given a lusty welcome by the local fisher folk and then taken quickly to Aberdeen, where he was lodged near the Tolbooth but spared the frightful sight of one of Montrose's arms nailed to the city gate. From there he travelled south to Fife, to his new residence, the old Stewart hunting palace at Falkland in the lee of the Lomond Hills. It was a comfortable enough place, improved and beautified in the French style by his ancestor James V, but Charles was quickly subjected to a programme of severe religious indoctrination which undid any delight he might have taken in his new surroundings. Not for him the pleasures of court and hunting for which the lodge had been built or the 'dancin and deray' celebrated by James V in his poem 'Christ's Kirk on the Green'; instead he faced the wrath of fundamentalist clerics determined to purge his soul and bring him into the true faith. Later in life Gilbert Burnet remembered one Sunday when the young prince was forced to endure 'six sermons without intermission' while being exposed to a regime which disallowed any frivolity such as walking on the Sabbath 'and if at any time there had been gaiety at court, such as dancing or playing at cards, he was severely reproved for it.'[2] Worse was to follow: Charles was forced to denounce his parents, and on arriving at Falkland Palace he was informed that a new edict banished most of his followers and prevented his Scottish supporters from visiting him. Only Buckingham, his charming childhood companion and constant friend in exile, was allowed to remain.

It was a curious time. The Scots were determined to bring their Covenanted king into the true fold – one reason for housing him in Scotland was the need to indoctrinate him quickly and efficiently – but they also seemed unsure what to do next. Charles's presence north of the border was clearly a provocation to the Commonwealth at a time when part of their army was dealing with the Irish and the Council of State was tightening its grip on the country with measures designed to prevent any resurgence of Royalist support. The crackdown affected other walks of life, and state Puritanism was gradually coming into its own. Laws were passed to suppress Sabbath-breaking and to crack down on sexual excess (adultery and incest attracted the death penalty) and a revised High Court of Justice was given the power to punish traitors and other malignants without benefit of jury. Thomas Scot, one of the regicides, was given funds and the authority to recruit agents to infiltrate Royalist circles, and 'swarming all over England as lice and Frogs did in Egypt' his men acted as spies, decipherers and agents provocateurs. By the summer of 1650, when Charles was ensconced in Scotland, small groups of determined Royalists were gathering in former Royalist strongholds in England, the most notable being the foundation of a new Western Association in Salisbury, where a number of landowners led by Lord Beauchamp, son of the Marquis of Hertford, met under the guise of attending a race meeting. As Scot's men also knew that Charles and Henrietta Maria had been subsidising these groups with the hope of establishing a solid Royalist opposition, it was not to be wondered at that the Council of State fretted at Charles's arrival in Scotland, for it seemed to them to be a repeat of the events of 1648.

However, having landed the king, Argyll and his followers were not at all keen to repeat the invasion of England and to restore Charles to his throne. The failure of the disastrous Engager expedition had destroyed confidence and the remaining Army of the Covenants was a poor shadow of the force which had fought so resolutely at Marston Moor. Experienced soldiers who had been Engagers had long since been dismissed, and in a series of purges carried out by local Kirk sessions enthusiastic elders had expelled soldiers found guilty of any number of sins including profanity, drunkenness, fornication and general ungodliness, all of which were common enough vices in the armies of the day.* Most regiments underwent this ordeal of moral purification, and in the process many battle-hardened soldiers were given their marching orders so that, in the words of Samuel Rutherford, a new army could come into being to 'fight in faith and prevail with God', for the Almighty himself was on its side and would give its commanders 'a sword . . . and orders from heaven'. As religious exaltation overcame military commonsense, even David Leslie advised against invading England and taking on the professional New Model Army, by then five years into its existence.

Even so, the Scots still posed a threat to the Commonwealth. On three earlier occasions they had invaded England in pursuit of their

---

* Kirk session records from 1650 show that the two main reasons for purging regiments were the crime of fornication and evidence of adherence to the Engagers. Each was thought to be as bad as the other.

own interests, their Church and parliament still supported the aim of imposing Presbyterian Church government, and Argyll and his Covenanting supporters, civil and clerical, were not trusted in England. Then there was the presence of the dead king's son and the Scots' intention to crown him king; with evidence of growing Royalist support in England it all pointed to a new military threat to the body politic which would be launched from the north. That danger had brought Cromwell back from Ireland, but it was by no means clear what role he would be asked to play. On 20 June the Council of State decided that an invasion of Scotland was the only way to prevent the Scots from doing likewise to England and appointed a new committee to deal with the problem. It consisted of Cromwell, Lambert, Harrison, Bulstrode Whitelocke and Oliver St John, a long-time opponent of the Royalists, and it was given special powers to raise an army and decide its command structure.

On 24 June, the day that saw Charles being welcomed back to Scotland, the committee met Fairfax in a room in the palace of Whitehall and there was only one item on the agenda – the leadership of the Scottish invasion force and 'Black Tom's' command of it. Two days earlier Fairfax had signified his unwillingness to accept any new commission, but the scrupulous Cromwell still wanted the matter to be debated and hoped that a compromise might be reached. After earnest prayers Cromwell asked his old comrade-in-arms why a soldier such as he, the Lord General, should be so unwilling to take command of the army of invasion. Fairfax's reply was quite specific: as the English had signed the Solemn League and Covenant it would be morally and legally repugnant to breach the agreement and, besides, there was no evidence of any Scottish invasion threat. Cromwell was equally succinct in his reply: by invading England in 1648 the Scots had broken the treaty and the Council of State had intelligence that they were busy raising forces and money:

> I say, my Lord, that upon these grounds I think we have a most just cause to begin or rather to return and requite their hostility first begun upon us, and thereby to free our country – if God shall be pleased to assist us, and I doubt not but He will – from the great misery and calamity of having an army of Scots within our country. That there will be war between us I fear is unavoidable. Your

Excellency will soon determine whether it is better to have this war in the bowels of another country or our own, and that it will be one of them I think it without scruple.[3]

Cromwell was in a delicate position. After his successes in Ireland his reputation was riding high, yet he could still be accused of ambition if he did not try to convince Fairfax of his duty. Besides, the two men were old friends who had come through the test of battle, and as a soldier Cromwell genuinely wanted the Lord General to take this new command. Fairfax, though, was equally determined to stay out of the fray. During the trial of the king he had quietly distanced himself from the regicides and, privately, believed the execution to be morally repugnant, as did his wife, who had so noisily interrupted the proceedings in Westminster Hall. Religion also played a part. While Fairfax had sympathy for the demands made by the Independents and was a keen upholder of his soldiers' rights, he was a committed Presbyterian and could hardly applaud the demise of their political influence. The discussion continued over several hours, but in the end the committee bowed to Fairfax's conscience and to his assertion that 'human probabilities [the threat of a Scottish invasion] are not sufficient ground to make war upon a neighbouring nation'.

As Fairfax was a central figure in the English revolution his determination not to yield to such potent requests could have caused a breach in the fledgling republic, but he was too astute and too gentlemanly to allow his refusal to become a political football. The following day he wrote to Speaker Lenthall resigning his commission on the grounds of 'debilities both in body and mind' and shortly thereafter retired to his estates in Yorkshire. In his place the Council of State appointed Cromwell 'Captain-General and Commander-in-Chief of all the forces raised or to be raised within the Commonwealth of England'. Not unnaturally the appointment raised eyebrows. Cromwell was considered an opportunist, his performance in Ireland had been highly praised, and he had enemies in the ranks of the Levellers and other radical groups, yet even such a hostile witness as John Hutchinson admitted that Fairfax had come under sustained pressure from the committee members, not least Cromwell, to change his mind. In the best of all worlds Cromwell would have preferred to take an army to Scotland with a similar commission to his Irish operation. Fairfax would have remained commander-in-chief while he commanded the expeditionary force, but when 'Black Tom' proved to be so obdurate Cromwell recognised his duty to his country and saw in it God's providence. He accepted the commission and set about organising the force with his customary efficiency.

With equal vigour he also took steps to safeguard his own position while his attention was directed towards the Scots. Among his potential rivals the main threat came from Edmund Ludlow, the republican member of parliament who had criticised Cromwell's attempts to find an agreement with Charles I in 1647 and who had been equally vociferous in his disapproval of the treatment meted out to the army mutineers at Corkbush Field. Articulate, and held in high esteem by the more radical elements in the army, Ludlow was a tangible force in English politics and Cromwell was right to treat him with caution. Shortly after his appointment he arranged a meeting with him to clear the air and to underline his own resolution to maintain the Commonwealth as a means of giving England a democratic government and preventing the return of the Stewarts. Taking his text from Psalm 110 – 'The Lord at thy right hand shall strike through kings in the day of his wrath' – he convinced Ludlow that the Commonwealth would only thrive if it continued to address the needs of the people and to change the laws to meet that end. Ludlow was sufficiently charmed by this offensive to go to Ireland in the rank of Lieutenant-General of Horse to assist Ireton in his bloody endeavours.

The move suited Cromwell in two ways: he had found a replacement for the dependable Michael Jones and by removing Ludlow from England during his enforced absence he had covered his back. Other potential threats were also removed from the ranks. Cornet Joyce, the captor of Charles I and a noted agitator, was given command of the garrison of Portland in Dorset, and an overture was made to John Lilburne, with whom Cromwell dined on the eve of his departure, promising, albeit vaguely, to 'put forth all his power and interest that he had in the world, to make England enjoy the real fruit of all the Army's promises and declarations'. To complete his rear defences the redoubtable Harrison was given command of the home forces to deal with internal security in the event of trouble from Presbyterians or Royalist supporters.

Cromwell's invasion force was equally well supplied with reliable officers. His lieutenant-general was Charles Fleetwood, his major-general was John Lambert, and he had more than capable regimental commanders, among their number being his cousin Edward Whalley, Thomas Pride the purger of parliament and George Monck, fresh from his operations in Ulster.* The force consisted of 16,000 men, 5500 of them cavalry, and by July 19, taking the traditional east coast invasion route, it had reached Berwick, where Cromwell sent the first of three summons to the Scots to give up any thought of waging war, otherwise 'God shall please us to order the decision of this controversy by the sword'. Even at that stage Cromwell hoped that a peace could be negotiated and war avoided, but the Scots were not only implacable but equally convinced that as God was on their side they would surely triumph.

If Cromwell was affronted by the Scots' refusal to treat with him he was equally infuriated to hear that Scottish ministers were warning their congregations that they were about to face the same depre-dations that the Irish had faced, that savage English soldiers were about to lay waste to the country and 'to put all men to the sword, and to thrust hot irons through the women's breasts'. A counterblast was sent assuring all loyal Scots that they had nothing to fear, but no reply having been received, Cromwell's army streamed over the River Tweed on 22 July 1650. It being a Sunday, the move was swiftly condemned by the outraged Scottish clergy.

The English soldiers entered an empty landscape. In advance of the invasion most of the men of Berwickshire and East Lothian had moved out of the area to join the general muster, leaving behind empty houses and what one English soldier called a handful of 'Scotch women, pitiful sorry creatures, clothed in white flannel'. The Scots had long been expecting the attack. On paper they had a reasonable army made up of time-served regiments, many of whose soldiers had fought in the English campaigns or against Montrose, and in David Leslie, its field commander, they had a fine general. However, the

---

* Monck had originally fought on the Royalist side and was still considered suspect by many New Model Army soldiers. A new regiment was formed for him out of five composite companies drawn from men in Northumberland and Berwickshire. It laid the foundation for the later creation of the Coldstream Guards.

recent purges had reduced the number of trained personnel and the 20,000 eventually mustered contained many unlikely soldiers who were hardly suited to take on Cromwell's professionals. The best of their number were to be found in the horse regiments, which were commanded by officers of the calibre of Archibald Strachan, who had caught Montrose, and in regiments such as Pitscottie's Foot, which had managed to retain some of its Engagers, but according to one contemporary account far too many officers were 'ministers' sons, clerks and such sanctified creatures, who hardly ever saw or heard of any sword, but that of the Spirit'.[4] Alive to the danger of forcing a battle, Leslie decided to defend Edinburgh by creating a defensive line which stretched from the port of Leith and ran south to the Canongate, the city's main eastern entrance. Flanked by the estuary of the Forth and the heights of Arthur's Seat and St Leonard's Hill and backed by artillery, it provided a formidable obstacle, a fact acknowledged by Cromwell after he reached the outskirts of the city on 29 July. Following a brief exchange of artillery fire he withdrew five miles eastwards towards the small coastal town of Musselburgh.

During the move Major-General Robert Montgomery's Horse harried the English rear at Restalrig and Lambert was injured in the ensuing mêlée, but Leslie was in no mood to attempt any further engagement and ordered them to retire. This left Cromwell in a fix. Although his army was well supplied from the sea – the parliamentary navy had control of the coastal waters and could resupply the land forces at will – the Scottish summer was wet and cold and, lacking tents, many of his men succumbed to illness, forcing their evacuation. Still hoping that the two sides could reach a negotiated settlement, Cromwell produced another declaration attacking the Scots' stated principles as 'a covenant with death and hell', but neither the ministers nor the Committee of Estates were moved. Not only were they convinced that right was on their side but during the summer they were facing internal squabbles from two different directions.

Shortly after the first repulse of the English army Charles arrived in Leith at the invitation of the Earl of Eglinton, who had been made commander of the Royal Life Guards, and he received a warm welcome from the troops. However, his presence greatly discomfited the Kirk party, who believed that he was trying to gain control of the army, and the gloomy Wariston thought that no good would come of the visit as the soldiers were inviting God's retribution by according such honour to a living being and not to the Almighty. Given that Charles had already made contact with potential supporters such as Ogilvy, the Kirk party's fears were not groundless, and on 2 August Charles was ordered to leave Edinburgh and cross the Forth to his father's birthplace of Dunfermline. His ill-starred visit had an unlooked-for consequence. Fearing that the army might turn to the king, and bearing in mind the example of Gideon, the Commission of the General Assembly, its executive body, immediately urged a further purging of its ranks. In the days that followed, despite Leslie's protests, another 3000 men were dismissed as Engagers or malignants or both, all for the country's greater glory. One observer, James Kirkton, saw nothing wrong in this mood of exaltation: Scotland was 'Philadelphia' and the country 'seemed to be in her flower':

> Every minister was to be tried five times a year, both for his personal and ministerial behaviour; every congregation was to be visited by the presbytery that they might see how the vine flourished and how the pomegranate budded. Then was Scotland a heap of wheat set about with lilies, uniform, or a palace of silver beautifully proportioned. And this seems to me to have been Scotland's high noon. The only complaint of profane people was that the government was so strict that they had not liberty enough to sin.[5]

Unaware of these goings-on in the Scottish camp, Cromwell had taken his army further east along the coast to Dunbar, which had a better harbour and where they recuperated before marching back to Musselburgh. Under pressure from the Council of State to provoke a battle and aware that the longer his army remained unemployed the weaker it would become, Cromwell made one last appeal, this time to the religious sensibilities of his opponents' clergy:

> Your own guilt is too much to bear: bring not therefore upon yourselves the blood of innocent men, deceived with pretences of King and Covenant, from whose eyes you hide a better knowledge. I am persuaded that divers of you, who lead the people, have laboured to build in yourselves these things wherein you have

censured others, and established yourselves upon the Word of God. Is it therefore infallibly agreeable to the Word of God, all that you say? I beseech you, in the bowels of Christ, think it possible you may be mistaken.[6]

The ministers were not taken in by the appeal and replied tartly that he, Cromwell, was at fault, having broken his oath to obey unquestioningly the terms of the Solemn League and Covenant.

Having received that response Cromwell was left with no option but to try to force Leslie's army into what he hoped would be a decisive battle. In an attempt to draw the Scots out of Edinburgh Cromwell took his army around the south of the city on 13 August and camped on the Braid Hills, but Leslie refused to take the bait. A similar move to the western approaches a fortnight later brought no better result, as Leslie simply moved his defences to counter the threat. A desultory action took place at Gogar, to the south of the present-day airport, on 27 August but the wet ground hampered the New Model Army's horse and despite an exchange of artillery fire the action, such as it was, simply petered out. By that stage dysentery was present in the English camp to add to the discomfort of the wet summer weather, and there was a very real danger that the dispirited men would be too enfeebled to offer any opposition should Leslie ever opt for a set-piece battle – though the longer the stand-off continued the less likely was such an outcome. The only event of any significance occurred when rival patrols clashed near Colinton, the English group being led by Cromwell himself. A Scots dragoon fired a distant shot which had no hope of doing any damage, at which Cromwell shouted that, had the man been under his command, he would have had him punished. The Scot was unimpressed: he retorted that he knew who Cromwell was, having fought with him at Marston Moor.

With Leslie refusing to give battle Cromwell was running out of options, and all the time his casualty list was growing. He faced a much larger force and his supplies were finite; with little prospect of an engagement he ordered his army to move back towards Dunbar with its port and the prospect of fortifying it against Scottish attack. By then his army numbered little more than 12,000, at least a quarter having already fallen ill. To the Scots, this move on 31 August had all the aspects of a retreat. Rumours had reached Edinburgh of the problems facing Cromwell and to Leslie it made sense that a weakened opponent would disengage and try to regroup. Given the direction it had taken, the army might even be retreating back into England – now was the time to begin pursuit. Being a cautious man Leslie kept his forces at a discreet distance, for he knew that, even though he had numerical superiority, most of his men were raw and his officer corps had been further weakened by a fresh purge shortly before leaving Edinburgh. To keep the armies apart he marched to the south of Cromwell and on 1 September he reached Doon Hill, a high ridge on the Lammermuir Hills which overlooked Cromwell's army, encamped outside Dunbar between the high ground and the sea.

With its steep craggy slopes it was a well-nigh impregnable position, the slopes protected by a ravine through which ran a stream, the Brock Burn (today called Spott Burn), but useful though it was as a defensive feature Leslie knew it would never tempt Cromwell to attack him. He also realised that his own men were having problems with the wet weather and that the lack of fresh supplies was making them uneasy. To wait would achieve nothing other than enfeeble his army, while all the time the English army might be preparing to make their escape by sea from nearby Dunbar or getting ready for a break-out along the coast road. Fortune seemed to favour him. Below him lay an enemy whom he believed to have been seriously weakened while he enjoyed numerical and tactical superiority. With him too was a large collection of clerics, among them Wariston, who were keen to take immediate action against Cromwell's sectaries, and it is possible that he allowed his judgement to be affected by their exhortations. Robert Baillie certainly thought so, although he was not present and only reported hearsay, and in the aftermath of the battle a legend grew that Leslie surrendered his tactical advantage because he was told that the Lord of Hosts was with him.

It is quite likely that the ministers accompanying the army did enjoin him to strike, but Leslie was still a soldier with a soldier's instincts. The next day he summoned his senior officers, among them old Leven and the experienced James Lumsden, veterans of the German wars and the first fighting in England, and their unanimous decision was to take the battle to Cromwell while his army seemed to be in such a weak state. Had he been a suspicious man Leslie might have noted that the site was not exactly a place of good omen – a mile to the west was the field where a Scottish army was defeated in the opening battle of the Wars of Independence in 1296 – but Leslie still thought that the odds were stacked in his favour. Within hours of the war council's decision the Scots were streaming down the hill to take up new positions on the lower ground in a great arc below the escarpment, with the bulk of the cavalry on the right by the ravine cut by the Brock Burn. Watching from his headquarters at Broxmouth House to the north Cromwell was moved to say: 'God is delivering them into our hands, they are coming down to us.'

Indeed they were, but Cromwell was still outnumbered and his opponents were fighting on their home ground, an important consideration. He was also facing defeatism from some of his regimental colonels who believed that the only way out of the fix was to order the cavalry to break out along the coast and to ship out the foot soldiers as best they could. To them the position appeared hopeless: to the south of their forces they could see the strength in numbers of the Scottish army and they worried how their men would cope after the previous weeks' marching and counter-marching. It was at this point that Cromwell showed true genius as a commander. Watching the deployment in Lambert's company he noted that Leslie was over-extending his line as it stretched along the southern edge of the burn and arced round towards the coast over the present A1 trunk road. This gave him an unforeseen opportunity: with the left wing pinned in below Doon Hill where the ravine was narrow, a determined attack on the over-extended right could force the Scots to wheel round and fall back on the rest of their army. Even then manoeuvre would be difficult as there was little room for the regimental commanders to traverse their formations. Lambert agreed with Cromwell, telling his commander that 'he had thought to have said the same thing to me'.

To give him the force to attack the Scottish right, Cromwell had to reposition his army, at that time facing the Scots in the traditional cavalry–infantry–cavalry formation, and it also meant making the moves in darkness, never an easy manoeuvre. The guns remained in the centre in front of the burn, on a jut of land where they could both fire directly into the Scottish lines and enfilade them, while the main bulk of the attacking force moved to the low ground on the left before

Broxmouth House. Led by Lambert, it consisted of six regiments of horse supported by a brigade of three and a half foot regiments under Monck's command. Behind them, acting as a reserve, was Pride's brigade and two further regiments of horse. All through the wet night the men moved into their new positions, with Cromwell riding in their midst on a Scottish nag, biting his lip in his anxiety. By four o'clock the new dispositions had been completed and the attack was ready to go in shortly before sunrise, just as Cromwell planned. He could not have known it, but the advantage had already passed to him. In the Scots ranks men had gone to sleep as best they could, huddling down on the wet earth and extinguishing their musket matches as they did so. Some of the officers had even left their posts to take shelter in the nearby farm buildings, so confident were they that they faced a demoralised army. Cromwell was now confronting an enemy who was not only wet and tired but supremely confident that they held the upper hand. It was a dangerous combination.

When the attack began before first light the Scots were taken completely by surprise as Lambert's horse began pushing across the burn and assaulting their dumbfounded opponents. At the same time the artillery opened up, causing further dismay, as the Scots were unaware of its presence on the battlefield: the first they knew of it was the shot ripping into their ranks. On the right, having recovered their poise, the Scots horse counter-attacked, followed by the pikemen, charging down the slope towards the English line and getting in among Monck's infantry, where there was 'a very hot dispute at sword point'. It was a crucial point in the battle: only one part of the Scottish army was engaged, but if it checked the English attack and drove it back across the burn the way would be open for the left to join the battle.

Cromwell, though, was aware of the danger and he decided to use his reserve, not in support of Lambert and Monck but to attack from the left to outflank the Scottish line. 'And we did so,' recalled John Hodgson, one of their number, 'and horse and foot were engaged all over the field: and the Scots in confusion: And, the sun appearing upon the sea, I heard Noll [Cromwell] say "Now let God arise, and his enemies be scattered".'[7] As they pushed home their assault Lambert regrouped his horse for a counter-charge with the infantry which pushed the Scots back up the slopes. In the confusion the

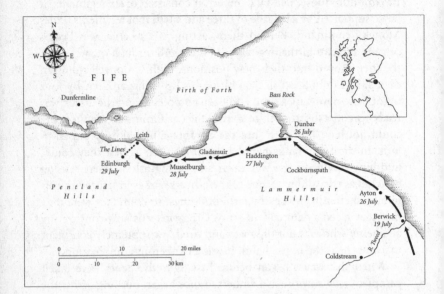

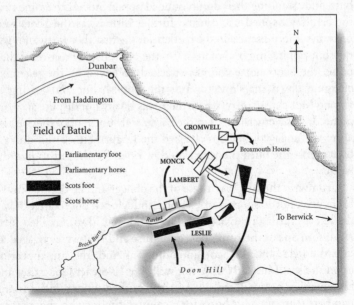

Field of Battle

- ☐ Parliamentary foot
- ▱ Parliamentary horse
- ■ Scots foot
- ◤ Scots horse

Scottish horse broke and fled, a move which condemned the rest of the army to a disorderly defeat. God's enemies, the Army of the Covenant, were about to be scattered, in Hodgson's words, 'all in disorder and running, both right wing and left'.

What followed next was a complete rout. As Cromwell had foreseen, the left broke as the English regiments wheeled round and began the business of rolling up the Scottish right flank. In the close-quarters fighting hundreds died where they stood while others, those on the flanks, made good their escape as best they could, running off in the direction of Edinburgh or pushing slowly back up the hill to the open countryside beyond. Later Cromwell reported that the Scots fell like stubble to English swords and the slaughter was indeed great, some 3000, perhaps more, being killed on the battlefield or cut down as they fled westwards towards Haddington. The main part of the battle had lasted little more than an hour. Not many Scottish formations behaved well; most were caught up by the panic and lacking firm control quickly broke; only two Highland regiments, Gleneagle's Foot and Lawer's Foot, held their ground and died to a man where they stood. Eight thousand made good their escape and the rest, some 10,000, were marched into captivity in England. It was not the end of their troubles: lacking food and suffering from dysentery, many died on the road south and those who lived were transported as slaves to work in the colonies or were pressed into English service.

For Leslie, a good soldier who had allowed himself to be out-manoeuvred and out-thought, Dunbar was a terrible stain on his career. Under his command a Scottish army had been destroyed, and although he accepted the responsibility, telling Argyll that he should accept his own 'share of the salt by many for drawing them [his men] so near the enemy', the defeat effectively put paid to his country's military ambitions. Fortunately for him the accompanying ministers did not apportion any blame and Leslie's offer of resignation was curtly rejected. Instead they heaped coals on the heads of the Scottish people, claiming that the setback was due to their own wickedness and that perhaps the association with the king was the reason for the downfall of an ungodly army which needed to be purged further to bring it to a state of much-needed purity.

The battle did not signify the end of the war, but Cromwell was right to report to the Council of State that it had been 'a signal mercy'.

With East Lothian open to him he took his army briskly to Edinburgh, entering it on 7 September and quickly taking possession of Leslie's old defensive positions. Although the castle did not surrender immediately the city gave itself up to its latest conqueror. Cromwell was accorded a civic welcome at the Nether Bow and took up residence in Moray House in the Canongate while the bulk of his army based themselves in and around Holyroodhouse. Instead of punishing the city and its inhabitants he was keen to win over Scottish public opinion and wanted to build bridges with the clergy, treating them as errant brothers, but despite the threat of punishment his army's stay in Edinburgh resulted in a good deal of damage. Royal arms and portraits on public buildings were destroyed, part of Holyroodhouse was accidentally burned down, and according to the diarist John Nicoll other notable buildings were also badly damaged:

> The College kirk, the Greyfriars kirk and that kirk called Lady Yester's [by the High School Wynd], the High school, and a greater part of the College of Edinburgh were all wasted, their pulpits, desks, lofts, seats, windows, doors, bands [hinges], and all other decorments [ornaments], were all dung [knocked] down to the ground by these English soldiers and burned to ashes.[8]

However, Cromwell did not want to tarry in the capital. Shortly before his arrival Leslie had gathered together the remnants of his army and taken them to Stirling, where they established themselves in a strong defensive position based on the castle. In vain did Cromwell pursue them. The weather was worsening and he was worried that any attempt to dislodge the Scots would drive them north into the Highlands, where they would regroup for a guerrilla war. Having spent one night outside Stirling in St Ninian's Church after summoning Leslie to surrender, he decided to back off and by 21 September had returned to Edinburgh, where according to Whitelocke he 'sought to win them [the Scots] by fair means rather than punish them'.

Chapter Eleven

HAMMER OF THE SCOTS

'I am more and more in the mind, that it were for the good of
the world, that Churchmen did meddle with Ecclesiastical affairs
only.'

Robert Baillie, letter to William Spang, March 1648

In dealing with the Scots Cromwell's main problem was that he was
not able to negotiate with a single faction. In the aftermath of Dunbar
the Kirk party began to lose ground; its military commander Leslie
was holed up in Stirling together with an array of politicians and
ministers, and the national mood was turning away from support for
the Covenant towards the patriotic duty of countering the English
invasion. Much of this feeling was centred on Charles, who was said
to have fallen on his knees in gratitude when the news of the defeat
reached him in Perth.* As Charles could still count on support from
Episcopalian magnates in Angus and the north-east he had grounds
for optimism that his former Royalist backers might rally once again
to his aid and that the defeat at Dunbar might give them new heart.
Shrewdly, Cromwell reckoned on that possibility when he wrote to
Hesilrige on the day after his victory: 'Surely, it's probable the Kirk has

---

* More to the point was the remark made by a New Model Army officer: 'Upon the rout
at Dunbar the Royal party were much comforted in seeing us destroy their enemy, as
well as ours.'

done their do. I believe their King will set up upon his own score now, wherein he will find many friends.'[1] The impetus to do just that came a month later when Charles received word that his household was to face a purge and he would lose most of his guards and closest servants.

By then he had already been in contact with the Earl of Airlie and his son Lord David Ogilvy and with the Earl of Atholl and the Marquis of Huntly, all of whom offered to provide men to rise in his support. The planned coup would have seen Perth and Dundee being seized as a prelude to a general Highland rising north of the Tay, but it went off at half-cock. Men failed to materialise, there was a display of outstanding incompetence by the noblemen concerned and Charles himself exhibited all his father's old habits of half-heartedness and indecision. Somewhat aimlessly he left Perth on 4 October, ostensibly on a hunting expedition, and rode the forty-two miles to Cortachy Castle in Angus, the seat of the Earl of Airlie, only to find that the revolt had failed. That night was spent disconsolately in a dingy shepherd's cottage in nearby Glen Cally, which lies between Glen Prosen and Glen Clova in the Braes of Angus. It was an ignominious end to the expedition, and further opprobrium came with the dawn, when a troop of horse appeared outside the house under the command of Lieutenant-Colonel Sir Thomas Nairn of Montgomery's Horse. The Start, as the incident is known in Scottish history, was over, and Charles was taken back to Perth to be admonished for his 'unexpected behaviour' by Chancellor Loudoun and the Committee of the Estates.

It was not the end of the Royalist uprising but it was the beginning of the end – a few weeks later a force led by Lord Ogilvy attacked one of Leslie's regiments under the command of Sir John Brown of Fordell at Newtyle in Strathmore. This could have ignited a wider revolt, but without Charles the northern Royalists lacked cohesion and on 4 November Ogilvy's men agreed to disband following a meeting with Leslie at Strathbogie. The only other place to witness an outbreak of serious Royalist support was in the south-east, where small bands of guerrilla forces had started harassing Cromwell's forces and threatening his lines of communication. Known as moss-troopers and led by two determined commanders, Augustine Hoffman, a German mercenary, and Sandy Kerr, a local man, they caused all manner of mischief for Cromwell, who responded by threatening reprisals against what remained of the civilian population. Although these guerrilla forces offered little more than a general nuisance they had to be subdued, and the task was given to Lambert and Monck. As happens in any guerrilla war the English commanders found it difficult to engage an enemy who relied on hit-and-run tactics, and their difficulties were compounded by the fact that the moss-troopers were operating out of secure bases – a number of heavily fortified houses which dotted the landscape of Midlothian and East Lothian. Over a thousand English soldiers were tied up besieging Dirleton Castle in East Lothian, and it did not fall until early November when Monck brought up two mortars which fired shells over the walls into the garrison's living quarters. The guerrilla commander, one Captain Watt, was shot by firing squad and by the end of the month the remaining strongholds had either been subdued or forced to surrender.[2]

By then the need for national unity was overwhelming, because the Kirk party was facing determined opposition from a new military cabal which had been formed in the south-west. Known as the Western Association, or western army, it was led by Archibald Strachan, Gilbert Ker and Sir John Chiesley, all of whom had served under Leslie but who now believed that their cause was best served by a new force of godly men freed from any contagious contact with the king. Its origins lay in the Whiggamore Raid of 1648 and it drew its support from the Covenanting counties of the south-west – Lanark, Ayr, Renfrew, Wigton, Kirkcudbright. It also enjoyed the backing of Wariston and other fundamentalist ministers such as James Guthrie of Stirling and Patrick Gillespie, who had recently come to the fore as a candidate for the post of principal of Glasgow University.

On 2 October the Western Association set out their stall at a meeting of the Glasgow synod where they produced a 'remonstrance' addressed to the Committee of Estates, placing the blame for Dunbar on those who had brought Charles into the Treaty of Breda 'before sufficient trial was taken and evidences had that his Majesty had changed his corrupt principles'. According to Baillie, who was present, the leaders claimed that Charles had failed to expel from his presence 'all disaffected and profane persons' and that as a result of that failing Scotland had been visited by the wrath of God.[3] A second remonstrance was produced a fortnight later at Dumfries, signalling their refusal to support the king until 'he had given satisfactory evidence of sincere repentance and of honest intention to abandon the company of Malignants'. Both remonstrances were sent to Stirling, where the parliament and the Church commissioners were sitting. The resulting schism helped no one: it deprived Leslie of an army, for the Remonstrants refused to serve under him, and that refusal to accept the king placed them on a collision course with the Kirk party.

Not unnaturally Cromwell took advantage of the confusion. On 9 October he marched his army, now reinforced by fresh regiments, to Linlithgow, where he sent a message to the Committee of Estates placing the blame for Scotland's woes on the presence of the king. From there he moved west to Glasgow, at that time a small and compact town which he and his men preferred to Edinburgh. In pursuit of his policy of pacification and conciliation he tried to win over the local clergy, even to the point of sitting through a lengthy sermon given by Zachary Boyd in the High Church of Glasgow. Despite the fact that Boyd, a sturdy preacher but a bad poet, railed against the English during the course of his sermon, Cromwell invited him back to his lodgings for a further three hours of prayer.* It is a tribute to Cromwell's resilience that the next day, 14 October, he rose early to march his army back to Edinburgh following receipt of intelligence that Leslie was about to attack the city to relieve the castle. By the time they had reached Linlithgow the rumour had been proved wrong but Cromwell had made a serious military point to the Scots. Lowland Scotland was an open country and he and his army were free to come and go as they pleased.

That freedom of movement also underlined the absence of any plan in the Scottish camp. Only the Kirk party and the Royalists wanted to rid the country of Cromwell's army, while the Remonstrants in Dumfries only desired a purged Scotland, freed from the taint of popish kings and others who doubted God's word as it

---

* Boyd was the author of *Zion's Flowers* (1644), a collection of Old Testament stories rendered into verse, much of it execrable:

'There was a man called Job,
Dwelt in the land of Uz;
He had the gift of the gob;
The same thing happen us!'

had been revealed to them. For a time Cromwell thought that he might find an accommodation with the latter party, as they were clearly opposed to the Royalists and might be persuaded to throw in their lot with the English. After all, Strachan had served under him at Preston and had attempted a parley earlier in the year during the siege of Edinburgh, but Wariston and Gillespie forbade any engagement with sectaries: in their opinion Cromwell and his soldiers were as dangerous as any Royalist. The only return Cromwell received was the defection of Strachan, leaving Ker in command of the Western Association's armed forces.

The Kirk party also needed the support of the Remonstrants and were greatly irked by the failure of the Western Association to do anything except keep their army in the south-west, where it posed no threat, other than to persuade Cromwell to strengthen Carlisle with Hacker's and Whalley's regiments. However, the production of the two remonstrances decided the issue: if the Western Association would not hand over their military power it would be taken from them. By then, the middle of November, the Kirk party had entered into an agreement with the northern Royalists and the need to settle Scotland's internal affairs was paramount. On the receipt of the remonstrances, which were condemned as scandalous to the king, the Committee of Estates decided to send Colonel Robert Montgomery and 3000 men to remove Ker and take over command of the western forces. As the son of the Earl of Eglinton, a leading Covenanter with interests in the south-west, Montgomery had a reasonable chance of fulfilling his commission. He was also convinced he was doing the right thing, as Ker had recently refused a request from the Committee of Estates to take his army to relieve Borthwick Castle outside Edinburgh, one of the fortified houses holding out against Monck and Lambert. However, nothing came of Montgomery's expedition as Cromwell had himself decided to destroy Ker's little army. On 27 November he left Edinburgh with eight regiments and marched west by way of Shotts towards Rutherglen, where the Western Association's army was quartered.

Ker was in a difficult position. Strachan had deserted him, he knew that he faced replacement once Montgomery arrived, and he must have realised he had attracted opprobrium for refusing to support the Estates. His only hope was to win credit by taking on and defeating Cromwell in Lanarkshire, and at first he seemed to hold the upper hand. When he first learned of Cromwell's approach he held the bridge over the River Clyde at Bothwell, a move which forced Cromwell to halt and allowed the Scots to retire in good order to the south. At that point Ker was in a commanding position and luck appeared to be his companion – on the night of 30 November he learned that a force commanded by Lambert had entered Hamilton and first reports indicated that it was considerably smaller than his.

Ker decided to attack immediately, sending an advance guard of troopers under the command of Colonel William Ralston into the town, where they met little or no opposition. However, it was a cold moonlit night and from the clatter of horses being driven over the frosty ground Lambert was given advance warning of the Scots' attack. Before they arrived he withdrew the greater part of his force out of Hamilton, leaving behind a small rearguard, and the move tricked Ralston into believing that he had won control of the town and that the English had fled. Encouraged, Ker brought up the rest of the force, only to be ambushed as they were crossing the nearby Cadzow Burn. Despite putting up fierce resistance – Ker had his horse shot from under him and was badly wounded – the Scots were badly mauled and by the time day broke they were in full retreat. Around a hundred were killed, Ker and several score were taken prisoner but the rest, over one thousand, melted away from the area and went back to their homes. The army of the Western Association had been destroyed.

Three weeks later, on Christmas Eve, another obstacle was removed for Cromwell when the garrison of Edinburgh Castle agreed to surrender even though it could have held out much longer. Cromwell had ordered up miners from Derbyshire to help him break the siege, but they were not needed as the governor, Sir Walter Dundas, obviously believed that after the defeat at Hamilton it was pointless to continue holding out against the English.

Ker's defeat had another unexpected consequence. With the loss of the Western Association army it was made clear to the Kirk party and its followers that they had no other means of raising a force capable of defeating Cromwell. Concessions had to be made and, given the need to find soldiers, they came on the grounds of conscience. On 12

December the Church commissioners assembled in Perth and the following question was put to them: 'What persons are to be admitted to rise in Arms, and join with the forces of the Kingdom, and in what capacity, for defence thereof against the Army of Sectaries, who (contrary to the Solemn League and Covenant and Treaties) have most unjustly invaded and destroyed the Kingdom?' In other words, the ministers were being asked to find a way of reversing the purges which had driven so many Engagers and Malignants, out of Scotland's army. Two days later they replied with a 'first resolution' which paved the way for 'the raising of all fensible persons [capable of serving] in the land, and permitting them to fight against this enemy for the defence of the Kingdom, except such as are excommunicated, forfaulted, notoriously profane or flagitious [guilty of criminal behaviour]'. No mention was made of Engagers or Malignants, and that same day the process began of recalling to the colours trained soldiers who had been victims of the infamous purges. Provided that they offered abject apologies to their local presbyteries – Middleton made his dressed in sackcloth, an ignominy he never forgot – they were welcomed back into the fold.[4]

The change of heart deepened the gulf with the Remonstrants, who remained a potent political force despite the military defeat, but the decision to include Royalists gave additional weight to the moderates, who became known as Resolutioners. It also paved the way for Charles's coronation, which took place on New Year's Day 1651 at Scone outside Perth, the traditional place of coronation for Scotland's kings. In keeping with the mood of the times the ceremony was a curious mixture of pomp and Presbyterianism. Charles was allowed to wear a rich robe and was seated beneath a velvet canopy accompanied by pages drawn from the sons of the nobility. There was a feast of some magnificence, but although he was crowned king by Argyll, with Loudoun offering the crown to him, he was not anointed, the act being considered too superstitious and therefore popish, and he had to endure a lengthy sermon from Robert Douglas, the moderator, who preached on the perils of a fading crown. It made a brave show, one that was designed to produce a sense of national unity, but as Robert Baillie noted on the last day of 1650 Scotland was still a long way from solving its problems:

It cannot be denied but our miseries and dangers of ruin are greater nor for many ages have been; a potent victorious enemy master of our seas, and for some good time of the best part of our land; our standing forces against this his imminent invasion, few, weak and inconsiderable; our Kirk, State, Army, full of divisions and jealousies; the body of our people be-south [river] Forth spoiled, and near starving; they be-north Forth extremely ill used by a handful of our own; many inclining to treat and agree with Cromwell, without care either of King or Covenant; none of our neighbours called upon by us, or willing to give us any help, though called. What the end of all shall be the Lord knows.[5]

Subsequent events showed that Baillie's pessimism was not misplaced but, as 1651 began, there was a feeling abroad that matters could only get better. The return of the purged soldiers permitted the creation of a new army, the Army of the Kingdom, its regiments rich with aristocratic and Highland clan names. In Edinburgh, for all his military successes, Cromwell had fallen ill and was incapable of directing further military operations. As for Charles, he was enjoying a popularity denied to his father and as his authority increased so did that of Argyll wane. Having opposed the Engagers he was now forced to concede his support for the king, and his last attempt to gain influence was an ill-starred proposal to marry off his daughter, Lady Anne Campbell, to Charles.

Yet for all the demonstrations of support which the new king received when he visited major towns such as St Andrews and Aberdeen, both within his bailiwick of personal influence, there was no coherent idea about what should be done next. Charles's aim was the restoration of his crown, but that could only be achieved by invading England and defeating the forces of the Commonwealth. To accomplish that he would have to rely on the backing of an army of Presbyterians which was still intent on upholding the terms of the Solemn League and Covenant. So far he had managed to convince the Scots of his earnestness – those who attended his coronation were impressed by the zeal with which he reaffirmed his adherence to the Covenants – but the unity of his supporters was paper-thin. Former Engagers might have done their penance and been accepted back into the fold, but there was the danger, ever-present in Scotland's history, that traditional enemies such as Argyll, representing the Covenanters, and Hamilton, the Royalists, would strive to gain a political advantage and in so doing split the king's supporters.

Matters came to a head in mid-March when Charles tried to persuade parliament that repentant Engagers should be allowed to sit on the Committee of Estates, a move which would have given him more power at the expense of the Covenanters. Unwilling to respond, parliament passed the question over to the Church commissioners, who hedged their bets by proposing that a new committee be formed to direct military affairs. This was approved, much to Wariston's anger – he likened the move to making an alliance with the devil ('all Jews, Turks, all Rome, but not Protestants') – and the way was open for the Act of Classes (which had demanded the employment in public office or the army of only the most rigorous supporters of the Covenant) to be repealed at the beginning of June. Within days former Engagers and suspected Malignants had been brought back into Scottish public and clerical life. At the same time, the Church's General Assembly, meeting in St Andrews and Dundee in mid-July, voted to deprive extremists such as Guthrie and Gillespie of their livings. The decision split the Church – the assembly was something of a farce, with rival groups of Resolutioners and Remonstrants meeting separately – but within the space of a few heady months Charles appeared to have won control of Scottish political and clerical life.

It was, of course, all veneer. Such as it was, Charles's writ did not run very far: his Scotland was the country beyond the central lowlands – Fife, the north-east and the Highlands – while Cromwell controlled the capital and the routes into England. At the same time Cromwell had thrown off his illness – once again he saw the hand of God in his recovery – and his army had been reinforced. Facing him was a Scottish army, 18,000 strong, which was lined up behind a line of fortified positions which stretched along the north side of the Forth from Stirling into Fife. Most of the men were untrained and no match for the New Model Army but, once again, Leslie had adopted a defensive strategy and Cromwell realised that it would not be easy to crack it. In June and July English forces made a feint towards Stirling before heading south to ravage the area around Glasgow but, realising that a pitched battle would be fatal, Leslie would not be drawn, other than to move his army to a new defensive position at Torwood, south-east of Stirling. The only solution was an amphibious attack across the Forth, an operation which carried no guarantee of success, as it would take time to ferry sufficient men across the estuary to form a bridgehead before the defenders responded – an earlier attempt to take Burntisland had ended with Monck's men being repulsed.

But, if Cromwell wanted to avoid another period of stalemate, such an operation had to be attempted. His solution was startlingly simple, and it worked. Using specially constructed flat-bottomed boats, his men would cross the estuary at its narrowest point, the gap between South Queensferry and North Queensferry, the point at which the river is crossed by the modern rail and road bridges. Led by Colonel Robert Overton and under Lambert's overall command, the first units were taken over the crossing and formed a bridgehead on the small peninsula on the night of 16/17 July. Three days later 4500 of Lambert's men were on the Fife shore.

The Scots had to respond, and a force was hurriedly mustered under the command of Sir John Browne of Fordell and Sir James Holburn and including some seasoned regiments, among which might be mentioned Brechin's Horse and Buchanan's and Pitscottie's Foot. Attached to the force was a Highland regiment, Maclean's Foot, commanded by Sir Eachunn Ruadh (Red Hector) Maclean of Duart and consisting mainly of Macleans and Macquarries raised from Argyll and Bute. The Scots' task was simply stated – to prevent Lambert's force from breaking out of the peninsula and streaming into Fife – and the lie of the land favoured their accomplishing that aim. The North Queensferry peninsula is belted by a narrow isthmus and backed by some rising ground known as the Ferry Hills. On the other side to the north-west the land rises again to the prominent Castland Hill. If this point could be held Lambert would have difficulty breaking out of his defensive position.

Having arrived on 20 July the Scots deployed across the high ground to the west of the town of Inverkeithing, the cavalry under Browne on the left while Holburn commanded the foot on the right. Sensing the danger Lambert drew up his force on the reverse slopes of the Ferry Hills, the main strength a force of cavalry and dragoons on the right, with the foot in the centre. The clash lasted little more than a quarter of an hour and, as the battle-hardened English pikemen and musketeers collided with the raw Scottish soldiers, Holburn's lines broke, leaving the cavalry exposed. As Lambert's men drove on towards Castland Hill many Scots started throwing down their arms and fled the battlefield with the English horse troopers in full pursuit. Over 2000 Scots were killed at Inverkeithing, Browne was captured along with 1500 prisoners, and Lambert had Fife at his mercy. Not all Scots behaved less than heroically. On the right, brigaded with Buchanan's Foot, were the Macleans, who had come under intense artillery fire before the Scottish horse fled from the field. Although facing overwhelming odds, and with all hope of support gone, they made one last stand, the clansmen taking it in turns to place themselves as bodyguards between the attacking English soldiers and their chieftain. As each one fell another would take his place with the rallying call, 'Fear eil airson Eachuinn!' ('Another one for Hector!') Of the 800 who began the battle only 35 survived. Their valiant efforts failed to protect their clan chief: Red Hector Maclean of Duart was killed by a musket shot.

Inverkeithing destroyed all hope of further Scottish resistance. From Linlithgow Cromwell ordered the bulk of his army to cross into Fife, and by the month's end the English forces were outside Perth. Even as the General Assembly was disputing in St Andrews and Dundee their nemesis, Cromwell's army of sectaries, was within marching distance. With Scotland lying at his feet Cromwell had won the initiative. Leslie could not afford to move into Fife to force a battle, for he knew that to do so would only bring a repetition of Dunbar and Inverkeithing. Only one option remained: to march rapidly into England and to rally Royalist support while the main bulk of the New Model Army was tied down in operations in Scotland. This is what Charles wanted – ever since arriving in Scotland he had been itching to return to England – and it might also be what Cromwell intended, for he realised Leslie would never dare meet him in pitched battle without reinforcement. On 31 July the Scots took the fateful decision to invade England for the third time in ten years.

Not everyone was enamoured of the move. Leslie had wavered but he had been persuaded by Buckingham's enthusiasm. Argyll took himself off home and refused to have any part of the adventure, leaving Hamilton to gloat that 'all the rogues have left us'. Loudoun, too, remained behind, to head a rump Scottish government. In Edinburgh

Wariston prayed that the English sectaries would finally be defeated, although in his enemies' eyes his prayers were negated by the accusation that he had been over-familiar with Cromwell during the occupation of Edinburgh. Only Charles and his closest advisers were buoyant and confident of success. They also clung to hopes that their friends and associates in England would rally to the cause and that the support of latent Royalists would strengthen the Scottish army before Cromwell could intercede. However the portents were not good. In the previous December a local rebellion in Norfolk had fizzled out as soon as it began and the main participants were swiftly executed. Alarmed by the incident, pathetic though it had been, the Council of State ordered the arrest of suspected Royalists and the strengthening of militia forces in Lancashire, a county traditionally loyal to the Crown. They were also helped by the arrest of two Royalist agents, Isaac Birkenhead and Thomas Coke, who saved their lives by giving full details about the plans to support the king's cause, a betrayal which effectively put paid to English resistance groups such as the newly formed Western Association which had been formed by Royalist supporters in April 1650 under the pretext of holding race meetings.

Even so, when Charles crossed the border into England on 6 August 1651 he remained remarkably confident. Not only was he leaving Scotland, a country for which he had little enthusiasm or affection, but against all the odds he believed that his presence would rally support for his cause.* He had high hopes that Lancashire would rise and he had been told that the Earl of Derby planned to cross over from the Isle of Man with an invasion force. Apart from some levies from Manchester few recruits appeared – most of the gentry were unwilling to take the Covenant – and Derby's pathetically small army was overwhelmed by parliamentary forces outside Wigan on 25 August. By then Charles and the Scottish army had reached Worcester and it was horribly clear to the king that his English subjects were not interested in helping them. He was proclaimed king by the mayor at the town's cross but an attempt to muster men from the surrounding countryside ended ingloriously with the herding up of barely 200

---

* Charles never returned to his northern kingdom and it was not until 1822 that another British monarch, King George IV, saw fit to visit Scotland.

unwilling conscripts. Meanwhile Cromwell's army had arrived to the east and taken up position between Red Hill and Perry Wood, having marched down the east coast route from Scotland, while Lambert was to the south, having followed hot on the heels of the Royalist army. Charles and the Scots were now surrounded and vastly outnumbered.

In dealing with the new strategic situation posed by the Scottish invasion Cromwell had acted decisively. Monck was left behind in Scotland with a force of 6000 soldiers to complete the country's subjugation while he and Lambert marched south with the rest of the army, each commander taking a different route. As Lambert harried Charles's army, never being less than a day's march behind it, Cromwell took the eastern route, forcing his men to march an average of twenty miles a day. Before leaving Edinburgh he had written to the Council of State stiffening their resolve and reassuring them that theirs and the country's safety would not be compromised:

> I do appreciate that if he [Charles] goes for England, being some few days before us, it will trouble some men's thoughts, and may occasion some inconveniences; of which I hope we are deeply sensible, and have, and I trust shall be, as diligent to prevent as any: and indeed this is our comfort, that in simplicity of heart as to God, we have done to the best of our judgements, knowing that if some issue were not put to this business, it would occasion another winter's war, to the ruin of our soldiery . . .[6]

While Cromwell was right to steady nerves he was still the master of the situation. His army was larger, more experienced, and they had been joined by equally experienced units led by seasoned commanders – Fleetwood, Harrison, Grey of Groby and Robert Lilburne. They were also fighting to defeat invaders who commanded no local support. That was an important factor. Anti-Scottish feeling was running high, there was general dislike of the Solemn League and Covenant and government newspapers such as *Mercurius Politicus* never tired of jeering that Charles had come south with an army which had just suffered two crushing defeats at Cromwell's hands. Memories of 1648 and, earlier, of Leven's presence outside Hereford in 1645, remained strong: the Scots were unpopular, being regarded as an alien and untrustworthy race whose people were little better than uncouth savages. On the other hand the Commonwealth was secure, if not popular, and it could afford the upkeep of superior forces – in addition to the New Model Army Cromwell had the newly raised county militias at his disposal to guard key points.

And yet, all was not lost. Leslie hoped that in Worcester he might be able to repeat the tactics which had proved so successful in Edinburgh and Stirling – to construct a strong defensive position and provoke Cromwell into the kind of costly frontal attack which the Scot knew his opponent was loath to make. (For all his ruthlessness Cromwell was miserly with his men's lives.) There were grounds for thinking this might be successful. Worcester was already partially fortified, it sat astride the River Severn and its cathedral tower offered commanding views of the surrounding countryside, a tactical advantage which meant that every enemy move to the east could be observed by Charles's commanders. With the Welsh hinterland to the west, traditionally Royalist, the city offered several strategic advantages. Clarendon noted with more optimism than judgement that it was 'a good city, served by the noble river of Severn from all the adjacent counties; Wales behind it, from whence levies might be made of great numbers of stout men: it was a place whither the King's friends might repair if they had the affections they pretended to have'.[7] Within days of the arrival of the Royalist army, the southern bridges over the Severn were destroyed at Upton and Bewdley and the bridges over the River Teme at Powick and Bransford to the south of the city were also cut.

The move was designed to prevent any encirclement of the city and to keep the exit route to the west clear, but the guard posted on the bridge at Upton, which had been kept open by a plank across the broken arches, failed to keep adequate watch. Shortly before dawn on 29 August Lambert exploited this weakness by sending an advance guard across to create a diversion while his main force forded the river. The Scots put up a stout defence but they were driven back by force of numbers and lost heart when their commander, Major-General Edward Massey,* the former parliamentary governor of Gloucester,

---

* Massey had arrived in Scotland at the end of 1650. During the march south he had been commissioned to recruit English Royalists but, as he was forced to remind potential supporters of the requirement to sign the Solemn League and Covenant, he met with little success.

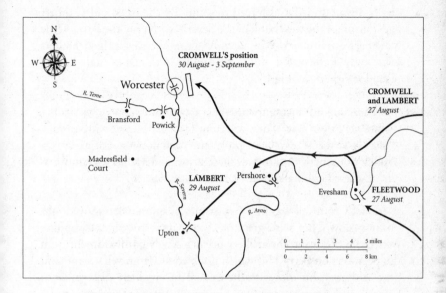

CROMWELL'S position
30 August - 3 September

Worcester

R. Teme

Bransford
Powick

Madresfield
Court

LAMBERT
29 August

R. Severn

Pershore

R. Avon

Upton

Evesham

CROMWELL
and LAMBERT
27 August

FLEETWOOD
27 August

0 1 2 3 4 5 miles
0 2 4 6 8 km

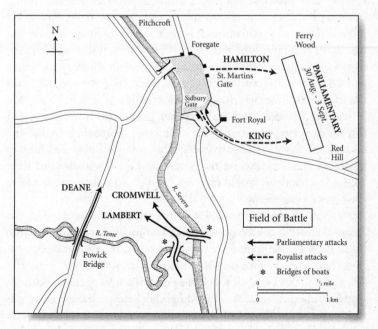

N

Pitchcroft

Foregate

Ferry
Wood

HAMILTON

St. Martins
Gate

PARLIAMENTARY
30 Aug.- 3 Sept.

Sidbury
Gate

Fort Royal

KING

Red
Hill

DEANE

CROMWELL

LAMBERT

R. Severn

R. Teme

Powick
Bridge

*

*

*

Field of Battle

Parliamentary attacks

Royalist attacks

Bridges of boats

0   ½ mile
0   1 km

was badly wounded and forced to retire. By the day's end Lambert had control of the west bank of the Severn, with only the River Teme lying between him and Worcester. As Cromwell saw it the defenders could only 'fight or fly', but as he told the Council of State he was ready for either eventuality:

> We are thus advancing towards that city. And I suppose we shall draw very close to it. If they will come forth and engage with us we shall leave the issue to God's providence, and doubt not to partake of glorious mercies. If they avoid fighting, and lead us a jaunt, we shall do as God shall direct.[8]

In fact Cromwell was in a very strong position. Men moved into position slowly but with great precision, ammunition and supplies were brought up and the artillery began a steady bombardment from the positions on Perry Hill which doubled as Cromwell's command post. Although his moves to the east of the city were discernible to Charles and his commanders, Cromwell possessed overwhelming strength: his army was 28,000 strong and growing daily, Fleetwood joining them at Evesham, and a force led by Lilburne was in the process of cutting off the routes into Wales. Cromwell had sufficient men for a long siege, but he was impatient to attack from the south and west, where the city's defences were weaker and the open fields on the left bank of the Severn offered a better line of attack. To do that he had to get his forces there in strength, because the Scots had placed three regiments to defend the southern approaches under the command of Robert Montgomery. One solution suggested itself, a bridge of boats to traverse the Severn and the Teme close to their confluence, but this would take time and could only be done under the noses of the enemy.

Nevertheless that is what Cromwell ordered to be done on 30 August, and the resulting delay had the fortuitous result that the Battle of Worcester took place on 3 September, exactly a year after the Scots had been crushed outside Dunbar. This was to be Cromwell's 'crowning mercy', and although the result was a foregone conclusion it still required three hours of hard fighting before Charles's army was finally defeated. The attack began in the morning with Fleetwood's men crossing the bridge of boats under covering fire while another force led by Colonel Richard Deane pressed home their attack over the Teme at Powick, where the first fighting of the war had taken place nine years earlier. The Scots, mainly Highlanders, put up a fierce resistance, using the hedgerows as cover and only retreating as the weight of Cromwell's men pushed them back. In so doing they also sucked more men on to the western bank, with the result that Fleetwood's investing force was suddenly exposed. From his eyrie on the cathedral tower Charles noted what was happening and acted.

As Montgomery's men withdrew in order back into Worcester Charles ordered two assaults to be made on the parliamentary lines to the east. The first, led by Hamilton, went from St Martin's Gate and attacked the northern section of the line at Perry Wood while Charles led a second charge out of Sidbury Gate towards the southern end at Red Hill. Although both were forced to attack uphill and lacked sufficient numbers to press home the advantage of surprise, the first stage of the assault succeeded in pushing the parliamentarians back. At this stage Leslie's cavalry could have lent support – they were watching from Pitchcroft meadow outside the town – but their orders were to pursue the enemy once they had broken and Leslie chose not to intervene. Had Cromwell not possessed sufficient reserves to bolster the line the Royalists' attack might have yielded a greater advantage, but once the momentum had gone they had no option but to retreat. Within an hour the withdrawal had turned into a rout, with both sides intermingled in close-quarters fighting as the beaten Scots tried to win back to the illusory safety of Worcester. At the same time Lambert's men were rolling up the Scots to the south, and by late afternoon the battle had turned into a vicious street-to-street and house-to-house encounter, with men fighting over corpses and dead horses until darkness fell.

It had been a bloody battle, and those who managed to escape death in the city fared little better as they fled from the scene of carnage. In Kidderminster, to the north of Worcester, Richard Baxter woke to find the remnants of the 'flying army' passing through the town:

> I was newly gone to bed when the noise of the flying Horse acquainted us of the Overthrow: and a piece of one of Cromwell's Troops that Guarded Bewdley-Bridge having tidings of it, came

into our Streets, and stood in the open Market-place before my Door, to surprise those that past by: And so when many hundreds of the flying Army came together, when the 30 troopers cryed stand, and fired at them, they hasted away, or cryed Quarter, not knowing in the Dark what Number it was that charged them: And so as many were taken there, as so few Men could lay hold on: and till Midnight the Bullets flying towards my Door and Windows, and the sorrowful Fugitives hasting by for their Lives, did tell me the Calamitousness of War.[9]

The Royalists had lost 3000 of their number, the majority Scots, 4000 managed to escape, but most of those were captured as they tried to make their way home to Scotland and a further 10,000 were taken prisoner. From Worcester they were marched to London or other provincial cities, where arrangements were made to sell them as slaves to landowners in New England, Bermuda and the Caribbean; those who survived the journey never saw their homes again. The English among their number fared little better: they were sent to join Ireton's forces in Ireland and one of their number, the Earl of Derby, was executed for treason. Of the leaders Hamilton (who died later of gangrene), Leslie, Middleton, Lauderdale and Montgomery were taken prisoner. Buckingham managed to escape, as, famously, did Charles himself, who managed to get to France on 16 October following an extraordinary journey around southern and south-western England in which luck, loyalty, a variety of disguises and a network of sound contacts combined to save him. During his wanderings he was constantly recognised, yet despite the lure of reward he was never betrayed and the story of his escape passed into English legend, not least because, 'in a manner sufficiently declared to the World' one of his hiding places was the oak tree at Boscobel, the home of the Penderells in Shropshire.[10] Charles was fortunate that his escape was eased by a number of Catholic families: they had more reason than most other English people of the period to possess long experience of concealment and subterfuge.

As for the New Model Army, their losses were counted in their hundreds and Cromwell was fully justified in telling the Council of State that he had acted in the name of the people and that God had rewarded that duty by once more revealing his providence:

The dimensions of this mercy are above my thoughts. It is, for aught I know, a crowning mercy. Surely if it be not, such a one we shall have if this provoke those that are concerned in it to thankfulness, and the Parliament to do the will of Him who hath done His will for it and for the nation and the change of government, by making the people so willing to the defence thereof, and so signally blessing the endeavours of your servants in this great work.[11]

Hugh Peters was more to the point but no less eloquent. Using language reminiscent of Shakespeare's *Henry V*, he reminded the soldiers that they were near Powick Bridge, the site of one of the first of those battles that had plunged the three kingdoms into a decade of chaos: 'When your wives and children shall ask you where you have been, and what news: say you have been at Worcester, where England's sorrows began, and where they are happily ended.'[12]

Chapter Twelve

HELL OR CONNACHT: THE SUBJUGATION OF SCOTLAND AND IRELAND

'We well understand the present condition of this nation is more inclining to ruin and despair than recovery.'

Declaration of Irish prelates, 12 August 1650

For the first time in nine years England was free of the scourge of war. During that period some 85,000 soldiers had died in battle, the majority of them (50,000) Royalists, and it has been estimated that one in four of the country's population of five million found themselves caught up in war in one way or another between 1642 and 1646. Civilians, too, became casualties as victims of siege warfare and disease, especially bubonic plague: the latest figures suggest that 40,000 fell victim to non-combat deaths during the conflict. One example will stand for many: almost 12,000 people died in Devon during the war, and a quarter of those were casualties of illnesses contracted during the siege of Plymouth.[1] Rape, often followed by murder, had been commonplace and soldiers indulged in casual plundering which usually involved equally offhand brutality. Prisoners, mainly Scots and Irish, were sold into slavery and although the war never produced the kind of mindless barbarity which was endemic in the Thirty Years War, there was a disturbing tendency among parliamentary commanders to hang Irish Catholic prisoners.

On the other hand soldiers requesting quarter were rarely refused and most were allowed to return home scot-free, but tribal animosities meant that amnesties of that kind were the exception in Scotland and Ireland. The landscape also suffered. Towns such as Bristol and Colchester were partially destroyed, crops were ruined as armies marched and counter-marched over the countryside, often in the atrocious weather which seemed to be commonplace in the 1640s, countless homes were wrecked, deserters became vagrant criminals and civilians had to endure the distress of seeing strange and frequently uncouth soldiers billeted upon them. Few were spared the experience of conflict: as Richard Baxter had put it in 1646: 'Oh the sad and heart-piercing spectacles that mine eyes have seen in four years space! Scarce a month, scarce a week without the sight or noise of blood.' And writing about the period many years later John Oglander said: 'you would think it strange if I should tell you there was a time in England when brothers killed brothers, cousins cousins, and friends their friends'.[2]

Clearly there was a need for stability; the world had been turned upside down and now it had to be righted. People wanted not just peace but a return to the old certainties – a settled government, a peaceable society, lower taxation and an end to militarism. Cromwell recognised the mood, telling Whitelocke in 1652 that the problem was 'how to make good our station, to improve the mercies and successes which God hath given us, and not be fooled out of them again, nor to be broken in pieces by our particular jarrings and animosities one against another but to unite our counsels'.[3] His aims could not be questioned, but the settlement of the new republic would not be easily accomplished. The army was still in being and remained a powerful factor in political life, a fact underlined by Cromwell's dual authority as a member of the Council of State and as Captain-General of the armed forces. For all that Royalist rule had been abolished, most of the army's claims, embodied in their earlier manifestos, had not been met and far from having a more democratic parliament England was still ruled by the Rump Parliament and its executive body, the Council of State. Change would be slow in coming as the earliest date for elections had been set for November 1654. Church governance had to be addressed, as did reform of the law. And hanging over all those issues was the matter of supreme power and who, if anyone, should hold it. As Whitelocke shrewdly put it, a decision had to be taken about what kind of settlement was required and what type of republic should be created.

Before any of those claims could be addressed adequately the situation in Scotland and Ireland had to be brought under control, because in both countries, in varying degrees, a state of warfare persisted. It was not as if either nation had been spared in the earlier fighting. For a country whose population numbered one million Scotland had suffered a higher proportion of casualties than her southern neighbour, mainly because quarter was rarely given to Highland soldiers and because internecine rivalries meant that, all too often, civilians were caught up in the fighting. The best estimate is that there were 28,000 Scottish military casualties and that a further 15,000 non-combatants were killed in incidents ranging from the destruction of the Campbells at Inverlochy, counted as a battle, to Alasdair MacColla's notorious 'Barn of Bones' massacre of Campbell women and children, which is properly accounted as an atrocity. With the undying enmity of Catholic and Protestant, Ireland fared even worse. Soldiers spoke of marching through empty countrysides – before his death Owen Roe O'Neill had likened parts of Donegal to hell – and the retribution visited on local communities meant that military and civilian casualties are difficult to disentangle. Lack of contemporary records and the production of rival propaganda cloud the issue, with the result that the estimated deaths from warfare in Ireland between 1641 and 1652 range from 192,000 to 618,000. Even the lower figure is far worse than anything suffered in the other two kingdoms.[4]

And even after the battle of Worcester brought the fighting in England to an end the killing was still going on as Commonwealth forces carried on the task of pacification and subjugation. Before Cromwell left Scotland in pursuit of Charles's Scottish army he left Monck to deal with the remaining Scottish resistance. Under Monck's command was a field force of 6000, together with the bulk of the artillery train, and he also enjoyed the support of further English troops in the main garrisons at Edinburgh, Leith and Perth. Ranged against him was a disparate grouping of Royalists, Covenanters and Highlanders who should have been able to offer a spirited opposition – after all they were facing unpopular English invaders –

Parliamentary commander and defender of Bristol, Nathaniel Fiennes was forced to surrender to Prince Rupert in 1643. *(Mary Evans Picture Library)*

Philip Skippon, the highly respected parliamentary commander of the London Trained Bands. *(Mary Evans Picture Library)*

Cromwell's son-in-law Henry Ireton, a key figure in the Putney Debates of 1647. *(Mary Evans Picture Library)*

A tough and popular parliamentary commander, John Lambert was considered a possible successor to Cromwell. *(Mary Evans Picture Library)*

Demands for better pay and a general indemnity led to mutinies in the parliamentary army in 1647. These were ruthlessly put down. *(Mary Evans Picture Library)*

'This is nothing but the hand of God.' The defeat of the Scots Engager army at Preston in 1648 sealed Charles I's fate. *(Private Collection/ Bridgeman Art Library)*

On the eve of his execution Charles I said a tearful farewell to his younger children, Prince Henry and Princess Elizabeth. *(Private Collection/ Bridgeman Art Library)*

Charles I was executed on 30 January 1649. 'Such a groan as I never heard before, and desire I may never hear again.' *(British Museum/Bridgeman Art Library)*

Cromwellian justice: the Irish town of Drogheda was put to the sword following a short and bloody siege, 11 September 1649. *(Mary Evans Picture Library)*

A signal mercy: the defeat of the Scottish Royalist army at Dunbar in 1650 allowed Cromwell to occupy Scotland. *(Mary Evans Picture Library)*

On New Year's Day 1651 Charles II was crowned at Scone, the ancient coronation place of Scottish kings. *(Private Collection/Bridgeman Art Library)*

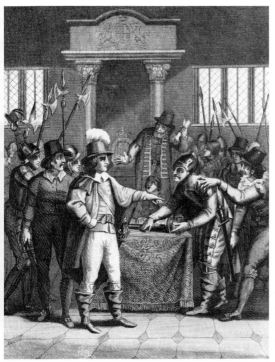

The Rump of the Long Parliament was dismissed by Cromwell on 20 April 1653. *(Private Collection/Bridgeman Art Library)*

The defeat of the Dutch navy at the Battle of Scheveningen in 1653 ended the first Anglo-Dutch naval war. *(Mary Evans Picture Library)*

Soldier turned sailor: Robert Blake commanded the Commonwealth navy in successful actions against the Netherlands and Spain. *(Mary Evans Picture Library)*

Tumbledown Dick: Richard Cromwell failed to live up to the reputation of his famous father. *(Mary Evans Picture Library)*

A good soldier but a headstrong king, James II lost his throne in 1688 after trying to impose Catholicism on his subjects. *(Mary Evans Picture Library)*

John Lilburne, the most prominent of the Leveller leaders who was imprisoned regularly for his radical beliefs. *(Mary Evans Picture Library)*

In writing her husband's memoirs Lucy Hutchinson produced a vivid description of the civil wars in England. *(Mary Evans Picture Library)*

Described as 'the first English woman writer', Margaret Cavendish was the wife of the Duke of Newcastle, a leading Royalist. *(Mary Evans Picture Library)*

A great naval administrator in the reign of Charles II, Samuel Pepys owes his place in history to his famous diary. *(Mary Evans Picture Library)* but only if they combined, and that outcome was unlikely. That perennial problem would be Scotland's undoing, but even without it Monck had no easy task ahead of him. A Scottish garrison still occupied Stirling, England's writ ran only in the central belt, and beyond that there was potential Royalist opposition in the north-east and the fastness of the Highlands. There was also an administration in place under Loudoun and his Committee of Estates – albeit in a fair state of disarray – and key centres such as St Andrews had held out against summons to surrender to the occupying forces.

The final subjection of Scotland was not a foregone conclusion, but in Monck the Commonwealth had the ideal soldier for a steady and deliberate campaign of attrition. A careful planner who was not given to impulsive gestures, he decided that his best hope lay in systematically reducing Scottish military strength and preventing the various oppositions from using their combined efforts against him. Within hours of the departure of the main bulk of the English army he parked his field force outside Stirling on 6 August. A summons to surrender was issued and the town council accepted it, allowing the Committee of Estates to make good their escape, while the garrison of 300 moved into the castle. For Monck this was a blow, as the ancient stronghold was well protected and he could not afford to be tied down by a lengthy and costly siege. One option was to ignore the obstacle and continue operations elsewhere, but Stirling's strategic position provided the link between the Highlands and the Lowlands and offered a rallying point for Scottish opposition. Monck took the second option of battering the castle into submission with his heavy mortars and great guns.

It took effort and patience to bring up the pieces and then to create the secure platforms required for their use but, within a week, following two days of bombardment, the garrison was ready to surrender. Under heavy and frightening mortar fire morale quickly collapsed and on 15 August 1651 the men, mainly Highlanders, led by Colonel William Cunningham, a former Engager, marched out of the castle and were allowed to go home. The collapse came at a good time. First, it removed a strategic obstacle and allowed Monck greater freedom of movement and, secondly, it freed up his forces to deal with pockets of resistance which were appearing elsewhere. From the west of Scotland had come rumours that the old Western Association forces might be revived: to counter that threat Monck dispatched two regiments under Colonel John Okey, a veteran of Naseby, with a show of overwhelming force. The sight of patrols of heavily armed cavalry troopers and dragoons did the trick and, having imposed fines on Glasgow and Paisley, Okey was able to tell Monck that the west was quiet. A second military demonstration in Fife led by Colonel Matthew Alured, once a Leveller, also kept the county quiet, although St Andrews, having just played host to the General Assembly, declined to submit until 30 August and was then heavily fined for its stubbornness.

By then Monck had capitalised on the fall of Stirling and had moved his forces north towards Perth with the intention of marching on Dundee, now the seat of the Scottish administration. The plan made sense. From his intelligence reports Monck had heard that fresh Royalist forces were being raised in the north-east by Balcarres and Huntly and the heavily defended Dundee was regarded by the Scots as the next centre of resistance. Monck's route out of Perth took him along the north bank of the Tay through the fertile Carse of Gowrie towards Dundee at the mouth of the river's estuary. On 20 August Loudoun issued a call to arms, but the Committee of Estates was unwilling to be taken captive and as Monck's army approached they rode north to the small town of Kirriemuir in the lea of the Braes of Angus. Although this was Ogilvy territory there was little local support or protection apart from that offered by the much-depleted regiment of Ogilvy's Horse commanded by Lieutenant-Colonel William Sinclair of Dun. From Kirriemuir the committee made its way to Alyth, ten miles to the west, and it was there on 28 August that they were surprised by Alured's regiment; among those taken into confinement were Leven, Earl Marischal, Lord Ogilvy and the Earl of Crawford-Lindsay, who had recently been given command of the forces in Scotland, a poisoned chalice if ever there was one. Any forces remaining in the area scattered and at one swoop Scottish political authority had been crushed.

Dundee went the same way two days later when Monck's artillery opened up a barrage, the town's governor Robert Lumsden having refused to surrender. Rain delayed the operation – once again the weather was dire – and following a second summons, which was also refused, the bombardment began again early in the morning of

1 September. By midday the walls had been breached and the attackers entered the city to begin the task of killing off the outnumbered defenders. Because quarter had been offered and refused the subsequent sacking of the city was carried out with more than usual ferocity and the casualties were unacceptably high – anything from one hundred to one thousand depending which side's figures are to be believed. Monck claimed 500 killed and 200 taken prisoner, his report noting by way of explanation that the inhabitants had 'paid dearly for their contempt'. Whatever the number, contemporary accounts make it clear that women and children were among the casualties and that during the twenty-fours of plunder permitted by Monck innocent lives were lost. John Nicoll, admittedly not present, claimed over 1000 casualties and placed the blame on Monck's soldiers who 'coming in furiously upon the people, put all that were found without [outside] doors to the sword, both men and women'.[5] While it was not Drogheda revisited, the sacking of Dundee was none the less a blot on the reputation of the New Model Army. At that stage an atrocity of that immensity would never have been visited upon an English city.

Two days later came the news of the defeat at Worcester, and with it Scotland had ceased to exist as a viable military power, its armies had been destroyed and apart from a few fortresses such as Dumbarton and Dunottar, to which the Scottish regalia had been taken, resistance was mainly confined to the Highland reaches which for the moment were beyond Monck's capabilities. Within the space of two months the country had lost its government, its army and its king, and with them removed from the equation Scotland was effectively rudderless. Not having been taken at Alyth, Loudoun attempted to arrange meetings of the Committee of Estates first at Killin and then at Dunkeld, both secure places in Perthshire, but his call was ignored. With Commonwealth soldiers occupying the main towns and cities the situation seemed hopeless. By November Huntly and Balcarres stood down their forces, mainly because they were outnumbered and also because it was becoming difficult to retain the support of the local population. It helped that Monck had put his house in order by instituting stricter measures of military discipline in the wake of the sacking of Dundee. Aberdeen was spared a similar fate and, recognising the general war-weariness, the Commonwealth army, effectively an army of garrison, set about enforcing strict military discipline and restoring law and order.

In Dundee, for instance, two drunken soldiers were court-martialled and flogged for assaulting a local woman, three others heard swearing were forced to sit astride 'the horse', a sharp-backed wooden frame, with weights attached to their legs to increase the pain by putting pressure on the genitals, and anyone caught robbing locals faced similar punishments.[6] Steps were also taken to prevent English soldiers becoming romantically involved with Scottish women, and any fornication was rooted out and punished as enthusiastically as it had been by the Kirk sessions. In Angus and the Mearns of the north-east the local lairds were encouraged to take responsibility for law and order within their own areas of influence, on pain of being fined if they failed in their duties. This not only freed up soldiers from security duties but encouraged a sense of responsibility and inclusiveness. In Edinburgh large numbers of prisoners were freed, a welcome amnesty, but leaders such as Ogilvy were sent south for further imprisonment in the Tower of London.

Much of this was done to make sure that Scotland functioned; the military were in effect the ruling authority, but there was also a political dimension to the English presence in the country. In the aftermath of the victory at Worcester the English parliament was minded to treat Scotland as a conquered and hostile country and to garrison it accordingly. Wariston feared as much, especially when lands of inheritance were granted to Lambert, Monck and other senior officers, and he saw this colonisation as God's reproach for the country's continuing wickedness. However, Cromwell had other ideas about how to deal with the Scots. All along he had tried to find common ground between the two countries – while in Edinburgh earlier that summer he had discussed with Wariston the possibility of a closer union – and that idea eventually prevailed. On 13 October the Council of State produced *A Declaration of the Parliament of the Commonwealth of England, concerning the Settlement of Scotland*, a document which outlined the provisions for the political, social and religious incorporation of Scotland with England. Over 2000 copies were printed and distributed throughout Scotland so that the people could be reliably informed about the nature of the English proposals. Briefly, the main points dealt with toleration of religion (bar

Episcopalians and Catholics), political union and the forfeiture of royal property and revenues as well as of those who had supported the Stewarts (only those who renounced their support after Dunbar were exempt). Under a separate agreement a new Court of Judicature was created, with seven judges, four of whom were English, but because of the differences between the legal systems of the two countries no attempt was made to incorporate Scots law.

The message was clear. Instead of being punished Scotland was to be treated not just leniently but almost as an equal partner; only the Royalist leaders, 'the chief Actors in these invasions and wars against England', were to be given harsher treatment by being proscribed and having their estates and revenues confiscated. By being brought into partnership with England, Scotland would become part of the Commonwealth and would benefit from the revolution which had swept away royal rule.[7] The Scots had no leeway and were bound to accept what was being offered. Their Covenanted king was in exile, the government was in disarray, the Church was bitterly divided between Resolutioners and Remonstrants and trade was at a standstill; to some contemporary observers the state of the nation was as bad as it had ever been since the fourteenth-century Wars of Independence and the reign of King Edward I. The only other option was to become a province of England, but the Council of State's declaration, soon to become a Tender of Union, offered the fig-leaf of political respectability by allowing the Scots to be 'one Commonwealth with this of England'.

To underline the fact that this was an English settlement commissioners were appointed to execute the policy contained in the declaration. Ostensibly they were appointed as negotiators, but because England held the reins of power, not least militarily, they were really there to implement a policy which had been agreed beforehand by the Council of State. In theory the Scots would be free to debate the main issues, but in practice they were being presented with a decision from which they would only be able to wring minor concessions. As the Rev. Robert Blair put it, the union was as unnatural an occurrence 'as when the poor bird is embodied into the hawk that hath eaten it up',[8] and many Scots were keenly aware that they were being forced into an agreement which had been imposed on them by the winning side. Even the English understood that they were pushing through a predetermined policy and that the Scots were in no position to object to the outcome. Robert Joyce, an officer accompanying the commissioners, said as much shortly after he arrived at Dalkeith, south of Edinburgh, in January 1652:

> The Scotch people know not what to say to them now that they are comed; some are glad and some are mad now that they see we are in earnest, and that their power is like to change. The Kirk and Cavalier cannot endure one another: each of them endeavours to ingratiate, but the latter is more rationally convinced; the other are yet much unsatisfied. I fear those that seem to have most religion will be most at a loss if they timely prevent it not by a free condescension. I think power will not early and hastily be given to either of them.[9]

It was a prescient observation. Although deputies from the shires and burghs were summoned to discuss the main points, the union was a settled issue and the subsequent act for incorporation was introduced in the English parliament on 18 March. Within a month it had become law and was read at the Mercat Cross in Edinburgh on 21 April, to no great enthusiasm from the watching crowd: 'scarce a man of them showed any sign of rejoicing, though the most flourishing of their kings would have given the best jewel in their crown to have procured a vote in Parliament for their equal shares in the laws of England'.[10] At one stroke the Scots were no longer a separate nation but united with England in a bond which was stronger than that produced by the Union of the Crowns. Paradoxically that state of affairs had been the aspiration of the supporters of the National Covenant when they attempted to impose Presbyterian Church government throughout the three kingdoms; now they found that while they were allowed to worship freely, so too were Independents, the very people whom they had opposed and detested. Only the regalia, the honours of Scotland, remained intact and they were jealously guarded. Before Dunottar Castle fell on 26 May the royal crown, sceptre and sword were smuggled out and taken to the village of Kineff, where they were buried under the floor of the church. By then Monck and Lambert had returned to England, leaving the English garrison under the command of one of the regicides, Major-General Richard Deane, who served until the end of the year, when he was replaced by Colonel Robert Lilburne, the Leveller's brother. The latter was soon involved in attempts to pacify the Highland areas outside Commonwealth control, where the last Royalist elements had assembled under William Cunningham, the Earl of Glencairn, a prominent Engager who had remained behind to raise levies after Charles took the Scottish army into England.* In time he would be replaced by John Middleton, an experienced soldier, but it would take time and much effort to get him back into Scotland from his exile in France.

Most Scots accepted the new order, but assent did not imply appreciation or welcome. This was especially true in the Church of Scotland, whose ministers, Resolutioner and Remonstrant alike, were appalled by the union with the Commonwealth because it broke the word and spirit of the National Covenant by introducing toleration and destroying the Church's relationship with the Crown. An attempt was made at healing the breach between the ecclesiastical rivals but, as Baillie noted, there was no common ground: 'We did declare our mind unanimously . . . they did declare their mind as unanimously in the rigour of all the other; so any drawing near to one another, while we remained in our present judgements, appeared desperate to us all'. Matters became so bad that the two groups held rival General Assemblies in Edinburgh in 1653, but these were destined to be the last meetings for thirty-seven years. Determined to suppress a Church which was regarded by many army officers as the instrument which had caused the war between the two countries, and which was suspected of covertly supporting the Stewarts' cause by offering prayers for the king, Lilburne decided to move against it. Under the new dispensation meetings of ministers were banned, and the order was implemented by English troops under the command of Lieutenant-Colonel Cotterell, who ignored claims that the assembly was 'a spiritual court of Jesus Christ' and ordered the ministers to disband as an illegal gathering.† For Baillie, who had attended the Glasgow assembly in 1638, it had been a long

---

* He had studied at Glasgow under Robert Baillie; a fellow student had been Archibald Johnston of Wariston.

† Synods and presbyteries were allowed to continue because they had no authority without the General Assembly.

journey with a tragic destination, the Church deeply divided and its ministers powerless:

> Thus our General Assembly, the glory and strength of our Church upon earth, is by your soldiery, crushed and trod under foot [he was writing to an English friend], without the least provocation from us, at this time, either in word or deed. For this our hearts are sad, our eyes run down with water, we sight a God against whom we have sinned, and wait for the help of his hand; but from those who oppressed us deserved no evil.[11]

Tears were also being shed in Ireland, but for different reasons. Firstly, before any settlement could be introduced, the violence had to be brought to an end. Following Cromwell's departure in the late spring of 1650 his son-in-law Ireton, as Lord Deputy, was left with the time-consuming and awkward business of reducing the remaining opposition in the west of the country. Limerick was his main objective, but he divided his forces, giving command of the besieging army to Sir Hardress Waller (another regicide) while he tried his luck against the town of Athlone with its strategically important bridges across the River Shannon. It was a mistake. Waller summoned Limerick on 9 September only to have the demand refused, but it took a further week for Ireton to bring his army to Athlone, to find the river crossing heavily defended. Leaving behind a force under Sir Charles Coote, a Leitrim landowner who had commanded the parliamentary army with no little success in Ulster, Ireton marched on Limerick to join Waller, but the late season of the year made a lengthy siege impractical. His father-in-law would never have acted so incompetently: had Cromwell still been in Ireland he would surely have dealt with Athlone before tackling the more difficult objective of Limerick.

With winter in the offing the only operations left to the Commonwealth army were confined to mopping up pockets of opposition in west Cork, undertaken by Waller and Cromwell's son Henry, and the clearing of the midland counties of Westmeath, Longford and Cavan. When the campaigning season reopened in the spring Irish opposition was confined to Connacht and to the mountainous areas of Wicklow, Donegal and Clare. There was also movement on the political front when parliamentary commissioners arrived to settle the civil administration, which was in a parlous state, the country having been engaged in warfare of one kind or another for the past ten years. There was a desperate need to put farming back on an even keel, to reopen trade and to make good the damage to the towns, but Ireton and his colleagues were dealing not with fallen brethren, as in Scotland, but with a defeated and sullen people who were not prepared to kowtow to foreign, that is English, rule. This led Ireton to use force if necessary to get his way, and as he warned the citizens of Waterford he was justified in so doing as they had brought punishment on their own heads by refusing to obey the new order:

I desire those that question it but to look upon the late actions of many of those that upon their fair professions to us, and our trust in them for faithfulness, or, at least, for innocent and peaceable demeanours towards us, have received protection from us; who notwithstanding do most of them make it their daily business to do us all the mischief they can wherever they see an opportunity, and for that purpose do harbour, entertain and encourage those many Tories* in every corner that otherwise durst not come into our quarters, nor could subsist in them undiscovered, or do that mischief that they do and escape yet from all our forces and garrisons in every corner ready to pursue them, but that as they are assured, and find the protected people are friends to them and, in their hearts, enemies and false to us, notwithstanding all their professions to the contrary; nay, many of the protected people themselves, upon every slight occasion or ground of hope of doing mischief to us, do frequently run from their habitations, join with the enemy in arms, and deliver up their castles to them.[12]

It was the classic dilemma facing military commanders opposed by guerrilla or terrorist forces who have the backing of the local population. Ideally Ireton would have liked to win hearts and minds, but faced by the obduracy of the Irish and their refusal to give up supporting the rebels he had to use force against them. While that

* From the Irish *toraidhe* ('raider'), a term of abuse for dispossessed Irish Catholics who became outlaws and harassed English forces.

worked in the short term it had the lasting effect of alienating the increasingly hostile Irish. In short, Ireton realised that his authority depended solely on the backing of superior military force – hardly the best way to control a country which in many areas was already contemptuous of English rule. Given the local tensions caused by the presence of the English army and the hostility it engendered, fraternisation was frowned upon and, as had happened in Scotland, soldiers were banned from marrying local Catholic girls even if they agreed to abandon their religion – Ireton believed that their decision in such cases could not 'flow from a real work of God upon their hearts'.

With the arrival of spring the English turned their attention once more to Limerick and reopened their siege at the beginning of June 1651. Ireton was in a strong position: he had placed his forces on both sides of the River Shannon and parliamentary warships guarded the lower reaches, deployments which meant that any relieving force would have to fight its way towards the city. Not that Clanricard was in any position to offer help: his dwindling forces were being harried by Coote in the midland counties and by Broghill in Cork. On 14 June the attack began, but Limerick was heavily defended and well stocked with provisions and ammunition. It also possessed a good military commander in its governor Hugh Dubh O'Neill, who had outwitted Cromwell at Clonmel. Within a fortnight the assaults had failed and when a further call to surrender was rejected Ireton decided to blockade the city into submission. It was to be a long process, and the longer it continued the more obstinate became the defenders, or at least those of them who were determined never to surrender.

Although plague broke out inside the city and although Ireton took to executing those who attempted to escape, Limerick remained secure, and might have held out for another winter but for divisions in the local population which led to an armed faction opposing O'Neill's orders. On 27 October the city capitulated and as had happened at Colchester a number of the leading defenders were sentenced to death for prolonging the siege. Among their number was O'Neill, but the sentence was not carried out and he was sent to London for imprisonment in the Tower of London. With him went a strange companion – the body of Henry Ireton, who died of plague on 7 November and whose body was returned to London in a lead coffin for a state funeral in Westminster Abbey, a transaction which many of his more robust colleagues and his many enemies thought scandalous.* For all that death brought Ireton unwanted honours – he was an austere man who had refused additional pay for his service in Ireland – that should not obscure the debt that the parliamentarians owed him. As Cromwell's friend, supporter and kinsman he provided intellectual backbone to the revolution and he was the outstanding moderator at the Putney debates. As a soldier he had his shortcomings in command but he was never less than brave and resourceful in the field, and John Owen was well within his rights for taking his funeral oration from the example of the prophet Daniel, 'a man greatly beloved'. Had he survived the operations in Ireland he could well have found himself succeeding Cromwell.

In his place Edmund Ludlow was appointed commander of the English forces in Ireland and the war turned into an operation to break down the remaining pockets of resistance. In an attempt to gain better terms Clanricard tried to negotiate with the new commander, but was bluntly told: 'The settlement of this nation doth of right belong to the Parliament of the Commonwealth of England, to whom we leave the same, being assured they will not therein capitulate with those who ought to be in subjection, yet stand in opposition to their authority.'[13] By the spring of 1652 a succession of surrenders saw Roscommon and Galway give up the fight, with both towns' garrisons granted quarter on condition that they surrender their arms or go into foreign service. Even so the last garrisons did not finally surrender until the following year – the island of Inishboffin off the Mayo coast on 14 February 1653 and a remote island fortress on Lough Oughter at the end of April.

Mostly the surrenders were achieved peacefully, but given the nature of the operations and the dislike of the English for the Catholic Irish, not to say the memories of 1641, there was a fair amount of violence. Houses were burned down, people were killed, and in so doing future animosities were kindled and lovingly fostered. Whereas Cromwell and his fellow army commanders had been determined to treat the Scots as sinners in need of reform, they looked on the Irish

---

* His chosen motto, *Dulce et decorum est pro patria mori*, was translated by Royalist wags as 'It is a good thing for his country that he died.'

Catholics as apostates who needed to be punished. In consequence the Commonwealth's settlement of Irish affairs was touched by a brutality that was not evident elsewhere. Under an Act of Settlement passed in August 1652 landowners were divided into two groups – those who had taken part in the 1641 rebellion and those who had not – and each was treated accordingly. For the first group, including those who had refused to surrender, the punishment was death or confiscation of property, while the second group became entitled to new land in Connacht and Clare, places so bare that Cromwell is supposed to have said that those dispatched there had the option of being sent to hell or Connacht. For example, in County Cork a local Catholic landowner, Donogh Callaghan, forfeited his 12,000-acre estate and in return was granted 3000 acres of poor farming land in East Clare. As for the rest of Ireland, it became government property to be used for settlement by Adventurers – those who had 'adventured' or lent money to parliament – and soldiers of the Commonwealth army. (See Part Four, Chapter Three.)

The only part of Britain which remained outside the writ of the new order was the Highlands of Scotland, which contained pockets of Royalist supporters. Allied to the region's traditional lawlessness and the capacity of the inhabitants to indulge in violence, this was a source of irritation to the Commonwealth forces of occupation, and Lilburne and Deane rightly feared that an insurrection could be launched from the remote hills and glens. Attempts at disarming suspected malcontents only added to the sense of grievance held by local clan leaders such as Angus Macdonald of Glengarry, who looked to the Stewart court in exile for support. For all his dislike of the Scots, whom he accused of betraying him at Worcester, Charles was still tempted to use the country as a springboard for a bid to reclaim his throne. Despite reverting to Anglican rites on arriving in Paris in October 1651, following his miraculous escape after the Battle of Worcester, he still found time to write to the Moderator of the Church of Scotland asking him to pray for his well-being. He also began the habit of maintaining what contact he could with those who were known to be loyal to him. But fine words and loyal sentiments were not enough. In Paris Charles had little money and French promises of financial support were tardily realised; his courtiers lived modestly in lodgings and were denied the use of carriages. Without the resources any attempt at reviving his fortunes was doomed to disappointment, and by the end of 1652, bar the fractious and uncertain Scottish Highland clan leaders, he was very much on his own. His three British kingdoms had come under the rule of the Commonwealth and even the English colonies of the Americas had sworn their allegiance to the Commonwealth – the last to hold out in supporting the Royalists was Maryland which, like Virginia,* had been loath to acknowledge the supremacy of parliament and did not submit until 12 March 1652. At long last the war was over and the settlement of the new order could begin.

---

* Its governor, Sir William Berkeley, a courtier and minor playwright, was simply removed from his post and allowed to retire to his plantations. He returned to his post in 1660 following the Restoration.

PART FOUR

THE PROTECTORATE
1653–1659

Chapter One

WINNING THE PEACE

'... Peace hath her victories
No less renowned than war'

*John Milton, 'To the Lord General Cromwell, May 1652,
on the proposals of certain ministers at the
Committee for Propagation of the Gospel'*

By the end of 1651 the fighting was over, apart from continued Royalist skirmishing in the Highlands of Scotland and the mopping-up operations in Ireland, but the matter of the governance of England was still an open question. Elections were not due to be held for another three years, leaving the Rump Parliament in being and the Council of State re-elected on an annual basis with Cromwell regularly heading the list of elected members. In a changed world the arrangement represented security and succession, but that came at a price, as its very existence was a block to changes in the franchise which many radicals wanted to be carried through in the post-war settlement. At the same time the army remained ominously in the background, still potent and still a force demanding respect and attention. Also, and this counted for much, it was still the main engine for social change, many of its members being radicals who were anxious to see the introduction of wider reforms in the law and the Church. At its head, as Lord-General, Cromwell was in a powerful position, and in recognition of that pre-eminence he summoned a meeting of leading politicians and army officers on 10 December to discuss what he called 'the settlement of the nation'.

The conference, which took place in Speaker Lenthall's residence in London, was dominated by what form of government England should adopt now that the old king had been executed and his son defeated in battle and sent into exile. Essentially the country had become a republic, but there was an uneasy realisation that the hegemony of the House of Commons (the Lords having been abolished) had to be curbed by some other power, otherwise the rights of ordinary English people would be jeopardised. Obviously there had to be checks and balances of the kind imposed by the monarchy, but that could not be supplied by Charles II or his brother James, the Duke of York, as both were perceived to be the enemies of the Commonwealth. Bulstrode Whitelocke posed the question by asking if those present wanted an all-out republic or a new kind of government which would contain an admixture of monarchy. The point was conceded by Cromwell, who insisted that the question centred on 'whether a republic or a mixed monarchical government will be best to be settled; and if anything monarchical, then in whom that power shall be placed'. This allowed Sir Thomas Widdrington, formerly Commissioner of the Great Seal, to propose that if this course were accepted, the best thing would be to enter into an agreement with Henry, Duke of Gloucester, the king's youngest son, who had, of course, assured his father on the eve of execution that he would never treat with the regicides. By its nature the discussion was theoretical, but Cromwell's summing up encapsulated the dilemma facing the Commonwealth leadership: introducing a new monarch 'will be a business of more than ordinary difficulty; but really I think, if it may be done with safety and preservation of our rights both as Englishmen and Christians, that settlement of somewhat with monarchical power in it would be very effectual'.[1] This tallied with Cromwell's thinking prior to the execution, that the quarrel was with Charles I and not with the Crown, but it left the unspoken thought that, as the most powerful man in England, Cromwell might well be considered the best candidate for such a moderating role.

He was certainly the guiding light behind the Act of Oblivion, a reasonably lenient piece of legislation which pardoned those who had spoken out treasonably against the new order between the time of Charles I's execution and the Battle of Worcester. Those who had acted in the Royalist cause, delinquents all, were still liable to be punished by having their estates sequestrated or their funds confiscated – both sources of income being regarded as important additions to the impoverished national exchequer – but the move was a starting point in healing the raw wounds caused by the civil war. Under Cromwell's guidance the process of reconciliation had already started. In contrast to the savage reprisals of 1648, punishment of Royalists had been restrained in the wake of Worcester; Derby had been the most prominent victim of the executioner's axe but other notables, including the Scottish commanders David Leslie and the Earl of Lauderdale, had been merely confined. Although in most respects the Act of Oblivion turned out to be more symbolic of intention than an instrument of execution it was typical of Cromwell's desire for a peaceful settlement and a return to an ordered way of life.

By then, too, many of the veterans of the fighting in the three kingdoms were dead. After his defeat at Stow-on-the-Wold Sir Jacob Astley had been imprisoned at Warwick Castle before being released on bail to live in Kent, where he died in 1652. Sir John Byron (later Lord Byron), who had done so much to rally Wales and the north-west, died in exile that same year, as did Sir Ralph Hopton, the victor of Lansdown Hill, and Lord Eythin, who had fled to the Continent after Marston Moor. Patrick Ruthven, the Earl of Forth and Brentford, returned from exile to die in his native Scotland in 1650, having spent his last years in the service of the Prince of Wales.

The legislation also excluded from pardon those found guilty of sexual crimes such as bigamy, rape and sodomy. Added to laws passed in 1650 which made adultery and incest punishable by death and the introduction of new rules for the punishment of swearing under the Blasphemy Act, the dawn of the Commonwealth is often regarded as the beginning of a new Puritan age in English social life. While the laws were usually honoured in the breach – the death sentence for adultery was usually considered too extreme and the laws against swearing too cumbersome (there was a scale of fines according to sex and social class*) – added together they seem to suggest that the early legislators of the Commonwealth administration were more

---

* Thirty shillings for a nobleman, six shillings and eight pence for a gentleman and three shillings and four pence for lower orders. Husbands were expected to settle their wives' fines.

interested in the minutiae of introducing new standards of morality than they were in addressing the bigger issues of fiscal and religious reform. For example, under the Blasphemy Act a sailor was jailed for six months for gross blasphemy after writing a private letter to his girl friend saying that he would rather be in bed with her than in heaven with Jesus Christ. When informed against he uttered the exclamation which led to his trial and sentence: 'A pox on Jesus Christ!' This was hardly criminal behaviour, yet he found himself in Newgate prison for his pains.[2]

The laws also added to the impression that the new regime was joyless and humourless, and in time the catch-all word 'puritan' acquired a pejorative or derogatory meaning, with the adjective puritanical being used to describe any practice of strict religious or moral behaviour. Before the word was appropriated as a term of abuse, though, the early Puritans of the late sixteenth century, were simply disaffected Protestants who sought a purer form of religion freed from ceremony, ornamentation and episcopacy; they also favoured a plainer style of dress, and while they insisted on strict personal morality they were not opposed to enjoyment of the arts and entertainment. It is inaccurate to paint a picture of England in the 1650s as a country held in the grip of a gloomy fundamentalist regime bent on the destruction of any aspect of life which gave pleasure to the people. One of the most pertinent statements on the character of the typical English Puritan and what drove him was uttered in a sermon given at Tewkesbury by the Rev. John Geree in the summer of 1646:

He accounted religion an engagement to duty, that the best Christians should be best husbands, best wives, best parents, best children, best masters, best servants, best magistrates, best subjects, that the doctrine of God might be adorned, not blasphemed. His family he endeavours to make a church, both in regard of persons and exercises, admitting none into it but such as feared God; and labouring that those that were born in it, might be born again unto God. He blessed his family morning and evening by the word and prayer and took care to perform those ordinances in the best season. He brought up his children in the nurture and admonition of the Lord and commanded his servants to keep the way of the Lord. He set up discipline in his family, as he desired it in the church, not only reproving but restraining vileness in his. He was conscientious of equity as well as piety knowing that unrighteousness is abomination as well as ungodliness. He was cautious in promising, but careful in performing, counting his word no less engagement than his bond. He was a man of tender heart, not only in regard of his own sin, but others misery, not counting mercy arbitrary, but a necessary duty wherein as he prayed for wisdom to direct him, so he studied for cheerfulness and bounty to act. He was sober in the use of things of this life, rather beating down the body, than pampering it, yet he denied not himself the use of God's blessing, lest he should be unthankful, but avoid excess lest he should be forgetful of the Donor. In his habit he avoided costliness and vanity, neither exceeding his degree in civility, nor declining what suited with Christianity, desiring in all things to express gravity.[3]

Of course the picture was not all delineated in the black and white suggested by John Geree, and as the decade grew older restrictions became more prevalent. Among the shades of grey as the decade progressed, staged theatre was banned and many ale-houses were closed down, religious festivals such as Christmas were not celebrated, sabbatarianism was encouraged, maypoles disappeared from the greens of English villages lest they give rise to sexual licence, and marriages could be conducted through a justice of the peace – all considered to be revolutionary changes in English life – but not everything was turned upside down. In the early years of the Commonwealth newspapers could be printed under licence and some publications such as John Crouch's *Mercurius Democritus* and *Fumigosis* contained material which was not only scurrilous but indecent, yet neither was restrained by the public licenser, Gilbert Mabbott, the government official permitted to censor publications. On the other hand literature flourished, especially doctrinal and devotional books or biographical works which exemplified the practice of the art of saintly living. For Richard Baxter, a tireless promoter of the godly life yet aware of the temptation of pride, perusal of such volumes could be the key to salvation:

The true history of exemplary Lives, is a pleasant and profitable recreation to young persons; and may secretly work them to a liking of Godliness and value of good men, which is the beginning of saving Grace: O how much better is it, than Cards, Dice, Revels, Stage-Plays, Romances or idle Chat.[4]

Just as Cromwell had struggled through the dark night of the soul before finding himself, so too had Baxter gone through a similar conversion, in his case by reading 'an old torn book' at the age of fifteen, in which 'it pleased God to awaken my Soul, and show me the folly of Sinning, and the misery of the Wicked, and the inexpressible weight of things Eternal, and the necessity of resolving on a Holy Life'. That strain of illuminated awareness is central to the writings of the Puritan tradition – the desire to usurp sin and accept God's sovereignty and to embrace godliness, grace and humility. Added to the notion that black was black and white was white and that to compromise was the work of the devil, it was a heady message and one which was eagerly embraced by the writers of the immediate post-monarchical period. A moderate in an immoderate age, Baxter's interpretation of contemporary events appeared as *Reliquiae Baxterianae* in 1696, five years after his death, and his account is marked both by intellectual prudence and an inflexible religious understanding.

Other works which personified the spirituality of the age include Richard Norwood's *Confessions* and James Harrington's *Oceana*, which argued for liberty of conscience in matters of religion (while disallowing 'popish, Jewish or idolatrous' worship), but the greatest of the Puritan autobiographies is John Bunyan's *Grace Abounding to the Chief of Sinners*, which was not published until his imprisonment after the Restoration, in 1666. Having served as a soldier in the parliamentary army under Sir Samuel Luke at Newport Pagnell, Bunyan returned to his native village of Elstow near Bedford, where he married and seems to have undergone a mystical conversion after witnessing a heavenly vision. This led him to embrace the millenarian beliefs of the Fifth Monarchists, to embrace God and eschew the works of the devil, to put aside despair and to struggle towards a sense of personal righteousness freed from the claims of temptation:

If ever Satan and I did strive for any word of God in all my life, it was for this good word of Christ; he at one end and I at the other.

Oh, what work did we make! It was this in John, I say, that we did so tug and strive: he pulled and I pulled; but, God be praised, I got the better of him, I got some sweetness from it.[5]

Bunyan, of course, became better known as the author of *The Pilgrim's Progress,* but his spiritual autobiography tracing his journey towards grace was typical of the self-questioning among independent thinkers as they grappled with the questions thrown up by the new order and the need to understand the revelation of God's will. The chiliastic temper was heightened by other manifestations: an eclipse of the sun in March 1652 created widespread fear and enough panic to force many people to quit London during the so-called Black Monday when it occurred. There was also an outpouring of millennial visions and apocalyptic prophecies, the end of the world was forecast by various self-styled seers and prophets,* and in London two quacks called Lodowicke Muggleton and his cousin John Reeve caused outrage when they denied the doctrine of the Trinity and claimed to be the two witnesses cited in the Book of Revelation (11: 3–6): 'These have the power to shut heaven, that it rain not in the days of their prophecy: and have power over waters to turn them to blood, and to smite the earth with all plagues as often as they will.'

In many respects that spiritual chaos was a manifestation of England's state after nine years of warfare which had seen the country divided and destroyed and its anointed ruler executed. There was a general desire for a return to the remembered normality of Charles I's reign or for the implementation of a new form of governance based on constitutional principles. All that remained from the disorder was a purged unicameral government, itself a relic of the old parliament, which owed its existence not to the democratic vote but to the might of the New Model Army. Just as bad, it existed in a political vacuum with no checks or balances to keep it in order. Faced by that unjust arrangement, which bordered on tyranny, political thinkers tried to make sense of the situation by promoting new forms of government freed from the constitutional chains of the past. One of the most

---

* One of the best known utterances came from Thomas Beverley, who said that the world would end in 1697. Finding himself alive the following year he asserted that the event had in fact taken place unnoticed.

prominent was James Harrington, who had served as a groom to the bedchamber during the last two years of the reign of Charles I. Although he had revered the king and served him loyally, he realised that the regicide opened up opportunities for bringing in a new form of republican government based on the precepts of classical Greece or, in contemporary terms, the rule of the Venetian republic.

The result was *The Commonwealth of Oceana*, which was written in the aftermath of the king's execution and which attempts to redefine the governance of England as 'an equal commonwealth' with a two-chamber government and the electorate divided into three orders, 'the senate debating and proposing, the people resolving, and the magistracy executing by an equal rotation through the suffrage of the people given by the ballot'. Equally revolutionary, Harrington advocated the redistribution of land and the creation of a system of tenure which limited land ownership, because 'where there is inequality of estates there must be inequality of power, and where there is inequality of power there can be no commonwealth.' (Harrington explained the cause of the civil war as the result of a shift in the balance of property from kings and lords to the commoners.) And ruling over the new edifice was the figure of the Archon, Olpheus Megalator, a thinly disguised manifestation of Cromwell, to whom the work was dedicated when it finally appeared in 1656. Without the Archon there could be no good government, for the simple reason that when the times were out of joint strong leadership was required – 'a parliament of physicians would never have found out the circulation of the blood, nor would a parliament of poets have written Virgil's Aeneid'.[6]

It was not as if the Rump Parliament had nothing to do. In addition to pursuing a war against the Netherlands, a direct result of the passing of the Navigation Act in October 1651 (see following chapter), the executive spent 1652 fitfully toying with judicial and religious reform. A Committee for the Propagation of the Gospel was appointed in February, its task the settlement of the Church, and its main architect was Cromwell's Chaplain, John Owen, now the dean of Christ Church, who was in favour of an established Church and a fair degree of religious toleration. Its main recommendation was that candidates for the ministry should be examined by two sets of commissioners composed of laity and the clergy. The first, the 'Triers', would be responsible at local level for testing candidates for their 'piety and soundness of faith', while a second group, the 'Ejectors', would tour the country removing unsuitable ministers from their posts. On the question of tithes the committee hedged its bets and decided to keep in being this unpopular means of paying ministers whose abolition had been demanded in the Heads of the Proposals presented to Charles. Tithes were still an emotive issue, as they seemed to promote local vested interests, and many reformers such as George Fox preferred the payment of national stipends, but the forces of conservatism kept them in being when the matter was put to the vote on 29 April.

A collection of committees dealt with other reforms – for example the Sequestration Committee was concerned with confiscated Royalist estates while the Scandalous Ministers Committee engaged itself with moral delinquency within the clergy – but the system was sluggardly and the anticipated changes were slow in evolving. As the reforms ambled on, the army was still champing at the bit. Denied any role in the fighting against the Dutch and, barring operations in Ireland and Scotland, freed from general internal security duties, the New Model Army remained a hotbed of radicalism, especially in its junior ranks, and it quickly became a focus for dissent. By August its tolerance had reached breaking-point and the result was a fresh petition to parliament signed by its leading officers including Cromwell's cousin Edward Whalley and the commanding officer of his own regiment, Charles Worsley.

The demands were not particularly excessive and had been made before in earlier statements, notably the *Declaration of the Army* of 1647, but this time the army's patience was wearing thin. 'Speedy consideration' was requested for the main points contained in the petition, principally the dissolution of parliament, the settlement of arrears of pay, the establishment of a national Treasury with transparent accounts, the creation of work schemes for the poor and unemployed, the abolition of tithes and the pious hope that unfit men should be removed from positions of authority to make way for 'men of truth, fearing God and hating covetousness'.[7] At Cromwell's prompting – his name was not on the petition but his influence was obviously present – the demand for an immediate dissolution was replaced by a more general statement of intent to hold early elections, but the army's move did have repercussions. First, it prompted parliament to appoint a new Committee on Elections on 14 September and to think more urgently about its future; secondly it brought the debate into the open by instigating cooperation between the army and parliament; thirdly, it forced Cromwell to take stock of his position as the predominant man in the country. All were to affect the course of events during the months which followed.

On the question of collaboration between the army and parliament a dozen discussions took place, but they were hardly meetings of true minds. While the politicians were anxious to retain what remained of their power as the last survivors of constitutional authority, the army officers wanted radical change. (Even on this point the latter were divided: Harrison distrusted elections and wanted the creation of a perpetual parliament chosen from the godly.) As had happened so often in the past the committees became little more than debating chambers, and Cromwell was left to rue the lack of any impetus:

> I believe we had ten or twelve meetings, most humbly begging and beseeching of them that by their own means they would bring forth those good things which had been promised and expected; that so it might appear they did not do them by any suggestion from the army, but from their own ingenuity: so tender were we to preserve them in the reputation of the people.[8]

It was a familiar refrain – for all its superior power and authority the army had been remarkably unblest in pushing forward its programme of reforms – and the sense of impotence clearly irked Cromwell. Having fought for change and with the help of God's providence and mercy having achieved it on the battlefield, he and his fellow officers were left with a parliament which refused to reform itself. This was hardly a just reward for the sufferings at Naseby, Preston and Dunbar, and Cromwell would not have been human had he not mused long and deeply about his own position. He had already pondered the concept of the monarchy in relation to the new order and, although he had not as yet considered the prospect himself, parliament's obduracy was slowly forcing him to change his mind. Aware of the dilemma that whatever else it might be the Rump

Parliament at least had legal authority, he discussed the position in November 1652 while walking in St James's Park with Bulstrode Whitelocke, who later made a record of what had taken place.

Cromwell's first question set the tone for what followed: 'How to make good our station, to improve the mercies and successes which God hath given us, and not to be fooled out of them again, nor to be broken in pieces by our particular jarrings and animosities one against another, but to unite our counsels?' To the ever-cautious Whitelocke the danger seemed to come from the army, and the radical spirits within its ranks who were intent on enforcing change on the country. Not so, replied Cromwell, the army was easily restrained, but it was more difficult to deal with the corruption and unaccountability of politicians:

> As for members of Parliament, the army begins to have a strange distaste against them, and I wish there were not too much cause for it; and really their pride and ambition and self-seeking, ingrossing all places of honour and profit to themselves and their friends, and their daily breaking forth into new and violent parties and factions; their delay of business and design to perpetuate themselves, and to continue their power in their own hands; their meddling in private matters between party and party, contrary to the institution of Parliament, and their injustice and partiality in those matters, and the scandalous lives of some of the chief of them; these things, my lord, do give much ground for people to open their mouths against them and to dislike them, nor can they be kept within the bounds of justice and law or reason, they themselves being the supreme power of the nation, liable to no account to any, nor to be controlled or regulated by any other power; their being none superior or co-ordinate with them.

The inference was clear: Cromwell thought the parliament as it stood unaccountable and therefore liable to fall into greater 'exorbitances' (Cromwell's word) unless its power was checked. Whitelocke demurred, adding the thought that parliament had to reform itself, but Cromwell's stream of thought led him to pose the startling question: 'What if a man should take upon him to be king?' Showing unaccustomed deftness, Whitelocke replied that such a remedy would be worse than the disease, that the memory of Charles I was too recent to inspire any confidence and that the civil war would have been fought for nothing if it reduced itself to a question of Cromwell or Stewart. If that were the case then it would be preferable to enter into discussions with Charles II, a solution which Cromwell found unappealing, Whitelocke noting that 'by his countenance and carriage [he had] displeased' his companion. Although Whitelocke recalled the episode in the years following the Restoration,[9] apart from the introduction of felicitous phrases there is nothing to suggest that he was not being accurate in delineating Cromwell's frame of mind in the autumn and early winter of 1652. Whitelock was after all a sober lawyer, had nothing to gain by reporting the discussion in St James's Park – after the Restoration he enjoyed Charles II's favour – and although his memoirs appeared long after the event (1681–82) his text was based on notes made at the time. The resulting work does not make for exciting reading but it is a reliable record.

Even if Cromwell was not contemplating the crown, at the very least he had his eye on assuming the highest rank in the land – two months earlier he had suggested that it should be offered to Henry, Duke of Gloucester while he acted as Protector or regent until the boy came of age.* The main point which shines through Whitelocke's commentary is Cromwell's dissatisfaction with the parliament and his impatience to see change. While he understood that the times were out of joint as a result of the long and debilitating civil wars, that was all the more reason why there was a desperate need for an early and just settlement. If the parliament could not provide that, and if the army contained too many radicals to ensure public safety, then perhaps one man should assume control. That, too, might be God's providence; the cause might be greater than the man. Others comprehended his growing stature and realised that any settlement in the three kingdoms would depend on the judgement of this experienced leader who now believed himself to be a man of destiny. Shortly before Cromwell and Whitelocke conferred, the Venetian ambassador sent back a report which clearly demonstrated Cromwell's stature within the country:

---

* The following year the young prince applied to join his brother in France and the request was granted.

He is a man of great foresight, of a lofty spirit, and capable whatever happens of parrying blows directed against himself, and of retaining the affection and esteem of both parties, and, in fine, of preserving the independence of the authority which he exercises, disposing at his free will of all military offices, and influencing all by the modesty of his life, in which there is no display or magnificence. At present – it was otherwise formerly – he is applauded, but not loved by all; his riches, or, to speak more correctly, his treasures, increase daily through his conduct, and he thereby looks to maintain himself in augmented authority and power.[10]

Ambassador Pauluzzi was right to insist that Cromwell was not loved or respected by everyone – Lucy Hutchinson wrote at this time about his 'private ambition' – but, popular or not, he was in a powerful position. Better still, he had the wit to realise it.

Cromwell was also helped by the fact that he had no real rivals. Ireton, his son-in-law, had been his equal, perhaps his intellectual superior, but his death in 1651 had robbed Cromwell of much-needed support and friendship. His fellow regicide Thomas Harrison was too extreme, Whitelocke was never the same after the conversation on the monarchy, a coolness had developed between Cromwell and the other leading personality in parliament, the serious-minded Sir Henry Vane, over the future of the Rump Parliament, and older friends such as his cousin Oliver St John, the Chief Justice, were content with their lot. One man was capable of standing up to him – John Lambert, his cohort in Scotland and Ireland – but at the time his career was in a state of muddle which was not of his making. In January he had been appointed to the post of Lord Deputy for Ireland in succession to Ireton, but this had come to nothing four months later when parliament decided to abolish Cromwell's post as Lord Lieutenant. This was done in an attempt to cut costs and save money, but it put Lambert in an awkward position. He had spent considerable sums in advance of taking up the appointment and his wife had allowed herself to be over-impressed at her husband's advancement, so much so that she snubbed Ireton's widow in public in St James's Park (if Lucy Hutchinson is to be believed). To ease the pain of disappointment Cromwell encouraged parliament to make a financial grant to 'honest

John Lambert', but the damage had been done. Lambert became ever more contemptuous of parliament: according to Lucy Hutchinson, 'with a heart full of spite, malice and revenge' he 'retreated to his palace at Wimbledon, and sat there watching an opportunity to destroy the Parliament'.[11] Those misgivings were increased when Ireton's widow, Cromwell's daughter Bridget, married Charles Fleetwood, who went to Ireland as commander-in-chief of the Commonwealth forces there.

The year ended with army and parliament still at loggerheads over the matter of the latter's early dissolution and the new year began with the Council of Officers renewing their demands for the establishment of 'successive Parliaments consisting of men faithful to the interest of the Commonwealth, men of truth, fearing God and hating covetousness'. The mood in London became ever more tense, with only the naval war against the Dutch providing any optimism, and only Cromwell's influence prevented the army from acting unilaterally against parliament. At the beginning of April matters came to a head when a new Bill of Elections was debated. This allowed for a franchise of £200, one of the army's demands, and for the adjournment of the house with elections for a 'new representative' later in the year. However, no thought had been given to the interim government or its composition, and it was on this point that the two sides finally fell out because it seemed to the Council of Officers that parliament would simply perpetuate itself in the new body and then engineer the elections to their own advantage. Such an eventuality, argued Cromwell, would bring to power unwanted 'neuters' and Presbyterians and the army would have 'thrown away the liberties of the nation into the hands of those who had never fought for it'.

Only Cromwell could break the deadlock, but he was in a difficult position, for the longer the stand-off continued the less easy it was for him to retain the confidence of both sides. The key meeting came on 19 April when he met with senior army officers and members of parliament in Whitehall and put forward a compromise whereby a council of forty would be chosen and these would be men whose religious and political integrity was not in doubt. While this was not to parliament's liking – Whitelocke thought it unconstitutional – an agreement was patched up whereby further discussion of the bill would be halted until further notice. For Cromwell, who had not attended the house for a month, this was a much-needed breathing space:

> At the parting two or three of the chief ones, and the very chiefest of them [Vane] did tell us that they would endeavour to suspend further proceedings about the bill for a new representative until they had a further conference. And upon this we had great satisfaction, and we did acquiesce, and had hope, if our expedient would receive a loving debate, that the next day we should have some such issue thereof as would have given satisfaction to all.[12]

It was not to be. The next morning dawned with the astonishing news that parliament was already debating the bill, a move which suggested that it was about to adjourn itself without reaching any agreement on the composition of the interim council. Not only had the members broken their word but they were taking advantage of the broken promise to further their own interests. To Cromwell this was an outrageous breach of trust, and he acted with characteristic energy and decision. Soldiers were ordered to guard the approaches to the House of Commons and, dressed only in plain clothes, Cromwell entered the chamber shortly after eleven o'clock and took up his seat in the chamber. What followed next was one of the most electrifying episodes in English parliamentary history.

As the Speaker called for the bill to be passed Cromwell rose to his feet and addressed the house in what most contemporary observers described as a cold fury. If he felt betrayed, not just by the attempt to pass the bill but by the men who were doing it, men who had never fought for the liberties of the nation as he and others had, then his language and actions provided a full response. Casting his eyes around the crowded house he castigated some members as 'whoremasters', others as 'drunkards' or 'scandalous to the profession of the Gospel', and informed them that they were no longer fit to rule the country. His flow was interrupted by Sir Peter Wentworth, who protested at the abusive language, 'more horrid' in that it came from a man they trusted, but Cromwell was not to be stilled: 'Come, come, I will put an end to your prating. You are no Parliament. I say you are no Parliament. I will put an end to your sitting.' At that he called on Harrison to do his duty and some forty musketeers under Worsley's command entered the House of Commons to clear the members from the chamber. As they left, dazed by the sudden turn of events, Cromwell rounded on them once again: 'It's you that have forced me to do this, for I have sought the Lord night and day, that he would rather slay them than put me upon the doing of this work.' The last act came when he ordered Worsley to remove the mace, the symbol of the Speaker's authority, with the contemptuous words: 'What shall we do with this bauble? Here, take it away.'[13]

In the space of a few minutes the Rump of the Long Parliament was dismissed and England found itself without a legitimate government. Parliamentary democracy (however unpopular and misguided) had been unseated by a military coup and until a new administration could be put in place Cromwell was the uncontested ruler of England. That afternoon he cemented his position by telling a meeting of the Council of State that they had no further business to conduct as parliament had been dissolved. In vain did one of their number, the lawyer John Bradshaw, protest that 'no power under heaven can dissolve them [parliament] but themselves' and that Cromwell should note that well. The council had no option but to heed the warning and end its session. A revolution had taken place, but for all its violence it attracted no reaction and London and the rest of the country accepted parliament's dismissal with remarkable indifference. That evening someone scribbled an obsequy on the main door which seemed to reflect the general mood: 'This house to be let unfurnished'. Cromwell was equally phlegmatic about the turn of events. 'When they were dissolved,' he said later, 'there was not so much as the barking of a dog, or any general or visible repining at it.'[14]

Cromwell had come a long way in just under ten years. From being an obscure member of parliament dressed in a plain suit ill-cut by a country tailor he had risen to become the most influential man in the country. He had been central to the moves which had led to the overthrowing of the monarchy, he had reduced the authority of the episcopalian clergy, he had destroyed the Scottish Presbyterians, he had brought Ireland under control and now he had expelled the rump of the English parliament. All of England, Ireland and Scotland lay at his feet; Cromwell the destroyer was also Cromwell the breaker of nations. Now the question was, could he be the creator of a just and tolerant nation? It would not be an easy task. Peace had to be made with the Dutch and at home he had to satisfy the differing demands within the army as represented by Lambert, who wanted an elected government, and Harrison, who desired a chosen government of the saints, but first he had to find a means of governing the country.

The result was the Nominated Parliament which came into being on 4 July 1653 with 129 selected men 'fearing God and of approved fidelity and honesty' from England and Wales with a further five from Scotland and six from Ireland. It was also known as the Barebones Parliament, after one of its members, Praise-God Barbon, a London leather trader and Independent of Huguenot stock, and its members had been chosen by the Council of Officers to represent the cities and counties of England, a disparate grouping whom Clarendon later dismissed as 'a pack of weak, senseless fellows'. The final tally reflected the divisions within the army: some eighty were moderates while the remainder were radicals, many of them Harrison's Fifth Monarchists. That they were of the elect was made manifest by Cromwell when he addressed their first assembly, telling them that they were there by God's authority to do his great work. In the past the deity's purpose had been unclear, but now his will had been revealed and in the summer of 1653 these pious gentlemen, all carefully chosen with much to recommend them, found themselves 'at the edge of promises and prophecies'. It was announcing the beginning of a brave new world in which saints would rule the land, but its success or failure would depend on whether or not these hallowed men would have the moral strength to undertake their calling.

Chapter Two

MY DELIGHT AMONGST THE NATIONS: THE ANGLO-DUTCH WAR

'The Dutch have too much power and the English are resolved to take it from them.'

George Monck, on the passing of the Navigation Act,
October 1651

In addition to settling the civil administration of England, Cromwell had to deal with war as well as peace. Since the spring of 1652 a naval conflict had been raging against the Dutch United Provinces* in which English and Dutch warships had clashed in the English Channel. Its trigger was a row about the saluting of warships, but its longer-term causes were rooted in maritime rivalry; this was a trade war carried on, first intermittently and then enthusiastically, by the navy of the Commonwealth and with the wholehearted support of the Rump Parliament and the Council of State.

In theory the Dutch should have been natural allies of the new Commonwealth. They were Protestant, they had thrown off the hegemony of the Habsburgs in the previous century, and that struggle had acted as an inspiration to many in England who opposed the personal rule of Charles I. The Dutch were also a maritime people

---

* Holland, Zeeland, Utrecht, Overijssel, Gröningen, Gelderland and Friesland. Roughly the area contained by the modern Belgium and the Netherlands.

with lucrative trading interests and a large fishing fleet, and the two countries enjoyed close cultural and religious links – large numbers of English and Scottish ministers had preached in Dutch churches or were resident in Antwerp or Rotterdam – and everything pointed to an alliance against the threat posed by France and Spain. That was certainly Cromwell's point of view – at the back of his mind lay the bigger dream of creating a Protestant Europe – but the possibility of forging some kind of coalition was rendered impossible by years of tensions on the high seas.

Even before the civil conflict had broken out in Britain in 1638 there had been clashes between the ships of the two countries. These had ranged from skirmishing between fishing or merchant vessels in home waters to armed battles between rival traders in the spice islands of the East Indies – the Molucca group, which belong to modern Indonesia. It was in the latter locality that the worst clash took place in 1623; and even though thirty years had passed, few people in England had forgotten the notorious Amboina Massacre. Through pamphlets and broadsheets, the majority of them exaggerated to present the victims as martyrs, the memory of this outrage had been kept alive. In fact, the killings at Ambon in the Moluccas was a disgraceful episode by any standards. Fourteen English traders led by Gabriel Towerson, a tough no-nonsense factor, were arrested by the local Dutch garrison on trumped-up charges of fomenting a revolt and they were savagely tortured before going on trial – the favoured method being a water torture which left the victim with his 'body [. . .] swollen twice or thrice as big as before, his cheeks like great bladders, and his eyes staring and strutting out beyond his forehead'. Others had the soles of their feet burned, and ten of those who refused to confess or confessed under duress were subsequently hanged.[1] All died as martyrs and the massacre incited great anger at home, not least because Britain was unable to retaliate.

That distrust had been exacerbated more recently by other offences, namely the hospitality which the Dutch afforded to the Prince of Wales in the first years of his exile, the House of Orange's support for the Stewarts, and the failure to arrest the murderers of Dr Dorislaus, the regicide lawyer. There was also a difference of ideology. The Dutch believed in the freedom of the seas, a philosophy which allowed them to emerge as a formidable trading power with links to the east through their East India Company, control of Baltic commerce and supremacy in North Sea fishing. In contrast English expansion in those areas had been piecemeal and was stymied by Charles I's preference for granting restrictionist trading monopolies and an unwillingness to expand the Royal Navy for protection against privateering. At the same time Britain laid claim to sovereignty over the so-called 'British seas' – home waters which stretched from the North Sea to Cape Finisterre and required foreign ships to strike their flags to their warships as a matter of respect and, if necessary, to be searched for contraband. It was a proud philosophy but its implementation was hindered by the sorry state of the fleet. Ships were poorly designed and constructed, crews were badly paid and liable to desert and, although the imposition of Ship Money in 1634 had allowed the Channel fleet to be strengthened, it had been unable to intervene five years later when a Spanish fleet was destroyed by the Dutch under Lieutenant-Admiral Maarten Harpertszoon Tromp while it was sheltering in English territorial waters in the Downs, the anchorage for ships which was sheltered by the Goodwin Sands. With Sir John Pennington's squadron looking on impotently, the incident had been a humiliating blow to Britain's national pride and it sent a signal to the Dutch, who had been cheered on by the English sailors, that England had no pretension to be a first-rate naval power.

The onset of the civil wars and the decision of the navy to support parliament kept the country out of international affairs for over a decade, but during that time the fleet expanded and conditions of service were improved, all to the navy's benefit. It was money well spent too: parliamentary ships acted in support of land forces in the sieges of Hull, Plymouth and Bristol, they protected overseas trading links and cut off Continental support for the Royalist cause. This vigorous blockading policy and the successful engagement of privateering helped to turn the parliamentary navy into a useful instrument of policy – Clarendon called it 'a terrible addition of strength' – which survived the mutinies of 1648 and allowed the emergence of a New Model Navy the following year. Between then and 1651, at a cost of over £2 million (the money coming from the forfeiture of royal estates), 41 new ships were added to the fleet, more than doubling its previous size of 39 ships, and plans were laid for 200 more by the end of the decade.[2] The policy brought results too.

Under the command of Robert Blake, the hero of the sieges of Lyme and Taunton, and a soldier turned sailor who was one of three generals-at-sea appointed by parliament (the others being Richard Deane and Edward Popham), Prince Rupert's Royalist fleet was destroyed off the Portuguese coast at Cartagena in November 1650. The navy was also in a strong enough position to search ships suspected of helping the Stewart cause in the home waters of the North Sea, the English Channel and the Western Approaches.

The expansion of the navy coincided with a new mood in the mercantile community, which came to regard the warships as instrument of national policy. A strong naval presence made it easier to resist the threat of France and Spain, both thought to be potential enemies of the new republic; but there was more to the possession of warships than tactical necessity. With a powerful fleet England would be in a position to impose its will on Europe, and at the same time it could capitalise on overseas trade, especially with the colonies of North America and the West Indies, territories which were now being viewed as vital national assets possessing a limitless potential for growth. As such, they needed to be nurtured and protected, and the ships of the Commonwealth's navy were just what was needed. As one leading naval historian has put it, under the new dispensation 'the government would provide a legislative and power-political framework of support for trade, but individual merchants and firms would work out their own destiny'.[3] This was the beginning of the commercial policy of empire, the means by which Britain was able to extend its trading links with the fledgling colonies and protect them from the interference of other European powers.

The policy's glue was the Navigation Act of 1651. Under its terms only British ships (Scotland was included in the legislation) or ships of the country of origin could import goods into Britain; at the same time colonial exports could only be carried in English ships. Both were moves which effectively froze out the United Provinces. The sanctions hurt the Dutch by dislocating the trade which had brought them wealth and made them the fastest-growing country in Europe. They were bound to retaliate, either diplomatically or by using their own fleet to protect their interests: the Dutch were not only excellent sailors but the combined strength of their seagoing population was 168,000, their lines of communication stretched to the Baltic, the

Americas, India and the Far East, and the spice trade had brought the country fabulous wealth. It also has to be said that their reliance on the sea meant that they were fighting for their very lives.

And yet, for all their supremacy, the Dutch operated under several disadvantages, the principal one being that their entire economy was built on their position as traders to the world. Their ships carried the goods which their merchants bought and sold, their own East India Company had a virtual monopoly on spices, their financiers underwrote trading deals, in addition to their fishing and whaling fleets their merchant fleet was huge, and they possessed a number of sound naval commanders including the indefatigable Tromp, who had perfected the art of convoy protection. In short, mercantile trading was the mainstay of the Dutch people. As Adriaen Pauw, one of their diplomatic representatives, put it when war became inevitable: 'The English are about to attack a mountain of gold; we are about to attack a mountain of iron.'[4]

Their other main disadvantage was geographical: all the sea lanes to the Atlantic and beyond were covered by the British Isles. Dutch sailors had to use the Channel, which meant staying close to the English coast facing the prevailing westerly winds, or they had to take the longer and more hazardous route north around Scotland, either risking the stormy passage through the Pentland Firth, which lies between Orkney and the Scottish mainland, or skirting the seas further north around Shetland. The shallow coastal waters in the approaches to their ports also limited the size of their merchant and warships, most of which were significantly smaller than their English opposite numbers (Tromp's flagship *Brederode* carried only fifty-nine guns, while even a third-rate English warship carried between fifty-six and seventy guns), and the composition of the provinces with their internal jealousies meant that there was no unity of command in the fleet.

Alarmed by their neighbour's protectionist legislation, the Dutch sent emissaries to London in December 1651 and desultory negotiations continued throughout the winter, but the Council of State refused to budge from the main conditions of the new Navigation Act. With tensions running high and an increasing number of Dutch vessels being searched – 140 were stopped and searched in 1651 alone – a confrontation at sea was perhaps inevitable. It came in the middle of May 1652, when Tromp was in the Channel with a fleet of forty-two warships and a north-easterly gale forced him to take shelter in English waters in the lee of the Kentish coast. Although he was able to explain his position to the English commander, Nehemiah Bourne, a Massachusetts shipowner who had thrown in his lot with the parliamentary side, events elsewhere were soon to draw Tromp and his fleet into an unwanted and unnecessary battle.

A few days earlier a Dutch convoy inward-bound from Genoa had been intercepted by an English squadron, one of the Dutch warships had refused to strike its flag and shots had been fired as the English commander Captain Anthony Young attempted unsuccessfully to take one of the merchantmen into port. At the same time Tromp received the mistaken information that another Dutch convoy had been intercepted in the Channel by Blake on the pretext that they were carrying French goods. This was too much for the Dutch admiral, who sailed towards Dover, where the two battle fleets met in the waters just off the coast. With his blood up – he was under orders not to strike his flag unless outnumbered – and with a superior number of ships under his command, Tromp refused to give the required salute. Blake's flagship *James* opened fire, which was returned by the *Brederode*, and in the ensuing mêlée the Dutch lost two ships before retiring to the French coast. Sailors on both sides were killed and Blake's ship was badly damaged by Dutch cannon and musket fire but, as he told parliament in words that could have been uttered by Cromwell, he was justified in making the Dutch pay for their insolence:

> We have received above seventy great shot in our hull and masts, in our sail and rigging without number, being engaged with the whole body of the fleet for the space of four hours, and the mark at which they aimed. We must needs acknowledge a great mercy that we had no more harm, and our hope the righteous God will continue the same unto us if there do arise a war between us, they being first in the breach, and seeking an occasion to quarrel and watching, as it seems, an advantage to brave us upon our coast.[5]

When further Dutch merchant vessels were intercepted in the following weeks war between the two countries became inevitable.

Parliament was generally in favour of fighting the Dutch and crushing their trading superiority once and for all. Hesilrige said that it was God's will to do so, but in this instance Mammon was more influential than the Almighty's providence. A conflict was a convenient means of trouncing a commercial rival and defending colonial interests under the guise of national necessity, and it helped to cement the theory of mercantilism by which trade was protected through regulation and if necessary by military intervention. Alone among the Rump Parliament's policies the passing of the Navigation Act and the war which followed were driven more by cupidity and patriotism than by any belief that God's work was being furthered. But not everyone supported the conflict. Cromwell was ambivalent about going to war, as was Whitelocke. The closest Cromwell came to expressing a view came when he told a group of Dutch expatriates in London who were petitioning parliament for the resumption of peace talks: 'I do not like the war and I commend your Christian admonition. I will do everything in my power to bring about peace.'[6]

By then, though, peace was irretrievable, and it was also clear that the Commonwealth navy was gaining the upper hand. For a start it held the initiative: Blake and his fellow commanders had the luxury of operating out of the Channel ports and could decide when and where to take on the Dutch warships. As for the Dutch, their navy's first priority was to form the merchant ships into convoys as they ran the gauntlet through the Channel, and they found it difficult to take the battle to the English. Being bound to guard their convoys they were usually placed on the defensive and could not afford to release warships for other duties – the Dutch navy was divided into three squadrons to protect the Baltic trade, to convoy ships from the east and the Mediterranean in home waters and to guard the fishing and whaling fleet. That they were severely overstretched became clear during the summer when Blake took a 60-strong battle-fleet into the North Sea, first to attack the Dutch herring fleet which was operating off Orkney and Shetland and, secondly, to lay a trap for an inward-bound Dutch East India fleet which was taking the northerly route home. The first task presented few difficulties. With only twelve warships to protect them the Dutch fishermen were easily dispersed or destroyed by Blake's firepower while operating off Shetland on 12 July 1652. Operating in advance of the fleet, a flotilla of English frigates under the command of Vice-Admiral William Penn easily overwhelmed the escorts – three were sunk and the rest captured along with 900 crew – and the fishing busses were allowed to escape. It was a first and telling indication of the advantages of possessing faster and more powerful ships with a longer range.

While the survivors scattered Blake considered his next move. Judging that the Dutch merchantmen would attempt the passage between Orkney and Shetland, where they would most likely be met by Tromp's escorts, Blake headed for Fair Isle, the expected rendezvous point, where he hoped to attack the convoy and defeat the Dutch in a fleet action. It was a double gamble: not only was he relying on the Dutch ships to arrive at the same time but in the home waters of the Downs he had left behind a hostage in the shape of a small flotilla of 20 warships under the command of Sir George Ayscue. A veteran of the operations in the Irish Sea during the civil war, Ayscue was a pugnacious and experienced commander – in the previous year he had taken a small fleet to Barbados to impose parliament's authority on the colony – but despite his doubts about the wisdom of provoking a war with the Dutch he was not prepared to keep his ships in the safety of the Downs. That meant patrolling aggressively in the Channel, even though his tactics were bound to provoke a Dutch response. When Ayscue took the opportunity to attack a Dutch convoy in the Channel on 2 July, destroying three merchant ships, capturing seven and forcing the remainder, 26 ships, to run aground on the Calais shore, Tromp had no option but to deal with him. As the English were outnumbered four to one the odds were against them, but a change of wind from the south-west prevented Tromp from pressing home an attack on the smaller fleet. Besides, by then he had received intelligence that Blake was in the North Sea and in a position to threaten the incoming East India merchant ships he had been ordered to protect. On 12 July Ayscue's men woke to find the eastern horizon empty of masts as Tromp took his ships north.

If the two fleets had collided near Fair Isle, as Blake expected, the battle would probably have decided the issue, for both he and Tromp had the bulk of their respective fleets under their command, but once again the weather intervened. A fortnight later, on 26 July, as the fleets manoeuvred in the strait between Orkney and Shetland, a mighty gale blew up and Tromp's fleet bore the brunt of it. At least 16 ships sank at sea or were driven on to the Shetland shore and wrecked on the rocks around Sumburgh Head, none escaped damage and many were blown off course, some as far as the Norwegian coast. It took several weeks for the survivors to reach their home ports, and most arrived there to find that they had been given up as lost. A contemporary Dutch account described the atrocious weather conditions as being among the worst encountered by their crews:

> The wind shifted from one quarter to another, settling down at last to a storm from the NNW, and that with such a din that it was terrible to hear it; but what was far more awful was to see the boiling sea foaming and dashing to the height of a house upon the rocky cliffs of Shetland. Every one, thus seeing his graveyard before his eyes, did his best to save ship and life by keeping off the danger; while many of the Dutch ships had these rocks to the leeward, they all, except four or five (amongst which were some fire-ships, which, though destined to perish by fire, were now consumed by another element), were preserved though many ships appeared to sink than to drive through the great troughs of the sea, which seemed as if they would swallow up every ship. In the morning were seen two ships, almost uninjured, lying between the rocks, upon which they had been driven, and the hulls of three others and the corpses of their crews being dashed about.[7]

Blake's fleet fared better, having been able to take shelter in the sound between the mainland and the island of Bressay, but the decisive encounter between the two fleets had to be postponed. For his pains Tromp was blamed for the disaster and chose resignation before he could be dismissed from his post.

The next best chance for the two navies to engage in combat fell to Ayscue and to a younger Dutch naval commander, Michiel Adriaanszoon de Ruijter, a Zeelander who had gone to sea at the age of nine and who had risen through the service by way of the merchant marine. On 16 August he was shepherding through the Channel a convoy of 60 merchantmen from the West Indies bringing home a cargo of silver when it was raided by 40 English warships under Ayscue's command. The advantage lay with the attackers, not just because they outgunned their Dutch opponents but because de

Ruijter was placed in the difficult position of having to defend the merchantmen while trying to engage Ayscue's ships. The ensuing battle was keenly contested as Ayscue's ships smashed through the Dutch lines firing their heavier ordnance, but in the confusion most of the English ships failed to keep their station in the line of attack and quickly lost the advantage. What saved the Dutch was de Ruijter's order to fire at the enemy's sails and rigging and, as darkness fell, Ayscue's fleet was forced to limp into Plymouth harbour. No ships were lost on either side but each suffered heavy casualties among their crews; more to the point though, the Dutch admiral had the satisfaction of getting his convoy safely home. Three days later he even had the temerity to sail into the Plymouth roads to inflict further damage on the home fleet, and was only deterred from pressing home an attack by adverse winds.

For the rest of the summer the English fleet remained in port or in the Downs making good battle and storm damage – a game of cat and mouse between Blake and de Ruijter in mid-September came to nothing – and there was no further encounter until the end of September, when Tromp's replacement, Vice-Admiral Witte Corneliszoon de With, took a Dutch fleet into the Channel to meet up with de Ruijter's force off Ostende. Impatient, bad-tempered, a severe taskmaster and a Hollander who was unpopular with the Zeeland crews, de With had many defects as a naval commander, but he did possess aggression. On 2 October he took the combined Dutch fleet north towards the Downs, where Blake's ships were lying off a shoal in the Thames estuary known as the Kentish Knock. With the wind blowing from the south-west it took six days for de With to get his fleet to the north and to tack south in three lines towards Blake's fleet, which was stretched out over six miles of water with Bourne's flotilla lying to the south. Blake was also hampered when the mighty 88-gun *Sovereign* ran aground on the shoal together with the 66-gun *James*.

A confused and disorderly battle followed, with both sides showing a good deal of tactical naïveté. Even before the action began de With suffered a setback when out of loyalty to Tromp the crew of the *Brederode* refused to allow him to move his flag to it and he was forced to use the smaller armed merchantman *Prins Willem* – hardly a sign of the fleet's willingness to follow him in battle. The first stage of the battle saw an exchange of gunfire as the Dutch fleet passed Blake's ships and continued the attack towards Bourne's isolated ships. As they did so the *Sovereign* and the *James* were finally freed to attack from the flank with the rest of Penn's squadron while Blake's ships tacked back to the south in pursuit, and the fighting degenerated into a mêlée. With both sides firing at will, the main damage was done to the rigging, and afterwards de With confessed that he could see nothing but 'smoke, fire and the English'.

By nightfall the Dutch fleet was all but defeated. De With's flagship had been crippled, its rigging in tatters, and at least ten more were so disabled that they were unable to continue fighting. Typically the Dutch admiral wanted to restart the battle at daybreak, but the fight had gone out of his crews and he bowed to de Ruijter's advice to return to port – a route which the Zeeland ships had already taken. It was the correct decision. Badly mauled and unable to withstand the heavy pounding of the English guns, the ships were unequal to the task, and their crews had been demoralised both by the fighting and by the scurvy which had broken out before the battle. They were saved further damage when it became clear that Blake's fleet was too badly damaged to offer pursuit. Kentish Knock counted as a victory, and it was celebrated as such on Blake's return, but it left many issues unresolved. For all their superior firepower the English fleet lacked sufficient logistical support, it took time to replenish ships and repair battle damage – shortage of funds and slowness in settling accounts made contractors cautious – and there was a pressing need to produce more warships. These problems fell to the Council of State's Admiralty sub-committee, which was dominated by Sir Henry Vane the Younger, but it was large and unwieldy and too many of its members knew nothing about naval affairs. Tactics, too, were a problem. Ships' captains tended to act independently, and as many of them commanded their own armed merchantmen they were often loath to engage the enemy. There was no attempt to provide concerted firepower and the concept of squadrons attacking in line and maintaining their position was still in its infancy.*

In an attempt to raise more money for the navy, and to reduce the

---

* *Instructions for the better ordering of the Fleet in Fighting*, an attempt at clarifying tactics, was published in 29 March 1653.

deficit which stood at close under half a million pounds, parliament passed a fresh Confiscation Act on 18 November which produced a new list of Royalist 'traitors' whose properties were to be seized and sold off. This was expected to halve the deficit, but any advantage was offset by the chronic maladminstration of the naval dockyards at Chatham, Deptford and Woolwich and by the widespread embezzlement not just of naval property but also of prize ships taken into custody. So obvious was the corruption that Nehemiah Bourne was forced to complain to the Admiralty Committee that he could not keep silent, 'having no other design but to render myself faithful to my trust and to prevent unavoidable inconveniences that will follow upon such disorderly and preposterous courses'.[8] Being a New England Puritan who had put at risk much of his own fortune and career to support the parliamentary cause, Bourne had good reason to be incensed about this criminal profligacy and he remained a stern critic of the corruption in the naval dockyards – after retiring from active service he was appointed Commissioner at the port of Harwich. Part of the problem was that the Petts, the leading shipbuilding and victualling family at Chatham, operated a cartel which dominated the administration of the dockyards and allowed abuses to remain unchecked.

It was an uncomfortable situation. The navy had defeated the Dutch, yet it was in a state of disrepair and had little reason to feel complacent. At the same time, stung by their defeat, the Dutch recalled Tromp and set about an ambitious programme for the construction of 30 ships which would match the size and power of the first three English rates. Although this plan had to be modified as a result of bickering among the five naval boards – there were fears that the bigger ships would be unable to operate in coastal waters – the Dutch had finally taken on board the message that the only way to counter the English was to smash their navy. It would take time before these ships were ready, but Tromp was impatient to strike an early blow to retrieve the situation and started pressing men from merchant ships to fill the gaps left by death, illness and desertion. By mid-November he was ready to run a convoy through the Channel, and in the late afternoon of 24 November 1651 Blake received the astonishing news that some 500 sail had been observed by the lookouts in Margate. For the English admiral this was unwelcome information – his fleet was undergoing replenishment and repair and was not in a position to take on the Dutch navy – but he could hardly stay in the safety of the Downs while Tromp swept through the Channel.

Fortunately adverse winds hindered the Dutch progress and for two days the convoy was forced to heave to on the Flanders coast. A respite on 27 November allowed them to make further progress by tacking against the prevailing south-westerly wind, allowing Blake to intervene. The English fleet was outnumbered two to one – of the 500 Dutch sail 90 were warships – but against that Blake had the advantage of the English shore, and two days later the two fleets were racing through the Strait of Dover in parallel lines, their courses kept apart by a shoal known as the Rip-Raps. When they reached Dungeness Point Tromp swung his ships towards the English fleet, allowing the *Brederode* to engage the *Triumph*, Blake's flagship. Hampered by their proximity to the shore, the English captains had difficulty manoeuvring, but *Brederode* itself was soon in difficulties as the captain of *Garland* put his ship between it and *Triumph* while an armed merchantmen, *Anthony Bonaventure*, attacked from the other side. Their gallantry allowed Blake to slip away to the west, but both the English ships paid the price – *Anthony Bonaventure* was captured, *Garland* exploded and both captains were killed. As the short winter afternoon drew to a close the English fleet disengaged and made its way back to the safety of the Thames estuary.

A total disaster had been averted, but Dungeness was still a bad defeat, and had Tromp possessed more rigour and self-belief he could have returned to take on Blake's depleted fleet and perhaps even attacked London – the latter plan was debated but abandoned because the Dutch pilots were wary of taking their fleet through the shoal-ridden Thames estuary. Even so, he used his temporary advantage to attack English merchant ships and managed to land raiding parties on the Sussex coast, while Blake was forced to take his fleet out of the Downs to greater safety north of the Thames estuary.* While the English fleet licked its wounds the Council of State held a post-mortem conducted by three commissioners who investigated the

---

* It was at this time that Tromp was rumoured to have fastened a broom to his main masthead as a sign of his determination to sweep the English from the Channel.

conduct of the battle and the part played by individual commanders, Blake having already complained to the Council of State on 1 December that several ships held back during the fighting:

> In this account I am bound to let your Honours know in general that there was much baseness of spirit, not among the merchantmen only, but many of the State's [war] ships, and therefore I make it my humble request that your Honours would be pleased to send down some gentlemen to take an impartial and strict examination of the deportment of several commanders, that you may know who are to be confided in and who are not. It will then be time to take into consideration the grounds of some other errors and defects, especially the discouragement and want of seamen.[9]

As a result of the inquiries six captains were dismissed for cowardice, one of them being Blake's brother Benjamin, while the captains of *Victory* and *Vanguard* were commended for their efforts in defending *Triumph*. Blake's own offer to resign was refused, but his defeat at Dungeness was not wholly worthless because it ushered in a revolution in the way the navy was administered and controlled.

All the changes were far-reaching and each one affected the way in which the navy would develop into a modern fighting force. The three generals-at-sea – Popham had been replaced by Monck, fresh from his endeavours in Scotland – would be given greater authority, the fleet was divided into three divisions (red, white and blue), and at Bourne's suggestion armed merchantmen were phased out because their masters were often unwilling to engage the enemy for fear of damaging their property. Also, Articles of War were drawn up which provided for martial law at sea backed up by severe punishments in the event of crews refusing to do their duty. (These were published on 25 December 1652 as *Laws of War and Ordinances of the Sea, ordained and established by the Commonwealth of England*.) Just as importantly, the administration of the navy was improved by the creation of a smaller, independent and more authoritative Admiralty Committee which first met on 17 December under Vane's direction. Improvements followed rapidly, the most notable being 'inducements and encouragements to seamen cheerfully to engage in the service'. Rates of pay were increased and the victualling of ships improved, thereby removing the two main reasons for discontent within the fleet.

The first opportunity to test the new order came early in 1653 in the waters of the West Channel. On 10 February the fleet under the command of Blake, Deane and Monck put to sea, their mission being to engage Tromp as he ushered a large convoy through the Western Approaches. The English naval commanders' main problem was lack of intelligence information – Blake was unsure if Tromp would follow the English or the French coast – and he was forced to order his divisions to sweep backwards and forwards across the Channel, a time-consuming manoeuvre which also broke up the unity of his fleet. It was almost by accident that the two sides collided on 18 February south of Portland Bill. Everything then seemed to favour the Dutch – Monck's squadron lay to the south facing adverse winds while the two remaining squadrons, Penn's and Blake's, were scattered over a wide area of sea.

However, both commanders were eager for battle, and seeing that his 80-strong fleet vastly outnumbered Blake's squadron of some 20 ships the Dutch admiral turned towards his adversaries, attacking them in four lines abreast. Knowing that he could not retire towards the comparative safety of Penn's squadron and his rearguard under the command of John Lawson – any hint of retreat would have unsettled his inexperienced captains – Blake ordered his ships to turn into the wind and take up a defensive position around his flagship, *Triumph*, while Penn's ships tacked round to support them. At the same time, in a masterly move, Lawson took his ships westwards on a southerly bearing before joining the battle from the south-west while Monck's frigates moved to the west in support. As the ships opened fire a brisk engagement followed. This was one of the biggest naval battles ever seen in the Channel – the gunfire could be heard in the counties along the English coastline – and as darkness fell Tromp's ships were forced to retire in disarray.

By then the Dutch had lost eight ships, the English one, and they had also lost a golden opportunity to smash their opponents. The safety of his convoy now being paramount, Tromp put his ships into a defensive screen between the merchant ships and the English fleet. Fighting continued over the next two days as the English ships hounded the retreating convoy, and only an audacious piece of seamanship by Tromp saved what remained of his convoy and their escorts. With many of the ships dismasted and having to be towed, he took them into the shallow waters of the Flanders coast and at night slipped past Cape Gris Nez to safety. He had avoided total defeat but it was at a terrible cost – out of a total fleet of 230 ships only seventy remained, the rest having been sunk or captured. Later it was found that many of these lost ships had in fact scattered to other ports and, as Blake and Deane told the Council of State, the Dutch losses were seventeen warships and sixty merchantmen. It had been a bloody battle – *Mercurius Politicus* reported that 'all the men-of-war who are taken are much dyed with blood, their masts and tackle being moiled with brains, hair, pieces of skulls' – but the English had regained control of the Channel:

> Thus your Lordships see what the Lord hath done for us, and how far He brought us. We have taken and destroyed about seventeen of their men of war and have not lost any one ship as we know of, only one that was so torn that she was not fit to keep the seas and therefore we took out the men and sunk her. Yet we are miserably torn and have very many men slain and wounded, and therefore humbly desire provisions, surgeons, and all things needful may be had for the wounded men on the coast between Weymouth and the Downs, where we have been necessitated to land them. We are now hastening to Portsmouth and the Isle of Wight for our refitting.[10]

The English victory at Portland struck a heavy blow against the Dutch, who were forced to send their merchant ships on the northerly route around Scotland, but it was not a decisive action. The United Provinces were blockaded, a factor that increased calls for a negotiated peace, but Tromp had not given up the fight and spent the rest of the spring of 1653 overseeing the construction of new and larger ships and building up fresh crews. By mid-May he was in the North Sea again with a fleet of just under one hundred war and fire ships, but once again the superior firepower and discipline of the English navy told against him. On 2 June off the Gabbard Shoal to the east of Harwich the Dutch were engaged and defeated with the loss of twenty ships, and this was followed by the final battle of the war, fought off

Scheveningen at the end of July. With Blake ill, Monck commanded the fleet and gained a substantial victory: the Dutch lost about twenty ships and between 3000 and 4000 men killed, among them Tromp himself. By then Deane, too, had been killed but as a contemporary report made clear the Dutch had been forced to recognise the strength and power of the English fleet:

> But the truth is, the English have better ships, more power or money. The people here (chiefly the Zeelanders) who did boast that they alone would drive home the English, being ignorant of this ground, did build castles in the air, and did frame to themselves maxims which have prejudiced and will prejudice this State. The wise men know it well enough but they dare not speak it.[11]

Three things saved the Dutch from absolute ruin – the safe arrival of convoys from the northerly route, the need to replenish and repair Monck's fleet, and the political upheaval in England which saw Cromwell finally take power as Lord Protector. All were to lead to the negotiated peace which followed a year later. Having concluded the treaty, to show that they were now friends, the Dutch and English negotiators sat down to sing the 133rd psalm, with its sonorous lines on 'how good and how pleasant it is for brethren to dwell together in unity', but the mood was caught more precisely by the merging of triumphalism and humility in the official proclamation: 'the dispensations of the Lord have been as if he had said, England thou art my first-born, my delight amongst the nations'. A new age had dawned. England had demonstrated the first signs of becoming a world power, a Protestant country doing God's will while bettering itself and its people, and the navy had emerged as the main instrument of its commercial and colonial policies.

Chapter Three

CROMWELL, LORD PROTECTOR

'If these the times, then this must be the man.'

Andrew Marvell, 'The First Anniversary of the Government
under His Highness the Lord Protector', 1654

By the time that the Barebones Parliament began its work – its first sitting came between the naval battles of the Gabbard in early June and Scheveningen in late July – it was already clear that its programme of reforms would be slow in arriving. An expanded Council of State was formed to sit until 3 November 1653 and to deal with domestic and foreign policy, including the negotiations with the Dutch, while the parliament itself concentrated on addressing the policies put forward by the Heads of the Proposals and the *Agreement of the People*. At the opening session Cromwell had exulted that he was addressing a chosen body – 'you are as like the forming of God as ever people were' – but despite those heady words and the parliament's godly designs the membership was too riven by factions for their ideals to be translated into practice. Religious piety and an exalted conscience were no substitute for political experience and administrative energy, a point that was made, inadvertently perhaps, by one of the Scottish members, Andrew Jaffray, when he recollected his time as a member: 'I had there occasion to meet and be acquainted with many godly men; though I can say little of any good we did at that

Parliament; yet it was in the hearts of some there to have done good for the promoting of the kingdom of Christ.'[1]

The new body was not helped by the choice of speaker. Francis Rous was a formidable parliamentarian, having been a member since 1626, his former role as Provost of Eton College gave him moderating skills and intellectual respectability, his friendship with Cromwell provided him with powerful allies, and his relationship to Pym, his brother-in-law, brought a pedigree and connections, but against those attributes he was querulous and proved incapable of dealing with the sectaries, especially the Fifth Monarchist members. He was also in his seventies, and although age is no barrier in political life a younger man might have possessed the energy and commitment to keep the parliament busy and its members' minds concentrated. Being a Presbyterian, Rous was also counted a moderate.

As it was, the Barebones Parliament set about its initial tasks with a good deal of enthusiasm, and its willingness to attack problems was an immediate and welcome change from the lethargy of the previous administration. On law reform it busied itself by passing an act allowing for civil marriage, a sensible enough and popular reform, but the administration came to grief when it addressed the ancient Court of Chancery. Originally an office for keeping and maintaining state records, it had evolved into a court responsible for the law of equity, and in that time it had become notorious for its many self-perpetuating corruptions, its abuses of power and its jobbery in selling posts. Clearly it needed to be reformed, but the changes to such a venerable and complicated organisation could not be made overnight. But that is what Rous allowed to happen: an act was passed abolishing the court before steps had been taken to create a substitute body. The result, of course was further muddle.

Religious reform fared no better. The maintenance of tithes was no less popular than the Court of Chancery, the army had demanded their abolition and the creation of a state Church, yet the Barebones' response was equally unrealistic. On 15 July a motion was raised to abolish tithes forthwith, but this was defeated, as the moderate members were not minded to sweep them away before finding some other means of remunerating ministers. Fear of change and loss of income was one reason (tithes were a form of property and generated income), respect for patronage was another, but for the moderates it was a question of keeping the sectaries at bay and preserving the rights of the propertied classes – in their petition of 1647 Levellers had made it a credo that tithes should be abolished and parishioners given the liberty to choose their own clergy. Another sect proposed that 'mechanick ministers' should spend six days a week labouring to earn their keep, as Jesus had done as a carpenter. The matter was referred to a committee, but that did not stop it being a contentious issue; far from it, this would be the means of the Barebones Parliament's undoing.

It has to be said too that the parliament was not best served by those members who represented sects such as the Fifth Monarchists. In the aftermath of the execution of Charles I and the emergence of the English republic there had been varied outbreaks of radicalism and mysticism, and these were mirrored in parliament by some of its more extreme members. Although it would be easy to write off the Barebones Parliament as a congregation of fanatics – the committee system was businesslike and efficient and the civil administration had been improved and streamlined – many of its decisions were taken against a background of intense religious debate and a heightened belief that the world was going to end or that Christ was about to come into his own. One speaker proposed that the oceans should be secured 'in order to prepare for the coming of Christ', while another stated that the second coming would have to take place before Christmas or Jesus need not come at all. Writing about this nation of prophets and prophecies two years later, one observer judged that the mood was simply a product of the troubled times:

> Men variously impoverished by the long troubles, full of discontents, and tired by long expectation of amendment, must needs have great propensions to hearken to those that proclaim times of refreshing – a golden age at hand etc. Nor is it a wonder that some would willingly listen to those that publish such glad tidings, under the name of the kingdom of Christ and of the saints; especially when so many prophecies are cited and applied to these times.[2]

The Fifth Monarchists proved to be the most vocal within the chamber, and backed by their fiery preachers they enjoyed political power beyond their actual numbers. They supported the war against the Dutch and stood firmly against peace negotiations, their enthusiasm on both counts being heightened by the fact that many were traders and stood to gain from a Dutch defeat. They also wanted to export the revolution to other parts of Europe, and that idealism helps to explain their vociferous millenarian beliefs. Although they did not actually dictate policy, their numbers being small, their presence and their ability to make their feelings known certainly influenced the complexion of the Barebones Parliament – a contemporary account of a Fifth Monarchist church service complained about the sermon's 'most horrid trumpets of fire, murther and flame'.[3]

To add to the tumult John Lilburne, the leader of the Levellers, resurfaced and his presence also caused a diversion. Having been exiled by the previous parliament on charges of sedition, he had returned to England in the middle of June and had taken up residence in London, hoping no doubt to take advantage of the fall of the parliament which had exiled him and the arrival of this parliament of Barebones saints. His arrival was thoroughly unsettling, for not only was he one of the country's best-known and most widely admired political activists but he had also spent much of his exile in the company of Royalist sympathisers, a fact that must have been known to the authorities. Added to the fact that he enjoyed popular support for his straightforward radicalism he also provided a focus for discontent, an uncomfortable state of affairs for a parliament which had come into being at the behest of the army. By returning, Lilburne had given his enemies every opportunity to arrest him as a felon, and although he asked to be left alone he was taken into custody prior to being put on trial for his life.

What followed next only added to the general air of unease which gripped England during the brief period of the Barebones Parliament. Lilburne's detention sparked off a flurry of pamphlets, many of them written by himself, others by his supporters and all aimed at winning his release. One petition had 6000 signatures and the Venetian representative in London mused that if Lilburne were condemned 'his death would find 20,000 avengers'. So concerned was the Council of State that they ordered three regiments of horse to move into London to deal with the expected unrest. The trial was fixed for 13 July, but when it opened Lilburne defended himself with customary vigour.

Asked if he was the Lieutenant-Colonel John Lilburne mentioned in the act exiling him he replied in the negative, on the grounds that as he was no longer in the army the rank did not apply. Pursuing his own logic, he argued in his defence that he could not be held to book by the previous parliament as it had been dismissed as an illegal body by Cromwell. If the charge were to stand then that implied agreement with a discredited body and he should be freed forthwith. His trial attracted equal amounts of condemnation and support, further petitions were written in his favour and his supporters rallied round his cause with a jingle which soon had a wide currency:

> And what shall then honest John Lilburne die?
> Three thousand score will know the reason why.

At the end of the trial Lilburne was found 'not guilty of any crime worthy of death', and when the verdict was announced by the jury the whole court broke into applause, including the soldiers who were present to keep order. This was serious, as Lilburne had many supporters in the army, and the Council of State decided to bottle up the threat by keeping the prisoner in custody in the Tower of London 'for the peace of the nation'. There is little doubt that Lilburne had touched a nerve and that Cromwell was unsettled by the presence in London of such an awkward character who had made so many egalitarian demands in the past. Even though the Levellers were no longer the political force they had been in the previous decade, their leader enjoyed a good deal of popularity and the jury's verdict, plus the soldiers' demonstration of support, were powerful reminders of the administration's lack of popularity. The following year Lilburne was quietly removed to the island of Jersey, where he was kept under what amounted to house arrest. Later he was allowed to return to mainland England, where he died in Eltham on 29 August 1657, having embraced the Quaker faith. He died knowing that the Levellers' revolution had also crumbled.* In the wake of the not guilty

---

* One of the most prominent agitators was Colonel (formerly Cornet) George Joyce, who had arrested Charles I at Holmby House. For expressing the wish that Cromwell should have been shot by the army during the rendezvous at Triploe Heath in 1647 he was cashiered.

verdict there had been demonstrations and some agitation in the army, all of which was quickly repressed, and Lilburne's last pamphlet showed that the fire had gone out of his fight and that his enemies, not least Cromwell, had finally got the better of him:

> Frailties and infirmities I have and thick and threefold have been my provocations; he that hath not failed in his tongue, is perfect, so am not I. I dare not say, Lord I am not as other men; but, Lord be merciful to me a sinner; but I have been hunted like a partridge upon the mountains; my words and actions in the times of my trials and deepest distress and danger have been scanned with the spirit of Jobs comforters; but yet I know I have to do with a gracious God, I know that my redeemer liveth, and that he will bring light out of this darkness, and clear my innocency to all the world.[4]

Lilburne was right to be downcast about winning his trial but losing his fight to stay a free man. For all the trappings of democracy the parliament remained a creature of the army, and although it was tolerably efficient – during the five months of its existence it passed thirty ordinances – it was a spatchcock body which smacked of compromise. It suffered too from irregular attendance, and majority decisions were often a matter of chance or calculated design – knowing that radicals were at prayer on Monday mornings, moderates used that hour to push through an ordinance creating a new High Court of Justice for trying enemies of the state, a move which seemed to their opponents to have been inspired by Lilburne's acquittal.

Clearly such a haphazard means of administering the country could not work. Cromwell stayed away from the chamber (though not the Council of State), and as the year progressed the work of the parliament became increasingly disjointed. Even the man who gave the parliament its later nickname, Praise-God Barbon, never spoke in any of its meetings and had shown himself to be incapable of dealing with a deputation of women protesters during Lilburne's trial. And as the year grew older the great question of reform of religious patronage remained unanswered. The motion to abolish tithes might have been thrown out in midsummer, but the defeat had not silenced the radicals who wanted action from the investigating committee. Those who supported tithes, either because no other system of remuneration had been evolved or because they resented the loss of a valuable asset, were equally vocal. At the outset of their existence the Barebones members had been told by Cromwell that they stood on the verge of promises and prophecies, yet barely three months into their existence they were in danger of tearing themselves apart over a primitive form of clerical taxation. Matters came to a head at the beginning of December when the committee on tithes made its report; this came down on the side of retaining the system and allowing those who benefited to keep their legal title to tithes. However, when the proposition was put to the vote on 10 December it was rejected by a majority of four, the narrowness of the result being explained by the dissension of a number of moderates who felt that the proposal had failed to solve the issue and would only create further problems.

The decision plunged the parliament into crisis and forced the moderates to act. Two days later, another Monday when the radicals were again at prayer, forty members convened early in the house and by prior arrangement Sir Charles Worsley, a conservative member of the Council of State, rose to propose a motion that would spell the end of the Barebones Parliament. Powerful in his own right – he had married a daughter of Lord Saye and Sele, was close to Cromwell and enjoyed the support of Speaker Rous – Worsley mounted a vehement attack on the moves to change the Court of Chancery and to abolish tithes and ended by moving 'that the sitting of this parliament any longer as now constituted will not be for the good of the Commonwealth, and that therefore it is requisite to deliver up unto the Lord General Cromwell the powers they have received from him'. His motion was supported by others, but Rous was unwilling to have the issue debated and in an extraordinary move he led the members out of the chamber and the party made its way to Cromwell in Whitehall where, according to the Clerk of the House, 'they, being the Greater Number of the Members sitting in Parliament, did, by a Writing under their Hands, resign unto his Excellency their said powers'.[5] At the same time a troop of musketeers arrived in the chamber to clear it of the radicals who had arrived, too late, to protest against their own demise.

The move took Cromwell by surprise. The plans had been hatched over the weekend by Rous and the moderates and put into action by the formidable figure of Major-General John Lambert. Now aged thirty-three, Lambert was the coming man in the army, a popular commander who had helped to pacify Scotland, a moderate and no friend of extremists such as the Fifth Monarchists. He also had the ear of Cromwell, and although he had opposed the Barebones Parliament the two men had remained on terms friendly enough to survive Lambert's disappointment at losing the Irish Lord Deputyship. Ambitious, and spurred on by his equally determined wife Frances, who still nursed her wrath over the lost Irish opportunity, he represented that side of the army which had little truck with the more extreme demands of the sectaries and which wanted a solid constitutional settlement. An iron dreamer, Lambert had no time for saintly aspirations or for radical reforms to mend the fabric of English life, hence his opposition to the Barebones Parliament; his solution was the Instrument of Government, a constitutional document which he drew up with the help of fellow moderates in the Council of Officers. Rapidly finalised over the weekend between the vote on tithes and Worsley's motion, it allowed for a new constitution based on a titular leader and a reformed parliament. The document was presented to Cromwell on the same day that Rous delivered up the powers of parliament.

According to Cromwell, writing in 1657, he had already seen the Instrument but had rejected it because it would have offered him the king's crown, a move which would have alienated sections of the army. He was also shrewd enough to know that, had he accepted the offer, he would have been forced to dismiss the Barebones Parliament, a failed body which he had brought into being but which he now called 'a story of my own weakness and folly'. It seemed better to adopt the 'waiting posture' once more, just as he had done in Pontefract in the winter of 1647–48 when Colonel Pride purged parliament, and to await the outcome of events. When it became clear that the moderates were about to mount a coup Lambert reworked the Instrument and presented it timeously to Cromwell. Suddenly it all fell into place for the Lord General. The parliament he had created had proved to be a broken reed, its members had handed back those powers to him (within a few days the supporters of the move would grow to over eighty), and at the same time he had been presented with a constitutional document which would authorise and regulate the new powers given to him. It was a neat solution which was guaranteed to provide stability with sufficient checks and balances to reduce the danger of power being abused. Above all, at a time when the country was struggling to reinvent itself after the fall of the monarchy, the Instrument of Government produced respectability and a much-needed sense of coherence. In a letter to Whitelocke, now representing his country in Sweden, the new secretary to the Council, John Thurloe, made it clear that at long last conservative moderation had triumphed over an unfettered administration: 'This change . . . hath a very general acceptance, especially among the lawyers, the ministers and the merchants, who conceived themselves most in danger from the temper of the last Parliament.'[6]

Within three days the Instrument had been debated, amended and accepted; in place of the bogeyman 'king', Cromwell would be named His Highness the Lord Protector of the Commonwealth of England, Scotland and Ireland, a suitably sonorous title which made him Britain's ruler and monarch in all but name. On 16 December 1653 he was sworn into office in the Court of Chancery in a ceremony which had some of the trappings of royalty – a strong military presence and the production of the Great Seal – while rejecting others. Anxious not to display any hints of ostentation or pride, Cromwell wore a plain black suit and cloak (his black hat alone carried a gold band) and symbolically he unbuckled his soldier's sword in return for a civilian model handed over by Lambert. And on return to the Banqueting Hall there was a short peroration followed by a volley of three shots, the mixing of religion with the sword being as a good a way as any to welcome Britain's new ruler. Relief was the prevailing emotion. After the period of political uncertainty and the war against the Dutch there was an overwhelming need for settled continuity but, of course, not everyone was enamoured of the new order. Having prophesied a second coming in the wake of Charles's execution, the Fifth Monarchists were outraged to find that another ruler was in place before King Jesus. Other critics, such as Lucy Hutchinson, discerned the hand of personal ambition and aggrandisement:

In the interim Cromwell and his army grew wanton with their power, and invented a thousand tricks of government which, when nobody opposed, they themselves fell to dislike and vary every

[day]. First he calls a parliament out of his own pocket, himself nominating a sort of godly men for every country, who meeting and not agreeing, part of them, in the name of the people, gave up the sovereignty to him . . .[7]

Lucy Hutchinson was a hostile witness and throughout the Protectorate continued to criticise the new style of ruling ('full of sin and vanity'), but in the existing circumstances it is difficult to envisage any other outcome. Through his standing as the commander-in-chief of the army, his widely respected personal integrity and his unmatched authority, Cromwell was de facto ruler of the country, the strong man who would be king but feared the consequences of accepting the title. When Lambert produced his Instrument of Government he was simply providing a legal framework for a system of government which was awaiting constitutional respectability. Under its terms power was vested in the Lord Protector with the advice of fifteen members of an executive council, all appointed for life. A new parliament would come into being, but not until the following year, and it would be composed of four hundred members from England and Wales and thirty each from Scotland and Ireland, the franchise being £200 a year in personal property. Royalists and Engagers were debarred from the first four parliaments, while Roman Catholics were excluded permanently. They were also exempted from religious toleration, as were Anglicans who refused to forswear the Prayer Book, but nonconformists were admitted provided that they did not disturb the peace. Tellingly, the Lord Protector was left in control of the armed forces, which received a permanent revenue.

In many respects the Instrument was an imperfect document, based as much on the *Agreement of the People* and the Heads of the Proposals as anything else, but as Cromwell put it the new order avoided the worst excesses of hereditary monarchy and the unwieldiness of a unicameral parliament. The men who commissioned the document and benefited from it were close to Cromwell, another factor in making the new arrangement work. Through death, retirement or disagreement, Cromwell had lost several good friends and advisers – Fairfax, St John, Hampden and Holles – but the men who came to power through the Instrument were not unequal to the task of providing the Lord Protector with an efficient staff. Its author, Lambert, became a member of the council, as did Generals Skippon and Fleetwood. The latter was related by marriage to Cromwell, as were two other councillors, John Desborough and Henry Lawrence, both of whom were married to the Lord Protector's sisters. Rous and Worsley were also elected to the body and its other members were all solid moderates, some of whom had fought in the war or had served in administrative posts in the Commonwealth. Others, such as Viscount Lisle and Sir Anthony Ashley Cooper, represented the landed gentry and pointed the way ahead to a settlement which would embrace all classes.

Together they provided Cromwell with a solid power base, but even by the time he had accepted the Instrument he had managed to dispel most of his political rivals and enemies. By destroying the Rump of the Long Parliament he had broken the power of the radicals and sent into political exile Ludlow, Marten and the younger Henry Vane. This was followed by the immolation of the Barebones Parliament, which ended the authority wielded by Harrison (exiled to his father's house in Staffordshire), and the silencing of John Lilburne had broken any effectiveness the Levellers hoped to wield after their power had been broken in 1649. Now the country had returned to the safe hands of 'natural rulers' – those who preferred conservatism to the noisy upheavals threatened by the Levellers and others. Purged of the radicals the army supported Cromwell, as did the navy, and backed by them and by his friends and allies he was in a position to do what he had set out to do in the early days of the Commonwealth – to settle the country's affairs, reconcile old enemies and give much-needed stability to economic and foreign policies. That he succeeded in meeting those aims was given grudging acceptance by Hyde, who noted in the following spring that 'Cromwell proceeds with strange dexterity towards the reconciling all kinds of persons and chooses out those of all parties whose abilities are most eminent'.[8]

Despite the return to a settled form of government, the certainties were not evident everywhere. By 1655 press censorship had been instituted, with only two newspapers surviving, Nedham's *Mercurius Politicus* and *The Publick Intelligencer*, but even so they could publish nothing without the agreement of John Thurloe, now regarded as one of the most influential politicians in the inner circles of power. A lawyer by training, Thurloe had enjoyed the patronage of Oliver St

John and worked as a secretary in the Long Parliament. Able, loyal, discreet, committed to Cromwell and a skilled bureaucrat, he built up a professional intelligence service to observe and infiltrate the court of Charles II, by then in residence in much-reduced circumstances in Cologne. Agents were paid well and from them an accurate picture was built up of the difficulties facing the royal household as it attempted to maintain its existence with a semblance of style while existing on handouts from Royalist supporters and an uncertain grant from Cardinal Mazarin. 'How they all live, God knows!' exclaimed one agent after spying on Charles's impoverished court, 'I am sure I do not!' So successful was this network that Thurloe's agents were able to intercept correspondence between the exiled Royalists and their supporters in England and Scotland. Very little of what Hyde wrote was not passed on to Thurloe and then to Cromwell.

The agents also dealt with suspected conspiracies – at various stages Harrison and Ludlow were thought to be fomenting unrest and there was an assassination scare in the summer of 1654 – but although England had become a republic it was hardly a dictatorship. Enemies of the state were not executed: either they agreed to support the Protectorate or they suffered Lilburne's fate of internal banishment. There was also a fair degree of religious tolerance. Following a widespread ejection of unsuitable ministers in 1654, in which one-third of England's 9500 parishes saw their charges being expelled and replaced, the general rule was that congregations could practise according to their wishes provided they caused no scandal or public uproar. Because there was no prescription of worship they were free to use the prayer book or the precepts of the Covenant provided that they were discreet. Only the Catholics were proscribed, but Cromwell was often minded to bring them back into the fabric of English life. That summer he tried to save an elderly Jesuit priest from the awful punishment of being hanged, drawn and quartered, and by 1655 he was in secret discussions with the Vatican seeking a rapprochement which would have allowed English Catholics to conduct their worship in private. Nothing came of the move, which was condemned by Hyde as 'hypocrisy and juggling', but after Cromwell became Lord Protector he was generally minded to show tolerance to English Catholics, provided always that they maintained the laws of the land.

Before the election of parliament in September 1654 Cromwell and the council spent the first part of the year tackling a number of outstanding concerns, and in so doing passed over a hundred ordinances which affected social, legal and economic issues. Duelling and challenges were outlawed and sports involving gambling such as bear-baiting, cock-fighting and horse-racing were forbidden on the grounds that they created conditions which could lead to affray and could be used as cover for the meeting of Royalist conspirators.* For similar reasons stage plays were also banned, but the prohibition did not extend to opera, which flourished under the Protectorate because it was considered to have a high moral tone. Cromwell's interest in music might also have been a factor, and one of the first productions to be staged was *The Siege of Rhodes* in 1656, with a libretto by the poet Sir William Davenant. The governance of Scotland and Ireland was also taken in hand (see the following chapter) and a Treason Act was passed making it a capital offence to plot the death of the Protector or foment mutiny in the armed forces. The High Court of Justice was confirmed in its position and the post of Chief Justice was given to Matthew Hale, a moderate and a conciliator who made it a condition of acceptance that he would not be asked to prosecute Royalists.

Gradually the country was coming back under control – some measures were more welcome than others – but it was an authority which depended on the army's backing. Cromwell was still Lord General, and he had been able to push through his coup because he knew that the regiments would always march or ride in his support. He was their commander-in-chief and accepted as such, but now that he was also the country's Protector, a post more akin to a modern presidency, he had to alter his life-style to meet his obligations. Always a plain and unostentatious man – his first biographer Carlyle imagined him as 'a figure of sufficient impressiveness – not lovely to the man-milliner species, nor pretending to be so' – Cromwell had spent most of his middle life campaigning and had generally eschewed luxury. Now that he was the first man of his country he had to change his image to meet the new circumstances – he was not just a

---

* In his *History of England* Lord Macaulay noted wrongly but ironically: 'The Puritans hated bear-baiting, not because it gave pain to the bear, but because it gave pleasure to the spectators'.

Cambridgeshire soldier-squire but the holder of a post which demanded prestige and the trappings of power.

With no other model on which to base the creation of a dignified household for the Protector, his family and his advisers, and to give it the dignity expected by the ambassadors of foreign nations, the new administration had to turn to the workings of the royal courts, although any mention of regality was sedulously avoided. Fortunately the main buildings associated with Charles still stood and only required refurbishment. The royal chambers in the palace of Whitehall were redecorated, as were the other London residences at St James's and Somerset House. On the outskirts of the capital Hampton Court became a weekend retreat, and the Cromwells also had the keys to other royal residences at Windsor and Greenwich. The rehousing entailed some buying back of property, because in the brave new world of 1649 the leaders of the Commonwealth had vowed not only to abolish the office of king but to sell off royal property for the benefit of the people. It proved to be an expensive and time-consuming business, especially at Hampton Court, where the buildings and land had been sold off to private parties and had to be repurchased, one reason being that it was the one property which Cromwell loved. To add to the legal difficulties, squatters from nearby Kingston-on-Thames had to be cleared off land which they had claimed for themselves.

Naturally the process was the cause of some dismay among the sterner Puritans who preferred austerity and thought that the expense and pomp was vainglorious. If they had seen inside the properties their fears might have been justified, for the Protectorate administration was not sparing in its expenditure on the refurbishment. To cater to Cromwell's love of music an organ from Magdalen College, Oxford, was installed in the Great Hall at Hampton Court, furnishings from Charles's time were taken out of store, as were hangings and works of art including Titian's *Herodias with the Head of John the Baptist*, Romano's *The Burning of Rome* and the Raphael cartoons *The Acts of the Apostles*.* Judging from the contemporary

---

* Commissioned by Pope Leo X for the redecoration of the Vatican's Sistine Chapel and purchased by Charles in 1623.

inventories the use of the pieces from the royal collection was as
shrewd and judicious as the king's original purchases had been,
although care was taken to ensure that most of the hangings and
works of art were based on historical or biblical themes. The gardens
at all the residences were also redesigned, and no expense was spared
in providing them with ornamental fountains and statuary, another
enhancement which met with some disapproval, it being only twenty
years since the more extreme iconoclasts had destroyed similar
artefacts in England's churches. Still, the effort seemed to bear fruit.
In February 1656, for the first time in many years, the diarist John
Evelyn 'ventured to go to Whitehall . . . and found it very glorious
and well furnished'.⁹

To ensure the smooth running of the courts a household staff was
organised, and while it did not match Charles I's in size and lavishness
it was equal to the tasks it had to perform. An army of servants saw
to the day-to-day operation of the court's domestic needs, including
the entertainment of foreign dignitaries, an aspect of diplomacy which
was not overlooked by the Protectorate. A Master of Horse oversaw
the stables and managed the horses and coaches, while the chamber
or household above the stairs was managed by a chamberlain, Sir
Gilbert Pickering, who was appointed in 1655, and a Master of
Ceremonies ensured that protocol was observed during state
occasions. In short, Cromwell's households employed many of the
trappings and borrowed many of the observances of the old Stewart
court, but in most of its practices it had been slimmed down and
simplified to meet the changing needs of the Protectorate. The
watchword seems to have been that the court was the outward symbol
of the Commonwealth and that none of its power or pomp was vested
in the Lord Protector himself but in his great office. From all accounts
Cromwell's head was not turned by the ceremonial surrounding him
and neither was he particularly extravagant, managing to combine a
reasonably lavish public style of living with austerity in his private life.

It was a curious time. The Commonwealth was governed by a
Protectorate, and while there was a fair degree of control – the practice
of banning maypoles continued, theatrical performances were
prohibited and breaches in private morality were investigated and
punished – it would be wrong to regard this as a period of simple
austerity. After the Restoration Royalist supporters created a myth of

stern puritanical joylessness compared with the lively and fun-loving period which had gone before. In turn this was reduced to the simple equation that while Royalists were artistic free spirits Puritans and their supporters were dull dogs with a loathing of anything that smacked of fun. As with all stereotypes the creation is wide of the mark. Cromwell's government might have frowned on licence but it was not afraid of liberty, and during the period of the protectorate the musical arts flourished. When Cromwell's daughter Frances married Richard Rich, son of the Earl of Warwick, he entertained his guests with a large orchestra complete 'with forty-eight violins and much mirth with frolics'. And when Bulstrode Whitelocke was sent on his mission to Sweden in 1653 he took with him a party of musicians to entertain the Swedish court.

Literature, too, was encouraged, and not just the doctrinal works by Bunyan and others. In addition to the poetry of Milton and Marvell, both of whom enjoyed the not insignificant patronage of acting as secretary to the Council of State, the period also saw the publication of Izaak Walton's *The Compleat Angler*, a discourse on the art of fishing which was published in 1653 and again in an enlarged edition two years later. Walton's friend and collaborator Charles Cotton was also a prolific poet, although most of his best work appeared after the Restoration. In addition to promoting opera, Davenant, once Charles I's unofficial poet laureate, produced his epic poem *Gondibert* in 1651, a tale of chivalry which ran to 1700 quatrains. It has been said that Davenant's interest in opera was a means of avoiding the ban on stage plays and that he was merely producing an entertainment which combined words with music. The same point was made of his fellow writer for the stage, Richard Flecknoe, whose creation of *Ariadne* in 1654 could be the first English opera – the music has been lost – but there was more to both men's innovations than entrepreneurial enterprise. Both were familiar with the early development of Italian opera by Peri, Caccini and Monteverdi, and Davenant had lived for a time in France, where operatic performances were also in their infancy. This was hardly a nation groaning under the insupportable burden of a tyrannical government, but a sensible orderly country, at ease with itself and, as Marvell put it, with even greater glories lying ahead of it:

What may not then our isle presume
While victory his [Cromwell's] crest does plume!
    What may not others feare
    If thus he crown each yeare!
A Caesar he ere long to Gaul,
To Italy an Hannibal,
    And to all states not free
    Shall clymacterick be.

There were still causes to be fought for and worlds to win (Marvell's lines come from his 'Horatian Ode upon Cromwell's Return from Ireland', but the sentiment was still good three years later), and the opening of the new parliament on the fortuitous date of 3 September, the anniversary of Dunbar and Worcester, echoed that sentiment. At the opening ceremony the following day Cromwell reminded its members that their task was the 'healing and settling' of the nation and that they had upon their shoulders not only 'the interests of three great kingdoms' but also 'the interest of all the Christian people in the world'. It was a dignified speech with high rhetorical notes of soaring grandeur. Parliament was told that it was meeting 'on the greatest occasion that . . . England ever saw', that its responsibilities, political and spiritual, were onerous but the rewards would be greater. Sects were dismissed as a threat to 'the ranks and orders of men, whereby England hath been known for years' ('a nobleman, a gentleman, a yeoman'), and it was the members' duty to reach 'a sweet, gracious and holy understanding of one another'. Once again Cromwell's heart was in the right place, but events were to prove that spirited optimism was no armour for a body which soon showed that it was as incapable of ordering itself as any of its predecessors.

Chapter Four

THE CROMWELLIAN SETTLEMENT IN SCOTLAND AND IRELAND

'We always reckoned those eight years of usurpation a time of great peace and prosperity.'

Bishop Gilbert Burnet, History of His Own Time, *1724–37*

'The truth is, these people are abominable, false, cunning and perfidious people; and the best of them to be pitied, but not to be trusted.'

Sir Charles Fleetwood, Lord Deputy of Ireland,
to John Thurloe, 2 June 1654

In his opening speech to the first Protectorate parliament Cromwell's reference to 'the interests of three great kingdoms' is indicative of the way he viewed the future progress of the Commonwealth of England, Ireland and Scotland. Their common future was also part of the reconciliation process; everyone should benefit from the new order wherever they lived, and the presence of Scottish and Irish members attested to the willingness of the new administration that it should comprise a British union. But there were differences in approach in dealing with Scotland and Ireland. Both had been settled by military force under Cromwell's direction and he was keen to see the two countries settled forcibly and peaceably. Apart from the 'Tories' – disaffected Catholic outlaws who continued to attack settlers and local landowners – Fleetwood had put down any remaining resistance in Ireland by 1654, and in the post of Lord Deputy with a council to support him he had begun the process of land settlement which would see the country divided up and subjected to Protestant colonisation. That same year Monck returned to Scotland to push ahead with the task of absorbing the country into a more complete union with England, a process that had begun after Worcester with the 'Tender of Union' and had continued intermittently ever since. Both countries had been incorporated into this union and had been offered free trade, but there would be substantial variances in the settlement – whereas Ireland was to be colonised as a means of keeping it under control, Scotland would be offered a partnership which would eventually obliterate the distinctions, legal and ecclesiastical, separating the two countries.

Before that happy conjunction could take place, though, the Commonwealth had to deal with a Royalist insurrection which flared up in 1653 and lasted for two uneasy years. Led first by the Earl of Glencairn, who was succeeded by Middleton, and supported by prominent Royalist magnates such as Huntly, Macdonald of Glengarry and Seaforth, its main locus was the Highlands, which provided manpower from clans loyal to the Stewart cause and a safe retreat from which to mount raids into other parts of Scotland. Glencairn could not be compared to Montrose either in his military capacity or in his ability to inspire, but he did possess a rugged determination and a loyal conviction to the cause, virtues which were much needed, given his uncertain support. As a Lowlander his royal commission was questioned by the touchier Highland leaders and, this being Scotland, the attacks on him came from both sides: one of his biggest critics was Balcarres, who was a fellow Lowland magnate. Glencairn was also hobbled by the conflicting interests of the clan leaders and by the need to unite the different factions in common cause against the Commonwealth. Many Scots bridled against the occupation of their country by an English army and the gradual implementation of alien laws, and there was still loyal support for the king matched by a dislike of republican rule. Also there was widespread opposition to the whole notion of union with England, but all too often this nationalistic fervour was neutralised by internecine rivalry among the local clan and family leaders. It also extended to family allegiances: for example, Argyll's son and heir, Lord Lorne, had already thrown in his lot with the Royalists, despite paternal pleas to 'forbear such causes'. In an eerie echo of the outbreak of the civil war in England, in 1642 Argyll wrote a letter to his son's godfather virtually disowning Lorne for taking a decision which would split family loyalties:

> As for what you say about my son, though I know nothing of the particular yet I can believe your information for I trust nothing to him but that he will run to every excess of riot with the wildest that are his associates, and as I told you before I do still advise you not to suffer him nor any of his accomplices to enter into any of your houses, and I discharge you of any prejudice by me though you kill him in keeping him out by force.[1]

Although Argyll's longer-term interests rested with the king – at one point he had hoped to see Charles II marry his daughter – he was not prepared to follow his son's example in joining the rebels, and at one stage in the summer campaigning season of 1653 he sent Campbell soldiers to guard a Commonwealth force retreating to Dumbarton through his clan lands. With Argyll out of the equation for the time being, the trick for Glencairn was to marry those disparate Royalist interests and thereby to broaden the social and territorial spread of his support, not least between Highland and Lowland Scotland. But history was against him: warring elements within the Scottish camp had been the ruin of many another nationalist enterprise in the past and Glencairn's rising was to be no exception.

Initially Robert Lilburne, an experienced if ponderous commander who was the elder brother of John Lilburne the Leveller, thought that the trouble in the Highlands was little more than local unrest or criminal activity which could be contained, and it took him valuable time to realise that Glencairn was gathering together forces for a more general Royalist uprising. Lilburne's position was eroded further by the need to reduce his security forces to meet the expenses of the Dutch War, and he lacked the element needed by any independent commander – the support of his political superiors. Even though he was Free-Born John's brother, Lilburne was trusted by his fellow officers, but he did not possess the direct communications channels to London enjoyed by his predecessor, Deane, and his successor, Monck. That left him unable to put pressure on the government for additional supplies and pay for his men, and all too often he was unsure about what tactics he should use. Nor did it help that he was a colonel, a relatively junior rank for his command.

When Glencairn's forces began their operations Lilburne was aware of the need to win hearts and minds in Scotland. He did not want therefore to use undue force, but he also realised that he had to maintain law and order among a people who were skilled in the use of guerrilla tactics. In the previous year he had seen how pro-Royalist clansmen had been able to attack at will in the Highland areas, using their knowledge of the topography and local conditions to outwit the English patrols. When he started receiving intelligence reports of a Royalist conspiracy early in 1653 he decided on a policy of containment of the Highlands and protection of the vulnerable Lowlands. This meant mounting patrols in fragile areas and threatening to punish the local population if they offered support to the Royalist rebels. Lilburne also spent time successfully courting Argyll, a wise move given the marquis's influence in the West Highlands; his decision to remain loyal to the Commonwealth was one factor in the failure of Glencairn's revolt.

Given the prevailing circumstances Lilburne had made the right decision, although following it meant that he was damned if he acted aggressively towards the Scots and damned if he failed to contain Glencairn's rebels. For all that Glencairn held the king's commission his forces were overstretched, he had a huge area to cover and he was acting in a region where the local clan leaders expected to assume authority within their own bailiwicks. They were also tardy in obeying his orders. When Glencairn summoned a war council in June none of the main protagonists bothered to turn up, while other potential supporters hedged their bets for fear of attracting English reprisals. There was also a good deal of self-interest involved when deciding whether or not to support the Royalist cause: one clan chief wrote to Lilburne offering to cooperate with him but only on condition that he received financial recompense.[2]

As it turned out, the summer campaigns of 1653 did nothing to change the tactical situation in Scotland. Lilburne sent forces to secure the Hebridean islands of Lewis and Mull, both thought to be open to attack from the Dutch, while Lorne marched on Kintyre in his father's clan lands to harass a group of Lowland settlers loyal to the

Commonwealth. The year ended with the bulk of the forces loyal to Glencairn secured in Badenoch in the central Grampians. Apart from a number of raids, the Scottish Royalists had achieved nothing and their meanderings around the Highlands were as nothing compared to the earlier expeditions undertaken by Montrose. Glencairn remained in command until the early part of 1654, when Middleton eventually fetched up in Scotland, having landed with a small party of professional soldiers at Little Ferry, north of Dornoch, on 20 February. A loyal and steadfast soldier who had served at Preston and Worcester, Middleton was the king's man but, lacking any dazzling military successes to give him substance among the Highland clan leaders, he failed to produce any cohesion to the cause or to create a rallying point for Charles II. Appointing a Highland leader such as Glengarry might have been an option for the exiled king, but so bitter were the local antipathies that only a strong man could have hoped to produce the unity needed for a successful uprising: for all his virtues, Middleton was not that prodigy. It was not surprising that Charles felt let down by the lack of any tangible military activity in Scotland. With the Commonwealth getting the better of the Dutch at sea and with his own exchequer in desperate straits, he was at a low point and needed some signs of successful support. Showing more optimism than realism, Hyde offered the defiant hope that if all else failed, if 'no more probable adventure' emerged, Charles should try his luck in Scotland again, but in the summer of 1654 the exiled king was merely tilting at Caledonian windmills.

Middleton's arrival back in Scotland coincided with the return of Monck. In the final months of his command Lilburne had made little secret of his desire to leave the country, and the appearance of his successor in April signalled a turnaround in the fortunes of the Commonwealth's management of Scotland. Fresh from his success as a general-at-sea and blessed by easy access to Cromwell, Monck changed everything. The army was reinforced with regiments which had seen service in the Dunbar campaign, funds were made available in the shape of a grant of £30,000, and he brought with him a more robust approach to forging the political union between the two countries. As for his military objectives, these were similar to Lilburne's – aggressive patrolling of the Highland areas and the containment of the rebellion – but this time he had the troops and the political support to back him. It also helped that the Dutch war was almost at an end, but the deciding factor was the establishment of the Protectorate and the wholehearted backing of the new Council of State, with its firm intention of pushing through a lasting union with Scotland.

With him, too, Monck brought additional powers to deal with the revolt, which he found to be more serious than had first been thought. Because many Scottish families allowed their sons to support the Royalist cause as proxies, while their fathers stayed at home maintaining a semblance of loyalty to the Protectorate, Monck was provided with legislation to punish the family concerned or reward them if the recalcitrant surrendered within three weeks of being summoned. Further rewards were made available for the capture of rebel leaders and the regulations concerning the sequestration of rebel property were tightened. Wariston described the new policy as 'rigour and ruin', and it was a fair description of Monck's determination to crush the revolt once and for all by using a mailed fist while proffering the hand of friendship to potential allies. His tactics were simple but effective: the Lowlands would be kept quiet and secure while the Highlands would be cut off to prevent attacks being made from them. At the same time smaller mobile garrisons would be stationed in the upland areas at vital points to prevent any insurrection from spreading – Dornoch, Ruthven in Badenoch, Inverlochy, Inverness, Loch Tay, and in the area to the west of the Great Glen bounded by Glen Moriston and Glen Urquhart. It helped, too, that Monck had an effective second-in-command in Colonel Thomas Morgan, who knew the country well, having served in the post-Dunbar campaign, and who had command of the northern forces.

In common with most counter-insurgency wars it was a brutal and time-consuming business. While the Royalists had the benefit of local support and knew the lie of the land, Monck's men had to carry their own supplies and must operate over long lines of communication which were always open to attack and disruption. All too often, too, the security forces were working in the dark. It proved difficult to get accurate intelligence about the Royalists' intentions, locals either refused to hand over information or gave it inaccurately, and the long days spent marching or in the saddle left men exhausted and demoralised. None the less the English forces proved to be hardy and adaptable. Monck's first task was to secure the approaches to the Highlands from Loch Lomond and the Kilsyth Hills in the west to Perth and the main route north in the centre. Having accomplished that by the middle of June, he marched north towards Ruthven to attack Middleton's forces, which were supposed to be assembling to the west in the lands of Kintail and were rumoured to be 3000 strong. What followed typified that year's campaign: Monck's men were forced to march prodigious distances, the lands of suspected Royalist supporters were laid waste, but against those local successes the lack of intelligence prevented them from engaging decisively with Middleton's army.

Back and forwards they went. By the beginning of July Monck had met up with Morgan near Inverness only to learn that Middleton was further south in the lands of Atholl, near Blair Castle, Montrose's old stamping ground. Monck set off in pursuit, arriving in the Loch Tay area by the middle of July while Morgan remained at Ruthven, which guarded both the main north–south route and the westward route into the mountainous and glen-filled country of Kintail. As they marched the English troopers laid waste to the surrounding countryside, and that scorched-earth policy, combined with the sweeps and drives, reduced Middleton's options. Being forced to keep on the move and denied the opportunity to plunder – a powerful motivating factor for the clansmen – his Highland forces began slipping back to their homes, a common failing which had also beset Montrose. Monck's movement towards Loch Tay forced Middleton to retreat westwards towards Loch Awe, where the two armies almost collided, before heading north-east back towards Badenoch. For the Royalists the move was both decisive and disastrous, because it put them between two powerful English forces – Morgan's ahead of them and Monck's to the rear.

The result was the only fixed battle during the Glencairn uprising – Dalnaspidal, fought on the evening of 19 July – and it proved to be the last fought between Royalists and parliamentarians in Scotland during the wars of the three kingdoms. Like Newburn, the clash of arms during the Bishops' Wars which had triggered the conflict in 1640, it was less of a battle and more of a 'fight' – and not a very glorious one at that. The site lies at the northern end of Loch Garry, between the loch and the modern trunk road and railway line to

Inverness.* Overlooked by the heights of An Cearcall and Meall na Leitreach, it is a bleak and cheerless place, and the outcome for the Royalists was equally dismal. Under him Middleton had around 800 horse, but these had become separated from the foot which were commanded by Lieutenant-General Thomas Dalyell of the Binns, who had served under Monro in Ulster and under Charles II at Worcester. This division of forces was to cost Middleton the battle: as he and his horse pushed north they were met by Morgan's superior force on the flat ground at Dalnaspidal and quickly put to flight. Over 300 horses were captured, along with the baggage train, which contained valuable and incriminatory documents, but the biggest blow was to pride. Most of Middleton's horse simply ran away without offering any resistance – their flight spread out over half-a-dozen miles – and as a result Dalyell's infantry were left unprotected. Approached by Morgan's cavalry they turned tail and fled back to their homes. In the aftermath of the action their commander Dalyell managed to negotiate terms with Monck and a year later was allowed to leave Scotland to go into Russian service, Middleton was badly injured and managed to flee north into Sutherland before leaving Scotland to rejoin Charles II in Cologne, but the main result of Dalnaspidal was the destruction of his army and the final suppression of the Royalist cause. Although isolated groups remained in hiding to harry the English forces, they were in a sorry position, as the evergreen James Turner found later in the summer after he had returned to Scotland to try his luck once again in the Stewart cause:

> I had the bad fortune to see numbers of horsemen which belonged to the King's army pass that way [Loch Earn], seeking to get to their several homes; having taken a liberty to themselves to disband, after an unhappy encounter at Loch Garry between General Middleton and Morgan, wherein the Royal party was worsted, but with the loss of very few men . . . this made me sensible that the King's affairs in that country were all out of frame, and made me conclude it necessary, that he who was most concerned ought to know his own condition, and that it could be represented to him

---

* Until it was closed in May 1965 this was the highest station on any British railway line at 1420 feet above sea level.

by no fitter person than myself, who I found could do him no good
where I was. And hereupon I put on a resolution to get out of
Scotland as soon as I could.

Disheartened by the venture, Turner made his way back to the
Continent to live in Bremen, 'having [myself] passed the year 1654
with as much trouble and anxiety of mind, fatigue of body, and
danger both at land and sea, as any year I ever passed in my life'.
Within a year shortage of funds pushed him back into the Royalist
cause, but failing to make any progress he offered his sword to the
Danish Crown.

The rest of the summer was spent by the English forces sweeping
up isolated pockets of resistance, tightening the net around the main
lines of communication and, as Monck told Cromwell, 'reducing the
Highlands' – shorthand for bringing it under strict control and
extirpating the remaining resistance. It was a time-consuming and
expensive operation but it paid dividends. By the end of August
Atholl and Glencairn had surrendered in return for signing substantial
securities, and while Middleton remained at large his force was too
small and ineffectual to trouble English interests. Even Argyll joined
in the fray by sending forces to drive his son out of his lands, and by
the end of the year the Royalist revolt was over. Ferocious winter
weather, the worst seen for two decades, made life miserable for the
men still on the hills and while rumours abounded that Charles II was
about to land with French money and troops to back him, the Stewart
cause in the Highlands was dying on its feet. By the time spring
arrived (1655) the remaining Royalist clan leaders were starting to
capitulate, Seaforth in January followed by Lorne and Glengarry in
May, and the levies under their command broke up in disarray. All the
leaders were fined heavily but were offered amnesties on condition
that they kept the peace, an obliging piece of leniency which
encouraged landowners to be responsible for policing their own areas.
Summer saw Monck's army completely in control, with only the
traditional lawlessness north of the Highland line offering any
possibility of further trouble. By maintaining the garrisons or
strongholds at key points throughout the area and operating against
the opposition with mobile columns Monck ensured that any unrest
was easily contained, and this he was able to do by reducing the size

of his forces. At the height of the troubles he had 18,000 soldiers under his command: by the end of 1655 the figure had been reduced to 10,500. The Highlands might not have been occupied, but for the first time they had been pacified in a way that would have astonished the earlier kings of Scotland.

The subjugation of the Glencairn Revolt allowed Monck to turn to civil matters. Under his rule Scotland became a contributing member of the Protectorate, a partner which was separate but equal. In May 1655 a mild form of devolved authority came into being with the creation of a Council for Scotland which was chaired by the Irish magnate Lord Broghill, son of the Earl of Cork and a friend of Cromwell. Backed by the army, its rule was generally benevolent. Law and order returned to areas such as the Borders, where it had broken down, taxation was reformed largely to support the military presence, which cost £6000 a month, and steps were taken 'to encourage commerce, advance manufactures and fisheries'. The legal system was overhauled by the appointment of seven commissioners, four English and three Scots, who replaced the jurisdiction of the Privy Council and the Court of Session. Under their authority steps were taken to ban witch-hunting and the burnings which followed them. Only religion remained in chaos, the rift between Remonstrants and Resolutioners being as wide as ever it was at the beginning of the decade. Normally the occupying power might have wished to side with the majority faction, the Resolutioners, but because Cromwell was suspicious of a form of Presbyterianism which had supported the Stewarts and continued to pray for the king, he favoured the Remonstrants, who only made up twenty per cent of the ministry. One result was the extension of the universities of Glasgow and Aberdeen with funds from the vanished bishoprics and the appointment of leading Remonstrants as principals. Baillie's old nemesis Patrick Gillespie became principal of Glasgow, his alma mater, leaving the former to complain that the English response to toleration had been 'to plant our Universities with their own'.[4]

In a sense it was a classic case of divide and rule – one historian of the period claims that 'Remonstrant and Resolutioner hated and opposed each other with far greater bitterness than either side would show to Roman Catholic or Episcopal'[5] – but the Protectorate in Scotland was generally a tolerant, acquiescent and progressive period in the nation's politics. A regular stagecoach service was started between Edinburgh and London which ran every three weeks, and 1652 saw the publication of the first newspaper to be published in Scotland: *A Diurnal of a Passage of Affairs*, which was printed in Leith from London copy. Taxes were high, there was widespread dislike of the freedom given to Independents such as Quakers, and there was a feeling of resentment at the English usurpation of Scottish independence, but most Scots living through that period greeted the new order if not with respect then at least with resigned acceptance. Some Scots bettered themselves as a result – Wariston resurfaced in 1657 in the powerful position of Lord Clerk Register and as a member of the English Council of State – and the diarist John Nicoll spoke for many of his fellow countrymen when he admitted that, 'to speak the truth, the English were more indulgent and merciful to the Scots . . . and their justice exceeded the Scots in many things'.[6]

While Scotland was treated as a sullen partner, a more miserable fate awaited Ireland, where the epithet 'Cromwellian' was equated with 'the ruthless suppression of Catholic and Royalist resistance, the execution, transportation, or imprisonment of substantial numbers of Catholic clergy, and the wholesale confiscation of lands'.[7] It is not surprising that the period had acquired such a forlorn description. Although Cromwell spent little more than nine months in Ireland his name is for ever associated with the post-war land settlement which saw the parliament in London redraw the Irish map for the redeployment of the population and its own enrichment. The war had cost over £3 million pounds to prosecute, English soldiers were due back pay and these sums had to be made good from the land itself. In September 1653 four counties were set aside for the English government (Carlow, Cork, Dublin and Kildare) while ten were assigned for division between soldiers and those who had supported the Act for Adventurers, the legislation of 1642 whereby subscribers or adventurers received parcels of Irish land in return for financial support to fund military action in the country. These counties were: Antrim, Armagh, Down, Laois, Limerick, Offaly, Meath, Tipperary, Waterford and Westmeath. To the native Irish was apportioned the barren lands of Clare and Connacht where, as a local saying had it, there were neither trees to hang a man nor water in which to drown him.

Over a million pounds was the target for the adventurers, but little more than a third of that sum was ever raised; nonetheless the monies had to be repaid and the Cromwellian land settlement was designed to settle debts and to satisfy arrears of pay for the military. As a preliminary measure a Civil Survey was established to compute the lands in question and commissioners were appointed to oversee the division of the territory by lot. By the end of the process, Sir William Petty, the man responsible, estimated that of the country's 20 million acres some 11 million had been confiscated, a figure which suggests widespread disruption, but the effects of the settlement were uneven. Many soldiers sold their holdings to their officers (or in some instances were cheated out of them), eventually becoming more Irish than the Irish, some parcels of land were unproductive or barren and were soon abandoned and the main beneficiaries, the London merchants and English county towns, did not settle English people on their lands but preferred to milk them as absentee landlords. In this respect Sir William Petty, a doctor who had served as physician-general to the army in Ireland, did particularly well out of the arrangement and eventually came into the possession of most of Killarney. However, those who did settle were considered to be of poor quality, one contemporary report in Galway dismissing the incomers from Liverpool and Gloucester as 'a few mechanick barbers and tailors . . mean persons unfit to carry on the trade of so great a port'.[8] Other plans encouraged by Cromwell spoke of trying to encourage more promising settlers from New England and Huguenots from France, but few took up the offers.

In common with the sacking of Drogheda and Wexford the Cromwellian land settlement of the 1650s implanted itself on the Irish mind as a period when repression, brutality and English avarice were visited on the native, mainly Catholic population. It is easy to see why that point of view gained a wide currency. Catholic families were transplanted from their lands in Ulster, Leinster and Munster because they were on the losing side and the winners, the English Protestants, had to be rewarded. In pursuit of that policy many thousands of Catholic Irish were also sold into slavery in the West Indies; some of these were vagrants from the main towns, but because women and children were included in their number it added to the feelings of persecution. In keeping with the policy of corralling the Catholics in Clare and Connacht the religion itself was attacked. Catholic worship was outlawed, Catholics were forbidden to take any part in public life, and their priests were either executed, imprisoned or driven into exile under laws passed originally in the Elizabethan period – up to 40,000 are estimated to have been banished. Any person found harbouring priests or helping them to escape 'would incur the confiscation of his property, and be put to death without hope or mercy'. The use of Irish Gaelic was also banned under earlier statutes and the net aim was to produce an anglicised Protestant society in which all traces of traditional Irish life would eventually disappear. It was little wonder that when they fled to Europe to escape the prosecution Irish priests used the opportunity to produce propaganda attacking the intolerance and cruelties of Cromwellian rule in their country:

It is easy to imagine what whirlwinds of dangers then assailed the Catholic community in this island! and yet the assault evinced how little the persecutors gained by that edict, for the more their fury raged against the priests, the more courageous did these become to encounter every danger; and although very many of them in each of the kingdom [*sic*] were cast into prison, of whom some were hanged on gibbets, some expired, overcome by the sufferings of their filthy dungeons, some were sent into exile to Spain, and others transported as slaves to the Barbados, yet those who escaped from the enemy's pursuit were not deterred by such impending dangers from the discharge of their ministry; and others who, scattered through the various academies of Europe, were engaged preparing themselves for the Irish mission, on seeing the harvest now ripe for the sickle, and hoping for more abundant spiritual fruit amid these temporal disasters, in greater numbers than was known for many years, abandoned their studies and entered on their field of labour.

In the meantime the magistrates, lest the edict might fall into oblivion, and in order to strike greater terror into those who might give shelter to the clergy, caused it to be proclaimed anew each year throughout the entire kingdom; whence it happened that the greatest part of the priests, unwilling to create danger for their flocks, lived in caverns, or on mountains, or through the woods, or in remote hiding-places, and often, too, were obliged to pass the winter without any shelter, concealed amid the branches of the trees. This deplorable condition of the kingdom fills all the Catholics with terror.[9]

This makes sorry reading, and there are countless examples of priests facing cruel deaths or wasting 'away their life in the tedious and loathsome horrors of a dungeon' or simply being driven into unwelcome exile but, like the transplantations and the resettlements, the English policy did not produce uniform results. Much of it was driven by simple hatred of the Catholic Irish, who were regarded as an inferior race, and also present was a large slice of revenge for the uprising of 1641, but the picture of repression was unevenly drawn. Although the Catholic land-owning classes lost heavily, their holdings falling from 59 per cent in 1641 to 20 per cent in 1660, by the end of that period many tenants had returned to their holdings and at that time they still made up three-quarters of the country's population.[10] In spite of the edicts against them Catholic priests also started slipping back into the country, where they were generally shielded and protected. For their flocks, remaining Catholic and refusing to apostasise became both an article of faith and a statement of Irish patriotism; like the use of Irish it was a means of holding on to national identity in the face of encroaching anglicisation.

Many of the returning priests expressed surprise and understandable delight that the English had done so little to reduce their religion by persuading Catholics to convert to Protestantism. Divisions in the Irish Protestant Church provided one reason, shortage of funds for schools and the re-education of clergy another, but the plan to convert Ireland to Protestantism was in itself unrealistic, a result perhaps of growing English tolerance and indifference in the later part of the decade. One man alone was responsible for this growing policy of laissez faire – Henry Cromwell, the Protector's younger son. A young man – he was only twenty-six at the time of his appointment as army commander in July 1655 – he had no direct experience of the recent fighting and was untouched by the maelstrom of emotions which followed the 1641 uprising, both factors which gave him a relatively clean slate in dealing with the Irish.

Initially his position was anomalous, as Fleetwood, his brother-in-law, retained the title of Lord Deputy and remained in the country until September, but that did not stop the younger man from making his presence felt in Dublin. Easygoing (except in the case of Baptists, whom he abhorred) and amiable (Hyde called him 'gracious and popular'), he constructed good relationships with the Old Protestant landowners and quickly established a reputation for moderation. In November 1657 he was at last appointed Lord Deputy and a year later, following his father's death, he received the commission of Lord Lieutenant, appointments which simply consolidated what had gone before.

All this was in contrast to Fleetwood's reign. A strict Puritan with a tendency towards narrow-mindedness, Fleetwood was a thoroughly professional soldier who was wary of compromise. In his way of thinking the best settlement of Ireland lay in crushing resistance and then converting the people to Protestantism as a prelude to turning them into model English citizens. The first aim had been achieved but in the second he was to be confounded by lack of funds and the absence of any realisable policy. An independent who favoured religious tolerance (apart from Catholics), Fleetwood encouraged the growing numbers of Baptists who began to appear and flourish in Ireland during the first half of the 1650s – Ludlow was of their number, as were several highly placed army officers, and they came to be a dominant voice in the administration. While Fleetwood's tolerance was admirable he seemed to be unaware that the sect was no friend of Cromwell or the aims of the Protectorate, and it was that forbearance which led to him being replaced by the younger man. Henry Cromwell showed his mettle within a year of his arrival: the Baptists could expect 'liberty and countenance . . . but to rule me, or to rule with me, I should not approve', and pointedly, when his son Oliver was born he was christened while an infant, a move which publicly slighted Dublin's senior Baptists.[11]

The removal of the Baptist threat paved the way for Henry Cromwell to consolidate his rule in Ireland. Many of the senior members of the sect resigned and returned to England, the better to pursue their cause, leaving Cromwell with a free hand to pursue non-sectarian policies. He strengthened the Church of Ireland by appointing moderate and independent ministers, he restored much of the legal system and gave greater weight to municipal government and, although he pursued the policies of transplantation, he did so less vigorously than his predecessor. He even managed to reconcile the prickly Scots ministers of Ulster by offering them state salaries and by favouring the Remonstrants among them. It kept the peace, albeit grudgingly, but it came at a price: Henry admitted to his father that while he did not trust the Scots it was better to keep them under a watchful eye than to pursue a confrontation.

Under Henry Cromwell and George Monck, both of whom ruled their fiefdoms with little interference from London, Ireland and Scotland were kept relatively quiet during the reign of the Protectorate. Of the two, Scotland had the better deal, Bishop Burnet confiding to his memoirs that it was a time of peace and prosperity, but few in Ireland would echo that sentiment. Instead the country was affected in other and more deeply rooted ways. The transplantation policy failed either to anglicise Ireland or to prevent future revolts against English rule, the Catholic Church remained as strong as ever it had been, strengthened perhaps by the years of persecution, and Irish continued to be spoken. In the short term, with their estates and their trading monopolies, the Old Protestant ascendancy families prospered as an upper class while in the longer term the disinherited and disgruntled Catholics were left to struggle to recover their land and their influence. In that sense the Cromwellian settlement was not so much a matter of transplanting Catholics to hell or Connacht but of transferring power and wealth from Catholics to Protestants. Half a century later Jonathan Swift, Dean of St Patrick's, encapsulated their plight in words that are both melancholy and straight to the point:

> The Catholics of Ireland . . . lost their estates for fighting in defence of their king. Those who cut off the father's head, forced the son to fly for his life and overturned the whole ancient frame of government . . . obtained grants of those very states the Catholics lost in defence of the ancient constitution, and thus they gained by their rebellion what the Catholics lost by their loyalty.[12]

That clash of interests and the resentment it produced continued to colour the Irish political scene for many years to come:

Chapter Five

'SILLY MEAN FELLOWS': THE RULE OF THE MAJOR-GENERALS

'Our ministers of religion are bad, our magistrates idle, and the people all asleep: only these present actings have a little awakened them.'

James Berry, major-general of Herefordshire, Shropshire,
Worcestershire and Wales, writing from Shrewsbury,
September 1655

Three weeks after the Protectorate parliament opened in early September 1654 it was given a graphic demonstration of the frailty of the new order when Cromwell came close to losing his life, an eventuality for which there was no ordered succession under the Instrument of Government. On 29 September 1654 the Protector was enjoying a picnic in the grounds of Hyde Park in the company of John Thurloe. It was a common enough experience – he was seen regularly there or in St James's exercising both body and mind – but on this occasion disaster struck. He had been presented with six grey Friesland horses by the Count of Oldenburg, the gift made at a time of tension between Denmark and Sweden over trade in the Baltic, and Cromwell was keen to test his equestrian skills. All his life he had been a sound judge of horses and was a good rider, but on this occasion his experience was unequal to the horses' mettle. Unable to resist the challenge posed by this new gift, he had the horses reined up to his coach and set off to demonstrate his skills with Thurloe seated beside him. It was a disaster. The lively horses bolted, Cromwell was unable to control them and was flung to the ground with the reins caught up in one of his legs. Dragged along for several yards, he was saved when his shoe came off, releasing him from further damage. Thurloe also fell and accidentally discharged his pistol, narrowly missing his master.

Cromwell was not badly hurt, but he was sufficiently shaken for his doctors to recommend some bloodletting and a course of recuperation at home. Not unnaturally the incident caused mirth among Royalist supporters – several squibs appeared comparing the inadequate driving to bad government – but those close to Cromwell were alarmed and dismayed by the incident. Had the Lord Protector been killed there was no succession, and the Protectorate would never have survived the removal of its main architect and the emergence of the rivalries in its wake. By then it was already clear that the new parliament was emerging not as the agent of restitution and healing (as Cromwell hoped) but as a body which was as argumentative and divided as any that had preceded it. For a start a clique within it, led by Hesilrige and Thomas Scot, insisted on questioning the legality of the legislation which had brought it into being, the Instrument of Government, and the proper relationship between parliament and Protector. Those critical of the new administration had fought to remove the personal rule of the king, and now they saw parliament being subordinated to the will of one man, Cromwell, they were determined to question the limits of their respective powers. To them parliament was the supreme body and they did not take kindly to the fact that the Lord Protector seemed to be ruling by the authority provided by the army and his main supporters. That power had to be returned to the legislature.

Cromwell's own supporters countered that parliament was simply seeking self-perpetuation and on 12 September the Lord Protector spoke in his own defence by arguing that a combination of necessity and God's providence had taken him to an office which he had not sought but had been thrust upon him. Having the backing of the army helped his cause – there were files of soldiers present in Westminster on the day of his speech – but the defining moment was Cromwell's insistence on members signing their agreement to the Instrument of Government, a move known as the Recognition. About a hundred members refused that summons and lost the vote: Hesilrige and Scot were of that number. The power of the house had been effectively broken as parliament divided itself into those who supported Cromwell and the government and those who were too weak or ineffectual to resist. Cromwell's power-base was strengthened when he was named Protector for life, although a move by Lambert to fix the succession through his children was defeated. He was also given control of the militia and the armed forces, thereby cementing the Protectorate's power in a manner that would have astonished Charles I and making any coup impossible.

For the rest of its session the parliament continued to debate the terms of the Instrument of Government as if that were its sole reason for existence. Clauses were discussed issue by issue. The lack of progress troubled Cromwell, as did the fact that he was not involved in any of the deliberations, and his patience was tried by the avalanche of words inside the house and the consequent lack of action. There was no movement on taxation and legislation in hand was held up by the inexorable debating. Cromwell had promised to let parliament run for five months, but now he could see that all his hopes were being undermined. The riding accident had not helped his mood and the death of his mother at the grand age of eighty-nine in November also helped to unnerve him. A powerful upright character of decided opinions, she had been a great influence on his life and her last words only reinforced his belief that providence was guiding him: 'The Lord cause his face to shine upon you, and comfort you in all your adversities, and enable you to do great things for the glory of your most high God, and to be a relief unto his people; my dear son, I leave my heart with thee, a good night.'[1]

Elsewhere, in the country, the mood was equally out of joint. Confronted by a parliament which lacked the will to do anything other than to niggle about the constitution which had brought it into being, voices of public protest began to be heard, almost as if the disparate groups were filling the vacuum created by parliament. The Fifth Monarchists still controlled many pulpits and their ministers railed against the ungodly parliament and prophesied the Second Coming, there was a rise in support for Baptists and 'that damnable sect of Quakers' (the description used by the Edinburgh diarist John Nicoll who also noted their tendency to walk the streets 'all naked except their shirts'), and there was a recrudescence of Leveller pamphleteering. Calls were made for a full and free parliament, and in some publications Cromwell was branded a traitor. Lucy

Hutchinson went one stage further, noting that the Protector's 'court was full of sin and vanity, and the more abominable, because they had not yet quite cast away the name of God, but profaned it by taking it in vain upon them'.[2] Even the lower ranks of the army and navy were showing signs of dissent, not least because they were owed pay and parliament was unlikely to vote the necessary funds.

With the country losing patience and Cromwell anxious to settle the issue of government, matters came to a head when the parliament threatened to reduce religious tolerance by curtailing the activities of the Independents and imposing Presbyterianism. Then it voted that the militia 'ought not to be raised, formed or made use of, but by common consent of the people assembled in Parliament'. This was unacceptable. It struck at the heart of the Protectorate's power – the New Model Army, the protector of the sects – and Cromwell made use of an escape clause which allowed him to end parliamentary proceedings at the end of five lunar months instead of the traditional calendar months. On 22 January 1655 he summoned parliament to tell them that their services were no longer required, 'that it is not for the profit of these nations, nor for the common and public good, for you to continue here any longer, and therefore, I do declare unto you, that I do dissolve this Parliament'. It was not one of his longest speeches, it lasted little more than forty-five minutes, but it was one of his most powerful pieces of rhetoric, uttered more in sorrow than in anger. The tone was regretful, with scorn and anger never far away, as he chided the members for their dilatoriness and their many shortcomings.

Likening them to a man taking a thoughtless walk in the country while his house burned, he criticised their failure to make any arrangements to pay the army, a miscarriage of justice which encouraged thoughts of mutiny in the ranks and led to the misery of free-quartering. He denied his own ambition and chided them for enslaving others ('is it ingenuous to ask liberty and not give it?'), and he spoke of the regret that he felt in being forced to take an action which dashed all his earlier hopes:

> Instead of the peace and settlement, instead of mercy and truth being brought together, righteousness and peace kissing each other, by reconciling the honest people of these nations, and settling the

woeful distempers that are among us . . . weeds and nettles, briers and thorns, have thriven under your shadow, dissettlement and division, discontent and dissatisfaction together with real dangers to the whole.[3]

Behind the ringing biblical phrases the inference was obvious: the parliament had been given its chance but it had scorned it. Like God's judgement on sinners, as foreseen by the prophet Isaiah, it was being laid waste and reduced to 'briers and thorns'.[4] Once again Cromwell was forced to move against a body which was not only not acting in the best interests of the country but was standing in the way of the work of the Lord. Regrets he had a-plenty, but Cromwell could not stand by and let the country grind to a halt.

The constitutional experiment had failed, and in its place there came a period when the country was ruled by what amounted to a military dictatorship. Government was carried out by proclamation and Cromwell, backed by Thurloe's intelligence services, was able to take a tighter grip on the country's affairs. The army's support was still vital to him and his high reputation meant that he retained the affection and loyalty of most of its senior officers and the rank and file. Still a powerful factor in the nation's affairs, in 1655 the New Model Army was some 57,000 strong, with 23,000 soldiers in Ireland, 19,000 in Scotland, and of the remaining 11,000 in England, 3000 were stationed in London.[5] The mailed fist did not come cheaply: the defence budget was £90,000 a month, the funds raised from unpopular taxation, but Cromwell dared not cut back his main means of support. A firm hand was in fact needed for, although the universal desire for a return to the old certainties was as strong as ever, there was also a growing and vociferous opposition to what was happening at Westminster. It was hardly surprising that the repression would attract a counter-reaction; Levellers and Fifth Monarchists preached that the revolution had been betrayed and that the institutions had failed to bring about long-cherished reforms. Allied to this was a fear that the Protectorate might become more Royalist than the Royalists themselves and that new tyrants had simply driven out the older versions. Particularly distasteful to many was the emergence of the Cromwells' quasi-regal household, with its fripperies and pretension – what the Earl of Warwick called its 'resemblance to a court', with its 'liveries, lackeys and yeomen of the guard'.

Backed by the support of the army and Thurloe's network of spies Cromwell did not have much to fear from the simmering unrest, although he understood that he could not afford to ignore the opposition of republicans such as Hesilrige, Scot and Ludlow. It also helped that most of the protest was overt; indeed it was one of the saving graces of this period that most of the debate took place in the open, that ordinary people were able to voice their speculations in an atmosphere of tolerance which seems remarkable. Sects were allowed to flourish and their ideas were disseminated by debate and through an outpouring of pamphlets, freed from the 'tyrannical duncery' of the past and aware, in Christopher Hill's words, that in the aftermath of the toppling of kings and the creation of republics 'it seemed as though the world might have been turned upside down'.[6] For those who revelled in the new freedoms and who gave full expression to a bewildering number of contentions – the existence of God, man's right to freedom of thought and property, the second coming – it seemed to be a time when anything was possible.

True, there were hysterical counterblasts when liberty turned to licence and men were punished for stating beliefs that were deemed heretical. The Quakers were regarded as a threat, as were sects such as the Diggers and the Ranters, and the censorship of the press was a curb, but the existence of radical groups helps to put the failure of the Commonwealth and Protectorate parliaments into perspective. There had been considerable investment in the Instrument of Government and the administration it brought into being, but its inadequacy and collapse created a vacuum which its opponents were bound to exploit. Not least among these groups were those Royalists who still hoped that the Stewart cause might be revived and with it their own fortunes – over 4000 of Charles I's supporters had seen their lands and possessions sequestered and had been impoverished by heavy fines. These country gentlemen hoped that their cause would be helped by the unrest which followed parliament's dismissal and that the heightened atmosphere of intrigue and new beginnings would give them a head start. They had no interest in the rights of man or whether or not the sun or the moon was a true manifestation of God's existence, but in a haphazard and misguided way a handful of them believed that the time was right for restoration and that Cromwell had run his course.

One result had been the creation in 1653 of the Sealed Knot,* the name given to a secret but ineffective group of Royalist conspirators which was supposed to coordinate plans for Charles II's return. Composed mainly of the sons of former Royalists, its efforts were rendered useless when one of its members, Sir Richard Willis, started passing on information to Thurloe. One of its leading lights was Lord John Mordaunt, son of the Earl of Peterborough, who established the more radical Action Party. Typical of the Sealed Knot's lack of cohesion was Penruddock's Uprising, a tilt against the administration which owed more to the heart than to the head. On the night of 11 March 1655 a group of 400 horsemen assembled at Clarendon Park in Wiltshire and rode into Salisbury early next morning to arrest the local sheriff and the judges sitting at the Wiltshire Assizes. Their leaders were Colonel John Penruddock, a local man who had served in the earlier civil war on the king's side, and Sir Joseph Wagstaffe, the emissary of Charles II. Their supporters lacked nothing in enthusiasm (more sensible Royalists stayed at home, knowing that the enterprise was doomed) but they were woefully short of numbers. From Salisbury they headed west into Dorset and Somerset, ever hopeful of sparking a Royalist uprising, but few took up the challenge, not least the Marquis of Hertford, who had promised support but failed to show up. Within a fortnight it was all over, the final blow being struck by a New Model Army force under the overall command of John Desborough: at South Molton near Tiverton in Devon, the scene of spirited Royalist resistance twelve years earlier, Penruddock's force was crushed in a businesslike way and its leaders taken prisoner. Coming on top of a failed revolt in the north a few weeks earlier – two faint-hearted groups of Royalists had attempted to seize Newcastle and York before running away when support failed to arrive – the uprising gave a pretext for repression and Cromwell took it.

Of those captured thirty-three stood trial and were condemned to death, but of their number only twelve were executed, among them

---

* Its name lives on in the title of the modern organisation which is devoted to the re-enactment of civil war battles.

Penruddock, who met his death with grave composure. Those whose sentences were quashed did not go unpunished – they were transported to the West Indies. Although the sentences were reasonably lenient Cromwell's administration used the revolt (such as it was) to push through a number of security measures to strengthen the country's internal defences and tighten their grip on the government. Three additional infantry regiments were raised in London and on 20 March some 5000 militiamen were paraded in Finsbury to the north of the city; at the same time commissions were issued to raise militia forces in the English counties. Their task was to provide forces to deal with further insurrections, to maintain a watch on disaffected persons and potential enemies of the state and to 'kill and slay' those who resisted arrest, the idea being that the new militia forces would act as a reserve to the New Model Army's regiments. It was an overreaction – in the scale of things Penruddock's action had been a minor incident – but it paved the way for Cromwell to use the armed forces and their commanders to gain a greater degree of control over the country.

The result was the rule of Cromwell's major-generals, a period that has cast a long shadow over English history and one which has come to typify what are supposed to be the worst excesses of Puritan repression. In later times the major-generals were damned as 'bashaws' and their men as 'janissaries' (the comparison being with the forces of the nineteenth-century Ottoman empire) or even as Nazi Gauleiters in the Second World War, and their rule was generally held to be cruel, joyless and inhuman, 'the most intolerable experience England ever had'.[7] It is not difficult to see why the rule of the major-generals has attracted such bad publicity and is used as a reason why the British have entertained an historical dislike of standing armies. It came after the dissolution of parliament, at a time when the army was a real force in English life and Cromwell's own position was unassailable, but, because the major-generals were given added responsibility for civilian affairs, it seemed as if the country was under the heel of unelected military despots.

In recent years calmer voices have been heard and the period has come to be seen as less of a military junta and more of a necessary expedient to impose a form of settled rule on a country in danger of becoming ungovernable. The genesis of rule by major-generals lay in the raising of the militia forces which, it was hoped, would gradually take over from the more expensive regular regiments of the New Model Army, each one to be formed into ten regional associations commanded by a major-general. Initially it was a military solution to provide command and control for the new forces along strict territorial lines, the demarcation being as follows:

Cornwall, Devon, Somerset, Dorset, Wiltshire and Gloucestershire – John Desborough

Kent and Surrey – Thomas Kelsey

Hampshire, Sussex and Berkshire – William Goffe

Northamptonshire, Rutland, Huntingdonshire and Bedfordshire – William Boteler

Derbyshire, Leicestershire, Lincolnshire, Nottinghamshire, and Warwickshire – Edward Whalley

Herefordshire, Shropshire, Worcestershire and Wales – James Berry

Yorkshire, Durham, Northumberland, Westmorland and Cumberland – John Lambert

Norfolk, Suffolk, Essex, Hertfordshire, Cambridgeshire and the Isle of Ely, Oxfordshire and Buckinghamshire – Charles Fleetwood

Cheshire, Lancashire and Staffordshire – Charles Worsley (after his death in 1656, Tobias Bridge)

Middlesex and London – Philip Skippon[8]

Owing to their positions on the Council of State, Lambert had two deputies (Charles Howard and Robert Lilburne) and Fleetwood three (Hezekiah Haynes, William Packwood and George Fleetwood), while the elderly Skippon's work was largely undertaken by Sir John Barkstead, governor of the Tower of London. Later, Berry was given deputies for Wales in John Nicholas and Rowland Dawkins. Scotland and Ireland were omitted from the scheme, being under the control, respectively, of two other major-generals – Monck and Henry Cromwell (nominally Charles Fleetwood) – but during this period their own administrations had already been settled by Cromwell.

Among the major-generals were distinguished soldiers such as Fleetwood, Desborough, Whalley and Lambert, but others were less well-known and all too often their promotion to positions of authority angered those in the localities who felt that they had been saddled with men who had risen beyond their proper station in life. Having made her feelings plain about Cromwell's 'court', Lucy Hutchinson turned her venom to the new political set-up, railing against the establishment of 'a company of silly, mean fellows called major-generals, as governors in every county, who ruled according to their wills, by no law but what seemed good in their own eyes'.[9] It was also easy to poke fun at those who came from ordinary backgrounds – Barkstead and Kelsey had been in trade, Berry had worked as a clerk in an ironworks, Worsley's father had been a Lancashire merchant – but this was English snobbery speaking. Perhaps, too, it was another manifestation of a desire to see the old order returned, as the major-generals fulfilled many of the responsibilities of the lord lieutenants, the traditional intermediaries (usually aristocratic) between the Crown and the shires. Berry, for example, was supposed to have been 'scorned' by the local gentry in the Welsh marches who knew all about his background, but this had to be balanced by his own religious beliefs, which made light of such worldly matters.

As with any group of individuals from different backgrounds, each major-general had strengths and weaknesses. And, of course, some were better than others. Of their number, Lambert, Skippon and Charles Fleetwood are beyond praise or blame, as their work for the Council of State meant that their deputies handled day-to-day affairs and were the instruments of policy within their own regions. Contrary to the condescending opinions about their origins which grew up later, the majority of those selected enjoyed strong territorial links with the areas they represented. They might not have been aristocrats or gentry but some were well respected, Whalley being praised by his Nottinghamshire commissioners as coming from an old-established local family 'of singular justice and piety' while John Desborough, Cromwell's brother-in-law, won praise for his civility and natural good manners. As for Hezekiah Haynes, who served under Fleetwood, he came from an old Essex family which had emigrated to New England in the wake of the Laudian attacks on the Puritans and his father had been governor of both Massachusetts and Connecticut. The youngest of their number, Charles Howard, was a scion of an old-established Yorkshire family and had been brought up a Roman Catholic. Later he was raised to the peerage as the Earl of Carlisle.

All enjoyed close to links to Cromwell through their service with the New Model Army in the civil war, but some were closer than others. Berry, Desborough, Packer and Whalley had all served as 'Ironsides', fighting in the momentous battles which had destroyed the Royalist cause in England, and it was only natural that Cromwell should have smiled on such loyal and steadfast allies. Even Howard, only twenty-six at the time, had fought at Worcester and the rest all had a formidable accumulation of military experience – among them, Goffe had commanded a regiment at Dunbar, Lilburne the army in Scotland and Boteler a regiment of horse. All were godly soldiers of the elect, too, but some were more zealous than others in their approach to crushing Royalists and unearthing wickedness. Whalley and Desborough tended to be more temperate and inclined to mercy (the former permitted horse-racing to continue at Lincoln) while others, namely Boteler, adopted a hard-line approach to Royalists and to Quakers, both of whom he persecuted with relentless vigour. Whatever their backgrounds, though, there is little doubt that all were soldiers of the Lord, intent on doing his divine work for the good of the English people and for God's greater glory. They laboured long and hard, too, and it has been conjectured that it was overwork which led to Worsley's sudden death June 1656. In the summer of 1656 when their work was almost done, a letter from Kelsey to Cromwell set the seal on their endeavours:

> If the Lord shall take pleasure in us, he will cause his face to shine upon us and carry us through the seas of blood that are threatened against us and the vast howling wilderness of our straits and difficulties, and at length bring us to that blessed haven of reformation endeavoured by us, and cause all our troubles and disquiet to end in a happy rest and peace, when all his people shall be one and his name one in all your dominions.[10]

It could have been Cromwell himself speaking.

Having been given their military commissions, the remit of the major-generals was quickly extended to include civilian matters. In August and September the administrative details of the work to be undertaken by the major-generals were codified by a committee of the Council of State chaired by Lambert: in addition to supervising the militia and containing any hint of Royalist opposition they were to act, in broad terms, as tax collectors, commissioners of police and guardians of public morality. It was this aspect of their work which coloured their reputations in English history and which led the historian and philosopher David Hume to complain in the following century that the major-generals ruled 'not in the legal manner of European nations, but according to the maxims of eastern tyranny'.

In practice their duties amounted to administering the militia, overseeing local government and collecting taxes, including the highly unpopular Decimation Tax which took 10 per cent of the rental value of the lands of Royalist supporters as well as a smaller percentage of their personal assets, the task of assessment falling to local commissioners. The major-generals were also given extensive powers to arrest felons, investigate and restrain suspected enemies of the state, improve the local infrastructure, especially the highways, and to suppress any facility which hinted at enjoyment or over-indulgence. Brothels, gaming houses and taverns were closed down, further restrictions were placed on cock-fighting and horse-racing (primarily to deny Royalists a meeting place), and in many parts of the country steps were taken to punish adultery, poaching, Sabbath-breaking, swearing and public drunkenness, the aim being to restore order and to prevent the kind of sinful behaviour which, in the Puritan mind, led to civic disorder and unrest. More than anything else it was the suppression of excess that gave the major-generals such a dire name as killjoys, although with each official having different concepts of godliness the moral reform programme was unevenly enforced and its results equally patchy. Christopher Durston, the most recent historian of the period, has shown that the sum achievement of their repression was the closing of a few hundred alehouses, the rounding up of a small number of vagabonds and the ejection of a few ungodly ministers from their livings – 'a very modest achievement and one which fell far short of the religious and cultural transformation for which the major-generals had been aiming'.[11]

One of the problems facing the major-generals was the lack of focus in what was expected of them. Their main responsibilities lay in local administration and law enforcement, but this channelled too much power into their hands. Their task was to prevent insurrection and to extirpate the conditions which encouraged opposition to the Protectorate, and those aims allowed them to act as they pleased. In place of generosity and reconciliation, Cromwell's immediate aims in the aftermath of the fighting and the creation of the post-revolutionary parliaments, there was be a sustained campaign against the malignants and delinquents who refused to accept the settlement and continued to harbour Royalist sentiments. The civil war had ended, in that the Royalists had been defeated and the godly were in power, but the fight to win men's hearts and minds was far from over. Not unnaturally this hard-line policy appealed to those radicals who feared that the reforming zeal of the revolution had been dissipated and that supporters of the Stewarts were clawing their way back into public life while refusing to put aside immorality and ungodly behaviour. To them it was right that the major-generals had been ordered to protect 'the quiet and security of all that are godly in the land'.

Unfortunately the system itself was not efficient. Although individual major-generals carried out their tasks as best they could they did not receive much support from the centre and all too often their requests and recommendations were ignored. Taxes were collected, maypoles were torn down, beggars disappeared from the streets, suspected Royalist activists were interrogated and soldiers were employed to make sure that local restrictions were enforced, but the overall effect was inconsistent and the long-term effects disappointing. For a start the aims were far too ambitious and as the system itself only lasted for little over a year there was not enough time for results to be achieved and analysed. In contemporary terms the major-generals were overstretched and lacked support from central government. For this failing Cromwell must accept some of the blame. He had shown flair and ability on the battlefield and his political life demonstrated that he knew when to act decisively and when to hold his peace, but as an administrator he was lazy and disinclined to concern himself with the minutiae of government, preferring ideas and ideals to concrete action. It did not help that for much of the period Cromwell was in poor health, suffering variously from stones in his bladder, boils on his abdomen, and almost continuously from gout.

To many it seemed as if the major-generals were operating their own type of personal rule, obeying instructions from London and imposing conditions on a people who did not take kindly to rules and regulations, nor to what amounted to a police state. Taxes had to be paid, and the major-generals had the means of raising them together with the authority to punish those who evaded them. Royalists feared for their lives if they made their loyalties known and soldiers were on hand to shut down alehouses or arrest known fornicators and profaners. All this went against the grain of ordinary English life. The major-generals might not have subsumed the workings of local government – the local county committees, the justices of the peace and so on – but by reinforcing them and directing their work they helped to create a lasting dislike of military interference in civil affairs. Even a reduction in military expenditure, one of their avowed aims, proved to be beyond them. A Decimation Tax had been introduced to demand 10 per cent of Royalist incomes but, apart from being unpopular, it had not yielded the expected results, and the hoped-for reductions in the size of the New Model Army (and its consequent costs) did not take place until later.

For all that, Cromwell praised his major-generals for their constancy, telling them that they had 'done their parts well'. In the summer of 1656 he was confident enough of their success to claim that they had been 'more effective towards the discountenancing of vice and settling religion than anything done these fifty years', a bold assertion which would not be borne out by events, but their reign was almost at an end. By then the country was at crisis point in its relations with Spain (see next chapter) and its financial arrangements were haywire, with expenditure running so far ahead of income that the annual deficit stood at a quarter of a million pounds. The only solution was to recall parliament, a move that was permitted by the Instrument of Government. Although Cromwell was not persuaded, the previous experiments having taken away his enthusiasm, he realised that he could only raise taxes through a legal assembly and, encouraged by the enthusiasm of his major-generals, he recalled them to London for consultation in May 1656.

The election was called for in late August and following the meeting in London the consensus was that the major-generals would be able to fix the results within their own areas and keep out undesirable Independents. More than anything else Cromwell wanted a docile assembly whose term would be finite and which would raise the necessary sums of money to fund his armed forces and his foreign policy – Charles I had entertained similar hopes in 1640 – but his hopes were dashed. Despite the major-generals' optimism the second parliament of the Protectorate was little different from the one which preceded it. The absence of a unified plan, the disparity of seats within a major-general's jurisdiction, the determined opposition of the minorities and a widespread dislike of the system prevented Cromwell from realising his dream.

While all the major-generals were elected together with many placemen who promised to be loyal, among them the sixty Scottish and Irish members, the new parliament also included Presbyterians and Independents as well as those who had been excluded by the Recognition. Among their number were Hesilrige and Bradshaw, but this time Cromwell and his Council of State were taking no chances. The returns were carefully scrutinised and around one hundred of those elected were excluded from sitting in parliament; tickets were prepared and any member not given one would be prevented from entering the chamber by the military guards. It was a crude form of censorship but it did not stop the parliament from being as impetuous and single-minded as its predecessor, one of its first measures being to demand the reversal of the exclusions. It was also subjected to one of Cromwell's longest and least interesting opening speeches – three hours of muddled rhetoric on 17 September 1656 during which he expounded on the nation's debts and meandered from one subject to the next, ending with an exhortation to put their trust in God. Unfocused and preoccupied with hazily thought-out concepts – 'The mind is the man. If that be kept pure, a man signifies somewhat; if not, I would very fain see what difference there is between him and a beast' – it lacked inspiration and failed to address the underlying concern that many members were tiring of the oppressive and increasingly wasteful rule of the major-generals.[12] Their rule was not yet over – it lingered into the following year – but the election of the second Protectorate parliament was the beginning of the end.

Chapter Six

FIGHTING THE LORD'S BATTLES: THE WAR AGAINST SPAIN

'The Lord Himself hath a controversy with your enemies; even in that Romish Babylon of which the Spaniard is the great underpropper. In that respect we fight the Lord's battles.'

Oliver Cromwell, Instructions to his Admirals, 1656

There was another reason for urgency in implementing the rule of the major-generals in the summer of 1655. The Protectorate had just received news of a severe setback to its foreign policy after a naval and military expedition to the Spanish colony of Hispaniola (modern Haiti and the Dominican Republic) had been roundly defeated. To Cromwell this seemed an indication of divine displeasure and a punishment for untold sins within the body politic at home. God had set his heart against the chosen race and, having given them victory after victory over their enemies as a sign of his eternal providence, he had inflicted on them a painful reverse in the distant West Indies. Of all men Cromwell understood that sin was the cause of this unexpected downfall, and because of that the country and the people had to be purged. 'We think God has not brought us hither where we are but to consider the work we may do in the world, as well as at home,' Cromwell told the Army Council in 1654 when he was first thinking about exporting the revolution for God's purposes. The result of those deliberations was a scheme known as the 'Western Design', which had the aim of attacking Spain's possessions in the

West Indies and transforming them into English Protestant colonies. At the same time Spanish wealth from gold and silver would be diverted into the English Exchequer to help pay for the venture and also to break the power of Catholic Spain. But it had not turned out as planned. In a letter to Vice-Admiral William Goodson Cromwell made it clear that he knew where to place most of the blame: 'It is not to be denied but the Lord hath greatly humbled us in the sad loss sustained at Hispaniola; no doubt we have provoked the Lord, and it is good for us to know and be abased for the same.'[1]

Cromwell's Council of State had decided to attack Spain for several reasons. It was the strongest Catholic power in Europe, its possessions in the West Indies were extensive and hampered English trade, and there was the added danger that King Philip IV might lend aid to Charles II. There was also a slightly hysterical belief that England was doing the Lord's work by hitting at the centre of popish power in Europe – Cromwell himself had told his second parliament that Spain was 'papal and Antichristian'. Wilder preachers promoted the idea of an English army marching on Rome to drive out the pope and impose Protestantism on the world; even Cromwell is supposed to have said to Lambert: 'Were I as young as you, I should not doubt, ere I died, to knock at the gates of Rome.' And in Christopher Feake the Fifth Monarchists possessed a preacher who could rouse the dead, a man of contradictions who could slander Cromwell as a 'perjured villain' (for which Feake was jailed) yet could also praise him for taking the word to the benighted enemies of the revolution:

> Thou gavest a Cup into the hand of England and we drank of it. Now thou hast carried it to Holland and they are drinking of it. Lord, carry it also to France, to Spain, to Rome, and let it never be out of some or other of their hands, till they drink and be drunk and spew and fall and never rise any more.[2]

The collapse of the Nominated Parliament meant that such visionary rants were heeded only by the converted, but the idea of making war with Spain or, indeed, France remained central to Cromwell's foreign policy in 1654. It was a heady prospect, the opportunity to impose the will of England on Europe and promote lucrative trading links, but before embarking on such a grandiose scheme Cromwell had to make peace with the Dutch, the nation with whom he thought the English should never have been at war. This was achieved on 5 April 1654 by a treaty which imposed the Navigation Act on the Dutch and forced their ships to salute the flag in territorial waters. It also obliged them to expel Charles II's court and to exclude the House of Orange from any military or naval command. The treaty was followed by two other diplomatic initiatives which helped to cement the Protectorate's interests and laid the basis for the expansionist policies which followed – a treaty with Denmark which reopened the routes into the Baltic, closed as a result of the war against the Dutch, and an enforced treaty with Portugal which opened up trade with her colonies in the east and west.

That left France and Spain, Europe's two largest powers, both of which were in a state of conflict and keen to enter into a compact with the new English republicans – in 1650 a second Frondist revolt backed by the Duke of Lorraine had attracted Spanish military support. Although the revolt in France had been crushed early in 1653 after Turenne defeated the Frondists under Condé outside Paris, the war against Spain went on, its centre of operations the Spanish Netherlands. By then revulsion at the execution of Charles I had given way to a more pragmatic approach, namely the need to deal with a country which had powerful naval and military assets, and the ambassadors of both countries, Antoine de Bordeaux-Neufville of France and Alonso de Cardenas of Spain, worked assiduously for an alliance with Cromwell's England. A contemporary Dutch spoof medal caught the mood. On one side is a portrait of Cromwell while on the reverse he is seen kneeling before a seated Britannia with his 'nether end' bare. In the background stand the two ambassadors vying to kiss it. The accompanying verse is nothing if not explicit:

> Britannia's isle, like Fortune's Wheel,
> in Politicks does daily reel –
> What's up today, tomorrow down;
> And from a smile ensues a frown.
>
> She sits in pompous State you see –
> And bears HIS HEAD upon her knee;
> While two Ambassadors contend –
> Which first shall kiss his nether end.[3]

Flattering though these approaches were – Cromwell had boasted to his first parliament as Protector that they had nothing to fear in Europe as every country was 'willing to ask a good understanding of you' – the primary need was to protect England's financial and political interests and to dissuade France and Spain from offering support to Charles II. Unwilling to commit himself to either country, Cromwell allowed Thurloe to continue his discussions with the ambassadors while preparations were made to attack Spain's colonial interests in the West Indies. Not only would this create lucrative trading opportunities but the wealth produced would help to pay for the Protectorate's navy, an increasingly expensive national asset. An important side-issue was the requirement that Spain would have to permit freedom of worship for English merchants living and working within their country and their overseas territories.

As a prelude Cromwell summoned Cardenas in the summer of 1654 and put to him two demands – that Spain allow the right of free trade in the West Indies without danger of molestation, and that all English merchants be allowed to worship as their consciences dictated and not as the agents of the Inquisition insisted. This brought the riposte from the Spanish ambassador that were Philip IV to concede those points it would be akin 'to demand of his Master his two eyes'; but even as the two men spoke the plan known as the Western Design was already in full and secret discussion. Its main thrust was the creation of an expeditionary force of twenty warships and 2500 men which would be sent to attack Spanish holdings in the West Indies while a smaller battle fleet under Blake would sail into the Mediterranean as a deterrent force to protect British shipping. Cromwell believed that hostilities in the Caribbean would not cause a general conflict with Spain in Europe, but that hope was as unrealistic as the Caribbean campaign plans, which turned out to be ill-conceived and hopelessly over-optimistic.

John Desborough was put in charge of the committee charged with planning the expedition but, given his other responsibilities, he lacked the time and the application to impose his will on it. Worse, the advice provided by the experts proved to be both inadequate and unreliable. Most of the intelligence came from an adventurer called Thomas Gage, a former Catholic who had worked in the region earlier in the century and who had gained a wholly uncalled-for reputation as an authority on the Caribbean and Spain's colonial interests. Having changed his faith Gage had come to despise his former religion and, with all the fury of the convert, he poured scorn on the Catholic presence in the West Indies and succeeded in convincing Cromwell that the Spaniards were so weak and corrupt that they would surrender without putting up too much of a fight. Hispaniola would fall into English hands, followed by Cuba and the isthmus of Panama, and the Protectorate would be left in strategic control of the entire region. The expulsion of the Spaniards would be followed by the swift colonisation of the Caribbean. It was a tantalising prospect.

The overconfidence was not helped by a weak command structure and muddled thinking which would have been unthinkable when the conquest of Ireland was being undertaken earlier in the decade. In place of an overall commander five commissioners were appointed to provide a council of war, only one of whom, Edward Winslow, a Pilgrim Father and former governor of New Plymouth, had any experience. Naval and military control was divided between two men, neither of whom had any clear notion of their mission's objectives. Command at sea was given to Blake's subordinate William Penn, a capable sailor (as he had shown at the Battle of the Downs), while the military command was given to Robert Venables, a veteran of the Irish campaign. To compound the commanders' problems the men provided for them were the dregs of the New Model Army – criminals and misfits who had been 'volunteered' from regiments by colonels anxious to be rid of them – supplemented by godly people from Ulster and the offspring of the Pilgrim Fathers from New England. There was no regimental structure as such, and when the expedition eventually arrived Venables found that the promised local reinforcements were not much better, being both badly disciplined and cowardly. The numbers might have provided him with an impressive army of 9000 soldiers, but as a fighting force it was useless. And betraying a lack of judgement which was unthinkable in an army which had set new standards of military professionalism, the matter of supply and resupply of provisions was more or less ignored. Water bottles were noticeable by their absence, there was a shortage of pikes, and lack of pay did not encourage men to risk their lives. If God was really going to provide, a miracle would be needed.

So it proved. The fleet sailed from Spithead on Christmas Day 1654 and five weeks later it made landfall off Barbados, where it encountered its first setback. The island had been an English trading colony since 1627, but that did not ensure its loyalty: enriched by a flourishing export trade of cotton, tobacco and indigo its settlers were unwilling to make the expected contribution to the Western Design. They also wanted to maintain their right to free trade, even if that meant breaking the terms of the Navigation Act by using Dutch ships. The British force's arrival seemed to be an unnecessary encumbrance to those lucrative activities. As Venables plaintively put it in self-serving letters to London, all the promised manpower and provisions turned out to be little more than words. It did not help that there was a strong Royalist influence on the island, which at one point, in 1650, had declared for Charles II. Illness, too, weakened Venables's men and the shortfall in supplies added to their hardships. Nevertheless further recruits were eventually levied from the neighbouring islands of St Kitts and Nevis and by mid-April Venables was ready to begin his attack on Hispaniola. In fact he had been given a free hand to choose his objectives, when he was in the area of operations. This allowed him to consider Cuba or Puerto Rico as alternative objectives, and he was even given leave to attack the port of Cartagena on the Spanish Main* (in present-day Colombia), the starting point for the homeward-bound Spanish plate, or silver, fleets.

To make matters worse the exact plans were a matter for debate on the spot. Not even Penn had been made privy to them, and this lack of confidence did little to promote solidarity in the attacking forces. Eventually it was decided to land on Hispaniola and to attack the port of Santo Domingo as a prelude to taking the island, but Venables's army was in trouble as soon as it landed, and far from encountering the spineless Spanish Catholics described by Gage, they met determined resistance when they pushed home their first assault on 17 April. As Venables complained later, they knew nothing of the nature of their target until they were outside the town's defences:

---

* The coastal territory along South America's Caribbean coastline between Panama and the Orinoco, known to the Spanish as Tierra Firme. Cartagena was sacked by Sir Francis Drake in 1586.

The town of Santo Domingo is situated on a plain, next the seaside, in a bay to the westward of a river running by the eastward part thereof, a most safe and convenient harbour for shipping not drawing above 16 feet water. The town is walled to the westward, has the river to the eastward, the sea to the southward: but to the northward it has only a lime hedge growing thick above it, but since our men being there we doubt not but the enemy has perfected his line and breastworks of earth, which he was throwing up all the time we delayed coming down to the town. They shot upon us in the ships, and by land on our men in six several places, castles, forts and the town walls; what other places whence they might plant their cannon they had, we know not, only we believe they had one hundred piece of ordnance on carriage to annoy us if occasion were, as by them that came to us.

Their cause was not helped by being divided into two groups on opposite banks of the River Ozama and, unable to regroup, they were repulsed again a week later. Panic set in, as did dysentery, and the will to fight quickly evaporated. 'We were not able to do it,' reported Venables, 'our Army being then so weak, and no water to be had, and we nothing to carry it with us, were forced to draw off in the most private way that could be, lest we should there lose all.'[4] What had started as a rabble ended as a rout; over 1000 men were killed or died of disease, and only the presence of Penn's fleet lying offshore prevented further casualties by taking off the survivors.

It was an embarrassing defeat but one which was entirely predictable. The orders were too sketchy, the overall policy too far-fetched, Venables was no Cromwell and the men under his command were entirely unsuited to the task. To be fair to them, they hoped for plunder and for new lives in a tropical paradise, but no one told them that they would have to fight for those benefits and when the time came to show their mettle their shortcomings were uncovered. With good reason the name of Santo Domingo is largely unremembered in the annals of Britain's armed forces, and yet, out of disaster came a triumph of sorts. After leaving Hispaniola Venables decided to cut his losses and head for the island of Jamaica which lay a hundred miles to the west. Relatively undefended by the Spanish, it offered a rich prize and it quickly fell into English hands, its capture providing a good base for future operations in the Caribbean, not least in the slave trade. Many of the original settlers perished from illness and Spanish counter-attacks, but Jamaica remained solidly British, being ceded by the Spanish in 1671. By the middle of the following century its sugar plantations had developed to produce a lucrative export trade, and a major naval port and dockyard had come into being at Port Royal. The island had not been the primary target of Cromwell's policy but its acquisition pointed the way towards an ambitious global expansionist policy backed by the bold use of sea power.

As for Penn and Venables, each blamed the other for the failure to take Hispaniola and, anxious to excuse themselves, both made their separate ways back to London, where they were locked up in the Tower of London and made to explain themselves. Later they were released and dismissed from the service, but only after they had admitted their guilt and their professional shortcomings. In a self-serving comment Venables attempted to place the blame on the moral shortcomings of his men, perhaps hoping that the excuse would find favour with the Lord Protector:

> God was not pleased to deliver it up unto us though with 9500, and 80 sail of great ships and small vessels, so that never were men more disappointed than some of us, nor did the hearts of English men fail them more than in this attempt. There was nothing to be attributed to the valour of the Spaniard towards his own preservation in all this, for he was ready to fly when we ran not, but only to God, who respited the enemy, because perhaps he found the reformers worse than the unreformed themselves; and surely more ungodly army of professed Protestants this wicked world cannot afford (and 'twere pity it should), which I conceive to be the inward cause of our misfortune and disgrace.[5]

Cromwell was not impressed, and he was particularly incensed by Penn's failure to attack the Spanish plate fleet, not least because its capture would have helped to pay for the high costs of keeping the fleet at sea – by then the annual naval debt was over one million pounds. Fortunately Blake's presence in the Mediterranean had achieved better results. While Penn had been committed to an expedition which seemed aimless and was ill-equipped for its task, his old commander had enjoyed a fruitful cruise – an attempt by the French to take Spanish Naples had been foiled and he had some success in preventing privateers from operating out of Tunis and Algiers.

While Blake's fleet was serving in the Mediterranean he was allowed to victual his ships at Spanish ports as the representative of a friendly power – wisely so, Cromwell's musings on the Western Design had been kept a closely guarded secret – but the news from Hispaniola changed all that. Cardenas was ordered to return to Madrid, English ships were banned from entering Spanish ports, and a state of war was declared. It was to be a curious imitation of a conflict, lacking large-scale set-piece battles and being dominated by the wearisome business of blockade. It also took place at a time of rapprochement with France, Cromwell finally having come off the fence in October 1655 by entering into a commercial treaty with France. Part of the agreement was that the English court-in-exile should be expelled, a move that drove Charles into the arms of Spain – in return for Philip IV's promised support the young king happily signed away his country's rights in the Caribbean – but the main import of the alliance was to pave the way for future military co-operation between the two countries.

It was a logical move. France was still locked in conflict with Spain and the country had already sided with the Protestant powers against the Habsburgs in the Thirty Years War. Catholic it might have been, and a potential supporter of the Stewarts, but in Mazarin France had a chief minister who was as interested as Cromwell in preserving the forces of conservatism. Having survived the second Fronde, during which he had been expelled from Paris, Mazarin was keen to sustain the rule of the young Louis XIV and weaken the Paris Parlement, increasingly an anti-Royalist body. Central to that policy was the continuation of the war with Spain, for which the support of England's battle-hardened regiments would be useful. Mazarin had also made himself agreeable by intervening in a notorious dispute in Savoy which had seen the persecution of the Protestants of the Vaudois, an incident which had shocked Cromwell and which had provoked Milton's sonnet 'Avenge, O Lord, thy slaughtered saints!' There were calls in England for the New Model Army to intervene to help their fellow Protestants in Savoy, and at one stage Cromwell considered ordering Blake to bombard Nice, but in the end he decided on diplomacy. A stern letter to Louis XIV led to French intercession and the promise of freedom of religious conscience for the Vaudois Protestants. Another factor in the rapprochement with France was Cromwell's failure to create a northern European Protestant league which would be led by England and Sweden. However, the new Swedish king Charles X was more interested in getting English support to extend his possessions in Poland than in combining with England in an anti-Catholic crusade, and only a commercial treaty was agreed.

In creating the alliance with France Cromwell was served well by his choice of ambassador in Paris. Sir William Lockhart of Lee was a Scot 'known for his very great fidelity, valour and integrity of character' who had begun life as a Royalist. His father was Lord Lee, his mother had been a maid of honour to Henrietta Maria and he had fought for Charles I, being knighted at Newark in 1646, but had changed sides following a quarrel with Argyll. After his offers of help had been spurned by Charles II prior to the Worcester campaign in 1651, he threw in his lot with the Commonwealth, becoming one of the legal commissioners in Edinburgh, and later a member of the Scottish Council of State and one of Scotland's members in the Barebones Parliament. His career was not hindered when he married Cromwell's niece by marriage, Roberta Sewster – the Protector liked having family friends around him in positions of power. It also helped that Lockhart quickly built up a good understanding with Mazarin; having run away from home at the age of thirteen to serve in the French army as a captain of horse, he not only spoke the language well but understood the nuances and vagaries of French diplomacy. Even Clarendon was impressed, after the Restoration describing Lockhart as 'a man who could best cajole the cardinal, and knew well the intrigues of court'.

While the treaty with France was being negotiated the opening rounds of the naval war against Spain had already taken place in the Atlantic approaches. On 16 August Blake encountered the Spanish battle fleet off Cadiz, but a mixture of poor weather and ambiguous orders from London – the English admiral was only permitted to attack westward-bound Spanish ships – allowed the Spaniards to slip back into port and the moment was lost. Shortage of food and supplies obliged Blake to follow suit and take his fleet home, too, but the missed opportunity only hardened Cromwell's resolve to use sea power to enforce England's foreign policy. He had already seen off a near-mutiny by the Channel fleet – the sailors' discontent was caused by lack of pay and dislike of impressment – and he strengthened Blake's hand by appointing a new general-at-sea in Edward Mountagu, a cousin of the Earl of Manchester who had served on the parliamentary side, distinguishing himself as a soldier at Marston Moor and the siege of Bristol. The fact that Cromwell had known him since boyhood also helped, the families being Huntingdonshire neighbours, and although Mountagu retired from the army in 1645 following the Self-Denying Ordinance he remained close to the seat of power. He became a member of the Commonwealth's Council of State and prior to his appointment he was a member of the Admiralty Committee: that lifetime of service and his friendship with Cromwell were enough to justify his new sea-going appointment.

Blake would not have been human had he not pondered the arrival of this courteous and grave county gentleman who seemed to be more interested in managing his estates than in learning the business of seafaring. He might even have wondered if Mountagu were Cromwell's spy, or if he had been sent as a punishment for his failure to engage the Spanish fleet, but Blake need not have worried. Mountagu's easy access to Cromwell meant that naval problems needing a political fix could be dealt with quickly and easily and he proved to be a quick learner who became fascinated with the technicalities of life at sea and the components of naval warfare. In fact Blake was badly in need of support. His deputy, Richard Badily, an experienced seaman, was ill and he himself was exhausted, 'sick, tired and troubled both in mind and body' after the long years of campaigning on land and sea. An injection of new blood was needed, and it was all the better that it came from a man who enjoyed close links to political power.[6]

The two generals-at-sea had specific instructions to intercept the Spanish plate fleet and attack its defending warships, and that meant mounting a blockade outside Cadiz with a formidable fleet of 37 warships led by Blake in his flagship *Naseby*. It set sail in the middle of March 1656, but the commanders soon found that they had been handed a frustrating and time-consuming task. The stragglers from the previous year's plate fleet had reached port and the escorts for the 1656 plate fleet had already left Cadiz for the Caribbean. Although there were warships in Cadiz they were in the inner port, which was too strongly defended for a purely naval attack.

This was disappointing news, but Blake's fleet had to be employed while it waited for the plate fleet and, following a council of war, a force of fourteen frigates under Nehemiah Bourne continued the blockade to allow the remainder to be replenished in Tangier. Mountagu took the opportunity to reconnoitre Gibraltar, which Cromwell had presciently suggested as a base, but he found it too strongly defended for an attack without landing soldiers. The only action came in June, when King John of Portugal seemed to be on the point of abrogating his treaty with England and Blake was ordered to take his fleet into the River Tagus to encourage minds to be concentrated. Portugal conceded the point, and the agreement had the added bonus of allowing Lisbon to be used by the English warships during the Spanish blockade, an important consideration given the long lines of communication. It was going to be a lengthy business requiring patience and strong nerves: even a diversion into the Mediterranean to deal with privateers proved inconclusive.

The deadlock was broken on 8 September when a squadron of eight warships under the command of Captain Richard Stayner came across part of the plate fleet making its way unescorted towards Cadiz. The heavily armed and bigger English ships were too powerful for their prey, and during a sharp action two ships were captured, three were sunk and another three escaped into Cadiz. Taken by surprise, the Spanish ships had little chance: not only were they unescorted but their captains had been lulled into believing that Blake had lifted his blockade. Stayner took his prizes into Lisbon; from them he extracted prize silver worth a quarter of a million pounds and other goods which totalled almost a million.[7] The booty would have been greater if the other ships had not sunk or escaped, and the final amount was also reduced after the prizes had been plundered by Stayner's crews. Even so, 38 wagons were needed to carry the bullion to the Tower of London, and among them were more than 200 chests of silver. When the news reached London it caused a sensation. Not only had a blow been struck against Spain but it seemed as if the forecast of vast wealth from the Indies was about to be proved correct. Perhaps this was a war which would finally pay for itself and justify the huge cost of maintaining a large and modern navy at sea. In the aftermath Mountagu was recalled to England, leaving Blake in command of a smaller fleet to guard the approaches to Cadiz and to wait for the next wave of Spanish galleons.

By then the admiral was much enfeebled and was in no physical state to spend another winter at sea, but Blake was England's most experienced naval commander and from the captured crews he knew that another larger and richer fleet was about to appear in the New Year. Quite apart from his infirmities – he was suffering from stones in his kidneys – Blake knew that keeping his fleet at sea would be no easy task.[8] His ships were low on supplies and he was by no means sure that they would receive a regular supply of victuals for the winter. (He was right to worry: on his return Mountagu had to use all his influence to get money through to the agents in Portsmouth who were refusing to act without it.) Against that, being at sea and having to work hard, his crews were well trained and fit and would be in a better condition to take on the Spaniards who had spent the winter on shore in Cadiz. As ever, the main problem was getting accurate intelligence. It was all very well knowing that the plate fleet would arrive in the new year, but it was another matter discovering its route and its possible whereabouts. Blake also had to take into account the Spanish battle fleet in Cadiz. It was going to be a long and trying winter watch, hard on the ships and hard on their crews.

At the beginning of 1657 there was a sudden alarm when a Dutch squadron of nine warships arrived in the Gulf of Cadiz under de Ruijter's command, but it was bound for the Mediterranean to protect Dutch shipping. Wisely, de Ruijter was deaf to Spanish pleas to help, but at the time the threat of Dutch intervention was real enough for Blake to reposition his fleet off Cape St Vincent, where it ran into a storm which necessitated repairs serious enough for him to consider calling off the blockade. However, no sooner were his ships back on station than he received the breakthrough he had been seeking. On 19 February an English merchant ship arrived with the news that the plate fleet was indeed at sea, and judging by its direction it was heading for the island of Tenerife, whose port, Santa Cruz de Tenerife, was large enough and safe enough to harbour it. There it would wait for the escorts which would break out of Cadiz to bring it safely home. To Blake this seemed a credible plan: the plate fleet would hardly make the same mistake that had led the previous year's ships into Stayner's hands by sailing directly towards Cadiz. Instead, by sheltering in Tenerife to the south the galleons presented Blake with a tantalising problem. If he sailed to attack the plate fleet he would allow the Spanish battle fleet to break out unhindered or he would have to divide his forces, a move which might pass the initiative to the Spaniards. And the longer the stand-off continued the worse it would be for Blake, whose ships were again running short of supplies.

Blake's response was to wait and see, and for another eight weeks the English fleet maintained its blockade in the Gulf of Cadiz, sailing backwards and forwards between the Strait of Gibraltar and Cape St Vincent. Then in mid-April he had to act. Intelligence from an English privateer, William Saddleton, confirmed that the Spanish plate fleet was harboured at Santa Cruz de Tenerife waiting for the arrival of its escorts. It was now or never and Blake acted decisively. Leaving behind a token watch of three small warships he took his fleet south, flying his flag in the *George*. Landfall was made on 18 April, but bad weather and an opposing wind forced Blake to postpone the attack for forty-eight hours; the intervention of a Sunday may also have been a factor. He also needed time to assess the local situation, and found it not to be promising. The Spanish admiral Don Diego Diagues had positioned his big galleons in line abreast outside the harbour with their broadsides facing the sea, and behind them on land he had the covering fire provided by the guns of Fort St Philip and seven smaller forts linked by three lines of breastworks. As an added precaution the cargoes of the plate fleet sheltering behind the galleons had been unloaded and taken ashore.

Blake's plan was simple and direct. While he provided cover, a line of twelve ships led by Stayner in *The Speaker* would attack the galleons from the open sea side, getting as close to them as they dared before anchoring and firing their heavier and more powerful broadsides from the starboard. They would also have to leave enough sea room to swing round using their anchor lines so that the port guns could be fired.[9] It was a manoeuvre which demanded high standards of seamanship and courage, and it worked. The attack began at nine o'clock, and by midday the superior firepower of the attacking English ships had destroyed most of the Spanish galleons. Blake's ships also joined the battle, one, the *Bristol*, destroying a galleon after a lucky shot hit the magazine and, according to a witness, 'she blew up, not a man escaping'. The shore batteries were also hit and silenced, but their role had been minimised by the need to shoot over their own ships and by the smoke from the burning fleet. Not that Blake's ships escaped scot-free. *The Speaker* was so badly hit and holed that only good seamanship, luck and 'the good hand of God' saved her. An attempt to take her under tow by the *Swiftsure* failed, but once *The Speaker* reached open water the *Plymouth* was able to get a line to her. According to Blake's official dispatch the casualties were light:

> In this service we had not above fifty slain outright, and one hundred and twenty wounded, and the damage to our Ships was such as in two days time we indifferently well repaired for present security: Which we had no sooner done, but the Wind veered to the South West (which is rare among these Islands) and lasted just to bring us to our former Station near Cape Maries, where we arrived the second of May following: For which merciful appearance all along with us, we desire the Lord may have the praise and glory, to whom only it is due; and that all that hear of it may turn and say (as of a truth we have found) that among the gods there is none like unto Him, neither are there any works like unto His works.[10]

The destruction of the Spanish plate fleet was the decisive battle in the war with Spain, and it is one of the most complete victories in British naval history. By using a combination of guile, determination and quick thinking Blake outwitted the opposition and his superior naval artillery did the rest, thereby sending an unmistakable message to the other European powers. The Spanish had been outgunned and out-fought and their captains had no answer to the concentrated firepower which Blake's ships brought to bear on the outer defensive line of galleons. Even Royalists such as Clarendon were impressed:

> The whole action was so miraculous that all men who knew the place concluded that no sober men, with what courage soever endued, would ever undertake it; and they could hardly persuade

themselves to believe what they had done; while the Spaniards comforted themselves with the belief that they were devils, not men, which had destroyed them in such a manner.[11]

However, not everything went according to plan. At the height of the battle several captains disobeyed orders and tried to secure prizes, and Stayner was reckless with the safety of *The Speaker*. It is also true, as Thurloe admitted to parliament, that the victory failed to secure the Spanish silver and other rich cargoes, but against that it soon became clear that the wealth remained locked up in Tenerife for the rest of the war, where it was useless to the Spanish exchequer. The worst outcome came at the very end while the fleet was returning home. Death finally caught up with Blake, who succumbed to illness as the *George* entered Plymouth Sound on 7 August 1657. The old republican who had begun his career as a soldier, the saviour of Taunton, slipped away before he could receive the thanks of a grateful nation. But that was not the end. Even though he would have disapproved, Blake was granted a state funeral, full of pomp and solemnity, and his remains were buried in King Henry VII's chapel in Westminster Abbey.

Blake's victory ended any hope Spain had of securing mastery of the sea, and it changed the focus of the war to the land. One of the English war aims had been the reduction of the port of Dunkirk in the Spanish Netherlands, for many years a base for privateers to attack shipping in the Channel. To do that, the treaty with France would have to be extended and English troops sent to Flanders, but Cromwell was uncertain if France would keep her side of the bargain by paying for their use. He also began to harbour doubts if Catholic France were really a natural ally, but these were stilled when Spain decided to help the exiled Charles II and made threatening noises about supporting an invasion. In spring 1657 the alliance was extended and the Protectorate agreed to send 6000 troops to join the French army in Flanders under Turenne. In return England would take possession of the ports of Dunkirk and Mardyke, possessions which would provide a foothold in Continental Europe and hit hard at Spanish power and authority.

Although Cromwell was right to distrust French sincerity – it took all of Lockhart's diplomacy to keep Turenne's mind fixed during the fighting to take the Channel ports – the expeditionary force won a hard-fought battle outside Dunkirk on 14 June 1658, known as the Battle of the Dunes. The New Model Army regiments were commanded by Lockhart, who relished the idea of returning to his old profession, and they were central to Turenne's victory. Ordered to attack the Spanish right, they made their assault over the sandy terrain while the English warships offered covering fire offshore. At the same time the French infantry assaulted the centre while their horse attacked on the flanks. Under sustained pressure the Spanish infantry was pushed back and finally broke after their cavalry fled from the field. As a battle it was all over in four hours and, although some Spanish commanders tried to rally their men, notably the Duke of York, Charles II's brother, their army was easily routed. Again, the news sent a shock through Europe: the Spanish were supposed to possess the world's best infantry soldiers, yet they had succumbed to the professionalism of the New Model Army and the leadership of Turenne. English losses were around 100 men, a quarter of those suffered by Turenne's army, while the Spanish lost over 1000 as well as a good deal of military pride. Ten days later Dunkirk surrendered to Lockhart and the English moved in to take possession of the town and its vital port. For the first time since Calais was lost in 1558 the English were back on the European mainland.

In itself that was a useful achievement, but the main result of the two battles – Santa Cruz de Tenerife and the Dunes – was to reinforce the Protectorate's emergence as a major power and the beginning of Spain's decline. It had been an expensive war to fight, the expected Spanish silver failed to materialise and it almost bankrupted the country, but there were material results. The display of English authority put paid to Charles II's hopes of Spanish (or any other) support and, although it was not realised at the time, England had gained a foothold in the Caribbean in its possession of Jamaica and a useful long-term European ally in Portugal. The war might have raised taxes and crippled trade, but, as the poet Marvell put it, Cromwell had 'made England great and his enemies tremble'.

Chapter Seven

KING CROMWELL AND
TUMBLEDOWN DICK

'I was no private, but a person raised
With strength sufficient and command from heaven
To free my country.'

John Milton, Samson Agonistes, *1671*

Shortly after the announcement of Stayner's capture of a substantial part of the Spanish plate fleet, the poet Edmund Waller was moved to salute the triumph and to suggest how some of the treasure might be best employed:

> Let the rich ore be forthwith melted down
> And the state fixed by making him a crown
> With ermine clad and purple, let him hold
> A royal sceptre, made of Spanish gold[1]

The idea that Cromwell should be crowned king was not a new one; Cromwell himself had toyed with the idea, and those close to him had also suggested that such a transformation was in the country's best interests, but in this the fifty-seventh year of the Protector's life it was being openly discussed as a matter of urgency. Some who supported the idea wanted a return to the old constitutional certainties, a few disliked the term 'Protector', while others were concerned about the succession and the likelihood of further upheaval if Cromwell died before an heir had been chosen. Added to those concerns there was a growing belief that parliament needed a second house, if not the return of the House of Lords then at least an upper chamber which would act as a check on the administration. The times, too, seemed to be ripe for change and the creation of a new political settlement. The second Protectorate parliament was sitting, the unpopular major-generals were still in power, there was a war with Spain, the religious sects, especially the Quakers, were restless, and all the while Cromwell remained the most powerful man in England, his word well-nigh unassailable. Against that background something had to yield, and the call for change centred on the position of the Lord Protector.

Cromwell had not wanted the recall of parliament and now he blamed the major-generals for forcing it on him. He rebuked them, too, for not managing the election properly – that is by ensuring the election of acquiescent members, 'men chosen to your heart's desire' – and for allowing potential enemies to win seats. The major-generals had not only let him down but their failure had 'disobliged' the country by allowing the continued opposition of anti-Commonwealth Independents.[2] Despite that uneasy start, it had quickly proved itself to be a busy parliament. During its sitting money was voted for the war with Spain, the right of the Stewarts to the throne was annulled, individual members' private bills received attention and the house pushed ahead with measures to decentralise the justice system by creating a branch court of equity at York, but in common with its predecessors this parliament also proved irksome to Cromwell – doubtless as he had always expected.

The introduction of the ticketing system proved to be a poor deterrent to keeping out unwelcome members – some ignored the curbs, others just slipped past the guards – and parliament soon demonstrated that it was as disputatious and contrary as ever. Its smooth running was not helped by external events which impinged on its routine, notably the infamous case of James Nayler, a Yorkshireman who had served in the parliamentary army before discovering a gift for preaching. Converted to Quakerism by its founder, George Fox, in 1651 he emerged as a charismatic preacher and built up a substantial following in the West Country both for his ability to move people and for his ascetic bearded appearance. It was an age which had spawned many deluded Christians who fancied that they were the reincarnation of Jesus Christ or had been born to do God's great work. Most were charlatans, or simple-minded souls who created sects and enjoyed a small following, but Nayler was different. Not only did he have a Christlike bearing and an ability to hold audiences but his support was radical and it enjoyed a following all over England, many of them drawn from the ranks of the Levellers and Ranters. When he preached against 'covetous cruel oppressors who grind the faces of the poor and needy' he was not speaking metaphorically but stating his disappointment that parliament had not carried through the expected reforms demanded in documents such as the *Agreement of the People.*

That alone made him dangerous and encouraged conservatives to think that religious toleration had gone too far, but Nayler was eventually condemned by his own foolish actions. Following a preaching tour of the West Country he entered Bristol on a donkey with women throwing down palm leaves in his path and calling out 'hosanna' and 'holy, holy, holy, Lord God of Israel' in a ghastly parody of Christ's entry into Jerusalem prior to his crucifixion. The procession was accompanied by a good deal of hysteria and, while many bystanders were shocked by Nayler's blasphemy, those in authority were horrified. Far from being an absurd or quixotic gesture Nayler's entry into Bristol, a centre of Quaker support, hinted at revolution and parliament was determined to punish the man for his 'horrid blasphemies'. At the same time members hoped that by castigating Nayler they would be striking at Quakerism and dealing religious toleration a fatal blow. 'He writes all their books,' advised one member. 'Cut off this fellow and you will destroy the sect.'[3]

The analogy was obvious, but killing the serpent proved to be a tortuous business. In December 1656 parliament decided to put Nayler on trial, even though the exact judicial procedure remained unclear and without a precedent it could be a messy and time-consuming affair. That turned out to be the case. When Nayler was summoned before the house he showed no respect, refused to take off his hat and behaved in a disconnected and pious manner which only infuriated members further.('I was never guilty of lewdness; or so reputed,' he told them. 'I abhor filthiness.') A majority was determined to punish him and the sentence was suitably cruel. For his gross behaviour Nayler was to be pilloried, branded, his tongue bored, and then he was to be whipped through the streets, first in London and then in Bristol. As if that were not enough to deter him he would then be imprisoned at parliament's leisure. Parliament was in no doubt that it had the authority to hand down the sentence, its powers having been granted de facto by the absence of the House of Lords, but Cromwell disagreed.

It seemed to him that parliament lacked the jurisdiction to try Nayler in the first place and then to sentence him to such a terrible punishment; troubled by the action he demanded to know 'the grounds and reason whereupon they have proceeded'. To Cromwell, the members appeared to have acted beyond the authority provided by the Instrument of Government and they had consulted neither him nor the Council of State before proceeding. There was another reason for the Lord Protector's unease. Cromwell was anxious not to alienate the Quakers and could see that such an action would be perceived as an attack on religious toleration, a matter which was taken seriously by the army. However, his concerns were ignored and in vain did he question parliament's right to act in this way: its members refused to back down and Nayler was forced to suffer unbelievable pain by way of punishment. (No one seemed to be able to draw the biblical comparison with the crucifixion of Jesus after his entry to Jerusalem.) Later Nayler was banished to the Scilly Isles but was released in 1659, a broken man, and died a year later. To ease the conditions of his imprisonment Cromwell helped his wife and sent a doctor, an offer which Nayler refused as 'God was his physician and he needed no other', but the whole episode was a bitter reminder of the gulf that lay between the Lord Protector and parliament as he struggled towards the construction of a godly society.

Hard on the heels of the Nayler trial came another test of parliamentary authority. On Christmas Day Desborough took advantage of the low turnout to push through a bill for the continuation of the Decimation Tax, the 10 per cent levy forced on Royalists, which funded the militia. It was a tried and tested political ruse, one which had been used before during the Barebones Parliament when tithes were being debated, and Desborough hoped that the matter could be dealt with swiftly and efficiently. Although 25 December was a working day, large numbers of members stayed away to enjoy the seasonal festivities and Desborough believed that their absence would allow parliament to proceed with a tax which was far from popular. He got his majority but it was too narrow, 86 votes to 63, and when the motion was debated again on 29 January it was heavily defeated. The following day parliament voted to supply £400,000 for the Spanish war. Both decisions sealed the fate of the major-generals, for with no militia to command their roles had been ended and although, technically, they remained in office their influence had been stripped from them. When the major-generals complained, Cromwell, who had failed to interfere, laid the blame for their demise at their own feet. 'What would you have me do?' he asked them. 'Are they [members of parliament] not of your own garbling [choosing]? Did you not admit whom you pleased and keep out whom you pleased? And now do you complain to me. Did I meddle with it?'[4]

By entering into the war with Spain Cromwell had been obliged to recall parliament a year earlier than planned, and that necessity marked the beginning of the end of the major-generals. Firstly they failed to control the elections as Cromwell wanted and then Desborough, one of their number, botched the introduction of the legislation which gave them their authority. There is no evidence to suggest that Cromwell wanted the rule of the major-generals to end in this way, unpopular though it had become. He was fulsome in their praise and spoke of the excellence of their service, but the fact remains that he had done nothing to save them, remaining indecisive and aloof throughout the crisis. Coming on top of the Nayler debacle and parliament's increasing truculence, the toppling of the major-generals was a further reminder of the muddle which existed at the heart of the country's administration. Cromwell had also been left in little doubt that most members of parliament opposed the major-generals – the influential Denbighshire member, Sir John Trevor, called their rule 'a power too great to be bound within any law' and claimed that the major-generals had enjoyed 'a power that was never set up in any nation without dangerous consequences'. While Trevor was a conservative and later a prominent supporter of the restoration of the monarchy he was not alone in voicing concern about the constitutional legality of the major-generals' rule. Whitelocke was another prominent sceptic.

With parliament split on this matter, albeit with the supporters of the Decimation Tax being in a minority, the feeling began to grow that the only way to reconcile the country was to offer the crown to Cromwell. The supporters of such a move were influential enough to give it a good hearing. Among their number were close associates such as Broghill, Mountagu, St John and Whitelocke (formerly an opponent of such an elevation), and they formed a nucleus of power and influence known self-deprecatingly as 'Kinglings'. As happens so often in political life, their cause was helped by other events. At the beginning of 1657 a series of plots against Cromwell's life was uncovered, and from the evidence produced at the time these were considered serious enough to make parliament fear for the safety of the Lord Protector. Although Cromwell had a personal lifeguard his personal security was lax and an attempt had already been made on his life in 1654 when John Gerard, a Royalist colonel, plotted to seize him while travelling between Whitehall and Hampton Court. Thanks to Thurloe's intelligence services the conspirators were arrested before they could do anything, but the presence in England of Royalist supporters such as the Sealed Knot meant that Cromwell was always a potential target for assassination.

The latest attempt was also the most serious. The originator was Colonel Edward Sexby, a Leveller leader who had been one of the leading lights at the Putney Debates in 1647 and whose dissatisfaction with Cromwell's government had led him to conspire with the Royalists.* With another Leveller, Silas Titus, he had written a pamphlet called *Killing No Murder*, and his plot to assassinate Cromwell centred on three murder attempts to be carried out by two soldiers, Miles Sindercombe and John Cecil. The first plan was to shoot Cromwell as he left London for Hampton Court, the second would have the Lord Protector assassinated as he walked unguarded in Hyde Park, while the third was a more ambitious effort to blow up Whitehall. All failed or were uncovered. On the day appointed for the first assassination Cromwell took a different route to Hampton Court, the second attempt in Hyde Park was foiled when the horse chosen for Cecil's escape became ill, and the gunpowder plot was

---

* He was not captured until July and died in the Tower of London in January 1658.

discovered when guards were made suspicious by the smell of burning and Sindercombe was arrested. He escaped what would have been a traitor's fate (hanged, drawn and quartered) by taking poison which his sister smuggled into the Tower of London. Even Lucy Hutchinson was shocked by the news:

> The Cavaliers, seeing their victors thus beyond their hopes falling into their hands, had not patience to stay till things ripened of themselves, but were every day forming designs, and plotting for the murder of Cromwell, and other insurrections, which, being contrived in drink and managed by false and cowardly fellows, were still revealed to Cromwell, who had most excellent intelligence of all things that passed, even in the King's closet; and by these unsuccessful plots they were the only obstructers of what they sought to advance, while, to speak the truth, Cromwell's personal courage and magnanimity upheld him against all enemies and malcontents.[5]

The revelation was made to a shocked parliament on 19 January 1657 and four days later its members invited Cromwell to the Banqueting Hall for a service of thanksgiving. It was a memorable occasion. Cromwell spoke humbly of his 'unworthiness and unprofitableness' and tried to make light of his escape, but parliament had been badly shaken. Even though none of the three plots came close to achieving their aims, some members felt that they had glimpsed the narrow dividing line between the security of the Lord Protector's rule and the chaos that would result if he died intestate. It was not altogether surprising that the question of the crown should gain a new momentum or that John Ashe, a member for Somerset, rose to propose that Cromwell should 'take upon him the government according to our ancient constitution'. The suggestion was soon followed up with a positive proposal. On 23 February parliament was presented with a *Humble Address and Remonstrance* which later became the *Humble Petition and Advice*, the constitutional instrument for the return of monarchical rule and the creation of an upper house and the granting of the crown to Cromwell. It was presented to the house by Sir Christopher Packe, formerly Lord Mayor of London, a wealthy and influential politician in his own right, but clearly he was acting as a front for the Kinglings to bring the question out into the open.

Packe's intervention divided the government. It was supported by the Kinglings, Thurloe, most of the legal members and the Irish representatives but it was opposed by an equally powerful group of republicans, Fifth Monarchists, former Levellers and 'swordsmen' – army officers, notably Lambert, Desborough and Fleetwood – all of whom believed that they were confronting the beginning of the end of everything they had fought for. This latter group stood appalled by the suggestion that Cromwell might become king and angrily confronted him only to receive the cool reply that the offer had been made before and that he counted the title as little more than 'a feather in a cap'. On the creation of the upper house Cromwell was on surer ground: remembering his own inability to intervene in the Nayler case he supported such a check to parliament's authority. 'May it not be anyone's case another time?' he asked the major-generals when they came to complain to him.[6]

It came as no surprise that this vital constitutional change was hotly debated. Throughout the month and well into March the discussion raged as parliament deliberated the terms of the *Humble Petition and Advice* and tried to weld it into a constitutional device which would provide the country with the permanent settlement which many craved after the unstable years following the regicide. Everyone wanted to have a say and, as the man who would decide the petition's fate, Cromwell was bombarded with argument and counter-arguments, all of which he had to take into account as he still could not afford to offend either side. On the question of the second house he supported Thurloe's assertion that its creation would be 'a great security and bulwark to the common interest'; while he was not interested in bringing back the old House of Lords Cromwell was keen to see a nominated upper chamber consisting of the great and good who would, as he put it, provide 'a balancing power'. On 11 March 1657 parliament fell in with the proposal that a second house of up to seventy members be created and that Cromwell should nominate its membership.

The change was achieved relatively painlessly but the central question of kingship proved to be a more complex issue. Everything hinged on Cromwell, who was facing a dilemma, and a very human one at that. He knew that the proposal enjoyed powerful support and understood the widespread hunger for a peaceful settlement and an end to the country's upheavals. He understood, too, that the transformation would benefit his family, for the title would pass to his eldest son Richard and would also benefit his other children. There were even rumours that his daughter Frances might make a match for Charles II, a move which would allow him to accept the crown and then pass it back to the Stewarts. As for himself, he had always been a man of simple tastes and although he had created a splendid court he was still very much the Huntingdonshire squire. If he did become king it would be the culmination of his service to the country and not a means of aggrandisement; at his stage of life he was hardly likely to be swayed by the baubles of kingship. Only duty would take him to the crown and the responsibilities which went with it; he must have given the possibility the fullest consideration, not least because age had not been kind to him and in his late fifties his body was weakening.

On the other hand Cromwell realised that his acceptance would offend the men who had marched with him from Edgehill to Worcester and whose counsels he still heeded. Two of them, Fleetwood and Desborough, were related to him by marriage, another, Lambert, was almost a second son, perhaps even a successor. To take the crown without their blessing would be to forsake principles which had been won on the battlefield and honed in the years of political struggle leading to the fateful decision to execute the king. And then there was the army itself, led by those honest men in russet coats who had given him the muscle to do his political work. They still lurked in the background fearing that should 'Old Noll' take the crown their influence would wane and their sacrifices would have been in vain. Cromwell was not just being sentimental when he considered the army and all that it had done for him: he had fashioned it into a useful instrument of policy which had helped to bring him to where he stood in the spring of 1657, and he would be loath to offend it. His conscience also played on him. How could he ignore the army or the voices of those soldiers who could not understand why he was even considering the offer? One veteran wrote to him begging him not to take the crown, for if he did he would 'provoke the vials of God's wrath', and reminding him that just as any other man, at his death he would have to face eternal justice.[7]

However, a decision had to be taken. Parliament's work would not wait on moral or religious considerations. When the *Humble Petition and Advice* was finally debated on 25 March it was agreed by 123 votes to 62 to offer the crown to Cromwell and that he should be allowed the right to name his successor. The motion was presented to Cromwell in the Banqueting Hall six days later, on the last day of the month, with the sonorous words that the office of king was both a Christian duty and a title which was not only legal and constitutional but 'most agreeable . . . to the temper of the people'. Cromwell must have known that the offer would be made, but he chose to prevaricate, telling the assembled parliament that he needed more time 'to deliberate and consider what particular answer I may return to so great a business as this'. He added the thought – this was pure Cromwell – that he had to 'ask counsel of God and of my own heart', to seek the providence of the former and to deliberate the matter with his conscience. All his life he had pondered God's great mercies and had looked for signs and signals which would tell him what God expected of him. Now that he was facing the greatest crisis of his life he needed all the spiritual grace and refreshment he could get ahead of the struggle to come.[8]

Everything in his life seemed to have led to this moment, yet Cromwell felt ill-equipped to deal with the challenge, and this affected him physically and mentally. As he had done so often in the past in times of crisis, he developed a psychosomatic illness, breaking down with 'some infirmity of body' which was so stressful that he was forced to prevaricate. A committee was appointed to help him with his deliberations and to settle constitutional questions, but his dealings with them proved to be long and rambling. It met half a dozen times in April but Cromwell refused to come to a decision and used delaying tactics – illness, doubts, fears and scruples – while London held its breath. Throughout the period Cromwell swithered from one extreme to the other. One day Thurloe felt confident enough to report that Cromwell was ready to concede, on another Ludlow remembered that the Lord Protector had appeared contrite and would refuse. Eventually, acting on the hunch that Cromwell would accept, 7 May was settled as the day when Cromwell would meet the committee and accept the crown. It would be known ever after as the Accession Day of King Oliver I.

It came and went without the king-apparent arriving in Whitehall; instead that evening he stated that he would attend the meeting the following day. So he did, but he brought with him the unexpected answer: 'I cannot undertake this Government with that title of king. And that's my answer to this great and weighty business.'[9]

The announcement came as a mighty shock. Primed by Thurloe, the committee thought that Cromwell would accept the crown and that the previous day's failure to appear was the result of nerves or a need for further prayer and cogitation. That was probably the case, but they could not have divined Cromwell's reasons. Unknown to parliament he had been subjected to an unwelcome but fateful meeting on the day before he was supposed to accept the crown. While walking alone in St James's Park on 6 May in an attempt to clear his head and put the great question in perspective he encountered Desborough, Fleetwood and Lambert, the prickers of his conscience and men whom he still trusted. Their message was unequivocal: if Cromwell accepted the crown they would resign their commissions and with them the bonds of friendship and loyalty would be shattered. In itself their warning would not have dissuaded Cromwell at that juncture, for he knew their feelings only too well, but it was a last straw. He already knew that a petition was being prepared against the monarchy for circulation among the army's regiments. That move was also no surprise, but the two men behind it were also cemented into Cromwell's past. The petition had been drawn up by John Owen, his former chaplain and companion from the campaigns in Scotland and Ireland, whom he had raised to the vice-chancellorship of Oxford University, and it was being organised by Colonel Thomas Pride, the officer who had taken his troopers to purge the last Royalist parliament. Faced by the disapproval of two such compelling figures and by the opposition of the army, acceptance of the crown was simply unwelcome and too great a burden to bear. Even if he were still swithering on 6 May – the odds are that he had made up his mind to accept – the meeting with his old unforgiving comrades must have concentrated his mind. Perhaps this was God's providence at work, the sign he had been seeking; acceptance of the offer was vainglorious, and not the solution to the correct governance of the Protectorate.

The decision also concentrated the minds of those who had been astonished by its announcement – the authors of the *Humble Petition*. Having recovered their wits they set about reworking the bill, and in its new form it was presented to Cromwell again on 25 May. This time he accepted and in effect the *Humble Petition and Advice* became the new constitution. Cromwell remained as Lord Protector but became king in all but name – the trappings of monarchy would be his on state occasions – and he was allowed to name his successor. The other main points were that parliament would meet every three years, an upper house consisting of 40 to 70 members was confirmed, members of the Council of State were obliged to take an oath and parliament would be able to veto its membership. For the first time since the regicide, governance of the country originated from parliamentary statute and not the rule of force. There were changes in the balance of power – parliament gained at the council's expense – but the biggest loser was John Lambert, whose Instrument of Government had been superseded.

The earnest major-general might still have survived the blow – Desborough and Fleetwood both accepted places in the upper house – but Lambert was now on collision course with the new order. He opposed the new upper chamber, he was hostile to the war with Spain and he disliked Cromwell's new status. For everyone concerned this was an intolerable situation, and when Lambert refused to take the new oath he was obliged by Cromwell to resign all his public commissions, a decision the young soldier accepted with commendable grace. He retired once again to his estate in Wimbledon to follow his interests in gardening and painting and to await future developments. For Lambert the fall had been hard. One of the New Model Army's most capable soldiers, and an astute politician, he had been spoken of as a successor to Cromwell, yet now at his patron's bidding he had been cast into political darkness. Cromwell softened the blow by awarding him a pension, perhaps as a reward for that last service in St James's Park, but Lambert remained that dangerous creature – a politician on the fringes with a grudge.

He was not the only man to decline a position in government – Hesilrige refused a place in the upper house on grounds of conscience, as did the Earl of Manchester – but before the new order could come into being Cromwell had to be sworn into his new office on 26 June. In all but name the ceremony was a coronation: the English throne with the Scottish Stone of Destiny was taken out of Westminster Abbey and placed in Westminster Hall, eight years earlier the scene of Charles I's trial, velvet drapes with gold fringes were used as decorations, and in front of the throne stood a table with an embossed bible, a huge golden sceptre and a great sword of state which had been born in by the Earl of Warwick. Apart from the anointing and the crowning the ceremony itself contained most of the elements of a coronation. According to a contemporary report published in *Mercurius Politicus*, Cromwell entered the hall with a full entourage of 'divers of the nobility and other persons of great quality', he was dressed in a robe of purple velvet lined with ermine, 'being the habit anciently used at the investiture of princes', he was girt with the sword of state, he was handed the sceptre and then swore a coronation oath to preserve the peace and safety of the people 'as Chief Magistrate of these three nations'. After an exhortatory prayer he sat down on the throne and 'while his Highness thus sat a Herald stood up aloft, giving a signal to a trumpet to sound three times, after which he did by authority and direction of Parliament there publish and proclaim his Highness Lord Protector of the Commonwealth of England, Scotland and Ireland and the dominions and territories thereunto belonging, requiring all persons to yield him due obedience. Hereupon the trumpets sounded and the people made several great acclamations with loud shouts, "God save the Lord Protector".'[10]

Apart from the crown Cromwell was king, and he was not tardy in exercising his new powers. Parliament was adjourned and among the new appointments to the Council of State was his son Richard, a weak-willed but pleasant young man, fond of country pursuits – Lucy Hutchinson astutely called him 'a peasant in his nature, yet gentle and virtuous, but became not greatness' – and with an unfortunate penchant (much abhorred by his father) for getting into debt.[11] By then aged thirty-one, Dick had become a member of parliament in 1654 and was slowly being groomed for greater things, but in his father he had a stern taskmaster who had once written of him from Ireland: 'as for Dick, I do not expect it from him, knowing his idleness'. Crucially, apart from a brief commission in 1647 before he entered Lincoln's Inn, he had not served as a soldier and that absence in his life meant that the army would be at best suspicious, at worst downright hostile if he ever succeeded his father as Lord Protector.

Under the terms of the Humble Address and Remonstrance Cromwell had been given the authority to name his successor, but although he prevaricated most of his closest advisers thought that the choice would fall on his eldest son. Following Oliver Cromwell would never be easy, but for Richard, soon to be laughed at as 'Tumbledown Dick', it would be a rough apprenticeship.

In the aftermath of his elevation Cromwell turned his mind to other family matters. Following a lengthy and troubled courtship with Robert Rich, grandson of the Earl of Warwick and a man whom Cromwell disliked, being 'a vicious man given to play and such like things', Frances his youngest daughter was allowed to marry. The wedding on 11 November 1657 was an extravagant affair complete with music and dancing and 'much mirth and frolic'. The party went on until five o'clock the following morning but the merry-making did not end there: ahead lay a week of festivities as the wedding party made a stately peregrination from Whitehall to Warwick House. Hard on its heels there was a second family wedding when another daughter, Mary, married Thomas Belayse, Viscount Fauconberg, a man of great personal charm whose links with the Stewarts were overlooked on account of his abilities – many of his family were Catholics and an uncle was one of the founders of the Sealed Knot. In contrast to Frances's wedding the ceremony was private, and Fauconberg quickly became established in Cromwell's inner circle of advisers, his fluency in French making him a useful addition in the country's diplomatic policy. If there was any criticism of either union or of Cromwell's burgeoning aristocratic connections, it was never voiced in public.

Unfortunately the same calm acceptance of social change could not be said of the new political order. It had proved difficult to fill the upper house: of the 63 nominees invited to join only 42 accepted, and of that number 37 came to the first meeting. Some of the absentees could not attend owing to their public duties – Henry Cromwell, Monck, Mountagu and Lockhart – but it was not just the membership which was creating uncertainty; it was the presence of the house itself. When parliament reassembled on 20 January 1658 it became clear that its republican members were determined to wreck the *Humble Petition and Advice* and to kill off the upper house even before it had decided on its name. (The only business debated by that august body was whether or not it should be called the House of Lords or the Other House.) Five days later Cromwell addressed both houses in the Banqueting House, and although he warned them about Royalist threats to the established order and 'another more bloody civil war', parliament was not minded to be acquiescent, Scot setting the mood with his thunderous rebuke: 'Shall I that sat in a parliament that brought a king to the bar, and to the block, not speak my mind freely here?' Urged on by Hesilrige the debate had only one topic – the abolition of the upper chamber and the return to the Commonwealth.

In fact the threats to the body politic were exaggerated: the main danger came from parliament itself. A petition was being organised to demand the primacy of parliament and the dismantling of the upper house, questions were being asked about Cromwell's right to command the army, rumours abounded that the army was on the verge of mutiny, and more restive voices began calling for Cromwell to intervene. By then it was almost inevitable that the Lord Protector would act. Appalled by the incessant bickering, alarmed by the expression of republican sentiments and concerned about the army's loyalty, Cromwell decided that enough was enough. On 4 February, a bitterly cold winter's morning, he went to the old House of Lords, informed its members that he was about to dismiss parliament and then called on Black Rod to summon its members. Before they arrived Fleetwood remonstrated with his father-in-law, but Cromwell was in a mighty rage. 'You are milksop,' he thundered. 'By the living God I will dissolve the house.' And so he did, telling parliament that he dismissed them with a heavy heart. Having chided them for causing so much mischief in so short a time – sixteen days – he offered a sturdy defence of the upper house and its right to exist before reminding them again that a Royalist army was 'at the waterside, drawn down towards the waterside, ready to be shipped to England'. It was hyperbole but Cromwell was in no mood to mince his words and his dismissal of this, the shortest Protectorate parliament contained echoes of his abrupt dissolution of the Rump: 'I think it high time that an end be put to your sitting and I do declare to you here that I do dissolve this parliament.'[12]

Anticlimax followed. The members returned to their homes, there was no revolution, the Royalists failed to materialise, thanks mainly to Thurloe's efficiency and the ineffectiveness of plotters such as the Sealed Knot, the army remained loyal and closed ranks and Cromwell was left in supreme control of the three countries. That summer was marked by Lockhart's triumphs in Flanders and by a strengthening of the French alliance, thanks in part to a successful diplomatic mission led by Fauconberg, but Cromwell was left with little time to enjoy his continuing good fortune. Family tragedies were beginning to intrude. Poor sickly Robert Rich died in February, just four months after his marriage, Warwick followed him three months later, a grandson died in June and Cromwell's favourite daughter Bettie was found to be dying slowly of cancer. Her death at the beginning of August was a tremendous blow and it is doubtful if Cromwell ever recovered. George Fox saw him a few days later at Hampton Court and 'felt a great waft of death go forth against him and when I came to him he looked like a dead man'. In fact Cromwell was a very sick man indeed. Gout was a long-standing affliction, kidney stones were causing problems, a boil on his neck refused to heal and by the third week of August he had been stricken with a malarial fever.

For a change of air he was ordered to return to Whitehall, where he entered a swift decline. Although there were moments when he rallied and seemed to be improving, Cromwell was dying, and those around him sensed it. For them the immediate problem was the succession, but a search for a sealed envelope naming the heir proved fruitless. Pressed to reveal his wishes on 2 September Cromwell eventually whispered the word 'Richard', but that deathbed admission did not still rumours that he had wanted to nominate his soldier-son Henry or his son-in-law Fleetwood. The apocalyptic tidings from Whitehall were not lessened in any way by the unseasonable weather. At the end of August England was gripped by one of the biggest storms in living memory, a mighty hurricane which tore up trees and damaged buildings up and down the country. To the superstitious it seemed to presage terrible events and perhaps it did. After a fitful few days Cromwell died in the afternoon of 3 September, his last words being a simple desire 'to make what haste I can to be gone'.

The date of death had a resonance: it was the anniversary of two of Cromwell's greatest triumphs, Dunbar and Worcester, and it also gave rise to a fantastic but widely believed tale which had been retailed by one of his officers. According to a Captain Lindsay, who claimed to have witnessed the scene, Cromwell had sold his soul to the Devil shortly before the Battle of Worcester. In return for victory and 'all things else for seven years' Cromwell would pay back what he owed on 3 September 1658, the date of his death, and so it transpired – the tremendous storm was nothing less than Satan announcing his arrival to carry off the Lord Protector's soul.[13] And if it were not the devil's work then the high winds must signify God's anger: in distant Aberdeen both the hurricane and the news of Cromwell's death arrived like a celestial thunderclap in the sin-fearing mind of Alexander Jaffray:

> There being also at this time, very sad evidences of the Lord's anger against this land, by unseasonable weather, so that the fruits of the earth are threatened to be destroyed; this thought of the abuse of so much peace and plenty, as formerly we have been enjoying, did much continue on my heart – and that we were, in the righteous judgement of God, to be exercised with famine and war; and a sharper trial to pass over such as fear the Lord, than they had ever met with; especially their unthankfulness for the peace we have been enjoying these years by-gone.[14]

Richard Cromwell was quietly informed that evening that he was the new Lord Protector, and Thurloe noted that after the storm and the momentous tidings the country was completely calm. Royalist supporters did not take advantage of the situation, neither did the Scots or the Irish, the death being announced in Edinburgh and Dublin with scarcely a murmur. In Scotland there could have been trouble – taxes were high, quartering was unpopular and Monck had warned his officers to 'have a special eye over the Scots' – but there were no outbreaks of unrest. During Cromwell's illness Robert Baillie 'feared for trouble' and claimed that the Protector's death would be a great misfortune, and in many respects he was right, for despite being 'exceedingly poor', his country had been reasonably secure and well-ordered during its union with England. The most sincere mourning was done in private. Cromwell's immediate family and friends had not expected his death and had difficulty accepting that a summer fever should have taken away such a tough old soldier. His wife Elizabeth, the Lady Protectress, was distraught, having lost a husband, a daughter and a grandchild in quick succession and having enjoyed a long and fruitful marriage, but friends like Thurloe and Fleetwood were equally distressed, seeing in Cromwell's death evidence of their own shortcomings. The great captain was no longer at the helm and they were determined to mark his passing with a fanfare.

Like a king, Cromwell was buried in Westminster Abbey at a service which was based on the funeral of James I, complete with a lying-in-state prior to it and interment in the chapel of Henry VII on 23 November. (Poor embalming meant that a life-size model had to be used, the decomposing corpse having been buried earlier.) One observer, the poet Abraham Cowley, thought the funeral 'a great show' but 'an ill sight', and many were to be found who deprecated the extravagance and the popish elements which found their way into the last rites – at one stage the effigy was hauled up and a crown placed on its head to represent the passing of the soul out of Purgatory. Painful for Puritans it must have been to witness such a scene and at such a cost (at least £50,000), but in a sense the people were simply being allowed to pay their last respects to a much-respected ruler. Cromwell had not been crowned monarch but for the last seven years he had been the country's most powerful figure, a man who in death was hailed as the people's saviour and redeemer.

In some respects he was just that. At the end of his life Cromwell was still the same country gentleman in a 'plain cloth suit' noticed by Sir Philip Warwick in the days of the Long Parliament. Even though a critic such as the Quaker Edward Burough complained that Cromwell had embraced too easily 'the greatness and honour of the world' he still conceded that at his best Cromwell was 'a gallant instrument for the Lord'. A member of the Lord Protector's household was no less acute when he mourned his lost leader with the words, 'a larger soul, I think, hath seldom dwelt in a house of clay than his was'.[15] That observation gets close to the heart of the man: he was out of the ordinary. Under his guidance the countries of the British Isles had been transformed and, although the revolution was far from complete or permanent, the monarchy could never again assume unchallenged primacy and parliament would be the main executive authority determining national policies. As a soldier Cromwell emerged on the battlefield as a natural leader of men and a commander with an uncanny ability to read a battle and a capacity to know when to act decisively. In his treatment of parliament he demonstrated a less sure touch, showing himself impatient of the slow speed of their deliberations and fearing any outbreak of republicanism. In that sense he was a conservative, and his crushing of the Levellers and other sects put paid to contemporary demands for universal suffrage and the reform of property law. It would be another two centuries before they became political issues again.

At times driven by the belief that his actions were guided by God's providence, at times fearful that he had fallen from grace, Cromwell was not a man of iron but a human being, like any other, full of paradox. While he was one of the regicides who had turned the world upside down, a deed requiring courage and conviction, he could be querulous and uncertain, much given to periods of doubt and bouts of imagined illness. He could be stern and unbending, with a bad temper which shocked even such seasoned commanders as Fleetwood and Fairfax, yet he had a gentle side and was not above playing practical jokes on his subordinates. No intellectual, he was widely read in the scriptures; no killjoy, he took pleasure in music and dancing; no statesman (as his handling of his parliaments revealed), he had the politician's knack of knowing when to act. History has not always been kind to him, seeing in him the extremes of the republican who helped to kill a king and the conservative who helped to kill off the reformers of his age. As a character who changed the course of British history he is not only difficult to ignore but equally difficult to pin down. A century after his death the poet Alexander Pope came closest to doing that in his long poem *An Essay on Man*, posing the question 'Say where Greatness lies?' he exclaimed: 'See Cromwell, damned to everlasting fame!'

Chapter Eight

THE KING COMES INTO HIS OWN

'Boys do now cry "Kiss my Parliament" instead of "Kiss my arse," so great and general contempt is the Rump come to among all men, good and bad.'

Samuel Pepys, Diary, 7 February 1660

In the first months of his reign Richard Cromwell made a good attempt at filling his father's ample boots. His position was not easy. Doubts lingered about his right to the succession, the army was dubious about his capacity to do anything for their benefit – that is, to pay them, clear arrears, protect the sects and provide them with indemnity against future prosecution – and he was surrounded by advisers much given to plotting in order to better themselves. Shortly after being appointed he told his brother Henry that security within his household was so lax that he dared not commit his innermost thoughts to paper. On the credit side he had the support of his brother-in-law Fleetwood, loyal Thurloe with his intelligence service remained to hand, as did his father's closest advisers Broghill, Lockhart and Mountagu. In Scotland Monck kept his own counsel but had announced his determination to protect the succession. Being aware that some Scots hoped that the English would now start falling out among themselves, Monck ordered his regimental officers to be alert for Royalist plots and also to clamp down on any dissent shown by the men in the junior ranks. In return Richard Cromwell rewarded his circle of supporters. Brother Henry became Lord Lieutenant of Ireland and continued his policy of supporting the Old Protestants at the expense of the sects, Fleetwood was given command of the army in the rank of lieutenant-general, Lockhart remained at Dunkirk and Mountagu was confirmed as general-at-sea in charge of the fleet in addition to being given command of a regiment, the latter promotion being greatly resented by junior army officers. Wisely, the new Protector retained supreme command of the armed forces with the power to award or withhold commissions.

By making himself agreeable and demonstrating tact and charm, Richard Cromwell enjoyed a brief honeymoon, and for a while it seemed that, guided by the Council and parliament, his position and the succession would be secure. It was not to be. The country was deeply in debt, its accumulated deficit almost £2,500,000, and in 1659 the annual shortfall was over £300,000. As ever, the armed forces were in the worst straits. Pay was months in arrears, the total shortfall being around £900,000, and the men were restless. The navy was in a similar state of financial disrepair. For the armed forces this was not new – throughout the Commonwealth and the Protectorate the regiments had complained long and hard about lack of pay – but at least in the days of their fame they had trusted Old Noll and had respected officers such as Fleetwood and Desborough. Theirs was a long history of hardship and shared dangers, of common cause and righteous convictions, but of Richard Cromwell they were not so sure. They knew nothing of him except that he had not served as a soldier (apart from a brief period in 1647) and the more radical among their number disliked the fact that he had succeeded as Lord Protector. Not only did they have no liking for the post itself but they resented Richard Cromwell's easy acceptance of it. At least his father had earned the right to the title and the trappings which went with it.

No fool, Richard Cromwell understood their grievances and tried to alleviate them by ordering back payments, but it was not enough to win over the soldiers. Obdurate and unwelcoming at the beginning of the second Protectorate, their feelings hardened over the winter of 1658–59 and by spring the New Model Army, once the administration's main prop, had become its main critic. The ever-prescient Thurloe got close to the heart of the problem when he noted the army's misgivings: 'There are some secret murmurings in the army, as if his highness were not general of the army as his father was.'[1] Parliament, too, was being difficult. Recalled at Henry Cromwell's suggestion on 27 January 1659 to deal with the country's financial problems, it was soon back in its usual state of turmoil. With Scots and Irish members present it numbered 549 members, many of whom were inexperienced, while others were old republicans from the Purged Parliament of 1648 and, as Lucy Hutchinson could see from the outset, it was clearly and decisively divided:

> Now the Parliament were sat, and no sooner assembled but were invaded by several enemies. The Presbyterians had long since espoused the royal interest, and forsaken God and the people's cause when they could not obtain the reins of government in their own hands, and exercise dominion over all their brethren. It was treason, by the law of those men in power to talk of restoring the King; therefore the Presbyterians must face the design, and accordingly all the members ejected in 1648 now came to claim their seats in the house, whom Colonel Pride, that then guarded the Parliament, turned back.[2]

On the one hand were those who accepted the Protectorate and were opposed to making any concessions to the army, an unexpected supporter being John Lambert, who represented Pontefract; on the other were those who wanted to destroy the Protectorate and to return to the Commonwealth. The latter grouping, republican by inclination and iconoclastic by nature, was determined to put a stop to the upper chamber and they also resisted the inclusion of the Scottish and Irish members on the grounds that they should withdraw until the constitutional question had been settled. On 21 March grudging acceptance was given to the Celtic presence, but that was only a brief reprieve. By the time Monck received the news in Edinburgh parliament had once more been dismissed.

Although the administration had started well it foundered on the familiar rocks of religious discord and insolvency. Gone were the days when deficits could be made good by the sale of Royalist lands or by the confiscation of Catholic lands in Ireland; if parliament wanted funds to pay for the armed forces these would have to come from taxes, but instead of acting decisively parliament was gripped by terminal lassitude. Worse, the republican elements had bent their energies to stirring up the army with rumours of its impending disbandment and a further suppression of the sects, notably the Quakers and the Baptists. The stories were not true, they did not need to be true, but they were widely believed and the army quickly became a hotbed of gossip and intrigue, just as it had been in 1647 in the wake of the Putney Debates. 'For this cause we have covered ourselves with blood,' was the soldiers' cry. 'We shudder when we think of the account which we must one day give if we suffer the blood-bought liberties of the people to again be destroyed.' However, this time there was no Oliver Cromwell to settle the issue by rooting out the troublemakers and dismissing the radicals from positions of command. Against a background of further unrest fomented by Fifth Monarchists and old Digger groups attacking land ownership, tithes and the landed gentry, the country was in danger of falling into political, social and religious anarchy.

The flashpoint came when Richard Cromwell ordered the Council of Officers, the army's ruling body, to return to their regiments and to sign a declaration of loyalty that they would not interfere in the business of parliament. This was a challenge to their authority, for it would have brought the regiments under civilian control, and it was met in full. Regiments in the London area marched on Westminster and those officers still loyal to the Protectorate found that the rank and file refused to obey them and preferred to join what was later described as 'a giddy, hot-tempered, bloody multitude'. With Richard Cromwell's control of the army compromised – the troops had followed Fleetwood, not him – he was in a desperate position. Once the upholders of the state, the soldiers of the New Model Army were now playing for everything that made them what they were: they wanted to be paid, but more than that they did not want to come under the control of an administration which would disband them, persecute the sects and perhaps even bring back the Stewart monarchy. When Fleetwood and Desborough demanded the dissolution of parliament Richard Cromwell had no option but to concur, and troops turned away members attempting to enter the chamber. On 22 April parliament was dissolved and the two generals strengthened their position by packing the Council of Officers with purged officers and replacing those thought to be loyal to Richard

Cromwell. By taking that step the army was now on its own and had become virtually a state within a state.

This was the chaos which many had feared, and in the fortnight that followed, England was on the brink of falling apart. Parliament was replaced by the Council of Officers, but it was hardly a united body and its debates were shrill and hot-headed. Fleetwood wanted to keep things as they were but he was outnumbered by the vociferous majority and was outfought by those junior to him. A radical spirit was surging through the army; it demanded nothing less than the abolition of the Protectorate and a return to 'the good old cause' of republicanism. In this brave new world there would be pay for all, the army would remain in being, and there would be tolerance for all sects. Like the children of Israel they would soon be marching 'from a land of bondage and intolerance to a land of liberty and rest'. Few could resist the call and the Council of Officers found itself being swept along in an hysterical mood of self-righteousness and heady prophecies. At the beginning of May it agreed to dismiss the Protectorate and the upper house, but to give the decision a semblance of constitutional legality the council also decided to bring back the Rump of the Long Parliament, which had last sat six years earlier before being sent packing by Oliver Cromwell. A further throwback to the past came in the invitation to William Lenthall, long retired, to be its Speaker, a post he had first held under Charles I in 1640.

Richard Cromwell was now on his own, and the army was in complete control, free to issue its own demands – freedom of religious belief (bar Catholics), exclusion of all Royalists from office, the recognition of Fleetwood as commander-in-chief and the creation of a new Council of State whose leading lights would be Hesilrige, Scot, Ludlow, Wariston and Sir Henry Vane the Younger. No ruler could continue with that arrangement, and Richard Cromwell bowed to the inevitable during the last week in May 1659. Promised a pension he retired to his estates in Hampshire, having been in office less than half a year. (His departure was not without pathos: fear of debt forced him to remain in the Palace of Whitehall and he was loath to leave that immunity to return to his estates.) For all his weaknesses Richard was blameless, and he does not deserve history's ill opinion of him (later John Dryden portrayed him as 'foolish Ishbosheth' in his long poem *Absalom and Achitophel*); he was mildly popular and showed himself to be capable but, dangerously, he failed to build up powerful political allies. Henry followed him into political exile and returned to England, leaving Ireland increasingly in the grip of a class which would emerge as the Protestant ascendancy. Another casualty was John Thurloe, who lost his post as secretary, but due to his absence abroad Lockhart escaped censure, as did Mountagu,* who was commanding the fleet in the approaches to the Baltic: the rout of the Cromwellians was almost complete. A sign of the uncertain times was the appointment of Archibald Johnston of Wariston to the presidency of the Council of State. For the peevish Edinburgh lawyer this was the sign of God's pleasure, but he was little more than a catspaw, given the job because no one else wanted it and, as one member put it, so that 'they might be rid of his multiloquy and impertinent motions'.

That left Monck in Scotland, but he was playing his cards close to his chest. On 12 May he assured the Speaker that his regiments were loyal to the Rump – 'obedience is my great principle' – and added the hope that this support would be 'adequate to the Nature and being of a Commonwealth', but already his position was anomalous.[3] Once the Rump came into being the union with Scotland was dissolved, as all legislation passed since April 1653 was declared null and void. As that period included the Ordinance of Union a new bill had to be introduced by a committee whose deliberations were to be so slow and longwinded that they failed to arrive at a solution within the course of the parliament. Faced by that vacuum Monck continued to rule with a rod of iron, putting down a spate of summertime incidents, mainly cattle rustling and criminal disturbances which threatened the peace. Under his watchful eye Scotland remained calm and his forces relatively untainted by the turmoil in England. Such circumspection would stand him in good stead in the months ahead. 'He is a black Monck,' said Lord Mordaunt, now acting as an intermediary for Charles II, 'and I cannot see through him.'

Monck's absence also kept him clear of the clash which was about

---

* He was already in bad odour, having been accused with Fauconberg of fomenting a plot to murder Fleetwood and Desborough. On his return to England in September he was relieved of all his commissions.

to break out between the army and the new parliament. Nothing had been achieved by the dismissal of the Protectorate and its Cromwellian supporters. The army thought that the Rump Parliament would be its creature and would do its bidding, while the members firmly believed that they could control the soldiers. Other misunderstandings abounded: the army hoped for speedy reforms while the parliament treated the soldiers' demands with scant attention. All the while both bodies were extremely unpopular, parliament because it excluded elected members and the army because of its physical presence in the country and the vast expense of maintaining it. Neither side seemed to realise that in those circumstances both were so dependent on the other for their survival that it was madness to march towards confrontation and discord.

Something had to give, but before it did the army had to deal with a Royalist uprising which flared up at the end of July 1659. The product of plotting by the Sealed Knot, it envisaged a series of uprisings across northern England, but lack of security meant that its secrets were divulged to parliament and it went off at half-cock. An attempt was made to call off the revolt but the orders failed to reach the main protagonists in Cheshire, Lancashire and north Wales. Most of them were not old Royalists but a mixture of disaffected parliamentarians who had been expelled and Royalist supporters who believed that the restoration of the Stewarts was the best way forward for the country. In Wrexham Sir Thomas Myddleton proclaimed Charles II king of England; the Earl of Derby, whose father had been executed in 1651, called on Lancashire to rise; Chester's mayor threw in his support and on 1 August a local landowner, Sir George Booth, appeared at the head of an army some 4000 strong, his aim being the restoration of parliament. The cause was already hopeless. Everything depended on other Royalist groups rising with him, and that failure to achieve solidarity meant that Booth and his army were doomed even before their campaign began. Dithering was also his undoing. When news reached him that the revolt had been called off he could have dispersed his army and fled into exile or into the mountains of north Wales. He might even have forced the issue by seizing Chester, which was garrisoned by a small force under Colonel Thomas Croxton, but Booth seemed to be paralysed. Meanwhile parliament had ordered Lambert to deal with the revolt and he was marching north with an army of 2000 foot and horse which would be joined by experienced troops from Ireland and Yorkshire under the command of Robert Lilburne.

Not wanting to be caught between the advancing parliamentary army and the walls of Chester, on 7 August Booth took his army to Manchester, where he made further attempts to gather support, but by 18 August Lambert's forces had reached Weaverham to the west of Northwich, where Booth's army was preparing for battle. The following day saw a series of running skirmishes over the maze of enclosure land at Hartford Beech and Booth's unprepared and largely amateur force soon started withdrawing in disarray towards the River Weaver. Their one hope lay in reaching the hilly ground to the north and in securing the only river crossing at Winnington Bridge. Unable to cope with the sheer weight of Lambert's attack, the volley of fire from the parliamentary dragoons and musketeers, Booth's men started retiring as best they could. Panic quickly set in. Those defending the bridge were swept aside while those attempting to reach the high ground at Barnton were chased off the field by the parliamentary horse, and the pursuit was continued as far as Warrington and Manchester. Thirty Royalists were killed and one parliamentary soldier, but Lambert was inclined to be merciful. Booth's foot soldiers were allowed to escape back to their homes, as in the parliamentary general's words, they were only 'forced and hired'. The last set-piece battle of the wars of three kingdoms had been fought and won.*

In the aftermath Myddleton surrendered after his home at Chirk Castle was surrounded by parliamentary troopers and Booth escaped south, disguised as a woman. He got as far as Newport Pagnell, where an innkeeper became suspicious of 'Mistress Dorothy's' big frame and a request for a razor. Booth was arrested and might have expected a traitor's sentence but was simply incarcerated in the Tower of London and later released. His adversary was a winner in more ways than one – Lambert's military success paved the way for his return to public life and he made full use of the opportunity. At Derby his regiments sent a petition to parliament requesting that all their demands should be met and that 'malignants' should be purged from public life. The

---

* The site of the battle is now covered by the industrial development of Northwich; most of the fighting took place on ground now owned by the Moss Farm Sports Ground.

call had been made before, but this time Lambert was using his military muscle to remind members of parliament that they owed their positions not to the electorate but to the soldiers of the New Model Army.

If part of the Derby Petition's purpose was to provoke parliament, it succeeded. Lambert was rebuked for his presumptuous actions and when he protested parliament stripped him of his rank, expelled him from parliament and on 5 October ordered Fleetwood to arrest him. At the same time a bill was introduced making void all acts and ordinances of the Protectorate unless they had already been confirmed by the Rump. Members also insisted that no taxes could be raised without the assent of parliament, a declaration which reminded the army that the country's survival depended on the continuation of a legislative body. This was a direct challenge, and a clash became inevitable when Lenthall summoned the London-based regiments to protect Whitehall. The soldiers refused and threw in their lot with Lambert. On 13 October Whitehall was surrounded, parliament was once more dismissed and the governance of England passed back into military hands in the shape of the Council of Officers.

To give the coup a figleaf of political respectability the senior officers appointed a Committee of Safety to run the country, but it could only be a stopgap arrangement. While it included some civilians it was powerless to raise taxes, and without income the country was slowly foundering amid a welter of confusion and conflicting loyalties. In theory there was an administration, however flawed it might be, but the real power lay with Fleetwood and Lambert, who had engineered the coup. Using Fleetwood's London residence in the Strand as their headquarters the leaders of the coup became known as the Wallingford House Party. According to Lucy Hutchinson 'they there began their arbitrary reign, to the joy of all the vanquished enemies of the parliament and to the amazement and terror of all men that had any honest interest. And now they were all devising governments; and some honourable members, I know not through what fatality of the times, fell in with them.'4

Among those castigated by Lucy were Sir Henry Vane the Younger and Bulstrode Whitelocke, both polar opposites in their outlook, and the committee also included representatives of the City of London, but the leading lights were the two generals. Lambert and Fleetwood were capable soldiers and strong-minded men who tried to do their best according to their consciences, but they were not Cromwell and would never be able to impose their will on the army, the radicals or those who wanted a return to normality. Even the instrument of their power, the army, was in trouble, with disaffected regiments demanding an end to the turmoil and the restitution of parliament. As things fell apart ever more rapidly thoughts turned to the possibility of bringing Charles II back but, in the autumn of 1659, the time was not yet ripe for any direct approach to be made to the exiled court, by then in residence in the Spanish Netherlands, in Brussels. For Charles himself the year had produced an emotional helter-skelter. At first elated by Cromwell's death, he was cast down by the appointment of Richard Cromwell as Lord Protector; the military coups had raised expectations so much so that he was fully prepared to go back to England, but Booth's heavy defeat killed off those hopes. Later, his brother James, Duke of York, would recall that during the winter of 1659-60 the court was at its 'lowest ebb'.

Only one man seemed capable of acting decisively – George Monck. In distant Edinburgh he was more or less a Protector in his own right, with a large, disciplined and well-trained army under his command and a settled administration in place. Good general that he was, he had rooted out over a hundred troublesome disaffected sectaries and had rearranged the composition of the regiments to make sure that they remained at full strength, an important consideration in maintaining morale. By paying his soldiers regularly and keeping them in quarantine from the chaos breaking out in England he ensured their absolute loyalty. As to his own thoughts, on the surface these were remarkably straightforward. On hearing the news of the expulsion of the Rump he made it clear to Lenthall that he supported parliamentary rule and would defend it, if need be, 'to the last drop of my blood'. On 20 October he issued a proclamation to that effect, demanding the recall of parliament, and two days later he issued a proclamation for four days of fasting in Edinburgh so that he might 'seek the Lord for his blessing in this great affair'.[5] Fleetwood and Lambert also received letters in which Monck reinforced his belief in parliamentary rule and his willingness to protect it, if need be by bringing his army into England. As the correspondence became more acrimonious a clash between the two armies seemed inevitable, and in mid-November representatives from both sides met in Newcastle to discuss constitutional matters and to find a way out of the impasse. It was a welcome break, for not only did it put off the awful prospect of a fresh civil war but it allowed Monck to put his house in order in Scotland before marching south. The démarche proved remarkably easy to organise. Representatives of the Estates were summoned to Edinburgh to be told that Monck had heard a call from God and intended 'to March into England' and that he required them to keep the peace while he was absent. With no demur they agreed, and it was a sign of the times that among those elected to make the necessary arrangements was the Earl of Glencairn, only five years previously leader of a Royalist revolt against Cromwell.

In November Lambert left London to take over command of the army in northern England, first at York and then at Newcastle, his commission being 'to use all endeavours to beget an understanding between the army here and the forces in Scotland, that they may become one in heart and hand for defence against the common enemy who waits for the ruin of both'.[6] All his previous experience and his local knowledge – he was a Yorkshireman – made him the ideal commander, but the great days of Preston and the defeat of the Scottish Royalists were long gone. A decade later the times were out of joint and the soldiers responded to the changing situation by behaving in ways that would have been unthinkable in Cromwell's time. Already infuriated by the lack of pay and the deteriorating conditions, many regiments in the north were disaffected and their calls for the return of parliament were shrill and insistent. It was not yet mutiny but a rot was setting in: discipline became difficult to impose, morale was low and there was widespread criticism of the leadership offered by the Wallingford House Party. Lambert was a battle-hardened soldier whose support among the soldiers had been absolute in the past, but during his 'exile' in Wimbledon the army had deteriorated and he was slow to recognise the drift. He was sluggish too in recognising that the rule of the swordsmen had entered its dying days.

That winter the country's fate lay in the hands of the two generals who owed everything to Cromwell – Monck, the hard-bitten and cautious soldier and sailor, and Lambert, the aesthetic cavalryman who nurtured ambitions of high office. If the latter brought Monck to heel his position would be strengthened immeasurably and the protectorship would not have been beyond him. Before leaving London, friends noticed that Lambert was trying to sideline Fleetwood in much the same way that Cromwell had Fairfax in 1648, and even an anonymous Royalist supporter was sufficiently convinced that he was the coming man to publish a public address to him on 14 October:

> We look upon you at this instant as having the whole strength of the nation in your hands, but if you expect to hold it long, you will be miserably deceived. Therefore I beseech you make good use of this happy opportunity, and consider how great you may make yourself, and how glorious you will be to posterity, if you be the means of laying the government on the shoulders of him who ought to bear it, which will in an instant restore a happy peace and settlement to this distracted nation.[7]

For a while Lambert, too, put his trust in that evaluation. Regiments from the south arrived to reinforce his army and there was a trickle of desertions from Scotland, but this advantage was negated by the heavy winter, the poor quartering conditions and the lack of pay. On 15 November Lambert thought that he had got the better of Monck when he forced the latter's commissioners to back down on the demand for parliament's immediate recall but, a fortnight later, Monck tore up the agreement and continued his silent waiting game: all he had to do was to do nothing but keep Lambert tied down in the north of England and isolated from events in London. At the beginning of December Monck's patience was rewarded when the south of England erupted. First the garrison at Portsmouth added their weight to the demand for parliament to be recalled and the security forces sent to repress them quickly defected, then the army in Ireland repeated the demand in Dublin; the fleet under the command of Admiral John Lawson also joined the call, adding the threat that it would blockade the Thames until parliament was recalled. There was rioting in London which the army failed to quell and even though Lambert hurried south to take command of the situation there was little he could do. All around him men were deserting, and then, in the first days of the new year, 1660, came news from Yorkshire that spelled the end for him – Fairfax had emerged from retirement and had raised Yorkshire for the cause of restoring parliament. Long unsure of their position and fearful of the future, men from Lambert's regiments flocked to join the veteran commander – Cromwell's old favourite was now in command of a shadow army.

Faced by the breakdown of their authority the Wallingford House men panicked. There was talk of making contact with Charles II, and this might have happened had not Fleetwood refused permission for Whitelocke to undertake the mission; various constitutional changes, all fanciful, were bandied about, but in effect Fleetwood and his cohorts were only playing out their allotted time. On Christmas Eve the regiments in the London district declared for parliament and the members of the Rump, all fifty-five of them, started arriving back in London. That same day Wariston lost his position as president of the council, and as his life fell apart he wrote disconsolately in his diary: 'And hereupon some heavy, bitter words of my wifes to me for my meddling with this Committee, and my passionate repart[ee] that I found her often a miserable comforter to me in the day of my calamity; my heart was like to break and burst with grief and anguish.'[8] Two days later, on 26 December, Fleetwood and Lambert had no other option but to recall the Rump Parliament and in so doing to concede to Monck's stubborn demands. Immediately, the Rump (soon to become a term of obloquy) set about establishing its authority. Republicans such as Vane were expelled, and having finally brought the army under civilian control there was a large-scale pogrom of officers and senior soldiers who had supported the Wallingford House Party. Over 500 of their number were cashiered and many more were dispersed by being transferred to different regiments, the better to dilute their capacity to cause trouble. With Fairfax in command in Yorkshire the army's political complexion had changed. In vain did Lambert make one final journey north to rally support against the military threat from Scotland: there was nothing left to command, and when he fled back to London this most capable of Cromwell's lieutenants was arrested and imprisoned in the Tower. 'He was a person of great parts and good courage, and as fit for the Protectorship as Oliver, and some think fitter,' remembered Dr Gumble, Monck's chaplain, 'but that foolish comedy was not to be acted upon again.'[9]

Behind Lambert came the army of Scotland under Monck's command, intent on playing out the final act. In December it had moved to Coldstream in Berwickshire on the River Tweed, and there Monck had awaited the outcome of events to the south. On New Year's Day 1660 the regiments started crossing the Tweed and headed south, first six regiments of foot followed by four regiments of horse.

Throughout the early months of winter Monck had been bombarded with requests and words of advice; Charles had also written to him through Sir John Grenville, a fellow Devonshire man and the son of the Royalist commander Beville Grenville, but Monck had put the letter to one side until events became clearer. His sole intention, he said, was to restore parliament, everything in his correspondence points to that fact, but even on that score he was vague about recalling the expelled members. First he had to test the waters. During his march south Monck was bombarded with petitions from leading figures in London demanding a free parliament, and by the time he reached Fairfax in York it was clear that the country wanted him to march on London. A number of factors urged him on. From the enthusiasm of his reception he could see that the demand for the recall of parliament was just, the absence of military opposition and the flight of Lambert meant that there would be no internecine fighting, and when parliament reassembled members made it clear that they wanted him to return to the capital. It remained to be seen what he would do when he got there, but by then some problems had been settled – parliamentary rule had been restored, the army was under control and the republicans within its ranks had been neutralised. The question of what to do with the king was less apparent; his restoration was being openly discussed but everything still hung on Monck.

On 2 February his regiments reached London and entered Whitehall. Among those watching the procession of smart disciplined soldiers was Samuel Pepys, a protégé of Edward Mountagu whose diary illuminates so many of the events of the restoration and of the reign of Charles II. In Whitehall he looked on as soldiers in 'very good plight' marched by amid 'calls to him [Monck] for a free Parliament, but little other welcome'. In the days that followed Pepys's observations would provide a good barometer of the reception given to Monck – from the initial wariness to the heady moments a month later when the king's health was being drunk openly in the streets of the capital. On 5 March Pepys visited George Pinkney, later to be the king's embroiderer, and the entry read: 'To Westminster by water, seeing Mr Pinkney at his own house, where he showed me how he had always kept the Lion and Unicorn in the back of his chimney bright, in expectation of the King's coming again.'[10]

Before that could happen – and it is important to realise that at this stage the restoration of Charles II was by no means a foregone conclusion – Monck had to deal with the unruly Rump, which was busily squabbling over its future. Clearly it could not remain a small disunited body, yet the readmission of members could take months to achieve and that tardiness was unhelpful at such a fractious time. To complicate matters Hesilrige had gained an ascendancy in the house and was intent on imposing parliament's will on the country and, foolishly, also on Monck. When the City of London announced its intention to withhold the payment of taxes until the expelled members were recalled Monck was ordered to take his men into the city to secure its gates. This he did with some reluctance, but the furious opposition to the move only demonstrated to the soldiers the government's unpopularity and the recklessness of its policies. The demonstrations also proved to Monck that he alone could restore order: that was underlined on 11 February when Hesilrige pushed through a bill depriving him of command of the army. That night Monck's regiments moved on the city and Monck himself presented parliament with an ultimatum giving it six days to dissolve itself and issue the writs for a new election. Hearing the news Pepys went to the Guildhall just as Monck was leaving to be met with 'such a shout I never heard in all my life, crying out, "God bless your Excellence"'. Elsewhere soldiers were being given drinks, bells were rung and bonfires blazed in the Strand and on Ludgate Hill, 'a whole lane of fire', many of them roasting rumps in a grim parody of the end of the hated administration.[11] Ten days later, on 21 February, just under half the number of excluded members entered the house and the Long Parliament was allowed to come into being again to make the necessary arrangements for its dissolution and the calling of an early election. It took only three weeks to put that design into effect: on 16 March, some twenty years after it first met, the Long Parliament consigned itself to history. The rebellion was now in its terminal stages.

Monck had played his cards well. First, by getting rid of agitators and imposing firm discipline, he had ensured the absolute loyalty of the forces under his command. Then he had responded to public opinion by putting pressure on parliament to dissolve itself, a move which was facilitated by the insensitive behaviour of men like Hesilrige, and finally he displayed the successful politician's knack of knowing when to act and when to hold back. No doubt there was an element of personal ambition. Monck was, after all, a professional soldier and he possessed the good commander's ability to make the best use of the forces at his disposal, but he was not yet vying for public office himself. Throughout this momentous period when a false move could have reignited passions and plunged the country into a fresh bout of internecine fighting Monck seemed to realise that he was marching with destiny and that he alone could decide events. Later Hyde said of him: 'It was the king's great happiness that he [Monck] never had it in his purpose to serve him till it fell to be in his power, and indeed till he had nothing else to do.' With people clamouring about the next leadership – Pepys noted on 2 March 'Great is the talk of a single person, and that it would now be Charles, George or Richard again' – Monck made the decisive move and contacted the exiled court of Charles II.

Heartened by Cromwell's death the king had moved his court to Brussels, but one of Monck's first recommendations was to quit it for the more neutral setting of Breda, the Dutch town where Charles had once negotiated with the Scots. From there Charles issued the Declaration of Breda on 4 April, a masterly and tactful statement of intent which paved the way for a swift rapprochement with parliament. Drawn up by Hyde, with Monck's blessing, it was a remarkably tolerant manifesto. A free and general pardon was offered to those who had fought against the Crown (there would be exceptions, mainly regicides), all sales of Royalist lands made during that period were confirmed, there would be a large measure of religious tolerance ('a liberty to tender consciences') and the army's arrears would be swiftly paid. This generous and statesmanlike document paved the way to an early settlement. There was a brief period of alarm a week later when Lambert escaped from the Tower, but his attempt at a republican revolt was nipped in the bud by forces led by Colonel Ingoldsby, one of the regicides. Bizarrely, Lambert was arrested at his chosen rendezvous of Edgehill.* Not only was Monck in full control of the country but the country itself wanted no more war. Even Cromwell's Thurloe saw the drift, noting in a letter to one of his agents: 'I do not see, but that the next parliament will endeavour to settle the nation by the king; but certainly great difficulties will attend it.'[12]

He was both right and wrong. Elections were held, the first free vote for twenty years, and on 25 April the new parliament assembled, but, not having the king's writ, the restored house was known as the 'Convention Parliament'. The 'good old cause' was in tatters, with no republicans left to cause 'difficulties', great or small. Charles's emissary Sir John Grenville then arrived in London to present the declaration of Breda, which was read to both houses on 1 May, and together with the king's letter this formed the basis of the lasting settlement, 'that, according to the ancient and fundamental laws of this kingdom, the Government is, and ought to be, by Kings, Lords and Commons'. Money was set aside to bring the king back to his country and commissioners were chosen to collect him from the Netherlands. Among the party was Samuel Pepys, who recorded the unstinted enthusiasm of the day after the 'welcome news' had been announced: 'Great joy all yesterday at London, and at night more bonfires than ever, and ringing of bells, and drinking of the King's health upon their knees, which methinks is a little too much. But everybody seems to be very joyful in the business.'[13] By then the court had moved to The Hague, and it was from there that Charles made his triumphal return to his kingdom, arriving at Dover on 25 May on board the *Royal Charles*, formerly the *Naseby*, one of a flotilla of New Model Navy

---

* This gave rise to one of the most famous Cromwellian quotations. Led back to Northampton Lambert was jeered by the crowds and told Ingoldsby: 'This puts me in mind of what Cromwell said to us both near this very place in the year 1650, when we, with a body of soldiers, were going down after the enemy that was marching into Scotland, the people all the while shouting and wishing us success. I said to Cromwell, "I was glad to see we had the nation on our side." He answered, "Do not trust to that; for these very persons would shout as much if you and I were going to be hanged." I now look upon myself as in a fair way to that, and begin to think Cromwell was a prophet.'

warships hastily renamed to meet the occasion. (*The Speaker*, heroine of Santa Cruz, became the *Mary*.) Among those who accompanied the king was Ann Fanshawe, whose husband Sir Richard had remained in the king's service as Treasurer for the Royalist fleet in Ireland. Ten years earlier they had been forced to flee from Galway to Spain; now they were coming home with the king:

> The king embarked at four of the clock, upon which we set sail, the shore being covered with people, and shouts from all places of a good voyage, which was seconded with many volleys of shot interchanged. So favourable was the wind, that the ships' wherries went from ship to ship to visit their friends all night long. But who can sufficiently express the joy and gallantry of that voyage, to see so many great ships, the best in the world, to hear the trumpets and all other music, to see near a hundred brave ships sail before the wind with the vast cloths and streamers, the neatness and cleanness of the ships, the strength and jollity of the mariners, the gallantry of the commanders, the vast plenty of all sorts of provisions. Above all, the glorious Majesties of the king and his two brothers were so beyond man's expectation and expression. The sea was calm, the moon shone at full, and the sun offered not a cloud to hinder his prospect of the best sight, by whose light and the merciful bounty of God he was set safely ashore at Dover, in Kent, upon the 25th of May, 1660.[14]

The king's triumphant return took him through Kent by way of Canterbury and Rochester – 'the shouting and joy expressed by all is past imagination' noted Pepys – and on 29 May he finally arrived in London, entering the city through Southwark before crossing London Bridge in the company of the Lord Mayor. Among those who witnessed the moment was the Royalist diarist John Evelyn, who 'stood in the Strand and beheld it, and blessed God':

> This day, his Majesty, Charles the Second came to London, after a sad and long exile and calamitous suffering both of the King and Church, being seventeen years. This was also his birth-day, and with a triumph of above 20,000 horse and foot, brandishing their swords, and shouting with inexpressible joy; the streets strewed

with flowers, the bells ringing, the streets hung with tapestry, fountains running with wine; the Mayor, Aldermen, and all the Companies, in their liveries, chains of gold and velvet; the windows and balconies, all set with ladies; trumpets, music and myriads of people flocking, even so far as from Rochester, so as they were seven hours in passing the city, even from two in the afternoon till nine at night.[15]

All this had been done, Evelyn noted, 'without one drop of blood shed, and by that very army which rebelled against him'. Not everyone was pleased by the turn of events – in Nottingham Lucy Hutchinson noted 'the mutability of some, and the hypocrisy of others, and the servile flattery of all' – but even she could not disguise the 'universal joy and triumph' which greeted the king's return.[16] That evening Charles received loyal addresses from both houses, the Lords being represented by the Earl of Manchester and the Commons by the Speaker. The king, soon to be the 'Merry Monarch', had finally come into his own; the republic was dead and, best of all, the revolution, such as it was, had been bloodless. As Pepys prepared to make his own way back to London he made his last entry for that momentous month of May: 'This day the month ends, I in very good health. And all the world in a merry mood because of the King's coming.' He was not alone in expressing his delight. In Edinburgh, where the conflagration had been sparked twenty-two years ago with the signing of the National Covenant,* Charles was proclaimed king at the Mercat Cross with, according to Nicoll, 'all solemnities requisite, by ringing of bells, setting out of bonfires, sounding of trumpets, roaring of cannons, beating of drums, dancing about the fires, and using all other tokens of joy for the advancement and preference of their native King to his crown and inheritance'.[17]

---

* It is fitting perhaps that the last word should be left with one of its authors, Johnston of Wariston, by then back in Edinburgh, who remained suitably acerbic and disapproving of such levity: 'At the time of the bonfires there was great riot, excess, extravagance, superfluity, naughtiness, profanity, drinking of healths; the Lord be merciful to us.' *Diary*, III, 183.

PART FIVE

RESTORATION

1660

Chapter One

REVENGE AND RESTRAINT

'Never was any king endued
With so much grace and gratitude.'

John Wilmot, Earl of Rochester,
'A Satire on King Charles II', *1697*

Charles II would not have been human had he wanted simply to forgive and forget. As a young and impressionable man he had lived through a period of revolution which had seen his father executed and his kingdoms placed under the rule of unelected swordsmen intent on preserving their own power and authority at the expense of the common good. Living in exile he had known the misery of poverty and the contempt of his fellow sovereigns; his position had been placed in jeopardy and his pride had been dented. He had aged, too, and there was a certain melancholia in his personality which others noted – Pepys thought him 'a very sober man' – as well as a good deal of circumspection in his response to the new situation. That his people were pleased to see his return was beyond doubt. The cheering crowds, the roaring cannons, the service of thanksgiving all spoke of relief and pleasure at the turn of events, but he still had to come to terms with the management of his restored monarchy.

Fortunately he was well served by the inner circle which advised him. Hyde, who had shared the perils and hardships of exile and as the leading personality of the court, became Secretary of State. The

764 of Clarendon. Ormond

following year he was ennobled as the Earl of Clarendon. Ormond became Lord Steward of the Household and would soon return to Ireland in his old office of Lord Lieutenant, the Earl of Southampton became Lord Treasurer and his nephew Anthony Ashley Cooper, a member of the former Council of State, was appointed Chancellor of the Exchequer. As for parliament, an election had been held in April, but not having the king's writ, the restored house was known as the 'Convention Parliament'; it had come into being in April and sat until December 1660, when it dissolved itself and the first true parliament of the king's reign immediately confirmed all its legislation. The Convention Parliament's most important bill was the Act of Indemnity and Oblivion, passed in June, which pardoned all the king's enemies, bar fifty named persons, restored royal and Church lands to their owners and settled an income of £1.2 million a year on the king, the money to be found from taxation and hereditary revenues. It also began the long task of winding down the army through the Act for Speedy Disbanding, and the cost to the Exchequer was put at £835,819, eight shillings and ten pence, but it was money well spent, parliament noting that 'so long as the soldiery continued, there would be a perpetual trembling in the nation, for they are inconsistent with the happiness of the Kingdom'. By the end of the year only two regiments remained in being – Monck's Regiment and the Duke of York's Life Guards, which had accompanied the king from Flanders.

The temptation to punish those who had toppled the monarchy must have been very great; at the same time Charles II was under immediate pressure to reward those who had supported his cause, notably those who had suffered as a result. Both matters would take up time and weighty consideration, but on the first point, the persecution of the leading Cromwellians, Charles was minded not to be over-zealous in exacting revenge. By the Act of Oblivion and Indemnity, hastily pushed through to prevent it becoming a political football for those Royalists who were demanding vengeance, all those who had fought in the armed forces of the Commonwealth and Protectorate were pardoned. This was a wise move, because prosecution would have been a difficult and divisive device; but for the regicides, those who had put their names to his father's execution, there could be no pity. Charles left the business of prosecution to parliament and in so doing spared himself the difficult duty of determining who should face trial and possible execution and who should be sentenced to terms of imprisonment or spared.

Of the fifty exempted by the Act, forty-one were regicides or had shown too much vindictiveness to King Charles I to expect any mercy from his son. Most stood trial and were executed during the months which followed the Restoration. Of these six were army officers, including Colonels Axtell, Hunks and Hacker, who had overseen the king's execution, but the most senior was Thomas Harrison, the Fifth Monarchist, who was the first to be executed on 13 October. The veteran of Edgehill, Marston Moor, Naseby and Worcester impressed the watching crowd by his bearing on the scaffold, his words displaying an undaunted courage: 'By God, I have leaped over a wall; by God, I have run through a troop; and by God I will go through this death, and he will make it easy for me.' Among the inquisitive bystanders was Samuel Pepys, who had been in the crowd when Charles I was beheaded at Whitehall eleven years earlier:

> I went out to Charing Cross, to see Maj-Gen Harrison hanged, drawn and quartered – which was done there – he looking as cheerful as any man could do in that condition. He was presently cut down, and his head and his heart shown to the people, at which there was great shouts of joy. It is said that he was sure to come shortly at the right hand of Christ to judge them that now had judged him. And that his wife did expect his coming again.[1]

Their deaths were horrible. Reserved for traitors, the execution was by being hanged, drawn and quartered – first hung until barely conscious, then cut down to have the genitals cut off and stuffed in the victim's mouth, followed by evisceration. Finally the corpse was butchered, the head and limbs being cut off. Hugh Peters, Cromwell's chaplain, was unmanned by the sight but found his courage when the gloating hangman asked him how the bloody knife suited him. 'Well enough,' he replied. Others executed in that way included John Cook, who had conducted the prosecution of the king, Thomas Scot, who had been one of the first to call for the execution of Charles I in 1648, 'he being the only cause of all the bloodshed through the three kingdoms', and Adrian Scrope, who had left public life after the king's execution but was damned by his assertion that the action was justified. Although there were calls for more bloodshed, the scenes at Charing Cross proved to be counter-productive, and later executions were confined to beheading or hanging. That fate awaited Sir Henry Vane the Younger, who had already been imprisoned by Cromwell but returned to parliament after his death. He put up a stout defence, and might have been pardoned but for his involvement in the moves which led to Strafford's execution twenty years earlier – it had been he who had shown Pym the notes of a Privy Council meeting which seemed to show that Strafford wanted to bring an Irish army into England. The verdict was helped by refusing the jury food and drink until it made the right decision. While Vane was not a regicide Charles was disinclined to show him mercy: 'He is too dangerous to let live if we can honestly put him out of the way.' He was beheaded on Tower Hill in June 1662, on the anniversary of Naseby and two months after the executions of John Barkstead and John Okey, two regicide army officers who had fled to the Continent at the time of the Restoration.

Barkstead, who had commanded the Tower of London in Richard Cromwell's administration, was the only one of the major-generals to face the ultimate penalty. Thomas Kelsey was also sentenced to death as a regicide in October, but his sentence was commuted to life imprisonment on St Nicholas Island in Plymouth Sound where he died five years later. George Fleetwood also faced the death sentence, despite a last-minute conversion to the Royalist cause by joining Monck, and only escaped death by arguing that he had been coerced into signing the king's death warrant. Monck's support also helped him and, after a period of imprisonment, he disappeared from public life.

Apart from Charles Howard, who was appointed to Charles II's Privy Council on account of his Royalist sympathies (later as the Earl of Carlisle he served as Governor of Jamaica), the rest of the major-generals were all arrested or fled into exile. James Berry was imprisoned at Scarborough Castle, where a fellow prisoner was George Fox; he died in 1691, having been released some years earlier. Hezekiah Haynes was arrested in November but was released eighteen months later; he died in 1693. William Packer endured a short term of imprisonment and had his Crown lands confiscated. Lambert's close associate John Desborough fled to the Netherlands, where he was accused of plotting with fellow republicans and was forced to return to England to face trial; later he was released on condition he retired from public life. He agreed and retired to live in Hackney. Tobias Bridge was governor of Dunkirk at the time of the Restoration and his support for Monck kept him in the king's employment; his subsequent career included service in Tangier and Barbados. Rowland Dawkins also escaped censure and retired to live in Wales, where he died in 1691.

The most curious fate fell on Edward Whalley and his son-in-law William Goffe. As a regicide and a close associate of Cromwell, Whalley was a prime candidate for the death sentence and he and Goffe decided to seek sanctuary in New England in the summer of 1660. Boston was their first home, but their presence attracted the interest of English agents who been dispatched to arrest them. Fortunately Whalley and Goffe enjoyed the support of the local community, and when they were forced into hiding in the countryside near New Haven they managed to avoid arrest. Both men were known locally for their piety – they both expected the imminent Second Coming – and at one point they were able to use their military skills to help the local community ward off an attack by Native Americans. Both appear to have died by 1679.[2]

For many more who had served the Commonwealth and Protectorate or had fought in the civil wars there were different degrees of mercy. Thomas Fairfax received a royal pardon, for he had opposed the execution of Charles I and his decision to support Monck had ensured the success of the Restoration; he retired from public life to breed horses and died in 1671.* The lawyer Bulstrode Whitelocke was left alone and retired to live in Wiltshire (but only after he had paid Hyde £250); his memorials provided a vivid first-hand account of the period from the outbreak of the war to the restoration of the king. Charles Fleetwood was allowed to retire to live out his life at Stoke Newington with his wife Bridget, Cromwell's daughter and Ireton's widow. His rival John Lambert was sentenced

---

* When Charles II was crowned in April 1661 Fairfax presented him with a splendid horse to ride to his coronation: its dam was the horse the general had ridden at Naseby sixteen years earlier.

to life imprisonment, first on Guernsey and then on St Nicholas Island; he lost his mind and died in 1683, the best years of his life long behind him. The man who stopped his attempted uprising earlier in the year, Richard Ingoldsby, was a regicide but his service to the Royalist cause allowed him to be exonerated. Ingoldsby's escape was also engineered by his untrue declaration that he had been forced to sign the death warrant. That excuse was in stark contrast to John Hutchinson's bold statement that he would gladly share the fate of his fellow regicides, but he was dissuaded from his ambitions to be 'a public sacrifice' by the intervention of his wife Lucy. Instead he was imprisoned at Sandown Castle, 'a lamentable ruined place' in Kent where he died in 1664, still certain that he had been right to support the parliamentary cause:

> His wife bore all her own toils joyfully enough for the love of him, but could not but be very sad at the sight of his undeserved sufferings; and he would very sweetly and kindly chide her for it, and tell her that if she were but cheerful, he should think his suffering the happiest thing that ever befell him. He would also bid her consider what reason she had to rejoice that the Lord supported him, and how much more intolerable it would have been if their Lord had suffered his spirit to have sunk or his patience to have been lost under this. One day when she was weeping, after he had said many things to comfort her, he gave her reasons why she should hope and be assured that this cause would revive, because the interest of God was so much involved in it that he was entitled to it. She told him she did not doubt but that the cause would revive. 'But,' said she, 'notwithstanding all your resolution, I know this will conquer the weakness of your constitution, and you will die in prison.' He replied, 'I think I shall not, but if I do, my blood will be so innocent I shall advance the cause more by my death, hasting the vengeance of God upon my unjust enemies, than I could do by all the actions of my life.'[3]

Sir Arthur Hesilrige was also imprisoned but died a year later in the Tower of London. Edmund Ludlow was a prime candidate for punishment, being a regicide and a republican, but he managed to escape to Switzerland, where he lived under the protection of the

Council of Bern at Vevey on Lake Geneva. Encouraged by the
accession of William of Orange in 1689 he returned to England, but
he found that he still stood accused of high treason and was forced to
go back to Vevey, where he died three years later. As for the
Cromwells, Richard lived abroad for a time, but when he returned to
England in 1680 he was left in peace and died at Cheshunt in
Buckinghamshire in 1712. His brother Henry was allowed to keep his
Irish lands and died a wealthy landowner in 1674. Their mother was
also left unmolested and died in Northamptonshire in 1665. There
was no clemency, though, for those had died before the Restoration:
the bodies of Oliver Cromwell, Henry Ireton, Thomas Pride, Robert
Blake and John Bradshaw were exhumed and placed on public display
at Westminster Hall.

Death and disgrace were not reserved just for the English and the
Welsh – the Scots also suffered. Archibald Johnston of Wariston tried
to avoid his fate by going into hiding and escaping to France, but in
1662 he was arrested and extradited. In a pitiful mental state he
begged for mercy, but Charles II was determined that this thorn in his
father's flesh should not be excused and Wariston was duly hanged.
James Guthrie, the Remonstrant minister, was also done to death, but
the most prominent Scot to be executed was the Earl of Argyll, who
had hastened south to present himself to the king and to declare his
loyalty. His protests were ignored and Charles refused to see him;
instead Argyll was imprisoned in the Tower of London before being
sent back to Edinburgh to face trial for collaborating with Cromwell.
Not even the fact that he had crowned Charles in 1651 could save
him – his treatment of Montrose precluded mercy – and as he awaited
trial in the confines of Edinburgh Castle he knew that all was lost.
'They are very miserable who have nothing but a heap of years to
prove they have lived long,' he told his son, who had been pardoned
on account of his support for the Glencairn Rising. 'There is no better
defence against the injuries of fortune and vexation than death.'[4] His
end came on 24 May 1661 at the Mercat Cross and his head was fixed
above the Tolbooth to take the place of Montrose's skull.

Before his execution Argyll had to endure the further indignity of
knowing that Montrose was undergoing ceremonial rehabilitation at
the command of the king. His remains had been disinterred and reassembled that January and amid great pomp the coffin had been

deposited in the Abbey Church of Holyrood as trumpets blew fanfares and cannons roared out a last salute to one of the greatest of the Royalist military leaders. A year later the coffin was moved to the High Kirk of St Giles in a lavish procession which included the heads of Scotland's greatest families, all dressed in solemn mourning, and led by the Lord Lyon King of Arms. It lies beneath a splendid marble effigy in repose: Charles had finally repaid his debt to one of his most unswerving supporters. For the anonymous writer in *Mercurius Caledonius* the rehabilitation of Montrose cancelled all of Scotland's debts – partly caused, he wrote smugly, by 'rebellious Confederates in England':

> It is well known to the world that since the year 1648, there was never a people enterprised such honourable and probable ways to redeem former Escapes than we did; and though it was the pleasure of providence to disappoint our designs, yet we never grudged neither at our Imprisonments, the loss of the dearest of our blood, nor devastation of our Fortunes.[5]

In fact all over the three kingdoms people were trying to cover the traces of past actions and allegiances. Extremists of any kind were most at risk, as were those who had espoused anti-monarchical politics, but there was no widespread persecution of the sectaries. George Fox, the Quaker leader, was imprisoned briefly at Scarborough, but that was not a new experience as he had spent time in confinement during the Commonwealth and Protectorate, and it was not until later in the decade that he was able to consolidate his work from his headquarters at Swarthmore Hall near Ulverstone in Cumberland. John Milton also endured a brief period of confinement, but the intercession of Andrew Marvell allowed him to be released and he used the first years of Charles II's reign to complete his *Paradise Lost*, which he had begun in 1642. He had held the post of Latin secretary right up to the Restoration and showed that he had lost none of his conviction by publishing a tract, *The Ready and Easy Way to Establish a Free Commonwealth*, which made a last-minute appeal to support the republic and to halt the swing towards the monarchy by 'the misguided and abused multitude'.

A wretched fate awaited John Bunyan: he was arrested in

November 1660 for preaching without a licence and spent the next twelve years in jail in Bedford. During that period he produced nine works, the most notable being *Grace Abounding to the Chief of Sinners*, which appeared in 1666, but he also used the time to start his greatest work, *The Pilgrim's Progress*, which was published in two parts in 1678 and 1684. As for the others, the army radicals, the Levellers and the Diggers, the men and women who had wanted to turn the world upside down, the Restoration called a halt to their activities but their dreams did not die; they lived on, albeit fitfully and hidden from view. Their revolution had failed before it had begun, nipped in the bud by Cromwell when the Levellers were levelled at Corkbush Field. There was to be no Second Coming and no New Jerusalem. The Restoration marked the end of their hopes but, as Christopher Hill reminds us, 'if we stand back to look at the beginning and the end of the revolution, if we can use such inaccurate terms about something which is always beginning and never ends . . . we can, perhaps, extend a little gratitude to all those nameless radicals who foresaw and worked for – not our modern world, but something far nobler, something yet to be achieved – the upside-down world.'[6] Hill, who died in 2003, wrote from a Marxist standpoint and offered an interpretation of the civil wars as a failed revolution in which radicals such as the Levellers anticipated the development of socialism.

For those who had stood by the king or had engineered his return there were rewards and honours, although the level of recompense was not always uniform. Monck, the son of a modest Devon squire, was made the Duke of Albemarle and remained close to the king he had returned to the throne; in later life Charles would call the old general 'uncle'. He died in 1670. Mountagu was also rewarded for his loyalty: he was created Earl of Sandwich. He continued in royal service as an admiral and as ambassador to Madrid and was drowned in 1672 when his warship the *Royal James* caught fire at the Battle of Solebay during the Third Dutch War. His cousin, the Earl of Manchester, Cromwell's general in the Eastern Association army, was appointed Lord Chamberlain and made a Knight of the Garter; he died in 1671. Another Cromwellian aristocrat who did not fall foul of his previous associations was Lord Saye and Sele, who became Lord Privy Seal, while two senior New Model Army officers, Richard Browne and Edward Massey, were knighted and became members of parliament.

Other soldiers rewarded were Sir Marmaduke Langdale, the stalwart commander of the Northern Horse, who only lived for a year to enjoy his ennoblement (he died in Germany claiming that he was too poor to attend the coronation), while the Scots General David Leslie was created Lord Newark and awarded a pension. The mercenary soldier Sir James Turner also received a reward by being appointed Sergeant-Major of the King's Foot Guards in Scotland, but he tarnished his reputation by ruthlessly putting down religious dissidents later in the decade; he died in 1685 having completed his memoirs and *Pallas Armata, Military Essays of the Ancient Grecian, Roman and Modern Arts of War*. For Sir William Waller, though, there was to be nothing. Despite having endured imprisonment for his suspected Royalist sympathies he was ignored, just as he had been by Cromwell, and he died in obscurity in 1668.

Lack of available funds circumscribed any largesse which Charles might have wanted to give those noblemen who had freely given of their fortunes for his father's cause. The Marquess of Newcastle was made a duke, but that was a poor return for his efforts in raising the Army of the North and paying to keep it in the field between 1642 and 1645. The Somerset family also received nothing for the large sums of money raised by the first Marquess of Worcester, and the Marquess of Winchester received nothing for the losses he had incurred during the ruinous siege of Basing House. Other lesser claims were also ignored. There were numerous petitions for appointments including ecclesiastical preferments, recompense for non-payment of bills, and requests for pensions, some going back to the reign of James I. All had to be tested, but the shortage of funds meant that many of the payments were niggardly and it proved impossible to reward everyone who had served Charles II or his father. There were some notable and deserved exceptions – the sister of Sir George Lisle, executed after the siege of Colchester, was rescued from poverty with a grant made from 'Royal bounty' – but between 1660 and 1667 the average spent on 'loyal and indigent' supporters was a modest £31,600 a year.[7]

Demobilising the army was the main expense on the Exchequer. The cost of maintaining the New Model Army had been a heavy burden for the Commonwealth and Protectorate and no less of a charge for the Convention Parliament. By dint of taxation some two-thirds of the arrears had been raised and paid and hundreds of soldiers flocked back into English society. At first it was feared that they would provide a locus for troublemaking, but the concern proved to be groundless. Thanks to Monck's ruthless purge of potential trouble-makers in the run-up to the Restoration most of the demobbed soldiers were simply trained men who wanted to get back to their civilian lives and occupations. The payment of arrears also helped, and within three years Pepys was able to note in conversation with his colleague Robert Blackeburne that the retired soldiers were the 'most substantial sort of people, and the soberest':

Of all the old army now, you cannot see a man begging about the street. But what? You shall see this Captain turned a shoemaker; the lieutenant, a Baker; this, a brewer; that, a haberdasher; this common soldier, a porter; and every man in his apron and frock, & c., as if they had never done anything else – whereas the [Royalists] go with their belts and swords, swearing and cursing and stealing – running into people's houses, by force oftentimes.[8]

The process nonetheless had been orderly, much to most people's surprise, but the reduction in the size of the army did not mean the complete demilitarisation of the three kingdoms. The New Model Army had disappeared but there remained garrisons in Ireland, Scotland and in the ports of Dunkirk and Mardyck (Lockhart's Brigade). All were kept in existence. Around 7500 soldiers comprised the Restoration army in Ireland, and it was officered mainly by former New Model Army officers who had gained land in the country; only later, in the following reign, would its complexion be changed as Catholics were promoted to key posts. In Scotland the size of the army was reduced dramatically, to some 2200 men consisting of two regiments of foot and a troop of horse, but the changes also allowed the formation of regiments which survive to this day. A regiment of foot guards consisting of five companies was formed in 1662, and in time (1678) it became the Scots Guards, while Sir John Hepburn's regiment, the Régiment de Douglas (The Royal Scots), was brought home briefly from France to help with internal security duties. The garrison in Dunkirk and Mardyke proved more troublesome: numbering 6600, it consisted of an amalgamation of Royalists and

New Model Army and it could have proved troublesome but for the acquisition of Tangier in 1662 following Charles II's marriage to Catherine of Braganza of Portugal. Under the settlement Britain received the North African port as well as Bombay in India, and among the forces sent to Tangier from Dunkirk were one regiment of horse (later to become the Royal Dragoons) and one of foot (later to become the Queen's Royal West Surrey Regiment). As for Dunkirk, it was sold to the French in October that same year.

Even before Charles II had dealt with the garrisons outside England he and Clarendon had decided that the king needed a personal life-guard, a small force which would owe its loyalty to the Crown – Charles had seen how his father had been weakened by the lack of a reliable force in 1641. As a result a regiment of foot guards was formed in November under the command of Colonel John Russell; known as the first foot guards, it later became the Grenadier Guards, and one of its first duties was to put down an attempted Fifth Monarchist insurrection in January 1661. Led by a wine cooper called John Venner, who believed that Christ's return was imminent, about fifty of his followers, including one woman dressed in armour, marched to Westminster Hall on 6 January 1661 to try to recover the heads of the regicides which were on public display. The militia was hard pressed to deal with the situation and in the aftermath parliament agreed to the formation of more guards regiments. In a symbolic move on 14 February 1661, Monck's regiment laid down its arms on Tower Hill and immediately took them up again to be reconstituted as the Lord General's Regiment of Foot in the service of the Crown; thus was born the regiment which lives on as the Coldstream Guards. Two regiments of horse guards were added: the Duke of York's and the Duke of Albemarle's Life Guards and the Earl of Oxford's regiment, formed largely out of Cromwell's old Life Guard of Horse, the renowned 'Lobsters' formerly commanded by Hesilrige. Later the latter regiment would become the Royal Horse Guards or the 'Blues' (from the colour of the uniform). Britain might have been demilitarised but Charles still had 7000 loyal soldiers at his disposal

---

* Later in his reign they were joined by the Scots Guards and the Royal Scots, and in 1684 by the regiments of the Tangier Garrison. They were known not as the army but as the king's 'guards and garrisons'.

and in those regiments the modern British army can trace its origins.*

The home army was the servant of the king; he was its head – its commander was Albemarle in the rank of Lord General – and it was counted as part of the king's household, hence its size was limited. Overseas Charles also had substantial forces on which he could call. A British brigade, under the command of Inchiquin, served in the Portuguese war of independence from 1662 to 1668, several regiments remained in French service, a joint Anglo-Scottish brigade was on loan to the Stadtholder of the United Provinces and, until Tangier was abandoned in 1684, its garrison was also available to the king. In addition to these regulars, by virtue of 'An Act declaring the sole right of the Militia to be in the King' he also had control of the militia through the lord lieutenants of the counties. All those soldiers provided Charles II with a military resource which his father had never enjoyed. The country might have been weary of the presence of the army but Charles and his supporters were determined that the Crown should be protected by fully equipped and fully manned security forces. The New Model Navy also remained in being, its ships were tactfully renamed and although some were laid up, naval construction was planned to resume as soon as funds permitted. The Royal Navy was a formidable force – 32 ships out of a fleet of 156 had brought the king home in May 1660 – and all the bigger warships were more powerful than any other in service in Europe. Soon it would be required to fight another two wars against the Dutch, the first in 1665–67 and then a second in 1672–74.

The armed forces' backing for the king was a powerful incentive to keep the peace but, in truth, the country was tired of both war and the experience of the republic. That much became clear at the coronation which took place on 23 April 1661 at the end of a fortnight of ceremonial designed to reinforce the majesty of the king's restoration. Over a three-day period beginning on 15 April the new Knights of the Garter had been installed at Windsor in an elaborate ceremony which harked back to medieval times, but this was merely a prelude to the greater ostentation of the crowning of the king in Westminster Abbey. It was a ceremony designed to impress, not just Charles's subjects but also the attending ambassadors. The streets were decorated with triumphal arches, Charles himself was dressed in gold and crimson velvet, the foot and horse guards were in attendance to reinforce the king's authority, and when the crown was placed on Charles's head there was a 'a great shout' before the nobility swore their oath of allegiance. Even the specially cast coronation medal pointed to new beginnings from established traditions: it showed an oak tree bursting into leaf with the motto *Iam Florescit* (Now It Flourishes). To complete the symmetry the coronation feast was held in the same Westminster Hall which had witnessed the trial of the king's father. But this time the ceremony spoke not of treason but of loyalty, as the King's Champion, Sir Edward Dymoke, appeared armed and mounted on a charger while a page read out the solemn declaration, 'That if any dare deny Charles Stewart to be the lawful King of England, here was a Champion that would fight with him.' There were no takers and the watching Samuel Pepys was left to conclude that it was 'a brave sight'. Later it rained and the fireworks display had to be postponed, but that could not put a damper on the private celebrations enjoyed by Pepys and his neighbours and thousands more unknown citizens of London:

[To] Mr [William] Bowyer's [where] a great deal of company; some I knew, others I did not. Here we stayed upon the leads and below till it was late, expecting to see the Fireworks, but they were not performed tonight: only the City had a light like a glory round about it with bonfires. To Axe Yard [Pepys' residence], in which at the further end there were three great bonfires, and a great many great gallants, men and women; and they laid hold of us, and would have us drink the King's health upon our knee, kneeling upon a faggot, which we all did, they drinking to us one after another, which we thought a strange Frolique. But these gallants continued thus a great while, and I wondered to see how the ladies did tipple. At last I sent my wife and her bedfellow to bed, and Mr Hunt [John, a neighbour] and I went in with Mr [Gilbert] Thornbury (who did give the company all their wine, he being yeoman of the wine-cellar of the King) to his house; and there . . . we drank the King's health and nothing else, till one of the gentlemen fell down stark drunk, and lay spewing. And I went to my Lord's pretty well. But no sooner a-bed with Mr Shipley [Edward, steward to the Earl of Sandwich] but my head began to hum, and I to vomit, and if ever I was foxed it was now – which I cannot say yet, because I fell asleep, and slept till morning – only, when I waked I found myself wet with my spewing. Thus did the day end with joy everywhere.

Now, after all this, I can say that besides the pleasure of the sight of these glorious things, I may now shut my eyes against any other objects, or for the future trouble myself to see things of state and show, as being sure never to see the like again in this world.[9]

For Pepys and his friends it had been a long two days of celebration to welcome back the king after an eleven-year absence. The following day he woke to ashes 'with my head in a sad taking through last night's drink', but there were compensations – the Restoration helped to make his name and his fortune. Through the patronage of his kinsman Mountagu, Pepys became Clerk of the Acts to the Navy Board in 1660 and emerged as an outstanding administrator of Charles's navy – 'the right hand of the Navy,' according to Albemarle. He remained in public life (with varying degrees of success) until the end of the reign of King James II in 1689, having enjoyed a long and prosperous career in public service. Fear of going blind forced him to close his diary on 31 May 1669, but its six volumes, all written in shorthand, produced a wonderfully vivid picture of events such as the Great Fire of London as well as intimate and frequently rueful portraits of the social and sexual mores of the day. He died in 1703, having bequeathed to the nation a solid foundation for running the Royal Navy and to posterity a lively record of his life and times.

Of the other diarists and writers of memorials whose work illuminates the period, all lived into the Restoration. Lucy Hutchinson survived her husband and completed the production of the memoirs of his life between 1664 and 1671. In so doing she produced a social document which not only charted the progress of the civil wars but also gave her response to it; and one of its many delights is the astringency she brings to her defence of her husband's role on the losing side. The Duchess of Newcastle's memoirs of her own husband might have been a spur; both women lived into the middle of the following decade (and their work was first published two centuries later). By then Robert Baillie was also dead, his last letter being written to his cousin William Spang in May 1662, and although Thomas Carlyle would castigate his fellow countryman's correspondence and journals as 'mere hasty babblements', Baillie's observations as a participator in great events provide enlightening reading. The same is true of another contemporary clerical record – Richard Baxter's autobiography. Although increasingly regarded as a moderate after 1649, when he returned to his charge in Kidderminster, Cromwell's old confederate fell foul of the Church of England after the Restoration and became a leading Dissenter, the alliance of Protestants who refused to accept the reimposition of the episcopacy and the Prayer Book after 1662. He died in 1691, having built up a reputation for a tumultuous demotic preaching style which won him many admirers.

Most of the memoirs, letters and journals were written for private circulation or personal consumption, yet this first great stirring of British autobiographical writing allowed later generations to understand more fully the contrasting emotions which lay behind the wars of the three kingdoms. In some cases the passing of the years allowed memories to be selective or recast in a better light, but there is little doubt that the turbulent nature of the times helped to ignite a period which Prince Rupert was moved to call 'this scribbling age'. They wrote from both sides of the divide, and while there is an understandable tendency to be partisan or, in the case of writers such as Wariston, extreme, the majority of the texts are remarkably even-handed and free of rancour. In telling her husband's story Lucy Hutchinson was convinced of 'the righteousness of the Parliament's cause' and saw in it the hand of God's providence, but she was still determined to be scrupulously fair: 'A naked, undressed narrative, speaking the truth of him, will deck him with more substantial glory, than all the panegyrics that the best pens could ever consecrate to the virtues of the best men.'[10]

On one matter they were agreed: Waller's 'war without an enemy' had been wasteful and the Restoration was a logical conclusion to those long years of upheaval. Order had returned but, as Clarendon told parliament in 1661, the claims of the Commonwealth died with the king's restoration; now it was the people of England's privilege 'to be represented by the greatest, and learnedest, and wealthiest and wisest persons that can be chosen out of the nation'. This was not what men like Thomas Rainsborough had fought for when he declared at the Putney Debates thirteen years earlier: 'I think that the poorest he that is in England has a life to live as the greatest he.' For the Puritans and the sectaries there were also losses, God's kingdom had not been revealed, leaving only bewilderment and disillusion. The republican experiment had also failed: the swordsmen who had seized power after killing the king had spent the next decade fighting to defend their gains and the political and constitutional achievements of the Commonwealth and Protectorate were limited. King Charles I's concessions of 1642 were upheld by the new administration and the Long Parliament's reforms were retained, but the Court of Chancery remained unreformed, as did the franchise. As time passed people looked back to the wars of the three kingdoms and its aftermath as an expensive and unnecessary anomaly, a period of confusion, destruction of property, loss of life and upheaval which had brought few gains and much misery. In the aftermath it was referred to as a 'rebellion' or less precisely as 'the troubles'; only later would it be called a 'revolution', a term which is still hotly debated by historians.[11]

But that was for the future to wrangle over. As the first year of the Restoration drew to a close and the next year of Charles II's reign began, Pepys computed his gains and losses and declared himself and the country to be in credit: 'Myself in constant good health – and in a most handsome and thriving condition. Blessed be God for it . . . As to things of State – the King settled and loved of all.'[12]

Chapter Two

THE SETTLEMENT OF THE THREE KINGDOMS

'His lazy, long, lascivious reign.'

Daniel Defoe, The True-Born Englishman, *1701*

To reinforce the idea that things had returned to normal after the Restoration, Charles's reign was back-dated to his father's funeral and all acts and ordinances passed since 1641 were removed from the statute book. Divine right was re-established – in practice by the Church, which wanted to strengthen the links with Crown which it had enjoyed since the Reformation, but in theory Charles found that his regal office was not to be imbued with the same authority that had been enjoyed by his father.

That much was made clear when the first parliament of his reign opened in May 1661. It was known as the Cavalier Parliament – many of its first members were Royalist supporters or soldiers who had fought on the side of Charles I – and it was destined to sit for eighteen years until January 1679, the longest sitting in English history. (It was dissolved in the wake of the Popish Plot, a period of anti-Catholic hysteria occasioned by a fictitious intrigue to murder Charles II and place his Catholic brother James, Duke of York, on the throne.) The administration was conservative and measured, and from the outset it was determined to ensure its own survival: while it supported the king, it had no intention of allowing him to get the upper hand as his father had done twenty years earlier. Loyal monarchists its members might have been, but they were also anxious to preserve the rights and privileges which parliament had won in the struggle with Charles I.

The two courts which stood outside common law, the Star Chamber and the Council of the North, were abolished. The Triennial Act of 1641 was upheld – this had removed from the Crown the ability to dismiss parliaments at will – and the right to arrest members of parliament, enforced so dramatically and recklessly in January 1642, was quietly removed. At the same time parliament got rid of measures which were regarded as being inimical to the security of the three kingdoms. The statute banning bishops from the House of Lords was repealed, as was the Solemn League and Covenant which committed the country to Presbyterian Church government. So unpopular was this Scottish declaration of intent that parliament ordered it to be burned in public, a move which Charles chose to ignore despite the fact that he had promised to uphold the Covenant when he was crowned King of Scots at Scone a decade earlier. In return parliament gave the Crown control of the militia and other forces and the act enabling the measure insisted that 'both or either of the houses of Parliament cannot nor ought to pretend to the same'. While this gave Charles the security of having the armed forces under his personal control, the legislation also removed one of the main reasons for the dispute between Charles I and the Long Parliament.

Religion, too, had to be addressed, and this parliament of Royalist landowners, county gentry and former soldiers was determined to go back to the old ways. It had the rightful king back on the throne and now its members wanted to return to the calmer waters of episcopalian rule. Although Charles was largely indifferent to the imposition of a state Church – he was prepared to accommodate Presbyterians provided they accepted bishops – and although the Breda agreement had promised religious toleration regulated by the Crown, the Cavalier Parliament resolved to re-establish the Church of England and to sideline nonconformists. Partly the policy was driven by a desire to return to the status quo after the years of internecine warfare and religious upheaval; partly, too, it arose from a lingering dislike of Catholicism, but the main spur was an unyielding repugnance for the Puritans. Put simply, parliament loathed all sectaries, dissenters and Protestant extremists, and the legislation re-establishing the Anglican Church along Laudian lines was correspondingly severe.

Loosely known as the Clarendon Code, after the king's first minister, who preached toleration but was vehement in his private support of Anglicanism, the measures were codified by the following pieces of legislation: the Corporation Act (1661), which excluded from public office anyone who refused to take communion in the Church of England or to swear the oath of allegiance and reject the Solemn League and Covenant; the Act of Uniformity (1662), which introduced a revised prayer book and liturgy; the Conventicle Act (1664), which forbade religious meetings of more than five people; and the Five Mile Act (1665), which barred nonconformist preachers from going within five miles of their former ministries or towns. Each act hit at the spirit of reconciliation which had underpinned the Breda agreement and, taken together, they marked the beginning of a permanent breach between the Church of England and the nonconformist faiths. As a result of the new order over 2000 Anglican clergy lost their livings and the dissenters were left as a persecuted minority subject to sporadic bouts of harassment and punishment for many years to come. Clarendon's role in the code named for him has been much debated. Although he was not the main author and was held to be more tolerant than the laws supposed, he greatly disliked religious radicalism of any kind, holding sectaries and others to be 'fanatics' unworthy of leniency.[1] As for Charles, his belief in toleration was ignored by the new parliament and a Declaration of Indulgence, an attempt by him to repeal the laws against Catholics, had to be dropped due to lack of support. Charles had Catholic sympathies, and rumours abounded that he worshipped in that faith in secret, but beyond his feeling that he had a duty to reward those Catholics who had supported his father, he realised that his interests were best preserved by sustaining the Church of England. Only on his death-bed in 1685 was he received into his mother's Church, largely, it has to be admitted, at the behest of his brother James, Duke of York.

Religious affairs also dominated the settlement in Scotland. At first the Scots believed that their Covenanted king's return was the beginning of a new golden age and that they would be rewarded for their support in making his Restoration possible. John Nicoll caught the mood at the time of Montrose's rehabilitation in 1661:

> At this time, our gentry did look with such gallant and joyful countenances, as if they had been the sons of princes; the beasts also of the field, the numbers of the fishes in the sea, and flowers of the field, did manifest God's goodness towards this kingdom; and it was the joy of this nation to behold the flower of this kingdom, which for so many years had been overclouded and now to see them upon brave horses, prancing in their accustomed places, in tilting, running of races and suchlike.[2]

However, Nicoll's vision was all fancy. The Scots were soon to discover that the Restoration settlement had been engineered solely by English politicians to suit the English people and that they would have little say in its fashioning. They were sidelined in more ways than one. Remembering the interminable sermons at Falkland Palace and the constant lecturing by Presbyterian divines, Charles had no intention of revisiting his northern kingdom – he informed his new Scottish secretary, the Earl of Lauderdale, that Presbyterianism was no religion for a gentleman – and was destined never again to wear the royal regalia which had been rescued from Dunottar Castle. He was hardly likely to listen to the appeals of the Resolutioners who had supported him in 1650 but who wanted to impose Presbyterianism on his kingdoms. To begin with, Lauderdale was minded to be in favour of a Presbyterian settlement, but when it became clear to him that Clarendon wanted to subordinate Scotland to England through the creation of a London-based Scottish Council and to reimpose episcopalianism, he bent with the wind and withdrew his earlier endorsement of the Presbyterian cause. In any case the Resolutioners' cause was already lost. Shortly after the king's Restoration they had dispatched to London the devious and self-serving figure of James Sharp,* minister of Crail in Fife, to argue their case. Supposed to act as an advocate of Presbyterian Church governance, he saw at an early

---

* Earlier, Cromwell had noted Sharp's feline character, dubbing him 'Sharp of that Ilk'. In 1679 he was murdered at Magus Muir outside St Andrews by a party of Covenanters led by John Barbour of Kinloch and David Hackston of Rathillet.

stage that the cause was hopeless and abandoned any attempt to convince the king that bishops should not be reimposed. Although he insisted later that he had fought hard to protect the Church of Scotland's interests and had put the case for a moderate episcopacy, the truth is that he had quickly fallen in with Clarendon's policies.

At the beginning of January 1661 the Scottish parliament reopened in Edinburgh with the newly appointed Earl of Middleton as commissioner, and the Estates set about the process of aligning themselves to the king. As solidly Royalist in composition and aspiration as the Cavalier Parliament, the body immediately put its support into practice with a sweeping programme of legislation which returned power to the Crown. The king was given the right to appoint privy councillors, judges and officers of state, the right to call parliaments was also ceded to him and a new oath of allegiance was instituted requiring office-holders to acknowledge Charles as the 'only Supreme Governor of this Kingdom, over all persons and all causes'. Finally, an Act Recissory was passed on 28 March annulling all legislation passed since 1633. As Rosalind Mitchison put it: 'Scotland was legally back where she had been before the Great Rebellion, as if nothing had happened.'[3] The Cromwellian union was over and Scotland was once more back at the stage where a king (James I) had been able to boast that he ruled it with his pen or, in Charles's case, with the help of powerful henchmen like Lauderdale, who was soon boasting to his master, 'Never was king so absolute as you are in poor old Scotland.'[4]

The return to the old days gave the Scottish parliament much work to do in restoring twenty-eight years of legislation; it also paved the way for the return of episcopalian Church government, albeit one which was much modified. In the summer of 1661, at a time when the Cavalier Parliament was setting about the restitution of the Church of England, Scotland moved in a similar direction. At a meeting held between the Scottish Council and English ministers including Clarendon it was agreed that an episcopalian form of Church government should be restored and that it would be superimposed on the presbyteries. There would be no return of the hated liturgy and prayer book but the General Assembly would not be allowed to convene and a new bishopric would be appointed. Those who spoke against the move included Lauderdale and the Duke of Hamilton, but it was strongly supported by Middleton and the new Chancellor, Glencairn. Sharp, too, was in favour and benefited as a result: he was appointed Archbishop of St Andrews and Primate of Scotland, a promotion which won him a deserved Judas reputation.

Robert Baillie also found himself in troubled waters. Elderly and in bad health he had spent most of the previous decade embroiled in the religious squabbles which had threatened to tear apart the Church of Scotland and he had opposed the Cromwellian occupation of Scotland. While he welcomed the Restoration, he feared, rightly, that the new order would bring the return of rule by bishops, a position he deplored, yet he had been offered the post of principal of Glasgow University, a post he had long coveted. His inclination was to refuse on the grounds of 'age and weakness', but as it was the king's wish that he accept the appointment he had no room for manoeuvre. Perhaps, too, he realised that his acceptance signified support for episcopalian rule. He was after all an early supporter of the National Covenant, and as he reminded Lauderdale on 16 June 1660, the return of the bishops would strain his loyalty not just to the king but to the great events of 1638:

Is Cromwell, the great enemy of our Covenant, so soon arisen out of his grave? Can our gracious Prince ever forget his solemn oath and subscription? He is a better man than to do it, for these about him be not very faithful servants. For myself, such as are my rooted respects, both to his person and place, that do what he will, and tolerate what he will, I purpose while I live to be his most loving and loyal subject. But believe me, if I were beside him I would tell him sadly, and with tears, oaths to the Almighty are not to be broken, and least of all by him whom the Lord has wrought at this very time a more marvellous mercy than he has done for any or all of the princes in Europe these hundred years. Bishops were the very fountain of all our mischiefs: will they ever change their nature? Will God ever bless that plant which himself never planted? It's a scorn to tell us of moderate Episcopacy, a moderate Papacy! The world knows that Bishops and Popes could never keep caveats: the Episcopal faction were never more immoderate than this day . . . Be assured, whatever surprise be for the time, this so hideous a breach to god and man can not fail to produce the wrath of God in the end. Shall all our blood and labour for that Covenant be so easily buried?[5]

Despite Baillie's fears, though, the move was accepted in Scotland, not least in the Highlands and the north-east, where episcopalianism was strong, but it was not universally popular. It was also imposed with a heavy hand. Presbyteries were prevented from meeting until the bishops had been appointed, those who opposed the move or upheld the Covenant were themselves removed from office, and there was a widespread purge in the south-west, which became once more a hotbed of radicals. Some 262 ministers were 'outed' in this way, most of them Protesters, and many of them turned to the practice of holding illegal field conventicles in the remote hills of Dumfries and Galloway. They became known as Covenanters and continued to administer to their parishioners in the old way, despite government repression. Theirs was an austere and unyielding form of religion which demanded discipline and obedience: in Burnet's memoirs the Covenanting ministers seem to have had more in common with the Old Testament prophets:

> They prayed long and with much fervour. They preached twice on Sunday and for most part once on a week day. They catechised all their people at least once a year in their communions, and they used to visit the families in their parishes oft and to pray to them and exhort them in secret. They had also frequent private meetings, where those that were of a higher dispensation than the rest met, sometimes without the minister and sometimes with him, and used to propose their cases and discourse about them and pray concerning them. And by these means the people, especially in the west, where those practices were frequenter, grew to that readiness, both in discoursing about sacred things and in praying, that it has astonished me to overhear them at these exercises; not but that they had many impertinences among them, yet it was a wonderful thing to me, and perhaps not to be paralleled anywhere, that the generality of the commons should have been able to pray extempore something for a whole hour together.[6]

Attempts were made to repress the sect and to force them to conform to episcopalian practices, but resistance was equally committed. Five years later, in November 1666, a group of 900 supporters captured Sir James Turner who was commanding the security forces in Dumfries and marched on Edinburgh. Most of them were simply deluded or religious fanatics who believed in the Second Coming, and all were badly armed. At Rullion Green in the lea of the Pentland Hills outside the Scottish capital their rebellion, such as it was, met its end in a short and bloody action against government security forces under the command of General Tam Dalyell. Fifty of their number were taken prisoner and thirty-three were executed in Edinburgh, going to their deaths in a mood of religious exaltation. Although the rising prompted Lauderdale to adopt a policy of moderation through indulgences which allowed worship under strict control, savage repression of Covenanters returned in the following two decades. Known to Scottish history as the 'Killing Times', the main target was the radical Cameronian sect, named after its leader Richard Cameron, who were quickly mythologised as godly 'martyrs' and entered the folk memory as saints fighting in the cause of liberty. In fact fewer than eighty Cameronians were illegally killed or executed in Scotland during the mid-1680s.

Bishops were also returned in Ireland, with Royalist clergy quickly being appointed in the summer of 1660, most of them on the recommendation of Ormond, who came back to Dublin as Lord Lieutenant in succession to Monck two years later. Henry Cromwell's administration did not survive the last days of Cromwellian rule, having been overthrown in December 1659, and replaced by a convention. Its key personalities were Sir Charles Coote, an Old Protestant planter who had defected to the parliamentary side after Ormond's negotiations with the Confederates, and Lord Broghill, Cromwell's old favourite, who had supported the move to make Cromwell king in 1657. Both men had combined in February 1660 to put down a last-ditch revolt in Limerick led by the regicide Sir Hardress Waller; this was the final Irish military action of the wars of the three kingdoms and it was accompanied by a rapid purge of radicals within the army. That late action aside, which secured Ireland for the king, neither man should really have been a natural ally of the Stewarts – Broghill had been close to Cromwell and Coote was a turncoat – but Charles was anxious not to upset Ireland. The two men were kept on as regional administrators – Coote of Connacht and Broghill of Munster – while Monck was appointed Lord Lieutenant. Later in the year all three, plus Sir Maurice Eustace, a former Speaker of the Irish parliament, were named as Lords Justices and in December an Irish Privy Council was formed to deal with the country's affairs.

On 8 May 1661 the Irish parliament reassembled in Dublin and immediately the lot of the Catholics and of the land loomed large on its agenda. As a result of the confiscations of the previous two decades both subjects were connected, but the position was complicated by Charles's desire to be even-handed – in November 1660 he had issued a declaration confirming the new owners of confiscated land but demanding the return of Church lands as well as the properties of families who had not taken part in the rebellion of the 1640s. Although principled, the scheme proved difficult to operate, not least because Charles was in the habit of unilaterally restoring lands to Catholics who had supported him in exile – men such as Taaffe, who was given back his lands at Clancarty and provided with the earldom of Carlingford. A compromise was reached in the Act of Settlement, passed the following year, which allowed dispossessed landowners to appeal to a court of claims, but it failed to achieve much. Over 800 cases were heard – successful applicants had to prove that they were innocent of participation in the rebellion or had served the king during his exile – and of that number 707 were found to be innocent. As 566 were Catholic, and as there were many more cases to be heard, the mainly Protestant parliament took fright, fearing a Catholic resurgence, and the hearings ended in August 1663. A subsequent Act of Explanation required landowners who had benefited from the Cromwellian land settlement to surrender one-third of their holdings, but Catholics were still the losers – their holdings amounted to only 20 per cent of Irish land, compared to 59 per cent in 1641.[7] Dislike of the land issue was hardened by the discovery of a plot by disaffected Protestants to seize Dublin Castle in the spring of 1663; as a result eight members of parliament were arrested and one of their number, Colonel Alexander Jephson, was executed. Ireland was still an unquiet place.

Religion was the main stumbling block. The Irish parliament was at a loss to know how to deal with Catholics, many of whom expected to be rewarded for supporting Charles and to have their lands restored. Protestant landowners feared a reprise of 1641 and the release of a letter in December 1661 hinting at a new uprising led to a flurry of arrests of priests in and around Dublin. The scare also prompted the creation of the Irish Remonstrance, a declaration of loyalty to the king supported by Taaffe and Inchiquin and other Old English Catholic landowners and by some clergy who signed it to remind Charles of their loyalty and to secure their own position. As a result there were concessions, including the release of clergy and the relaxation of laws against the mass, but there were checks and balances. Ormond was determined to impose this 'loyal formulary of Irish Remonstrance' as a means of keeping Catholics in check and rewarded those who signed it. Those who refused he harassed, and the resulting split in Catholic opinion was as deep as any experienced during the years of the Confederation of Kilkenny.

By this time Charles's honeymoon was all but over in all three of his kingdoms, and 1663 was to be the beginning of the first low watermark in his relationship with his subjects. Pepys noted a diminution of interest in the holiday kept for the king's Restoration and birthday (29 May) and, within the next two years, London was to suffer two disasters in the shape of the Great Plague of 1665, which carried off 68,000 lives, and the Great Fire of September 1666, which destroyed 80 per cent of the capital. Dissatisfaction with the king's rule was fuelled by the retailing of colourful accounts of scandalous behaviour at Charles's court – Pepys was told that the king spent too much time 'employing his lips and his prick about the Court and has no other employment'. The sober king of 1660 had given way to a far merrier monarch who encouraged licence in his entourage and saw no reason to restrict his own appetites. Life at court was one long round of pleasure – 'more resembling a luxurious and abandoned rout than a Christian court' according to John Evelyn – and debauchery was not frowned upon.

Shortly after returning to England Charles had embarked on a passionate love affair with Barbara Villiers, the wife of Roger Palmer, a young Royalist squire who had been obliged to condone the unwelcome intrusion in his marriage. In return Palmer was created Earl of Castlemaine, but his wife's open relationship with the king, by whom she was to have five children, was the cause of a good deal of hostile gossip. Even after Charles had married Catherine of Braganza he continued to flaunt the adulterous affair, and his new wife was forced to accept Lady Castlemaine into her household. (Other royal mistresses included Louise de Kéroualle, Moll Davis, Winifred Wells and, famously, Nell Gwyn.) All this might not have mattered – Charles had already fathered a love-child while in exile whom he ennobled as the Duke of Monmouth – but in the summer of 1663 he became enamoured of a new favourite whom he wanted to make his mistress. This was Frances Stuart, a young Scottish beauty who aroused a number of conflicting emotions. Some thought her disingenuous, others believed her to be driven by ambition. Even Pepys, no saint, was scandalised when he heard the news from the distinguished naval surgeon James Pearce, and not just because Lady Castlemaine was his favourite ('though I know well enough she is a whore'):

> He told me how loose the Court is, nobody looking after business but every man his lust and gain; and how the King is now become besotted upon Mrs Steward, [sic] that he gets into corners and will be with her half an hour together, kissing her to the observation of all the world; and now she stays by herself and expects it, as my Lady Castlemaine used to do; to whom the King, he says, is still kind, so as now and then he goes to have a chat with her as he believes, but with no such fondness as he used to. But yet it is thought that this new wench is so subtle, that she lets him not do anything more than is safe to her.[8]

The température was heightened by the fact that Catherine of Braganza had failed to conceive and the marriage remained childless. This caused numerous problems. Lady Castlemaine did not restrict her favours to the king – among her other lovers was the dramatist William Wycherley – there was the worrying presence of the royal bastards, and the next-in-line, brother James, was also promiscuous and unsettled in his private life. In September 1660 James had entered into a secret marriage with Anne Hyde, the plain but spirited daughter of the Earl of Clarendon, having made her pregnant. In vain did he try to wriggle out of the match – Charles refused to allow parliament to annul the marriage. Although their son died the couple went on to have two daughters, Mary and Anne, both of whom were destined to become queens of Britain in their own right following the

'Glorious Revolution' of 1688–89. Catherine's failure to provide a legal heir would have unforeseen consequences – in 1668 she produced a first child, but it was still-born, as was another a year later.

There was another side to the court's licentiousness. With the return of the royal household there was renewed patronage of the arts, and although Charles was no aesthete he was intellectually curious. In his early years he encouraged the creation of the Royal Society, and he retained a lifelong interest in the sciences, mathematics and navigation; while this decreased later in his life, the Restoration period can lay claim to being a time of advancement in the arts and sciences. His court, too, was a lively place, and not just on account of its permissiveness. Perhaps because they were the most boisterous the most influential were the so-called 'Wits', a group of high-spirited younger courtiers who included the rake-hell poet John Wilmot, Earl of Rochester. The theatre was their special delight and they encouraged playwrights such as Wycherley, John Dryden, George Etherege and others. Restoration comedy, as it came to be known, was witty, bawdy, frequently obscene, and the plots were convoluted and reflected the permissive manners of the day. Not unnaturally they came under public attack for corrupting morals, and for most upright citizens theatres became places of ill repute. Equally unsurprisingly, the plays were popular. After seeing Nell Gwyn's performance in Dryden's *The Maiden Queen* in March 1667 Pepys was moved to note: 'mightily commended for the regularity of it and the strain and wit; and the truth is, there is a comical part done by Nell, which is Florimell, that I can hope never to see the like done again by man or woman.'[9]

Nell Gwyn's arrival at court was the cause of a good deal of public distaste. Reviled as a common actress, she had been set up in a house in Pall Mall and bore Charles two children, but her shrillness and avarice made her many enemies – the Earl of Arlington, who succeeded Clarendon, called her a 'lewd and bouncing orange girl', a reference to her earlier employment selling refreshments in the theatre. Unlike Charles's aristocratic mistresses, who knew and valued their place in society, Nell Gwyn was loud and cared little about discretion, one of her most famous utterances coming when a crowd mistook her for Louise de Kéroualle and began to taunt her on account of her Catholicism. 'Good people, be civil,' responded Nell,

'I am the Protestant whore!' Stories like that add to a perception that the early years of Charles's reign were a time of unadulterated pleasure and that the Restoration was one long sigh of relief after the dark night of Cromwell's rule. It was almost as if the country wanted to forget a period which seemed to be an aberration or a nightmare and was now minded to tolerate its merry monarch's excesses, almost as if they were a much-needed antidote to puritanical restraint. There is some truth to the conceit. Charles was a passionate man who gave full rein to his hedonistic side and encouraged enjoyment in those around him, but there was more to his twenty-five-year-long reign than a succession of pleasures patiently borne by his tolerant subjects.

It is true that his reign got off to the best of all possible starts because England was tired of conflict and the rule of the swordsmen, and wanted to return to the older certainties of settled rule. Charles was also reasonably popular, not just among his inner circle but also with a wider public. He enjoyed company and being no mean wit himself, he relished discourse, preferring the spoken to the written word. Coupled with his known physical courage and traditional love of field sports this made him an attractive monarch, endowed with no little charm and capable of using it to good advantage. As a ruler, though, the results were less promising, largely due to his insistence on pursuing an unpopular and unsuccessful foreign policy. His position was weakened by the failure of two wars against the Dutch and by entering into a secret treaty with the French in May 1670. Its intention was to collaborate with Charles's cousin, Louis XIV, in a new campaign against the Dutch, but the deal was known only to an inner circle. Charles also signed confidential clauses promising to re-establish Catholicism in return for French funds and support.

By then Clarendon had gone. He was made the scapegoat for the failure of the Dutch war in 1667 when the Medway had been attacked and the Royal Navy humbled as Dutch ships made free with the Kentish anchorage. Facing impeachment for treason – the charge was made by Arlington, a new favourite and shortly to replace him as Chancellor* – Clarendon went into exile in France, where he used his

---

* Henry Bennet, Earl of Arlington (1672) was an established Royalist courtier and Charles II's ambassador to Spain when in exile. At the Restoration he became Keeper of the Privy Purse and led the opposition to Clarendon.

time to write his great *History of the Rebellion and Civil Wars.* He died seven years later, in 1674. New men and new faces appeared in the administration – the Duke of Buckingham, son of Charles I's favourite, Anthony Ashley Cooper, soon to be Earl of Shaftesbury; and Thomas Clifford, the pro-Catholic Lord Treasurer. Gradually the links with the civil wars were being eased as a younger generation came to the fore, most notably the grouping which gave their initials to the Cabal, Charles' inner cabinet of advisers – Clifford, Arlington, Buckingham, Ashley and Lauderdale. They steered Charles through the greatest threat to this throne, the Popish Plot and Exclusion crisis of 1679 to 1681 when the king dismissed three parliaments in rapid succession after each one had introduced legislation to bar the Catholic James, Duke of York, from the succession. During the squabble between king and parliament there were uneasy echoes of Charles I's reign and the rift opened up serious divisions in English political life. The most dangerous instance was the Rye House Plot of 1683, a badly planned attempt to kidnap the king at the Newmarket home of Richard Rumbold, a former parliamentary soldier. Associated with it were Monmouth (by then an enemy of his father), Essex, Algernon Sidney and a mixter-maxter gang of criminals, radicals and malcontents, but it went off at half-cock when a fire at Newmarket made the royal party leave the house before the conspirators were ready to act.

Two years later Charles II died, struck down by a painful kidney disease which killed him at the beginning of February 1685, his death being as much due to the illness as to the barbaric methods used by the doctors. He died having been received into the Catholic Church by Father John Huddleston, who had helped him escape in the aftermath of Worcester and who had gone on to serve Queen Catherine, the conversion being carried out simply and secretly on the last night of his life. The news of the king's death was greeted with great sadness, not just in the immediate court but as it spread out in waves of grief also by the wider public. Charles had brought peace to a country racked by divisions and bitter memories of an internecine war; while he had many imperfections these were not wholly vicious and he possessed many human virtues which were loved or admired in varying degrees of intensity. During the long years of exile – an exhausting and frequently depressing period – he had shown resilience and courage. He was loyal to those who served him, rewarded those who merited it and frequently refused to exact extreme punishments from those who turned against him.

Not that he was virtue personified. In his public dealings he was inclined to sloth and prevarication, his mind wandered in political discourse and he was much given to pursuing personal policies without informing his ministers. And like any absolute ruler he was possessed by caprice and megalomania, at times demanding that his will had to obeyed whatever the consequences, as in his acceptance of the French subsidies for the war against the Dutch. His flirtation with Catholicism and his eventual conversion also leaves a questionmark over his attitudes to the religious tensions which existed in each of his three kingdoms throughout his reign. He was certainly attracted to the religion, he counted Catholics among his advisers, notably Arlington, and was prepared to enter into a détente with Louis XIV, the persecutor of the Huguenots. He also promised his French cousin that he would return at some future date to the old faith, but that was realpolitik. Charles was driven to accept subsidies and to make a worthless pledge by the need to overcome perennial money problems and to prosecute a badly run war against the Dutch.

On the other hand, he bent with parliament's wishes when he realised the unpopularity of his proposals to bring Catholics back into the fold and he was not slow to repeal the Declaration of Indulgence, restoring rights to Catholics and nonconformists alike, when it suited him. True, he was received into the Catholic Church on his deathbed, but that was largely at his brother's bidding and, in any case, a person's actions at that time of extremity are not always subject to rational thought. None of this makes him a closet Catholic as many have suggested; rather, while not embracing the religion during his lifetime, he seems to have maintained a healthy respect for it, rewarding those Catholics who had helped his father and, whenever possible, trying to encourage acceptance and toleration. His watchword on religion was quite simple: as long as Catholics and others not of the Church of England accepted his authority then he was prepared to live and let live. Those who refused or set themselves up against him could only expect retaliation – his reign saw the savage repression of the Covenanters in Scotland and the imprisonment of hundreds of Quakers in England.

A similar belief guided his attitude to his advisers and to parliament. Determined to reassert the monarchy and the Stewart succession, he had to find an arrangement with those close to him, first with Clarendon, whom he grew to detest, tiring of his avuncular style, and then with the Cabal, which shared with him the guilty secret of the treaty with France. Charles's final years were dominated by an increasingly combative political arena in which it was impossible to find any consensus on the religious issue. Following the dissolution of the Cavalier Parliament in February 1679 and the moves to exclude James from the throne, England was plunged into a series of crises which recalled the attainder of Strafford and it was a measure of Charles's statesmanship that he was able to resolve the crisis without the country falling again into civil war. This period also saw the beginnings of party political wrangling over the succession: the Whigs, led by Anthony Ashley Cooper, now Earl of Shaftesbury, supported exclusion of Catholics from the succession, notably James, while the Tories were in favour of a hereditary monarchy, although not always ready to include Catholics and nonconformists. During the debate on the Exclusion Bill between 1679 and 1681 Charles dissolved parliament four times, but even with tempers running as high as they had done forty years earlier there was no descent into warfare.

One reason was the fear of revisiting the horrors of the conflict between the Crown and parliament: none of the adversaries had the stomach for going down that particular road. Another was the king's diplomacy and willingness to make concessions: at the height of the Exclusion crisis he persuaded James to go into temporary exile in the Netherlands. Nonetheless for all the successes of his reign and for all that he settled his three kingdoms – the position being helped by having strong men in Scotland (Lauderdale) and Ireland (Ormond) to keep both countries in order – the unresolved matter of the succession clouded his last years.

As it turned out, James II's reign got off to a reasonably happy beginning; his predominantly Royalist Tory parliament voted a generous financial settlement and on his succession the new monarch made it clear that he had no interest in arbitrary power, pointing to his service as Lord High Admiral as evidence of his determination to preserve the liberties of his kingdoms. Scotland, too, was minded to be generous – they had had experience of James in 1681 after Charles sent him to Edinburgh as commissioner to parliament – and the exclusionists were in a minority. Not even a revolt in the opening months of his reign could unsettle him or disrupt the calm which greeted his reign. Led in England by Charles's bastard son Monmouth and in Scotland by the Earl of Argyll, the uprising was quickly and ruthlessly put down. Far from detracting from James's popularity it only added to it.

But in that challenge and in the Crown's response to it lay the seeds of the new king's downfall. In the aftermath of Monmouth's rebellion supporters were punished mercilessly by Lord Chief Justice Jeffreys, whose 'Bloody Assizes' passed into folk memory as hundreds of West Country peasants were sent to the gallows. The Scots were equally brutal: Argyll was guillotined and his supporters were shipped out to Barbados. Inevitably there was a reaction – Jeffreys's persecution rekindled memories of Queen Mary I's mass burnings of Protestants in the 1550s – and those who already disliked the idea of a Catholic on the throne began to look to the king's Protestant nephew and son-in-law, William of Orange, Stadtholder of the Netherlands and the husband of Mary, James's daughter by Anne Hyde. At first this opposition was muted but its aims were helped by James's own intemperate policies to obtain emancipation for Catholics. Just as Charles I had failed to understand that there were limits to the royal prerogative and to his subjects' willingness to tolerate unpopular legislation, so too did his second son push ahead with policies that quickly attracted dissatisfaction and general loathing.

After the Monmouth uprising James demanded a standing army to replace the militias, which he held to be useless. Furthermore he insisted that he meant to retain officers who could not conform to the regulations of the Test Acts of 1673 and 1678, an earlier measure designed to exclude Catholics from public life. This was followed by a reckless promotion of Catholic allies – including the Earl of Tyrconnell as Lord Lieutenant in Ireland, Jeffreys as Lord Chancellor, and the ambitious Earl of Sunderland as joint secretary of state. Slowly, an inner circle of Catholic advisers ring-fenced the king and England became increasingly Catholic in complexion. A papal nuncio was received, new friaries and monasteries were opened in London, a Jesuit school appeared at the Savoy, the army welcomed Catholic chaplains and James began taking soundings among Justices of the Peace and deputy lieutenants of the counties about repealing the Test Act. A first Declaration of Indulgence ending laws against Catholics was passed in April 1687 (in Scotland the legislation appeared as Letters of Indulgence) and a second in May the following year. Similar steps were taken in Ireland to unstitch the Protestant ascendancy: Catholics were granted key political and legal appointments and the Irish parliament threatened to pass legislation to reverse the Cromwellian land settlement. To the watching Irish Protestants the situation seemed ripe for a Catholic takeover. James was now on the same kind of collision course as his father had been when he defied parliament in 1642.

This time the flashpoint was provided by the Church. In May James ordered the second Declaration of Indulgence to be read in all churches; six bishops refused and were put on trial for seditious libel, together with the archbishop of Canterbury. (They were acquitted amid great public jubilation at the end of June.) With the king and the Church in direct confrontation, a group of conspirators made contact with William of Orange and invited him to intervene to save parliament and religion, 'if the circumstances stand so with your Highness that you believe that you can get here time enough, in a condition to give assistance this year'. This was the message James's son-in-law had been waiting for, and he immediately began raising an invasion force. William's decision was prompted by one further event – the birth of a son and heir, James Edward Stewart, to his father-in-law and his second wife Mary of Modena. It was inconceivable that the new prince would not be raised in the Catholic faith.

James attempted to make concessions, but it was too late and he knew it. Following the bishops' acquittal James had been surprised to see his soldiers cheering and was equally astonished when an officer told him not to concern himself. 'Do you call that nothing?' he asked. Things were falling apart, and when William landed at Torbay on 5 November 1688 support began drifting away from the Crown towards the invading saviour. The magnates who had invited William began seizing the key cities, two senior army commanders, the Duke of Grafton and Colonel John Churchill, turned coat and, with no army to defend him, James was left with no option but to escape to France.

Even that proved difficult. The fishermen taking him uncovered his identity and brought him back and it was not until the year's end that he was allowed to leave openly through the port of Rochester. The last Stewart king had departed and the dynasty finally ended with the reign of his daughter, Anne, between 1702 and 1714.

With French help James made an attempt to reclaim his crown through Ireland in 1689 but was heavily defeated the following year at the Battle of the Boyne while his son and grandson made equally fruitless efforts to invade Britain through Scotland in 1715 and 1745. James II's last hopes were effectively crushed on 12 July 1691 when his forces, under the command of the Marquis de Saint-Ruth, were destroyed in Ireland at the Battle of Aughrim.

The end of the Stewarts and the arrival of the Protestant house of Orange finally settled the relationship between the monarch, parliament and the people, and in that sense the arrival of William and Mary put a final gloss on the arrangements which followed the demise of the Commonwealth and Protectorate. The new settlement was enshrined in the Declaration of Rights. This was presented to William and Mary on 13 February 1689 together with the offer of the crown. This stated that parliaments must be held regularly, that elections must be free, and its debates free and not questioned in any place other than parliament, that only parliament could give consent to statutes and levy taxation, and that 'raising and keeping a standing army within the kingdom in time of peace unless it be with consent of parliament is illegal'. The declaration also limited the succession to the heirs of William and Mary.

The wheel had come full circle. Just as had happened in 1638 when the English parliament had asked the Scots to intervene to help bring Charles I under control, so too had a group of English magnates looked outside their country, to the Netherlands, for a means of protecting parliament and the Protestant ascendancy. This time, however, there was no bloodshed and the event became known to English history as the 'Glorious Revolution'. Only in Scotland and Ireland was there violence: in July 1689 a pro-James or Jacobite Highland force led by John Graham of Claverhouse, Viscount Dundee, was defeated by a government army under General Hugh Mackay of Scourie at Killiecrankie in Perthshire, and the following year Ireland was once more the theatre of James's unsuccessful attempt to win back his throne, the Cogadh an Dá Rí, or War of the Two Kings. Ahead lay an unsettled history for both Celtic kingdoms. Scotland's economy was poor, its trade was limited by the Navigation Acts and punitive taxes on exports, and by the time of the reign of Queen Anne, which began in 1702, union with England was inevitable if the country was to survive. Although the move was unpopular in Scotland a Treaty of Union was pushed through in May 1707 against a background of political chicanery and opportunism. For Ireland, the succession of the House of Orange reinforced the Protestant ascendancy, and savage penal laws were enacted against Catholics, turning them into second-class citizens. James II had given the Protestants a fright and they were determined to protect what they held: it would take many generations for the religious apartheid to decrease in intensity; indeed it was not until 1829 that Catholic emancipation became a reality with the passing of the final Catholic Relief Act.

And yet, despite the killing and the continuing bad blood, which was a reflection of the greater violence perpetrated in the Celtic regions during the wars of the three kingdoms, the settlement of 1689 was not altogether inglorious. (In Edmund Burke's telling phrase it was a 'a revolution not made but prevented'.) It produced a solution which had evaded Crown and parliament fifty years earlier and which had plunged the British Isles into conflict, and it placed executive authority in the hands of the king's ministers, who in turn depended on the support of the House of Commons which could never again be ignored. In that sense at least the settlement was a fulfilment of the hopes which had sent Cromwell and others to war in the reign of Charles I: 'I profess I could never satisfy myself of the justness of this war but from the authority of the Parliament to maintain itself in its rights,' Cromwell had told his brother-in-law Valentine Walton in 1644, 'and in this cause I hope to approve myself an honest man and single-hearted.'

Chapter Three

THE CIVIL WARS AND MODERN MEMORY

'The Cavaliers (Wrong but Wromantic) and the Roundheads (Right but Repulsive).'

W.C. Sellar and R.J. Yeatman, 1066 and All That, 1930

In 1700 Richard Gough started writing down everything that he could bring to mind about his native village of Myddle, a small and not untypical English settlement north of Shrewsbury, not far from the Welsh border. The population of Myddle was around 450; the economy was dominated by agriculture, mainly the cultivation of cattle; the people were neither better nor worse than their neighbours, neither richer nor poorer than others in the district, but their lives had been circumscribed by the area and the events of the past hundred or so years. Gough was aged sixty-six at the time and he drew not only on his own memories but also on the stories that had been handed down to him and which he was anxious to record. Not all of the tales were edifying. There was a good deal of casual violence and heavy drinking, the two vices often arriving hand-in-hand, and the lives of many of the villagers were frequently venal and self-serving. What makes the story of Myddle so memorable is its sheer humanity: here is life as experienced by ordinary people laid bare in a state of heightened self-awareness. Banal in places, touching in others, the narrative is at once disarmingly simple and yet revealingly complex.

The people of Myddle lived pretty much for themselves and the immediate area. Outside their environs the world of far-off England was glimpsed but dimly, travellers arrived and departed, villagers left, some never to return, and great events were few and far between. Except, of course, there was the struggle between the king and his parliament: among the deepest memories recorded by Richard Gough were those of the fighting between 1642 and 1651, and for them he devoted a section entitled 'Some accidents which happened in the Parish of Myddle in the Time of the Wars':

King Charles set up his standard at Nottingham, AD 1642, and because few there resorted to him, he removed thence to Shrewsbury about the latter end of summer 1642, in hopes that this country and Wales would soon furnish him with an army, and he was not disappointed in his expectation, for multitudes came to him daily. And out of these three towns, Myddle, Marton and Newton, there went no less than twenty men, of which number thirteen were killed in the wars. (vizt.)

First, Thomas Formeston, of Marton, a very hopeful young man, but at what place he was killed I cannot say.

Secondly, Nathaniel, the son of John Owen of Myddle, the father was hanged before the wars, for he was a Catiline to his own country.* His common practice was to come by night with a party of horses to some neighbour's house and break open the doors, take what they pleased, and if the man of the house was found, they carried him to prison, from whence he could not be released without a ransom in money; so that no man here about was safe from him in his bed; and many did forsake their own houses. This Nat. Owen was mortally wounded by some of his own party in an alehouse quarrel, near Bridgenorth [sic], and was carried in a cart to Bridgenorth to be healed, but in the mean time the parliamentary party laid siege to Bridgenorth, and the garrison soldiers within the town set the town on fire, and fled into the

* The Catiline Conspiracy of 62 BC: an attempt to gain political power by Lucius Sergius Catilina, who conspired to plunder the Roman treasury and destroy Rome as part of a political revolution. The plot was uncovered by the consul Cicero, whose Orations led to the suppression of the revolt and to Catiline's death in battle.

castle, in which fire, this Owen (being unable to help himself), was burnt to death.

Thirdly, Richard Chaloner of Myddle, bastard son of Richard Chaloner, brother of Allen Chaloner, blacksmith. This bastard was partly maintained by the parish, and being a big lad, went to Shrewsbury, and was there listed, and went to Edgehill fight (which was October 23rd, 1642), and was never heard of afterwards in this country.

Fourthly, Reece Vaughan, he was brother to William Vaughan a weaver in Myddle, and brother to Margaret the wife of Francis Cleaton. He was killed at Hopton Castle in this county, where the garrison soldiers refusing fair quarter, when they might have had it, were afterward cut in pieces when the castle was taken by storm.

Fifthly, John Arthurs, a servant of my father's who was killed at the same castle.

Sixthly, Thomas Hayward, brother to Joseph Hayward the innkeeper then in Myddle was killed in the wars, but I cannot say where.

Seventhly, Thomas Taylor, son of Henry Taylor of Myddle, was killed, I think at Oswestry.

Eighthly and ninethly, William Preece of the cave (who was commonly called Scogan of the Goblin Hole) went for a soldier in the king's service and three of his sons (i.e.) Francis, Edward and William, two of them viz Francis and William were killed at High Ercall. The old man died in his bed, and Edward was hanged for stealing horses.

Tenthly and eleventhly, Richard Jukes and Thomas Jukes, sons of Roger Jukes, sometime innkeeper in Myddle.

Twelfthly, John Benion, a tailor, who lived in Newton in the house where Andrew Paine lives.

Thirteenthly, an idle fellow, who was a tailor and went from place to place to work in this parish, but had no habitation. These four last named went for soldiers, when the king was at Shrewsbury, and were heard of no more, so that it was supposed that they all died in the wars. And if so many died out of these towns, we may reasonably guess that many thousands died in England in that war.

There were but few that went out of this parish to serve the parliament, and of them, there was none killed (as I know of) nor wounded except John Mould of Myddle Wood. He was a pretty little fellow, and a stout adventurous soldier. He was shot through the leg with a musket bullet, which broke the master bone of his leg and slew his horse under him. His leg was healed but was very crooked as long as he lived.[1]

Myddle was not published until 1834, yet it is not fanciful to believe that the village's experience was not uncommon and that what Gough recorded would have been repeated elsewhere in any part of the three kingdoms which had been visited by the fighting. By the time of its publication the people of Britain looked back on the English Civil War, as it was always known, as an unnecessary and unwelcome period of religious and political disruption which had resulted in the execution of a king and the imposition of a military dictatorship. At the Restoration the Stewarts had been given a second chance, but it had taken the revolution settlement of 1688–89 to curb the dynasty and its propensity for non-parliamentary rule. For many people the French revolution of the late eighteenth century had been a good example of what Britain had been lucky to avoid in 1649. In that sense the earlier fighting between king and parliament had been an aberration, the king had been wilful and foolish and those who opposed him had been equally irresponsible to kill him unlawfully and then plunge the country into the chaos of rule by unelected swordsmen.

Around the time that Gough started his composition about everyday life in Myddle, the first history of the conflict was about to be published. Written by Clarendon over the long period that he shared his king's exile – he began writing in the Scilly Isles in March 1646 – it was printed from a transcript under the direction of his son and published between 1702 and 1704 under the title *The True Historical Narrative of the Rebellion and Civil Wars in England*. When Clarendon was forced to flee England in 1667 he had left behind his many manuscripts, including the sections written twenty years earlier, and at that stage he regarded the work as a private vindication of his own life and career set against the main events he had witnessed. Four years later one of his sons, Laurence, later first Earl of Rochester, travelled to Montpellier bringing with him the manuscripts. It was at that stage that Clarendon began the massive task of editing and rewriting which resulted in the first account of a confrontation which he described as being both a civil war and a rebellion. In his own words in his preface it was the best time to attempt the task: he had learned more, knew himself and other men much better, and served God and his country with more devotion, and he hoped more effectually, than in all his life:

> As I may not be thought altogether an incompetent person for this communication, having been present as a member of Parliament in those councils before and till the breaking out of the Rebellion, and having since had the honour to be near two great kings in some trust, so I shall perform the same with all faithfulness and ingenuity, with an equal observation of the faults and infirmities of both sides, with their defects and oversights in pursuing their own ends; and shall not otherwise mention small and light occurrences than as they have been introductions to matters of the greatest moment; nor speak of persons otherwise than as the mention of their virtues or vices is essential to the work in hand: in which as I shall have the fate to be suspected rather for malice to many than of flattery to any, so I shall, in truth, preserve myself from the least sharpness that may proceed from private provocation or a more public indignation; in the whole observing the rules that a man should, who deserves to be believed.[2]

In many respects it is an uncertain history. For all that the narrative flows easily enough and that Clarendon's own voice and thinking informs everything that he wrote, it is not always accurate and in some episodes it is alarmingly prolix. Partly the fault lies in the nature of the composition. The history was written over a long period and in circumstances which were not always suitable for measured thought and objective analysis. For two of those years in exile Clarendon acted as Charles's ambassador in Madrid, and the work was completed when he had fallen from grace and was forced to leave England for ever, friendless and bereft of his monarch's support. Clarendon had shared many of the dangers and discomforts of the war itself and had been Charles II's constant companion during a long and daunting exile, and that knowledge must have weighed heavily on him as he began writing his other great work *The Life of Edward, Earl of*

Clarendon. Partly, too, the history was written as the author's own 'lest we forget' record, in the hope that it would shed light on a cataclysmic event 'when the passion, rage and fury of the time shall be forgotten'. Nonetheless, it is enthralling first-hand-account history, made memorable by Clarendon's ability to encompass the events of the war and to make them comprehensible and also by his capacity to breathe life into the main protagonists, many of whom owe their historical permanence to Clarendon's powers of observation.* Both the *Life* and the *History* contain elaborate portraits of the men and women he had known during his long and eventful life. Some he had respected even though they had not belonged to the Royalist camp, Blake being a good example; others he had despised, not least the regicides Bradshaw and Harrison, but all spring easily to life in his huge gallery of characters. Among the most enduring is the account of his close friend Lucius Cary, Viscount Falkland, the 'cavalier sans rapproche' who was transmogrified in death into everything that Clarendon believed to be fine and noble about the Royalist cause:

> In this unhappy battle [Newbury] was slain the lord viscount Falkland; a person of such prodigious parts of learning and knowledge, of that inimitable sweetness and delight in conversation, of so flowing and obliging a humanity and goodness to mankind, and of that primitive simplicity and integrity of life, that if there were no other brand upon this odious and accursed civil war, than that single loss, it must be most infamous, and execrable to all posterity.[3]

On the Stewarts themselves Clarendon was as just as a state servant in their employment could be. His reading of Charles I is sympathetic but he was not without insight into the king's personal foibles, his tendency to follow the last advice given to him, his wilfulness, his blindness to public opinion and his unwillingness to surrender the royal prerogative. Not surprisingly, Charles II is given a more critical treatment, and Clarendon would not have been the man he was had

---

* Wit too is present. Of Sir John Coke, a secretary of state to Charles I, Clarendon wrote that his 'cardinal perfection was industry, and his most eminent infirmity covetousness'.

he not taken the opportunity to give a good (but long-winded) account of his own downfall. He was also critical of divine right and had harsh words to say about Laud and the encroachment of the episcopacy in lay affairs. For him religion was a private matter, and as for the position of the Church of England, it should have been beyond politics and its reform external to the body politic. As long as the Church went about its business quietly and without challenging the accepted order, it was 'constituted for the splendour and security of the Crown'. In Clarendon's *History* religion was not deemed to be a prime factor in causing the war, although he underestimated the strength of feeling caused by the Scottish Presbyterians and their commitment to the National Covenant, which provided a trigger well before the crisis developed in England and Ireland in 1641. For him the deciding factor was the king's peremptory decision to arrest the five members, because it alienated many moderates and made a confrontation with parliament inevitable.

Clarendon also saw the conflict in terms of a social and economic divide which cut across British life, or as Christopher Hill put it, he 'makes no bones about describing the line-up in the Civil War as a class division'.[4] The Royalist party was composed mainly of people of 'prime quality', they have good lineages, own inherited property and, in short, are 'persons of honour'. On the other hand parliament enjoyed the support of a meaner sort of person, natural malignants who had made their fortunes only recently and were jealous of their social superiors, 'common people', obscure men 'of no name' without any military traditions who made reckless demands for change. As a contemporary witness Clarendon's interpretation must command respect, but his severe black-and-white synthesis was wide of the mark even at the time and owes more to his own experiences than to any contemporary reality. Under his rule of thumb, Cromwell's landed background and connections should have made him a natural Royalist.

Clarendon came from a similar kind of family. The son of a small Wiltshire landowner, he was educated at Magdalen Hall, Oxford, and was later called to the bar. Ambitious and something of a snob, he was anxious to advance and through his uncle's influence became a member of Buckingham's entourage. Elected to parliament in 1640, he supported the impeachment of Strafford and came to royal notice by helping to produce the king's response to the *Grand Remonstrance* in 1641. At the outbreak of the fighting he became one of Charles I's principal advisers, and after the defeat he transferred his loyalties to the Prince of Wales and quickly established himself as effective head of the government in exile. Perhaps his prejudices were strengthened by that long absence from London and his proximity to the court-in-exile; perhaps he hoped that the Restoration would bring about a return to the values he extolled, instead of ushering in a new world in which property and money would be as important as 'great honour and fortune'.

That simple division left a long shadow over English memory, of a struggle between aristocratic or at least conservative Royalists and vulgar opportunists of a radical persuasion. From there it was a short step to Cavaliers and Roundheads, a clash as persuasive and partisan as Cowboys and Indians would be to later generations, the polarisation being as complete as any that existed during the fighting. It lasted a long time, too, and was soon to be readapted in the political squabbles of the eighteenth century between Whigs (natural successors to the Roundheads) and Tories (natural conservatives just as the Royalists had been). As Whigs gave way to Liberals in the following century the difference remained part of the political scheme of things and according to Blair Worden, who has conducted an invigorating investigation into the phenomenon, the civil war stereotypes continued to dominate English history in the next two centuries and even infiltrated that most English of games, cricket. Amateur players were 'gentlemen' while professionals were 'players', and 'when, towards that [twentieth] century's end, reporters portrayed the rivals for the England captaincy, the dashing David Gower and the pertinacious Graham Gooch, as the Cavalier and the Roundhead, their readers knew that they meant'.[5] The comparison could just as easily have been made about the rival claims of a Prince Rupert and a John Lambert as military commanders.

Central to the split between Cavalier and Roundhead was the difference between the character of Charles I with his long aristocratic Stewart nose and Oliver Cromwell with his homelier features and familiar wart. Following the Restoration the executed king was well-nigh sanctified, so much so that a statute was passed marking 30 January as a day of fasting and contemplation while the dead Lord

Protector was condemned to oblivion as a monstrous dictator and regicide. (Radicals also excoriated him, but for the quite different reason that he had failed to complete the political revolution.) It was not until the middle of the nineteenth century that the position began to change. In 1858 the law marking 30 January was quietly removed from the statute books and thirteen years earlier Cromwell's rehabilitation had begun with the publication of an edition of his *Letters and Speeches*. Its editor was Thomas Carlyle, a Scottish writer and historian who could have stepped out of the same religious mould which had produced the Huntingdonshire squire.

Born in Ecclefechan in Dumfriesshire on 4 December 1795, the son of a stonemason, Carlyle was raised on the Old Testament and the precepts of Calvinism and went on to study at the University of Edinburgh. At the time of his interest in Cromwell he was living in London following a series of single-minded attempts to become a professional writer and having dabbled in the waters of German Romanticism. In 1840 he was in middle life when he came upon the claims of Cromwell, one of the 'strong men' who plays a central role in his series of lectures, *On Heroes, Hero-Worship and the Heroic in History*:

> Poor Cromwell, – Great Cromwell! The inarticulate Prophet; Prophet who could not *speak*. Rude, confused, struggling to utter himself, with his strange depth, with his wild sincerity; and looked so strange among the elegant Euphuisms; dainty little Falklands, didactic Chillingworths, diplomatic Clarendons? Consider him. An outer-hall of chaotic confusion, visions of the Devil, nervous dreams, almost semi-madness; and yet such a clear determinate man's energy working in the heart of that. A kind of chaotic man. The ray as of pure starlight and fire, working in such an element of boundless hypochondria, what was it but the very greatness of the man? The depth and tenderness of his wild affections; the quantity of *sympathy* he had with things, – the quantity of insight he would yet get into the heart of things, the mastery he would yet get into the heart of things: this was hypochondria. The man's misery, as man's misery always does, came of his greatness. Samuel Johnson too is that kind of man. Sorrow-stricken, half-distracted; the wide element of mournful *black* enveloping him, – wide as the

world. It is the character of a prophetic man; a man with his whole soul *seeing* and struggling to see.[6]

Carlyle explained his interest in the heroic by claiming that 'no sadder proof can be given by a man of his own littleness than disbelief in great men' and in Cromwell he believed that he had found his own exemplar. The Lord Protector came to him as if in a dream, an 'armed Soldier, terrible as Death, relentless as Doom; doing God's judgements on the Enemies of God!' but he proved difficult to pin down. As was his habit Carlyle read voluminously around his subject and it was not until the beginning of 1842 that he began writing what he hoped would be the life of a 'living God-inspired soul'. Even then his subject proved elusive. He complained that his research was not taking him in any fixed direction, Cromwell refused to come into focus and on more than one occasion he confided to friends that he was close to abandoning the project as a hopeless cause. Shortly before Christmas 1843 Carlyle burned most of his research papers and read instead a copy of *A Christmas Carol* which Charles Dickens had presented to him.

The new year brought new hope: either Carlyle would finish Cromwell or Cromwell would finish him. Instead of writing a life he decided to produce an edition of Cromwell's letters and speeches and set about trying to gather them together from the state papers and from private archives up and down the country. From Carlyle's own account and the memories of his friends the composition of the Cromwell volumes was a Sisyphean task which almost broke him and his marriage, yet the result produced one of the most extraordinary books in British historiography. The text is largely Cromwell's but it is enlivened by Carlyle's commentary, almost as if the nineteenth-century historian was shadowing his seventeenth-century subject and interpolating to explain his thoughts and actions to a later generation. Sometimes Carlyle seemed almost to be at Cromwell's side, imaginatively recreating and reporting great events such as the dismissal of the Rump in 1653:

'You call yourself a Parliament,' continues my Lord General in a clear blaze of conflagration: 'You are no Parliament; I say you are no Parliament! Some of you are drunkards,' and his eye flashes on poor Mr Chaloner, an official man of some value, addicted to the bottle; 'some of you are –' and glares into Harry Marten, and the poor Sir Peter who rose to order, lewd livers both; 'living in open contempt of God's Commandments. Following your own greedy appetites, and the Devil's Commandments . . . how can you be a Parliament for God's people? Depart, I say; and let us have done with you. In the name of God – go!'[7]

The tortured prose notwithstanding, this is high drama and it appealed to Carlyle's readership. The first edition of 1200 copies sold out quickly when it appeared at the end of 1845 and the reviews were encouraging. Readers flocked to buy the book for several reasons. First and foremost it is an enthralling account, enlivened by Carlyle's contribution, not least his many asides, which help to give life to Cromwell's experiences and to guide the reader through the complexities of the period. Secondly, the bulk of the material was fresh and it helped to put Cromwell, a hitherto despised figure, in a new and encouraging light for nineteenth-century readers – in the introduction Carlyle sees his hero as 'the last glimpse of the Godlike vanishing from this England; conviction and veracity giving place to hollow cant and formulism'. Thirdly, there was Carlyle's preoccupation with Puritanism and his rewriting of history to give a heroic emphasis to its 'God-given precepts', its virtues outweighing its vices and the lessons it contains for a modern age ('we have wandered far away from the ideas which guided us in that Century'). Fourthly, and this is pure Carlyle, for he took great pains to make sure that he understood the subject, there is the vividness of his descriptions of battle, especially the fighting at Dunbar, the field of which he walked in 1844.[8]

Carlyle informed his mother that his book on Cromwell was the 'usefullest business I shall ever do in the world', and although he was wrong on that score – ahead lay his great work on Frederick the Great – his study of Cromwell helped to rehabilitate the Lord Protector not just for the Victorians but also for the modern age. It also acted as a corrective to Clarendon and introduced the notion that the wars had been a 'Puritanic revolt', a concept which was taken up by the next great historian of the war, Samuel Rawson Gardiner, who provided the bedrock on which all future historians would base their work. A product of Winchester and Christ Church, Oxford, and the son of a family which worshipped in the Irvingite or Catholic Apostolic Church whose members believed in the Second Coming, Gardiner devoted his working life to the seventeenth century from the accession of James I to the establishment of the Protectorate and the Restoration of Charles II. His education was interrupted by the decision to become a deacon in the Church which Carlyle, a friend of the founder Edward Irving, described as being 'deep in prophecy and other aberrations'. Irving, a fellow Scot from Dumfriesshire, had taught Jane Welsh (later Carlyle's wife) and was one of the most striking preachers in an age which produced many powerful performers, but his ability to create an atmosphere bordering on hysteria and his reliance on the 'gift of tongues' was deeply distrusted by his fellow churchmen.

Gardiner's involvement in the Church and his marriage to one of Irving's daughters kept him outside the mainstream of academic life, but that did not stop him producing the first volumes of his projected history or from undertaking voluminous research at the British Museum and the Public Record Office. His methodology was simple and direct: 'It seemed to me,' he wrote later, 'that it was the duty of a serious inquirer to search into the original causes of great events rather than, for the sake of catching at an audience, to rush unprepared on the great events themselves.' Unfortunately, his efforts were not rewarded and his early books did not sell well – *A History of England from the Accession of James I to the Disgrace of Lord Justice Coke* sold less than one hundred copies and according to a friend 'most of the edition went for wastepaper'. Undeterred, at the end of the 1860s he parted company with the Irvingites and was appointed to the staff of King's College, London, becoming Professor of Modern History in 1877, and continued his career as a prolific author. He became the director of the Camden Society, which had been founded in 1838 to reproduce vital historical documents, and was also editor of the authoritative *English Historical Review*. In all these guises he promoted the cause of seventeenth-century studies, his interest being quickened by the fact that through his paternal grandmother, May Boddam, he was descended from Cromwell's eldest daughter, Bridget. His *History of the Great Civil War* appeared between 1886 and 1891 and his *History* *of the Commonwealth and Protectorate* followed between 1895 and 1901. Unfortunately Gardiner died a year later and the last section from 1658 was completed by his student Charles Harding Firth,* his protégé and another noted scholar of the same period.[9]

Contemporaries were not always kind to Gardiner. His outside interests in the extension of adult education and his sheer productivity told against him, and although he was elected a fellow of All Souls his reputation dipped after his death. One contemporary account complained that he lacked the verve of a Thomas Babington Macaulay and damned him with faint praise. While his research efforts were lauded his literary style was disparaged, one critic writing that 'Gardiner was not, and, if his method of composition be taken into account, hardly could be, a brilliant writer; as with his lecturing, so his written narrative seemed to spin itself continuously out of a full store of maturely considered facts and necessary comments, reaching, without strain, the end of chapter or volume, as of lecture or course.'[10] Gardiner was also chided for failing to take into account economic factors and for his insistence on the civil war conflict being propelled by the Puritans' search for political and religious liberties but, as Christopher Hill has pointed out in recent times, it is impossible to ignore his labours: 'Gardiner's immense learning and mastery of the then available sources, his narrative gifts and his knack of hitting on the telling quotation – all this has made his authority very difficult to overthrow.'[11]

It was also one of Gardiner's achievements to put the war in its British context – the religious, political and military facts were explained by him in Scottish and Irish terms as well as in English. Towards the end of the twentieth century the idea resurfaced and historians began discussing the conflict in terms of 'the British civil war' or as 'the wars of the three kingdoms'. While this inclusive approach has been welcomed in that it has rescued the conflict from the straitjacket of 'the English Civil War' and has helped to give substance to the role played by Scotland and Ireland, both of which provided flashpoints and influenced events in England throughout

---

* Charles Harding Firth, 1857–1936, Regius professor of history at Oxford from 1904. The son of a wealthy Sheffield steel manufacturer, a contemporary critic said of Firth that he possessed three disadvantages: 'bad health, a private income and a single subject'.

the period, it also produced a reaction from other historians who were cautious of subsuming the period under a single umbrella, arguing that it was too simplistic to talk only of a pan-British dimension.[12] Nonetheless, for all that the conflict produced different experiences and different outcomes in each of the three kingdoms there was sufficient interaction for the wars of 1638–60 to possess British as well as English, Scottish and Irish dimensions. As Peter Gaunt points out, at best the historians have produced a hung verdict: 'The wars which rent that [Atlantic] archipelago in the mid-seventeenth century were Irish, Scottish, English and Welsh, and British. It would be as misleading to ignore British history and British problems as it would be to deny the separate histories of each of the component kingdoms and to tell only an archipelagic account.'[13]

The British civil wars of the seventeenth century are Janus-like. They look back to an older world of the absolute power of kings and queens, to the Middle Ages and the old certainties of land and aristocratic wealth; at the same time they heralded a new beginning in the political life of Britain's nations. While the end of the fighting in 1651 did not produce a lasting solution other than the rule by unelected swordsmen, which was not workable, and while the Stewarts were given a second chance in the reign of Charles II, the events of 1641 and 1642 helped to fashion the future condition of Britain. When the Stewarts were dethroned for a second time in 1688 the subsequent revolution meant that the parliamentary privileges won half a century earlier would be written into the constitution and the absolute authority of the Crown would be curbed. These were the principles which had to be defended and which had pitched the Westminster parliament into conflict with the king. By 1689 the balance of power had shifted and authority lay in the hands of ministers whose own authority was determined by members of the House of Commons.

It was still an oligarchy, but no longer could monarchs rule by whim and no longer could ministers ignore the voice of parliament. Ahead lay the emergence of a party political system determined by vote, and although it would not be until the nineteenth century that the difficult questions of the suffrage would be addressed – concerns which had already been raised by the Levellers and others – the accession of the House of Orange and the demise of the House of Stewart, both results of the civil war, put Britain on the course which

would make it a great power. In the century which followed the civil
wars, commercial and colonial interests encouraged the expansion of
Britain's overseas possessions, war with France and Spain augmented
them, the Royal Navy was expanded and the country prospered.
Scotland, too, was changed inexorably by the turmoil. In 1707 its
parliament entered into a union with England to complete the
process begun by King James VI and I in 1603 and although it took
another fifty years for the policy to bear fruit, by the second half of
the eighteenth century Scotland was beginning to share its
neighbour's growing prosperity and industrial progress. From being
one of the poorest countries in Europe it had become part of a union
which would make it the industrial workshop of the world and a
substantial contributor to, and beneficiary of, the colonial empire.
Only Ireland failed to benefit in any meaningful way. The wars of the
three kingdoms and the settlements which followed had left the Irish
Catholics excluded from public life. Although there were advances
in trade under the Protestant ascendancy the lot of the rural Catholic
poor was wretched – Dean Swift declared that the poverty was such
that any visitor to Ireland would 'hardly think himself in a land
where law, religion and common humanity is professed' – and it was
not until the end of the eighteenth century that a political front
emerged to fight for the repeal of the penal laws and the reform of
parliament. There was not only a difference between Protestant and
Catholic but a huge gulf between rich and poor, and that split would
colour the complexion of Irish society and politics for many years to
come.

Few people escaped the scourge of the fighting and the sieges which
dominated the British landscape between 1641 and 1651 – the period
when the war was at its most ferocious – and many more suffered
from the aftermath of battle, the pillaging and plundering and the
diseases following in the soldiers' wake. Large numbers of people were
killed or dispossessed, property was damaged and families split apart
by supporting the opposing sides. The first settlement ended in the
unlawful killing of the king and the rule of men determined to hold
what they had gained, whatever the cost to the country. The second
settlement returned the monarchy but failed to solve the problem of
the succession and plunged the country into a crisis which many
thought was a reprise of the first. As for the Levellers and other

radicals who hoped that the agitation of the 1640s would help to extend the franchise and make Britain a democracy, their claims would have to wait until well into the Victorian period and beyond that into the twentieth century. It took the revolution settlement of 1688 and 1689 to create a workable means of ruling the country, an oligarchy which balanced the power of Crown and parliament. Against that background the wars of the three kingdoms were not an end in themselves, nor even the beginning of the end, but the beginning of an age far more settled than anything that had preceded it.

Epilogue

Lexington and Concord, 1775

'By the rude bridge that arched the flood,
Their flag to April's breeze unfurled,
Here once the embattled farmers stood,
And fired the shot heard round the world.'

Ralph Waldo Emerson, Concord Hymn, *19 April 1836*

During the night of 18/19 April 1775 a force of 800 heavily armed British infantrymen made their way through the dark and unfamiliar Massachusetts countryside. Being a night march the going was not easy. As the soldiers were being ferried out of Boston to reach Cambridge they had been forced to wade the last few yards through freezing water, but they made good time, marching at an unaccustomed four miles an hour. Every attempt had been made to maintain security – orders were given at the last minute and these were few and far between, oars had been muffled – but the soldiers' target, the small town of Concord to the north, was obvious. No one marches through a seemingly dead countryside at night without being noticed and, even before leaving, the reasons for the military expedition were common knowledge in Boston. The British force under Lieutenant-Colonel Francis Smith, 10th Regiment, had been ordered to march to Concord, seat of the Provisional Congress, and once there to seize its arsenal.

As the column approached the town shortly before dawn, Smith sent a party of some 200 light infantrymen ahead of the main force under the command of Major John Pitcairn to seize the bridges at Concord. To do that they had to pass through Lexington, and as Pitcairn's men approached the town they realised that their arrival was expected. Church bells tolled, on the surrounding ridges warning beacons had been lit, and as day began to break they could make out parties of local militia, known as minutemen, scurrying through the countryside. A few hours earlier, Paul Revere, the son of a French Huguenot, had galloped out of Boston with the news of the British approach, and despite being captured and interrogated by a British patrol he had managed to raise the alarm. By the time that the British advance party reached Lexington Green they were confronted by fewer than one hundred militiamen under the command of Captain John Parker, a local farmer.

Both sides were under strict orders not to fire. As the red-coated British troops approached the green Parker told his men to stand their ground and not to open fire unless provoked. 'If they want to have a war,' he shouted, 'let it begin here!' Pitcairn, too, was anxious to avoid a confrontation. Before leaving Boston the British commander, General Thomas Gage, had specifically warned the British commanders to 'take care that the soldiers do not plunder the inhabitants or hurt private property', but he was with the rearguard and as the British column swung into Lexington a collision on the green was inevitable. All might still have been well had the column halted, but in circumstances which have never been fully explained a shot rang out and the British infantrymen responded, firing at will into the ranks of the militia. Later, men remembered hearing British officers shouting 'by God fire' and 'fire, damn you, fire' but this might have been selective hearing as Pitcairn and his officers attempted to restore order. Eight militiamen were killed in the shooting or when the British charged them with the bayonet. Only the arrival of a horrified Colonel Smith restored order, and by beat of drum the British column reformed to march the last ten miles into Concord.

By now the surrounding countryside was ablaze, not with fire but with the response of angry Massachusetts militiamen who were determined to protect their homeland and to avenge the deaths at Lexington. Smith's men marched unopposed into Concord and managed to round up a few weapons from the surrounding farms, including an ancient cannon, but militiamen were already gathering in a well defended position by the North Bridge. Just as had happened at Lexington, a single shot rang out, starting a vigorous skirmish, but this time the casualties were on the British side. Seven soldiers, including four officers, were killed and, falling into a panic, the infantrymen began to withdraw. As they did so Smith was wounded in the leg, and to add to the soldiers' dismay they came across one of their number who had not only been badly wounded but seemed to have been scalped as well. Suddenly retreat turned into a panic-stricken rout and officers were forced to line the road back to Lexington, threatening to kill their men unless they regrouped and restored order. But for the arrival of a fresh force of infantry and marines sent to rescue Smith's column the pride of the British army could have faced an ignominious defeat at the hands of a local militia dressed in drab working clothes, broad-brimmed hats and equipped with weapons little more lethal than fowling pieces.[1]

It was not the end of the affair – the British retreated towards Boston and the militiamen followed to besiege the town from Bunker Hill – but it was the beginning of the American War of Independence or the American Revolution, the next great confrontation between a British people and their king and parliament. The men who fired on the redcoated soldiers at Lexington and Concord were residents of the American colonies; the majority were of British descent, and even at that time most considered themselves to belong to an offshoot of the mother country, sharing with it the common inheritance of constitutional freedoms won in the previous century. Only five years earlier a Boston politician, Benjamin Franklin, had said as much when he wrote about the 'love and honour' which his fellow countrymen felt for Britain, arguing that his fellow countrymen had no desire to break the connection. The British had been in the American continent since the early seventeenth century, and in that time the relationship had become that of a vigorous young man struggling to break away from the family's apron-strings, but there was still a widespread feeling that America and Britain were one family. Small wonder that the events at Lexington and Concord were considered so shocking: this was the war which many colonists had long expected, now the world had been turned upside down at the sight of country boys attacking and killing their red-coated cousins. The fire which had been ignited that spring morning was to go on burning until 1781, when the British forces surrendered at Yorktown, in its later stages the struggle was to be fanned by the interference of the European powers, notably France, and the war eventually ended with America's independence from London rule.

In that sense many in Britain saw it as a civil war – the poet William Cowper described it in those terms, as did the future American commander George Washington – and it is not difficult to regard the war for independence as a family squabble.[2] The rebellion had been started by the imposition of British taxes and restrictions on land settlement and by the American colonists' insistence that these moves were illegal and could only be imposed by their own elected assemblies. Dissatisfaction with supervision by London rule throughout the middle years of the century also played its part, as did misguided rumours that the British were about to impose popery on the country, but the British reaction was as much to blame. As American colonists kicked against the imposition of taxes they thought to be unfair and unjust, the government in London responded by closing ranks, avoiding compromise and planning to contain the problem with the resident armed forces which had helped to secure the American colonies during Britain's recently ended Seven Years War with France, 1757–63. Confrontation became unavoidable. At a meeting of a Continental Congress in the autumn of 1774 the leaders of the 'patriots' rejected parliamentary sovereignty and declared that they would not accept British legislation which alienated their rights. Finally, they also called for a boycott of British trade.

It is easy to overstate the colonists' connections with Britain. By the late eighteenth century the thirteen colonies had received large numbers of immigrants from Europe, and with them the newcomers brought not just a desire for social change but also a need for land. Both aims seemed to be stymied by the far-off London government whose local garrison was not only thought to be repressive but was known to be expensive as well. (One reason for the taxation was the maintenance of the red-coated regiments to protect the colonies.) As the protests grew and spread to the main areas – New York, Philadelphia, New Jersey – the local governing classes realised that they could be the target of that dissatisfaction, and most decided to swim with the tide, becoming the leaders of the rebellion that was sure to break out. While that prevented the American uprising from becoming an internecine quarrel of the kind which had divided Britain a century earlier, if the argument about consanguinity is accepted the men who fired the first shots in 1775 were impelled by motives very similar to those which had sent soldiers to fight at Edgehill in 1642 – the refusal to accept an authority over which they had no control and in which they played no part. The colonists' cry of 'no taxation without representation' would certainly have been understood by the Levellers who debated the issue at Putney in 1647. In that respect, at least, some of their idealism lived on and found an echo in the Declaration of Independence which brought the United States of America into being on 4 July 1776.*

The main difference on this occasion was that the colonists were not just fighting against a king who was determined to use his prerogative; they were also fighting against a parliament which believed that it and it alone should raise taxes and control revenues, rights which had been won in the previous century. Even so, despite that difference, there were many parallels between the wars of the three kingdoms and the American War of Independence. Many Americans sided with Britain and were known as Loyalists, and families were often divided as a result – Benjamin Franklin was a signatory to the Declaration of Independence while his son William supported Britain. Men changed sides throughout the conflict, often on a whim but usually because they had been offered inducements, and thousands of ordinary people found themselves caught up in the fighting. Local scores were settled and in places lawlessness was commonplace. Although British soldiers were under strict instructions not to plunder, the aim being to encourage support from local communities, the orders were frequently disobeyed. The need to forage and the sheer scale of the operations meant that forces in remote areas simply took what they could get from the local population. There was no shortage of casual violence and American soldiers often behaved just as badly as the British.

---

* In April 1786 John Adams and Thomas Jefferson, respectively the second and third US presidents, visited the Edgehill battlefield and were much moved by what they saw. Adams scolded locals for not knowing its history – 'Tell your neighbours and your children that this is holy ground!' – and noted in his diary that he had witnessed 'scenes where farmers had fought for their rights'.

In George Washington the Americans found their Oliver
Cromwell. Both men came from similar backgrounds, both had to
forge armies out of unpromising material and then had to urge them
not to intervene in civil government, both were fine horsemen, both
were disciplinarians, both were intensely patriotic, both won
important victories and both lived to be reviled by their enemies in
later life – Cromwell as Lord Protector and Washington as the
president who was upbraided as being no better than a king.
(Washington was in fact offered the 'crown' but had the moral
courage to refuse it.) The difference was that whereas Britain's
republic ended with Cromwell's death, the American revolution
worked, and from Washington sprang the long succession of
presidential rule which saw the United States becoming a world
power by the end of the nineteenth century and in time the most
powerful country in the world. Not that it was always a glorious
progression. For the first half-century of its existence the United
States had to struggle with a weak economy, its constitution might
have declared men to be free but that emancipation did not extend
to the black slaves, nor to the native Americans, and there was to be
no tolerance for the Loyalists, who either escaped to Canada or
returned home to Britain. From that vantage point the struggle for
freedom loses some of its gloss.

And yet, this greatest of the wars between two anglophone peoples
lived up to the hopes of the men who fashioned the revolt and who
dreamed of creating a better world for themselves and their children.
It broke the umbilical cord with Britain, and for better or for worse
the constitutional changes made the United States the country which
it eventually became. In so doing the revolt provided an example of
what could be achieved by a free people united in common cause and
determined to protect their freedoms. Cromwell had presaged those
sentiments when he told the Speaker following the battle of Naseby:
'He that ventures his life for the liberty of his country, I wish he trust
God for the liberty of his conscience.' Just as Britain had been
fashioned by the events which took the people from a war against an
anointed king through an uncertain republic to the fashioning of a
Bill of Rights which safeguarded constitutional rights, so too was the
United States of America created by a war which began with shots
ringing out at an unplanned ambush in Massachusetts and proceeded

to produce the great statement of intent contained within the Declaration of Independence.

Over a century later, its words and its message would surely have been understood by any of those russet-clad soldiers who stood alongside Cromwell during the wars of the three kingdoms: 'whenever any form of government becomes destructive . . . it is the right of the people to alter or to abolish it, and to institute new government, laying its foundation on such principles, and organising its powers in such form, as to them shall seem most likely to effect their safety and happiness.'

Bibliography

The bibliography of the period 1603 to 1660 is one of the largest in British history, and as historians continue the task of placing the seventeenth-century Civil War in its British context the list of books will continue to grow. The following represents the main texts consulted, and to anyone familiar with the period my debt to previous historians is obvious.

PRIMARY SOURCES AND CONTEMPORARY ACCOUNTS

Calendar of State Papers, Domestic (CSPD)

Calendar of State Papers, Ireland (CSPIr)

Calendar of State Papers, Venice (CSPV)

State Papers, James I, SP 14–15

State Papers, Charles I, SP 16

State Papers, Council of State (1649–60), SP 18

State Papers, Books and Accounts, SP 25

Somers Tracts, Collection of scarce and valuable Tracts, on the most interesting and entertaining subjects: but chiefly as relate to the history and constitution of these kingdoms . . . particularly of the late Lord Somers, revised by eminent hands, 4 vols (London, 1748–51)

Thomason Tracts, ed. George Thomason, Catalogue of Pamphlets, Books and Newspapers relating to the Civil War, the Commonwealth and Restoration, 2 vols (London, British Museum, 1908)

Abbott, W. C., *Writings and Speeches of Oliver Cromwell*, 4 vols (Cambridge, Massachusetts, 1937–47)

Atkyns, Richard, ed. Peter Young, *The Vindication of Richard Atkyns and the Military Memoirs of John Gwyn* (London, 1967)

Aubrey, John, ed. Oliver Lawson Dick, *Brief Lives, Chiefly of Contemporaries* (London, 1949)

Baillie, Robert, ed. David Laing, *The Letters of and Journals of Robert Baillie*, 3 vols (Edinburgh, Maitland Club, 1724–37)

Baxter, Richard, *Reliquiae Baxterianae, or Mr Richard Baxter's Narrative of the Most Memorable Passages of His Life and Times, Faithfully Publish'd from His Own Original Manuscript* (London, 1696)

Bulstrode, Sir Richard, *Memoirs* (London, 1971)

Burnet, Gilbert, Bishop, *History of His Own Time*, 2 vols (London, 1727); *Memoirs of the Lives and Actions of James and William, Dukes of Hamilton and Castlehead* (London, 1677)

Carlyle, Thomas, *The Letters and Speeches of Oliver Cromwell*, 3 vols (London, 1845)

Cavendish, Margaret, Duchess of Newcastle, ed. C. H. Firth, *The Life of the Thrice Noble, High and Puissant Prince William Cavendish* (London, 1886)

Cholmley, Sir Hugh, *Memoirs* (London, 1787)

Clarendon, see below, Hyde, Edward

Clifford, Lady Anne, ed. D. J. H. Clifford, *The Diaries of Lady Anne Clifford* (Gloucester, 1990)

D'Ewes, Sir Symonds, ed. Wallace Notestein, *The Journals of Symonds D'Ewes*, I, November 1640–March 1641 (New Haven, 1923); ed. Willson H. Coates, *The Journals of Sir Symonds D'Ewes*, II, October 1641–January 1642 (New Haven, 1942)

Dugdale, Sir William, ed. William Hamper, *Life, Diary and Correspondence* (London, 1827)

Ellis, Sir Henry, *Original Letters Illustrative of English History*, 11 vols (London, 1824–1846)

Evelyn, John, ed. E. S. de Beer, *The Diary of John Evelyn*, 6 vols (Oxford, 1955)

Fairfax, Sir Thomas, ed. Robert Bell, *Memorials of the Civil War, Comprising the Correspondence of the Fairfax Family*, 2 vols (London, 1849)

Fanshawe, Ann, Lady, and Halkett, Anne, Lady, ed. John Loftis, *Memoirs* (Oxford, 1979)

Gordon, James, of Rothiemay, *A History of Scots Affairs 1637–1641* (Aberdeen, Spalding Club, 1841)

Gordon, Patrick, of Ruthven, *A Short Abridgement of Britane's Distemper 1639–1649* (Aberdeen, Spalding Club, 1844)

Gough, Richard, ed. Peter Razzell, *The History of Myddle* (Firle, Sussex, 1979)

Harley, Lady Brilliana, *The Letters of Lady Brilliana Harley* (London, Camden Society, 1854)

Herbert, Sir Thomas, ed. Roger Lockyer, *Memoirs of the Last Years of the Reign of King Charles* (London, 1959)

Hodgson, Captain John, see below, Slingsby, Henry

Hudson, Roger, ed., *The Grand Quarrel: Women's Memoirs of the English Civil War* (London, 1993)

Hutchinson, Lucy, ed. N. H. Keeble, *Memoirs of the Life of Colonel Hutchinson, with a fragment of autobiography* (London, 1995)

Hyde, Edward, Earl of Clarendon, ed. W. D. Macray, *The History of the Rebellion and Civil War in England*, 6 vols (Oxford, 1888, 1992)

Iain Lom (John Macdonald), ed. Annie M. Mackenzie, *Orain Iain Luim* (Songs of John MacDonald Bard of Keppoch), (Edinburgh, Scottish Gaelic Texts Society, 1964)

Jaffray, Alexander, ed. John Barclay, *Diary of Alexander Jaffray, Provost of Aberdeen* (Aberdeen, 1856)

Johnston, Sir Archibald, ed. George M. Paul, *Diary of Sir Archibald Johnston, Lord Wariston*, vol. I (Edinburgh, Scottish History Society, 1911); ed. David Hay Fleming, vol. II (Edinburgh, Scottish History Society, 1919); ed. J. D. Ogilvie, vol. III (Edinburgh, Scottish History Society, 1940)

Lister, John, ed. Thomas Wright, *Autobiography of John Lister of Bradford* (1842)

Ludlow, Edmund, ed. C. H. Firth, *Memoirs*, 2 vols (Oxford, 1894)

Luke, Sir Samuel, ed. I. G. Philip, *The Journal of Sir Samuel Luke*, 3 vols (Oxford, 1874)

McCrie, Thomas, ed., *The Life of Mr Robert Blair, Minister of St Andrews, Containing His Autobiography from 1593 to 1636, with Supplement to His Life and Continuation of the History of the Times to 1680 by His Son-in-Law, Mr William Row, Minister of Ceres* (Edinburgh, Wodrow Society, 1848)

Montreui, Jean de, ed. J. T. Fotheringham, *Diplomatic Correspondence 1645–48*, 2 vols (Edinburgh, Scottish History Society, 1899)

Oglander, Sir John, ed. Francis Bamford, *A Royalist's Notebook: The Commonplace Book of Sir John Oglander of Nunwell* (London, 1936)

Pepys, Samuel, ed. Robert Latham, *The Shorter Pepys* (London, 1985); ed. Robert Latham and William Matthews, *The Diary of Samuel Pepys*, vol. X Companion (London, 1983)

Petrie, Sir Charles, ed., *The Letters of King Charles I* (London, 1935)

Powell, J. R., ed., *The Letters of Robert Blake* (London, Navy Records Society, 1937)

Rushworth, John, *Historical Collections of Private Passages of State*, 7 vols (London, 1659–1701)

Rutherford, Samuel, ed. Rev. Andrew Bonar, *Letters of Samuel Rutherford* (Edinburgh, 1891)

Slingsby, Henry, *Original Memoirs Written During the Great Civil War, being the Life of Sir Henry Slingsby and the Memoirs of Captain Hodgson* (Edinburgh and London, 1806)

Slingsby, Walter, ed. C. E. H. Chadwyck-Healey, *Bellum Civile* (Somerset Record Society, 1902)

Somerville, James, *Memory of the Somervilles* (Edinburgh, 1815)

Spalding, John, *Memorials of the Troubles in Scotland and England 1624–1645*, vols 1 and 2 (Aberdeen, Spalding Club, 1850)

Sprigge, Joshua, ed. Ken Trotman, *Anglia Rediviva* (London, 1647, 1984)

Stuart, J., ed., *Extracts from the Council Register of the Burgh of Aberdeen*, 2 vols (Edinburgh, Scottish Record Society, 1871–72)

Symonds, Richard, ed. C. E. Long, *Diary of the Marches of the Royal Army* (London, the Camden Society, 1859)

Thurloe, John, *A Collection of the State Papers of John Thurloe Esq, secretary, first, to Council of State, and afterwards to the two protectors, Oliver and Richard Cromwell*, 7 vols (London, 1742)

Turner, Sir James, *Memoirs of His Own Life and Times* (Edinburgh, Bannatyne Club, 1829)

Venables, Robert, ed. C. H. Firth, *The Narrative of General Venables* (London, Royal Historical Society, 1900)

Verney, F. J., ed., *Memoirs of the Verney Family*, 2 vols (London, 1892)

Wallington, Nehemiah, *Historical Notes of Events Occurring Chiefly in the Reign of Charles I*, 2 vols (London, 1869)

Warwick, Sir Philip, *Memoirs of the Reign of King Charles* (London, 1813)

Wentworth, Thomas, ed. W. Knowler, *The Earl of Strafford's Letters and Dispatches*, 2 vols (London, 1739)

Wharton, Nehemiah, 'Letters from a Subaltern Officer in the Earl of Essex's Army', *Archaeologia*, vol. XXXV, 1853

Whitelocke, Bulstrode, *Memorials of the English Affairs from the Beginnings of the Reign of Charles I to King Charles II's Happy Restoration* (London, 1722)

Wishart, George, ed. A. D. Murdoch and H. F. M. Simpson, *The Memoirs of James, Marquis of Montrose* (London, 1893)

SECONDARY SOURCES

General

Adair, John, *Roundhead General: A Military Biography of Sir William Waller* (London, 1969); *By the Sword Divided: Eyewitness Accounts of the English Civil War* (London, 1983)

Ashley, Maurice, *General Monck* (London, 1977)

Ashton, Robert, *The English Civil War: Conservatism and Revolution* (London, 1989)

Aylmer, Gerald, *The State's Servants: The Civil Service of the English Republic 1649–1660* (London, 1973); *Rebellion or Revolution?* (London, 1986)

Barnett, Correlli, *Britain and Her Army 1509–1970* (London, 1970)

Baumber, Michael, *General at Sea: Robert Blake and the Seventeenth Century Revolution in Naval Warfare* (London, 1989)

Bayley, A. R., *The Civil War in Dorset 1642–1660* (London, 1910)

Bennett, Martyn, *The Civil Wars in Britain and Ireland* (London, 1997); *The Civil Wars Experienced: Britain and Ireland 1638–1661* (London, 2000)

Bowle, John, *Charles the First* (London, 1975)

Buchan, John, *Oliver Cromwell* (London, 1934)

Burne, Alfred H. and Young, Peter, *The Great Civil War* (London, 1959)

Capp, Bernard, *Cromwell's Navy: The Fleet and the English Revolution 1648–1660* (Oxford, 1990)

Carlton, Charles, *Charles I: Personal Monarch* (London, 1983); *Archbishop William Laud* (London, 1988); *Going to the Wars: The Experience of the British Civil Wars* (London, 1992)

Davies, Godfrey, *The Restoration of Charles II 1658–1660* (San Marino, California, 1955)

Davies, Stevie, *Unbridled Spirits: Women of the English Revolution 1640–1660* (London, 1998)

Dawson, W. H., *Cromwell's Understudy: The Life and Times of General John Lambert* (London, 1938)

Durston, Christopher, *Cromwell's Major-Generals: Godly Government during the English Revolution* (Manchester, 2001)

Everitt, Alan, *The Community of Kent and the Great Rebellion 1640–60* (Leicester, 1966)

Firth, C. H., *History of the Commonwealth and Protectorate*, 2 vols (London, 1909); *Cromwell's Army* (new edition London, 1962)

Firth, C. H. and Davies, G., *A Regimental History of Cromwell's Army*, 2 vols (Oxford, 1940)

Fraser, Antonia, *Cromwell: Our Chief of Men* (London, 1973); *King Charles II* (London, 1979)

Gardiner, S. R., *The Constitutional Documents of the Puritan Revolution 1626–60* (London, 1889); *History of the Great Civil War 1642–1649*, 4 vols (London, 1893); *History of the Commonwealth and Protectorate 1649–1656*, 4 vols (London, 1903)

Gardiner, S. R. and Atkinson, C. T., eds., *Letters and Papers Relating to the First Dutch War*, 6 vols (London, Navy Records Society, 1899–1930)

Gaunt, Peter, *The Cromwellian Gazetteer* (Stroud, 1987); *The British Wars 1637–1651* (London, 1987); *A Nation Under Siege* (London, 1991); *Oliver Cromwell* (London, 1996); ed., *The English Civil War: The Essential Readings* (London, 2001)

Gentles, Ian, *The New Model Army in England, Ireland and Scotland 1645–1653* (London, 1992)

Gregg, Pauline, *Free-Born John: A Biography of John Lilburne* (London, 1961)

Hainsworth, Roger, *The Swordsmen in Power: War and Politics under the English Republic 1649–1660* (Stroud, 1997)

Hainsworth, Roger and Churches, Christine, *The Anglo-Dutch Naval Wars 1652–1674* (Stroud, 1998)

Harris, R. W., *Clarendon and the English Revolution* (London, 1983)

Hibbert, Christopher, *Cavaliers and Roundheads: The English at War 1642–1649* (London, 1993)

Hill, Christopher, *Puritanism and Revolution: Studies in Interpretation of the English Revolution of the 17th Century* (London, 1958); *God's Englishman: Oliver Cromwell and the English Revolution* (London, 1970); *The World Turned Upside Down: Radical Ideas during the English Revolution* (London, 1972)

Hirst, Derek, *Authority and Conflict: England 1603–1658* (London, 1986)

Hobman, D. L., *Cromwell's Spymaster: A Study of John Thurloe* (London, 1961)

Hutton, Ronald, *The Royalist War Effort 1642–1646* (London, 1982); *The Restoration: A Political and Religious History of England and Wales 1658–1667* (Oxford, 1985); *Charles II, King of England, Scotland and Ireland* (Oxford, 1989)

James, Lawrence, *Warrior Race: A History of the British at War* (London, 2001)

Kennedy, Paul, *The Rise and Fall of British Naval Mastery* (London, 1976)

Kenyon, John, *The Stuart Constitution: Documents and Commentary* (Cambridge, 1966); *The Civil Wars of England* (London, 1988)

Kenyon, John and Ohlmeyer, Jane, eds., *The Civil Wars: A Military History of England, Scotland and Ireland 1638–1660* (Oxford, 1998)

Kishlansky, Mark, *The Rise of the New Model Army* (London, 1979); *A Monarchy Transformed* (London, 1996)

Leach, Arthur Leonard, *The History of the Civil War (1642–1649) in Pembrokeshire and its Borders* (London, 1937)

Lindley, Keith, *The English Civil War and Revolution* (London, 1998)

Morrill, John, *The Revolt of the Provinces: Conservatives and Radicals in the English Civil War 1630–1650* (London, 1980); ed., *Reactions to the English Civil War* (London, 1982); ed., *Oliver Cromwell and the English Revolution* (London, 1990); ed., *The Impact of the English Civil War* (London, 1991); ed., *Revolution and Restoration: England in the 1650s* (London, 1992); *The Nature of the English Revolution* (London, 1993)

Newman, P. R., *Royalist Officers in England and Wales 1641–1660* (New York, 1981); *Atlas of the English Civil Wars* (London, 1988)

Ollard, Richard, *This War without an Enemy: A History of the English Civil Wars* (London, 1976); *Cromwell's Earl* (London, 1994)

Phillips, J. R., *Memoirs of the Civil War in Wales and the Marches*, 2 vols (London, 1874)

Powell, J. R., *The Navy in the English Civil War* (London, 1962)

Roots, Ivan, *The Great Rebellion* (London, 1966)

Russell, Conrad, *The Causes of the English Civil War* (Oxford, 1990); *Unrevolutionary England 1603–1642* (Oxford, 1990); *The Fall of the British Monarchies* (Oxford, 1991)

Sharpe, Kevin, *The Personal Rule of Charles I* (London, 1992)

Sherwood, Roy, *The Court of Oliver Cromwell* (London, 1977); *The Civil War in the Midlands 1642–1651* (Stroud, 1997)

Stone, Lawrence, *Causes of the English Revolution* (London, 1972)

Trease, Geoffrey, *Portrait of a Cavalier: William Cavendish, 1st Duke of Newcastle* (London, 1979)

Underdown, David, *Royalist Conspiracy in England* (New Haven, 1960); *Pride's Purge: Politics in the English Revolution* (Oxford, 1971); *Somerset in the Civil War and Interregnum* (Newton Abbot, 1973)

Warburton, Eliot, *Memoirs of Prince Rupert and the Cavaliers*, 3 vols (London, 1849)

Wedgwood, C. V., *The King's Peace 1637–1641* (London, 1955); *The King's War 1641–1647* (London, 1958); *Thomas Wentworth, First Earl of Strafford 1593–1641* (London, 1961); *The Trial of Charles I* (London, 1964)

Woodhouse, A. P. ed., *Puritanism and Liberty* (London, 1938)

Woolrych, Austin, *England without a King* (London, 1983); *Soldiers and Statesmen* (London, 1987); *Battles of the English Civil War* (London, 1991)

Worden, Blair, *Roundhead Reputations: The English Civil Wars and the Passions of Posterity* (London, 2001)

Young, Peter and Holmes, Richard, *The English Civil War 1642–1651* (London, 1974)

Ireland

Aiazza, Giuseppe, trs. A. Hutton, *The Embassy in Ireland of Monsignor G.B. Rinuccini* (Dublin, 1873)

Bagwell, Richard, *Ireland under the Stuarts during the Interregnum*, 3 vols (London, 1909–1916)

Barnard, T. C., *Cromwellian Ireland: English Government and Reform in Ireland 1649–1660* (Oxford, 1975)

Bartlett, Thomas, and Jeffrey, Keith, *A Military History of Ireland* (Cambridge, 1996)

Beckett, J. C., *The Making of Modern Ireland 1603–1923* (London, 1966)

Bottigheimer, K. G., *English Money and Irish Land: the 'Adventurers' in the Cromwellian Settlement of Ireland* (Oxford, 1971)

Canny, Nicholas, *From Reformation to Restoration: Ireland 1534–1660* (London, 1987); *Making Ireland British, 1580–1650* (Oxford, 2001)

Carte, Thomas, *History of the Life of James, First Duke of Ormonde*, 6 vols (Oxford, 1851)

Clarke, Aidan, *Prelude to Restoration in Ireland: The End of the Commonwealth* (Cambridge, 1999)

Gilbert, J. T., *History of the Irish Confederation and the War in Ireland 1641–1643*, 7 vols (Dublin, 1882–1891); *A Contemporary History of Affairs in Ireland*, 3 vols (Dublin, Irish Archaeological and Celtic Society, 1879)

Hayes-McCoy, G. A., *Irish Battles: A Military History of Ireland* (Belfast, 1981)

Mac Cuarta, Brian, ed., *Ulster 1641* (Belfast, 1993)

MacCurtain, Margaret, *Tudor and Stewart Ireland* (Dublin, 1972)

Meehan, C. P., *The Confederation of Kilkenny* (Dublin, 1905)

Moody, T. W., Martin, F. X. and Byrne, F. J., eds., *A New History of Ireland*, vol. III, 1534–1691 (Oxford, 1976)

Murphy, Denis, *Cromwell in Ireland* (Dublin, 1883)

Ohlmeyer, Jane, *Civil War and Restoration in the Three Stuart Kingdoms: The Career of Ranald MacDonnell, Earl of Antrim* (Cambridge, 1993); ed., *Ireland from Independence to Occupation 1641–1660* (Cambridge, 1995)

Perceval-Maxwell, Michael, *The Outbreak of the Irish Rebellion of 1641* (Montreal, 1995)

Prendergast, J. P., *The Cromwellian Settlement of Ireland* (Dublin, 1865)

Reilly, Tom, *Cromwell: An Honourable Enemy* (London, 1999)

Wheeler, James Scott, *Cromwell in Ireland* (London, 1999)

Scotland

Akerman, J. Y., ed., *Letters from Roundhead Officers written from Scotland and chiefly addressed to Captain Adam Baynes* (Edinburgh, Bannatyne Club, 1856)

Balfour, Sir John, *Historical Works*, 4 vols (Edinburgh, 1824–1825)

Brown, Keith, *Kingdom or Province? Scotland and the Regal Union 1603–1715* (Basingstoke, 1992)

Buchan, John, *Montrose* (London, 1928)

Cowan, Edward J., *Montrose: For Covenant and King* (London, 1977)

Dickinson, W. C. and Donaldson, Gordon, eds., *A Source Book of Scottish History*, vol. III (Edinburgh, 1961)

Donald, Peter, *An Uncounselled King: Charles I and the Scottish Troubles 1637–1641* (Cambridge, 1990)

Douglas, W. S., *Cromwell's Scotch Campaigns 1650–1651* (London, 1898)

Dow, Frances, *Cromwellian Scotland* (Edinburgh, 1979)

Ferguson, William, *Scotland's Relations with England: A Survey to 1707* (Edinburgh, 1977)

Firth, C. H., ed., *Scotland and the Commonwealth* (Edinburgh, Scottish History Society, 1895); *Scotland and the Protectorate* (Edinburgh, Scottish History Society, 1899)

Fissel, Mark, *The Bishops' Wars* (1994)

Fugol, Edward M., *A Regimental History of the Covenanting Armies* (Edinburgh, 1990)

Grainger, John D., *Cromwell against the Scots: The Last Anglo-Scottish War* (East Linton, 1997)

Lee, Maurice J., *The Road to Revolution: Scotland under Charles I* (Chicago, 1985)

Levack, B. P., *The Formation of the British State: England, Scotland and the Union 1603–1707* (Oxford, 1987)

McCoy, F. N., *Robert Baillie and the Second Scots Reformation* (Berkeley and Los Angeles, 1974)

Macinnes, Allan I., *Charles I and the Making of the Covenanting Movement 1625–1641* (Edinburgh, 1991)

Marren, Peter, *Grampian Battlefields* (Aberdeen, 1990)

Mathew, David, *Scotland under Charles I* (London, 1955)

Meikle, H. W., ed., *Correspondence of Scots Commissioners in London 1644–1646* (Edinburgh, Roxburghe Club, 1917)

Mitchison, Rosalind, *History of Scotland* (London, 1970); *Lordship to Patronage: Scotland 1603–1745* (Edinburgh, 1983)

Morrill, John, ed., *The Scottish National Covenant in its British Context* (Edinburgh, 1990)

Napier, Mark, *Memorials of Montrose and his Times*, 2 vols (Edinburgh, Maitland Club, 1848–1850)

Preston, Raymond Campbell, *A Land Afflicted: Scotland and the Covenanter Wars 1638–1690* (Edinburgh, 1998)

Rothes, Earl of, ed. David Laing, *A Relation of Proceedings concerning the Affairs of the Kirk of Scotland* (Edinburgh, Bannatyne Club, 1830)

Row, John, *Historie of the Kirk of Scotland*, vol. 2 (Edinburgh, Maitland Club, 1842)

Stevenson, David, *The Scottish Revolution 1637–1644* (Newton Abbot, 1973); *Revolution and Counter-Revolution in Scotland 1644–1651* (London, 1977); *Scottish Covenanters and Irish Confederates* (Belfast, 1981); *Alasdair MacColla and the Highland Problem in the 17th Century* (Edinburgh, 1980); *King or Covenant: Voices from Civil War* (East Linton, 1996)

Terry, Charles Sanford, *The Life and Campaigns of Alexander Leslie* (London, 1899); *The Cromwellian Union* (Edinburgh, Scottish History Society, 1902); *The Army of the Covenant*, 2 vols (Edinburgh, Scottish History Society, 1917)

Wedgwood, C. V., *Montrose* (London, 1952)

Young, J. R., *Celtic Dimensions of the British Civil Wars* (Edinburgh, 1997)

Notes and References

PROLOGUE: LÜTZEN, 1632

1. Fuller, J. F. C., *The Decisive Battles of the Western World* (London 1954–56), I, 68–75
2. Terry, *Leslie*, 30–31
3. CSPD, 1640–41, 212
4. Grant, James, *Sir John Hepburn* (Edinburgh, 1851), 201

PART ONE: THE DESCENT TO WAR 1638–1642

CHAPTER ONE: THE ILLUSTRIOUS HOPE OF GREAT BRITAIN

1. Ellis, *Original Letters*, III, 92
2. James Craigie, ed., *The Basilikon Doron of King James VI*, 1 (Edinburgh, Scottish Texts Society, 1944), 7–8
3. Ellis, *Original Letters*, III, 112
4. Petrie, *Letters of King Charles I*, 26
5. Clarendon, *History*, I, 22
6. Firth, *Cromwell's Army*, 3
7. Petrie, *Letters of King Charles I*, 45
8. Kenyon, *The Civil Wars of England*, 11
9. Petrie, *Letters of King Charles I*, 77

CHAPTER TWO: THE PERSONAL RULE

1. Carlton, *Charles I*, 131
2. Williams, *Capuchin Friars*, II, 313–314
3. Sharpe, 'Halcyon Days?', *The Personal Rule of Charles I*, 608–611
4. Williams, *Capuchin Friars*, II, 309
5. Thomas Carew, *Poems* (Oxford, 1949), 77
6. CSPV, 1636–1639, 242
7. Carlton, *Charles I*, 160–170
8. William Laud, ed. W. Scott and J. Bliss, *Works*, VII (Oxford, 1847–1860), 382
9. Clarendon, *History* I, 342
10. Perceval-Maxwell, *The Outbreak of the Irish Rebellion of 1641*, 311
11. Wentworth, *Strafford's Letters*, I, 450
12. ibid.

CHAPTER THREE: THE CROWN AND THE KIRK

1. Baillie, *Letters and Journals*, I, 4
2. Stevenson, *Scottish Revolution*, 15

3. CSPV, 1626–1628, 615
4. Burnet, *History*, I, 34
5. Balfour, *Historical Works*, II, 128
6. ibid., II, 131
7. Sir William Fraser, *The Sutherland Book*, II (Edinburgh, 1892), 357
8. William Lithgow, 'Scotland's Welcome to her Native Son and Soveraigne Lord, King Charles', *Poetic Remains* (Edinburgh, 1832) (1633)
9. Spalding, *Memorials*, I, 39
10. W. K. Tweedie, *Select Biographies* (Edinburgh, Wodrow Society, 1845–47), I, 397
11. Baillie, *Letters and Journals*, I, 4–5
12. David Masson, *Drummond of Hawthornden* (Edinburgh, 1873), 250

CHAPTER FOUR: 'THAT GLORIOUS MARRIAGE OF THE KINGDOM WITH GOD'

1. Rutherford, *Letters*, to Lady Kenmure, xi, 53
2. 'The Stoneyfeild Saboth Day', Advocates Manuscript, 33.2.32, 47–48
3. Stevenson, *Scottish Revolution*, 74
4. Spalding, *Memorials*, I, 82
5. Johnston of Wariston, *Diary*, I, 369
6. Stevenson, *Scottish Revolution*, 64–79; Gordon of Rothiemay, *History*, I, 31
7. Baillie, *Letters and Journals*, I, 23
8. Row, *History of the Kirk*, II, 268
9. Johnston of Wariston, *Diary*, I, 254
10. Baillie, *Letters and Journals*, I, 28
11. Carlton, *Charles I*, 198–199
12. Samuel Rutherford to Lord Loudoun, 4 January 1638, David Reid, *The Party-Coloured Mind: Selected Prose relating to the conflict between Church and State in Seventeenth Century Scotland* (Edinburgh, Association for Scottish Literary Studies, 1982), 46–47
13. Rothes, *A Relation of Proceedings concerning the Kirk of Scotland from August 1637 to July 1638*, 69
14. The entire text is in Dickinson and Donaldson, *Source Book of Scottish History*, III, 93–104
15. Cowan, Macinnes, Morrill, Stevenson et al.
16. Johnston of Wariston, *Diary*, I, 327–328
17. James Row, 'The Red-Shankes Sermon or Pockmanty Preaching', R. D. S. Jack, *Scottish Prose 1500–1700* (London, 1971), 137

CHAPTER FIVE: THE ASSEMBLY IN GLASGOW

1. Baillie, *Letters and Journals*, I, 83
2. Burnet, *History*, I, 76
3. Baillie, *Letters and Journals*, I, 211
4. Samuel Rutherford to John Fennick, 13 February 1640, Reid, op. cit., 48–52
5. Firth, *Cromwell's Army*, 8–9
6. Cowan, *Montrose*, 49–54
7. Johnston of Wariston, *Diary*, I, 92
8. Wentworth, *Strafford's Letters*, II, 257
9. Baillie, *Letters and Journals*, I, 104

10. Macinnes, *Charles I and the Making of the Covenanting Movement*, 86
11. J. D. Marwick, ed., *Extracts from the Records of the Burgh of Glasgow 1573–1642* (Glasgow, 1876), 391–393
12. Baillie, *Letters and Journals*, I, 63
13. Alexander Peterkin, ed., *Records of the Kirk of Scotland* (Edinburgh, 1838), 146
14. ibid., 147
15. Robert Baillie: History of the General Assembly in Glasgow in 1638, letter to William Spang, *Letters and Journals*, I, 118–175
16. 'Some special arguments which warranted the Scottish subjects lawfully to take up arms in defence of their religion and liberty when they are in danger', Andrew Stevenson, *History of the Church and State in Scotland* (Edinburgh, 1840), 356–360
17. CSPD, 1639, 243

CHAPTER SIX: FOR CHRIST'S CROWN AND COVENANT:
THE FIRST BISHOPS' WAR

1. Firth, *Cromwell's Army*, 13
2. Turner, *Memoirs*, 14
3. CSPD, 1639, 210, 243
4. Rutherford to Fennick, Reid, op. cit., 48–52
5. Spalding, *Memorials*, I, 154
6. ibid., I, 1867; CSPD, 1639, 165
7. CSPD, 1639, 189
8. Baillie's description of the military preparations takes up the bulk of his letter to William Spang, 28 September 1639, *Letters and Journals*, I, 211–216
9. Baillie, *Letters and Journals*, II, 442
10. CSPD, 1639, 303
11. CSPD, 1639, 367–370
12. Johnston of Wariston, *Diary*, I, 64
13. Abraham Cowley, *Poems* (Cambridge, 1905), 22
14. Burnet, *Hamilton*, 144

CHAPTER SEVEN: FOUL AND HORRID TREASON: THE SECOND BISHOPS' WAR

1. Burnet, *Hamilton*, 112
2. Wentworth, *Strafford's Letters*, II, 393–398
3. ibid.
4. Gordon, *History*, III, 112–114, Stevenson, *Scottish Revolution*, 179–184
5. CSPD, 1639, 608
6. CSPD, 1640, 112–113
7. CSPD, 1640, 189
8. Cowan, *Montrose*, 93; Balfour, *Historical Works*, II, 379
9. Spalding, *Memorials*, I, 291–292
10. The version is from R. A. Smith's *The Scottish Minstrel*, II (Edinburgh, 1820–1824)
11. CSPD, 1640, 548
12. CSPD, 1640, 612
13. Terry, *Leslie*, 128

14. Zachary Boyd, *The Battle of Newburne: where the Scots armie obtained a notable victorie against the English papists, prelats, and Arminians, the* 28 *day of August,* 1640 (Glasgow, 1643)

CHAPTER EIGHT: THE GATHERING STORM

1. Wedgwood, *Wentworth*, 311
2. Baillie, *Letters and Journals*, I, 271, 274
3. CSPD, 1640, 255
4. Baillie, *Letters and Journals*, I, 200–201
5. Stevenson, *Scottish Revolution*, 221
6. Cowan, *Montrose*, 96–98
7. Baillie, *Letters and Journals*, I, 354
8. Keith M. Brown, 'Courtiers and Cavaliers', Morrill, ed., *The Scottish National Covenant in its British Context*, 155–192
9. Wedgwood, *Wentworth*, 326
10. Baillie, *Letters and Journals*, I, 347
11. Thomas Stanley, *Poems* (London, 1818), 88–89
12. Terry, *Leslie*, 154
13. Baillie, *Letters and Journals*, I, 385–386
14. Baillie, *Letters and Journals*, I, 391
15. Hilary L. Rubenstein, *Captain Luckless, First Duke of Hamilton 1606–1649* (Edinburgh, 1975), 134

CHAPTER NINE: IRELAND IN FLAMES

1. Beckett, *Making of Modern Ireland*, 65
2. Wentworth, *Letters*, II, 93
3. Gilbert, *Irish Confederation*, I, 244–245
4. ibid., II, 4
5. Russell, *Fall of the British Monarchies*, 384
6. Gilbert, *Irish Confederation*, I, 255
7. The depositions are held in the library of Trinity College, Dublin and formed the basis for Sir John Temple's lurid *History of the Irish Rebellion* (1646), which greatly exaggerated the death toll.
8. Bagwell, *Ireland under the Stuarts*, I, 333
9. Stevenson, *Scottish Revolution*, 245–246
10. Turner, *Memoirs*, 19
11. Gilbert, *Irish Confederation*, I, 38
12. Kenyon and Ohlmeyer, *The Civil Wars*, 77
13. Baillie, *Letters and Journals*, II, 104
14. Lindley, *English Civil War and Revolution*, 81–82
15. Clarendon, *History*, VI, 2–3

CHAPTER TEN: THE STORM FINALLY BREAKS

1. Carlton, *Charles I*, 230–233; Clarendon, *History*, I, 434–435
2. Warwick, *Memoirs*, 193–194
3. Abbott, *Speeches and Writings of Oliver Cromwell*, IV, 452
4. ibid., I, 97

5. Fraser, *Cromwell*, 77
6. Gardiner, *Constitutional Documents*, 233–235
7. Barnett, *Britain and Her Army*, 34–35
8. D'Ewes, *Journals*, 381–383
9. Wallington, *Historical Notes*, I, 280
10. John Bruce, ed., *Letters of King Charles I to Queen Henrietta Maria* (London, Camden Society, 1856), 55–56
11. Baillie, *Letters and Journals*, II, 9
12. Spalding, *Memorials*, II, 141
13. Clarendon, *History*, II, 135
14. Rushworth, *Historical Recollections*, IV, 626
15. Hibbert, *Cavaliers and Roundheads*, 43

PART TWO: THE FIRST CIVIL WAR 1642–1647

CHAPTER ONE: FATHER AGAINST SON, BROTHER AGAINST BROTHER

1. Wharton, *Letters, Archaeologia*, XXXV, 315
2. Hutchinson, *Memoirs*, 86–87
3. Wharton, *Letters, Archaeologia*, XXXV, 316
4. Whitelocke, *Memorials*, I, 188–189
5. Firth, *Cromwell's Army*, 276–277
6. Hibbert, *Cavaliers and Roundheads*, 39
7. Carlton, *Going to the Wars*, 46
8. Carlton, *Charles I*, 249
9. D'Ewes, *Journals*, 346–347
10. Hodgson, *Memoirs*, 89
11. State Papers, 16/491/17; Buchan, *Cromwell*, 99
12. Everitt, *Community of Kent*, 120
13. Carlton, *Charles I*, 248
14. Verney, *Memoirs*, I, 282–283
15. Whitelocke, *Memorials*, I, 131
16. Baxter, *Reliquiae*, 40
17. CSPD, 1641–1643, 395
18. Stevenson, *Scottish Revolution*, 248–261
19. Cowan, *Montrose*, 135

CHAPTER TWO: FIRST SHOTS: EDGEHILL

1. Peter Edwards, 'Logistics and Supply', Kenyon and Ohlmeyer, *The Civil Wars*, 256–257
2. 'True and Happy News from Worcester', read in the House of Commons, 24 September 1642
3. Wharton, *Letters, Archaeologia*, XXXV, 317
4. Baxter, *Reliquiae*, 42
5. Warwick, *Memoirs*, I, 229
6. Bulstrode, *Memoirs*, 84
7. *A Relation of the Battle Fought between Keynton and Edgehill by His Majesty's Army and that of the Rebels* (Oxford, 1647)

8. Warwick, *Memoirs*, I, 228–232
9. *A Relation of the Battle Fought between Keynton and Edgehill by His Majesty's Army and that of the Rebels* (Oxford, 1647)
10. Ludlow, *Memoirs*, I, 45
11. Clarendon, *History*, II, 373
12. Aubrey, *Brief Lives*, 128–129

CHAPTER THREE: THE FAILURE TO TAKE LONDON

1. *A Relation of the Battle Fought between Keynton and Edgehill by His Majesty's Army and that of the Rebels* (Oxford, 1647)
2. Stevenson, *Scottish Revolution*, 267–270
3. Wallington, *Historical Notes*, II, 156
4. Samuel Butler, ed. John Wilders, *Hudibras*, Second Part, Canto II (Oxford, 1967), 148–149
5. Warwick, *Memoirs*, I, 228–232
6. Clarendon, *History*, II, 483
7. Sir John Denham, 'Western Wonder', *Mercurius Aulicus*, 25 April 1643
8. Fanshawe, *Memoirs*, 56
9. Stevenson, *Scottish Revolution*, 258–259
10. Baillie, *Letters and Journals*, II, 66–67
11. Napier, *Memorials of Montrose*, II, 77–78
12. Spalding, *Memorials*, II, 53
13. Baillie, *Letters and Journals*, II, 150; Napier, *Memorials of Montrose*, II, 119–121

CHAPTER FOUR: HEARTS AND CITIES: THE WAR TO WIN THE CENTRE

1. Hutchinson, *Memoirs*, 101–102
2. Hibbert, *Cavaliers and Roundheads*, 112
3. Abbott, *Writings and Speeches of Oliver Cromwell*, I, 204
4. Whitelocke, *Memorials*, I, 193
5. Baxter, *Reliquiae*, 98
6. Clarendon, *History*, II, 483
7. 'Prince Rupert's Burning Love to England, Discovered in Birmingham's Flames', Sherwood, *Civil War in the Midlands*, 36–37
8. Adair, *By the Sword Divided*, 56
9. Luke, *Journal*, 117
10. William Lithgow, 'The Present Survey of London and England's State', Somers Tracts, IV, 536–537
11. Spalding, *Memorials*, II, 151

CHAPTER FIVE: WESTERN WONDER: THE WAR IN THE WEST COUNTRY

1. Burne and Young, *The Great Civil War*, 39–41
2. Adair, *By the Sword Divided*, 88
3. Burne and Young, *The Great Civil War*, 44–46
4. Rushworth, *Collections*, V, 272
5. Waller to Hopton, 16 June 1643, Adair, *By the Sword Divided*, 92
6. Atkyns, *Vindication*, 19
7. Walter Slingsby, ed., C. E. H. Chadwyck-Healey, *Bellum Civile, Hopton's*

Narrative of his Campaign in the West Country (Somerset Record Society, 1902); Adair, *By the Sword Divided*, 94

8. Atkyns, *Vindication*, 20
9. Slingsby, op. cit.
10. Adair, *By the Sword Divided*, 99
11. Wallington, *Historical Notes*, II, 87–90

CHAPTER SIX: CHANGING FORTUNES: THE WAR IN THE NORTH

1. Ben Jonson, 'An Epigram to William, Earl of Newcastle', ed. C. H. Herford and Percy and Evelyn Simpson, *Ben Jonson: Poems and Prose Works*, VIII (Oxford, 1947), 228
2. Cavendish, *Life*, 10
3. Warburton, *Prince Rupert and the Cavaliers*, II, 437
4. Hutchinson, *Memoirs*, 104
5. Rushworth, *Historical Collections*, V, 269
6. Carlyle, *Cromwell*, I, 141
7. Aubrey, *Brief Lives* 43; Fraser, *Cromwell*, 102–106
8. Cavendish, *Life*, 179–180; Trease, *Portrait of a Cavalier*, 117–119
9. Lister, *Autobiography*, 6
10. Charles Carlton, 'Civilians', Ohlmeyer and Kenyon, *Civil Wars*, 280
11. Abbott, *Writings and Speeches of Oliver Cromwell*, I, 240
12. ibid., 204
13. Hutchinson, *Memoirs*, 117

CHAPTER SEVEN: STALEMATE

1. Abbott, *Writings and Speeches of Oliver Cromwell*, I, 256
2. From *Biblioteca Gloucestrensis: A collection of scarce and curious tracts relating to the county and city of Gloucester*, ed. John Washbourne, quoted in Adair, *By the Sword Divided*, 102–103
3. Henry Foster, 'A True and Exact Relation of the marchings of the two regiments of the Trained Bands of the City of London, being the Red and Blue Regiments', Adair, *By the Sword Divided*, 105–108
4. Clarendon, *History*, III, 178–179
5. Foster, op. cit.
6. Elias Archer, 'A True Relation of the trained-bands of Westminster, the Green Auxiliaries of London and the Yellow Auxiliaries of Tower Hamlets', Adair, *By the Sword Divided*, 119–121
7. Sir William Springate, *Sussex in the Great Civil War and Interregnum*, ibid., 123–126
8. Hibbert, *Cavaliers and Roundheads*, 156
9. Gough, *Myddle*, 46
10. Baillie, *Letters and Journal*, II, 109
11. ibid., 186
12. ibid., 164

CHAPTER EIGHT: KEEP YOUR POWDER DRY: MARSTON MOOR

1. *Parliament Scout*, 5–12 January 1644

2. Terry, *Leslie*, 188
3. Turner, *Memoirs*, 31
4, Cavendish, *Life*, 348
5. Carlton, *Charles I*, 266–270
6. Clarendon, *History*, III, 327
7. Burne and Young, *Great Civil War*, 129–131
8. Hibbert, *Cavaliers and Roundheads*, 159–160
9. Clarendon, *History*, III, 327
10. Adam Martindale, ed. Parkinson, *The Life of Adam Martindale* (Chetham Society), quoted in Adair, *By the Sword Divided*, 175–178
11. Warburton, *Memoirs of Prince Rupert*, II, 415
12. Burne and Young, *Great Civil War*, 149–152
13. Woolrych, *Battles of the English Civil War*, 68; the most complete description of the battle is Peter Young, *Marston Moor, 1644: The Campaign and the Battle* (London, 1970)
14. Young, *Marston Moor*, 123, 230
15. Sir Arthur Trevor to Ormonde, 10 July 1644, Carte, *Letters*, I, 56
16. Terry, *Leslie*, 251–252
17. Somerville, *Memory of the Somervilles*, II, 343

CHAPTER NINE: THE PITY OF WAR

1. Fraser, *Cromwell*, 130; Woolrych, *Battles of the English Civil War*, 77–78
2. Baillie, *Letters and Journals*, II, 170
3. Burne and Young, *Great Civil War*, 178
4. Symonds, *Diary*, 66
5. ibid.
6. CSPD, 1644–45, 150–151
7. John Bruce and David Masson, *The Quarrel between the Earl of Manchester and Oliver Cromwell* (London, the Camden Society, 1875)
8. Baillie, *Letters and Journals*, II, 168
9. Fraser, *Cromwell*, 71
10. Abbott, *Writings and Speeches of Oliver Cromwell*, I, 314
11. Spalding, *Memorials*, II, 406–413
12. Gordon of Ruthven, *Britane's Distemper*, 80–84
13. Spalding, *Memorials*, II, 265; Aberdeen Council Register, x
14. Cowan, *Montrose*, 152

CHAPTER TEN: SMILE OUT TO GOD IN PRAISES: NASEBY

1. Baillie, *Letters and Journals*, II, 164
2. Adair, *Roundhead General*, 179–180
3. Henry Townshend, *Diary* (Worcestershire Historical Society, 1920); Adair, *By the Sword Divided*, 172–173
4. Their rival prophecies can be found in Wharton's 'An Astrological Judgement upon his Majesties present March from Oxford, May 7 1645' and Lilly's 'An Examination of an Astrological Judgement upon his Majesties March . . . being a Postscript to the Starry Messenger', CSPD, 1645, 128–130.
5. Clarendon, *History*, IV, 34–40

6. Symonds, *Diary*, 180–181; Hutchinson, *Memoirs*, 196
7. Woolrych, *Battles of the English Civil War*, 122
8. Abbott, *Writings and Speeches of Oliver Cromwell*, I, 365
9. Sir Edward Walker, *Historical Discourses upon Several Occasions* (1705); Adair, *By the Sword Divided*, 194–195
10. Sprigge, *Anglia Rediviva*, 87
11. Hibbert, *Cavaliers and Roundheads*, 214
12. Warburton, *Memoirs of Prince Rupert*, III, 149
13. Fraser, *Cromwell*, 165

CHAPTER ELEVEN: MONTROSE'S ANNUS MIRABILIS

1. Terry, *Leslie*, 377; CSPD, 1645, 127
2. Gordon of Ruthven, *Britane's Distemper*, 94–96
3. Napier, *Memorials*, I, 172–173
4. Mackenzie, *Orain Iain Luim*, 21–25; the verse translation is from Derick Thomson, *An Introduction to Gaelic Poetry* (London, 1974)
5. Napier, *Memorials*, II, 175–179
6. In his chapter 'Auldearn Refought' (*Alasdair MacColla and the Highland Problem in the 17th Century*, 166–192), David Stevenson demolishes the theory that Montrose mounted his attack from the left flank: 'In reality it never took place; it is a nineteenth-century fantasy.'
7. Wishart, *Montrose*, 108–111
8. 'The Battle of Alford', Alexander Laing, *The Thistle of Scotland: A Selection of Ancient Ballads* (Aberdeen, 1823)
9. Gordon of Ruthven, *Britane's Distemper*, 160
10. 'The Battle of Philiphaugh', Sir Walter Scott, *Minstrelsy of the Scottish Border* (Edinburgh, 1802)

CHAPTER TWELVE: THINGS FALL APART

1. Warburton, *Memoirs of Prince Rupert*, II, 149
2. Rushworth, *Historical Collections*, IV, 132
3. Clarendon, *History* IV, 93
4. Henry Slingsby, *Original Memoirs*, 169
5. Hibbert, *Cavaliers and Roundheads*, 237–238
6. Sprigge, *Anglia Rediviva*, 149
7. ibid.
8. Clarendon, *History*, IV, 93
9. Wilson, *Fairfax*, 89
10. Sherwood, *Civil War in the Midlands*, 145
11. Dugdale, *Life*, 257

CHAPTER THIRTEEN: THE BEGINNING OF THE END

1. Carte, *Ormond*, VI, 305
2. ibid., 7–8
3. Clarendon, *History* II, 481
4. John Lowe, 'The Glamorgan Mission to Ireland, 1645–6', *Studia Hibernica*, 14 (1964)

5. Aiazza, *Embassy*, 94
6. Baillie, *Letters and Journals*, II, 338
7. CSPIr, 1646, 300
8. Carte, *Ormond*, VI, 349
9. John Lowe, 'The Glamorgan Mission to Ireland, 1645–6', *Studia Hibernica*, 14 (1964)
10. Lindley, *The English Civil War and Revolution*, 125
11. Gilbert, *Affairs*, I, 678

CHAPTER FOURTEEN: THE BEGINNING OF THE END

1. Montereul, *Diplomatic Correspondence*, I, 6
2. Baillie, *Letters and Journals*, II, 337
3. Montereul, *Diplomatic Correspondence*, I, 152
4. Terry, *Leslie*, 402–405
5. Turner, *Memoirs*, 41
6. *Weekly Intelligencer*, 19–26 May 1646
7. Cowan, *Montrose*, 248–249
8. Baillie, *Letters and Journals*, II, 374
9. ibid., 385–392
10. Montereul, *Diplomatic Correspondence*, I, 295
11. ibid., 444
12. Turner, *Memoirs*, 239–241
13. Baxter, *Reliquiae*, 50
14. Whitelocke, *Memorials*, II, 85

CHAPTER FIFTEEN: THE LEVELLERS AND THE PUTNEY DEBATES

1. 'A Solemn Engagement of the Army', Thomason Tracts, E.401 (24)
2. Rushworth, *Historical Collections*, VI, 515–517
3. Abbott, *Writings and Speeches of Oliver Cromwell*, I, 453
4. Berkeley, *Memoirs*, 30–34
5. ibid.
6. William Haller, ed., *Tracts on Liberty in the Puritan Revolution*, III (New York, 1934), 195
7. Hutchinson, *Memoirs*, 222
8. Baillie, *Letters and Journals*, II, 361
9. Woodhouse, *Puritanism and Liberty*, 52–53
10. ibid.
11. Rushworth, *Historical Collections*, VII, 875–6
12. ibid., 871–2

CHAPTER SIXTEEN: THE KING'S ENGAGEMENT

1. John Ashburnham, *A Narrative of his Attendance on King Charles the First from Oxford to the Scotch Army and from Hampton-Court to the Isle of Wight* (London, 1830), II, 108
2. Oglander, *Commonplace Book*, 112–117
3. Fraser, *Cromwell*, 225
4. ibid., 225–226

5. Hutchinson, *Memoirs*, 223
6. Dickinson and Donaldson, *Source Book of Scottish History*, III, 134–139
7. The terms of the Engagement are in Gardiner, *Constitutional Documents*, 259–264
8. Ludlow, *Memoirs*, I, 183
9. Baillie, *Letters and Journals*, III, 15
10. McCoy, *Baillie and the Second Scots Reformation*, 115–125
11. Baillie, *Letters and Journals*, III, 24–31
12. Montereul, *Diplomatic Correspondence*, II, 402

PART THREE: THE SECOND AND THIRD CIVIL WARS 1648–1651

CHAPTER ONE: WALES RISES FOR THE KING

1. 'Resolution of the Army', Somers Tracts, VI, 500
2. Whitelocke, *Memorials*, II, 287
3. Horton to Lenthall, April, 1647, Phillips, *Memoirs of the Civil War in Wales and the Marches*, II, 354
4. Leach, *Pembrokeshire and its Borders*, 183
5. Abbott, *Writings and Speeches of Oliver Cromwell*, I, 606
6. Phillips, *Memoirs of the Civil War in Wales and the Marches*, II, 359
7. Horton to Lenthall, May 1647, ibid., 367
8. Leach, *Pembrokeshire and its Borders*, 196
9. Cromwell to Lenthall, 1647, Leach, 196; Phillips, I, 411

CHAPTER TWO: A SUMMER OF DISCONTENT

1. Woodhouse, *Puritanism and Liberty*, 52–53
2. Hutchinson, *Memoirs*, 230
3. Barkstead to Fairfax, 29 May 1648, Gardiner, *Civil War*, IV, 136–137
4. Gardiner, *Civil War*, IV, 150–151
5. 'A True and Correct Relation of the Taking of Colchester', Gardiner, *Civil War*, IV, 199
6. Clarendon, *History*, IV, 388–389
7. Everitt, *Community of Kent*, 269
8. Articles of Capitulation, 26 August 1648, Gardiner, *Civil War*, IV, 201-202
9. Clarendon, *History*, IV, 388
10. Fairfax to Lenthall, 29 August 1648, Gardiner, *Civil War*, IV, 205

CHAPTER THREE: NOTHING BUT THE HAND OF GOD: PRESTON

1. Turner, *Memoirs*, 53–54
2. Baillie, *Letters and Journals*, III, 54
3. Burnet, *Hamilton*, 432
4. Turner, *Memoirs*, 57–58
5. Oglander, *Commonplace Book*, 121–122
6. Turner, *Memoirs*, 62
7. Hodgson, *Autobiography*, 120
8. Abbott, *Writings and Speeches of Oliver Cromwell*, I, 639

9. ibid., 653
10. Turner, *Memoirs*, 69; Gardiner, *Civil War*, IV, 227–231

CHAPTER FOUR: PRIDE'S PURGE

1. Turner, *Memoirs*, 77
2. *Mercurius Pragmaticus*, 2 October 1648, Gardiner, *Civil War*, IV, 219
3. Charles I to William Hopkins, 9 October 1648, ibid., 220–221
4. Carte, *Ormond*, V, 24
5. Abbott, *Writings and Speeches of Oliver Cromwell*, I, 676
6. Gardiner, *Civil War*, IV, 241–246
7. Hutchinson, *Memoirs*, 231
8. Whitelocke, *Memorials*, II, 472
9. Adair, *By the Sword Divided*, 229
10. Davies, *Unbridled Spirits*, 136–141
11. Ludlow, *Memoirs*, I, 211
12. Hill, *God's Englishman*, chapter 9

CHAPTER FIVE: THAT MEMORABLE SCENE

1. *Mercurius Pragmaticus*, 3 January 1649, Gardiner, *Civil War*, IV, 289
2. Resolutions, 4 January 1649, Thomason Tracts, E357, 35
3. David Masson, *Life of John Milton*, IV (Edinburgh, 1859–1880), 600
4. Wedgwood, *Trial of Charles I*, 108–110
5. State Trials, V, 1201
6. The text of the king's trial was published in John Nalson, *A True Copy of the Journal of the High Court of Justice for the Trial of King Charles I* (1684)
7. Gardiner, *Civil War*, IV, 301
8. The death warrant was later lodged in the library of the House of Lords and first reprinted in *Notes and Queries* in July 1872.
9. Hutchinson, *Memoirs*, 252–253
10. Herbert, *Memoirs*, 247–254
11. Rushworth, *Historical Collections*, Adair, *By the Sword Divided*, 234–237
12. Joseph Spence, *Anecdotes, Observations and Characters of Books and Men* (London, 1820), 286
13. Hutchinson, *Memoirs*, 305

CHAPTER SIX: THE CREATION OF A COMMONWEALTH

1. 'The Act abolishing the Office of King', 17 March 1649, Gardiner, *Constitutional Documents*, 384–7
2. 'The Hunting of the Foxes . . .' D. M. Wolfe, ed., *Leveller Manifestos of the Puritan Revolution* (New York, 1944), 369–372
3. Gardiner, *Commonwealth and Protectorate*, I, 35–36
4. Report from *The Moderate*, Thomason Tracts, E.556,3
5. 'The Declaration and Standard of Levellers', Gardiner, *Commonwealth and Protectorate*, I, 43
6. 'A Plea for the King and Kingdom', *Mercurius Pragmaticus*, November 1648, Wedgwood, *Trial of Charles I*, 10

7. CSPD, 1649, 39
8. 'Light Shining in Buckinghamshire', December 1648, G. H. Sabine, ed., *The Works of Gerard Winstanley* (Cornell, 1941), 611

CHAPTER SEVEN: THOSE BARBAROUS WRETCHES: DROGHEDA AND WEXFORD

1. *The Moderate Intelligencer*, 10 July 1649, Murphy, *Cromwell in Ireland*, 70
2. Hill, *God's Englishman*, 108–112
3. *Perfect Diurnal*, 23 August, 1649, Reilly, *Cromwell*, 50–51
4. Gardiner, *Commonwealth and Protectorate*, I, 114–115
5. Gilbert, *Contemporary History*, II, 233–236
6. Murphy, *Cromwell in Ireland*, 96
7. Rev. Patrick Francis Moran, *Persecutions suffered by the Catholics of Ireland under the rule of Cromwell and the Puritans* (Dublin, 1903), 51
8. Gilbert, *Contemporary History*, 275; Gardiner, *Commonwealth and Protectorate*, I, 120–121
9. Gardiner, *Commonwealth and Protectorate*, I, 121
10. Reilly, *Cromwell*, chapters 2 and 3. This is the most solidly researched and trenchantly argued account of the battle for Drogheda and its aftermath.
11. Gardiner, *Commonwealth and Protectorate*, I, 124–125
12. Abbott, *Writings and Speeches of Oliver Cromwell*, II, 138
13. Reilly, *Cromwell*, 185
14. Abbott, *Writings and Speeches of Oliver Cromwell*, II, 146
15. Thomas Davis, 'Lament for the Death of Owen Roe O'Neill', *The Poems of Thomas Davis* (Dublin, 1846)

CHAPTER EIGHT: THE CURSE OF CROMWELL

1. The declarations and Cromwell's responses are reproduced in full in Reilly, *Cromwell*, Appendix 6, 292–300
2. Murphy, *Cromwell in Ireland*, 261. Antonia Fraser also attributes the saying to Prince William of Orange, *Cromwell*, 352
3. Ferguson, *Scotland's Relations with England*, 134
4. Baillie, *Letters and Journals*, III, 66
5. Gardiner, *Commonwealth and Protectorate*, I, 26
6. 'The History of the War in Ireland from 1641 to 1653', quoted in full, Reilly, *Cromwell*, Appendix 7
7. Severall Proceedings, 23 May – 6 June 1650, Reilly, *Cromwell*, 245–246
8. Murphy, *Cromwell in Ireland*, 349

CHAPTER NINE: PRINCE OF WALES, KING OF SCOTLAND

1. Baillie, *Letters and Journals*, III, 90
2. Napier, *Memorials of Montrose*, II, 375
3. McCoy, *Baillie and the Second Scots Reformation*, 128
4. Ferguson, *Scotland's Relations with England*, 135–137
5. Gardiner, *Commonwealth and Protectorate*, I, 184–185
6. Napier, *Memorials of Montrose*, II, 752
7. ibid., 411–412

8. Jaffray, *Diary*, 56
9. James Fraser, ed. William Mackay, *Chronicles of the Frasers, the Wardlaw Manuscript* (Edinburgh, Scottish History Society), 353–354

CHAPTER TEN: A SIGNAL MERCY: DUNBAR

1. CSPD, 1650, 256
2. Burnet, *History*, I, 53
3. Whitelocke, *Memorials*, III, 207
4. Gardiner, *Commonwealth and Protectorate*, I, 292
5. James Kirkton, ed. Charles Kirkpatrick Sharpe, *The True and Secret History of the Church of Scotland* (Edinburgh, 1817)
6. Abbott, *Writings and Speeches of Oliver Cromwell*, II, 325
7. Hodgson, *Autobiography*, 143
8. Nicoll, *Diary*, 33

CHAPTER ELEVEN: HAMMER OF THE SCOTS

1. Abbott, *Writings and Speeches of Oliver Cromwell*, II, 314
2. Grainger, *Cromwell Against the Scots*, 51–75
3. Baillie, *Letters and Journals*, III, 115–116
4. Preston, *A Land Afflicted*, 205–207
5. Baillie, *Letters and Journals*, III, 127–128
6. Abbott, *Writings and Speeches of Oliver Cromwell*, II, 444
7. Clarendon, *History*, V, 180–181
8. Abbott, *Writings and Speeches of Oliver Cromwell*, II, 455
9. Baxter, *Reliquiae*, 69
10. ibid. For a complete account of this romantic and much-mythologised episode see Richard Ollard, *The Escape of King Charles II after the Battle of Worcester* (London, 1966)
11. Carlyle, *Letters*, III, 183
12. Gardiner, *Commonwealth and Protectorate*, II, 46–47

CHAPTER TWELVE: HELL OR CONNACHT: THE SUBJUGATION OF SCOTLAND AND IRELAND

1. Charles Carlton, 'Civilians', in Kenyon and Ohlmeyer, *The Civil Wars*, 272–305
2. Baxter, *Reliquiae*, 55; Oglander, *Commonplace Book*, 103
3. Whitelocke, *Memorials*, III, 372
4. Carlton, 'Civilians', in Kenyon and Ohlmeyer, *The Civil Wars*, 278; Reilly, *Cromwell*, 228
5. Nicoll, *Diary*, 54–58
6. James, *Warrior Race*, 189–190
7. Dow, *Cromwellian Scotland*, 46–51
8. McCrie, *Life of Blair*, 291
9. Akerman, *Letters from Roundhead Officers*, 43
10. *Perfect Diurnal*, Gardiner, *Commonwealth and Protectorate*, II, 135–136
11. Baillie, *Letters and Journals*, III, 200 and 255–256
12. Proclamation to the people of Waterford, 10 February 1651, Gardiner, *Commonwealth and Protectorate*, II, 117

13. Ludlow, *Memoirs*, I, 504

PART FOUR: THE PROTECTORATE 1653–1659

CHAPTER ONE: WINNING THE PEACE

1. Whitelocke, *Memorials*, III, 272
2. Middlesex County Records III, 215–216; Aylmer, *The State's Servants*, 159
3. John Geree, 'The Character of the Old English Puritan or Non-Conformist', printed by W. Wilson for Christopher Meredith at the Crane in Paul's Churchyard, 1646 (Grace Chapel, Spokane, 1995)
4. 'Epistle to the Reader', Samuel Clarke, *Lives of Sundry Eminent Persons* (London, 1683)
5. John Bunyan, ed. S. C. Freer, *Grace Abounding to the Chief of Sinners*, part 5, 215 (London, 1903), 114–115
6. Hill, 'James Warrington and the People', *Puritanism and Revolution*, 269–281
7. 'Petition of the Army', Gardiner, *Commonwealth and Protectorate*, II, 167
8. ibid., 227
9. Whitelocke, *Memorials*, III, 468 seq.
10. Gardiner, *Commonwealth and Protectorate*, II, 226
11. Hutchinson, *Memoirs*, 252
12. Abbott, *Writings and Speeches of Oliver Cromwell*, III, 59
13. Whitelocke, who was present throughout, is the most reliable source.
14. Abbott, *Writings and Speeches of Oliver Cromwell*, III, 453

CHAPTER TWO: MY DELIGHT AMONGST THE NATIONS: THE ANGLO-DUTCH WAR

1. There is a good account of the action in John Keay, *The Honourable Company: A History of the English East India Company* (London, 1991), 47–51
2. The best account is contained in Capp, *Cromwell's Navy*
3. Paul Kennedy, *The Rise and Fall of British Naval Mastery* (London, 1976), 47
4. Gardiner, *Commonwealth and Protectorate*, II, 119
5. Blake to the Speaker 20 May 1652, Powell, ed., *The Letters of Robert Blake*, 159
6. Abbott, *Writings and Speeches of Oliver Cromwell*, II, 588
7. Extract from *Hollandsche Mercurius* 1652, 78, Gardiner, ed., *Letters and Papers Relating to the First Dutch War*, I, 403–404
8. Bourne to Admiralty Committee, 24 February 1653, Aylmer, *The State's Servants*, 159
9. Blake to Council of State, 1 December 1652, Powell, ed., *The Letters of Robert Blake*, 185
10. Blake and Deane to Council of State, 22 February 1653, ibid., 205
11. *Mercurius Politicus*, 22 February 1653, C. T. Atkinson, ed., *Letters and Papers Relating to the First Dutch War*, IV, 111; A Letter of Intelligence from the Hague, 2 September 1653, C. T. Atkinson, ed., *Letters and Papers Relating to the First Dutch War*, VI, 48

CHAPTER THREE: CROMWELL, LORD PROTECTOR

1. Jaffray, *Diary*, 51

2. John Pell to John Thurloe, March 1655, Hill, *Puritanism and Revolution*, 293
3. Baumber, *General at Sea*, 188
4. 'The Just Defence of John Lilburn against such as charge him with Turbulency of Spirit, 25 August 1653', Gregg, *Freeborn John*, 335
5. Fraser, *Cromwell*, 447
6. John Thurloe to Bulstrode Whitelocke, 23 December 1653, Hill, *God's Englishman*, 143
7. Hutchinson, *Memoirs*, 256
8. Hyde to Rochester, 4 March 1654, Abbott, *Writings and Speeches of Oliver Cromwell*, III, 208
9. The best account of this process is Roy Sherwood, *The Court of Oliver Cromwell* (London, 1977)

CHAPTER FOUR: THE CROMWELLIAN SETTLEMENT IN SCOTLAND AND IRELAND

1. Argyll to John Campbell of Glenorchy, 13 August 1653, Dow, *Cromwellian Scotland*, 93
2. Dow, *Cromwellian Scotland*, 78–98
3. Turner, *Memoirs*, 109–110
4. Baillie, *Letters and Journals*, III, 247–253
5. Mitchison, *History of Scotland*, 236
6. Nicoll, *Diary*, 104
7. Hiram Morgan, 'Cromwellian Land Settlement', S. J. Connolly, ed., *The Oxford Companion to Irish History* (Oxford, 1998)
8. CSPIr, 1660, 325; Barnard, *Cromwellian Ireland*, 56–57
9. Jesuit correspondence, 1662, Rev. Patrick Francis Moran, *Persecutions suffered by the Catholics of Ireland under the rule of Cromwell and the Puritans* (Dublin, 1903)
10. Bottigheimer, *English Money and Irish Land*, 141–142
11. L. F. Brown, *The Political Activities of the Baptist and Fifth Monarchy Men in England during the Interregnum* (London, 1912), 149–152
12. Jonathan Swift, ed. T. Scott, *Works*, IV (Dublin, 1910), 94

CHAPTER FIVE: 'SILLY MEAN FELLOWS': THE RULE OF THE MAJOR-GENERALS

1. Abbott, *Writings and Speeches of Oliver Cromwell*, II, 261
2. Nicoll, *Diary*, 148; Hutchinson, *Memoirs*, 257
3. Abbott, *Writings and Speeches of Oliver Cromwell*, III, 579
4. Fraser, *Cromwell*, 516
5. John Morrill, 'Postlude: Between War and Peace, 1651–1662', Kenyon and Ohlmeyer, *Civil Wars*, 306–309
6. Hill, *The World Turned Upside Down*, 361–386
7. The description is John Buchan's in his biography of Cromwell, but similar sentiments were expressed by Samuel Rawson Gardiner and others. Durston, *Cromwell's Major-Generals*, 5–12
8. ibid., *Cromwell's Major-Generals*, 22
9. Hutchinson, *Memoirs*, 257
10. Durston, *Cromwell's Major-Generals*, 199

11. ibid., 53–54
12. ibid., 179

CHAPTER SIX: FIGHTING THE LORD'S BATTLES: THE WAR AGAINST SPAIN

1. Abbott, *Speeches and Writings of Oliver Cromwell*, III, 859
2. Baumber, *General-at-Sea*, 188
3. John Morrill, 'Postlude: Between War and Peace 1651–1662', Kenyon and Ohlmeyer, *The Civil Wars*, 317
4. *The Narrative of General Venables*, ed. C. H. Firth (London, Royal Historical Society, 1900), 136
5. ibid., 44
6. Ollard, *Cromwell's Earl*, 40–44
7. Baumber gives the figure as £200,000, *General-at-Sea*, 224; Hainsworth as £2 million, *The Swordsmen in Power*, 213
8. Baumber, *General-at-Sea*, 225–226
9. The exact details are ambiguous: Stayner's battle plan has been lost and he wrote his account later.
10. 'Narrative of Action at Santa Cruz', Blake, *Letters*, 387
11. Clarendon, *History*, VI, 36

CHAPTER SEVEN: KING CROMWELL AND TUMBLEDOWN DICK

1. Edmund Waller, 'On a War with Spain, and a Fight at Sea', *Poems* (London, 1840), 164
2. Durston, *Cromwell's Major-Generals*, 215–220
3. Hill, 'Ranters and Quakers', *World Turned Upside Down*, 231–258; Davies, *Unbridled Spirits*, 235–240
4. Abbott, *Writings and Speeches of Oliver Cromwell*, IV, 414
5. Hutchinson, *Memoirs*, 257–258
6. Abbott, *Writings and Speeches of Oliver Cromwell*, IV, 418
7. Fraser, *Cromwell*, 605
8. Sherwood, 'Oliver Cromwell and Regality', *Court of Oliver Cromwell*, 158–167
9. Hutchinson, *Memoirs*, 256
10. Abbott, *Writings and Speeches of Oliver Cromwell*, IV, 728
11. Fraser, *Cromwell*, 387
12. Bennett, *Civil Wars Experienced*, 186
13. Hill, *God's Englishman*, 183–184
14. Jaffray, *Diary*, 119–20
15. Fraser, *Cromwell*, 706

CHAPTER EIGHT: THE KING COMES INTO HIS OWN

1. Thurloe, *State Papers*, VII, 379
2. Hutchinson, *Memoirs*, 264
3. Dow, *Cromwellian Scotland*, 233–240
4. Hutchinson, *Memoirs*, 268–269
5. *Clarke Papers*, ed. C. H. Firth (London, 1901), IV, 69
6. Dawson, *Cromwell's Understudy*, 362
7. Somers Tracts, VI, 538

8. Johnston of Wariston, *Diary*, III, 163
9. Dawson, *Cromwell's Understudy*, 380
10. Pepys, *Diary*, 25
11. ibid., 15
12. Hobman, *Cromwell's Spymaster*, 167
13. Pepys, *Diary*, 2 May 1660, 39
14. Fanshawe, *Memoirs*, 140–141
15. Evelyn, *Diary*, 406
16. Hutchinson, *Memoirs*, 278
17. Nicoll, *Diary*, 283

PART FIVE: RESTORATION 1660

CHAPTER ONE: REVENGE AND RESTRAINT

1. Pepys, *Diary*, 86
2. Durston, *Cromwell's Major-Generals*, 234–239
3. Hutchinson, *Memoirs*, 321–322
4. Cowan, *Montrose*, 299
5. *Mercurius Caledonius*, 7 January 1661
6. Hill, *The World Turned Upside Down*, 384
7. Kenyon, *Civil Wars*, 233–234
8. Pepys, *Diary*, 319
9. Pepys, *Diary*, 132
10. Hutchinson, *Memoirs*, 16
11. Gardiner, Hill, Stone, Kenyon, Morrill, Gaunt et al.
12. Pepys, *Diary*, 107

CHAPTER TWO: THE SETTLEMENT OF THE THREE KINGDOMS

1. Hutton, *Charles II*, 180–184
2. Nicoll, *Diary*, 322
3. Mitchison, *History of Scotland*, 242
4. Ferguson, *Scotland's Relations with England*, 148
5. Baillie, *Letters and Journal*, III, 406–407
6. Burnet, *History*, II, 157
7. Hutton, *Charles II*, 196–201
8. Pepys, *Diary*, 319
9. Pepys, *Diary*, 735

CHAPTER THREE: THE CIVIL WARS AND MODERN MEMORY

1. Gough, *Myddle*, 5–6
2. Clarendon, *History*, I, 1–3
3. Clarendon, *History*, III, 178–179
4. Hill, 'Lord Clarendon and the Puritan Revolution', *Puritanism and Revolution*, 181–194
5. Worden, *Roundhead Reputations*, 7. This chapter could not have been attempted without a reading of this brilliant study.

6. Thomas Carlyle, *On Heroes, Hero-Worship and the Heroic in History* (London, 1841), 249–250

7. Carlyle, *Cromwell*, III, 35

8. Simon Heffer, *Moral Desperado: A Life of Thomas Carlyle* (London, 1995); Dale Trela, *A History of Carlyle's 'Oliver Cromwell's Letters and Speeches'* (New York, 1992)

9. Charles Harding Firth, 'Samuel Rawson Gardiner', *Dictionary of National Biography 1931–1940*

10. 'Samuel Rawson Gardiner', *The Cambridge History of English and American Literature in 18 Volumes* (London, 1907–1921), XIV, *The Victorian Age,* Part Two

11. Hill, 'Recent Interpretations of the Civil War', *Puritanism and Revolution*, 181–194

12. Gaunt, *The British Wars*, Select Bibliography, 86–88

13. ibid., 80

EPILOGUE: LEXINGTON AND CONCORD, 1775

1. Good recent accounts from a British perspective include Robert Harvey, *A Few Bloody Noses: The American War of Independence* (London, 2001) and Christopher Hibbert, *Redcoats and Rebels: The War for America 1770–1781* (London, 1990)

2. J. G. A. Pocock, *Three British Revolutions, 1641, 1688 and 1776* (Princeton, 1980)

Index

/